ENCYCLOPEDIA OF TARIFFS AND TRADE IN U.S. HISTORY

Volume II. Debating the Issues:
Selected Primary Documents

ENCYCLOPEDIA OF TARIFFS AND TRADE IN U.S. HISTORY

Volume II. Debating the Issues: Selected Primary Documents

Edited by Cynthia Clark Northrup and
Elaine C. Prange Turney

GREENWOOD PRESS
Westport, Connecticut • London

Library of Congress Cataloging-in-Publication Data

Encyclopedia of tariffs and trade in U.S. history / edited by Cynthia Clark Northrup
and Elaine C. Prange Turney.
    p. cm.
    Includes bibliographical references and index.
    ISBN 0–313–32789–0 (set : alk. paper)—ISBN 0–313–31943–X (v. 1 : alk. paper)—ISBN 0–313–31944–8
(v. 2 : alk. paper)—ISBN 0–313–31945–6 (v. 3 : alk. paper)
    1. Tariff—United States—History—Encyclopedias.   2. Taxation—United
States—History—Encyclopedias.   3. United States—Commercial
policy—History—Encyclopedias.   4. Free trade—United States—History—Encyclopedias.
5. Protectionism—United States—History—Encyclopedias.   6. United States—History—
Encyclopedias. I. Title: Encyclopedia of tariffs and trade in US history.   II. Northrup,
Cynthia Clark, 1959–   III. Turney, Elaine C. Prange, 1957–
HF1705.T37   2003
382'.7'097303—dc21   2002019506

British Library Cataloguing in Publication Data is available.

Library of Congress Catalog Card Number: 2002019506
ISBN: 0–313–32789–0 (set)
        0–313–31943–X (Vol. I)
        0–313–31944–8 (Vol. II)
        0–313–31945–6 (Vol. III)

First published in 2003

Greenwood Press, 88 Post Road West, Westport, CT 06881
An imprint of Greenwood Publishing Group, Inc.
www.greenwood.com

Printed in the United States of America

The paper used in this book complies with the
Permanent Paper Standard issued by the National
Information Standards Organization (Z39.48–1984).

10 9 8 7 6 5 4 3 2 1

Every reasonable effort has been made to trace the owners of copyright materials in this book, but in some instances
this has proven impossible. The editors and publisher will be glad to receive information leading to more complete
acknowledgments in subsequent printings of the book and in the meantime extend their apologies for any
omissions.

Contents

Contents

The Index for this volume appears at the end of Encyclopedia of Tariffs and
Trade in U.S. History: Volume III. The Texts of the Tariffs.

Preface

Whereas the first volume of this work contains information on specific individuals, acts, or events associated with tariffs and trade in U.S. history, this volume contains primary historical documents. Works illustrate particular arguments or positions on significant tariffs or the issue of trade and illustrate the passion and conviction in the words of the contemporary participants.

The documents appear in chronological order, spanning all of American history from 1776 to the present. While space prohibits the inclusion of all sources on the subject, we have chosen these thirty-six documents because of their importance or representative nature.

When at all possible, we have attempted to replicate the document, including the format, as close to the original as possible. Some formats appear slightly different from the source material; in these cases, the style was changed for consistency and to make it easier for the reader to follow the author's organization. The words and content, however, remain those of the original author.

The Wealth of Nations

Scottish economist Adam Smith addressed numerous topics, including tariffs and trade, in his 1776 work An Inquiry into the Nature and Causes of the Wealth of Nations. *Written at the onset of the American Revolution, Smith's argument that trade should remain unrestricted except in cases of national defense was embraced by many Americans such as Benjamin Franklin and Alexander Hamilton. After the revolution, Franklin continued to espouse Smith's theories, whereas Hamilton sought to modify the argument in an effort to strengthen American economic independence. Smith's work remains the principal document arguing for a shift from a mercantile society to a capitalist one with free trade.*

Of Treaties of Commerce

When a nation binds itself by treaty either to permit the entry of certain goods from one foreign country which it prohibits from all others, or to exempt the goods of one country from duties to which it subjects those of all others, the country, or at least the merchants and manufacturers of the country, whose commerce is so favoured, must necessarily derive great advantage from the treaty. Those merchants and manufacturers enjoy a sort of monopoly in the country which is so indulgent to them. That country becomes a market both more extensive and more advantageous for their goods: more extensive, because the goods of other nations being either excluded or subjected to heavier duties, it takes off a greater quantity of theirs: more advantageous, because the merchants of the favoured country, enjoying a sort of monopoly there, will often sell their goods for a better price than if exposed to the free competition of all other nations.

Such treaties, however, though they may be advantageous to the merchants and manufacturers of the favoured, are necessarily disadvantageous to those of the favouring country. A monopoly is thus granted against them to a foreign nation; and they must frequently buy the foreign goods they have occasion for dearer than if the free competition of other nations was admitted. That part of its own produce with which such a nation purchases foreign goods must consequently be sold cheaper, because when two things are exchanged for one another, the cheapness of the one is a necessary consequence, or rather the same thing with the dearness of the other. The exchangeable value of its annual produce, therefore, is likely to be diminished by every such treaty. This diminution, however, can scarce amount to any positive loss, but only to a lessening of the gain which it might otherwise make. Though it sells its goods cheaper than it otherwise might do, it will not probably sell them for less than they cost; nor, as in the case of bounties, for a price which will not replace the capital employed in bringing them to market, together with the ordinary profits of stock. The trade could not go on long if it did. Even the favouring country, therefore, may still gain by the trade, though less than if there was a free competition.

Some treaties of commerce, however, have been supposed advantageous upon principles very different from these; and a commercial country has sometimes granted a monopoly of this kind against itself to certain goods of a foreign nation, because it expected that in the whole commerce between them, it would annually sell more than it would buy, and that a balance in gold and silver would be annually returned to it. It is upon this principle that the treaty of commerce between England and Portugal, concluded in 1703 by Mr.

Methuen, has been so much commended. The following is a literal translation of that treaty, which consists of three articles only.

ARTICLE I

His sacred royal majesty of Portugal promises, both in his own name, and that of his successors, to admit, for ever hereafter, into Portugal, the woollen cloths, and the rest of the woollen manufactures of the British, as was accustomed, till they were prohibited by the law; nevertheless upon this condition:

ARTICLE II

That is to say, that her sacred royal majesty of Great Britain shall, in her own name, and that of her successors, be obliged, for ever hereafter, to admit the wines of the growth of Portugal into Britain; so that at no time, whether there shall be peace or war between the kingdoms of Britain and France, anything more shall be demanded for these wines by the name of custom or duty, or by whatsoever other title, directly or indirectly, whether they shall be imported into Great Britain in or hogsheads, or other casks, than what shall be demanded for the like quantity or measure of French wine, deducting or abating a third part of the custom or duty. But if at any time this deduction or abatement of customs, which is to be made as aforesaid, shall in any manner be attempted and prejudiced, it shall be just and lawful for his sacred royal majesty of

Portugal, again to prohibit the woollen cloths, and the rest of the British woollen manufactures.

ARTICLE III

The most excellent lords the plenipotentiaries promise and take upon themselves, that their above named masters shall ratify this treaty; and within the space of two months the ratifications shall be exchanged.

By this treaty the crown of Portugal becomes bound to admit the English woollens upon the same footing as before the prohibition; that is, not to raise the duties which had been paid before that time. But it does not become bound to admit them upon any better terms than those of any other nation, of France or Holland for example. The crown of Great Britain, on the contrary, becomes bound to admit the wines of Portugal upon paying only two-thirds of the duty which is paid for those of France, the wines most likely to come into competition with them. So far this treaty, therefore, is evidently advantageous to Portugal, and disadvantageous to Great Britain.

It has been celebrated, however, as a masterpiece of the commercial policy of England. Portugal receives annually from the Brazils a greater quantity of gold than can be employed in its domestic commerce, whether in the shape of coin or of plate. The surplus is too valuable to be allowed to lie idle and locked up in coffers, and as it can find no advantageous market at home, it must, notwithstanding any prohibition, be sent abroad, and exchanged for something for which there is more advantageous market at home. A large share of it comes annually to England, in return either for English goods, or for those of other European nations that receive their returns through England. Mr. Baretti was informed that the weekly packet-boat from Lisbon brings, one week with another, more than fifty thousand pounds in gold to England. The sum had probably been exaggerated. It would amount to more than two millions six hundred thousand pounds a year, which is more than the Brazils are supposed to afford.

Our merchants were some years ago out of humour with the crown of Portugal. Some privileges which had been granted them, not by treaty, but by the free grace of that crown, at the solicitation indeed, it is probable, and in return for much greater favours, defence and protection, from the crown of Great Britain had been either infringed or revoked. The people, therefore, usually most interested in celebrating the Portugal trade were then rather disposed to represent it as less advantageous than it had commonly been imagined. The far greater part, almost the whole, they pretended, of this annual importation of gold, was not on account of Great Britain nearly compensating the value of the British goods sent thither.

Let us suppose, however, that the whole was on account of Great Britain, and that it amounted to a still greater sum than Mr. Baretti seems to imagine; this trade would not, upon that account, be more advantageous than any other in which, for the same value sent out, we received an equal value of consumable goods in return.

It is but a very small part of this importation which, it can be supposed, is employed as an annual addition either to the plate or to the coin of the kingdom. The rest must all be sent abroad and exchanged for consumable goods of some kind or other. But if those consumable goods were purchased directly with the produce of English industry, it would be more for the advantage of England than first to purchase with that produce the gold of Portugal, and afterwards to purchase with that gold those consumable goods. A direct foreign trade of consumption is always more advantageous than a round-about one; and to bring the same value of foreign goods to the home market, requires a much smaller capital in the one way than in the other. If a smaller share of its industry, therefore, had been employed in producing goods fit for the Portugal market, and a greater in producing those fit for the other markets, where those consumable goods for which there is a demand in Great Britain are to be had, it would have been more for the advantage of England. To procure both the gold, which it wants for its own use, and the consumable goods, would, in this way, employ a much smaller capital than at present. There would be a spare capital, therefore, to be employed for other purposes, in exciting an additional quantity of industry, and in raising a greater annual produce.

Though Britain were entirely excluded from the Portugal trade, it could find very little difficulty in procuring all the annual supplies of gold which it wants, either for the purposes of plate, or of coin, or of foreign trade. Gold, like every other commodity, is always somewhere or another to be got for its value by those who have that value to give for it. The annual surplus of gold in Portugal, besides, would still be sent abroad, and though not carried away by Great Britain, would be carried away by some other nation, which would be glad to sell it again for its price, in the same manner as Great Britain does at present. In buying gold of Portugal, indeed, we buy it at the first hand; whereas, in buying it of any other nation, except Spain, we should buy it at the second, and might pay somewhat dearer. This difference, however, would surely be too insignificant to deserve the public attention.

Almost all our gold, it is said, comes from Portugal. With other nations the balance of trade is either against us, or not much in our favour. But we should remember that the more gold we import from one country, the less we must necessarily import from all others. The effectual demand for gold, like that for every other commodity, is in every country limited to a certain quantity. If nine-tenths of this quantity are imported from one country, there remains a tenth only to be imported from all others. The more gold besides that is annually imported from some particular countries, over and above what is requisite for plate and for coin, the more must necessarily be exported to some others; and the more that most insignificant object of modern policy, the balance of trade, appears to be in our favour with some particular countries, the more it must necessarily appear to be against us with many others.

It was upon this silly notion, however, that England could not subsist without the Portugal trade, that, towards the end of the late war, France and Spain, without pretending either offence or provocation, required the King of Portugal to exclude all British ships from his ports, and for the security of this exclusion, to receive into them French or Spanish garrisons. Had the king of Portugal submitted to those ignominious terms which his brother-in-law the king of Spain proposed to him, Britain would have been freed from a much greater inconveniency than the loss of the Portugal trade, the burden of supporting a very weak ally, so unprovided of everything for his own defence that the whole power of England, had it been directed to that single purpose, could scarce perhaps have defended him for another campaign. The loss of the Portugal trade would, no doubt, have occasioned a considerable embarrassment to the merchants at that time engaged in it, who might not, perhaps, have found out, for a year or two, any other equally advantageous method of employing their capitals; and in this would probably have consisted all the inconveniency which England could have suffered from this notable piece of commercial policy.

The great annual importation of gold and silver is neither for the purpose of plate nor of coin, but of foreign trade. A round-about foreign trade of consumption can be carried on more advantageously by means of these metals than of almost any other goods. As they are the universal instruments of commerce, they are more readily received in return for all commodities than any other goods; and on account of their small bulk and great value, it costs less to transport them backward and forward from one place to another than almost any other sort of merchandise, and they lose less of their value by being so transported. Of all the commodities, therefore, which are

bought in one foreign country, for no other purpose but to be sold or exchanged again for some other goods in another, there are none so convenient as gold and silver. In facilitating all the different round-about foreign trades of consumption which are carried on in Great Britain consists the principal advantage of the Portugal trade; and though it is not a capital advantage, it is no doubt a considerable one.

That any annual addition which, it can reasonably be supposed, is made either to the plate or to the coin of the kingdom, could require but a very small annual importation of gold and silver, seems evident enough; and though we had no direct trade with Portugal, this small quantity could always, somewhere or another, be very easily got.

Though the goldsmith's trade be very considerable in Great Britain, the far greater part of the new plate which they annually sell is made from other old plate melted down; so that the addition annually made to the whole plate of the kingdom cannot be very great, and could require but a very small annual importation.

It is the same case with the coin. Nobody imagines, I believe, that even the greater part of the annual coinage, amounting, for ten years together, before the late reformation of the gold coin, to upwards of eight hundred thousand pounds a year in gold, was an annual addition to the money before current in the kingdom. In a country where the expense of the coinage is defrayed by the government, the value of the coin, even when it contains its full standard weight of gold and silver, can never be much greater than that of an equal quantity of those metals uncoined; because it requires only the trouble of going to the mint, and the delay perhaps of a few weeks, to procure for any quantity of uncoined gold and silver an equal quantity of those metals in coin. But, in every country, the greater part of the current coin is almost always more or less worn, or otherwise degenerated from its standard. In Great Britain it was, before the late reformation, a good deal so, the gold being more than two per cent and the silver more than eight per cent below its standard weight. But if forty-four guineas and a half, containing their full standard weight, a pound weight of gold, could purchase very little more than a pound weight could of uncoined gold, forty-four guineas and a half wanting a part of their weight could not purchase a pound weight, and something was to be added in order to make up the deficiency. The current price of gold bullion at market, therefore, instead of being the same with the mint price, or #46 14s. 6d., was then about #47 14s. and sometimes about #48. When the greater part of the coin, however, was in this degenerate condition, forty-four guineas and a half, fresh from the mint, would purchase no more goods in the market than any other ordinary guineas, because when they came into the coffers of the merchant, being confounded with other money, they could not afterwards be distinguished without more trouble than the difference was worth. Like other guineas they were worth no more than #46 14s. 6d. If thrown into the melting pot, however, they produced, without any sensible loss, a pound weight of standard gold, which could be sold at any time for between #47 14s. and #48 either of gold or silver, as fit for all the purposes of coin as that which had been melted down. There was an evident profit, therefore, in melting down new coined money, and it was done so instantaneously, that no precaution of government could prevent it. The operations of the mint were, upon this account, somewhat like the web of Penelope; the work that was done in the day was undone in the night. The mint was employed, not so much in making daily additions to the coin, as in replacing the very best part of it which was daily melted down.

Were the private people, who carry their gold and silver to the mint, to pay themselves for the coinage, it would add to the value of those metals in the same manner as the fashion does to that of plate. Coined gold and silver would be more valuable than uncoined. The seignorage, if it was not exorbitant, would add to the bullion the whole value of the duty; because, the government having everywhere the exclusive privilege of coining, no coin can come to market cheaper than they think proper to afford it. If the duty was exorbitant indeed, that is, if it was very much above the real value of the labour and expense requisite for coinage, false coiners, both at home and abroad, might be encouraged, by the great difference between the value of bullion and that of coin, to pour in so great a quantity of counterfeit money as might reduce the value of the government money. In France, however, though the seignorage is eight per cent, no sensible inconveniency of this kind is found to arise from it. The dangers to which a false coiner is everywhere exposed, if he lives in the country of which he counterfeits the coin, and to which his agents or correspondents are exposed if he lives in a foreign country, are by far too great to be incurred for the sake of a profit of six or seven per cent.

The seignorage in France raises the value of the coin higher than in proportion to the quantity of pure gold which it contains. Thus by the edict of January 1726, the mint price of fine gold of twenty-four carats was fixed at seven hundred and forty livres nine sous and one denier one-eleventh, the mark of eight Paris ounces. The gold coin of France, making an allowance for the remedy of the mint, contains twenty-one carats and three-fourths of fine gold, and two carats one fourth of alloy. The mark of standard gold, therefore, is worth no more than about six hundred and seventy-one livres ten deniers. But in France this mark of standard gold is coined into thirty Louis d'ors of twenty-four livres each, or into seven hundred and twenty livres. The coinage, therefore, increases the value of a mark of standard gold bullion, by the difference between six hundred and seventy-one livres ten deniers, and seven hundred and twenty livres; or by forty-eight livres nineteen sous and two deniers.

A seignorage will, in many cases, take away altogether, and will, in all cases, diminish the profit of melting down the new coin. This profit always arises from the difference between the quantity of bullion which the common currency ought to contain, and that which it actually does contain. If this difference is less than the seignorage, there will be loss instead of profit. If it is equal to the seignorage, there will neither be profit nor loss. If it is greater than the seignorage, there will indeed

be some profit, but less than if there was no seignorage. If, before the late reformation of the gold coin, for example, there had been a seignorage of five per cent upon the coinage, there would have been a loss of three per cent upon the melting down of the gold coin. If the seignorage had been two per cent there would have been neither profit nor loss. If the seignorage had been one per cent there would have been a profit, but of one per cent only instead of two per cent. Wherever money is received by tale, therefore, and not by weight, a seignorage is the most effectual preventative of the melting down of the coin, and, for the same reason, of its exportation. It is the best and heaviest pieces that are commonly either melted down or exported; because it is upon such that the largest profits are made.

The law for encouragement of the coinage, by rendering it duty-free, was first enacted during the reign of Charles II for a limited time; and afterwards continued, by different prolongations, till 1769, when it was rendered perpetual. The Bank of England, in order to replenish their coffers with money, are frequently obliged to carry bullion to the mint; and it was more for their interest, they probably imagined, that the coinage should be at the expense of the government than at their own. It was probably out of complaisance to this great company that the government agreed to render this law perpetual. Should the custom of weighing gold, however, come to be disused, as it is very likely to be on account of its inconveniency; should the gold coin of England come to be received by tale, as it was before the late recoinage, this great company may, perhaps, find that they have upon this, as upon some other occasions, mistaken their own interest not a little.

Before the late recoinage, when the gold currency of England was two per cent below its standard weight, as there was no seignorage, it was two per cent below the value of that quantity of standard gold bullion which it ought to have contained. When this great company, therefore, bought gold bullion in order to have it coined, they were obliged to pay for it two per cent more than it was worth after coinage. But if there had been a seignorage of two per cent upon the coinage, the common gold currency, though two per cent below its standard weight, would notwithstanding have been equal in value to the quantity of standard gold which it ought to have contained; the value of the fashion compensating in this case the diminution of the weight. They would indeed have had the seignorage to pay, which being two per cent, their loss upon the whole transaction would have been two per cent exactly the same, but no greater than it actually was.

If the seignorage had been five per cent, and the gold currency only two per cent below its standard weight, the bank would in this case have gained three per cent upon the price of the bullion; but as they would have had a seignorage of five per cent to pay upon the coinage, their loss upon the whole transaction would, in the same manner, have been exactly two per cent.

If the seignorage had been only one per cent and the gold currency two per cent below its standard weight, the bank would in this case have lost only one per cent upon the price of the bullion; but as they would likewise have had a seignorage of one per cent to pay, their loss upon the whole transaction would have been exactly two per cent in the same manner as in all other cases.

If there was a reasonable seignorage, while at the same time the coin contained its full standard weight, as it has done very nearly since the last recoinage, whatever the bank might lose by the seignorage, they would gain upon the price of the bullion; and whatever they might gain upon the price of the bullion, they would lose by the seignorage. They would neither lose nor gain, therefore, upon the whole transaction, and they would in this, as in all the foregoing cases, be exactly in the same situation as if there was no seignorage.

When the tax upon a commodity is so moderate as not to encourage smuggling, the merchant who deals in it, though he advances, does not properly pay the tax, as he gets it back in the price of the commodity. The tax is finally paid by the last purchaser or consumer. But money is a commodity with regard to which every man is a merchant. Nobody buys it but in order to sell it again; and with regard to it there is in ordinary cases no last purchaser or consumer. When the tax upon coinage, therefore, is so moderate as not to encourage false coining, though everybody advances the tax, nobody finally pays it; because everybody gets it back in the advanced value of the coin.

A moderate seignorage, therefore, would not in any case augment the expense of the bank, or of any other private persons who carry their bullion to the mint in order to be coined, and the want of a moderate seignorage does not in any case diminish it. Whether there is or is not a seignorage, if the currency contains its full standard weight, the coinage costs nothing to anybody, and if it is short of that weight, the coinage must always cost the difference between the quantity of bullion which ought to be contained in it, and that which actually is contained in it.

The government, therefore, when it defrays the expense of coinage, not only incurs some small expense, but loses some small revenue which it might get by a proper duty; and neither the bank nor any other private persons are in the smallest degree benefited by this useless piece of public generosity.

The directors of the bank, however, would probably be unwilling to agree to the imposition of a seignorage upon the authority of a speculation which promises them no gain, but only pretends to insure them from any loss. In the present state of the gold coin, and as long as it continues to be received by weight, they certainly would gain nothing by such a change. But if the custom of weighing the gold coin should ever go into misuse, as it is very likely to do, and if the gold coin should ever fall into the same state of degradation in which it was before the late recoinage, the gain, or more properly the savings of the bank, in consequence of the imposition of a seignorage, would probably be very considerable. The Bank of England is the only company which sends any considerable quantity of bullion to the mint, and the burden of the annual coinage falls entirely, or almost entirely, upon it. If this annual coinage had nothing to do but to repair the unavoidable losses and necessary wear and tear of the coin, it

could seldom exceed fifty thousand or at most a hundred thousand pounds. But when the coin is degraded below its standard weight, the annual coinage must, besides this, fill up the large vacuities which exportation and the melting pot are continually making in the current coin. It was upon this account that during the ten or twelve years immediately preceding the late reformation of the gold coin, the annual coinage amounted at an average to more than eight hundred and fifty thousand pounds. But if there had been a seignorage of four or five per cent upon the gold coin, it would probably, even in the state in which things then were, have put an effectual stop to the business both of exportation and of the melting pot. The bank, instead of losing every year about two and a half per cent upon the bullion which was to be coined into more than eight hundred and fifty thousand pounds, or incurring an annual loss of more than twenty-one thousand two hundred and fifty pounds, would not probably have incurred the tenth part of that loss.

The revenue allotted by Parliament for defraying the expense of the coinage is but fourteen thousand pounds a year, and the real expense which it costs the government, or the fees of the officers of the mint, do not upon ordinary occasions, I am assured, exceed the half of that sum. The saving of so very small a sum, or even the gaining of another which could not well be much larger, are objects too inconsiderable, it may be thought, to deserve the serious attention of government. But the saving of eighteen or twenty thousand pounds a year in case of an event which is not improbable, which has frequently happened before, and which is very likely to happen again, is surely an object which well deserves the serious attention even of so great a company as the Bank of England.

Some of the foregoing reasonings and observations might perhaps have been more properly placed in those chapters of the first book which treat of the origin and use of money, and of the difference between the real and the nominal price of commodities. But as the law for the encouragement of coinage derives its origin from those vulgar prejudices which have been introduced by the mercantile system, I judged it more proper to reserve them for this chapter. Nothing could be more agreeable to the spirit of that system than a sort of bounty upon the production of money, the very thing which, it supposes, constitutes the wealth of every nation. It is one of its many admirable expedients for enriching the country.

Conclusion of the Mercantile System

Though the encouragement of exportation and the discouragement of importation are the two great engines by which the mercantile system proposes to enrich every country, yet with regard to some particular commodities it seems to follow an opposite plan: to discourage exportation and to encourage importation. Its ultimate object, however, it pretends, is always the same, to enrich the country by an advantageous balance of trade. It discourages the exportation of the materials of manufacture, and of the instruments of trade, in order to give our own workmen an advantage, and to enable them to undersell those of other nations in all foreign markets;

and by restraining, in this manner, the exportation of a few commodities, of no great price, it proposes to occasion a much greater and more valuable exportation of others. It encourages the importation of the materials of manufacture in order that our own people may be enabled to work them up more cheaply, and thereby prevent a greater and more valuable importation of the manufactured commodities. I do not observe, at least in our Statute Book, any encouragement given to the importation of the instruments of trade. When manufactures have advanced to a certain pitch of greatness, the fabrication of the instruments of trade becomes itself the object of a great number of very important manufactures. To give any particular encouragement to the importation of such instruments would interfere too much with the interest of those manufactures. Such importation, therefore, instead of being encouraged, has frequently been prohibited. Thus the importation of wool cards, except from Ireland, or when brought in as wreck or prize goods, was prohibited by the 3rd of Edward IV; which prohibition was renewed by the 39th of Elizabeth, and has been continued and rendered perpetual by subsequent laws.

The importation of the materials of manufacture has sometimes been encouraged by an exemption from the duties to which other goods are subject, and sometimes by bounties.

The importation of sheep's wool from several different countries, of cotton wool from all countries, of undressed flax, of the greater part of dyeing drugs, of the greater part of undressed hides from Ireland or the British colonies, of sealskins from the

British Greenland fishery, of pig and bar iron from the British colonies, as well as of several other materials of manufacture, has been encouraged by an exemption from all duties, if properly entered at the custom house. The private interest of our merchants and manufacturers may, perhaps, have extorted from the legislature these exemptions as well as the greater part of our other commercial regulations. They are, however, perfectly just and reasonable, and if, consistently with the necessities of the state, they could be extended to all the other materials of manufacture, the public would certainly be a gainer.

The avidity of our great manufacturers, however, has in some cases extended these exemptions a good deal beyond what can justly be considered as the rude materials of their work. By the 24th George III, c. 46, a small duty of only one penny the pound was imposed upon the importation of foreign brown linen yam, instead of much higher duties to which it had been subjected before, viz. of sixpence the pound upon sail yarn, of one shilling the pound upon all French and Dutch yarn, and of two pounds thirteen shillings and fourpence upon the hundredweight of all spruce or Muscovia yarn. But our manufacturers were not long satisfied with this reduction. By the 29th of the same king, c. 15, the same law which gave a bounty upon the exportation of British and Irish linen of which the price did not exceed eighteenpence the yard, even this small duty upon the importation of brown linen yarn was taken away. In the different operations, however, which are necessary for the preparation of linen yarn, a good deal more industry is employed than in the subsequent operation of preparing linen cloth from linen yarn. To say nothing of the industry of the flax-growers and flax-dressers, three or four spinners, at least, are necessary in order to keep one weaver in constant employment; and more than four-fifths of the whole quantity of labour necessary for the preparation of linen cloth is employed in that of linen yarn; but our spinners are poor people, women commonly scattered about in all different parts of the country, without support or protection. It is not by the sale of their work, but by that of the complete work of the weavers, that our great master manufacturers make their profits. As it is their interest to sell the complete manufacture as dear, so is it to buy the materials as cheap as possible. By extorting from the legislature bounties upon the exportation of their own linen, high duties upon the importation of all foreign linen, and a total prohibition of the home consumption of some sorts of French linen, they endeavour to sell their own goods as dear as possible. By encouraging the importation of foreign linen yarn, and thereby bringing it into competition with that which is made by our own people, they endeavour to buy the work of the poor spinners as cheap as possible. They are as intent to keep down the wages of their own weavers as the earnings of the poor spinners, and it is by no means for the benefit of the workman that they endeavour either to raise the price of the complete work or to lower that of the rude materials. It is the industry which is carried on for the benefit of the rich and the powerful that is principally encouraged by our mercantile system. That which is carried on for the benefit of the poor and the indigent is too often either neglected or oppressed.

Both the bounty upon the exportation of linen, and the exemption from duty upon the importation of foreign yarn, which were granted only for fifteen years, but continued by two different prolongations, expire with the end of the session of Parliament which shall immediately follow the 24th of June 1786.

The encouragement given to the importation of the materials of manufacture by bounties has been principally confined to such as were imported from our American plantations.

The first bounties of this kind were those granted about the beginning of the present century upon the importation of naval stores from America. Under this denomination were comprehended timber fit for masts, yards, and bowsprits; hemp; tar, pitch, and turpentine. The bounty, however, of one pound the ton upon masting-timber, and that of six pounds the ton upon hemp, were extended to such as should be imported into England from Scotland. Both these bounties continued without any variation, at the same rate, till they were severally allowed to expire; that upon hemp on the 1st of January 1741, and that upon masting-timber at the end of the session of Parliament immediately following the 24th June 1781.

The bounties upon the importation of tar, pitch, and turpentine underwent, during their continuance, several alterations. Originally that upon tar was four pounds the ton; that upon pitch the same; and that upon turpentine, three pounds the ton. The bounty of four pounds the ton upon tar was afterwards confined to such as had

been prepared in a particular manner; that upon other good, clean, and merchantable tar was reduced to two pounds four shillings the ton. The bounty upon pitch was likewise reduced to one pound; and that upon turpentine to one pound ten shillings the ton.

The second bounty upon the importation of any of the materials of manufacture, according to the order of time, was that granted by the 21st George II, c. 30, upon the importation of indigo from the British plantations. When the plantation indigo was worth three-fourths of the price of the best French indigo, it was by this act entitled to a bounty of sixpence the pound. This bounty, which, like most others, was granted only for a limited time, was continued by several prolongations, but was reduced to fourpence the pound. It was allowed to expire with the end of the session of Parliament which followed the 25th March 1781.

The third bounty of this kind was that granted (much about the time that we were beginning sometimes to court and sometimes to quarrel with our American colonies) by the 4th George III, c. 26, upon the importation of hemp, or undressed flax, from the British plantations. This bounty was granted for twenty-one years, from the 24th June 1764 to the 24th June 1785. For the first seven years it was to be at the rate of eight pounds the ton, for the second at six pounds, and for the third at four pounds. It was not extended to Scotland, of which the climate (although hemp is sometimes raised there in small quantities and of an inferior quality) is not very fit for that produce. Such a bounty upon the importation of Scotch flax into England would have been too great a discouragement to the native produce of the southern part of the United Kingdom.

The fourth bounty of this kind was that granted by the 5th George III, c. 45, upon the importation of wood from America. It was granted for nine years, from the 1st January 1766 to the 1st January 1775. During the first three years, it was to be for every hundred and twenty good deals, at the rate of one pound, and for every load containing fifty cubic feet of other squared timber at the rate of twelve shillings. For the second three years, it was for deals to be at the rate of fifteen shillings, and for other squared timber at the rate of eight shillings; and for the third three years, it was for deals to be at the rate of ten shillings, and for other squared timber at the rate of five shillings.

The fifth bounty of this kind was that granted by the 9th George III, c. 38, upon the importation of raw silk from the British plantations. It was granted for twenty-one years, from the 1st January 1770 to the 1st January 1791. For the first seven years it was to be at the rate of twenty-five pounds for every hundred pounds value; for the second at twenty pounds; and for the third at fifteen pounds. The management of the silk worm, and the preparation of silk, requires so much hand labour, and labour is so very dear in America that even this great bounty, I have been informed, was not likely to produce any considerable effect.

The sixth bounty of this kind was that granted by 2nd George III, c. 50, for the importation of pipe, hogshead, and barrel staves and heading from the British plantations. It was granted for nine years, from 1st January 1772 to the 1st January 1781. For the first three years it was for a certain quantity of each to be at the rate of six pounds; for the second three years at four pounds; and for the third three years at two pounds.

The seventh and last bounty of this kind was that granted by the 19th George III, c. 37, upon the importation of hemp from Ireland. It was granted in the same manner as that for the importation of hemp and undressed flax from America, for twenty-one years, from the 24th June 1779 to the 24th June 1800. This term is divided, likewise, into three periods of seven years each; and in each of those periods the rate of the Irish bounty is the same with that of the American. It does not, however, like the American bounty, extend to the importation of undressed flax. It would have been too great a discouragement to the cultivation of that plant in Great Britain. When this last bounty was granted, the British and Irish legislatures were not in much better humour with one another than the British and American had been before. But this boon to Ireland, it is to be hoped, has been granted under more fortunate auspices than all those to America.

The same commodities upon which we thus gave bounties when imported from America were subjected to considerable duties when imported from any other country. The interest of our American colonies was regarded as the same with that of the mother country. Their wealth was considered as our wealth. Whatever money was sent out to them, it was said, came all back to us by the balance of trade, and we could never become a farthing the poorer by any expense which we could lay out upon them. They were our own in every respect, and it was an expense laid out upon the improvement of our own property and for the profitable employment of our own people. It is necessary, I apprehend, at present to say anything further in order to expose the folly of a system which fatal experience has now sufficiently exposed. Had our American colonies really been a part of Great Britain, those bounties might have been considered as bounties upon production, and would still have been liable to all objections to which such bounties are liable, but to no other.

The exportation of the materials of manufacture is sometimes discouraged by absolute prohibitions, and sometimes by high duties.

Our woollen manufacturers have been more successful than any other class of workmen in persuading the legislature that the prosperity of the nation depended upon the success and extension of their particular business. They have not only obtained a monopoly against the consumers by an absolute prohibition of importing woollen cloths from any foreign country, but they have likewise obtained another monopoly against the sheep farmers and growers of wool by a similar prohibition of the exportation of live sheep and wool. The severity of many of the laws which have been enacted for the security of the revenue is very justly complained of, as imposing heavy penalties upon actions which, antecedent to the statutes that declared them to be crimes, had always been understood to be innocent. But the cruellest of our revenue laws, I will venture to affirm, are mild and gentle in comparison of some of those which the clamour of

our merchants and manufacturers has extorted from the legislature for the support of their own absurd and oppressive monopolies. Like the laws of Draco, these laws may be said to be all written in blood.

By the 8th of Elizabeth, c. 3, the exporter of sheep, lambs, or rams was for the first offence to forfeit all his goods for ever, to suffer a year's imprisonment, and then to have his left hand cut off in a market town upon a market day, to be there nailed up; and for the second offence to be adjudged a felon, and to suffer death accordingly. To prevent the breed of our sheep from being propagated in foreign countries seems to have been the object of this law. By the 13th and 14th of Charles II, c. 18, the exportation of wool was made felony, and the exporter subjected to the same penalties and forfeitures as a felon.

For the honour of the national humanity, it is to be hoped that neither of these statutes were ever executed. The first of them, however, so far as I know, has never been directly repealed, and Serjeant Hawkins seems to consider it as still in force. It may however, perhaps, be considered as virtually repealed by the 12th of Charles II, c. 32, sect. 3, which, without expressly taking away the penalties imposed by former statutes, imposes a new penalty, viz, that of twenty shillings for every sheep exported, or attempted to be exported, together with the forfeiture of the sheep and of the owner's share of the ship. The second of them was expressly repealed by the 7th and 8th of William III, c. 28, sect. 4. By which it is declared that, "Whereas the statute of the 13th and 14th of King Charles II, made against the exportation of wool, among other things in the said act mentioned, doth enact the same to be deemed felony; by the severity of which penalty the prosecution of offenders hath not been so effectually put in execution: Be it, therefore, enacted by the authority aforesaid, that so much of the said act, which relates to the making the said offence felony, be repealed and made void."

The penalties, however, which are either imposed by this milder statue, or which, though imposed by former statues, are not repealed by this one, are still sufficiently severe. Besides the forfeiture of the goods, the exporter incurs the penalty of three shillings for every pound weight of wool either exported or attempted to be exported, that is about four or five times the value. Any merchant or other person convicted of this offence is disabled from requiring any debt or account belonging to him from any factor or other person. Let his fortune be what it will, whether he is or is not able to pay those heavy penalties, the law means to ruin him completely. But as the morals of the great body of the people are not yet so corrupt as those of the contrivers of this statute, I have not heard that any advantage has ever been taken of this clause. If the person convicted of this offence is not able to pay the penalties within three months after judgment, he is to be transported for seven years, and if he returns before the expiration of that term, he is liable to the pains of felony, without benefit of clergy. The owner of the ship, knowing this offence, forfeits all his interest in the ship and furniture. The master and mariners, knowing this offence, forfeit all their goods and chattels, and suffer three months' imprisonment. By a sub-

sequent statute the master suffers six months' imprisonment.

In order to prevent exportation, the whole inland commerce of wool is laid under very burdensome and oppressive restrictions. It cannot be packed in any box, barrel, cask, case, chest, or any other package, but only in packs of leather or pack-cloth, on which must be marked on the outside the words wool or yam, in large letters not less than three inches long, on pain of forfeiting the same and the package, and three shillings for every pound weight, to be paid by the owner or packer. It cannot be loaden on any horse or cart, or carried by land within five miles of the coast, but between sun-rising and sun-setting, on pain of forfeiting the same, the horses and carriages. The hundred next adjoining to the sea-coast, out of or through which the wool is carried or exported, forfeits twenty pounds; if the wool is under the value of ten pounds; and if of greater value, then treble that value, together with treble costs, to be sued for within the year. The execution to be against any two of the inhabitants, whom the sessions must reimburse, by an assessment on the other inhabitants, as in the cases of robbery. And if any person compounds with the hundred for less than this penalty, he is to be imprisoned for five years; and any other person may prosecute. These regulations take place through the whole kingdom.

But in the particular counties of Kent and Sussex, the restrictions are still more troublesome. Every owner of wool within ten miles of the sea-coast must given an account in writing, three days after shearing to the next officer of the customs, of the number of his fleeces, and of the places where they are lodged. And before he removes any part of them he must give the like notice of the number and weight of the fleeces, and of the name and abode of the person to whom they are sold, and of the place to which it is intended they should be carried. No person within fifteen miles of the sea, in the said counties, can buy any wool before he enters into bond to the king that no part of the wool which he shall so buy shall be sold by him to any other person within fifteen miles of the sea. If any wool is found carrying towards the sea-side in the said counties, unless it has been entered and security given as aforesaid, it is forfeited, and the offender also forfeits three shillings for every pound weight. If any person lays any wool not entered as aforesaid within fifteen miles of the sea, it must be seized and forfeited; and if, after such seizure, any person claim the same, he must give security to the Exchequer that if he is cast upon trial he shall pay treble costs, besides all other penalties.

When such restrictions are imposed upon the inland trade, the coasting trade, we may believe, cannot be left very free. Every owner of wool who carries or causes to be carried any wool to any port or place on the seacoast, in order to be from thence transported by sea to any other place or port on the coast, must first cause an entry thereof to be made at the port from whence it is intended to be conveyed, containing the weight, marks, and number of the packages, before he brings the same within five miles of that port, on pain of forfeiting the same, and also the horses, carts, and other carriages; and also of suffering and forfeiting as by the other laws in force against the ex-

portation of wool. This law, however (1st William III, c. 32), is so very indulgent as to declare that, "This shall not hinder any person from carrying his wool home from the place of shearing, though it be within five miles of the sea, provided that in ten days after shearing, and before he remove the wool, he do under his hand certify to the next officer of the customs, the true number of fleeces, and where it is housed; and do not remove the same, without certifying to such officer, under his hand, his intention so to do, three days before." Bond must be given that the wool to be carried coastways is to be landed at the particular port for which it is entered outwards; and if any part of it is landed without the presence of an officer, not only the forfeiture of the wool is incurred as in other goods, but the usual additional penalty of three shillings for every pound weight is likewise incurred.

Our woollen manufacturers, in order to justify their demand of such extraordinary restrictions and regulations, confidently asserted that English wool was of a peculiar quality, superior to that of any other country; that the wool of other countries could not, without some mixture of it, be wrought up into any tolerable manufacture; that fine cloth could not be made without it; that England, therefore, if the exportation of it could be totally prevented, could monopolize to herself almost the whole woollen trade of the world; and thus, having no rivals, could sell at what price she pleased, and in a short time acquire the most incredible degree of wealth by the most advantageous balance of trade. This doctrine, like most other doctrines which are confidently asserted by any considerable number of people, was, and still continues to be, most implicitly believed by a much greater number- by almost all those who are either unacquainted with the woollen trade, or who have not made particular inquiries. It is, however, so perfectly false that English wool is in any respect necessary for the making of fine cloth that it is altogether unfit for it. Fine cloth is made altogether of Spanish wool. English wool cannot be even so mixed with Spanish wool as to enter into the composition without spoiling and degrading, in some degree, the fabric of the cloth.

It has been shown in the foregoing part of this work that the effect of these regulations has been to depress the price of English wool, not only below what it naturally would be in the present times, but very much below what it actually was in the time of Edward III. The price of Scots wool, when in consequence of the union it became subject to the same regulations, is said to have fallen about one half. It is observed by the very accurate and intelligent author of the *Memoirs of Wool*, the Reverend Mr. John Smith, that the price of the best English wool in England is generally below what wool of a very inferior quality commonly sells for in the market of Amsterdam. To depress the price of this commodity below what may be called its natural and proper price was the avowed purpose of those regulations; and there seems to be no doubt of their having produced the effect that was expected from them.

This reduction of price, it may perhaps be thought, by discouraging the growing of wool, must have reduced very much the annual produce of that commodity, though not below what it formerly was, yet below what, in the present state of things, it probably would have been, had it, in consequence of an open and free market, been allowed to rise to the natural and proper price. I am, however, disposed to believe that the quantity of the annual produce cannot have been much, though it may perhaps have been a little, affected by these regulations. The growing of wool is not the chief purpose for which the sheep farmer employs his industry and stock. He expects his profit not so much from the price of the fleece as from that of the carcass; and the average or ordinary price of the latter must even, in many cases, make up to him whatever deficiency there may be in the average or ordinary price of the former. It has been observed in the foregoing part of this work that, "Whatever regulations tend to sink the price, either of wool or of raw hides, below what it naturally would be, must, in an improved and cultivated country, have some tendency to raise the price of butcher's meat. The price both of the great and small cattle which are fed on improved and cultivated land must be sufficient to pay the rent which the landlord, and the profit which the farmer has reason to expect from improved and cultivated land. If it is not, they will soon cease to feed them. Whatever part of this price, therefore, is not paid by the wool and the hide must be paid by the carcass. The less there is paid for the one, the more must be paid for the other. In what manner this price is to be divided upon the different parts of the beast is indifferent to the landlords and farmers, provided it is all paid to them. In an improved and cultivated country, therefore, their interest as landlords and farmers cannot be much affected by such regulations, though their interest as consumers may by the rise in the price of provisions." According to this reasoning, therefore, this degradation in the price of wool is not likely, in an improved and cultivated country, to occasion any diminution in the annual produce of that commodity, except so far as, by raising the price of mutton, it may somewhat diminish the demand for, and consequently the production of, that particular species of butcher's meat. Its effect, however, even in this way, it is probable, is not very considerable.

But though its effect upon the quantity of the annual produce may not have been very considerable, its effect upon the quality, it may perhaps be thought, must necessarily have been very great. The degradation in the quality of English wool, if not below what it was in former times, yet below what it naturally would have been in the present state of improvement and cultivation, must have been, it may perhaps be supposed, very nearly in proportion to the degradation of price. As the quality depends upon the breed, upon the pasture, and upon the management and cleanliness of the sheep, during the whole progress of the growth of the fleece, the attention to these circumstances, it may naturally enough be imagined, can never be greater than in proportion to the recompense which the price of the fleece is likely to make for the labour and expense which that attention requires. It happens, however, that the goodness of the fleece depends, in a great measure, upon the health, growth, and bulk of the animal; the same attention which is necessary for the improvement of the carcase is, in some respects, sufficient for that of the fleece. Notwithstanding the degradation of price, English wool is said to have been improved considerably during the course even of the present century. The improvement might perhaps have been greater if the price had been better; but the lowness of price, though it may have obstructed, yet certainly it has not altogether prevented that improvement.

The violence of these regulations, therefore, seems to have affected neither the quantity nor the quality of the annual produce of wool so much as it might have been expected to do (though I think it probable that it may have affected the latter a good deal more than the former); and the interest of the growers of wool, though it must have been hurt in some degree, seems, upon the whole, to have been much less hurt than could well have been imagined.

These considerations, however, will not justify the absolute prohibition of the exportation of wool. But they will fully justify the imposition of a considerable tax upon that exportation.

To hurt in any degree the interest of any one order of citizens, for no other purpose but to promote that of some other, is evidently contrary to that justice and equality of treatment which the sovereign owes to all the different orders of his subjects. But the prohibition certainly hurts, in some degree, the interest of the growers of wool, for no other purpose but to promote that of the manufacturers.

Every different order of citizens is bound to contribute to the support of the sovereign or commonwealth. A tax of five, or even of ten shillings upon the exportation of every ton of wool would produce a very considerable revenue to the sovereign. It would hurt the interest of the growers somewhat less than the prohibition, because it would not probably lower the price of wool quite so much. It would afford a sufficient advantage to the manufacturer, because, though he might not buy his wool altogether so cheap as under the prohibition, he would still buy it, at least, five or ten shillings cheaper than any foreign manufacturer could buy it, besides saving the freight and insurance, which the other would be obliged to pay. It is scarce possible to devise a tax which could produce any considerable revenue to the sovereign, and at the same time occasion so little inconveniency to anybody.

The prohibition, notwithstanding all the penalties which guard it, does not prevent the exportation of wool. It is exported, it is well known, in great quantities. The great difference between the price in the home and that in the foreign market presents such a temptation to smuggling that all the rigour of the law cannot prevent it. This illegal exportation is advantageous to nobody but the smuggler. A legal exportation subject to a tax, by affording a revenue to the sovereign, and thereby saving the imposition of some other, perhaps, more burdensome and inconvenient taxes might prove advantageous to all the different subjects of the state.

The exportation of fuller's earth or fuller's clay, supposed to be necessary for preparing and cleansing the woolen manufacturers, has been subjected to nearly the same penalties as the exportation of wool. Even tobacco-pipe clay, though acknowledged to be different from fuller's clay, yet, on account of their resemblance, and because fuller's clay might sometimes be exported as tobacco-pipe clay, has been laid under the same prohibitions and penalties.

By the 13th and 14th of Charles II, c. 7, the exportation, not only of raw hides, but of tanned leather, except in the shape of boots, shoes, or slippers, was prohibited; and the law gave a monopoly to our bootmakers and shoemakers, not only against our graziers, but against our tanners. By subsequent statutes our tanners have got themselves exempted from this monopoly upon paying a small tax of only one shilling on the hundred-weight of tanned leather, weighing one hundred and twelve pounds. They have obtained likewise the drawback of two-thirds of the excise duties imposed upon their commodity even when exported without further manufacture. All manufacturers of leather may be exported duty free; and the exporter is besides entitled to the drawback of the whole duties of excise. Our graziers still continue subject to the old monopoly. Graziers separated from one another, and dispersed through all the different corners of the country, cannot, without great difficulty, combine together for the purpose either of imposing monopolies upon their fellow citizens, or for exempting themselves from such as may have been imposed upon them by other people. Manufacturers of all kinds, collected together in numerous bodies in all great cities, easily can. Even the horns of cattle are prohibited to be exported; and the two insignificant trades of the horner and combmaker enjoy, in this respect, a monopoly against the graziers.

Restraints, either by prohibitions or by taxes, upon the exportation of goods which are partially, but not completely manufactured, are not peculiar to the manufacture of leather. As long as anything remains to be done, in order to fit any commodity for immediate use and consumption, our manufacturers think that they themselves ought to have the doing of it. Woolen yarn and worsted are prohibited to be exported under the same penalties as wool. Even white cloths are subject to a duty upon exportation, and our dyers have so far obtained a monopoly against our clothiers. Our clothiers would probably have been able to defend themselves against it, but it happens that the greater part of our principal clothiers are themselves likewise dyers. Watch cases, clockcases, and dial-plates for clocks and watches have been prohibited to be exported. Our clock-makers and watch-makers are, it seems, unwilling that the price of this sort of workmanship should be raised upon them by the competition of foreigners.

By some old statutes of Edward III, Henry VIII, and Edward VI, the exportation of all metals was prohibited. Lead and tin were alone expected probably on account of the great abundance of those metals, in the exportation of which a considerable part of the trade of the kingdom in those days consisted. For the encouragement of the mining trade, the 5th of William and Mary, c. 17, exempted from the prohibition iron, copper, and mundic metal made from British ore. The exportation of all sorts of copper bars, foreign as well as British, was afterwards permitted by the 9th and 10th of William III, c. 26. The exportation of unmanufactured brass, of what is called gun-metal, bell-metal, and shroff-metal, still continues to be pro-

hibited. Brass manufactures of all sorts may be exported duty free.

The exportation of the materials of manufacture, where it is not altogether prohibited, is in many cases subjected to considerable duties.

By the 8th George I, c. 15, the exportation of all goods, the produce or manufacture of Great Britain, upon which any duties had been imposed by former statutes, was rendered duty free. The following goods, however, were excepted: alum, lead, lead ore, tin, tanned leather, copperas, coals, wool cards, white woolen cloths, lapis calaminaris, skins of all sorts, glue, coney hair or wool, hares' wool, hair of all sorts, horses, and litharge of lead. If you expect horses, all these are either materials of manufacture, or incomplete manufactures (which may be considered as materials for still further manufacture), or instruments of trade. This statute leaves them subject to all the old duties which had ever been imposed upon them, the old subsidy and one per cent outwards.

By the same statute a great number of foreign drugs for dyers' use are exempted from all duties upon importation. Each of them, however, is afterwards subjected to a certain duty, not indeed a very heavy one, upon exportation. Our dyers, it seems, while they thought it for their interest to encourage the importation of those drugs, by an exemption from all duties, thought it likewise for their interest to throw some small discouragement upon their exportation. The avidity, however, which suggested this notable piece of mercantile ingenuity, most probably disappointed itself of its object. It necessarily taught the importers to be more careful than they might otherwise have been that their importation should not exceed what was necessary for the supply of the home market. The home market was at all times likely to be more scantily supplied; the commodities were at all times likely to be somewhat dearer there than they would have been had the exportation been rendered as free as the importation.

By the above-mentioned statute, gum senega, or gum arabic, being among the enumerated dyeing drugs, might be imported duty free. They were subjected, indeed, to a small poundage duty, amounting only to threepence in the hundredweight upon their re-exportation. France enjoyed, at that time, an exclusive trade to the country most productive of those drugs, that which lies in the neighbourhood of the Senegal; and the British market could not easily be supplied by the immediate importation of them from the place of growth. By the 25th George II, therefore, gun senega was allowed to be imported (contrary to the general dispositions of the Act of Navigation) from any part of Europe. As the law, however, did not mean to encourage this species of trade, so contrary to the general principles of the mercantile policy of England, it imposed a duty of ten shillings the hundredweight upon such importation, and no part of this duty was to be afterwards drawn back upon its exportation. The successful war which began in 1755 gave Great Britain the same exclusive trade to those countries which France had enjoyed before. Our manufacturers, as soon as the peace was made, endeavoured to avail themselves of this advantage, and to establish a monopoly in their own favour both against the growers and against the importers of this commodity. By the 5th George III, therefore, c. 37, the exportation of gum senega from his Majesty's dominions in Africa was confined to Great Britain, and was subjected to all the same restrictions, regulations, forfeitures, and penalties as that of the enumerated commodities of the British colonies in America and the West Indies. Its importation, indeed, was subjected to a small duty of sixpence the hundredweight, but its re-exportation was subjected to the enormous duty of one pound ten shillings the hundredweight. It was the intention of our manufacturers that the whole produce of those countries should be imported into Great Britain, and, in order that they themselves might be enabled to buy it at their own price, that no part of it should be exported again but at such an expense as would sufficiently discourage that exportation. Their avidity, however, upon this, as well as upon many other occasions, disappointed itself of its object. This enormous duty presented such a temptation to smuggling that great quantities of this commodity were clandestinely exported, probably to all the manufacturing countries of Europe, put particularly to Holland, not only from Great Britain but from Africa. Upon this account, by the 14th George III, c. 10, this duty upon exportation was reduced to five shillings the hundredweight.

In the book of rates, according to which the Old Subsidy was levied, beaver skins were estimated at six shillings and eightpence a piece, and the different subsidies and imposts, which before the year 1722 had been laid upon their importation, amounted to one-fifth part of the rate, or to sixteen-pence upon each skin; all of which, except half the Old Subsidy, amounting only to twopence, was drawn back upon exportation. This duty upon the importation of so important a material of manufacture had been thought too high, and in the year 1722 the rate was reduced to two shillings and sixpence, which reduced the duty upon importation to sixpence, and of this only one half was to be drawn back upon exportation. The same successful war put the country most productive of beaver under the dominion of Great Britain, and beaver skins being among the enumerated commodities, their exportation from America was consequently confined to the market of Great Britain. Our manufacturers soon bethought themselves of the advantage which they might make of this circumstance, and in the year 1764 the duty upon the importation of beaver-skin was reduced to one penny, but the duty upon exportation was raised to sevenpence each skin, without any drawback of the duty upon importation. By the same law, a duty of eighteenpence the pound was imposed upon the exportation of beaverwool or wombs, without making any alteration in the duty upon the importation of that commodity, which, when imported by Britain and in British shipping, amounted at that time to between fourpence and fivepence the piece.

Coals may be considered both as a material of manufacture and as an instrument of trade. Heavy duties, accordingly, have been imposed upon their exportation, amounting at present (1783) to more than five shillings the ton, or to more than fifteen shillings the chaldron, Newcastle measures, which is in most cases more than the original value of the commodity at the coal pit, or even at the shipping port for exportation.

The exportation, however, of the instruments of trade, properly so called, is commonly restrained, not by high duties, but by absolute prohibitions. Thus by the 7th and 8th of William III, c. 20, sect. 8, the exportation of frames or engines for knitting gloves or stockings is prohibited under the penalty, not only of the forfeiture of such frames or engines so exported, or attempted to be exported, but of forty pounds, one half to the king, the other to the person who shall inform or sue for the same. In the same manner, by the 14th George III, c. 71, the exportation to foreign parts of any utensils made use of in the cotton, linen, woollen, and silk manufactures is prohibited under the penalty, not only of the forfeiture of such utensils, but of two hundred pounds, to be paid by the person who shall offend in this manner, and likewise of two hundred pounds to be paid by the master of the ship who shall knowingly suffer such utensils to be loaded on board his ship.

When such heavy penalties were imposed upon the exportation of the dead instruments of trade, it could not well be expected that the living instrument, the artificer, should be allowed to go free. Accordingly, by the 5th George I, c. 27, the person who shall be convicted of enticing any artificer of, or in any of the manufactures of Great Britain, to go into any foreign parts in order to practise or teach his trade, is liable for the first offence to be fined in any sum not exceeding one hundred pounds, and to three months' imprisonment, and until the fine shall be paid; and for the second offence, to be fined in any sum at the discretion of the court, and to imprisonment for twelve months, and until the fine shall be paid. By the 23rd George II, c. 13, this penalty is increased for the first offence to five hundred pounds for every artificer so enticed, and to twelve months' imprisonment, and until the fine shall be paid; and for the second offence, to one thousand pounds, and to two years' imprisonment, and until the fine shall be paid.

By the former of those two statutes, upon proof that any person has been enticing any artificer, or that any artificer has promised or contracted to go into foreign parts for the purposes aforesaid, such artificer may be obliged to give security at the discretion of the court that he shall not go beyond the seas, and may be committed to prison until he give such security.

If any artificer has gone beyond the seas, and is exercising or teaching his trade in any foreign country, upon warning being given to him by any of his Majesty's ministers or consuls abroad, or by one of his Majesty's Secretaries of State for the time being, if he does not, within six months after such warning, return into this realm, and from thenceforth abide and inhabit continually within the same, he is from thenceforth declared incapable of taking any legacy devised to him within this kingdom, or of being executor or administrator to any person, or of taking any lands within this kingdom by descent, device, or purchase. He likewise forfeits to the king all his lands, goods, and chattels, is declared an alien in every respect, and is put out of the king's protection.

It is unnecessary, I imagine, to observe how contrary such regulations are to the boasted liberty of the subject, of which we affect to be so very jealous; but which, in this case, is so plainly sacrificed to the futile interests of our merchants and manufacturers.

The laudable motive of all these regulations is to extend our own manufacturers, not by their own improvement, but by the depression of those of all our neighbours, and by putting an end, as much as possible, to the troublesome competition of such odious and disagreeable rivals. Our master manufacturers think it reasonable that they themselves should have the monopoly of the ingenuity of all their countrymen. Though by restraining, in some trades, the number of apprentices which can be employed at one time, and by imposing the necessity of a long apprenticeship in all trades, they endeavour, all of them, to confine the knowledge of their respective employments to as small a number as possible; they are unwilling, however, that any part of this small number should go abroad to instruct foreigners.

Consumption is the sole end and purpose of all production; and the interest of the producer ought to be attended to only so far as it may be necessary for promoting that of the consumer. The maxim is so perfectly self evident that it would be absurd to attempt to prove it. But in the mercantile system the interest of the consumer is almost constantly sacrificed to that of the producer; and it seems to consider production, and not consumption, as the ultimate end and object of all industry and commerce.

In the restraints upon the importation of all foreign commodities which can come into competition with those of our own growth or manufacture, the interest of the home consumer is evidently sacrificed to that of the producer. It is altogether for the benefit of the latter that the former is obliged to pay that enhancement of price which this monopoly almost always occasions.

It is altogether for the benefit of the producer that bounties are granted upon the exportation of some of his productions. The home consumer is obliged to pay, first, the tax which is necessary for paying the bounty, and secondly, the still greater tax which necessarily arises from the enhancement of the price of the commodity in the home market.

By the famous treaty of commerce with Portugal, the consumer is prevented by high duties from purchasing of a neighbouring country a commodity which our own climate does not produce, but is obliged to purchase it of a distant country, though it is acknowledged that the commodity of the distant country is of a worse quality than that of the near one. The home consumer is obliged to submit to this inconveniency in order that the producer may import into the distant country some of his productions upon more advantageous terms than he would otherwise have been allowed to do. The consumer, too, is obliged to pay whatever enhancement in the price if those very productions this forced exportation may occasion in the home market.

But in the system of laws which has been established for the management of our American and West Indian colonies, the interest of the home consumer has been sacrificed to that of the producer with a more extravagant profusion than in all our other commercial regulations. A great empire has been established for the sole purpose of raising up a nation of customers who should be obliged to buy from the shops of our different producers all the goods with which these could supply them. For the sake of that little enhancement of price which this monopoly might afford our producers, the home consumers have been burdened with the whole expense of maintaining and defending that empire. For this purpose, and for this purpose only, in the two last wars, more than two hundred millions have been spent, and a new debt of more than a hundred and seventy millions has been contracted over and above all that had been expended for the same purpose in former wars. The interest of this debt alone is not only greater than the whole extraordinary profit which it ever could be pretended was made by the monopoly of the colony trade, but than the whole value of that trade, or than the whole value of the goods which at an average have been annually exported to the colonies.

It cannot be very difficult to determine who have been the contrivers of this whole mercantile system; not the consumers, we may believe, whose interest has been entirely neglected; but the producers, whose interest has been so carefully attended to; and among this latter class our merchants and manufacturers have been by far the principal architects. In the mercantile regulations, which have been taken notice of in this chapter, the interest of our manufacturers has been most peculiarly attended to; and the interest, not so much of the consumers, as that of some other sets of producers, has been sacrificed to it.

See also: **Vol. I**: American Revolution; Capitalism; Colonial administration; Free trade; Franklin, Benjamin; Great Britain; Mercantilism; Navigation and Trade Acts; Smith, Adam. **Vol. III**: Tariff of 1789.

The Federalist (Federalist Papers)

While the states debated and examined the proposed U.S. Constitution, many New Yorkers resisted the idea of forming a stronger centralized government. To persuade fellow citizens of the strengths of a federal governing body versus the weaknesses of the Articles of Confederation, Alexander Hamilton, along with James Madison and John Jay, wrote a series of eighty-five articles that collectively became known as The Federalist. *The following articles, all written by Hamilton (as "Publius"), deal with issues involving commerce, trade, or forms of taxation including tariffs. Although* The Federalist *had little effect on the ratification process, the documents illustrate the impact of Adam Smith's ideas on Hamilton during this early period.*

Federalist No. 11

The Utility of the Union in Respect to Commercial Relations and a Navy

For the *Independent Journal.*

Author: Alexander Hamilton

To the People of the State of New York:

THE importance of the Union, in a commercial light, is one of those points about which there is least room to entertain a difference of opinion, and which has, in fact, commanded the most general assent of men who have any acquaintance with the subject. This applies as well to our intercourse with foreign countries as with each other.

There are appearances to authorize a supposition that the adventurous spirit, which distinguishes the commercial character of America, has already excited uneasy sensations in several of the maritime powers of Europe. They seem to be apprehensive of our too great interference in that carrying trade, which is the support of their navigation and the foundation of their naval strength. Those of them which have colonies in America look forward to what this country is capable of becoming, with painful solicitude.

They foresee the dangers that may threaten their American dominions from the neighborhood of States, which have all the dispositions, and would possess all the means, requisite to the creation of a powerful marine. Impressions of this kind will naturally indicate the policy of fostering divisions among us, and of depriving us, as far as possible, of an ACTIVE COMMERCE in our own bottoms. This would answer the threefold purpose of preventing our interference in their navigation, of monopolizing the profits of our trade, and of clipping the wings by which we might soar to a dangerous greatness. Did not prudence forbid the detail, it would not be difficult to trace, by facts, the workings of this policy to the cabinets of ministers.

If we continue united, we may counteract a policy so unfriendly to our prosperity in a variety of ways. By prohibitory regulations, extending, at the same time, throughout the States, we may oblige foreign countries to bid against each other, for the privileges of our markets. This assertion will not appear chimerical to those who are able to appreciate the importance of the markets of three millions of people— increasing in rapid progression, for the most part exclusively addicted to agriculture, and likely from local circumstances to remain so—to any manufacturing nation; and the immense difference there would be to the trade and navigation of such a nation, between a direct communication in its own ships, and an indirect conveyance of its products and returns, to and from America, in the ships of another country. Suppose, for instance, we had a government in America, capable of excluding Great Britain (with whom we

have at present no treaty of commerce) from all our ports; what would be the probable operation of this step upon her politics? Would it not enable us to negotiate, with the fairest prospect of success, for commercial privileges of the most valuable and extensive kind, in the dominions of that kingdom? When these questions have been asked, upon other occasions, they have received a plausible, but not a solid or satisfactory answer. It has been said that prohibitions on our part would produce no change in the system of Britain, because she could prosecute her trade with us through the medium of the Dutch, who would be her immediate customers and paymasters for those articles which were wanted for the supply of our markets. But would not her navigation be materially injured by the loss of the important advantage of being her own carrier in that trade? Would not the principal part of its profits be intercepted by the Dutch, as a compensation for their agency and risk? Would not the mere circumstance of freight occasion a considerable deduction? Would not so circuitous an intercourse facilitate the competitions of other nations, by enhancing the price of British commodities in our markets, and by transferring to other hands the management of this interesting branch of the British commerce?

A mature consideration of the objects suggested by these questions will justify a belief that the real disadvantages to Britain from such a state of things, conspiring with the pre-possessions of a great part of the nation in favor of the American trade, and with the importunities of the West India islands, would produce a relaxation in her present system, and would let us into the enjoyment of privileges in the markets of those islands and elsewhere, from which our trade would derive the most substantial benefits. Such a point gained from the British government, and which could not be expected without an equivalent in exemptions and immunities in our markets, would be likely to have a correspondent effect on the conduct of other nations, who would not be inclined to see themselves altogether supplanted in our trade.

A further resource for influencing the conduct of European nations towards us, in this respect, would arise from the establishment of a federal navy. There can be no doubt that the continuance of the Union under an efficient government, would put it in our power, at a period not very distant, to create a navy which, if it could not vie with those of the great maritime powers, would at least be of respectable weight if thrown into the scale of either of two contending parties. This would be more peculiarly the case in relation to operations in the West Indies. A few ships of the line, sent opportunely to the reinforcement of either side, would often be sufficient to decide the fate of a campaign, on the event of which interests of the greatest magnitude were suspended. Our position is, in this respect, a most commanding one. And if to this consideration we add that of the usefulness of supplies from this country, in the prosecution of military operations in the West Indies, it will readily be perceived that a situation so favorable would enable us to bargain with great advantage for commercial privileges. A price would be set not only upon our friendship, but upon

our neutrality. By a steady adherence to the Union, we may hope, erelong, to become the arbiter of Europe in America, and to be able to incline the balance of European competitions in this part of the world as our interest may dictate.

But in the reverse of this eligible situation, we shall discover that the rivalships of the parts would make them checks upon each other, and would frustrate all the tempting advantages which nature has kindly placed within our reach. In a state so insignificant our commerce would be a prey to the wanton intermeddlings of all nations at war with each other; who, having nothing to fear from us, would with little scruple or remorse supply their wants by depredations on our property as often as it fell in their way. The rights of neutrality will only be respected when they are defended by an adequate power. A nation, despicable by its weakness, forfeits even the privilege of being neutral.

Under a vigorous national government, the natural strength and resources of the country, directed to a common interest, would baffle all the combinations of European jealousy to restrain our growth. This situation would even take away the motive to such combinations, by inducing an impracticability of success. An active commerce, an extensive navigation, and a flourishing marine would then be the offspring of moral and physical necessity. We might defy the little arts of the little politicians to control or vary the irresistible and unchangeable course of nature.

But in a state of disunion, these combinations might exist and might operate with success. It would be in the power of the maritime nations, availing themselves of our universal impotence, to prescribe the conditions of our political existence; and as they have a common interest in being our carriers, and still more in preventing our becoming theirs, they would in all probability combine to embarrass our navigation in such a manner as would in effect destroy it, and confine us to a PASSIVE COMMERCE. We should then be compelled to content ourselves with the first price of our commodities, and to see the profits of our trade snatched from us to enrich our enemies and persecutors. That unequaled spirit of enterprise, which signalizes the genius of the American merchants and navigators, and which is in itself an inexhaustible mine of national wealth, would be stifled and lost, and poverty and disgrace would overspread a country which, with wisdom, might make herself the admiration and envy of the world.

There are rights of great moment to the trade of America which are rights of the Union—I allude to the fisheries, to the navigation of the Western lakes, and to that of the Mississippi. The dissolution of the Confederacy would give room for delicate questions concerning the future existence of these rights; which the interest of more powerful partners would hardly fail to solve to our disadvantage. The disposition of Spain with regard to the Mississippi needs no comment. France and Britain are concerned with us in the fisheries, and view them as of the utmost moment to their navigation. They, of course, would hardly remain long indifferent to that decided mastery, of which experience has shown us to be possessed in this valuable branch

of traffic, and by which we are able to undersell those nations in their own markets. What more natural than that they should be disposed to exclude from the lists such dangerous competitors?

This branch of trade ought not to be considered as a partial benefit. All the navigating States may, in different degrees, advantageously participate in it, and under circumstances of a greater extension of mercantile capital, would not be unlikely to do it. As a nursery of seamen, it now is, or, when time shall have more nearly assimilated the principles of navigation in the several States, will become, a universal resource. To the establishment of a navy, it must be indispensable.

To this great national object, a NAVY, union will contribute in various ways. Every institution will grow and flourish in proportion to the quantity and extent of the means concentred towards its formation and support. A navy of the United States, as it would embrace the resources of all, is an object far less remote than a navy of any single State or partial confederacy, which would only embrace the resources of a single part. It happens, indeed, that different portions of confederated America possess each some peculiar advantage for this essential establishment. The more southern States furnish in greater abundance certain kinds of naval stores—tar, pitch, and turpentine. Their wood for the construction of ships is also of a more solid and lasting texture. The difference in the duration of the ships of which the navy might be composed, if chiefly constructed of Southern wood, would be of signal importance, either in the view of naval strength or of national economy. Some of the Southern and of the Middle States yield a greater plenty of iron, and of better quality. Seamen must chiefly be drawn from the Northern hive. The necessity of naval protection to external or maritime commerce does not require a particular elucidation, no more than the conduciveness of that species of commerce to the prosperity of a navy.

An unrestrained intercourse between the States themselves will advance the trade of each by an interchange of their respective productions, not only for the supply of reciprocal wants at home, but for exportation to foreign markets. The veins of commerce in every part will be replenished, and will acquire additional motion and vigor from a free circulation of the commodities of every part. Commercial enterprise will have much greater scope, from the diversity in the productions of different States. When the staple of one fails from a bad harvest or unproductive crop, it can call to its aid the staple of another. The variety, not less than the value, of products for exportation contributes to the activity of foreign commerce. It can be conducted upon much better terms with a large number of materials of a given value than with a small number of materials of the same value; arising from the competitions of trade and from the fluctuations of markets. Particular articles may be in great demand at certain periods, and unsalable at others; but if there be a variety of articles, it can scarcely happen that they should all be at one time in the latter predicament, and on this account the operations of the merchant would be less liable to any considerable obstruction or stagnation. The speculative trader will at once perceive the force of

these observations, and will acknowledge that the aggregate balance of the commerce of the United States would bid fair to be much more favorable than that of the thirteen States without union or with partial unions.

It may perhaps be replied to this, that whether the States are united or disunited, there would still be an intimate intercourse between them which would answer the same ends; this intercourse would be fettered, interrupted, and narrowed by a multiplicity of causes, which in the course of these papers have been amply detailed. A unity of commercial, as well as political, interests, can only result from a unity of government.

There are other points of view in which this subject might be placed, of a striking and animating kind. But they would lead us too far into the regions of futurity, and would involve topics not proper for a newspaper discussion. I shall briefly observe, that our situation invites and our interests prompt us to aim at an ascendant in the system of American affairs. The world may politically, as well as geographically, be divided into four parts, each having a distinct set of interests. Unhappily for the other three, Europe, by her arms and by her negotiations, by force and by fraud, has, in different degrees, extended her dominion over them all. Africa, Asia, and America, have successively felt her domination. The superiority she has long maintained has tempted her to plume herself as the Mistress of the World, and to consider the rest of mankind as created for her benefit. Men admired as profound philosophers have, in direct terms, attributed to her inhabitants a physical superiority, and have gravely asserted that all animals, and with them the human species, degenerate in America—that even dogs cease to bark after having breathed awhile in our atmosphere.[1] Facts have too long supported these arrogant pretensions of the Europeans. It belongs to us to vindicate the honor of the human race, and to teach that assuming brother, moderation. Union will enable us to do it. Disunion will add another victim to his triumphs. Let Americans disdain to be the instruments of European greatness! Let the thirteen States, bound together in a strict and indissoluble Union, concur in erecting one great American system, superior to the control of all transatlantic force or influence, and able to dictate the terms of the connection between the old and the new world!

PUBLIUS.

1. "Recherches philosophiques sur les Americains."

Federalist No. 12

The Utility of the Union In Respect to Revenue

From the *New York Packet*.

Tuesday, November 27, 1787.

Author: Alexander Hamilton

To the People of the State of New York:

THE effects of Union upon the commercial prosperity of the States have been sufficiently delineated. Its tendency to promote the interests of revenue will be the subject of our present inquiry.

The prosperity of commerce is now perceived and acknowledged by all enlightened statesmen to be the most useful as well as the most productive source of national wealth, and has accordingly become a primary object of their political cares. By multiplying the means of gratification, by promoting the introduction and circulation of the precious metals, those darling objects of human avarice and enterprise, it serves to vivify and invigorate the channels of industry, and to make them flow with greater activity and copiousness. The assiduous merchant, the laborious husbandman, the active mechanic, and the industrious manufacturer,—all orders of men, look forward with eager expectation and growing alacrity to this pleasing reward of their toils. The often-agitated question between agriculture and commerce has, from indubitable experience, received a decision which has silenced the rivalship that once subsisted between them, and has proved, to the satisfaction of their friends, that their interests are intimately blended and interwoven. It has been found in various countries that, in proportion as commerce has flourished, land has risen in value. And how could it have happened otherwise? Could that which procures a freer vent for the products of the earth, which furnishes new incitements to the cultivation of land, which is the most powerful instrument in increasing the quantity of money in a state—could that, in fine, which is the faithful handmaid of labor and industry, in every shape, fail to augment that article, which is the prolific parent of far the greatest part of the objects upon which they are exerted? It is astonishing that so simple a truth should ever have had an adversary; and it is one, among a multitude of proofs, how apt a spirit of ill-informed jealousy, or of too great abstraction and refinement, is to lead men astray from the plainest truths of reason and conviction.

The ability of a country to pay taxes must always be proportioned, in a great degree, to the quantity of money in circulation, and to the celerity with which it circulates. Commerce, contributing to both these objects, must of necessity render the payment of taxes easier, and facilitate the requisite supplies to the treasury. The hereditary dominions of the Emperor of Germany contain a great extent of fertile, cultivated, and populous territory, a large proportion of which is situated in mild and luxuriant climates. In some parts of this territory are to be found the best gold and silver mines in Europe. And yet, from the want of the fostering influence of commerce, that monarch can boast but slender revenues. He has several times been compelled to owe obligations to the pecuniary succors of other nations for the preservation of his essential interests, and is unable, upon the strength of his own resources, to sustain a long or continued war.

But it is not in this aspect of the subject alone that Union will be seen to conduce to the purpose of revenue. There are other points of view, in which its influence will appear more immediate and decisive. It is evident from the state of the country, from the habits of the people, from the experience we have had on the point itself, that it is impracticable to raise any very considerable sums by direct taxation. Tax laws have in vain been multiplied; new methods to enforce the collection have in vain been tried; the public expectation has been uniformly disappointed, and the treasuries of the States have remained empty. The popular system of administration inherent in the nature of popular government, coinciding with the real scarcity of money incident to a languid and mutilated state of trade, has hitherto defeated every experiment for extensive collections, and has at length taught the different legislatures the folly of attempting them.

No person acquainted with what happens in other countries will be surprised at this circumstance. In so opulent a nation as that of Britain, where direct taxes from superior wealth must be much more tolerable, and, from the vigor of the government, much more practicable, than in America, far the greatest part of the national revenue is derived from taxes of the indirect kind, from imposts, and from excises. Duties on imported articles form a large branch of this latter description.

In America, it is evident that we must a long time depend for the means of revenue chiefly on such duties. In most parts of it, excises must be confined within a narrow compass. The genius of the people will ill brook the inquisitive and peremptory spirit of excise laws. The pockets of the farmers, on the other hand, will reluctantly yield but scanty supplies, in the unwelcome shape of impositions on their houses and lands; and personal property is too precarious and invisible a fund to be laid hold of in any other way than by the inperceptible agency of taxes on consumption.

If these remarks have any foundation, that state of things which will best enable us to improve and extend so valuable a resource must be best adapted to our political welfare. And it cannot admit of a serious doubt, that this state of things must rest on the basis of a general Union. As far as this would be conducive to the interests of commerce, so far it must tend to the extension of the revenue to be drawn from that source. As far as it would contribute to rendering regulations for the collection of the duties more simple and efficacious, so far it must serve to answer the purposes of making the same rate of duties more productive, and of putting it into the power of the government to increase the rate without prejudice to trade.

The relative situation of these States; the number of rivers with which they are intersected, and of bays that wash their shores; the facility of communication in every direction; the affinity of language and manners; the familiar habits of intercourse;—all these are circumstances that would conspire to render an illicit trade between them a matter of little difficulty, and would insure frequent evasions of the commercial regulations of each other. The separate States or confederacies would be necessitated by mutual jealousy to avoid the temptations to that kind of trade by the lowness of their duties. The temper of our governments, for a long time to come, would not permit those rigorous precautions by which the European nations guard the avenues into their respective countries, as well by land as by water; and which, even there, are found insufficient obstacles to the adventurous stratagems of avarice.

In France, there is an army of patrols (as they are called) constantly employed to secure their fiscal regulations against the inroads of the dealers in contraband trade. Mr. Neckar computes the number of these patrols at upwards of twenty thousand. This shows the immense difficulty in preventing that species of traffic, where there is an inland communication, and places in a strong light the disadvantages with which the collection of duties in this country would be encumbered, if by disunion the States should be placed in a situation, with respect to each other, resembling that of France with respect to her neighbors. The arbitrary and vexatious powers with which the patrols are necessarily armed, would be intolerable in a free country.

If, on the contrary, there be but one government pervading all the States, there will be, as to the principal part of our commerce, but ONE SIDE to guard—the ATLANTIC COAST. Vessels arriving directly from foreign countries, laden with valuable cargoes, would rarely choose to hazard themselves to the complicated and critical perils which would attend attempts to unlade prior to their coming into port. They would have to dread both the dangers of the coast, and of detection, as well after as before their arrival at the places of their final destination. An ordinary degree of vigilance would be competent to the prevention of any material infractions upon the rights of the revenue. A few armed vessels, judiciously stationed at the entrances of our ports, might at a small expense be made useful sentinels of the laws. And the government having the same interest to provide against violations everywhere, the co-operation of its measures in each State would have a powerful tendency to render them effectual. Here also we should preserve, by Union, an advantage which nature holds out to us, and which would be relinquished by separation. The United States lie at a great distance from Europe, and at a considerable distance from all other places with which they would have extensive connections of foreign trade. The passage from them to us, in a few hours, or in a single night, as between the coasts of France and Britain, and of other neighboring nations, would be impracticable. This is a prodigious security against a direct contraband with foreign countries; but a circuitous contraband to one State, through the medium of another, would be both easy and safe. The difference between a direct importation from abroad, and an indirect importation through the channel of a neighboring State, in small parcels, according to time and opportunity, with the additional facilities of inland communication, must be palpable to every man of discernment.

It is therefore evident, that one national government would be able, at much less expense, to extend the duties on imports, beyond comparison, further than would be practicable to the States separately, or to any partial confederacies. Hitherto, I believe, it may safely be asserted, that these duties have not upon an average exceeded in any State three per cent. In France they are estimated to be about fifteen per cent., and in Britain they exceed this proportion.[1] There seems to be nothing to hinder their being increased in this country to at least treble their present amount. The single article of ardent spirits, under federal regulation, might be made to furnish a considerable revenue. Upon a ratio to the importation into this State, the whole quantity imported into the United States may be estimated at four millions of gallons; which, at a shilling per gallon, would produce two hundred thousand

pounds. That article would well bear this rate of duty; and if it should tend to diminish the consumption of it, such an effect would be equally favorable to the agriculture, to the economy, to the morals, and to the health of the society. There is, perhaps, nothing so much a subject of national extravagance as these spirits.

What will be the consequence, if we are not able to avail ourselves of the resource in question in its full extent? A nation cannot long exist without revenues. Destitute of this essential support, it must resign its independence, and sink into the degraded condition of a province. This is an extremity to which no government will of choice accede. Revenue, therefore, must be had at all events. In this country, if the principal part be not drawn from commerce, it must fall with oppressive weight upon land. It has been already intimated that excises, in their true signification, are too little in unison with the feelings of the people, to admit of great use being made of that mode of taxation; nor, indeed, in the States where almost the sole employment is agriculture, are the objects proper for excise sufficiently numerous to permit very ample collections in that way. Personal estate (as has been before remarked), from the difficulty in tracing it, cannot be subjected to large contributions, by any other means than by taxes on consumption. In populous cities, it may be enough the subject of conjecture, to occasion the oppression of individuals, without much aggregate benefit to the State; but beyond these circles, it must, in a great measure, escape the eye and the hand of the tax-gatherer. As the necessities of the State, nevertheless, must be satisfied in some mode or other, the defect of other resources must throw the principal weight of public burdens on the possessors of land. And as, on the other hand, the wants of the government can never obtain an adequate supply, unless all the sources of revenue are open to its demands, the finances of the community, under such embarrassments, cannot be put into a situation consistent with its respectability or its security. Thus we shall not even have the consolations of a full treasury, to atone for the oppression of that valuable class of the citizens who are employed in the cultivation of the soil. But public and private distress will keep pace with each other in gloomy concert; and unite in deploring the infatuation of those counsels which led to disunion.

PUBLIUS.

1. If my memory be right they amount to twenty per cent.

Federalist No. 30

Concerning the General Power of Taxation

From the *New York Packet.*

Friday, December 28, 1787.

Author: Alexander Hamilton

To the People of the State of New York:

IT HAS been already observed that the federal government ought to possess the power of providing for the support of the national forces; in which proposition was intended to be included the expense of raising troops, of building and equipping fleets, and all other expenses in any wise connected with military arrangements and operations. But these are not the only objects to which the jurisdiction of the Union, in respect to revenue, must necessarily be empowered to extend. It must embrace a provision for the support of the national civil list; for the payment of the national debts contracted, or that may be contracted; and, in general, for all those matters which will call for disbursements out of the national treasury. The conclusion is, that there must be interwoven, in the frame of the government, a general power of taxation, in one shape or another.

Money is, with propriety, considered as the vital principle of the body politic; as that which sustains its life and motion, and enables it to perform its most essential functions. A complete power, therefore, to procure a regular and adequate supply of it, as far as the resources of the community will permit, may be regarded as an indispensable ingredient in every constitution. From a deficiency in this particular, one of two evils must ensue: either the people must be subjected to continual plunder, as a substitute for a more eligible mode of supplying the public wants, or the government must sink into a fatal atrophy, and, in a short course of time, perish.

In the Ottoman or Turkish empire, the sovereign, though in other respects absolute master of the lives and fortunes of his subjects, has no right to impose a new tax. The consequence is that he permits the bashaws or governors of provinces to pillage the people without mercy; and, in turn, squeezes out of them the sums of which he stands in need, to satisfy his own exigencies and those of the state. In America, from a like cause, the government of the Union has gradually dwindled into a state of decay, approaching nearly to annihilation. Who can doubt, that the happiness of the people in both countries would be promoted by competent authorities in the proper hands, to provide the revenues which the necessities of the public might require?

The present Confederation, feeble as it is, intended to repose in the United States an unlimited power of providing for the pecuniary wants of the Union. But proceeding upon an erroneous principle, it has been done in such a manner as entirely to have frustrated the intention. Congress, by the articles which compose that compact (as has already been stated), are authorized to ascertain and call for any sums of money necessary, in their judgment, to the service of the United States; and their requisitions, if conformable to the rule of apportionment, are in every constitutional sense obligatory upon the States. These have no right to question the propriety of the demand; no discretion beyond that of devising the ways and means of furnishing the sums demanded. But though this be strictly and truly the case; though the assumption of such a right would be an infringement of the articles of Union; though it may seldom or never have been avowedly claimed, yet in practice it has been constantly exercised, and would continue to be so, as long as the revenues of the Confederacy should remain dependent on the intermediate agency of its members. What the consequences of this system have been, is within the knowledge of every man the least conversant in our public affairs, and has been amply unfolded in different parts of these inquiries. It is this which has chiefly contributed to reduce us to a situation, which affords ample cause both of mortification to ourselves, and of triumph to our enemies.

What remedy can there be for this situation, but in a change of the system which has produced it—in a change of the fallacious and delusive system of quotas and requisitions? What substitute can there be imagined for this ignis fatuus in finance, but that of permitting the national government to raise its own revenues by the ordinary methods of taxation authorized in every well-ordered constitution of civil government? Ingenious men may declaim with plausibility on any subject; but no human ingenuity can point out any other expedient to rescue us from the inconveniences and embarrassments naturally resulting from defective supplies of the public treasury.

The more intelligent adversaries of the new Constitution admit the force of this reasoning; but they qualify their admission by a distinction between what they call *internal* and *external* taxation. The former they would reserve to the State governments; the latter, which they explain into commercial imposts, or rather duties on imported articles, they declare themselves willing to concede to the federal head. This distinction, however, would violate the maxim of good sense and sound policy, which dictates that every POWER ought to be in proportion to its OBJECT; and would still leave the general government in a kind of tutelage to the State governments, inconsistent with every idea of vigor or efficiency. Who can pretend that commercial imposts are, or would be, alone equal to the present and future exigencies of the Union? Taking into the account the existing debt, foreign and domestic, upon any plan of extinguishment which a man moderately impressed with the importance of public justice and public credit could approve, in addition to the establishments which all parties will acknowledge to be necessary, we could not reasonably flatter ourselves, that this resource alone, upon the most improved scale, would even suffice for its present necessities. Its future necessities admit not of calculation or limitation; and upon the principle, more than once adverted to, the power of making provision for them as they arise ought to be equally unconfined. I believe it may be regarded as a position warranted by the history of mankind, that, *in the usual progress of things, the necessities of a nation, in every stage of its existence, will be found at least equal to its resources.*

To say that deficiencies may be provided for by requisitions upon the States, is on the one hand to acknowledge that this system cannot be depended upon, and on the other hand to depend upon it for every thing beyond a certain limit. Those who have carefully attended to its vices and deformities as they have been exhibited by experience or delineated in the course of these papers, must feel invincible repugnancy to trusting the national interests in any degree to its operation. Its inevitable tendency, whenever it is brought into activity, must be to enfeeble the Union, and sow the seeds of discord and contention between the federal head and its members, and between the members themselves. Can it be expected that the deficiencies would be better supplied in this mode than the total wants of the Union have heretofore been supplied in the same mode? It ought to be rec-

ollected that if less will be required from the States, they will have proportionably less means to answer the demand. If the opinions of those who contend for the distinction which has been mentioned were to be received as evidence of truth, one would be led to conclude that there was some known point in the economy of national affairs at which it would be safe to stop and to say: Thus far the ends of public happiness will be promoted by supplying the wants of government, and all beyond this is unworthy of our care or anxiety. How is it possible that a government half supplied and always necessitous, can fulfil the purposes of its institution, can provide for the security, advance the prosperity, or support the reputation of the commonwealth? How can it ever possess either energy or stability, dignity or credit, confidence at home or respectability abroad? How can its administration be any thing else than a succession of expedients temporizing, impotent, disgraceful? How will it be able to avoid a frequent sacrifice of its engagements to immediate necessity? How can it undertake or execute any liberal or enlarged plans of public good?

Let us attend to what would be the effects of this situation in the very first war in which we should happen to be engaged. We will presume, for argument's sake, that the revenue arising from the impost duties answers the purposes of a provision for the public debt and of a peace establishment for the Union. Thus circumstanced, a war breaks out. What would be the probable conduct of the government in such an emergency? Taught by experience that proper dependence could not be placed on the success of requisitions, unable by its own authority to lay hold of fresh resources, and urged by considerations of national danger, would it not be driven to the expedient of diverting the funds already appropriated from their proper objects to the defense of the State? It is not easy to see how a step of this kind could be avoided; and if it should be taken, it is evident that it would prove the destruction of public credit at the very moment that it was becoming essential to the public safety. To imagine that at such a crisis credit might be dispensed with, would be the extreme of infatuation. In the modern system of war, nations the most wealthy are obliged to have recourse to large loans. A country so little opulent as ours must feel this necessity in a much stronger degree. But who would lend to a government that prefaced its overtures for borrowing by an act which demonstrated that no reliance could be placed on the steadiness of its measures for paying? The loans it might be able to procure would be as limited in their extent as burdensome in their conditions. They would be made upon the same principles that usurers commonly lend to bankrupt and fraudulent debtors,—with a sparing hand and at enormous premiums.

It may perhaps be imagined that, from the scantiness of the resources of the country, the necessity of diverting the established funds in the case supposed would exist, though the national government should possess an unrestrained power of taxation. But two considerations will serve to quiet all apprehension on this head: one is, that we are sure the resources of the community, in their full extent, will be brought into activity for the benefit of the Union; the other is, that whatever deficiencies there may be, can without difficulty be supplied by loans.

The power of creating new funds upon new objects of taxation, by its own authority, would enable the national government to borrow as far as its necessities might require. Foreigners, as well as the citizens of America, could then reasonably repose confidence in its engagements; but to depend upon a government that must itself depend upon thirteen other governments for the means of fulfilling its contracts, when once its situation is clearly understood, would require a degree of credulity not often to be met with in the pecuniary transactions of mankind, and little reconcilable with the usual sharp-sightedness of avarice.

Reflections of this kind may have trifling weight with men who hope to see realized in America the halcyon scenes of the poetic or fabulous age; but to those who believe we are likely to experience a common portion of the vicissitudes and calamities which have fallen to the lot of other nations, they must appear entitled to serious attention. Such men must behold the actual situation of their country with painful solicitude, and deprecate the evils which ambition or revenge might, with too much facility, inflict upon it.

PUBLIUS.

Federalist No. 31

Concerning the General Power of Taxation

From the *New York Packet.*

Tuesday, January 1, 1788.

Author: Alexander Hamilton

To the People of the State of New York:

IN DISQUISITIONS of every kind, there are certain primary truths, or first principles, upon which all subsequent reasonings must depend. These contain an internal evidence which, antecedent to all reflection or combination, commands the assent of the mind. Where it produces not this effect, it must proceed either from some defect or disorder in the organs of perception, or from the influence of some strong interest, or passion, or prejudice. Of this nature are the maxims in geometry, that "the whole is greater than its part; things equal to the same are equal to one another; two straight lines cannot enclose a space; and all right angles are equal to each other." Of the same nature are these other maxims in ethics and politics, that there cannot be an effect without a cause; that the means ought to be proportioned to the end; that every power ought to be commensurate with its object; that there ought to be no limitation of a power destined to effect a purpose which is itself incapable of limitation. And there are other truths in the two latter sciences which, if they cannot pretend to rank in the class of axioms, are yet such direct inferences from them, and so obvious in themselves, and so agreeable to the natural and unsophisticated dictates of common-sense, that they challenge the assent of a sound and unbiased mind, with a degree of force and conviction almost equally irresistible.

The objects of geometrical inquiry are so entirely abstracted from those pursuits which stir up and put in motion the unruly passions of the human heart, that mankind, without difficulty, adopt not only the more simple theorems of the science, but even those abstruse paradoxes which, however they may appear susceptible of demonstration, are at variance with the natural conceptions which the mind, without the aid of philosophy, would be led to entertain upon the subject. The INFINITE DIVISIBILITY of matter, or, in other words, the INFINITE divisibility of a FINITE thing, extending even to the minutest atom, is a point agreed among geometricians, though not less incomprehensible to common-sense than any of those mysteries in religion, against which the batteries of infidelity have been so industriously leveled.

But in the sciences of morals and politics, men are found far less tractable. To a certain degree, it is right and useful that this should be the case. Caution and investigation are a necessary armor against error and imposition. But this untractableness may be carried too far, and may degenerate into obstinacy, perverseness, or disingenuity. Though it cannot be pretended that the principles of moral and political knowledge have, in general, the same degree of certainty with those of the mathematics, yet they have much better claims in this respect than, to judge from the conduct of men in particular situations, we should be disposed to allow them. The obscurity is much oftener in the passions and prejudices of the reasoner than in the subject. Men, upon too many occasions, do not give their own understandings fair play; but, yielding to some untoward bias, they entangle themselves in words and confound themselves in subtleties.

How else could it happen (if we admit the objectors to be sincere in their opposition), that positions so clear as those which manifest the necessity of a general power of taxation in the government of the Union, should have to encounter any adversaries among men of discernment? Though these positions have been elsewhere fully stated, they will perhaps not be improperly recapitulated in this place, as introductory to an examination of what may have been offered by way of objection to them. They are in substance as follows:

A government ought to contain in itself every power requisite to the full accomplishment of the objects committed to its care, and to the complete execution of the trusts for which it is responsible, free from every other control but a regard to the public good and to the sense of the people.

As the duties of superintending the national defence and of securing the public peace against foreign or domestic violence involve a provision for casualties and dangers to which no possible limits can be assigned, the power of making that provision ought to know no other bounds than the exigencies of the nation and the resources of the community.

As revenue is the essential engine by which the means of answering the national exigencies must be procured, the power of procuring that article in its full extent must necessarily be comprehended in that of providing for those exigencies.

As theory and practice conspire to prove that the power of procuring revenue is unavailing when exercised over the States in their collective capacities, the federal government must of necessity be invested with an unqualified power of taxation in the ordinary modes.

Did not experience evince the contrary, it would be natural to conclude that the propriety of a general power of taxation in the national government might safely be permitted to rest on the evidence of these propositions, unassisted by any additional arguments or illustrations. But we find, in fact, that the antagonists of the proposed Constitution, so far from acquiescing in their justness or truth, seem to make their principal and most zealous effort against this part of the plan. It may therefore be satisfactory to analyze the arguments with which they combat it.

Those of them which have been most labored with that view, seem in substance to amount to this: "It is not true, because the exigencies of the Union may not be susceptible of limitation, that its power of laying taxes ought to be unconfined. Revenue is as requisite to the purposes of the local administrations as to those of the Union; and the former are at least of equal importance with the latter to the happiness of the people. It is, therefore, as necessary that the State governments should be able to command the means of supplying their wants, as that the national government should possess the like faculty in respect to the wants of the Union. But an indefinite power of taxation in the *latter* might, and probably would in time, deprive the *former* of the means of providing for their own necessities; and would subject them entirely to the mercy of the national legislature. As the laws of the Union are to become the supreme law of the land, as it is to have power to pass all laws that may be NECESSARY for carrying into execution the authorities with which it is proposed to vest it, the national government might at any time abolish the taxes imposed for State objects upon the pretense of an interference with its own. It might allege a necessity of doing this in order to give efficacy to the national revenues. And thus all the resources of taxation might by degrees become the subjects of federal monopoly, to the entire exclusion and destruction of the State governments."

This mode of reasoning appears sometimes to turn upon the supposition of usurpation in the national government; at other times it seems to be designed only as a deduction from the constitutional operation of its intended powers. It is only in the latter light that it can be admitted to have any pretensions to fairness. The moment we launch into conjectures about the usurpations of the federal government, we get into an unfathomable abyss, and fairly put ourselves out of the reach of all reasoning. Imagination may range at pleasure till it gets bewildered amidst the labyrinths of an enchanted castle, and knows not on which side to turn to extricate itself from the perplexities into which it has so rashly adventured. Whatever may be the limits or modifications of the powers of the Union, it is easy to imagine an endless train of possible dangers; and by indulging an excess of jealousy and timidity, we may bring ourselves to a state of absolute scepticism and irresolution. I repeat here what I have observed in substance in another place, that all observations founded upon the danger of usurpation ought to be referred to the composition and structure of the government, not to the nature or extent of its powers. The State governments, by their original constitutions, are invested with complete sovereignty. In what does our security consist against usurpation from that

quarter? Doubtless in the manner of their formation, and in a due dependence of those who are to administer them upon the people. If the proposed construction of the federal government be found, upon an impartial examination of it, to be such as to afford, to a proper extent, the same species of security, all apprehensions on the score of usurpation ought to be discarded.

It should not be forgotten that a disposition in the State governments to encroach upon the rights of the Union is quite as probable as a disposition in the Union to encroach upon the rights of the State governments. What side would be likely to prevail in such a conflict, must depend on the means which the contending parties could employ toward insuring success. As in republics strength is always on the side of the people, and as there are weighty reasons to induce a belief that the State governments will commonly possess most influence over them, the natural conclusion is that such contests will be most apt to end to the disadvantage of the Union; and that there is greater probability of encroachments by the members upon the federal head, than by the federal head upon the members. But it is evident that all conjectures of this kind must be extremely vague and fallible: and that it is by far the safest course to lay them altogether aside, and to confine our attention wholly to the nature and extent of the powers as they are delineated in the Constitution. Every thing beyond this must be left to the prudence and firmness of the people; who, as they will hold the scales in their own hands, it is to be hoped, will always take care to preserve the constitutional equilibrium between the general and the State governments.

Upon this ground, which is evidently the true one, it will not be difficult to obviate the objections which have been made to an indefinite power of taxation in the United States.

PUBLIUS.

Federalist No. 32

Concerning the General Power of Taxation

From the *Daily Advertiser*.

Thursday, January 3, 1788.

Author: Alexander Hamilton

To the People of the State of New York:

ALTHOUGH I am of opinion that there would be no real danger of the consequences which seem to be apprehended to the State governments from a power in the Union to control them in the levies of money, because I am persuaded that the sense of the people, the extreme hazard of provoking the resentments of the State governments, and a conviction of the utility and necessity of local administrations for local purposes, would be a complete barrier against the oppressive use of such a power; yet I am willing here to allow, in its full extent, the justness of the reasoning which requires that the individual States should possess an independent and uncontrollable authority to raise their own revenues for the supply of their own wants. And making this concession, I affirm that (with the sole exception of duties on imports and exports) they would, under the plan of the convention, retain that authority in the most absolute and unqualified sense; and that an attempt on the part of the national government to abridge them in the exercise of it, would be a violent assumption of power, unwarranted by any article or clause of its Constitution.

An entire consolidation of the States into one complete national sovereignty would imply an entire subordination of the parts; and whatever powers might remain in them, would be altogether dependent on the general will. But as the plan of the convention aims only at a partial union or consolidation, the State governments would clearly retain all the rights of sovereignty which they before had, and which were not, by that act, *exclusively* delegated to the United States. This exclusive delegation, or rather this alienation, of State sovereignty, would only exist in three cases: where the Constitution in express terms granted an exclusive authority to the Union; where it granted in one instance an authority to the Union, and in another prohibited the States from exercising the like authority; and where it granted an authority to the Union, to which a similar authority in the States would be absolutely and totally *contradictory* and *repugnant*. I use these terms to distinguish this last case from another which might appear to resemble it, but which would, in fact, be essentially different; I mean where the exercise of a concurrent jurisdiction might be productive of occasional interferences in the *policy* of any branch of administration, but would not imply any direct contradiction or repugnancy in point of constitutional authority. These three cases of exclusive jurisdiction in the federal government may be exemplified by the following instances: The last clause but one in the eighth section of the first article provides expressly that Congress shall exercise "*exclusive legislation*" over the district to be appropriated as the seat of government. This answers to the first case. The first clause of the same section empowers Congress *"to lay and collect taxes, duties, imposts and excises"*; and the second clause of the tenth section of the same article declares that, *"no state shall*, without the consent of Congress, *lay any imposts or duties on imports or exports*, except for the purpose of executing its inspection laws." Hence would result an exclusive power in the Union to lay duties on imports and exports, with the particular exception mentioned; but this power is abridged by another clause, which declares that no tax or duty shall be laid on articles exported from any State; in consequence of which qualification, it now only extends to the *duties on imports*. This answers to the second case. The third will be found in that clause which declares that Congress shall have power "to establish an UNIFORM RULE of naturalization throughout the United States." This must necessarily be exclusive; because if each State had power to prescribe a DISTINCT RULE, there could not be a UNIFORM RULE.

A case which may perhaps be thought to resemble the latter, but which is in fact widely different, affects the question immediately under consideration. I mean the power of imposing taxes on all articles other than exports and imports. This, I contend, is manifestly a concurrent and coequal authority in the United States and in the individual States. There is plainly no expression in the granting clause which makes that power *exclusive* in the Union. There is no independent clause or sentence which prohibits the States from exercising it. So far is this from being the case, that a plain and

conclusive argument to the contrary is to be deduced from the restraint laid upon the States in relation to duties on imports and exports. This restriction implies an admission that, if it were not inserted, the States would possess the power it excludes; and it implies a further admission, that as to all other taxes, the authority of the States remains undiminished. In any other view it would be both unnecessary and dangerous; it would be unnecessary, because if the grant to the Union of the power of laying such duties implied the exclusion of the States, or even their subordination in this particular there could be no need of such a restriction; it would be dangerous, because the introduction of it leads directly to the conclusion which has been mentioned, and which, if the reasoning of the objectors be just, could not have been intended; I mean that the States, in all cases to which the restriction did not apply, would have a concurrent power of taxation with the Union. The restriction in question amounts to what lawyers call a NEGATIVE PREGNANT—that is, a *negation* of one thing, and an *affirmance* of another; a negation of the authority of the States to impose taxes on imports and exports, and an affirmance of their authority to impose them on all other articles. It would be mere sophistry to argue that it was meant to exclude them *absolutely* from the imposition of taxes of the former kind, and to leave them at liberty to lay others *subject to the control* of the national legislature. The restraining or prohibitory clause only says, that they shall not, *without the consent of congress*, lay such duties; and if we are to understand this in the sense last mentioned, the Constitution would then be made to introduce a formal provision for the sake of a very absurd conclusion; which is, that the States, *with the consent* of the national legislature, might tax imports and exports; and that they might tax every other article, *unless controlled* by the same body. If this was the intention, why not leave it, in the first instance, to what is alleged to be the natural operation of the original clause, conferring a general power of taxation upon the Union? It is evident that this could not have been the intention, and that it will not bear a construction of the kind.

As to a supposition of repugnancy between the power of taxation in the States and in the Union, it cannot be supported in that sense which would be requisite to work an exclusion of the States. It is, indeed, possible that a tax might be laid on a particular article by a State which might render it *inexpedient* that thus a further tax should be laid on the same article by the Union; but it would not imply a constitutional inability to impose a further tax. The quantity of the imposition, the expediency or inexpediency of an increase on either side, would be mutually questions of prudence; but there would be involved no direct contradiction of power. The particular policy of the national and of the State systems of finance might now and then not exactly coincide, and might require reciprocal forbearances. It is not, however, a mere possibility of inconvenience in the exercise of powers, but an immediate constitutional repugnancy that can by implication alienate and extinguish a pre-existing right of sovereignty.

The necessity of a concurrent jurisdiction in certain cases results from the division of the sovereign power; and

the rule that all authorities, of which the States are not explicitly divested in favor of the Union, remain with them in full vigor, is not a theoretical consequence of that division, but is clearly admitted by the whole tenor of the instrument which contains the articles of the proposed Constitution. We there find that, notwithstanding the affirmative grants of general authorities, there has been the most pointed care in those cases where it was deemed improper that the like authorities should reside in the States, to insert negative clauses prohibiting the exercise of them by the States. The tenth section of the first article consists altogether of such provisions. This circumstance is a clear indication of the sense of the convention, and furnishes a rule of interpretation out of the body of the act, which justifies the position I have advanced and refutes every hypothesis to the contrary.

PUBLIUS.

Federalist No. 33

Concerning the General Power of Taxation

From the *Daily Advertiser.*

Thursday, January 3, 1788.

Author: Alexander Hamilton

To the People of the State of New York:

THE residue of the argument against the provisions of the Constitution in respect to taxation is in grafted upon the following clause. The last clause of the eighth section of the first article of the plan under consideration authorizes the national legislature "to make all laws which shall be *necessary* and *proper* for carrying into execution the *powers* by that Constitution vested in the government of the United States, or in any department or officer thereof"; and the second clause of the sixth article declares, "that the Constitution and the laws of the United States made *in pursuance thereof*, and the treaties made by their authority shall be the *supreme law* of the land, any thing in the constitution or laws of any State to the contrary notwithstanding."

These two clauses have been the source of much virulent invective and petulant declamation against the proposed Constitution. They have been held up to the people in all the exaggerated colors of misrepresentation as the pernicious engines by which their local governments were to be destroyed and their liberties exterminated; as the hideous monster whose devouring jaws would spare neither sex nor age, nor high nor low, nor sacred nor profane; and yet, strange as it may appear, after all this clamor, to those who may not have happened to contemplate them in the same light, it may be affirmed with perfect confidence that the constitutional operation of the intended government would be precisely the same, if these clauses were entirely obliterated, as if they were repeated in every article. They are only declaratory of a truth which would have resulted by necessary and unavoidable implication from the very act of constituting a federal government, and vesting it with certain specified powers. This is so clear a proposition, that moderation itself can scarcely listen to the railings which have been so copiously vented against this part of the plan, without emotions that disturb its equanimity.

What is a power, but the ability or faculty of doing a thing? What is the ability to do a thing, but the power of employing the *means* necessary to its execution? What is a LEGISLATIVE power, but a power of making LAWS? What are the *means* to execute a LEGISLATIVE power but LAWS? What is the power of laying and collecting taxes, but a *legislative power*, or a power of *making laws*, to lay and collect taxes? What are the proper means of executing such a power, but *necessary* and *proper* laws?

This simple train of inquiry furnishes us at once with a test by which to judge of the true nature of the clause complained of. It conducts us to this palpable truth, that a power to lay and collect taxes must be a power to pass all laws *necessary* and *proper* for the execution of that power; and what does the unfortunate and calumniated provision in question do more than declare the same truth, to wit, that the national legislature, to whom the power of laying and collecting taxes had been previously given, might, in the execution of that power, pass all laws *necessary* and *proper* to carry it into effect? I have applied these observations thus particularly to the power of taxation, because it is the immediate subject under consideration, and because it is the most important of the authorities proposed to be conferred upon the Union. But the same process will lead to the same result, in relation to all other powers declared in the Constitution. And it is *expressly* to execute these powers that the sweeping clause, as it has been affectedly called, authorizes the national legislature to pass all *necessary* and *proper* laws. If there is any thing exceptionable, it must be sought for in the specific powers upon which this general declaration is predicated. The declaration itself, though it may be chargeable with tautology or redundancy, is at least perfectly harmless.

But SUSPICION may ask, Why then was it introduced? The answer is, that it could only have been done for greater caution, and to guard against all cavilling refinements in those who might hereafter feel a disposition to curtail and evade the legitimate authorities of the Union. The Convention probably foresaw, what it has been a principal aim of these papers to inculcate, that the danger which most threatens our political welfare is that the State governments will finally sap the foundations of the Union; and might therefore think it necessary, in so cardinal a point, to leave nothing to construction. Whatever may have been the inducement to it, the wisdom of the precaution is evident from the cry which has been raised against it; as that very cry betrays a disposition to question the great and essential truth which it is manifestly the object of that provision to declare.

But it may be again asked, Who is to judge of the *necessity* and *propriety* of the laws to be passed for executing the powers of the Union? I answer, first, that this question arises as well and as fully upon the simple grant of those powers as upon the declaratory clause; and I answer, in the second place, that the national government, like every other, must judge, in the first instance, of the proper exercise of its powers, and its constituents in the last. If the federal government should overpass the just bounds of its authority and make a tyrannical use of its powers, the people, whose creature it is, must ap-

peal to the standard they have formed, and take such measures to redress the injury done to the Constitution as the exigency may suggest and prudence justify. The propriety of a law, in a constitutional light, must always be determined by the nature of the powers upon which it is founded. Suppose, by some forced constructions of its authority (which, indeed, cannot easily be imagined), the Federal legislature should attempt to vary the law of descent in any State, would it not be evident that, in making such an attempt, it had exceeded its jurisdiction, and infringed upon that of the State? Suppose, again, that upon the pretense of an interference with its revenues, it should undertake to abrogate a land tax imposed by the authority of a State; would it not be equally evident that this was an invasion of that concurrent jurisdiction in respect to this species of tax, which its Constitution plainly supposes to exist in the State governments? If there ever should be a doubt on this head, the credit of it will be entirely due to those reasoners who, in the imprudent zeal of their animosity to the plan of the convention, have labored to envelop it in a cloud calculated to obscure the plainest and simplest truths.

But it is said that the laws of the Union are to be the *supreme law* of the land. But what inference can be drawn from this, or what would they amount to, if they were not to be supreme? It is evident they would amount to nothing. A LAW, by the very meaning of the term, includes supremacy. It is a rule which those to whom it is prescribed are bound to observe. This results from every political association. If individuals enter into a state of society, the laws of that society must be the supreme regulator of their conduct. If a number of political societies enter into a larger political society, the laws which the latter may enact, pursuant to the powers intrusted to it by its constitution, must necessarily be supreme over those societies, and the individuals of whom they are composed. It would otherwise be a mere treaty, dependent on the good faith of the parties, and not a government, which is only another word for POLITICAL POWER AND SUPREMACY. But it will not follow from this doctrine that acts of the large society which are *not pursuant* to its constitutional powers, but which are invasions of the residuary authorities of the smaller societies, will become the supreme law of the land. These will be merely acts of usurpation, and will deserve to be treated as such. Hence we perceive that the clause which declares the supremacy of the laws of the Union, like the one we have just before considered, only declares a truth, which flows immediately and necessarily from the institution of a federal government. It will not, I presume, have escaped observation, that it *expressly* confines this supremacy to laws made *pursuant to the Constitution*; which I mention merely as an instance of caution in the convention; since that limitation would have been to be understood, though it had not been expressed.

Though a law, therefore, laying a tax for the use of the United States would be supreme in its nature, and could not legally be opposed or controlled, yet a law for abrogating or preventing the collection of a tax laid by the authority of the State, (unless upon imports and exports), would not be the supreme law of the land, but a usurpation of power not granted by the Constitution. As far as an improper accumulation of taxes on the same object might tend to render the collection difficult or precarious, this would be a mutual inconvenience, not arising from a superiority or defect of power on either side, but from an injudicious exercise of power by one or the other, in a manner equally disadvantageous to both. It is to be hoped and presumed, however, that mutual interest would dictate a concert in this respect which would avoid any material inconvenience. The inference from the whole is, that the individual States would, under the proposed Constitution, retain an independent and uncontrollable authority to raise revenue to any extent of which they may stand in need, by every kind of taxation, except duties on imports and exports. It will be shown in the next paper that this CONCURRENT JURISDICTION in the article of taxation was the only admissible substitute for an entire subordination, in respect to this branch of power, of the State authority to that of the Union.

PUBLIUS.

Federalist No. 34

Concerning the General Power of Taxation

From the *New York Packet.*

Friday, January 4, 1788.

Author: Alexander Hamilton

To the People of the State of New York:

I FLATTER myself it has been clearly shown in my last number that the particular States, under the proposed Constitution, would have COEQUAL authority with the Union in the article of revenue, except as to duties on imports. As this leaves open to the States far the greatest part of the resources of the community, there can be no color for the assertion that they would not possess means as abundant as could be desired for the supply of their own wants, independent of all external control. That the field is sufficiently wide will more fully appear when we come to advert to the inconsiderable share of the public expenses for which it will fall to the lot of the State governments to provide.

To argue upon abstract principles that this co-ordinate authority cannot exist, is to set up supposition and theory against fact and reality. However proper such reasonings might be to show that a thing *ought not to exist*, they are wholly to be rejected when they are made use of to prove that it does not exist contrary to the evidence of the fact itself. It is well known that in the Roman republic the legislative authority, in the last resort, resided for ages in two different political bodies—not as branches of the same legislature, but as distinct and independent legislatures, in each of which an opposite interest prevailed: in one the patrician; in the other, the plebian. Many arguments might have been adduced to prove the unfitness of two such seemingly contradictory authorities, each having power to *annul* or *repeal* the acts of the other. But a man would have been regarded as frantic who should have attempted at Rome to disprove their existence. It will be readily understood that I allude to the COMITIA CENTURIATA and the COMITIA TRIBUTA. The former, in which the people voted by centuries, was so arranged as to give a superiority to the patrician interest; in the latter, in which numbers prevailed, the plebian interest had an entire predominancy. And yet these two legislatures coexisted for ages, and the Roman republic attained to the utmost height of human greatness.

In the case particularly under consideration, there is no such contradiction as appears in the example cited; there is no power on either side to annul the acts of the other. And in practice there is little reason to apprehend any inconvenience; because, in a short course of time, the wants of the States will naturally reduce themselves within *a very narrow compass*; and in the interim, the United States will, in all probability, find it convenient to abstain wholly from those objects to which the particular States would be inclined to resort.

To form a more precise judgment of the true merits of this question, it will be well to advert to the proportion between the objects that will require a federal provision in respect to revenue, and those which will require a State provision. We shall discover that the former are altogether unlimited, and that the latter are circumscribed within very moderate bounds. In pursuing this inquiry, we must bear in mind that we are not to confine our view to the present period, but to look forward to remote futurity. Constitutions of civil government are not to be framed upon a calculation of existing exigencies, but upon a combination of these with the probable exigencies of ages, according to the natural and tried course of human affairs. Nothing, therefore, can be more fallacious than to infer the extent of any power, proper to be lodged in the national government, from an estimate of its immediate necessities.

There ought to be a CAPACITY to provide for future contingencies as they may happen; and as these are illimitable in their nature, it is impossible safely to limit that capacity. It is true, perhaps, that a computation might be made with sufficient accuracy to answer the purpose of the quantity of revenue requisite to discharge the subsisting engagements of the Union, and to maintain those establishments which, for some time to come, would suffice in time of peace. But would it be wise, or would it not rather be the extreme of folly, to stop at this point, and to leave the government intrusted with the care of the national defense in a state of absolute incapacity to provide for the protection of the community against future invasions of the public peace, by foreign war or domestic convulsions? If, on the contrary, we ought to exceed this point, where can we stop, short of an indefinite power of providing for emergencies as they may arise? Though it is easy to assert, in general terms, the possibility of forming a rational judgment of a due provision against probable dangers, yet we may safely challenge those who make the assertion to bring forward their data, and may affirm that they would be found as vague and uncertain as any that could be produced to establish the probable duration of the world. Observations confined to the mere prospects of internal attacks can deserve no weight; though even these will admit of no satisfactory calculation: but if we mean to be a commercial people, it must form a part of our policy to be able one day to defend that commerce. The support of a navy and of naval wars would involve contin-

gencies that must baffle all the efforts of political arithmetic.

Admitting that we ought to try the novel and absurd experiment in politics of tying up the hands of government from offensive war founded upon reasons of state, yet certainly we ought not to disable it from guarding the community against the ambition or enmity of other nations. A cloud has been for some time hanging over the European world. If it should break forth into a storm, who can insure us that in its progress a part of its fury would not be spent upon us? No reasonable man would hastily pronounce that we are entirely out of its reach. Or if the combustible materials that now seem to be collecting should be dissipated without coming to maturity, or if a flame should be kindled without extending to us, what security can we have that our tranquillity will long remain undisturbed from some other cause or from some other quarter? Let us recollect that peace or war will not always be left to our option; that however moderate or unambitious we may be, we cannot count upon the moderation, or hope to extinguish the ambition of others. Who could have imagined at the conclusion of the last war that France and Britain, wearied and exhausted as they both were, would so soon have looked with so hostile an aspect upon each other? To judge from the history of mankind, we shall be compelled to conclude that the fiery and destructive passions of war reign in the human breast with much more powerful sway than the mild and beneficent sentiments of peace; and that to model our political systems upon speculations of lasting tranquillity, is to calculate on the weaker springs of the human character.

What are the chief sources of expense in every government? What has occasioned that enormous accumulation of debts with which several of the European nations are oppressed? The answers plainly is, wars and rebellions; the support of those institutions which are necessary to guard the body politic against these two most mortal diseases of society. The expenses arising from those institutions which are relative to the mere domestic police of a state, to the support of its legislative, executive, and judicial departments, with their different appendages, and to the encouragement of agriculture and manufactures (which will comprehend almost all the objects of state expenditure), are insignificant in comparison with those which relate to the national defense.

In the kingdom of Great Britain, where all the ostentatious apparatus of monarchy is to be provided for, not above a fifteenth part of the annual income of the nation is appropriated to the class of expenses last mentioned; the other fourteen fifteenths are absorbed in the payment of the interest of debts contracted for carrying on the wars in which that country has been engaged, and in the maintenance of fleets and armies. If, on the one hand, it should be observed that the expenses incurred in the prosecution of the ambitious enterprises and vainglorious pursuits of a monarchy are not a proper standard by which to judge of those which might be necessary in a republic, it ought, on the other hand, to be remarked that there should be as great a disproportion between the profusion and extravagance of a wealthy

kingdom in its domestic administration, and the frugality and economy which in that particular become the modest simplicity of republican government. If we balance a proper deduction from one side against that which it is supposed ought to be made from the other, the proportion may still be considered as holding good.

But let us advert to the large debt which we have ourselves contracted in a single war, and let us only calculate on a common share of the events which disturb the peace of nations, and we shall instantly perceive, without the aid of any elaborate illustration, that there must always be an immense disproportion between the objects of federal and state expenditures. It is true that several of the States, separately, are encumbered with considerable debts, which are an excrescence of the late war. But this cannot happen again, if the proposed system be adopted; and when these debts are discharged, the only call for revenue of any consequence, which the State governments will continue to experience, will be for the mere support of their respective civil list; to which, if we add all contingencies, the total amount in every State ought to fall considerably short of two hundred thousand pounds.

In framing a government for posterity as well as ourselves, we ought, in those provisions which are designed to be permanent, to calculate, not on temporary, but on permanent causes of expense. If this principle be a just one our attention would be directed to a provision in favor of the State governments for an annual sum of about two hundred thousand pounds; while the exigencies of the Union could be susceptible of no limits, even in imagination. In this view of the subject, by what logic can it be maintained that the local governments ought to command, in perpetuity, an EXCLUSIVE source of revenue for any sum beyond the extent of two hundred thousand pounds? To extend its power further, in *exclusion* of the authority of the Union, would be to take the resources of the community out of those hands which stood in need of them for the public welfare, in order to put them into other hands which could have no just or proper occasion for them.

Suppose, then, the convention had been inclined to proceed upon the principle of a repartition of the objects of revenue, between the Union and its members, in *proportion* to their comparative necessities; what particular fund could have been selected for the use of the States, that would not either have been too much or too little—too little for their present, too much for their future wants? As to the line of separation between external and internal taxes, this would leave to the States, at a rough computation, the command of two thirds of the resources of the community to defray from a tenth to a twentieth part of its expenses; and to the Union, one third of the resources of the community, to defray from nine tenths to nineteen twentieths of its expenses. If we desert this boundary and content ourselves with leaving to the States an exclusive power of taxing houses and lands, there would still be a great disproportion between the *means* and the *end*; the possession of one third of the resources of the community to supply, at most, one tenth of its wants. If any fund could have been selected and appropriated, equal to and not greater than the object, it

would have been inadequate to the discharge of the existing debts of the particular States, and would have left them dependent on the Union for a provision for this purpose.

The preceding train of observation will justify the position which has been elsewhere laid down, that "A CONCURRENT JURISDICTION in the article of taxation was the only admissible substitute for an entire subordination, in respect to this branch of power, of State authority to that of the Union." Any separation of the objects of revenue that could have been fallen upon, would have amounted to a sacrifice of the great INTERESTS of the Union to the POWER of the individual States. The convention thought the concurrent jurisdiction preferable to that subordination; and it is evident that it has at least the merit of reconciling an indefinite constitutional power of taxation in the Federal government with an adequate and independent power in the States to provide for their own necessities. There remain a few other lights, in which this important subject of taxation will claim a further consideration.

PUBLIUS.

Federalist No. 35
Concerning the General Power of Taxation
From the *Independent Journal*.
Author: Alexander Hamilton

To the People of the State of New York:

BEFORE we proceed to examine any other objections to an indefinite power of taxation in the Union, I shall make one general remark; which is, that if the jurisdiction of the national government, in the article of revenue, should be restricted to particular objects, it would naturally occasion an undue proportion of the public burdens to fall upon those objects. Two evils would spring from this source: the oppression of particular branches of industry; and an unequal distribution of the taxes, as well among the several States as among the citizens of the same State.

Suppose, as has been contended for, the federal power of taxation were to be confined to duties on imports, it is evident that the government, for want of being able to command other resources, would frequently be tempted to extend these duties to an injurious excess. There are persons who imagine that they can never be carried to too great a length; since the higher they are, the more it is alleged they will tend to discourage an extravagant consumption, to produce a favorable balance of trade, and to promote domestic manufactures. But all extremes are pernicious in various ways. Exorbitant duties on imported articles would beget a general spirit of smuggling; which is always prejudicial to the fair trader, and eventually to the revenue itself: they tend to render other classes of the community tributary, in an improper degree, to the manufacturing classes, to whom they give a premature monopoly of the markets; they sometimes force industry out of its more natural channels into others in which it flows with less advantage; and in the last place, they oppress the merchant, who is often obliged to pay them himself without any retribution from the consumer. When the demand is equal to the quantity of goods at market, the consumer generally pays the duty; but when the markets happen to be over-stocked, a great proportion falls upon the merchant, and sometimes not only exhausts his profits, but breaks in upon his capital. I am apt to think that a division of the duty, between the seller and the buyer, more often happens than is commonly imagined. It is not always possible to raise the price of a commodity in exact proportion to every additional imposition laid upon it. The merchant, especially in a country of small commercial capital, is often under a necessity of keeping prices down in order to a more expeditious sale.

The maxim that the consumer is the payer, is so much oftener true than the reverse of the proposition, that it is far more equitable that the duties on imports should go into a common stock, than that they should redound to the exclusive benefit of the importing States. But it is not so generally true as to render it equitable, that those duties should form the only national fund. When they are paid by the merchant they operate as an additional tax upon the importing State, whose citizens pay their proportion of them in the character of consumers. In this view they are productive of inequality among the States; which inequality would be increased with the increased extent of the duties. The confinement of the national revenues to this species of imposts would be attended with inequality, from a different cause, between the manufacturing and the non-manufacturing States. The States which can go farthest towards the supply of their own wants, by their own manufactures, will not, according to their numbers or wealth, consume so great a proportion of imported articles as those States which are not in the same favorable situation. They would not, therefore, in this mode alone contribute to the public treasury in a ratio to their abilities. To make them do this it is necessary that recourse be had to excises, the proper objects of which are particular kinds of manufactures. New York is more deeply interested in these considerations than such of her citizens as contend for limiting the power of the Union to external taxation may be aware of. New York is an importing State, and is not likely speedily to be, to any great extent, a manufacturing State. She would, of course, suffer in a double light from restraining the jurisdiction of the Union to commercial imposts.

So far as these observations tend to inculcate a danger of the import duties being extended to an injurious extreme it may be observed, conformably to a remark made in another part of these papers, that the interest of the revenue itself would be a sufficient guard against such an extreme. I readily admit that this would be the case, as long as other resources were open; but if the avenues to them were closed, HOPE, stimulated by necessity, would beget experiments, fortified by rigorous precautions and additional penalties, which, for a time, would have the intended effect, till there had been leisure to contrive expedients to elude these new precautions. The first success would be apt to inspire false opinions, which it might require a long course of subsequent experience to correct. Necessity, especially in politics, often occasions false hopes, false reasonings, and a system of measures correspondingly erroneous. But even if this supposed excess should not be a consequence of the limitation of the federal power of taxation, the inequalities spoken of would still ensue, though not in the same degree, from the other causes that have been noticed. Let us now return to the examination of objections.

One which, if we may judge from the frequency of its repetition, seems most to be relied on, is, that the House of Representatives is not sufficiently numerous for the reception of all the different classes of citizens, in order to combine the interests and feelings of every part of the community, and to produce a due sympathy between the representative body and its constituents. This argument presents itself under a very specious and seducing form; and is well calculated to lay hold of the prejudices of those to whom it is addressed. But when we come to dissect it with attention, it will appear to be made up of nothing but fair-sounding words. The object it seems to aim at is, in the first place, impracticable, and in the sense in which it is contended for, is unnecessary. I reserve for another place the discussion of the question which relates to the sufficiency of the representative body in respect to numbers, and shall content myself with examining here the particular use which has been made of a contrary supposition, in reference to the immediate subject of our inquiries.

The idea of an actual representation of all classes of the people, by persons of each class, is altogether visionary. Unless it were expressly provided in the Constitution, that each different occupation should send one or more members, the thing would never take place in practice. Mechanics and manufacturers will always be inclined, with few exceptions, to give their votes to merchants, in preference to persons of their own professions or trades. Those discerning citizens are well aware that the mechanic and manufacturing arts furnish the materials of mercantile enterprise and industry. Many of them, indeed, are immediately connected with the operations of commerce. They know that the merchant is their natural patron and friend; and they are aware, that however great the confidence they may justly feel in their own good sense, their interests can be more effectually promoted by the merchant than by themselves. They are sensible that their habits in life have not been such as to give them those acquired endowments, without which, in a deliberative assembly, the greatest natural abilities are for the most part useless; and that the influence and weight, and superior acquirements of the merchants render them more equal to a contest with any spirit which might happen to infuse itself into the public councils, unfriendly to the manufacturing and trading interests. These considerations, and many others that might be mentioned prove, and experience confirms it, that artisans and manufacturers will commonly be disposed to bestow their votes upon merchants and those whom they recommend. We must therefore consider merchants as the natural representatives of all these classes of the community.

With regard to the learned professions, little need be observed; they truly form no distinct interest in society, and according to their situation and talents, will be indiscriminately the objects of the confidence and choice of each other, and of other parts of the community.

Nothing remains but the landed interest; and this, in a political view, and particularly in relation to taxes, I take to be perfectly united, from the wealthiest landlord down to the poorest tenant. No tax can be laid on land which will not affect the proprietor of millions of acres as well as the proprietor of a single acre. Every landholder will therefore have a common interest to keep the taxes on land as low as possible; and common interest may always be reckoned upon as the surest bond of sympathy. But if we even could suppose a distinction of interest between the opulent landholder and the middling farmer, what reason is there to conclude, that the first would stand a better chance of being deputed to the national legislature than the last? If we take fact as our guide, and look into our own senate and assembly, we shall find that moderate proprietors of land prevail in both; nor is this less the case in the senate, which consists of a smaller number, than in the assembly, which is composed of a greater number. Where the qualifications of the electors are the same, whether they have to choose a small or a large number, their votes will fall upon those in whom they have most confidence; whether these happen to be men of large fortunes, or of moderate property, or of no property at all.

It is said to be necessary, that all classes of citizens should have some of their own number in the representative body, in order that their feelings and interests may be the better understood and attended to. But we have seen that this will never happen under any arrangement that leaves the votes of the people free. Where this is the case, the representative body, with too few exceptions to have any influence on the spirit of the government, will be composed of landholders, merchants, and men of the learned professions. But where is the danger that the interests and feelings of the different classes of citizens will not be understood or attended to by these three descriptions of men? Will not the landholder know and feel whatever will promote or insure the interest of landed property? And will he not, from his own interest in that species of property, be sufficiently prone to resist every attempt to prejudice or encumber it? Will not the merchant understand and be disposed to cultivate, as far as may be proper, the interests of the mechanic and manufacturing arts, to which his commerce is so nearly allied? Will not the man of the learned profession, who will feel a neutrality to the rivalships between the different branches of industry, be likely to prove an impartial arbiter between them, ready to promote either, so far as it shall appear to him conducive to the general interests of the society?

If we take into the account the momentary humors or dispositions which may happen to prevail in particular parts of the society, and to which a wise administration will never be inattentive, is the man whose situation leads to extensive inquiry and information less likely to be a competent judge of their nature, extent, and foundation than one whose observation does not travel beyond the circle of his neighbors and acquaintances? Is it not natural that a man who is a candidate for the favor of the people, and who is dependent on the suffrages of his fellow-citizens for the continuance of his public honors, should take care to inform himself of their dispositions and inclinations, and should be willing to allow them their proper degree of influence upon his conduct? This dependence, and the necessity of being bound himself, and his posterity, by the laws to which he gives his assent, are the true, and they are the strong chords of sympathy between the representative and the constituent.

There is no part of the administration of government that requires extensive information and a thorough knowledge of the principles of political economy, so much as the business of taxation. The man who understands those principles best will be least likely to resort to oppressive expedients, or sacrifice any particular class of citizens to the procurement of revenue. It might be demonstrated that the most productive system of finance will always be the least burdensome. There can be no doubt that in order to a judicious exercise of the power of taxation, it is necessary that the person in whose hands it should be acquainted with the general genius, habits, and modes of thinking of the people at large, and with the resources of the country. And this is all that can be reasonably meant by a knowledge of the interests and feelings of the people. In any other sense the proposition has either no meaning, or an absurd one. And in that sense let every considerate citizen judge for himself where the requisite qualification is most likely to be found.

PUBLIUS.

Federalist No. 36

Concerning the General Power of Taxation

From the *New York Packet.*

Tuesday, January 8, 1788.

Author: Alexander Hamilton

To the People of the State of New York:

WE HAVE seen that the result of the observations, to which the foregoing number has been principally devoted, is, that from the natural operation of the different interests and views of the various classes of the community, whether the representation of the people be more or less numerous, it will consist almost entirely of proprietors of land, of merchants, and of members of the learned professions, who will truly represent all those different interests and views. If it should be objected that we have seen other descriptions of men in the local legislatures, I answer that it is admitted there are exceptions to the rule, but not in sufficient number to influence the general complexion or character of the government. There are strong minds in every walk of life that will rise superior to the disadvantages of situation, and will command the tribute due to their merit, not only from the classes to which they particularly belong, but from the society in general. The door ought to be equally open to all; and I trust, for the credit of human nature, that we shall see examples of such vigorous plants flourishing in the soil of federal as well as of State legislation; but occasional instances of this sort will not render the reasoning founded upon the general course of things, less conclusive.

The subject might be placed in several other lights that would all lead to the same result; and in particular it might be asked, What greater affinity or relation of interest can be conceived between the carpenter and blacksmith, and the linen manufacturer or stocking weaver, than between the merchant and either of them? It is notorious that there are often as great rivalships between different branches of the mechanic or manufacturing arts as there are between any of the departments of labor and industry; so that, unless the representative body were to be far more numerous than would be consistent with any idea of regularity or wisdom in its deliberations, it is impossible that what seems to be the spirit of the objection we have been considering should ever be realized in practice. But I forbear to dwell any longer on a matter which has hitherto worn too loose a garb to admit even of an accurate inspection of its real shape or tendency.

There is another objection of a somewhat more precise nature that claims our attention. It has been asserted that a power of internal taxation in the national legislature could never be exercised with advantage, as well from the want of a sufficient knowledge of local circumstances, as from an interference between the revenue laws of the Union and of the particular States. The supposition of a want of proper knowledge seems to be entirely destitute of foundation. If any question is depending in a State legislature respecting one of the counties, which demands a knowledge of local details, how is it acquired? No doubt from the information of the members of the county. Cannot the like knowledge be obtained in the national legislature from the representatives of each State? And is it not to be presumed that the men who will generally be sent there will be possessed of the necessary degree of intelligence to be able to communicate that information? Is the knowledge of local circumstances, as applied to taxation, a minute topographical acquaintance with all the mountains, rivers, streams, highways, and bypaths in each State; or is it a general acquaintance with its situation and resources, with the state of its agriculture, commerce, manufactures, with the nature of its products and consumptions, with the different degrees and kinds of its wealth, property, and industry?

Nations in general, even under governments of the more popular kind, usually commit the administration of their finances to single men or to boards composed of a few individuals, who digest and prepare, in the first instance, the plans of taxation, which are afterwards passed into laws by the authority of the sovereign or legislature.

Inquisitive and enlightened statesmen are deemed everywhere best qualified to make a judicious selection of the objects proper for revenue; which is a clear indication, as far as the sense of mankind can have weight in the question, of the species of knowledge of local circumstances requisite to the purposes of taxation.

The taxes intended to be comprised under the general denomination of internal taxes may be subdivided into those of the *direct* and those of the *indirect* kind. Though the objection be made to both, yet the reasoning upon it seems to be confined to the former branch. And indeed, as to the latter, by which must be understood duties and excises on articles of consumption, one is at a loss to conceive what can be the nature of the difficulties apprehended. The knowledge relating to them must evidently be of a kind that will either be suggested by the nature of the article itself, or can easily be procured from any well-informed man, especially of the mercantile class. The cir-

cumstances that may distinguish its situation in one State from its situation in another must be few, simple, and easy to be comprehended. The principal thing to be attended to, would be to avoid those articles which had been previously appropriated to the use of a particular State; and there could be no difficulty in ascertaining the revenue system of each. This could always be known from the respective codes of laws, as well as from the information of the members from the several States.

The objection, when applied to real property or to houses and lands, appears to have, at first sight, more foundation, but even in this view it will not bear a close examination. Land-taxes are commonly laid in one of two modes, either by *actual* valuations, permanent or periodical, or by *occasional* assessments, at the discretion, or according to the best judgment, of certain officers whose duty it is to make them. In either case, the EXECUTION of the business, which alone requires the knowledge of local details, must be devolved upon discreet persons in the character of commissioners or assessors, elected by the people or appointed by the government for the purpose. All that the law can do must be to name the persons or to prescribe the manner of their election or appointment, to fix their numbers and qualifications and to draw the general outlines of their powers and duties. And what is there in all this that cannot as well be performed by the national legislature as by a State legislature? The attention of either can only reach to general principles; local details, as already observed, must be referred to those who are to execute the plan.

But there is a simple point of view

in which this matter may be placed that must be altogether satisfactory. The national legislature can make use of the *system of each State within that State*. The method of laying and collecting this species of taxes in each State can, in all its parts, be adopted and employed by the federal government.

Let it be recollected that the proportion of these taxes is not to be left to the discretion of the national legislature, but is to be determined by the numbers of each State, as described in the second section of the first article. An actual census or enumeration of the people must furnish the rule, a circumstance which effectually shuts the door to partiality or oppression. The abuse of this power of taxation seems to have been provided against with guarded circumspection. In addition to the precaution just mentioned, there is a provision that "all duties, imposts, and excises shall be UNIFORM throughout the United States."

It has been very properly observed by different speakers and writers on the side of the Constitution, that if the exercise of the power of internal taxation by the Union should be discovered on experiment to be really inconvenient, the federal government may then forbear the use of it, and have recourse to requisitions in its stead. By way of answer to this, it has been triumphantly asked, Why not in the first instance omit that ambiguous power, and rely upon the latter resource? Two solid answers may be given. The first is, that the exercise of that power, if convenient, will be preferable, because it will be more effectual; and it is impossible to prove in theory, or otherwise than by the experiment, that it

cannot be advantageously exercised. The contrary, indeed, appears most probable. The second answer is, that the existence of such a power in the Constitution will have a strong influence in giving efficacy to requisitions. When the States know that the Union can apply itself without their agency, it will be a powerful motive for exertion on their part.

As to the interference of the revenue laws of the Union, and of its members, we have already seen that there can be no clashing or repugnancy of authority. The laws cannot, therefore, in a legal sense, interfere with each other; and it is far from impossible to avoid an interference even in the policy of their different systems. An effectual expedient for this purpose will be, mutually, to abstain from those objects which either side may have first had recourse to. As neither can *control* the other, each will have an obvious and sensible interest in this reciprocal forbearance. And where there is an *immediate* common interest, we may safely count upon its operation. When the particular debts of the States are done away, and their expenses come to be limited within their natural compass, the possibility almost of interference will vanish. A small land tax will answer the purpose of the States, and will be their most simple and most fit resource.

Many spectres have been raised out of this power of internal taxation, to excite the apprehensions of the people: double sets of revenue officers, a duplication of their burdens by double taxations, and the frightful forms of odious and oppressive poll-taxes, have been played off with all the ingenious dexterity of political legerdemain.

As to the first point, there are two cases in which there can be no room for double sets of officers: one, where the right of imposing the tax is exclusively vested in the Union, which applies to the duties on imports; the other, where the object has not fallen under any State regulation or provision, which may be applicable to a variety of objects. In other cases, the probability is that the United States will either wholly abstain from the objects preoccupied for local purposes, or will make use of the State officers and State regulations for collecting the additional imposition. This will best answer the views of revenue, because it will save expense in the collection, and will best avoid any occasion of disgust to the State governments and to the people. At all events, here is a practicable expedient for avoiding such an inconvenience; and nothing more can be required than to show that evils predicted to not necessarily result from the plan.

As to any argument derived from a supposed system of influence, it is a sufficient answer to say that it ought not to be presumed; but the supposition is susceptible of a more precise answer. If such a spirit should infest the councils of the Union, the most certain road to the accomplishment of its aim would be to employ the State officers as much as possible, and to attach them to the Union by an accumulation of their emoluments. This would serve to turn the tide of State influence into the channels of the national government, instead of making federal influence flow in an opposite and adverse current. But all suppositions of this kind are invidious, and ought to be banished from the consideration of the great question before the people. They can answer no other end than to cast a mist over the truth.

As to the suggestion of double taxation, the answer is plain. The wants of the Union are to be supplied in one way or another; if to be done by the authority of the federal government, it will not be to be done by that of the State government. The quantity of taxes to be paid by the community must be the same in either case; with this advantage, if the provision is to be made by the Union—that the capital resource of commercial imposts, which is the most convenient branch of revenue, can be prudently improved to a much greater extent under federal than under State regulation, and of course will render it less necessary to recur to more inconvenient methods; and with this further advantage, that as far as there may be any real difficulty in the exercise of the power of internal taxation, it will impose a disposition to greater care in the choice and arrangement of the means; and must naturally tend to make it a fixed point of policy in the national administration to go as far as may be practicable in making the luxury of the rich tributary to the public treasury, in order to diminish the necessity of those impositions which might create dissatisfaction in the poorer and most numerous classes of the society. Happy it is when the interest which the government has in the preservation of its own power, coincides with a proper distribution of the public burdens, and tends to guard the least wealthy part of the community from oppression!

As to poll taxes, I, without scruple, confess my disapprobation of them; and though they have prevailed from an early period in those States[1] which have uniformly been the most tenacious of their rights, I should lament to see them introduced into practice under the national government. But does it follow because there is a power to lay them that they will actually be laid? Every State in the Union has power to impose taxes of this kind; and yet in several of them they are unknown in practice. Are the State governments to be stigmatized as tyrannies, because they possess this power? If they are not, with what propriety can the like power justify such a charge against the national government, or even be urged as an obstacle to its adoption? As little friendly as I am to the species of imposition, I still feel a thorough conviction that the power of having recourse to it ought to exist in the federal government. There are certain emergencies of nations, in which expedients, that in the ordinary state of things ought to be forborne, become essential to the public weal. And the government, from the possibility of such emergencies, ought ever to have the option of making use of them. The real scarcity of objects in this country, which may be considered as productive sources of revenue, is a reason peculiar to itself, for not abridging the discretion of the national councils in this respect. There may exist certain critical and tempestuous conjunctures of the State, in which a poll tax may become an inestimable resource. And as I know nothing to exempt this portion of the globe from the common calamities that have befallen other parts of it, I acknowledge my aversion to every project that is calculated to disarm the government of a single weapon, which in any possible contingency might be usefully employed for the general defense and security.

I have now gone through the examination of such of the powers proposed to be vested in the United States, which may be considered as having an immediate relation to the energy of the government; and have endeavored to answer the principal objections which have been made to them. I have passed over in silence those minor authorities, which are either too inconsiderable to have been thought worthy of the hostilities of the opponents of the Constitution, or of too manifest propriety to admit of controversy. The mass of judiciary power, however, might have claimed an investigation under this head, had it not been for the consideration that its organization and its extent may be more advantageously considered in connection. This has determined me to refer it to the branch of our inquiries upon which we shall next enter.

PUBLIUS.
1. The New England States.

See also: **Vol. I**: American Revolution; Anti-Federalists; Articles of Confederation; *Cato's Letters*; *The Federalist* (Federalist Papers); Federalists; Hamilton, Alexander; Madison, James. **Vol. III**: Tariff of 1789.

Report on Manufactures

Submitted to Congress by Secretary of the Treasury Alexander Hamilton on January 15, 1790, the Report on Manufactures *addressed differences between agricultural and manufacturing interests. Although the United States had historically focused on agriculture and supplying raw materials to European nations, particularly Great Britain, Hamilton argued that the economic stability of the nation depended on the encouragement of industry. He pointed out that whereas agricultural countries remained dependent on manufacturing nations for their livelihood and survival, a nation as rich in natural resources as the United States could achieve economic freedom by utilizing domestic products for internal manufacturing. Hamilton also viewed the rise of industry as a means of attracting labor from the Old World because the United States continued to experience a "scarcity of hands." Although Congress failed to act on his recommendations at the time, in 1816 the government began encouraging the growth of domestic industry by passing the first protective tariff in the wake of the War of 1812.*

The Secretary of the Treasury, in obedience to the order of the House of Representatives, of the 15th day of January 1790, has applied his attention, at as early a period as his other duties would permit, to the subject of Manufactures; and particularly to the means of promoting such as will tend to render the United States, independent of foreign nations, for military and other essential supplies. And he there(upon) respectfully submits the following Report.

The expediency of encouraging manufactures in the United States, which was not long since deemed very questionable, appears at this time to be pretty generally admitted. The embarrassments, which have obstructed the progress of our external trade, have led to serious reflections on the necessity of enlarging the sphere of our domestic commerce: the restrictive regulations, which in foreign markets abridge the vent of the increasing surplus or our Agricultural produce, serve to beget an earnest desire, that a more extensive demand for that surplus may be created at home: And the complete success, which has rewarded manufacturing enterprise, in some valuable branches, conspiring with the promising symptoms, which attend some less mature essays, in others, justify a hope, that the obstacles to the growth of this species of industry are less formidable that they were apprehended to be; and that it is not difficult to find, in its further extension: a full indemnification for any external disadvantages, which are or may be experienced, as well as an accession of resources, favorable to national independence and safety.

There still are, nevertheless, respectable patrons of opinions, unfriendly to the encouragement of manufacturers. The following are, substantially, the arguments, by which these opinions are defended.

"In every country (say those who entertain them) Agriculture is the most beneficial and *productive* object of human industry. This position, generally, if not universally true, applies with peculiar emphasis to the United States, on account of their immense tracts of fertile territory, uninhabited and unimproved. Nothing can afford so advantageous an employment for capital and labour, as the conversion of this extensive wilderness into cultivated farms. Nothing equally with this, can contribute to the population, strength and real riches of the country."

"To endeavor by the extraordinary patronage of Government, to accelerate the growth of manufactures, is in fact, to endeavor, by force and art, to transfer the natural current of industry, from a more, to a less beneficial channel. Whatever has such a tendency must necessarily be unwise. Indeed it can hardly ever be wise in a government, to attempt to give a direction to the industry of its citizens. This, under the quick-sighted guidance of private interest, will, if left to itself, infallibly find its own way to the most profitable employment: and 'tis by such employment, that the public prosperity will be more effectually promoted. To leave industry to itself, therefore, is, in almost every case, the soundest as well as the simplest policy."

"This policy is not only recommended to the United States, by considerations which affect all nations, it is, in a manner, dictated to them by the imperious force of a very peculiar situation. The smallness of their population compared with their territory—the constant allurements of emigration from the settled to the unsettled parts of the country—the facility with which the less independent condition of a artisan can be exchanged for the more independent condition of a farmer, these and similar causes conspire to produce, and for a length of time must continued to occasion, a scarcity of hands for manufacturing occupation, and dearness of labor generally. To these disadvantages for the prosecution of manufactures, a deficiency of pecuniary capital being added, the prospect of a successful competition with the manufactures of Europe must be regarded as little less than desperate. Extensive manufactures can only be the offspring of a redundant, at least of a full population. Till the latter shall characterise the situation of the county, 'tis vain to hope for the former."

"If, contrary to the natural course of things, an unseasonable and premature spring can be given to certain fabrics, by heavy duties, prohibitions, bounties, or by other forced expedients; this will only be to sacrifice the interests of the community to those of particular classes. Besides the misdirection of labour, a virtual monopoly will be given to the persons employed on such fabrics: and an enhancement of price, the inevitable consequence of every monopoly, must be defrayed at the expence of the other parts of society. It is far preferable, that those persons should be engaged in the cultivation of the earth, and that we should procure, in exchange for its productions, the commodities, with which foreigners were able to supply us in greater perfection, and upon better terms."

This mode of reasoning is founded upon facts and principles, which have certainly respectable pretensions. If it had governed the conduct of nations, more generally than it has done, there is room to suppose, that it might have carried them faster to prosperity and greatness, than they have attained by the pursuit of maxims too widely opposite. Most general theories, however, admit of numerous exceptions, and there are few, if any, of the political kind, which do not blend a considerable portion of error, with the truths they inculcate.

In order to an accurate judgment how far that which has been just stated ought to be deemed liable to a similar imputation, it is necessary to advert carefully to the considerations, which plead in favor of manufactures, and which appear to recommend the special and positive encouragement of them; in certain cases, and under certain reasonable limitations.

It ought readily to be conceded that the cultivation of the earth—as the primary and most certain source of national supply—as the immediate and chief source of subsistence to a man—as the principal source of those materials which constitute the nutriment of other kinds of labor—as including a state more favourable to the freedom and independence of the human mind—one, perhaps, most conducive to the multiplication of the human species—has *intrinsically a strong claim to preeminence over every other kind of industry.*

But, that is has a title to any thing like an exclusive predilection, in any country, ought to be admitted with great caution. That is even more productive than every other branch of Industry requires more evidence, than has yet been given in support of the position. That its real interests, precious and important as without the help of exaggeration and importance, they truly are, will be advantaged, rather than injured by the due encouragement of manufactures, may, it is believed, be satisfactorily demonstrated. And it is also believed that the expediency of such encouragement in a general view may be shewn to be recommended by the most cogent and persuasive motives of national policy.

It has been maintained, that Agriculture is, not only, the most productive, but the only productive species of industry. The reality of this suggestion in either aspect has, however, not been verified by any accurate detail of facts and calculations; and the general arguments, which are adduced to prove

Debating the Issues: Selected Primary Documents

it, are rather subtil and paradoxical, than solid or convincing.

Those which maintain its exclusive productiveness are to this effect.

Labour, bestowed upon the cultivation of land produces enough, not only to replace all the necessary expences incurred in the business, and to maintain the persons who are employed in it, but to afford together with the *ordinary profit* on the stock and capital of the Farmer, a nett surplus, or *rent* for the landlord or proprietor of the soil. But the labor of Artificers does nothing more, than replace the Stock which employs them (or which furnishes materials tools and wages) and yield the *ordinary profit* of that Stock. It yields nothing equivalent to the *rent* of the land and labour of the country. The additional value given to those parts of the produce of land, which are wrought into manufacturers, is counterbalanced by the value of those other parts of that produce, which are consumed by the manufacturers. It can therefore only be by saving, or *parsimony*, not by the positive *productiveness* of their labour, that the classes of Artificers can in any degree augment the revenue of the Society.

To this it has been answered—

I "That inasmuch as it is acknowledged, that manufacturing labour reproduces a value equal to that which is expended or consumed in carrying it on, and continues in existence the original Stock or capital employed—it ought on that account alone, to escape being considered as wholly unproductive: That though is should be admitted, as alleged, that the consumption of the produce of the soil, by the classes of Artificers or Manufacturers, is exactly equal to the value added by there

labour to the materials upon with it is exerted; yet it would not thence follow, that it added nothing to the Revenue of the Society, or to the aggregate value of the annual produce of its land and labour. If the consumption for any given period amounted to a *given sum* in the *increased* value of the produce manufactured, in the same period, to a *like sum*, the total amount of the consumption and production during that period, will be equal to the *two sums*, and consequently double the value of the agriculture produce consumed. And though the increment of value produced by the classes of Artificers should at no time exceed the value of the produce of the land consumed by them, yet there would be at every moment, in consequence of labour, a greater value of goods in the market then would exist independent of it."

II—"That the position, that Artificers can augment the revenue of a Society, only by parsimony, is true, in no other sense, than in one, which is equally applicable to Husbandmen or Cultivators. It may be alike affirmed of all these classes, that the fund acquired by there labor destined for their support is not, in an ordinary way, more than equal to it. And hence it will follow, that augmentations of the wealth or capital of the community (except in the instances of some extraordinary dexterity or skill) can only proceed, with respect to any of them, from the savings of the more thrifty and parsimonious."

III—"That the annual produce of the land and labour of a country can be encreased, in two ways—by some improvement in the *productive powers* of the useful labour, which actually exists within it, or by some increase in the quantity of such labour: That with regard to the first, the labour of Artificers being capable of greater subdivision in simplicity of operation, within that of Cultivators, it is susceptible, in a proportionably greater degree, of improvement in its *productive powers*, whether to be derived from an accession of Skill, or from the application of ingenious machinery; in which particular, therefore, the labour employed in the cultural of land can pretend to no advantage over that engaged in manufactures: That with regard to an augmentation of the quantity of useful labuor, this, excluding adventitious circumstances, must depend essentially upon an increase of *capital*, which again must depend upon the savings made out of the revenues of those, who furnish or manage *that*, which is at any time employed, whether in Agricultural or Manufactures, or in any other way."

But while the *exclusive* productiveness of Agricultural labour has been thus denied and refuted, the superiority of its productiveness has been conceded without hesitation. As this concession involves a point of considerable magnitude, in relation to maxims of public administration, the grounds which it rests are worthy of a distinct and particular examination.

One of the arguments made use of, in support of the idea maybe pronounced both quaint and superficial. It amounts to this—That in the productions of the soil, nature co-operates with man; and that the effect of their joint labour must be greater than that of the labour of man alone.

This, however, is far from being a necessary inference. It is very conceivable, that the labor of man alone laid out upon a work, requiring great skill and art to bring it to perfection, may be more productive, *in value*, than the labour of nature and man combined, when directed toward more simple operations and objects: And when it is recollected to what an extent the Agency of nature, in the application of the mechanical powers, is made auxiliary to the prosecution of manufactures, the suggestion, which has been noticed, loses even the appearance of plausibility.

It might also be observed, with a contrary view, that the labour employed in Agriculture is in a great measure periodical and occasional, depending on the seasons, liable to various and long intermissions; while that occupied in many manufactures is constant and regular, extending through the year, embracing in some instances night as well as day. It is also probable, that there are among the cultivators of land more examples of remissness, than among artificers. The farmer, from the peculiar fertility of his land, or some other favorable circumstance, may frequently obtain a livelihood, even with a considerable degree of carelessness in the mode of cultivation; but the artisan can with difficulty effect the same object, without exerting himself pretty equally with all those, who are engaged in the same pursuit. And if it may likewise be assumed as a fact, that manufactures open a wider field to exertions of ingenuity than agriculture, it would not be a strained conjecture, that the labour employed in the former, being at once more *constant*, more uniform, and more ingenious, than that which is employed in the latter, will be found at the same time more productive.

But it is not meant to lay stress on

observations of this nature—they ought only to serve as a counterbalance to those of a similar complexion. Circumstances so vague and general, as well as so abstract, can afford little instruction in a matter of this kind.

Another, and that which seems to be the principal argument offered for the superior productiveness of Agricultural labour, turns upon the allegation, that labour employed on manufactures yields nothing equivalent to the rent of land; or to that nett surplus, as it is called, which accrues to the proprietor of the soil.

But this distinction, important as it has been deemed, appears rather *verbal* than *substantial*.

It is easily discernable, that what in the first instance is divided into two parts under the denominations of the *ordinary profit* of the Stock of the farmer and *rent* to the landlord, is in the second instance united under the general appellation of the *ordinary profit* on the Stock of the Undertaker; and that this formal or verbal distribution constitutes the whole difference in the two cases. It seems to have been overlooked, that the land is itself a Stock or capital, advanced or lent by its owner to the occupier or tenant, and that the rent he receives is only the ordinary profit of a certain Stock in land, not managed by the proprietor himself, but by another to whom he leads or lets it, and who on his part advances a second capital to stock & improve the land, upon which he also receives the usual profit. The rent of the landlord and the profit of the farmer are therefore nothing more than the *ordinary profits* of *two* capitals, belonging to *two* different persons, and united in the cultivation of a farm: As in the other case, the surplus which arises upon any manufactory, after replacing the expences of carrying it on, answers to the ordinary profits of *one* or *more* capitals engaged in the persecution of such manufactory. It is said *one* or *more* capitals; because, in fact the same thing which is contemplated, in the case of the farm, sometimes happens in that of a manufactory. There is one, who furnishes a part of the capital, or lends a part of the money, by which it is carried on, and another, who carries it on, with the addition of his own capital. Out of the surplus, which remains, after defraying expences, an interest is paid to the money-lender for the portion of the capital furnished by him, which exactly agrees with the rent paid to the landlord; and the residue of that surplus constitutes the profit of the undertaker or manufacturer, and agrees with what is denominated the ordinary profits on the Stock of the farmer. Both together make the ordinary profits of two capitals (employed in a manufactory; as in the other case the rent of the landlord and the revenue of the farmer compose the ordinary profits of two Capitals) employed in the cultivation of a farm.

The rent therefore accruing to the proprietor of the land, far from being a criterion of *exclusive* productiveness, as has been argued, is no criterion even of superior productiveness. The question must still be, whether the surplus, after defraying expences of a *given capital* employed in the *purchase* and *improvement* of a piece of land, is greater or less, than that of a like capital employed in the prosecution of a manufactory: or whether the *whole value produced* from a *given capital* and a *given quantity* of *labour*, employed in one way, be greater or less, than the *whole value produced* from an *equal capital* and an *equal quantity* of *labour* employed in the other way: or rather, perhaps whether the business of Agriculture or that of Manufactures will yield the greatest product, according to a *compound ratio* of the quantity of the Capital and the quantity of labour, which are employed in the one or in the other.

The solution of either of these questions is not easy; it involves numerous and complicated details, depending on an accurate knowledge of the objects to be compared. It is not known that the comparison has ever yet been made upon sufficient data properly ascertained and analised. To be able to make it on the present occasion with satisfactory precision would demand more previous enquiry and investigation, than there has been hitherto either leisure or opportunity to accomplish.

Some essays however have been made towards acquiring the requisite information; which have rather served to throw doubt upon, than to confirm the Hypothesis, under examination: But it ought to be acknowledged, that they have been too little diversified, and are too imperfect, to authorise a definitive conclusion either way; leading rather to probable conjecture than to certain deduction. They render it probable, there are various branches of manufactures, in which a given Capital will yield a greater *total* product, and a considerably greater *nett* product, than an equal capital invested in the purchase and improvement of lands; and that there are also *some* branches, in which both the *gross* and the *nett* produce will exceed that of Agricultural industry; according to a compound ratio of capital and labour: But it is on

this last point, that there appears to be the greatest room for doubt. It is far less difficult to infer generally, that the *nett produce* of Capital engaged in manufacturing enterprises is greater than that of Capital engaged in Agriculture.

In stating these results, the purchase and improvement of lands, under previous cultivation are alone contemplated. The comparison is more in favour of Agriculture, when it is made with reference to the settlement of new and waste lands; but an argument drawn from so temporary a circumstance could have no weight in determining the general question concerning the permanent relative productiveness of the two species of industry. How far it ought to influence the policy of the United States, on the score of particular situation, will be averted to in another place.

The foregoing suggestions are *not designed to inculcate an opinion that manufacturing industry is more productive than that of Agriculture.* They are intended rather to shew that the reverse of this proposition is not ascertained; that the general arguments which are brought to establish it are not satisfactory; and consequently that a supposition of the superior productiveness of Tillage ought to be no obstacle to listening to any substantial inducements to the encouragement of manufactures, which may be otherwise perceived to exist, through an apprehension, that they may have a tendency to divert labour from a more to a less profitable employment.

It is extremely probable, that on a full and accurate devellopment of the matter, on the ground of fact and calculation, it would be discovered that there is no material difference between the aggregate productiveness of the one, and of the other kind of industry; and that the propriety of the encouragements, which may in any case be proposed to be given to either ought to be determined upon considerations irrelative to any comparison of that nature.

II But without contending for the superior productiveness of Manufacturing Industry, it may conduce to a better judgment of the policy, which ought to be pursued respecting its encouragement, to contemplate the subject, under some additional aspects, tending not only to confirm the idea, that this kind of industry has been improperly represented as unproductive in itself; but [to] evince in addition that the establishment and diffusion of manufactures have the effect of rendering the total mass of useful and productive labor in a community, *greater than it would otherwise be*. In prosecuting this discussion, it may be necessary briefly to resume and review some of the topics, which have been already touched.

To affirm, that the labour of the Manufacturer is unproductive, because he consumes as much of the produce of land, as he adds value to the raw materials which he manufactures, is not better founded, than it would be to affirm, that the labour of the farmer, which furnishes materials to the manufacturer, is unproductive, *because he consumes an equal value of manufactured articles*. Each furnishes a certain portion of the produce of his labor to the other, and each destroys a correspondent proportion of the produce of the labour of the other. In the mean time, the maintenance of two Citizens, instead of one, is going on; the State has two members instead of one; and they together consume twice the value of what is produced from the land.

If instead of a farmer and artificer, there were a farmer only, he would be under the necessity of devoting a part of his labour to the fabrication of cloathing and other articles, which he would procure of the artificer, in the case of there being such a person; and of course he would be able to devote less labor to the cultivation of his farm; and would draw from it a proportionably less product. The whole quantity of production, in this state of things, in provisions, raw materials and manufactures, would certainly not exceed in value the amount of what would be produced in provisions and raw materials only, if there were an artificer as well as a farmer.

Again—if there were both an artificer and a farmer, the latter would be left at liberty to pursue exclusively the cultivation of his farm. A greater quantity of provisions and raw materials would of course be produced—equal at least—as has been already observed, to the whole amount of the provisions, raw materials and manufactures, which would exist on a contrary supposition. The artificer, at the same time would be going on in the production of manufactured commodities; to an amount sufficient not only to repay the farmer, in those commodities, for the provisions and materials which were procured from him, but to furnish the Artificer himself with a supply of similar commodities for his own use. Thus then, there would be two quantities or values in existence, instead of one; and the revenue and consumption would be double in one case, what it would be in the other.

If in place of both these suppositions, there were supposed to be two farmers, and no artificer, each of whom applied a part of his labour to the culture of land, and another part to the fabrication of Manufactures—in this case, the portion of the labour of both bestowed upon land would produce the same quantity of provisions and raw materials only, as would be produced by the intire sum of the labour of one applied in the same manner, and the portion of the labour of both bestowed upon manufactures, would produce the same quantity of manufactures only, as would be produced by the intire sum of the labour of one applied in the same manner. Hence the produce of the labour of the two farmers would not be greater than the produce of the labour of the farmer and artificer; and hence, it results, that the labour of the artificer is as possitively productive as that of the farmer, and, as positively, augments the revenue of the Society.

The labour of the Artificer replaces to the farmer that portion of his labour, with which he provides the materials of exchange with the Artificer, and which he would otherwise have been compelled to apply to manufactures: and while the Artificer thus enables the farmer to enlarge his stock of Agricultural industry, a portion of which he purchases for his own use, *he also supplies himself with the manufactured articles of which he stands in need.*

He does still more—Besides this equivalent which he gives for the portion of Agricultural labour consumed by him, and this supply of manufactured commodities for his own consumption—he furnishes still a surplus, which compensates for the use of the Capital advanced either by himself or

some other person, for carrying on the business. This is the ordinary profit of the Stock employed in the manufactory, and is, in every sense, as effective an addition to the income of the Society, as the rent of land.

The produce of the labour of the Artificer consequently, may be regarded as composed of three parts; one by which the provisions for his subsistence and the materials for his work are purchased of the farmer, one by which he supplies himself with manufactured necessaries, and a third which constitutes the profit on the Stock employed. The two last portions seem to have been overlooked in the system, which represents manufacturing industry as barren and unproductive.

In the course of the preceding illustrations, the products of equal quantities of the labour of the farmer and artificer have been treated as if equal to each other. But this is not to be understood as intending to assert any such precise equality. It is merely a manner of expression adopted for the sake of simplicity and perspicuity. Whether the value of the produce of the labour of the farmer be somewhat more or less, than that of the artificer, is not material to the main scope of the argument, which hitherto has only aimed at shewing, that the one, as well as the other, occasions a positive augmentation of the total produce and revenue of the Society.

It is now proper to proceed a step further, and to enumerate the principal circumstances, from which it may be inferred—That manufacturing establishments not only occasion a possitive augmentation of the Produce and Revenue of the Society, but that they contribute essentially to rendering then greater than they could possibly be, without such establishments. These circumstances are—

1. The division of Labour.

2. An extension of the use of Machinery.

3. Additional employment to classes of the community not ordinarily engaged in the business.

4. The promoting of emigration from foreign Countries.

5. The furnishing greater scope for the diversity of talents and dispositions which discriminate men from each another.

6. The affording a more ample and various field of enterprize.

7. The creating in some instances a new, and securing in all, a more certain and steady demand for the surplus produce of the soil.

Each of these circumstances has a considerable influence upon the total mass of industrious effort in a community. Together, they add to it a degree of energy and effect, which are not easily conceived. Some comments upon each of them, in the order in which they have been stated, may serve to explain their importance.

I. As to the Division of Labour.

It has justly been observed, that there is scarcely any thing of greater moment in the œconomy of a nation, than the proper division of labour. The seperation of occupations causes each to be carried to a much greater perfection, than it could possible acquire, if they were blended. This arises principally from three circumstances.

Ist—The greater skill and dexterity naturally resulting from a constant and undivided application to a single object. It is evident, that these properties must increase, in proportion to the separation and simplification of objects and the steadiness of the attention devoted to each; and must be less, in proportion to the complication of objects, and the number among which the attention is distracted.

2nd. The economy of time—by avoiding the loss of it, incident to a frequent transition from one operation to another of a different nature. This depends on various circumstances—the transition itself—the orderly disposition of the implements, machines and materials employed in the operation to be relinquished—the preparatory steps to the commencement of a new one—the interruption of the impulse, which the mind of the workman acquires, from being engaged in a particular operation—the distractions hesitations and reluctances, which attend the passage from one kind of business to another.

3rd. An extension of the use of Machinery. A man occupied on a single object will have it more in his power, and will be more naturally led to exert his imagination in devising methods to facilitate and abrige labour, than if he were perplexed by a variety of independent and dissimilar operations. Besides this, the fabrication of Machines, in numerous instances, becoming itself a distinct trade, the Artist who follows it, has all the advantages which have been enumerated, for improvement in his particular art; and in both ways the invention and application of machinery are extended.

And from these causes united, the mere separation of the occupation of the cultivator, from that of the Artificer, has the effect of augmenting the *productive powers* of labour, and with them, the total mass of the produce or revenue of a Country. In this single view of the subject, therefore, the utility of Artificers or Manufactures, towards promoting an increase of productive industry, is apparent.

II. As to an extension of the use of Machinery a point which though partly anticipated requires to be placed in one or two additional lights.

The employment of Machinery forms an item of great importance in the general mass of national industry 'Tis an artificial force brought in aid of the natural force of man; and, to all the purposes of labour, is an increase of hands; an accession of strength, *unencumbered too by the expence of maintaining the laborer.* May it not therefore be fairly inferred, that those occupations, which give greatest scope to the use of this auxiliary, contribute most to the general Stock of industrious effort, and, in consequence, to the general product of industry?

It shall be taken for granted, and the truth of the position referred to observation, that manufacturing pursuits are susceptible in a greater degree of the application of machinery, than those of Agriculture. If so all the difference is lost to a community, which, instead of manufacturing for itself, procures the fabrics requisite to its supply from other Countries. The substitution of foreign for domestic manufactures is a transfer to foreign nations of the advantages accruing from the employment of Machinery, in the modes in which it is capable of being employed, with most utility and to the greatest extent.

The Cotton Mill invented in England, within the last twenty years, is a signal illustration of the general proposition, which has been just advanced. In consequence of it, all the different processes for spining Cotton are performed by means of Machines, which are put in motion by water, and attended chiefly by women and Children; [and by a smaller] number of [persons, in the whole, than are] requisite in the ordinary mode of spinning. And it is an advantage of great moment that the operations of this mill continue with convenience, during the night, as well as through the day. The prodigious affect of such a Machine is easily conceived. To this invention is to be attributed essentially the immense progress, which has been so suddenly made in Great Britain in the various fabrics of Cotton.

III. As to the additional employment of classes of the community, not ordinarily engaged in the particular business.

This is not among the least valuable of the means, by which manufacturing institutions contribute to augment the general stock of industry and production. In places where those institutions prevail, besides the persons regularly engaged in them, they afford occasional and extra employment to industrious individuals and families, who are willing to devote the leisure resulting from the intermissions of their ordinary pursuits to collateral labours, as a resource of multiplying their acquisitions or [their] enjoyments. The husbandman himself experiences a new source of profit and support from the encreased industry of his wife and daughters; invited and stimulated by the demands of the neighboring manufactories.

Besides this advantage of occasional employment to classes having different occupations, there is another of a nature allied to it [and] of a similar tendency. This is—the employment of persons who would otherwise be idle (and in many cases a burthen on the community), either from the byass of temper, habit, infirmity of body, or some other cause, indisposing, or disqualifying them for the toils of the Country. It is worthy of particular remark, that, in general, women and Children are rendered more useful and the latter more early useful by manufacturing establishments, than they would otherwise be. Of the number of persons employed in the Cotton Manufactories of Great Britain, it is computed the 4/7 nearly are women and children; of whom the greatest proportion are children and many of them of a very tender age.

And thus it appears to be one of the attributes of manufactures, and one of no small consequence, to give occasion to the exertion of a greater quantity of Industry, even by the *same number* of persons, where they happen to prevail, than would exist, if there were no such establishments.

IV. As to the promoting of emigration from foreign Countries.

Men reluctantly quit one course of occupation and livelihood for another, unless invited to it by very apparent and proximate advantages. Many, who would go from one country to another, if they had a prospect of continuing with more benefit the callings, to which they have been educated, will often not be tempted to change their situation, by the hope of doing better, in some other way. Manufacturers, who listening to the powerful invitations of a better price for their fabrics, or their labour, of greater cheapness of provisions and raw materials, of an exemption from the chief part of the taxes burthens and restraints, which they endure in the old world, of greater personal independence and consequence, under the operation of a more equal government, and of what is far more precious than mere religious toleration—a perfect equality of religious privileges; would probably flock from Europe to the United States to pursue their own trades or professions, if they were once made sensible of the advantages they would enjoy, and were inspired with an assurance of encouragement and employment, will, with difficulty, be induced to transplant themselves, with a view to becoming Cultivators of Land.

If it be true then, that it is the interest of the United States to open every possible [avenue to] emigration from abroad, it affords a weighty argument for the encouragement of manufactures; which for the reason just assigned, will have the strongest tendency to multiply the inducements to it.

Here is perceived an important resource, not only for extending the population, and with it the useful and productive labour of the country, but likewise for the prosecution of manufactures, without deducting from the number of hands, which might otherwise be drawn to tillage; and even for the indemnification of Agriculture for such as might happen to be diverted from it. Many, whom Manufacturing views would induce to emigrate, would afterwards yield to the temptations, which the particular situation of this Country holds out to Agricultural pursuits. And while Agriculture would in other respects derive many signal and unmingled advantages, from the growth of manufactures, it is a problem whether it would gain or lose, as to the article of the number of persons employed in carrying it on.

V. As to the furnishing greater scope for the diversity of talents and dispositions, which discriminate men from each other.

This is a much more powerful mean of augmenting the fund of national Industry than may at first sight appear. It is a just observation, that minds of the strongest and most active powers for their proper objects fall below mediocrity and labour without effect, if confined to uncongenial pursuits. And it is thence to be inferred, that the results of human exertion may be immensely increased by diversifying its objects. When all the different kinds of industry obtain in a community, each individual can find his proper element, and can call into activity the whole vigour of his nature. And the community is benefitted by the services of its respective members, in the manner in which each can serve it with most effect.

If there be any thing in a remark often to be met with—namely that there is, in the genius of the people of this country, a peculiar aptitude for mechanic improvements, it would operate as a forcible reason for giving opportunities to the exercise of that species of talent, by the propagation of manufactures.

VI. As to the affording a more ample and various field for enterprise.

This also is of greater consequence in the general scale of national exertion, than might perhaps on a superficial view be supposed, and has effects not altogether dissimilar from those of the circumstance last noticed. To cherish and stimulate the activity of the human mind, by multiplying the objects of enterprise, is not among the least considerable of the expedients, by which the wealth of a nation may be promoted. Even things in themselves not positively advantageous, sometimes becomes so, by their tendency to provoke exertion. Every new scene which is opened to the busy nature of man to rouse and exert itself, is the addition of a new energy to the general stock of effort.

The spirit of enterprise, useful and prolific as it is, must necessarily be contracted or expanded in proportion to the simplicity or variety of the occupations and productions, which are to be found in a Society. It must be less in a nation of mere cultivators, than in a nation of cultivators and merchants; less in a nation of cultivators and merchants, than in a nation of cultivators, artificers and merchants.

VII. As to the creating, in some instances, a new, and securing in all a more certain and steady demand, for the surplus produce of the soil.

This is among the most important of the circumstances which have been indicated. It is a principal mean, by which the establishment of manufactures contributed to an augmentation of the produce or revenue of a country, and has an immediate and direct relation to the prosperity of Agriculture.

It is evident, that the exertions of the husbandman will be steady or fluctuating, vigorous or feeble, in proportion to the steadiness or fluctuation, adequateness, or inadequateness of the markets on which he must depend, for the vent of the surplus, which may be produced by his labour; and that such surplus in the ordinary course of things will be greater or less in the same proportion.

For the purpose of this vent, a domestic market is greatly to be preferred to a foreign one; because it is in the nature of things, far more to be relied upon.

It is a primary object of the policy of nations, to be able to supply themselves with subsistence from their own soils; and manufacturing nations, as far as circumstances permit, endeavor to procure, from the same source, the raw materials necessary for their own fabrics. This disposition, urged by the spirit of monopoly, is sometimes even carried to an injudicious extreme. It seems not always to be recollected, that nations, who have neither mines nor manufactures, can only obtain the manufactured articles, of which they stand in need, by an exchange of the products of their soils; and that, if those who can best furnish them with such articles are unwilling to give a due course to this exchange, they must of necessity make every possible effort to manufacture for themselves, the effect of which is that the manufacturing nations abrige the natural advantages of their situation, through an unwillingness to permit the Agricultural countries to enjoy the advantages of theirs, and sacrifice the interests of a mutually beneficial intercourse to the vain project of *selling every thing and buying nothing*.

But it is also a consequence of the policy, which has been noted, that the foreign demand for the products of Agricultural Countries, is, in a great degree, rather casual and occasional, than certain or constant. To what extent injurious interruptions of the demand for some of the staple commodities of the United States, may have been experienced, from that cause, must be referred to the judgment of those who are engaged in carrying on the commerce of the country; but it may be safely assumed, that such interruptions are at times very inconveniently felt, and that cases not unfrequently occur, in which markets are so confined and restricted, as to render the demand very unequal to the supply.

Independently likewise of the artificial impediments, which are created by the policy in question, there are natural causes tending to render the external demand for the surplus of Agricultural nations a precarious reliance. The differences of seasons, in the countries, which are the consumers make immense differences in the produce of their own soils, in different years; and consequently in the degrees of their necessity for foreign supply. Plentiful harvests with them, especially if similar ones occur at the same time in the countries, which are the furnishers, occasion of course a glut in the markets of the latter.

Considering how fast and how much the progress of new settlements in the United States must increase the surplus produce of the soil, and weighing seriously the tendency of the system, which prevails among most of the commercial nations of Europe; whatever dependence may be placed on the force of national circumstances to counteract the effects of an artificial policy; there appear strong reasons to regard the foreign demand for that surplus as too uncertain a reliance, and to desire a substitute for it, in an extensive domestic market.

To secure such a market, there is no other expedient, than to promote manufacturing establishments. Manufacturers who constitute the most numerous class, after the Cultivators of land, are for that reason the principal consumers of the surplus of their labour.

This idea of an extensive domestic market for the surplus produce of the soil is of the first consequence. It is of all things, that which most effectually conduces to a flourishing state of Agriculture. If the effect of manufactories should be to detach a portion of the hands, which would otherwise be engaged in Tillage, it might possibly cause a smaller quantity of lands to be under cultivation but by their tendency to procure a more certain demand for the surplus produce of the soil, they would, at the same time, cause the lands which were in cultivation to be better improved and more productive. And while, by their influence, the condition of each individual farmer would be meliorated, the total mass of Agricultural production would probably be increased. For this must evidently depend as much, if not more, upon the degree of improvement; than upon the number of acres under culture.

It merits particular observation, that the multiplication of manufactories not only furnishes a Market for those articles, which have been accustomed to be produced in abundance, in a country; but it likewise creates a demand for such as were either unknown or produced in inconsiderable quantities. The bowels as well as the surface of the earth are ransacked for articles which were before neglected. Animals, Plants and Minerals acquire an utility and value, which were before unexplored.

The foregoing considerations seem sufficient to establish, as general propositions, That it is the interest of nations to diversify the industrious pursuits of the individuals, who compose them—That the establishment of manufactures is calculated not only to increase the general stock of useful and productive labour; but even to improve the state of Agriculture in particular; certainly to advance the interests of those who are engaged in it. There are other views, that will be hereafter taken of the subject, which it is conceived, will serve to confirm these inferences.

III Previously to a further discussion of the objections to the encouragement of manufactures which had been stated, it will be of use to see what can be said, in reference to the particular situation of the United States, against the conclusions appearing to result from what has been already offered.

It may be observed, and the idea is of no inconsiderable weight, that however true it might be, that a State, which possessing large tracts of vacant and fertile territory, was at the same time secluded from foreign commerce, would find its interest and the interest of Agriculture, in diverting a part of its population from Tillage to Manufactures; yet it will not follow, that the same is true of a State, which having such vacant and fertile territory, has at the same time ample opportunity of procuring from abroad, on good terms, all the fabrics of which it stands in need, for the supply of its inhabitants.

The power of doing this at least secures the great advantage of a division of labour; leaving the farmer free to pursue exclusively the culture of his land, and enabling him to procure with its products the manufactured supplied requisite either to his wants or to his enjoyments. And though it should be true, that in settled countries, the diversification of Industry is conducive to an increase in the productive powers of labour, and to an augmentation of revenue and capital; yet it is scarcely conceivable that there can be any [thing] of so solid and permanent advantage to an uncultivated and unpeopled country as to convert its wastes into cultivated and inhabited districts. If the Revenue, in the mean time, should be less, the Capital, in the event, must be greater.

To these observations, the following appears to be a satisfactory answer—

I. If the system of perfect liberty to industry and commerce were the prevailing system of nations—the arguments which dissuade a country in the predicament of the United States, from the zealous pursuits of manufactures would doubtless have great force. It will not be affirmed, that they might not be permitted, with few exceptions, to serve as a rule of national conduct. In such a state of things, each country would have the full benefit of its peculiar advantages to compensate for its deficiencies or disadvantages. If one nation were in condition to supply manufactured articles on better terms than another, that other might find an abundant indemnification in a superior capacity to furnish the produce of the soil. And a free exchange, mutually beneficial, of the commodities which each was able to supply, on the best terms, might be carried on between them, supporting in full vigour the industry of each. And though the circumstances which have been mentioned and others, which will be unfolded hereafter render it probable, that nations merely Agricultural would not enjoy the same degree of opulence, in proportion to their numbers, as those united manufactures with agriculture: yet the progressive improvement of the lands of the former might, in the end, atone for an inferior degree of opulence in the mean time: and in a case in which opposite considerations are pretty equally balanced, the option ought perhaps always to be, in favour of leaving Industry to its own direction.

But the system which has been mentioned, is far from characterising the general policy of Nations. [The prevalent one has been regulated by an opposite spirit.]

The consequence of it is, that the United States are to a certain extent in the situation of a country precluded from foreign Commerce. They can indeed, without difficulty obtain from abroad the manufactured supplies, of which they are in want; but they experience numerous and very injurious impediments to the emission and vent of their own commodities. Nor is this the case in reference to a single foreign nation only. The regulations of several countries, with which we have the most extensive intercourse, throw serious obstructions in the way of the principal staples of the United States.

In such a position of things, the United States cannot exchange with Europe on equal terms; and the want of reciprocity would render them the victim of a system, which should induce them to confine their views to Agriculture and refrain from Manufactures. A constant and encreasing necessity, on their part, for the commodities of Europe, and only a partial and occasional demand for their own, in return, could not but expose them to a state of impoverishment, compared with the opulence to which their political and natural advantages authorise them to aspire.

Remarks of this kind are not made in the spirit of complaint. 'Tis for the nations, whose regulations are alluded to, to judge for themselves, whether, by aiming at too much they do not lose more than they gain. 'Tis for the United States to consider by what means they can render themselves least dependent, on the combinations, right or wrong of foreign policy.

It is no small consolation, that already the measures which have embarrassed our Trade, have accelerated internal improvements, which upon the whole have bettered our affairs. To diversify and extend these improvements is the surest and safest method of indemnifying ourselves for any inconveniences, which those or similar measures have a tendency to beget. If Europe will not take from us the products of our soil, upon terms consistent with out interest, the natural remedy is to contract as fast as possible our wants of her.

2. The conversion of their waste into cultivated lands is certainly a point of great moment in the political calculations of the United States. But the degree in which this may possibly be retarded by the encouragement of manufactories does not appear to countervail the powerful inducements to affording that encouragement.

An observation made in another place is of a nature to have great influence upon this question. If it cannot be denied, that the interests even of Agriculture may be advanced more by having such of the lands of a state as are occupied under good cultivation, than by having a greater quantity occupied under a must inferior cultivation, and if Manufactories, for the reasons assigned, must be admitted to have a tendency to promote a more steady and vigorous cultivation of the lands occupied than would happen without them—it will follow, that they are capable of indemnifying a country for a diminution of the progress of new settlements; and may serve to increase both the capital [value] and the income of its lands, even though they should abrige the number of acres under Tillage.

But it does, by no means, follow, that the progress of new settlements would be retarded by the extension of Manufactures. The desire of being an independent proprietor of land is founded on such strong principles in the human breast, that where the opportunity of becoming so is as great as it is in the United States, the proportion will be small of those, whose situations would otherwise lead to it, who would be diverted from it towards Manufactures. And it is highly probable, as already intimated, that the accessions of foreigners, who originally drawn over by manufacturing views would afterwards abandon them for Agricultural, would be more than equivalent for those of our own Citizens, who might happen to be detached from them.

The remaining objections to a particular encouragement of manufactures in the United States now require to be examined.

One of these turns on the proposition, that Industry, if left to itself, will naturally find its way to the most useful and profitable employment: whence it is inferred, that manufactures without the aid of government will grow up as soon and as fast, as the natural state of things and the interest of the community may require.

Against the solidity of this hypothesis, in the full latitude of the terms, very cogent reasons may be offered. These have relation to—the strong influence of habit and the spirit of imitation—the fear of want of success in untried enterprises—the intrinsic difficulties incident to first essays towards a competition with those who have previously attained to perfection in the business to be attempted—the bounties premiums and other artificial encouragements, with which foreign nations second the exertions of their own Citizens in the branches, in which they are to be rivalled.

Experience teaches, that men are often so much governed by what they are accustomed to see and practice, that the simplest and most obvious improvements, in the [most] ordinary occupations, are adopted with hesitation, reluctance and by slow graduations. The spontaneous transition to new pursuits, in a community long habituated to different ones, may be expected to be attended with proportionably greater difficulty. When former occupations ceased to yield a profit adequate to the subsistence of their followers, or when there was an absolute deficiency of employment in them, owing to the superabundance of hands, changes would ensue; but these changes would be likely to be more tardy than might consist with the interest either of individuals or of the Society. In many cases they would not happen, while a bare support could be ensured an adherence to ancient courses; though a resort to a more profitable employment might be practicable. To produce the desireable changes, as early as may be expedient, may therefore require the incitement and patronage of government.

The apprehension of failing in new attempts is perhaps a more serious impediment. There are dispositions apt to be attracted by the mere novelty of an undertaking—but these are not always those best calculated to give it success. To this, it is of importance that the confidence of cautious sagacious capitalists both citizens and foreigners, should be excited. And to inspire this description of persons with confidence, it is essential, that they should be made to see in any project, which is new, and for that reason alone, if, for no other, precarious, the prospect of such a degree of countenance and support from government, as may be capable of overcoming the obstacles, inseperable from first experiments.

The superiority antecedently enjoyed by nations, who have preoccupied and perfected a branch of industry, constitutes a more formidable obstacle, than either of those, which have been mentioned, to the introduction of the same branch into a country, in which it did not before exist. To maintain between the recent establishments of one country and the long matured establishments of another country, a competition upon equal terms, both as to quality and price, is in most cases impracticable. The disparity in the one, or in the other, or in both, must necessarily be so considerable as to forbid a successful rivalship, without the extraordinary aid and protection of government.

But the greatest obstacle of all to the successful prosecution of a new branch of industry in a country, in which it was before unknown, consists, as far as the instances apply, in the bounties premiums and other aids which are granted, in a variety of cases, by the nations, in which the establishments to be imitated are previously introduced. It is well known (and particular examples in the course of this report will be cited) that certain nations grant bounties on the exportation of particular commodities, to enable their own workmen to undersell and supplant all competitors, in the countries to which those commodities are sent. Hence the undertakers of a new manufacture have to contend not only with the natural disadvantages of a new undertaking, but with the gratuities and remunerations which other governments bestow. To be enabled to contend with success, it is evident, that the interference and aid of their own government are indispensable.

Combinations by those engaged in a particular branch of business in one country, to frustrate the first efforts to introduce it into another, by temporary sacrifices, recompensed perhaps by extraordinary indemnifications of the government of such country, are believed to have existed, and are not to be regarded as destitute of probability. The existence or assurance of aid from the government of the country, in which the business is to be introduced, may be essential to fortify adventurers against the dread of such combinations, to defeat their effects, if formed and to prevent their being formed, by demonstrating that they must in the end prove fruitless.

Whatever room there may be for an expectation that the industry of a people, under the direction of private interest, will upon equal terms find out the most beneficial employment for itself, there is none for a reliance, that it will struggle against the force of unequal terms, or will of itself surmount all the adventitious barriers to a successful competition, which may have been erected either by the advantages naturally acquired from practice and previous possession of the ground, or by those which may have sprung from positive regulations and an artificial policy. This general reflection might alone suffice as an answer to the objection under examination; exclusively of the weighty considerations which have been particularly urged.

The objections of the pursuit of manufactures in the United States, which next present themselves to discussion, represent an impracticability of success, arising from three causes—scarcity of hands—dearness of labour—want of capital.

The two first circumstances are to a certain extent real, and within due limits, ought to be admitted as obstacles to the success of manufacturing enterprize in the United States. But there are various considerations, which lessen their force, and tend to afford an assurance that they are not sufficient to prevent the advantageous prosecution of many very useful and extensive manufactories.

With regard to scarcity of hands, the fact itself must be applied with no small qualification to certain parts of the United States. There are large districts, which may be considered as pretty fully peopled; and which notwithstanding a continual drain for distant settlement, are thickly interspersed with flourishing and increasing towns. If these districts have not already reached the point, at which the complaint of scarcity of hands ceases, they are not remote from it, and are approaching fast towards it: And having perhaps fewer attractions to agriculture, than some other parts of the Union, they exhibit a proportionally stronger tendency towards other kinds of industry. In these districts, may be discerned, no inconsiderable maturity for manufacturing establishments.

But there are circumstances, which have been already noticed with another view, that materially diminish every where the effect of a scarcity of hands. These circumstances are—the great use which can be made of women and children; on which point a very pregnant and instructive fact has been mentioned—the vast extension given by late improvements to the employment of Machines, which substituting the Agency of fire and water, has prodigiously lessened the necessity for manual labor—the employment of persons ordinarily engaged in other occupations, during the seasons, or hours of leisure; which, besides giving occasion to the exertion of a greater quantity of labour by the same number of persons, and thereby encreasing the general stock of labour, as has been elsewhere remarked, may also be taken into the calculation, as a resource for obviating the scarcity of hands—lastly the attraction of foreign emigrants. Whoever inspects, with a careful eye, the composition of our towns will be

made sensible to what an extent this resource may be relied upon. This exhibits a large proportion of ingenious and valuable workmen, in different arts and trades, who, by expatriating from Europe, have improved their own condition, and added to the industry and wealth of the United States. It is a natural inference from the experience, we have already had, that as soon as the United States shall present the countenance of a serious prosecution of Manufactures—as soon as foreign artists shall be made sensible that the state of things here affords a moral certainty of employment and encouragement—competent numbers of European workmen will transplant themselves, effectually to ensure the success of the design. How indeed can it otherwise happen considering the various and powerful inducements, which the situation of this country offers; addressing themselves to so many strong passions and feelings, to so many general and particular interests?

It may be affirmed therefore, in respect to hands for carrying on manufactures, that we shall in a great measure trade upon a foreign Stock; reserving our own, for the cultivation of our lands and the manning of our Ships; as far as character and circumstances [shall] incline. It is not unworthy of remark, that the objection to the success of manufactures, deduced from the scarcity of hands, is alike applicable to Trade and Navigation; and yet these are perceived to flourish, without any sensible impediment from that cause.

As to the dearness of labour (another of the obstacles alledged) this has relation principally to two circumstances, one that which has been just discussed, or the scarcity of hands, the other, the greatness of profits.

As far as it is a consequence of the scarcity of hands, it is mitigated by all the considerations which have been adduced as lessening that deficiency.

It is certain too, that the disparity in this respect, between some of the most manufacturing parts of Europe and a large proportion of the United States, is not nearly so great as is commonly imagined. It is also much less in regard to Artificers and manufacturers than in regard to country labourers; and while a careful comparison shews, that there is, in this particular, much exaggeration; it is also evident that the effect of the degree of disparity, which does truly exist, is diminished in proportion to the use which can be made of machinery.

To illustrate this last idea—Let it be supposed, that the difference of price, in two Countries, of a given quantity of manual labour requisite to the fabrication of a given article is as 10; and that some *mechanic power* is introduced into both countries, which performing half the necessary labour, leaves only half to be done by hand, it is evident, that the difference in the cost of the fabrication of the article in question, in the two countries, as far as it is connected with the price of labour, will be reduced from 10. to 5, in consequence of the introduction of that *power*.

This circumstance is worthy of the most particular attention. It diminishes immensely one of the objections most strenuously urged, against the success of manufactures in the United States.

To procure all such machines as are known in any part of Europe, can only require a proper provision and due pains. The knowledge of several of the most important of them is already possessed. The preparation of them here, is in most cases, practicable on nearly equal terms. As far as they depend on Water, some superiority of advantages may be claimed, from the uncommon variety and greater cheapness of situations adapted to Mill seats, with which different parts of the United States abound.

So far as the dearness of labour may be a consequence of the greatness of profits in any branch of business, it is no obstacle of its success. The Undertaker can afford to pay the price.

There are grounds to conclude the undertakers of Manufacturers in this Country can at this time afford to pay higher wages to the workmen they may employ than are paid to similar workmen in Europe. The prices of foreign fabrics, in the markets of the United States, which will for a long time regulate the prices of the domestic ones, may be considered as compounded of the following ingredients—The first cost of materials, including the Taxes, if any, which are paid upon them where they are made: the expence of grounds, building machinery and tools: the wages of the persons employed in the manufactory: the profits on the capital or Stock employed: the commissions of Agents to purchase them where they are made; the expence of transportation to the United States [including insurance and other incidental charges;] the taxes or duties, if any [and fees of office] which are paid on their exportation: the taxes or duties [and fees of office] which are paid on their importation.

As to the first of these items, the cost of materials, the advantage upon the whole, is at present on the side of the

United States, and the difference, in their favor, must increase, in proportion as a certain and extensive domestic demand shall induce the proprietors of land to devote more of their attention to the production of those materials. It ought not to escape observation, in a comparison on this point, that some of the principal manufacturing Countries in Europe are much more dependent on foreign supply for the materials of the manufactures, than would be the United States, who are capable of supplying themselves, with a greater abundance, as well as a greater variety of the requisite materials.

As to the second item, the expence of grounds buildings machinery and tools, an equality at least may be assumed; since advantages in some particulars will counterbalance temporary disadvantages in others.

As to the third item, or the article of wages, the comparison certainly turns against the United States, though as before observed not in so great a degree as is commonly supposed.

The fourth item is alike applicable to the foreign and to the domestic manufacture. It is indeed more properly a *result* than a particular, to be compared.

But with respect to all the remaining items, they are alone applicable to the foreign manufacture, and in the strictest sense extraordinaries; constituting a sum of extra change on the foreign fabric, which cannot be estimated, at less than [from 15 to 30] per Cent. on the cost of it at the manufactory.

This sum of extra charge may confidently be regarded as more than a Counterpoise for the real difference in the price of labour; and is a satisfactory proof that manufactures may prosper in defiance of it in the United States. To the general allegation, connected with the circumstances of scarcity of hands and dearness of labour, that extensive manufactures can only grow out of a redundant or full population, it will be sufficient, to answer generally, that the fact has been otherwise— That the situation alleged to be an essential condition of success, has not been that of several nations, at periods when they had already attained to maturity in a variety of manufactures.

The supposed want of Capital for the prosecution of manufactures in the United States is the most indefinite of the objections which are usually opposed to it.

It is very difficult to pronounce any thing precise concerning the real extent of the monied capital of a Country, and still more concentrating the proportion which it bears to the objects that invite employment of Capital. It is not less difficult to pronounce how far the *effect* of any given quantity of money, as capital, or in other words, as a medium for circulating the industry and property of a nation, may be encreased by the very circumstance of the additional motion, which is given to it by the new objects of employment. That effect, like the momentum of descending bodies, may not improperly be represented, as in a compound ratio to *mass* and *velocity*. It seems pretty certain, that a given sum of money, in a situation, in which the quick impulses of commercial activity were little felt, would appear inadequate to the circulation of as great a quantity of industry and property, as in one, in which their full influence was experienced.

It is not obvious, why the same objection might not as well be made to external commerce as to manufactures; since it is manifest that our immense tracts of land occupied and unoccupied are capable of giving employment to more capital than is actually bestowed upon them. It is certain, that the United States offer a vast field for the advantageous employment of Capital; but it does not follow, that there will not be found, in one way or another, a sufficient fund for the successful prosecution of any species of industry which is likely to prove truly beneficial.

The following considerations are of a nature to remove all inquietude on the score of want of Capital.

The introduction of Banks, as has been shewn on another occasion has a powerful tendency to extend the active Capital of a Country. Experience of the Utility of these Institutions is multiplying them in the United States. It is probable that they will be established wherever they can exist with advantage; and wherever, they can be supported, if administered with prudence, they will add new energies to all pecuniary operations.

The aid of foreign Capital may safely, and, with considerable latitude be taken into calculation. Its instrumentality has been long experienced in our external commerce; and it has begun to be felt in various other modes. Not only our funds, but our Agriculture and other internal improvements have been animated by it. It has already in a few instances extended even to our manufactures.

It is a well known fact, that there are parts of Europe, which have more Capital, than profitable domestic objects of employment. Hence, among other proofs, the large loans continually furnished to foreign states. And it is equally certain that the capital of other parts may find more profitable employment in the United States, than at home. And notwithstanding there are weighty inducements to prefer the employment of capital at home even at less profit, to an investment of it abroad, though with greater gain, yet these inducements are overruled either by a deficiency of employment or by a very material difference in profit. Both these Causes operate to produce a transfer of foreign capital to the United States. 'Tis certain, that various objects in this country hold out advantages, which are with difficulty to be equalled elsewhere; and under the increasingly favorable impressions, which are entertained of our government, the attractions will become more and More strong. These impressions will prove a rich mine of prosperity to the Country, if they are confirmed and strengthened by the progress of our affairs. And to secure this advantage, little more is now necessary, than to foster industry, and cultivate order and tranquility, at home and abroad.

It is not impossible, that there may be persons disposed to look with a jealous eye on the introduction of foreign Capital, as if it were an instrument to deprive our own citizens of the profits of our own industry: But perhaps there never could be a more unreasonable jealousy. Instead of being viewed as a rival, it ought to be Considered as a most valuable auxiliary; conducing to put in Motion a greater Quantity of productive labour, and a greater portion of useful enterprise than could exist without it. It is at least evident, that in a Country situated like the United States, with an infinite fund of resources yet to be unfolded, every farthing of foreign capital, which is laid out in internal ameliorations, and in industrious establishments of a permanent nature, is a precious acquisition.

And whatever be the objects which originally attract foreign Capital, when once introduced, it may be directed towards any purpose of beneficial exertion, which is desired. And to detain it among us, there can be no expedient so effectual as to enlarge the sphere, within which it may be usefully employed: Though induced merely with views to speculations in the funds, it may afterwards be rendered subservient to the Interests of Agriculture, Commerce & Manufactures.

But the attraction of foreign Capital for the direct purpose of Manufactures ought not to be deemed a chimerial expectation. There are already examples of it, as remarked in another place. And the examples, if the disposition be cultivated can hardly fail to multiply. There are also instances of another kind, which serve to strengthen the expectation. Enterprises for improving the Public Communications, by cutting canals, opening the obstructions in Rivers and erecting bridges, have received very material aid from the same source.

When the Manufacturing Capitalist of Europe shall advert to the many important advantages, which have been intimated, in the Course of this report, he cannot but perceive very powerful inducements to a transfer of himself and his Capital to the United States. Among the reflections, which a most interesting peculiarity of situation is calculated to suggest, it cannot escape his observation, as a circumstance of Moment in the calculation, that the progressive population and improvement of the United States, insure a continually increasing domestic demand for the fabrics which he shall produce, not to be affected by any external casualties or vicissitudes.

But while there are Circumstances sufficiently strong to authorise a considerable degree of reliance on the aid of foreign Capital towards the attainment of the object in view, it is satisfactory to have good grounds of assurance, that there are domestic resources of themselves adequate to it. It happens, that there is a species of Capital actually existing within the United States, which relieves from all inquietude on the score of want of Capital—This is the funded Debt.

The effect of a funded debt, as a species of Capital, has been Noticed upon a former Occasion; but a more particular elucidation of the point seems to be required by the stress which is here laid upon it. This shall accordingly be attempted.

Public Funds answer the purpose of Capital, from the estimation in which they are usually held by Monied men; and consequently from the Ease and dispatch with which they can be turned into money. This capacity of prompt convertibility into money causes a transfer of stock to be in a great number of Cases equivalent to a payment in coin. And where it does not happen to suit the party who is to receive, to accept a transfer of Stock, the party who is to pay, is never at a loss to find elsewhere a purchaser of his Stock, who will furnish him in lieu of it, with the Coin of which he stands in need. Hence in a sound and settled state of the public funds, a man possessed of a sum in them can embrace any scheme of business, which offers, with as much confidence as if he were possessed of an equal sum in Coin.

This operation of public funds as capital is too obvious to be denied; but it is objected to the Idea of their operating as an *augmentation* of the Capital of the community, that they serve to occasion the *destruction* of some other capital to an equal amount.

The Capital which alone they can be supposed to destroy must consist of— The annual revenue, which is applied to the payment of Interest on the debt, and to the gradual redemption of the principal—The amount of the Coin, which is employed in circulating the funds, or, in other words, in effecting the different alienations which they undergo.

But the following appears to be the true and accurate view of this matter.

1st. As to the point of the Annual Revenue requisite for Payment of interest and redemption of principal.

As a determinate proportion will tend to perspicuity in the reasoning, let it be supposed that the annual revenue to be applied, corresponding with the modification of the 6 per Cent stock of the United States, is in the ratio of eight upon the hundred, that is in the first instance six on Account of interest, and two on account of Principal.

Thus far it is evident, that the Capital destroyed to the capital created, would bear no greater proportion, than 8 to 100. There would be withdrawn from the total mass of other capitals a sum of eight dollars to be paid to the public creditor; while he would be possessed of a sum of One Hundred dollars, ready to be applied to any purpose, to be embarked in any enterprize, which might appear to him eligible. Here then

the *Augmentation* of Capital, or the excess of that which is produced, beyond that which is destroyed is equal to Ninety two dollars. To this conclusion, it may be objected, that the sum of Eight dollars is to be withdrawn annually, until the whole hundred is extinguished, and it may be inferred, that in the process of time a capital will be destroyed equal to that which is at first created.

But it is nevertheless true, that during the whole of the interval, between the creation of the Capital of 100 dollars, and its reduction to a sum not greater than that of the annual revenue appropriated to its redemption—there will be a greater active capital in existence than if no debt had been Contracted. The sum drawn from other Capitals *in any one year* will not exceed eight dollars; but there will be *at every instance of time* during the whole period, in question a sum corresponding *with so much of the principal*, as remains *unredeemed*, in the hands of some person, or other, employed, or ready to be employed in some profitable undertaking. There will therefore constantly be more capital, in capacity to be employed, than capital taken from employment. The excess for the first year has been stated to be Ninety two dollars; it will diminish yearly, but there always will be an excess, until the principal of the debt is brought to a level with the *redeeming annuity*, that is, in the case which has been assumed by way of example, to *eight dollars*. The reality of this excess becomes palpable, if it is supposed, as often happens, that the citizen of a foreign Country imports into the United States 100 dollars for the purchase of an equal sum of public debt. Here is an absolute augmentation of the mass of Circulating Coin to the extent of 100 dollars. At the end of a year the foreigner is presumed to draw back eight dollars on account of his Principal and Interest, but he still leaves, Ninety two of his original Deposit in circulation, as he in like manner leaves Eighty four at the end of the second year, drawing back then also the annuity of Eight Dollars: And thus the Matter proceeds; The capital left in circulation diminishing each year, and coming nearer to the level of the annuity drawnback. There are however some differences in the ultimate operation of the part of the debt, which is purchased by foreigners, and that which remains in the hands of citizens. But the general effect in each case, though in different degrees, is to add to the active capital of the Country.

Hitherto the reasoning has proceeded on a concession of the position, that there is a destruction of some other capital, to the extent of the annuity appropriated to the payment of the Interest and the redemption of the principal of the deb(t) but in this, too much has been conceded. There is at most a temp(orary) transfer of some other capital, to the amount of the Annuity, from those who pay to the Creditor who receives; which he again restor(es) to the circulation to resume the offices of capital. This he does ei(ther) immediately by employing the money in some branch of Industry, or mediately by lending it to some other person, who does so employ (it) or by spending it on his own maintenance. In either sup(position) there is no destruction of capital, there is nothing more (than a) suspension of its motion for a time; that is, while it is (passing) from the hands of those who pay into the Public coffers, & thence (through) the public Creditor into some other Channel of circulation. (When) the payments of interest are periodical and quick and made by instrumentality of Banks the diversion or suspension of capita(l) may almost be denominated momentary. Hence the deduction on this Account is far less, than it at first sight appears to be.

There is evidently, as far as regards the annuity no destruction nor transfer of any other Capital, than that por(tion) of the income of each individual, which goes to make up the Annuity. The land which furnishes the Farmer with the s(um) which he is to contribute remains the same; and the like m(ay) be observed of other Capitals. Indeed as far as the Tax, w(hich) is the object of contribution (as frequently happens, when it doe(s) not oppress, by its weight) may have been a Motive to *greate(r) exertion* in any occupation; it may even serve to encrease the contributory Capital: This idea is not without importanc(e) in the general view of the subject.

It remains to see, what further deduction out to be mad(e) from the capital which is created, by the existence of the Debt; on account of the coin, which is employed in its circulation. This is susceptible of much less precise calculation, than the Article which has been just discussed. It is impossible to say what proportion of coin in necessary to carry on the alienations which any species of property usually undergoes. The quantity indeed varies according to circumstances. But it may still without hesitation be pronounced, from the quickness of the rotation, or rather of the transitions, that the *medium* of circulation always bears but a small proportion to the amount of the *property* circulated. And it is thence satisfactorily deductible, that the coin employed in the Negociations of the funds and which serves to give them activity, as capital, is incomparably less than the sum of the debt negotiated for the purposes of business.

It ought not, however, to be omitted, that the negotiation of the funds becomes itself a distinct business; which employs, and by employing diverts a portion of the circulating coin from other pursuits. But making due allowance for this circumstance there is no reason to conclude, that the effect of the diversion of coin in the whole operation bears any considerable proportion to the amount of the Capital to which it gives activity. The sum of the debt in circulation is continually at the Command, of any useful enterprise— the coin itself which circulates it, is never more than momentarily suspended from its ordinary functions. It experiences an incessant and rapid flux and reflux to and from the Channels of industry to those of speculations in the funds.

There are strong circumstances in confirmation of this Theory. The force of Monied Capital which has been displayed in Great Britain, and the height to which every species of industry has grown up under it, defy a solution from the quantity of coin which that kingdom has ever possessed. Accordingly it has been Coeval with its funding system, the prevailing opinion of the men of business, and of the generality of the most sagacious theorists of that country, that the operation of the public funds as capital has contributed to the effect in question. Among our-

selves appearances this far favour the same Conclusion. Industry in general seems to have been reanimated. There are symptoms indicating an extension of our Commerce. Our navigation has certainly of late had a Considerable spring, and there appears to be in many parts of the Union a command of capital, which till lately, since the revolution at least, was unknown. But it is at the same time to be acknowledged, that other circumstances have concurred, (and in a great degree) in producing the present state of things, and that the appearances are not yet sufficiently decisive, to be entirely relied upon.

In the question under discussion, it is important to distinguish between an *absolute increase of Capital, or an accession of real wealth*, and *an artificial increase of Capital*, as an engine of business, or as an instrument of industry and Commerce. In the first sense, a funded debt has no pretensions to being deemed an increase in Capital; in the last, it has pretensions which are not easy to be controverted. Of a similar nature is bank credit and in an inferior degree, every species of private credit.

But though a funded debt is not in the first instance, an absolute increase of Capital, or an augmentation of real wealth; yet by serving as a New power in the operation of industry, it has within certain bounds a tendency to increase the real wealth of a Community, in like manner as money borrowed by a thrifty farmer, to be laid out in the improvement of his farm may, in the end, add to his Stock of real riches.

There are respectable individuals, who from a just aversion to an accumulation of Public debt, are unwilling to concede to it any kind of utility, who can discern no good to alleviate the ill with which they suppose it pregnant; who cannot be persuaded that it ought in any sense to be viewed as an increase of capital lest it should be inferred, that the more debt the more capital, the greater the burthens the greater the blessings of the community.

But it interests the public Councils to estimate every object as it truly is; to appreciate how far the good in any measure is compensated by the ill; or the ill by the good, Either of them is seldom unmixed.

Neither will it follow, that an accumulation of debt is desirable, because a certain degree of it operates as capital. There may be a plethora in the political, as in the Natural body; There may be a state of things in which any such artificial capital is unnecessary. The debt too may be swelled to such a size, as that the greatest part of it may cease to be useful as a Capital, serving only to pamper the dissipation of idle and dissolute individuals: as that the sums required to pay the Interest upon it may become oppressive, and beyond the means, which a government can employ, consistently with its tranquility, to raise them; as that the resources of taxation, to face the debt, may have been strained too far to admit of extensions adequate to exigencies, which regard the public safety.

Where this critical point is, cannot be pronounced, but it is impossible to believe, that there is not such a point.

And as the vicissitudes of Nations beget a perpetual tendency to the accumulation of debt, there ought to be in every government a perpetual, anxious and unceasing effort to reduce that, which at any time exists, as fast as shall be practicable consistently with integrity and good faith.

Reasonings on a subject comprehending ideas so abstract and complex, so little reducible to precise calculation as those which enter into the question just discussed, are always attended with a danger of running into fallacies. Due allowance ought therefore to be made for this possibility. But as far as the Nature of the subject admits of it, there appears to be satisfactory ground for a belief, that the public funds operate as a resource of capital to the Citizens of the United States, and, if they are a resource at all, it is an extensive one.

To all the arguments which are brought to evince the impracticability of success in manufacturing establishments in the United States, it might have been a sufficient answer to have referred to the experience of what has been already done. It is certain that several important branches have grown up and flourished with a rapidity which surprises: affording an encouraging assurance of success in future attempts: of these it may not be improper to enumerate the most considerable.

I. Of Skins. Tanned and tawed leather dressed skins, shoes, boots and Slippers, harness and sadlery of all kinds. Portmanteau's and trunks, leather breeches, gloves, muffs and tippets, parchment and Glue.

II. Of Iron. Barr and Sheet Iron, Steel, Nail-rods & Nails, implem(ents) of husbandry, Stoves, pots and other household utensils, the steel and Iron work of carriages and for Shipbuildin(g,) Anchors, scale beams and

Weights & Various tools of Artificers, arms of different kinds; though the manufacture of these last has of late diminished for want of demand.

III. Of Wood. Ships Cabinet Wares and Turnery, Wool and Cotton ca(rds) and other Machinery for manufactures and husband(ry,) Mathematical instruments, Coopers wares of every kind.

IV. Of flax & Hemp. Cables, sailcloth, Cordage, Twine and packthread.

V. Bricks and course tiles & Potters Wares.

VI. Ardent Spirits, and malt liquors.

VII. Writing and printing Paper, sheathing and wrapping Paper, pasteboards, fillers or press papers, paper hangings.

VIII. Hats of furr and Wool and of mixtures of both, Womens Stuff and Silk shoes.

IX. Refined Sugars.

X. Oils of Animals and seeds; Soap, Spermaceti and Tallow Candles.

XI. Copper and brass wares, particularly utensils for distillers, Sugar refiners and brewers, And—Irons and other Articles for household Use, philosophical apparatus.

XII. Tin Wares, for most purposes of Ordinary use.

XIII. Carriages of all kinds

XIV. Snuff, chewing & smoking Tobacco.

XV. Starch and Hairpowder.

XVI. Lampblack and other painters colours.

XVII. Gunpowder.

Besides manufactories of these articles which are carried on as regular Trades, and have attained to a considerable degree of maturity, there is a vast scene of household manufacturing, which contributes more largely to the supply of the Community, than could be imagined; without having made it an object of particular enquiry. This observation is the pleasing result of the investigation, to which the subject of the report has led, and is applicable as well to the Southern as to the middle and Northern States; great quantities of coarse cloths, coatings, serges, and flannels, linsey Woolseys, hosiery of Wool, cotton & thread, coarse fustians, jeans and Muslins, check(ed) and striped cotton and linen goods, bed ticks, Coverlets and Counterpanes, Tow linens, coarse shirtings, sheetings, toweling and table linen, and various mixtures of wool and cotton, and of Cotton & flax are made in the household way, and in many instances to an extent not only sufficient for the supply of the families in which they are made, but for sale, and (even in some cases) for exportation. It is computed in a number of districts the $2/3$ $3/4$ and even $4/5$ of all the clothing of the Inhabitants are made by themselves. The importance of so great a progress, as appears to have been made in family Manufactures, within a few years, both in a moral and political view, renders the fact highly interesting.

Neither does the above enumeration comprehend all the articles, that are manufactured as regular Trades. Many others occur, which are equally well established, but which not being of equal importance have been omitted. And there are many attempts still in their Infancy, which though attended with very favorable appearances, could not have been properly comprized in an enumeration of manufactories, already established. There are other articles also of great importance, which tho' strictly speaking manufactures are omitted, as being immediately connected with husbandry: such are flour, pot & pearl ash, Pitch, tar, turpentine and the like.

There remains to be noticed an objection to the encouragement of manufactures, of a nature different from those which question the probability of success. This is derived from its supposed tendency to give a monopoly of advantages to particula(r) classes at the expence of the rest of the community, who, it is affirmed, would be able to procure the requisite supplies of manufactured articles on better terms from foreigners, than from our own Citizens, and who it is alledged, are reduced to a necessity of paying an enhanced price for whatever they want, by every measure, which obstructs the free competition of foreign commodi(es).

It is not an unreasonable supposition, that measures, which serve to abridge the free competition of foreign Articles, have a tendency to occasion an enhancement of prices and it is not to be denied that such is the effect in a number of Cases, but the fact does not uniformly correspond with the theory. A reduction of prices has in several instances immediately succeeded the establishment of a domestic manufacture. Whether it be that foreign Manufacturers endeavor to suppla(nt) by underselling our own, or whatever else be the cause, the effect has been such as is stated, and the reverse of what mig(ht) have been expected.

But though it were true, that the immedi(ate) and certain effect of regula-

tions controuling the competition of foreign with domestic fabrics was an increase of price, it is universally true, that the contrary is the ultimate effect with every successful manufacture. When a domestic manufacture has attainted to perfection, and has engaged in the prosecution of it a competent number of Persons, it invariably becomes cheaper. Being free from the heavy charges, which attend the importation of foreign commodities, it can be afforded, and accordingly seldom or never fails to be sold Cheaper, in process of time, than was the foreign Article for which it is a substitute. The internal competition, which takes place, soon does away every thing like Monopoly, and by degrees reduces the price of the Article to the *minimum* of a reasonable profit on the Capital employed. This accords with the reason of the thing and with experience.

Whence it follows, that it is the interest of a community with a view to eventual and permanent œconomy, to encourage the growth of manufactures. In a national view, a temporary enhancement of price must always be well compensated by a permanent reduction of it.

It is a reflection, which may with propriety be indulged here, that this eventual diminution of the prices of manufactured Articles; which is the result of internal manufacturing establishments, has a direct and very important tendency to benefit agriculture. It enables the farmer, to procure with a smaller quantity of his labour, the manufactured produce of which he stan(ds) in need, and consequently increases the value of his income and property.

The objections which are commonly

made to the expediency of encouraging, and to the probability of succeeding in manufacturing pursuits, in the United states, having now been discussed; the Considerations which have appeared in the Course of the discussion, recommending that species of industry to the patronage of the Government, will be materially strengthened by a few general and some particular topics, which have been naturally reserved for subsequent Notice.

I There seems to be a moral certainty, that the trade of a country which is both manufacturing and Agricultural will be more lucrative and prosperous, than that of a Counry, which is, merely Agricultural.

One reason for this is found in that general effort of nations (which has been already mentioned) to procure from their own soils, the articles of prime necessity requisite to their own consumption and use; and which serves to render their demand for a foreign supply of such articles in a great degree occasional and contingent. Hence, while the necessities of nations exclusively devoted to Agriculture, for the fabrics of manufacturing st(ates) are constant and regular, the wants of the latter for the products of the former, are liable to very considerable fluctuations and interruptions. The great inequalities resulting from difference of seasons, have been elsewhere remarked: This uniformity of deman(d) on one side, and unsteadiness of it, on the other, must necessarily ha(ve) a tendency to cause the general course of the exchange of commodit(ies) between the parties to turn to the disadvantage of the merely agricultural States. Peculiarity of situation, a climate and soil ada(pted) to the production of peculiar commodities, may, sometimes, contradi(ct) in the rule; but there is every reason to believe that it will be fou(nd) in the Main, a just one.

Another circumstance which gives a superiority of commercial advantages to states, that manufact(ure) as well as cultivate, consists in the more numerous attractions, which a more diversified market offers to foreign Customers, and greater scope, which it affords to mercantile enterprise. It is (a) position of indisputable truth in Commerce, depending too on very obvious reasons, that the greatest resort will ever be to those mar(ts) where commodities, while equally abundant, are most various. Each difference of kind holds out an additional inducement. And it is a position not less clear, that the field of enterprise must be enlarged to the Merchants of a Country, in proportion (to) the variety as well as the abundance of commodities which they find at home for exportation to foreign Markets.

A third circumstance, perhaps not inferior to either of the other two, conferring the superiority which has been stated has relation to the stagnations of demand for certain commodities which at some time or other interfere more or less with the sale of all. The Nation which can bring to Market, but few articles is likely to be more quickly and sensibly affected by such stagnations, than one, which is always possessed of a great variety of commodities. The former frequently finds too great a proportion of its stock of materials, for sale or exchange, lying on hand—or is obliged to make injurious sacrifices to supply its wants of foreign articles, which are *Numerous* and *urgent* in proportion to the smallness of the number of its own. The latter commonly finds itself indemnified, by the high prices of some articles, for the low prices of others—and the Prompt and advantageous sale of those articles which are in demand enables its merchant the better to wait for a favorable change, in respect to those which are not. There is ground to believe, that a difference of situation, in this particular, has immensely different effect(ts) upon the wealth and prosperity of Nations.

From these circumstances collectively, two important inferences are to be drawn, one, that there is always a higher probability of a favorable balance of Trade, in regard to countries in which manufactures founded on the basis of a thriving Agriculture flourish, than in regard to those, which are confined wholly or almost wholly to Agriculture; the other (which is also a consequence of the first) that countries of the former description are likely to possess more pecuniary wealth, or money, than those of the later.

Facts appear to correspond with this conclusion. The importations of manufactured supplies seem invariably to drain the merely Agricultural people of their wealth. Let the situation of the manufacturing countries of Europe be compared in this particular, with that of Countries which only cultivate, and the disparity will be striking. Other causes, it is true, help to Account for this disparity between some of them; and among these causes, the relative state of Agriculture; but between others of them, the most prominent circumstance of dissimilitude arises from the Comparative state of Manufactures. In corroboration of the same idea, it ought not to escape remark, that the West India Islands, the soils of which are the most fertile, and the Nation, which in the greatest degree supplies the rest of the world, with the precious metals, exchange to a loss with almost every other Country.

As far as experience at home may guide, it will lead to the same conclusion. Previous to the revolution, the quantity of coin, possessed by the colonies, which now compose the United states, appeared, to be inadequate to their circulation; and their debt to Great-Britain was progressive. Since the Revolution, the States, in which manufactures have most increased, have recovered fastest from the injuries of the late War, and abound most in pecuniary resources.

It ought to be admitted, however in this as in the preceding case, that causes irrelative to the state of manufactures account, in a degree, for the Phœnomena remarked. The continual progress of new settlements has a natural tendency to occasion an unfavorable balance of Trade; though it indemnifies for the inconvenience, by that increase of the national capital which flows from the conversion of waste into improved lands: And the different degrees of external commerce, which are carried on by the different States, may make material differences in the comparative state of their wealth. The first circumstance has reference to the deficien(cy) of coin and the increase of debt previous to the revolution; the last to the advantages which the most manufacturing states appear to have enjoyed, over the others, since the termination of the late War.

But the uniform appearance of an abundance of specie, as the concomitant of a flourishing state of manufacture(s) and of the reverse, where they do not prevail, afford a strong presumption of their favourable operations upon the wealth of a Country.

Not only the wealth; but the independence and security of a Country, appear to be materially connected with the prosperity of manufactures. Every nation, with a view to those great objects, ought to endeavor to possess within itself all the essentials of national supply. These comprise the means of *Subsistence habitation clothing* and *defence*.

The possession of these is necessary to the perfection of the body politic, to the safety as well as to the welfare of the society; the want of either, is the want of an important organ of political life and Motion; and in the various crises which await a state, it must severely feel the effects of such deficiency. The extreme embarrassments of the United States during the late War, from an incapacity of supplying themselves, are still matter of keen recollection: A future war might be expected again to exemplify the mischiefs and dangers of a situation, to which that incapacity is still in too great a degree applicable, unless changed by timely and vigorous exertion. To effect this change as fast as shall be prudent, merits all the attention and all the Zeal of our Public Councils; 'tis the next great work to be accomplished.

The want of a Navy to protect our external commerce, as long as it shall Continue, must render it a peculiarly precarious reliance, for the supply of essential articles, and must serve to strengthen prodigiously the arguments in favour of manufactures.

To these general Considerations are added some of a more particular nature.

Our distance from Europe, the great fountain of manufactured supply, subjects us in the existing state of things, to inconvenience and loss in two Ways.

The bulkiness of those commodities which are the chief productions of the soil, necessarily imposes very heavy charges on their transportation, to distant markets. These charges, in the Cases, in which the nations, to whom our products are sent, maintain a Competition in the supply of their own markets, principally fall upon us, and form material deductions from the primitive value of the articles furnished. The charges on manufactured supplies, brought from Europe are greatly enhanced by the same circumstance of distance. These charges, again, in the cases in which our own industry maintains no competition, in our own markets, also principally fall upon us; and are an additional cause of extraordinary deduction from the primitive value of our own products; these bei(ng) the materials of exchange for the foreign fabrics, which we consume.

The equality and moderation of individual prope(rty) and the growing settlements of new districts, occasion in this country an unusual demand for coarse manufactures; The charges of which being greater in proportion to their greater bulk augment the disadvantage, which has been just described.

As in most countries domestic supplie(s) maintain a very considerable competition with such foreign productions of the soil, as are imported for sale; if the extensive establishment of Manufactories in the United states does not create a similar competition in respect to manufactured articles, it appears to be clearly deducible, from the Considerations which have been mentioned, that they must sustain a double loss in their exchanges with foreign Nations; strongly conducive to an unfavorable balance of Trade, and very prejudicial to their Interests.

These disadvantages press with no small weight, on the landed interest of the Country. In seasons of peace, they cause a serious deduction from the intrinsic value of the products of the soil. In the time of a War, which shou'd either involve ourselves, or another nation, possessing a Considerable share of our carrying trade, the charges on the transportation of our commodities, bulky as most of them are, could hardly fail to prove a grievous burthen to the farmer; while obliged to depend in so great degree as he now does, upon foreign markets for the vent of the surplus of his labour.

As far as the prosperity of the Fisheries of the United states is impeded by the want of an adequate market, there arises another special reason for desiring the extension of manufactures. Besides the fish, which in many places, would be likely to make a part of the subsistence of the persons employed; it is known that the oils, bones and skins of marine animals, are of extensive use in various manufactures. Hence the prospect of an additional demand for the produce of the Fisheries.

One more point of view only remains in which to Consider the expediency of encouraging manufactures in the United states.

It is not uncommon to meet with an opin(ion) that though the promoting of manufactures may be the interest of a part of the Union, it is contrary to that of another part. The Northern & southern regions are sometimes represented as having adverse interests in this respect. Those are called Manufacturing, these Agricultural states; and a species of opposition is imagined to subsist between the Manufacturing a(nd) Agricultural interests.

This idea of an opposition between those two interests is the common error of the early periods of every country, but experience gradually dissipates it. Indeed they are perceived so often to succour and to befriend each other, that they come at length to be considered as one: a supposition which has been frequently abused and is not universally true. Particular encouragements of particular manufactures may be of a Nature to sacrifice the interests of landholders to those of manufacturers; But it is nevertheless a maxim well established by experience, and generally acknowledged, where there has been sufficient experience, that the *aggregate* prosperity of manufactures, and the *aggregate* prosperity of Agriculture are intimately connected. In the Course of the discussion which has had place, various weighty considerations have been adduced operating in support of that maxim. Perhaps the superior steadiness of the demand of a domestic market for the surplus produce of the soil, is alone a convincing argument of its truth.

Ideas of a contrariety of interests between the Northern and southern regions of the Union, are in the Main as unfounded as they are mischievious. The diversity of Circumstances on which such contrariety is usually predicated, authorises a directly contrary conclusion. Mutual wants constitute one of the strongest links of political connection, and the extent of the(se) bears a natural proportion to the diversity in the means of mutual supply.

In proportion as the mind is accustomed to trace the intimate connexion of interest, which subsists between all the parts of a Society united under the same government—the infinite variety of channels which serve to Circulate the prosper(ity) of each to and through the rest—in that proportion will it be little apt to be disturbed by solicitudes and Apprehensions which originate in local discriminations. It is a truth as important as it is agreeable, and one to which it is not easy to imagine exceptions, that every thing tending to establish *substantial* and *permanent order*, in the affairs of a Country, to increase the total mass of industry and opulence, is ultimately beneficial to every part of it. On the Credit of this great truth, an acquiescence may safely be accorded, from every quarter, to all institutions & arrangements, which promise a confirmation of public order, and an augmentation of National Resource.

But there are more particular considerations which serve to fortify the idea, that the encouragement of manufactures in the interest of all parts of the Union. If the Northern and middle states should be the principal scenes of such establishments, they would immediately benefit the more southern, by creating a demand for productions; some of which they have in common with the other states, and others of which are either peculiar to them, or more abundant, or of better quality, than elsewhere. These productions, principally are Timber, flax, Hemp, Cotton, Wool, raw silk, Indigo, iron, lead, furs, hides, skins and coals. Of these articles Cotton & Indigo are peculiar to the southern states; as are hitherto *Lead & Coal*. Flax and Hemp are or may be raised in greater abundance there, than in the More Northern states, and the Wool of Virginia is said to be of better quality than that of any other state: a Circumstance rendered the more probable by the reflection that Virginia embraces the same latitudes with the finest Wool Countries of Europe. The Climate of the south is also better adapted to the production of silk.

The extensive cultivation of Cotton can perhaps hardly be expected, but from the previous establishment of domestic Manufactories of the Article; and the surest encouragement and vent, for the others, would result from similar establishments in respect to them.

If then, it satisfactorily appears, that it is the Interest of the United states, generally, to encourage manufactures, it merits particular attention, that there are circumstances, which Render the present a critical moment for entering with Zeal upon the important business. The effort cannot fail to be materially seconded by a considerable and encreasing influx of money, in consequence of foreign speculations in the funds—and by the disorders, which exist in different parts of Europe.

The first circumstance not only facilita(tes) the execution of manufacturing enterprises; but it indicates them as a necessary mean to turn the thing itself to advantage, and to prevent its being eventually an evil. If useful employment be not found for the Money of foreigners brought to the country to be invested n purchase(s) of the public debt, it will quickly be reexported to defray the expence of an extraordinary consumption of foreign luxuries; and distressing drains of our specie may hereafter be experienced to pay the interest and redeem the principal of the purchased debt.

This useful employment too ought to be of a Nature to produce solid and permanent improvements. If the money merely serves to give temporary spring to foreign commerce; as it cannot procure new and lasting outlets for the products of the Country; there will be no real or durable advantage gained. As far as it shall find its way in Agricultural ameliorations, in opening canals, and in similar improvements, it will be productive of substantial utility. But there is reason to doubt, whether in such channels it is likely to find sufficient employment, and still more whether many of those who possess it, would be as readily attracted to objects of this nature, as to manufacturing pursuits; which bear greater analogy to those to which they are accustomed, and to the spirit generated by them.

To open the one field, as well as the other, will at least secure a better prospect of useful employment, for whatever accession of money, there has been or may be.

There is at the present juncture a certain fermentation of mind, a certain activity of speculation and enterprise which if properly directed may be made subservient to useful purposes; but which if left entirely to itself, may be attended with pernicious effects.

The disturbed state of Europe, inclining its citizens to emigration, the requisite workmen, will be more easily acquired, than at another time; and the effect of multiplying the opportunities of employment to those who emigrate, may be an increase of the number and extent of valuable acquisitions to the population arts and industry of the Country. To find pleasure in the calamities of other nations, would be criminal; but to benefit ourselves, by opening an asylum to those who suffer, in consequence of them, is as justifiable as it is pol(itic).

A full view having now been taken of the inducements to the promotion of Manufactures in the United states, accompanied with an examination of the principal objections which are commonly urged *in opposition*, it is proper in the next place, to consider the means, by which it may be effected, as introductory to a Specification of the objects which in the present state of things appear the most fit to be encouraged, and of the particular measures which it may be adviseable to adopt, in respect to each.

In order to a better judgment of the Means proper to be resorted to by the United states, it will be of use to Advert to those which have been employed with success in other Countries. The principal of these are.

I Protecting duties—or duties on those foreign articles which are the rivals of the domestic ones, intended to be encouraged.

Duties of this Nature evidently amount to a virtual bounty on the domestic fabrics since by enhancing the charges on foreign Articles, they enable the National Manufacturers to undersell all their foreign Competitors. The propriety of this species of encouragement need not be dwelt upon; as it is not only a clear result from the numerous topics which have been suggested, but is sanctioned by the laws of the

United states in a variety of instances; it has the additional recommendat(ion) of being a resource of revenue. Indeed all the duties imposed on imported articles, though with an exclusive view to Revenue, have the effect in Contemplation, and except where they fall on raw materials wear a beneficent aspect towards the manufactures of the Country.

II Prohibitions of rival articles or duties equivalent to prohibitions.

This is another and an efficacious mean of encouraging national manufactures, but in general it is only fit to be employed when a manufacture, has made such a progress and is in so many hands as to insure a due competition, and an adequate supply on reasonable terms. Of duties equivalent to prohibitions, there are examples in the Laws of the United States, and there are other Cases to which the principle may be advantageously extended, but they are not numero(us).

Considering a monopoly of the domestic market to its own manufacturers as the reigning policy of manufacturing Nations, a similar policy on the part of the United states in every proper instance, is directed, it might almost be said, by the principles of distributive justice; certainly by the duty of endeavouring to secure to their own Citizens a reciprocity of advantages.

III Prohibitions of the exportation of the materials of manufactures.

The desire of securing a cheap and plentiful supply for the national workmen, and, where the article is either peculiar to the Country, or a peculiar quality there, the jealousy of enabling foreign workmen to rival those of the nation, with its ow(n) Materials, are the leading motives to this species of regulation. (It) ought not to be affirmed, that it is in no instance proper, but it is certainly one which ought to be adopted with great circumspect(ion) and only in very plain Cases. It is seen at once, that its immedi(ate) operation, is to abridge the demand and keep down the price of the produce of some other branch of industry, generally speaking, of Agriculture, to the prejudice of those, who carry it on; and tho(ough) if it be really essential to the prosperity of any very important nati(onal) Manufacture, it may happen that those who are injured in the first instance, may be eventually indemnified, by the superior (steadiness) of an extensive domestic market, depending on that prosperity; yet in a matter, in which there is so much room for nice and difficult combinations, in which such considerations combat each other, prudence seems to dictate, that the expedient in question, ought to be indulged with a sparing hand.

IV Pecuniary bounties

This has been found one of the most efficacious means of encouraging manufactures, and it is in some views, the best. Though it has not yet been practiced by the Government of the United states (unless the allowance on the exportation of dried and pickled Fish and salted meat could be considered as a bounty) and though it is less favored by public opinion that some other modes.

Its advantages, are these—

I. It is a species of encouragement more positive and direct than any other, and for that very reason, has a more immediate tendency to stimulate and uphold new enterprises, increasing the chances of profit, and diminishing the risks of loss, in the first attempts.

2. It avoids the inconvenience of a temporary augmentation of price, which is incident to some other modes, or it produces it to a less degree; either by making no addition to the charges on the rival foreign article, as in the Case of protecting duties, or by making a small addition. The first happens when the fund for the bounty is derived from a different object (which may or may not increase the price of some other article, according to the nature of that object) the second, when the fund is derived from the same or a similar object of foreign manufacture. One per cent duty on the foreign article converted into a bounty on the domestic, will have an equal effect with a duty of two per Cent, exclusive of such bounty; and the price of the foreign commodity is liable to be raised, in the one Case, in the proportion of 1 per Cent; in the other, in that of two per Cent. Indeed the bounty when drawn from another source is calculated to promote a reduction of price, because without laying any new charge on the foreign article, it serves to introduce a competition with it, and to increase the total quantity of the article in the Market.

3. Bounties have not like high protecting duties, a tendency to produce scarcity. An increase of price is not always the immediate, though, where the progress of a domestic Manufacture does not counteract a rise, it is commonly the ultimate effect of an additional duty. In the interval, between the laying of the duty and a proportional increase of price, it may discourage importation, by interfering with the profits to be expected from the sale of the article.

4. Bounties are sometimes not only

the best, but the only proper expedient, for uniting the encouragement of a new object of agriculture, with that of a new object of manufacture. It is the Interest of the farmer to have the production of the raw material promoted, by counteracting the interference of the foreig(n) material of the same kind. It is the interest of the manufactu(rer) to have the material abundant and cheap. If prior to the domes(tic) production of the Material, in sufficient quantity, to supply the manufacturer on good terms; a duty be laid upon the importation of it from abroad, with a view to promote the raising of it at home, the Interests both of the Farmer and Manufacturer will be disserved. By either destroying the requisite supply, or raising the price of the article, beyond what can be afforded to be given for it, by the Conductor of an infant manufacture it is abandoned or fails; an(d) there being no domestic manufactories to create a demand for t(he) raw material, which is raised by the farmer, it is in vain, that the Competition of the like foreign articles may have been destroy(ed).

It cannot escape notice, that a duty upon the importation of (an) articles can not otherwise aid the domestic production of it, than giving the latter greater advantages in the home market. It ca(n) have no influence upon the advantageous sale of the article produced, in foreign markets; no tendency, there(fore) to promote its exportation.

The true way to conciliate these two interests, is to lay a duty on foreign manufactures of the material, the growth of which is desired to be encouraged, and to apply the produce of that duty by way of bounty, either upon the production of the material itself or upon its manufacture at home or upon both. In this disposition of the thing, the Manufacturer commences his enterprise under every advantage, which is attainable, as to quantity or price, of the raw material: And the Farmer if the bounty be immediately to him, is enabled by it to enter into a successful competition with the foreign material; if the bounty be to the manufacturer on so much of the domestic material as he consumes, the operation is nearly the same; he has a motive of interest to prefer the domestic Commodity, if of equal quality, even at a higher price than the foreign, so long as the difference of price is any thing short of the bounty which is allowed upon the article.

Except the simple and ordinary kinds of household Manufactures, or those for which there are very commanding local advantages, pecuniary bounties are in most cases indispensable to the introduction of a new branch. A stimulus and a support not less powerful and direct is generally speaking essential to the overcoming of the obstacles which arise from the Competitions of superior skill and maturity elsewhere. Bounties are especially essential, in regard to articles, upon which those foreigners, who have been accustomed to supply a Country, are in the practice of granting them.

The continuance of bounties on manufactures long established must almost always be of questionable policy: Because a presumption would arise in every such Case, that there were natural and inherent impediments to success. But in new undertakings, they are as justifiable, as they are oftentimes necessary.

There is a degree of prejudice against bounties from an appearance of giving away the pubic money, without an immediate consideration, and from a supposition, that they serve to enrich particular classes, at the expence of the Community.

But neither of these sources of dislike will bear a serious examination. There is no purpose, to which public money can be more beneficially applied, than to the acquisition of a new and useful branch of industry; no Consideration more valuable than a permanent addition to the general stock of productive labour.

As to the second source of objection, it equally lies against other modes of encouragement, which are admitted to be eligible. As often as a duty upon a foreign article makes an addition to its price, it causes an extra expence to the Community, for the benefit of the domestic manufacturer. A bounty does no more: But it is the Interest of the society in each case, to submit to a temporary expence, which is more than compensated, by an increase of industry and Wealth, by an augmentation of resources and independence; & by the circumstance of eventual cheapness, which has been noticed in another place.

It would deserve attention, however, in the employment of this species of encouragement in the United states, as a reason for moderating the degree of it in the instances, in which it might be deemed eligible, that the great distance of this country from Europe imposes very heavy charges on all the fabrics which are brought from thence, amounting from [15 to 30] per Cent on their value, according to their bulk.

A Question has been made concerning the Constitutional right of the Government of the United States to apply this species of encouragement, but there is certainly no good foundation for such a question. The National Legislature has express authority "To lay and Collect taxes, duties, imposts and excises, to pay the debts and provide for the *Common defence* and *general welfare*" with no other qualifications than that all duties, imposts and excises, shall be *uniform* throughout the United states, that no capitation or other direct tax shall be laid unless in proportion to numbers ascertained by a census or enumeration taken on the principles prescribed in the Constitution, and that "on tax or duty shall be laid on articles exported from any state." These three qualifications excepted, the power to *raise money* is *plenary*, and *indefinite*; and the objects to which it may be *appropriated* are no less comprehensive, than the payment of the public debts and the providing for the common defence and *"general Welfare."* The terms *"general Welfare"* were doubtless intended to signify more than was expressed or imported in those which Preceded; otherwise numerous exigencies incident to the affairs of a Nation would have been left without a provision. The phrase is as comprehensive as any that could have been used; because it was not fit that the constitutional authority of the Union, to appropriate its revenues shou'd have been restricted within narrower limits than the "General Welfare" and because this necessarily embraces a vast variety of particulars, which are susceptible neither of specification nor of definition.

It is therefore of necessity left to the discretion of the National Legislature, to pronounce, upon the subjects, which concern the general Welfare, and for which under that description, an appropriation of money is requisite and proper. And there seems to be no room for a doubt that whatever concerns the general Interests of *learning* of *Agriculture* of *Manufactures* and of *Commerce* are within the sphere of the national Councils *as far as regards an application of Money*.

The only qualification of the generallity of the Phrase in question, which seems to be admissible, is this—That the object to which an appropriation of money is to be made *General* and not *local*; its operation extending in fact, or by possibility, throughout the Union, and not being confined to a particular spot.

No objection ought to arise to this construction from a supposition that it would imply a power to do whatever else should appear to Congress conducive to the General Welfare. A power to appropriate money with this latitude which is granted too in *express terms* would not carry a power to do any other thing, not authorized in the constitution, either expressly or by fair implication.

V Premiums

These are of a Nature allied to bounties, though distinguishable from them, in some important features.

Bounties are applicable to the whole quantity of an article produced, or manufactured, or exported, and involve a correspondent expence. Premiums serve to reward some particular excellence or superiority, some extraordinary exertion or skill, and are dispensed on(ly) in a small number of cases. But their effect is to stimulate gener(al) effort. Contrived so as to be both honorary and lucrative, they address themselves to different passions; touching the chords as well of emulation as of Interest. They are accordingly a very economical mean of exciting the enterprise of a Whole Community.

There are various Societies in different countries, whose object is the dispensation of Premiums for the encouragemen(t) of *Agriculture Arts manufactures* and *Commerce*; and though they are for the most part voluntary associations, with comparatively slender funds, their utility has been immense. Much has been done by this mean in great Britain: Scotland in particular owes materially to it a prodigious amelioration of Condition. From a similar establishment in the United states, supplied and supported by the Government of the Union, vast benefits might reasonably be expected. Some further ideas on this head, shall accordingly be submitted, in the conclusion of this report.

VI   The Exemption of the Materials of manufactures from duty.

The policy of that Exemption as a general rule, particularly in reference to new Establishments, is obvious. It can hardly ever be advisable to add the obstructions of fiscal burthens to the difficulties which naturally embarrass a new manufacture; and where it is matured and in condition to become an object of revenue, it is generally speaking better that the fabric, than the Material should be the subject of Taxation. Ideas of proportion between the quantum of the tax and the value of the article, can be more easily adjusted, in the former, than in the latter case. An argument for exemptions of this kind in the United States, is to be derived from the practice, as far as their necessities have permitted, of those nations whom we are to meet as competitors in our own and in foreign Markets.

There are however exceptions to it; of which some examples will be given under the next head.

The Laws of the Union afford instances of the observance of the policy here recommended, but it will probably be found adviseable to extend it to some other Cases. Of a nature, bearing some affinity to that policy is the regulation which exempts from duty the tools and implements, as well as the books, cloths and household furniture of foreign artists, who come to reside in the United states; an advantage already secured to them by the Laws of the Union, and which, it is, in every view, proper to Continue.

VII   Drawbacks of the duties which are imposed on the Materials of Manufactures.

It has already been observed as a general rule that duties on those materials, ought with certain exceptions to be foreborne. Of these exceptions, three cases occur, which may serve as examples—one—where the material is itself, an object of general or extensive consumption, and a fit and productive source of revenue: Another, where a manufacture of a simpler kind [the competition of which with a like domestic article is desired to be restrained,] partakes of the Nature of a raw material, from being capable, by a further process to be converted into a manufacture of a different kind, the introduction of growth of which is desired to be encouraged; a third where the Material itself is a production of the Country, and in sufficient abundance to furnish cheap and plentiful supply to the national Manufacturer.

Under the first description comes the article of Molasses. It is not only a fair object of revenue; but being a sweet, it is just that the consumers of it should pay a duty as well as the Consumer(s) of sugar.

Cottons and linens in their White state fall under the second description. A duty upon such as are imported is proper to promote the domestic Manufacture of similar articles in the same state. A drawback of that duty is proper to encourage the printing and staining at home of those which are brought from abroad: When the first of these manufac(tures) has attained suficient maturity in a Country, to furnish a full supply for (the) second, the utility of the drawback ceases.

The article of Hemp either now does or may be expected soon to exemplify the third Case, in the United states.

Where duties on the materials of manufactures are not laid for the purpose of preventing a competition with some domestic production, the same reasons which recommend, as a general rule, the exemption of those materials from duties, would recommend as a like General rule, the allowance of draw backs, in favor of the manufacturer. Accordingly such drawbacks are familiar in countries which systematically pursue the business of manufactures; which furnishes an argument for the observance of a similar policy in the United states; and the Idea has been adopted by the laws of the Union in the stances of salt and Molasses. It is believed that it will be found advantageous to extend it to some other Articles.

VIII   The encouragement of new inventions and discoveries, at home, and of the introduction into the United States of such as may have been made in other countries; particularly those, which relate to machinery.

This is among the most useful and unexceptionable of the aids, which can be given to manufactures. The usual means of that encouragement are pecuniary rewards, and, for a time, exclusive privileges. The first must be employed, according to the occasion, and the utiity of the invention, or discovery: For the last, so far as respects "authors and inventors" provision has been made by Law. But it is desireable in regard to improvements and secrets of extraordinary value, to be able to extend the same benefit to Introducers, as well as Authors and Inventors; a policy which has been practiced with advantge in other countries. Here, however, as in some other cases, there is cause to regret, that the competency of the authority of the National Government to the good, which might be done, is not without a question. Many aids might be given to industry; many internal improvements of primary magnitude might be promoted, by an authority operating throughout the Union, which cannot be effected, as well, if at all, by an authority confined within the limits of a single state.

But if the legislature of the Union cannot do all the good, that might be wished, it is at least desirable, that all may be done, which is practicable. Means for promoting the introduction of foreign improvements, though less efficaciously than might be accomplished with more adequate authority, will form a part of the plan intended to be submitted in the close of this report.

It is customary with manufacturing nations to prohibit, under severe penalties, the exportation of implements and machines, which they have either invented or improved. There are already objects for a similar regulation in the United States; and others may be expected to occur from time to time. The adoption of it seems to be dictated by the principle of reciprocity. Great liberality, in such respects, might better comport with the general spirit of the country; but a selfish and exclusive policy in other quarters will not always permit the free indulgence of a spirit, which would place us upon an unequal footing. As far as prohibitions tend to prevent foreign competitors from deriving the benefit of the improvements made at home, they tend to increase the advantages of those by whom they may have been introduced; and operate as an encouragement to exertion.

IX Judicious regulations for the inspection of manufactured commodities.

This is not among the least important of the means, by which the prosperity of manufactures may be promoted. It is indeed in many cases one of the most essential. Contributing to prevent frauds upon consumers at home and exporters to foreign countries—to improve the quality & preserve the character of the national manufactures, it cannot fail to aid the expeditious and advantageous Sale of them, and to serve as a guard against successful competition from other quarters. The reputation of the flour and lumber of some states, and of the Pot ash of others has been established by an attention to this point. And the like good name might be procured for those articles, wheresoever produced, by a judicious and uniform system of Inspection; throughout the ports of the United States. A like system might also be extended with advantage to other commodities.

X The facilitating of pecuniary remittances from place to place is a point of considerable moment to trade in general, and to manufactures in particular; by rendering more easy the purchase of raw materials and provisions and the payment for manufactured supplies. A general circulation of Bank paper, which is to be expected from the institution lately established will be a most valuable mean to this end. But much good would also accrue from some additional provisions respecting inland bills of exchange. If those drawn in one state payable in another were made negotiable, everywhere, and interest and damages allowed in case of protest, it would greatly promote negotiations between the Citizens of different states, by rendering them more secure; and, with it the convenience and advantage of the Merchants and manufacturers of each.

XI The facilitating of the transportation of commodities.

Improvements favoring this object intimately concern all the domestic interests of a community; but they may without impropriety be mentioned as having an important relation to manufactures. There is perhaps scarcely any thing, which has been better calculated to assist the manufactures of Great Britain, then the ameliorations of the public roads of that Kingdom, and the great process which has been of late made in opening canals. Of the former, the United States stand much in need; and for the latter they present uncommon facilities.

The symptoms of attention to the improvement of inland Navigation, which have lately appeared in some quarters, must fill with pleasure every breast warmed with a true Zeal for the prosperity of the Country. These examples, it is to be hoped, will stimulate the exertions of the Government and the Citizens of every state. There can certainly be no object, more worthy of the cares of the local administrations; and it were to be wished, that there was no doubt of the power of the national Government to lend its direct aid, on a comprehensive plan. This is one of those improvements, which could be prosecuted with more efficacy by the whole, than by any part or parts of the Union. There are cases in which the general interest will be in danger to be sacrificed to the collission of some supposed local interests. Jealousies, in matters of this kind, are as apt to exist, as they are apt to be erroneous.

The following remarks are sufficiently judicious and pertinent to deserve a literal quotation:

"Good roads, canals, and navigable rivers, by diminishing the expence of carriage, put the *remote parts of a country* more nearly upon a level with those in the neighborhood of the town. They are *upon that account* the greatest of all improvements. They encourage the cultivation of the remote, which must always be the most extensive circle of the country. They are advantageous to the Town by breaking down the monopoly of the country in its neighborhood. They are advantageous *even to that part of the Country.* Though they introduce some rival commodities into the old Market, they open many new markets to its produce. Monopoly besides is a great enemy to good management, which can never be universally established, but in consequence of

that free and universal competition, which forces every body to have recourse to it for the sake of self defence. It is not more than Fifty years ago that *some of the countries in the neighborhood of London petitioned the Parliament, against the extension of the turnpike roads, into the remoter counties. Those remoter counties, they pretended, from the cheapness of Labor, would be able to sell their grass and corn cheaper in the London Market, than themselves, and they would thereby reduce their rents and ruin their cultivation.* Their rents however have risen and their cultivation has been improved, since that time."

Specimens of a spirit, similar to that which governed the counties here spoken of present themselves too frequently to the eye of an impartial observer, and render it a wish of patriotism, that the body in the Country, in whose councils a local or partial spirit is least likely to predominate, were at liberty to pursue and promote the general interest, in those instances, in which there might be danger of the interference of such a spirit.

The foregoing are the principal of the means, by which the growth of manufactures is ordinarily promoted. It is, however, not merely necessary, that the measures of government, which have a direct view to manufactures, should be calculated to assist and protect them, but that those which only collaterally affect them, in the general course of the administration, should be gaurded from any peculiar tendency to injure them.

There are certain species of taxes, which are apt to be oppressive to different parts of the community, and among other ill effects have a very unfriendly aspect towards manufactures.

All Poll or Capitation taxes are of this nature. They either proceed, according to a fixed rate, which operates unequally, and injuriously to the industrious poor; or they vest a discretion in certain officers, to make estimates and assessments which are necessarily vague, conjectural and liable to abuse. They ought therefore to be abstained from, in all but cases of distressing emergency.

All such taxes (including all taxes on occupations) which proceed according to the amount of capital *supposed* to be employed in a business, or of profits *supposed* to be made in it are unavoidably hurtful to industry. It is in vain, that the evil may be endeavoured to be mitigated by leaving it, in the first instance, in the option of the party to be taxed, to declare the amount of his capital or profits.

Men engaged in any trade of business have commonly weighty reasons to avoid disclosures, which would expose, with any thing like accuracy, the real state of their affairs. They most frequently find it better to risk oppression, than to avail themselves of so inconvenient a refuge. And the consequence is, that they often suffer oppression.

When the disclosure too, if made, is not definitive, but controulable by the discretion, or in other words, by the passions & prejudices of the revenue officers, it is not only an ineffectual protection, but the possibility of its being so is an additional reason for not resorting to it.

Allowing to the public officers the most equitable dispositions; yet where they are to exercise a discretion, without certain data, they cannot fail to be often misled by appearances. The quantity of business, which seems to be going on, is, in a vast number of cases, a very deceitful criterion of the profits which are made; yet it is perhaps the best they can have, and it is the one, on which they will most naturally rely. A business therefore which may rather require aid, from the government, than be in a capacity to be contributory to it, may find itself crushed by the mistaken conjectures of the Assessors of taxes.

Arbitrary taxes, under which denomination are comprised all those, that leave the *quantum* of the tax to be raised on each person, to the *discretion* of certain officers, are as contrary to the genius of liberty as to the maxims of industry. In this light, they have been viewed by the most judicious observers on government; who have bestowed upon them the severest epithets of reprobation; as constituting one of the worst features usually to be met with in the practice of despotic governments.

It is certain at least, that such taxes are particularly inimical to the success of manufacturing industry, and ought carefully to be avoided by a government, which desires to promote it.

The great copiousness of the subject of this Report has insensibly led to a more lengthy preliminary discussion, than was originally contemplated, or intended. It appeared proper to investigate principles, to consider objections, and to endeavour to establish the utility of the thing proposed to be encouraged; previous to a specification of the objects which might occur, as meriting or requiring encouragement, and of the measures, which might be proper, in respect to each. The first purpose having been fulfilled, it remains to pursue the second. In the selection of objects, five circumstances seem intitled to particular attention; the capacity of the Country to furnish the raw material—the degree in which the nature of the manufacture admits of a substitute for manual labour in machinery—the facility of execution—the extensiveness of the uses, to which the article can be applied—its subserviency to other interests, particularly the great one of national defence. There are however objects, to which these circumstances are little applicable, which for some special reasons, may have a claim to encouragement.

A designation of the principal raw material of which each manufacture is composed will serve to introduce the remarks upon it. As, in the first place—

Iron

The manufactures of this article are entitled to preeminent rank. None are more essential in their kinds, nor so extensive in their uses. They constitute in whole or in part the implements or the materials or both of almost every useful occupation. Their instrumentality is everywhere conspicuous.

It is fortunate for the United States that they have peculiar advantages for deriving the full benefit of this most valuable material, and that they have every motive to improve it, with systematic care. It is to be found in various parts of the United States, in great abundance and of almost every quality; and fuel the chief instrument in manufacturing, it is both cheap and plenty. This particularly applies to Charcoal; but there are productive coal mines already in operation, and strong indica-

tions, that the material is to be found in abundance, in a variety of places.

The inquiries to which the subject of this report has led have been answered with proofs that manufactories of Iron, though generally understood to be extensive, are far more so than is commonly supposed. The kinds, in which the greatest progress has been made, have been mentioned in another place, and need not be repeated; but there is little doubt that every other kind, with due cultivation, will rapidly succeed. It is worthy of remark that several of the particular trades, of which it is the basis, are capable of being carried on without the aid of large capitals.

Iron works have very greatly increased in the United States and are prosecuted, with much more advantage than formerly. The average price before the revolution was about Sixty four Dollars per Ton—at present it is about Eighty; a rise which is chiefly to be attributed to the increase of manufactures of the material.

The still further extension and multiplication of such manufactures will have the double effect of promoting the extraction of the Metal itself, and of converting it to a greater number of profitable purposes.

Those manufactures too united in a greater degree, than almost any others, the several requisites, which have been mentioned, as proper to be consulted in the selection of objects.

The only further encouragement of manufactories of this article, the propriety of which may be considered as unquestionable, seems to be an increase of the duties on foreign rival commodities.

Steel is a branch, which has already made a considerable progress, and it is ascertained that some new enterprizes, on a more extensive scale, have been lately set on foot. The facility of carrying it to an extent, which will supply all internal demands, and furnish a considerable surplus for exportation cannot be doubted. The duty upon the importation of this article, which is at present seventy five cents per Cwt., may it is conceived be safely and advantageously extended to 100 Cents. It is desirable, by decisive arrangements, to second the efforts, which are making in so very valuable a branch.

The United States already in a great measure supply themselves with Nails & Spikes. They are able, and ought certainly, to do it intirely. The first and most laborious operation, in this manufacture is performed by water mills; and of the persons afterwards employed a great proportion are boys, whose early habits of industry are of importance to the community, to the present support of this families, and to their own future comfort. It is not less curious than true, that in certain parts of the country, the making of Nails is an occasional family manufacture.

The expendiency of an additional duty on these materials is indicated by an important fact. About one million 800,000 pounds of them were imported into the United States in the course of a year ending the 30th. of September 1790. A duty of two Cents per lb would, it is presumable, speedily put an end to so considerable an importation. And it is in every view proper that an end should be put to it.

The manufacture of these articles, like that of some others, suffers from the carelessness and dishonesty of a part of those who carry it on. An inspection in certain cases might tend to correct the evil. It will deserve consideration whether a regulation of this sort cannot be applied, without inconvenience, to the exportation of the articles either to foreign countries, or from one state to another.

The implements of husbandry are made in several States in great abundance. In many places it is done by the common blacksmiths. And there is no doubt that an ample supply for the whole country can with great ease be procured among ourselves.

Various kinds of edged tools for the use of Mechanics are also made; and a considerable quantity of hollow wares; though the business of castings has not yet attained the perfection which might be wished. It is however improving, and as there are respectable capitals in good hands, embarked in the prosecution of those branches of iron manufactories, which are yet in their infancy, they may all be contemplated as objects not difficult to be acquired.

To ensure the end, it seems equally safe and prudent to extend the duty *ad valorem* upon all manufactures of Iron, or of which iron is the article of chief value, to ten per Cent.

Fire arms and other military weapons may it is conceived, be placed without inconvenience in the class of articles rates at 15 per Cent. There are already manufactories of these articles, which only require the stimulus of a certain demand to render them adequate to the supply of the United States.

It would also be a material aid to manufactories of this nature, as well as a mean of public security, if provision should be made for an annual purchase of military weapons, of home manufacture to a certain determinate extent, in order to the formation of Arsenals; and to replace from time to time such as should be withdrawn from use, so as always to have in store the quantity of each kinds, which should be deemed a competent supply.

But it may hereafter deserve legislative consideration, whether manufactories of all the necessary weapons of war ought not to be established, on account of the Government itself. Such establishments are agreeable on the usual practice of Nations and that practice seems founded on sufficient reason.

There appears to be an improvidence, in leaving these essential instruments of national defence to the casual speculations of individual adventure; a resource which can less be relied upon, in this case than in most others; the articles in question not being objects of ordinary and indispensable private consumption or use. As a general rule, manufactories on the immediate account of Government are to be avoided; but this seems to be one of the few exceptions, which that rule admits, depending on very special reasons.

Manufactures of Steel, generally, or of which steel is the article of chief value, may with advantage be placed in the class of goods rated at 7½ per Cent. As manufactures of this kind have not yet made any considerable progress, it is a reason for not rating them as high as those of iron; but as this material is the basis of them, and as their extension is not less practicable, than important, it is desirable to promote it by a somewhat higher duty than the present.

A question arises, how far it might be expedient to permit the importation of iron in pigs and bars free from duty.

It would certainly be favourable to manufactures of the article; but the doubt is whether it might not interfere with its production.

Two circumstances, however, abate if they do not remove apprehension, on this score; one is, the considerable increase of price, which has been already remarked, and which renders it probable, that the free admission of foreign iron would not be inconsistent with an adequate profit to the proprietors of Iron Works; the other is, the augmentation of demand, which would be likely to attend the increase in manufactures of the article, in consequence of the additional encouragements proposed to be given. But caution nevertheless in a matter of this kind is most adviseable. The measure suggested ought perhaps rather to be contemplated, subject to the lights of further experience, than immediately adopted.

Copper

The manufactures of which this article is susceptible are also of great extent and utility. Under this description, those of brass, of which it is the principal ingredient, are intended to be included.

The material is a natural production of the Country. Mines of Copper have actually been wrought, and with profit to the undertakers, though it is not known, that any are now in this condition. And nothing is easier, than the introduction of it, from other countries, on moderate terms, and in great plenty.

Coppersmiths and brass founders, particularly the former, are numerous in the United States; some of whom carry on business to a respectable extent.

To multiply and extend manufactories of the materials in question is worthy of attention and effort. In order to this, it is desireable to facilitate a plentiful supply of the materials. And a proper mean to this end is to place them in the class of free articles. Copper in plates and brass are already in this predicament, but copper in pigs and bars is not—neither is *lapis calaminaris*, which together with *copper* and *charcoal*, constitute the component ingredients of brass. The exemption from duty, by parity of reason, ought to embrace all such of these articles, as are objects of importation. An additional duty, on brass wares, will tend to the general end in view. These now stand at 5 per Cent, while those of tin, pewter and copper are rates at 7½. There appears to be a propriety in every view in placing brass wares upon the same level with them; and it merits consideration whether the duty upon all of them ought not to be raised to 10 per Cent.

Lead

There are numerous proofs, that this material abounds in the United States, and requires little to unfold it to an extent, more than equal to every domestic occasion. A prolific mine of it has long been open in the South Western parts of Virginia, and under a public administration, during the late war, yielded a considerable supply for military use. This is now in the hands of individuals, who not only carry it on with spirit; but have established manufactories of it, at Richmond, in the same State.

The duties, already laid upon the importation of this article, either in its unmanufactured, or manufactured state, ensure it a decisive advantage in the home market—which amounts to considerable encouragement. If the duty on pewter wares should be raised it would afford a further encouragement. Nothing else occurs as proper to be added.

Fossil Coal

This, as an important instrument of manufactures, may without impropriety be mentioned among the subjects of this Report.

A copious supply of it would be of great consequence to the iron branch: As an article of household fuel also it is an interesting production; the utility of which must increase in proportion to the decrease of wood, by the progress of settlement and cultivation. And its importance to navigation, as an immense article of transportation coastwise, is signally exemplified in Great Britain.

It is known, that there are several coal mines in Virginia, now worked; and appearances of their existence are familiar in a number of places.

The expediency of a bounty on all the species of coal of home production, and of premiums, on the opening of new mines, under certain qualifications, appears to be worthy of particular examination. The great importance of the article will amply justify a reasonable expence in this way, if it shall appear to be necessary to and shall be thought it likely to answer the end.

Wood

Several manufactures of this article flourish in the United States. Ships are no where built in greater perfection, and cabinet wares, generally, are made little if at all inferior to those of Europe. Their extent is such as to have admitted of considerable exportation.

An exemption from duty of the several kinds of wood ordinarily used in these manufactures seem to be all, that is requisite, by way of encouragement. It is recommended by the consideration of a similar policy being pursued in other countries, and by the expediency of giving equal advantages to our own workmen in wood. The abundance of Timber proper for ship building in the United States does not appear to be an objection to it. The increasing scarcity and the growing importance of that article, in the European countries, admonish the United States to commerce, and systematically to pursue, measures for the preservation of their stock. Whatever may promote the regular establishment of the Magazines of Ship Timber is in various views desirable.

Skins

There are scarcely any manufactories of greater importance, than of this article. Their direct and very happy influence upon Agriculture, by promoting the raising of Cattle of different kinds, is a very material consideration.

It is pleasing too, to observe the extensive progress they have made in their principal branches; which are so far matured as almost to defy foreign competition. Tanneries in particular are not only carried on as a regular business, in numerous instances and in various parts of the Country; but they constitute in some places a valuable item of incidental family manufactures.

Representations however have been made, importing the expediency of further encouragement to the Leather-Branch in two ways—one by increasing the duty on the manufactures of it, which are imported—the other by prohibiting the exportation of bark. In support of the latter it is alleged that the price of bark, chiefly in consequence of large exportations, has risen within a few years from [about three Dollars to four dollars and a half per cord].

These suggestions are submitted rather as intimations, which merit consideration, than as matters, the propriety of which is manifest. It is not clear, that an increase of duty is necessary: and in regard to the prohibition desired, there is no evidence of any considerable exportation hitherto; and it is most probable, that whatever augmentation of price may have taken place, is to be attributed to an extension of the home demand from the increase of manufactures, and to a decrease of the supply in consequence of the progress of Settlement; rather than to the quantities which have been exported.

It is mentioned however, as an additional reason for the prohibition, that one species of the bark usually exported is in some sort peculiar to the country, and the material of a very valuable dye, of great use in some other manufactures, in which the United States have begun a competition.

There may also be this argument in favor of an increase of duty. The object is of importance enough to claim decisive encouragement and the progress, which has been made, leaves no room to apprehend any inconvenience on the score of supply from such an increase.

It would be of benefit to this branch, if glue which is now rated at 5 perCent, were made the object of an excluding duty. It is already made in large quantities at various tanneries; and like paper, is an entire œconomy of materials, which if not manufactured would be left to perish. It may be placed with advantage in the class of articles paying 15 perCent.

Grain

Manufactures of the several species of this article have a title to peculiar favor; not only because they are most of them immediately connected with the subsistence of the citizens; but because they enlarge the demand for the most precious products of the soil.

Though flour may with propriety be noticed as a manufacture of Grain, it were useless to do it, but for the purpose of submitting the expediency of a general system of inspection, throughout the ports of the United states; which, if established upon proper principles, would be likely to improve the quality of our flour every where, and to raise its reputation in foreign markets. There are however considerations which stand in the way of such an arrangement.

Ardent spirits and malt liquors are, next to flour, the two principal manufactures of Grain. The first has made a very extensive, the last a considerable progress in the United States. In respect to both, an exclusive possession of the home market ought to be secured to the domestic manufacturers; as fast as circumstances will admit.

Nothing is more practicable & nothing more desireable.

The existing laws of the United States have done much towards attaining this valuable object; but some additions to the present duties, on foreign distilled spirits, and foreign malt liquors, and perhaps an abatement of those on home made spirits, would more effectually secure it; and there does not occur any very weighty objection to either.

An augmentation of the duties on imported spirits would favour, as well as the distillation of Spirits from molasses, as that from Grain. And to secure to the nation the benefit of the manufacture, even of foreign materials, is always of great, though perhaps of secondary importance.

A strong impression prevails in the minds of those concerned in distilleries (including too the mot candid and enlightened) that greater differences in the rates of duty on foreign and domestic spirits are necessary, completely to secure the successful manufacture of the latter; and there are fact which entitle this impression to attention.

It is known, that the price of molasses for some years past, has been successively rising in the West India Markets, owing partly to competition, which did not formerly exist, and partly to an extension of demand in this country; and it is evident, that the late disturbances in those Islands, from which we draw our principal supply, must so far interfere with the production of the article, as to occasion a material enhancement of price. The destruction and devastation attendant on the insurrection in Hispaniola, in particular, must not only contribute very much to that effect, but may be expected to give it some duration. These circumstances, and the duty of three cents per Gallon on molasses, may render it difficult for the distillers of that material to maintain with adequate profit a competition, with the rum brought from the West Indies, the quality of which is so considerably superior.

The consumption of Geneva or Gin in this country is extensive. It is not long since distilleries of it have grown up among us, to any importance. They are now becoming of consequence, but being still in their infancy, they require protection.

It is represented, that the price of some of the materials is greater here, than in Holland, from which place large quantities are brought, the price of labour considerably greater, the capitals engaged in the business there much larger, than those which are employed here, the rate of profits, at which the Undertakers can afford to carry it on, much less—the prejudices, in favor of imported Gin, strong. These circumstances are alleged to outweigh the charges, which attend the bringing of the Article, from Europe to the United states and the present difference of duty, so as to obstruct the prosecution of the manufacture, with due advantage.

Experiment could perhaps alone decide with certainty the justness of the suggestions, which are made; but in relation to branches of manufacture so important, it would seem inexpedient to hazard an unfavourable issue, and better to err on the side of too great, than of too small a difference, in the particular in question.

It is therefore submitted, that an addition of two cents per Gallon be made to the duty on imported spirits of the first class of proof, with a proportionable increase on those of higher proof; and that a deduction of one cent per Gallon be made from the duty on spirits distilled within the United states, beginning with the first class of proof, and a proportionable deduction from the duty on those of higher proof.

It is ascertained, that by far the greatest part of the malt liquors consumed in the United States are the produce of domestic breweries. It is desireable, and, in all likelihood, attainable, that the whole consumption should be supplied by ourselves.

The malt liquors, made at home, though inferior to the best are equal to a great part of those, which have been usually imported. The progress already made is an earnest of what may be accomplished. The growing competition is an assurance of improvement. This will be accelerated by measures, tending to invite a greater capital into this channel of employment.

To render the encouragement to domestic breweries decisive, it may be adviseable to substitute to the present rates of duty eight cents per gallon generally; and it will deserve to be considered as a guard against evasions, whether there ought not to be a prohibition of their importation, except in casks of considerable capacity. It is to be hoped, that such a duty would banish from the market, foreign malt liquors of inferior quality; and that the best kind only would continue to be imported till it should be supplanted, by the efforts of equal skill or care at home.

Till that period, the importation so qualified would be an useful stimulous to improvement: And in the mean time, the payment of the increased price, for the enjoyment of a luxury, in order to the encouragement of a most useful branch of domestic industry, could not reasonably be deemed a hardship.

As a further aid to the manufactures of grain, though upon a smaller scale, the article of Starch, hair powder and wafers, may with great propriety be placed among those, which are rate at 15 perCent. No manufactures are more simple, nor more completely within the reach of a full supply, from domestic sources, and it is a policy, as common as it is obvious, to make them the objects either of prohibitory duties, or of express prohibition.

Flax and Hemp

Manufactures of these articles have so much affinity to each other, and they are so often blended, that they many with advantage be considered in conjunction. The importance of the linnin branch to agriculture—its precious effects upon household industry—the ease, with which the materials can be produced at home to any requisite extend—the great advances, which have been already made, in the coarser fabricks of them, expecially in the family way, constitute claims, of peculiar force, to the patronage of the government.

This patronage may be afford in various ways; by promoting the growth of the materials; by increasing the impediments to an advantageous competition of rival foreign articles; by direct bounties or premiums upon the home manufacture.

First. As to promoting the growth of the materials.

In respect to hemp, something has been already done by the high duty upon foreign hemp. If the facilities for domestic production were not unusually great, the policy of the duty, on the foreign raw material, would be highly questionable, as interfering with the growth of manufactures of it. But making the proper allowances for those facilities, and with an eye to the future and natural progress, of the country, the measure does not appear, upon the whole, exceptionable. A strong wish naturally suggests itself, that some method could be devised of affording a more direct encouragement to the growth both of flax and hemp; such as would be effectual, and at the same time not attended with too great inconveniences. To this end, bounties and premiums offer themselves to *consideration*; but no modification of them has yet occurred, which would not either hazard too much expence, or operate unequally in reference to the circumstances of different parts of the Union, and which would not be attended with very great difficulties in the execution.

Secondly—

As to encreasing the impediments to an advantageous competition of rival foreign articles.

To this purpose, an augmentation of the duties on importation is the obvious expedient; which, in regard to certain articles, appears to be recommended by sufficient reasons.

The principal of these articles is Sail cloth; one intimately connected with navigation and defence; and of which a flourishing manufactory is established at Boston and very promising ones at several other places.

It is presumed to be both safe and adviseable to place this in the class of articles rated at 10 Per cent. A strong reason for it results from the consideration that a bounty of two pence sterling per ell is allowed, in Great Britain, upon the exportation of the sail cloth manufactured in that Kingdom.

It would likewise appear to be good policy to raise the duty to 7½ perCent on the following articles. Drillings, Osnaburghs, Ticklenburghs, Dowlas, Canvas, Brown Rolls, Bagging, and upon all other linnens the first cost of which at the place of exportation does not exceed 35 cents per yard. A bounty of 12½ perCent, upon an average on the exportation of such similar linens from Great-Britain encourages the manufacture of them in that country and increases the obstacles to a successful competition in the countries to which they are sent.

The quantities of tow and other household linnens manufactured in different parts of the United States and the expectations, which are derived from some late experiments, of being able to extend the use of labour-saving machines, in the coarser fabrics of linnen, obviate the danger of inconvenience, from an increase of the duty upon such articles, and authorize a hope of speedy and complete success to the endeavours, which may be used for procuring an internal supply.

Thirdly. As to direct bounties, or premiums upon the manufactured articles.

To afford more effectual encouragement to the manufacture, and at the same time to promote the cheapness of the article for the benefit of navigation, it will be of great use to allow a bounty of two Cents per yard on all Sail Cloth, which is made in the United States from materials of their own growth.

This would also assist the Culture of those materials. An encouragement of this kind if adopted ought to be established for a moderate term of years, to invite to new undertakings and to an extension of the old. This is an article of importance enough to warrant the employment of extraordinary means in its favor.

Cotton

There is something in the texture of this material, which adapts it in a peculiar degree to the application of Machines. The signal Utility of the mill for spinning of cotton, not long since invented in England, has been noticed in another place; but there are other machines scarcely inferior in utility which, in the different manufactories of this article are employed either exclusively, or with more than ordinary effect. This very important circumstance recommends the fabricks of cotton, in a more particular manner, to a country in which a defect of hands constitutes the greatest obstacles to success.

The variety and extent of the uses to which the manufactures of this article are applicable is another powerful argument in their favor.

And the faculty of the United States to produce the raw material in abundance, & of a quality, which though alledged to be inferior to some that is produced in other quarters, is nevertheless capable of being used with advantage, in many fabrics, and is probably susceptible of being carried, by a more experienced culture, to much greater perfection—suggests an additional and a very cogent inducement to the vigorous pursuit of the cotton branch, in its several subdivisions.

How much has been already done has been stated in a preceding part of this report.

In addition to this, it may be announced, that a society is forming with a capital which is expected to be extended to at lease half a million of dollars; on behalf of which measures are already in train for prosecuting on a large scale, the making and printing of cotton goods.

These circumstances conspire to indicate the expediency of removing any obstructions, which may happen to exist, to the advantageous prosecution of the manufactories in question, and of adding such encouragements, as may appear necessary and proper.

The present duty of three cents per lb. on the foreign raw material, is undoubtedly a very serious impediment to the progress of those manufactories.

The injurious tendency of similar duties either prior to the establishment, or in the infancy of the domestic manufacture, of the article, as it regards the manufacture, and their worse than inutility, in relation to the home production of the material itself, have been anticipated particularly in discussing the subject of pecuniary bounties.

Cotton has not the same pretensions, with hemp, to form an exception to the general rule.

Not being, like hemp an universal production of the Country it affords less assurance of an adequate internal supply; but the chief objection arises from the doubts; which are entertained concerning the quality of the national cotton. It is alledged, that the fibre of it is considerably shorter and weaker, than that of some other places; and it has been observed as a general rule, that the nearer the place of growth to the Equator, the better the quality of the cotton. That which comes from Cayenne, Surrinam and Demarara is said to be preferable, even at a material difference of price, to the Cotton of the Islands.

While a hope may reasonably be indulged, that with due care and attention the national cotton may be made to approach nearer than it now does to that of regions, somewhat more favored by climate; and while facts authorize an opinion, that very great use may be made of it, and that it is a resource which gives greater security to the cotton fabrics of this country, than can be enjoyed by any which depends wholly on external supply it will certainly be wise, in every view, to let our infant manufactures have the full benefit of the best materials on the cheapest terms.

It is obvious that the necessity of having such materials is proportioned to the unskilfulness and inexperience of the workmen employed, who if inexpert, will not fail to commit great waste, where the materials they are to work with are of an indifferent kind.

To secure to the national manufactures so essential an advantage, a repeal of the present duty on imported cotton is indispensible.

A substitute for this, far more encouraging to domestic production, will be to grant a bounty on the national cotton, when wrought at a home manufactory; to which a bounty on the exportation of it may be added. Either or both would do much more towards promoting the growth of the article, than the merely nominal encouragement, which it is proposed to abolish. The first would also have a direct influence in encouraging the manufacture.

The bounty which has been mentioned as existing in Great Britain, upon the exportation of coarse linnens not exceeding a certain vaue, applies also to certain discriptions of cotton goods of similar value.

This furnishes an additional argument for allowing to the national manufacturers the species of encouragement just suggested, and indeed for adding some other aid.

One cent per yard, not less than of a given width, on all goods of cotton, or of cotton and linnen mixed, which are manufactured in the United States; with the addition of one cent per lb weight of the material; if made of national cotton; would amount to an aid of considerable importance, both to the production and to the manufacture of that valuable article. And it is conceived, that the expence would be well justified by the magnitude of the object.

The printing and staining of cotton goods is known to be a distinct business from the fabrication of them. It is one easily accomplished and which, as it adds materially to the value of the article in its white state, and prepares it for a variety of new uses, is of importance to be promoted.

As imported cottons, equally with those which are made at home, may be objects of this manufacture, it will merit consideration, whether the whole, or a part of the duty, on the white goods, ought not to be allowed to be drawn back in favor of those, who print or stain them. This measure would certainly operate as a powerful encouragement to the business; and though it may in a degree counteract

the original fabrication of the articles it would probably more than compensate for this disadvantage, in the rapid growth of a collateral branch, which is of a nature sooner to attain to maturity. When a sufficient progress shall have been made, the drawback may be abrogated; and by that time the domestic supply of the articles to be printed or stained will have been extended.

If the duty of 7½ per Cent on certain kinds of cotton goods were extended to all goods of cotton, or of which it is the principal material, it would probably more than counterbalance the effect of the drawback proposed, in relation to the fabrication of the article. And no material objection occurs to such an extension. The duty then considering all the circumstances which attend goods of this description could not be deemed inconveniently high; and it may be inferred from various causes that the prices of them would still continued moderate.

Manufactories of cotton goods, not long since established at Beverly, in Massachusetts, and at Providence in the state of Rhode Island and conducted with a perseverence corresponding with the patriotic motives which began them, seem to have overcome the first obstacles to success; producing corduroys, velverets, fustians, jeans, and other similar articles of a quality, which will bear a comparison with the like articles brought from Manchester. The one at Providence has the merit of being the first in introducing [into the United States] the celebrated cotton mill; which not only furnishes materials for that manufactory itself, but for the supply of private families for household manufacture.

Other manufactories of the same material; as regular businesses, have also been begun at different places in the state of Connecticut, but all upon a smaller scale, than those above mentioned. Some essays are also making in the printing and staining of cotton goods. There are several small establishments of this kind already on foot.

Wool

In a country, the climate of which partakes of so considerable a proportion of winter, as that of a great part of the United States, the woolen branch cannot be regarded, as inferior to any, which relates to the cloathing of the inhabitants.

Household manufactures of this material are carried on, in different parts of the United States, to a very interesting extent; but there is only one branch, which, as a regular business, can be said to have acquired maturity. This is the making of hats.

Hats of wool, and of wool mixed with fur, are made in large quantities, in different States; & nothing seems wanting, but an adequate supply of materials, to render the manufacture commensurate with the demand.

A promising essay, towards the fabrication of cloths, cassimires and other woolen goods, is likewise going on at *Hartford* in Connecticut. Specimens of the different kinds which are made, in the possession of the Secretary, evince that these fabrics have attained a very considerable degree of perfection. Their quality certainly surpasses anything, that could have been looked for, in so short a time, and under so great disadvantages; and conspires with the scantiness of the means, which have been at the command of the directors, to form the eulogium of that public spirit, perseverance and judgment, which have been able to accomplish so much.

To cherish and bring to maturity this precious embryo must engage the most ardent wishes—and proportionable regret, as far as the means of doing it may appear difficult or uncertain.

Measures, which should tend to promote an abundant supply of wool, of good quality, would probably afford the most efficacious aid, that present circumstances permit.

To encourage the raising and improving the breed of sheep, at home, would certainly be the most desireable expedient, for the purpose; but it may not be alone sufficient, especially as it is yet a problem, whether our wool be capable of such a degree of improvement, as to render it fit for the finer fabrics.

Premiums would probably be found the best means of promoting the domestic, and bounties the foreign supply. The first may be within the compass of the institution hereafter to be submitted—The last would require a specific legislative provision. If any bounties are granted they ought of course to be adjusted with an eye to quality, as well as quantity.

A fund for the purpose may be derived from the addition of 2½ per Cent, to the present rate of duty, on Carpets and Carpeting; an increase, to which the nature of the Articles suggests no objection, and which may at the same time furnish a motive the more to the fabrication of them at home; towards which some beginnings have been made.

Silk

The production of this Article is attended with great facility in most parts of the United States. Some pleasing essays are making in Connecticut, as well towards that, as towards the Manufacture of what is produced. Stockings, Hankerchiefs Ribbons & Buttons are made though as yet but in small quantities.

A Manufactory of Lace upon a scale not very extensive has been long memorable at Ipswich in the State of Massachusetts.

An exemption of the material from the duty, which it now pays on importation, and premiums upon the production, to be dispensed under the direction of the Institution before alluded to, seem to be the only species of encouragement adviseable at so early a stage of the thing.

Glass

The Materials for making Glass are found every where. In the United States there is no deficiency of them. The sands and Stones called Tarso, which include flinty and chrystalline substances generally, and the Salts of various plants, particularly of the Sea Weed Kali or Kelp constitute the essential ingredients. An extraordinary abundance of Fuel is a particular advantage by this Country for such manufactures. They, however, require large Capitals and involve much manual labour.

Different manufactories of Glass are not on foot in the United States. The

present duty of 12½ per Cent on all imported articles of glass amount to a considerable encouragement of those Manufactories. If any thing in addition is judged eligible, the most proper would appear to be a direct bounty, on Window Glass and black Bottles.

The first recommends itself as an object of general convenience; the last adds to that character, the circumstance of being an important item in breweries. A Complaint is made of great deficiency in this respect.

Gun Powder

No small progress has been of late made in the manufacture of this very important article: It may indeed be considered as already established; but its high importance renders its further extension very desireable.

The encouragements, which it already enjoys, are a duty of 10 per Cent on the foreign rival article, and an exemption of Salt petre one of the principal ingredients of which it is composed, from duty. A like exemption of Sulphur, another chief ingredient, would appear to be equally proper. No quantity of this Article has yet been produced, from internal sources. The use made of it in finishing the bottoms of Ships, is an additional inducement to placing it in the class of free goods. Regulations for the careful inspection of the article would have a favourable tendency.

Paper

Manufactories of paper are among those which are Arrived at the greatest maturity in the United States, and are most adequate to national supply. That of paper hangings is a branch, in which respectable progress has been made.

Nothing material seems wanting to the further success of this valuable branch which is already protected by a competent duty on similar imported Articles.

In the enumeration of the several kinds, made subject to that duty, Sheathing and Cartridge paper have been omitted. These, being the most simple manufactures of the sort, and necessary to military supply, as well as Ship building, recommend themselves equally with those of other descriptions, to encouragement, and appear to be as fully within the compass of domestic exertions.

Printed Books

The great number of presses disseminated throughout the Union, seem to afford an assurance, that there is not need of being indebted to foreign Countries for the printing of the Books, which are used in the United States. A duty of ten per Cent instead of five, which is now charged upon the Article, would have a tendency to aid the business internally.

It occurs, as an objection to this, that it may have an unfavourable aspect towards literature, by raising the prices of Books in universal use in private families Schools and other Seminaries of learning. But the difference it is conceived would be without effect.

As to Books which usually fill the Libraries of the wealthier classes and of professional Men, such as Augmentation of prices, as might be occasioned by an additional duty of five per Cent would be too little felt to be an impediment to the acquisition.

And with regard to books which may be specially imported for the use of particular seminaries of learning, and of public libraries, a total exemption from duty would be adviseable, which would go far towards obviating the objection just mentioned. They are now subject to a duty of 5 per Cent.

As to the books in most general family use, the constancy and universality of the demand would insure exertions to furnish them at home and the means are compleatly adequate. It may also be expected ultimately, in this as in other cases, that the extension of the domestic manufacture would conduce to the cheapness of the article.

It ought not to pass unremarked, that to encourage the printing of books is to encourage the manufacture of paper.

Refined Sugars and Chocolate

Are among the number of extensive and prosperous domestic manufactures.

Drawbacks of the duties upon the materials, of which they are respectively made, in cases of exportation, would have a beneficial influence upon the manufacture, and would conform to a precedent, which has been already furnished, in the instance of molasses, on the exportation of distilled spirits.

Cocoa the raw material now pays a duty of one cent per lb., while chocolate which is a prevailing and very simple manufacture, is comprised in a mass of articles rated at no more tan five per Cent.

There would appear to be a propriety in encouraging the manufacture, by a somewhat higher duty, on its foreign rival, than is paid on the raw material.

Two cents per lb. on imported chocolate would, it is presumed, be without inconvenience.

The foregoing heads comprise the most important of the several kinds of manufactures, which have occurred as requiring, and, at the same time, as most proper for public encouragement; and such measures for affording it, as have appeared best calculated to answer the end, have been suggested.

The observations, which have accompanied this delineation of objects, supercede the necessity of many supplementary remarks. One or two however may not be altogether superfluous.

Bounties are in various instances proposed as one species of encouragement.

It is a familiar objection to them, that they are difficult to be managed and liable to frauds. But neither that difficulty nor this danger seems sufficiently great to countervail the advantages of which they are productive, when rightly applied. And it is presumed to have been shewn, that they are in some cases, particularly in the infancy of new enterprises indispensable.

It will however be necessary to guard, with extraordinary circumspection, the manner of dispensing them. The requisite precautions have been thought of; but to enter into the detail would swell this report, already voluminous, to a size too inconvenient.

If the principle shall not be deemed inadmissible the means of avoiding an abuse of it will not be likely to present insurmountable obstacles. There are useful guides from practice in other quarters.

It shall therefore only be remarked here, in relation to this point, that any

bounty, which may be applied to the *manufacture* of an article, cannot with safety extend beyond those manufactories, at which the making of the article is a *regular trade*.

It would be impossible to annex adequate precautions to a benefit of that nature, if extended to every private family, in which the manufacture was incidentally carried on, and its being a merely incidental occupation which engages a portion of time that would otherwise be lost, it can be advantageously carried on, without so special an aid.

The possibility of a diminution of the revenue may also present itself, as an objection to the arrangements, which have been submitted.

But there is no truth, which may be more firmly relied upon, than the interests of the revenue are promoted, by whatever promotes an increase of National industry and wealth.

In proportion to the degree of these, is the capacity of every country to contribute to the public Treasury; and where the capacity to pay is increased, or even is not decreased, the only consequence of measures, which diminish any particular resource is a change of the object. If by encouraging the manufacture of an article at home, the revenue, which has been wont to accrue from its importation, should be lessened, an indemnification can easily be found, either out of the manufacture itself, or from some other object, which may be deemed more convenient.

The measures however, which have been submitted, taken aggregately, will for a long time to come rather augment than decrease the public revenue.

There is little room to hope, that the progress of manufactures, will so equally keep pace with the progress of population, as to prevent, even, a gradual augmentation of the product of the duties on imported articles.

As, nevertheless, an abolition in some instances, and a reduction in others of duties, which have been pledged for the public debt, is proposed, it is essential, that is should be accompanied with a competent substitute. In order to this, it is requisite, that all the additional duties which shall be laid, be appropriated in the first instance, to replace all defalcations, which may proceed from any such abolition or diminution. It is evident, at first glance, that they will not only be adequate to this, but will yield a considerable surplus.

This surplus will serve.

First. To constitute a fund for paying the bounties which shall have been decreed.

Secondly. To constitute a fund for the operations of a Board, to be established, for promoting Arts, Agriculture, Manufactures and Commerce. Of this institution, different intimations have been given, in the course of this report. An outline of a plan for it shall now be submitted.

Let a certain annual sum, be set apart, and placed under the management of Commissioners, not less than three, to consist of certain Officers of the Government and their Successors in Office.

Let these Commissioners be empowered to apply the fund confided to them—to defray the expences of the emigration of Artists, and Manufacturers in particular branches of extraordinary importance—to induce the prosecution and introduction of useful discoveries, inventions and improvements, by proportionate rewards, judiciously held out and applied—to encourage by premiums both honorable and lucrative the exertions of individuals, And of classes, in relation to the several objects, they are charged with promoting—and to afford such other aids to those objects, as may be generally designated by law.

The Commissioners to render [to the Legislature] an annual account of their transactions and disbursements; and all such sums as shall not have been applied to the purposes of their trust, at the end of every three years, to revert to the Treasury. It may also be enjoined upon them, not to draw out the money, but for the purpose of some specific disbursement.

It may moreover be of use, to authorize them to receive voluntary contributions; making it their duty to apply them to the particular objects for which they may have been made, if any shall have been designated by the donors.

There is reason to believe, that the progress of particular manufactures has been much retarded by the want of skilful workmen. And it often happens that the capitals employed are not equal to the purposes of bringing from abroad workmen of a superior kind. Here, is case worthy of it, the auxiliary agency of Government would in all probability be useful. There are also valuable workmen, in every branch, who are prevented from emigrating solely by the want of means. Occasional aids to such persons properly administered might be a source of valuable acquisitions of the country.

The propriety of stimulating by rewards, the invention and introduction of useful improvements, is admitted without difficulty. But the success of attempts in this way must evidently depend much on the manner of conducting them. It is probable, that the placing of the dispensation of those rewards under some proper discretionary direction, where they may be accompanied by *collateral expedients*, will serve to give them the surest efficacy. It seems impracticable to apportion, by general rules, specific compensations for discoveries of unknown and disproportionate utility.

The great use which may be made of a fund of this mature to procure and import foreign improvements is particularly obvious. Among these, the article of machines would form a most important item.

The operation and utility of premiums have been adverted to; together with the advantages which have resulted from the dispensation, under the direction of certain public and private societies. Of this some experience has been had in the instance of the Pennsylvania society, [for the Promotion of Manufactures and useful Arts;] but the funds of that association have been too contracted to produce more than a very small portion of the good to which the principles of it would have led. It may confidently be affirmed that there is scarcely any thing, which has been devised, better calculated to excite a general spirit of improvement than the institutions of this nature. They are truly invaluable.

In countries where there is a great private wealth much may be effected by the voluntary contributions of patriotic individuals, but in a community situated like that of the United States, the public purse must supply the deficiency of private resource. In what can it be so useful as in prompting and improving the efforts of industry?

All which is humbly submitted

Alexander Hamilton
Secretary of the Treasury

See also: **Vol. I**: Hamilton, Alexander; Infant industries; Jefferson, Thomas; Labor; Protectionism; Tariff of 1789; Tariff of 1816; Washington, George; *The Wealth of Nations*. **Vol. III**: Tariff of 1789, Tariff of 1790; Tariff of 1792; Tariff of 1794; Tariff of 1796; Tariff of 1816.

Daniel Webster's Speech Defending His Support of the Tariff of 1828

The debate over the Tariff of 1828, also known as the "Tariff of Abominations," prompted Daniel Webster to give the following speech before the U.S. Senate on January 26, 1830, in response to his critics, specifically Senator Robert Young Hayne, who charged him with voting inconsistently on the tariff. His political opponents noted that he had voted against the Tariff of 1824, but for the Tariff of 1828. Webster eloquently pointed out that the shift in his position occurred not because he changed his mind about tariffs, but because the latter tariff corrected the worst abuses of the earlier act. He also argued that southerners saw the tariff as a political move by New England, no matter which position the regions representatives and senators assumed. The Tariff of 1828 divided the country geographically and threatened its unity.

I repeat, sir, that in adopting the sentiment of the framers of the Constitution I read their language audibly, and word for word, and I pointed out the distinction just as fully as I have now done, between the consolidation of the Union and that other obnoxious consolidation which I disclaimed. And yet the honorable member misunderstood me. The gentleman had said that he wished for no fixed revenue—not a shilling. If, by word, he could convert the capitol into gold, he would not do it. Why all this fear of revenue? Why, sir, because, as the gentleman told us, it tends to consolidation. Now, this can mean neither more nor less than that a common revenue is a common interest, and that all common interests tend to hold the Union of the states together. I confess I like that tendency; if the gentleman dislikes it, he is right in deprecating a shilling's fixed revenue. So much, sir, for consolidation.

As well as I recollect the course of his remarks, the honorable gentleman next recurred to the subject of the tariff. He did not doubt the word must be of unpleasant sound to me, and proceeded with an effort, neither new nor attended with new success, to involve me and my votes in inconsistency and contradiction. I am happy the honorable gentleman has furnished me an opportunity for a timely remark or two on that subject. I was glad he approached it, for it is a question I enter upon without fear from anybody. The strenuous toil of the gentleman has been to raise an inconsistency between my dissent to the tariff in 1824 and my vote in 1828. It is labor lost. He pays undeserved compliment to my speech in 1824; but this is to raise me high, that my fall, as he would have it, in 1828, may be more signal. Sir, there was no fall at all. Between the ground I stood on in 1824 and that I took in 1828 there was not only no precipice, but no declivity. It was a change of position, to meet new circumstances, but on the same level. A plain tale explains the whole matter. In 1816 I had not acquiesced in the tariff, then supported by South Carolina. To some parts of it, especially, I felt and expressed great repugnance. I held the same opinion in 1821, at the meeting in Faneuil Hall, to which the gentleman has alluded. I said then, and say now, that, as an original question, the authority of Congress to exercise the revenue power, with direct reference to the protection of manufactures, is a questionable authority, far more questionable, in my judgment, than the power of internal improvements. I must confess, sir, that, in one respect, some impression has been made on my opinions lately. Mr. Madison's publication has put the power in a very strong light. He has placed it, I must acknowledge, upon grounds of construction and argument which seem impregnable. But even if the power were doubtful, on the face of the Constitution itself, it had been assumed and asserted in the first revenue law ever passed under that same Constitution; and, on this ground, as a matter settled by contemporaneous practice, I had refrained from expressing the opinion that the tariff laws transcended constitutional limits, as the gentleman supposes. What I did say at Faneuil Hall, as far as I now remember, was that this was originally matter of doubtful construction. The gentleman himself, I suppose, thinks there is no doubt about it and that the laws are plainly against the Constitution. Mr. Madison's letter, already referred to, contain, in my judgment, by far the most able exposition extant of this part of the Constitution. He has satisfied me so far as the practice of the government had left it an open question.

With a great majority of the Representatives of Massachusetts I voted against the tariff in 1824. My reasons were then given, and I will not now repeat them. But, notwithstanding our dissent, the great states of New York, Pennsylvania, Ohio and Kentucky went for the bill, in almost unbroken column, and it passed Congress and the President sanctioned it, and it became the law of the land. What, then, are we to do? Our only option was either to fall in with this settled course of public policy, and accommodate ourselves to it as well as we could, or to embrace the South Carolina doctrine and talk of nullifying the statute by state interference.

This last alternative did not suit our principles and, of course, we adopted the former. In 1827 the subject came again before Congress on a proposition favorable to wool and woolens. We looked upon the system of protection as being fixed and settled. The law of 1824 remained. It had gone into full operation, and in regard to some objects intended by it, perhaps most of them, had produced all its expected effects. No man proposed to repeal it; no man attempted to renew the general contest on its principle. But, owing to subsequent and unforeseen occurrences, the benefit intended by it to wool and woolen fabrics had not been realized. Events, not known here when the law passed, had taken place, which defeated its object in that particular respect. A measure was accordingly brought forward to meet this precise deficiency; to remedy this particular defect. It was limited to wool and woolens. Was ever anything more reasonable? If the policy of the tariff laws had become established in principle, as the permanent policy of the government, should they not be revised and amended and made equal, like other laws, as exigencies should arise, or justice require? Because we had doubted about adopting the system were we to refuse to cure its manifest defects, after it became adopted, and when no one attempted its repeal? And this, sir, is the inconsistency so much bruited. I had voted against the tariff of 1824— but it passed; and in 1827 and 1828 I voted to amend it in a point essential to the interests of my constituents. Where is the inconsistency? Could I do otherwise? Sir, does a political consistency consist in always giving negative votes? Does it require of a public man to refuse to concur in amending laws, because they passed against his consent? Having votes against the tariff originally, does consistency demand that I should do all in my power to maintain an equal tariff, burdensome to my own constituents, and in many respects favorable to none? To consistency of that sort I lay no claim. And there is another sort to which I lay as little—and this a kind of consistency by which persons feel themselves as much bound to oppose a proposition, after it has become a law of the land, as before.

The bill of 1827, limited, as I have said, to the single object in which the tariff of 1824 had manifestly failed in its effect, passed the House of Representatives, but was lost here. We had then the Act of 1828. I need not recur to the history of a measure so recent. Its enemies spiced it with whatsoever they thought would render it distasteful; its friends took it, drugged as it was. Vast amounts of property, many millions, had been invested in manufactures under the inducements of the Act of 1824. Events called loudly, as I thought, for further regulation to secure the degree of protection intended by that Act. I was disposed to vote for such regulation, and desire nothing more; but certainly was not to be bantered out of my purpose by a threatened augmentation of duty on molasses, put into the bill for the avowed purpose of making it obnoxious. The vote may have been right or wrong, wise or unwise; but it is little less than absurd to allege against it an inconsistency with opposition to the former law.

Sir, as to the general subject of the tariff, I have little now to say. Another opportunity may be presented. I remarked the other day that this policy did not begin with us in New England; and yet, sir, New England is charged with vehemence as being favorable, or charged with equal vehemence as being unfavorable to the tariff policy, just as best suits the time, place and occasion for making some charge against her. The credulity of the public has been put to its extreme capacity of false impression relative to her conduct in this particular. Through all the South, during the late contest, it was New England policy and a New England administration that was afflicting the country with a tariff beyond all endurance; while on the other side of the Alleghany even the Act of 1828 itself, the very sublimated essence of oppression, according to Southern opinions, was pronounced to be one of these blessings for which the West was indebted to the "generous South."

With large investments in manufacturing establishments, and many and various interests connected with an dependent upon them, it is not expected that New England, any more than other portions of the country, will now consent to any measure, destructive or highly dangerous. The duty of the government, at the present time, would seem to be to preserve, not to destroy; to maintain the position which it had assumed; and, for one, I shall feel it an indispensable obligation to hold it steady, as far as in my power, to that degree of protection which it has undertaken to bestow.

See also: **Vol. I**: American System; Clay, Henry; Congress (United States); Hayne, Robert Y.; Tariff of 1824; Tariff of 1828 (Tariff of Abominations); Wool and woolens. **Vol. III**: Tariff of 1824; Tariff of 1828 (Tariff of Abominations).

Robert Young Hayne's 1832 Speech in Support of Free Trade

In January 1832, at the height of the Nullification Crisis brought on by the Tariff of Abominations, South Carolina Senator Robert Young Hayne argued for free trade before Congress in a debate with Massachusetts Senator Daniel Webster. In his moving oration Hayne pointed out that although countries had historically sought to restrict trade, the practice had led to the demise of great empires like Spain. He noted that the British Parliament had recently passed legislation that moved Great Britain toward a policy of free trade and recommended that the United States pursue a similar course to unfetter commerce and encourage economic growth. Following this speech Hayne returned to his home state, where he participated in the nullification convention of 1832; he later became the governor of the state.

Mr. President: The plain and seemingly obvious truth, that in a fair and equal exchange of commodities all parties gained, is a noble discovery of modern times. The contrary principle naturally led to commercial rivalries, wars and abuses of all sorts. The benefits of commerce being regards as a stake to be won, or an advantage to be wrested from others by fraud or by force, governments naturally strove to secure them to their own subjects; and when they once set out in this wrong direction it was quite natural that they should not stop short till they ended in binding, in the bonds of restriction, not only the whole country, but all of its parts. Thus we are told that England first protected by her restrictive policy her whole empire against all the world, then Great Britain against the Colonies, then the British Islands against each other, and ended by vainly attempting to protect all the great interests and employment of the state by balancing them against each other. Sir, such a system, carried fully out, is not confined to rival nations, but protects one town against another, considers villages and even families as rivals, and cannot stop short of "Robinson Crusoe" in his goatskins. It takes but one step further to make every man his own lawyer, doctor, farmer and shoemaker—and, if I may be allowed, an Irishman his own seamstress and washer woman. The doctrine of free trade, on the contrary, is founded on the true social system. It looks on all mankind as children of a common parent, and the great family of nations as linked together by mutual interests. Sir, as there is a religion, so I believe there is a politics of nature. Cast your eyes over this various earth, see its surface diversified by hills and valleys, rocks and fertile fields. Notice its difference productions, it infinite varieties of soil and climate. See the mighty rivers winding their way to the very mountain's base, and then guiding man to the vast ocean, dividing, yet connecting nations. Can any man who considers these things with the eye of a philosopher, not read the design of the great Creator (written legibly in His works) that His children should be drawn together in a free commercial intercourse and mutual exchanges of the various gifts with which a bountiful Providence has blessed them? Commerce, sir, restricted even as she has been, has been the great source of civilization and refinement all over the world. Next to the Christian religion, I consider free trade in its largest sense as the greatest blessing that can be conferred upon any people. Hear, sir, what Patrick Henry, the great orator of Virginia, whose soul was the very temple of freedom, says on this subject:

"Why should we fetter commerce? If a man is in chains he droops and bows to the earth, because his spirits are broken; but let him twist the fetters from his legs and he still stand erect. Fetter not commerce! Let her be as free as the air. She will range the whole creation, and return on the four winds of Heaven to bless the land with plenty."

But it has been said that free trade would do very well if all nations would adopt it; but as it is, every nation must protect itself from the effects of restrictions by countervailing measures. I am persuaded, sir, that this is a great, a most fatal error. If retaliation is resorted to for the honest purpose of producing a redress of the grievance, and while adhered to no longer than there is a hope of success, it may, like war itself, be sometimes just and necessary. But if it has no such object, "it is the unprofitable combat of seeing which can do the other most harm." The case can hardly be conceived in which permanent restrictions as a measure of retaliation could be profitable. In every possible situation a trade, whether more or less restricted, is profitable, or it is not. This can only be decided by experience, and if the trade be left to regulate itself, water would not more naturally seek its level than the intercourse adjust itself to the true interests of the parties. Sir, as to this idea of the regulation by government of the pursuits of men, I consider it as a remnant of barbarism disgraceful to an enlightened age and inconsistent with the first principles of rational liberty. I hold government to be utterly incapable, from its position, of exercising such a power wisely, prudently, or justly. Are the rulers of the world the depositories of its collected wisdom? Sir, can we forget the advice of the great statesman to his son—"Go, see the world, my son, that you may learn with how little wisdom mankind is governed." And is our own government an exception to this rule, or do we find here as everywhere else, that

> "Man, proud man,
> Robed in a little brief authority,
> Plays such fantastic tricks before high heaven,
> As make the angels weep."

The gentleman has appealed to the example of other nations. Sir, they are all against him. They have had restrictions enough to be sure; but they are getting heartily sick of them, and in England, particularly, would willingly get rid of them if they could. We have been assured, by the declaration of a minister of the crown, from his place in parliament, "that there is a growing conviction, among all men of sense and reflection" in that country, that the true policy of all nations is to be found in unrestricted industry. Sir, in England they are now retracing their steps and endeavoring to relieve themselves of the system as fast as they can. Within a few years past, upwards of three hundred statutes, imposing restrictions in that country, have been repealed; and a case has recently occurred there, which seems to leave no doubt that, if Great Britain has grown great, it is as Mr. Huskinson has declared, "not in consequence of, but in spite of their restrictions." The silk manufacture, pro-tected by enormous bounties, was found to be in such a declining condition, that the government was obliged to do something to save it from total ruin. And what did they do? They considerably reduced the duty on foreign silk, both on the raw material and the manufactured article. The consequence was the immediate revival of the silk manufacture, which has since been nearly doubled. Sir, the experience of France has been equally decisive. Bonaparte's efforts to introduce cotton and sugar has cost the country millions; and, but the other day, a foolish attempt to protect the iron mines spread devastation through half of France and nearly ruined the wine trade on which one-fifth of her citizens depend for subsistence. As to Spain, unhappy Spain, "fenced round with restrictions," her experience, one would suppose, would convince us, if anything could, that the protecting system in politics, like bigotry in religion, was utterly at war with sound principles and a liberal and enlightened policy. Sir, I may, in the words of the philosophical statesman of England, "Leave a generous nation free to seek their own road to perfection." Thank God, the night is passing away, and we have lived to see the dawn of a glorious day. The cause of free trade must and will prosper, and finally triumph. The political economist is abroad; light has come into the world; and, in this instance at least, men will not "prefer darkness rather than light." Sir, let it not be said in after times, that the statesmen of America were behind the age in which they lived—that they initiated this young and vigorous country into the enervating and corrupting practices of European nations—and that, at the moment when the whole world were looking to us for an example, we arrayed ourselves in the cast-off follies and exploded errors of the Old World, and, by the introduction of a vile system of artificial stimulants and political gambling, impaired the healthful vigor of the body politic, and brought on a decrepitude and premature dissolution.

See also: **Vol. I**. American System; Clay, Henry; Congress; Free Trade; Tariff of 1824; Tariff of 1828; Webster, Daniel; Wool and woolens. **Vol. III**: Tariff of 1824; Tariff of 1828 (Tariff of Abominations).

Henry Clay's 1832 Speech in Favor of the American System

Southern protests over the high rates passed under the Tariff of 1828 led Congress to address the issue again during the 1832 session. Whereas South Carolina's senator Robert Y. Hayne argued for free trade, Speaker of the House Henry Clay, in February 1832, argued for the maintenance of the American System with its protective tariffs. Clay noted that only domestic manufacturers stimulated competition; competition in turn, resulted in lower prices for the consumer. He also emphasized the necessity of self-sufficiency, especially if the United States should ever again enter into a war. He warned the senators of the danger that could arise from a fluctuating tariff policy.

The great law of price is determined by supply and demand. Whatever affects either affects the price. If the supply is increased, the demand remaining the same, the price declines; if the demand is increased, the supply remaining the same, the price advances; if both supply and demand are undiminished, the price is stationary, and the price is influenced exactly in proportion to the degree of disturbance to the demand or supply. It is, therefore, a great error to suppose that an existing or new duty necessarily becomes a component element to its exact amount of price. If the proportion of demand and supply are varied by the duty, either in augmenting the supply or diminishing the demand or vice versa, price is affected to the extent of that variation. But the duty never becomes an integral part of the price, except in the instances where the demand and the supply remain after the duty is imposed precisely what they were before, or the demand is increased, and the supply remains stationary.

Competition, therefore, wherever existing, whether at home or abroad, is the parent cause of cheapness. If a high duty excites production at home, and the quantity of the domestic article exceeds the amount which had been previously imported, the price will fall. This accounts for an extraordinary fact stated by a Senator from Missouri. Three cents were laid as a duty upon a pound of lead by the Act of 1828. The price at Galena, and the other lead mines, afterwards fell to one and a half cents per pound. Now it is obvious that the duty did not in this case enter into the price, for it was twice the amount of the price. What produced the fall? It was stimulated production at home, excited by the temptation of the exclusive possession of the home market. This state of things could not last. Men would not continue an unprofitable pursuit; some abandoned the business, or the total quantity was diminished and living prices have been the consequence. But, break down the domestic supply, place us again in a state of dependence on the foreign source, and can it be doubted that we should ultimately have to supply ourselves at dearer rates? It is not fair to credit the foreign market with the depression of prices produced there by the influence of our competition. Let the competition be withdrawn and their prices will instantly rise. But it is argued that if, by the skill, experience and perfection which we have acquired in certain branches of manufacture, they can be made as cheap as similar articles abroad, and enter fairly into competition with them, why not repeal the duties as to those articles? And why should we? Assuming the truth of the supposition, the foreign article would not be introduced in the regular course of trade, but would remain excluded by the possession of the home market which the domestic article had obtained. The repeal, therefore, would

have no legitimate effect. But might not the foreign article be imported in vast quantities to glut our markets, break down our establishments and ultimately to enable the foreigner to monopolize the supply of our consumption? America is the greatest foreign market for European manufactures. It is that to which European attention is constantly directed. If a great house becomes bankrupt there, its store houses are emptied and the goods are shipped to America, where, in consequence of our auctions and our custom house credits, the greatest facilities are afforded in the sale of them. Combinations among manufacturers might take place, or even the operations of foreign governments might be directed to the destruction of our establishments. A repeal, therefore, of one protecting duty, from some one or all of these causes, would be followed by flooding the country with the foreign fabric surcharging the market, reducing the price, and a complete prostration of our manufactories, after which the foreigner would leisurely look about to indemnify himself in the increased prices which he would be enabled to command by his monopoly of the supply of our consumption. What American citizen, after the government had displayed this vacillating policy, would again be tempted to place the smallest confidence in the public faith and adventure once more in the branch of industry?

Gentlemen have allowed to the manufacturing portions of the community no peace; they have been constantly threatened with the overthrow of the American system. From the year 1820, if not from 1816, down to this time, they have been held in a condition of constant alarm and insecurity. Nothing is more prejudicial to the great interests of a nation than unsettled and varying policy. Although every appeal to the national legislature has been responded to in conformity with the wishes and sentiments of the great majority of the people, measures of protection have only been carried by such small majorities as to excite hopes on the one hand and fears on the other. Let the country breathe, let its vast resources be developed, let its energies be fully put forth, let it have tranquillity, and my word for it, the degree of perfection in the arts which it will exhibit will be greater than that which has been presented, astonishing as our progress has been. Although some branches of our manufactures might, and in foreign markets now do, fearlessly contend with similar foreign fabrics, there are many others yet in their infancy struggling with the difficulties which encompass them. We should look at the whole system, and recollect that time when we contemplate the great movement of a nation is very different from the short period which is allotted for the duration of individual life. The honorable gentleman from South Carolina well and eloquently said in 1824: "No great interests of any country ever yet grew up in a day; no branch of industry can become firmly and profitably established but in a long course of years; everything, indeed, great or good, is matured by slow degrees; that which attains to speedy maturity is of small value and is destined to a brief existence. It is the order of providence that powers gradually developed shall alone attain permanency and perfection. Thus must it be with

our national institutions and the national character itself."

I feel most sensibly, Mr. President, how much I have trespassed upon the Senate. My apology is deep and deliberate conviction that the great cause under debate involves the prosperity and the destiny of the Union. But the best requital I can make for the friendly indulgence which has been extended to me by the Senate, and for which I shall ever retain sentiments of lasting gratitude, is to proceed, with as little delay as practicable, to the conclusion of the discourse which has not been more tedious to the Senate than exhausting to me. I have now to consider the remaining of the two propositions which I have already announced. That is:

Secondly. That under the operation of the American system the products of our agriculture command a higher price than they would do without it, by the creation of a home market, and by the augmentation of wealth produced by manufacturing industry, which enlarges our powers of consumption both of domestic and foreign articles. The importance of the home market is among the established maxims which are universally recognized by all writers and all men. However some may differ as to the relative advantages of the foreign and the home market, none deny to the latter great value and high consideration. It is nearer to us; beyond the control of foreign legislation and undisturbed by those vicissitudes to which all international intercourse is more or less exposed. The most stupid are sensible of the benefit of a residence in the vicinity of a large manufactory, or of a navigable stream, which connects their farms with some great capital. If the pursuits of all men were perfectly the same, although they would be in possession of the greatest abundance of the particular produce of their industry, they might, at the same time, be in extreme want of other necessary articles of human subsistence. The uniformity of the general occupation would preclude all exchanges, all commerce. It is only in the diversity of the vocations of the members of a community that the means can be found for those salutary exchanges which conduce to the general prosperity. And the greater that diversity the more expensive and the more animating is the circle of exchange. Even if foreign markets were freely and widely open to the reception of our agricultural produce, from its bulky nature and the distance of the interior, and the dangers of the ocean, large portions of it could never profitably reach the foreign market. But let us quit this field of theory, clear as it is, and look at the practical operations of the system of protection, beginning with the most valuable staple of our agriculture.

But if all this reasoning were totally fallacious—if the price of manufactured articles were really higher under the American system than without it, I should still argue that high or low prices were themselves relative—relative to the ability to pay them. It is in vain to tempt, to tantalize us with the lower prices of European fabrics than our own if we have nothing wherewith to purchase them. If, by the home exchanges, we can be supplied with necessary, even if they are dearer and worse, articles of American production than the foreign, it is better than not being supplied at all. And how would the large portion of our country which I have described be supplied but for the home exchanges? A poor people, destitute of wealth or of exchangeable commodities, has nothing to purchase foreign fabrics. To them they are equally beyond their reach, whether their cost be a dollar or a guinea. It is in this view of the matter that Great Britain, by her vast wealth—her excited and protected industry—is enabled to bear the burden of taxation which, when compared to that of other nations, appears enormous; but which, when her immense riches are compared to theirs, is light and trival. The gentleman from South Carolina has drawn a lively and flattering picture of our coasts, bays, rivers and harbors; and he argues that these proclaimed the design of Providence that we should be a commercial people. I agree with him. We differ only as to the means. He would cherish the foreign and neglect the internal trade. I would foster both. What is navigation without ships, or ships without cargoes? By pentrating the bosoms of our mountains and extracting from them their precious treasures; by cultivating the earth and securing a home market for its rich and abundant products; by employing the water power with which we are blessed; by stimulating and protecting our native industry. In all its forms, we shall but nourish and promote the prosperity of commerce, foreign and domestic. I have hitherto considered the question in reference only to a state at peace; but a season of war ought not to be entirely overlooked. We have enjoyed near twenty years of peace, but who can tell when the storm of war shall again break forth? Have we forgotten so soon the privations to which not merely our brave soldiers and our gallant tars were subjected, but the whole community during the last war for the want of absolute necessities? To what an enormous price they rose! And how inadequate the supply was at any price! The statesman who justly elevates his views will look behind, as well as forward, and at the existing state of things; and he will graduate the policy which he recommends to all the probable exigencies which may arise in the Republic. Taking this comprehensive range it would be easy to show that the higher prices of peace, if prices were higher in peace, were more than compensated by the lower prices of war, during which supplies of all essential articles are indispensable to its vigorous, effectual and glorious prosecution. I conclude this part of the argument with hope that my humble exertions have not been altogether unsuccessful in showing:

1. That the policy which we have been considering ought to continue to be regarded as a genuine American system.

2. That the free trade system, which is proposed as its substitute, ought really to be considered as the British Colonial system.

3. That the American system is beneficial to all parts of the Union, and absolutely necessary to much the larger portion.

4. That the price of the great staple of cotton, and of all our chief productions of agriculture, has been sustained and upheld and a decline averted by the protective system.

5. That if the foreign demand for cotton has been at all diminished by the operation of that system, the dim-

inution has been more than compensated in the additional demand created at home.

6. That the constant tendency of the system, by creating competition among ourselves, and between American and European industries, reciprocally acting upon each other, is to reduce prices of manufactured objects.

7. That in point of fact objects within the scope of the policy of protection have greatly fallen in price.

8. That if, in a season of peace, these benefits are experienced, in a season of war, when the foreign supply might be cut off, they would be much more extensively felt.

9. And, finally, that the substitution of the British Colonial system for the American system, without benefiting any section of the Union, by subjecting us to a foreign legislation, regulated by foreign interests, would lead to the prostration of our manufactures, general impoverishment and ultimate ruin.

The danger of our Union does not lie on the side of persistence in the American system, but on that of its abandonment. If, as I have supposed and believed, the inhabitants of all north and east of James river, and all west of the mountains, including Louisiana, are deeply interested in the preservation of that system, would they be reconciled to its overthrow? Can it be expected that two-thirds, if not three-fourths, of the people of the United States would consent to the destruction of a policy believed to be indispensable to their prosperity? When, too, the sacrifice is made at instance of a single interest, which they verily believe will not be promoted by it? In estimating the degree of peril which may be incident to two opposite portions of human policy, the statesman would be short-sighted who should content himself with viewing only the evils, real or imaginery, which belong to that course which is in practical operation. He should lift himself up to the contemplation of those greater and more certain dangers which might inevitably attend the adoption of the alternative course. What would be the condition of this Union if Pennsylvania and New York, were firmly persuaded that their industry was paralyzed, and their prosperity blighted, by the enforcement of the British Colonial system under the delusive name of free trade? They are now tranquil and happy, and contented, conscious of their welfare, and feeling a salutary and rapid circulation of the products of home manufactures and home industry through-

out all their great arteries. But let that be checked, let them feel that a foreign system is to predominate, and the sources of their subsistence and comfort dried up; let New England and the West and Middle States all feel that they, too, are the victims of a mistaken policy, and let these vast portions of our country despair of any favorable change, and then, indeed, might we tremble for the continuance and safety of this Union.

See also: **Vol. I**: American System; Calhoun, John Caldwell; Clay's Compromise; Force Act; Jackson, Andrew; Nullification; South Carolina *Exposition* and *Protest*; Tariff of 1816; Tariff of 1824; Tariff of 1828 (Tariff of Abominations); Tariff of 1832; Tariff of 1833 (Compromise Tariff). **Vol. III**: Tariff of 1824; Tariff of 1828 (Tariff of Abominations); Tariff of 1832; Tariff of 1833 (Compromise Tariff).

South Carolina *Exposition*

As southern tensions increased over the passage of the Tariff of 1828 the South Carolina House of Representatives appointed a special committee to draft a response to the act. On December 19, 1828, the committee presented the South Carolina Exposition, *drafted anonymously by Vice President John C. Calhoun, to the state legislature. The document, printed and distributed by the House, argued that the states retained the right to nullify federal law, basing their argument on James Madison's Virginia Resolution of 1798 and Thomas Jefferson's Kentucky Resolution of 1799. After reviewing the* Exposition, *the South Carolina Legislature then issued a formal protest to the U.S. Senate.*

[In the South Carolina House of Representatives, December 19, 1828]

The Committee have bestowed on the subject referred to them, the deliberate attention which its importance merits; and the result, on full investigation is, an unanimous opinion, that the Act of Congress of the last session, with the whole system of legislation imposing duties on imports, not for revenue, but for the protection of one branch of industry, at the expense of others, is unconstitutional, unequal and oppressive; calculated to corrupt the public morals, and to destroy the liberty of the country. These propositions they propose to consider in the order stated, and then to conclude their report, with the consideration of the important question of the remedy.

The Committee do not propose to enter into an elaborate, or refined argument on the question of the constitutionality of the Tariff system.

The General Government is one of specific powers, and it can rightfully exercise only the powers expressly granted, and those that may be "necessary and proper" to carry them into effect; all others being reserved expressly to the States, or to the people. It results necessarily, that those who claim to exercise a power under the Constitution, are bound to shew [*sic*], that it is expressly granted, or that it is necessary and proper, as a means to some of the granted powers.

The advocates of the Tariff have offered no such proof. It is true, that the third [*sic*] section of the first article of the Constitution of the United States authorizes Congress to lay and collect an impost duty, but it is granted as a tax power, for the sole purpose of revenue; a power in its nature essentially different from that of imposing protective or prohibitory duties. The two are incompatable [*sic*]; for the prohibitory system must end in destroying the revenue from impost. It has been said that the system is a violation of the spirit and not the letter of the Constitution. The distinction is not material. The Constitution may be as grossly violated by acting against its meaning as against its letter; but it may be proper to dwell a moment on the point, in order to understand more fully the real character of the acts, under which the interest of this, and other States similarly situated, has been sacrificed. The facts are few and simple. The Constitution grants to Congress the power of imposing a duty on imports for revenue; which power is abused by being converted into an instrument for rearing up the industry of one section of the country on the ruins of another. The violation then consists in using a power, granted for one object, to advance another, and that by the sacrifice of the original object. It is, in a word, *a violation of perversion*, the most dangerous of all, because the most insidious, and difficult to resist. Others cannot be perpetrated without the aid of the judiciary; this may be, by the executive

and legislative alone. The courts by their own decisions cannot look into the motives of legislators—they are obliged to take acts by their titles and professed objects, and if *they* be constitutional they cannot interpose their power, however grossly the acts may violate the Constitution. The proceedings of the last session sufficiently prove, that the House of Representatives are aware of the distinction, and determined to avail themselves of the advantage.

In the absence of arguments drawn from the Constitution itself, the advocates of the power have attempted to call in the aid of precedent. The committee will not waste their time in examining the instances quoted. If they were strictly in point they would be entitled to little weight. Ours is not a government of precedents, nor can they be admitted, except to a very limited extent, and with great caution, in the interpretation of the Constitution, without changing in time the entire character of the instrument. The only safe rule is the Constitution itself, or, if that be doubted, the history of the times. In this case, if doubt exists, the journals of the convention would remove them. It was moved in that body to confer on Congress, the very power in question; to encourage manufactures, but it was deliberately withheld, except to the extent of granting patent rights for new and useful inventions. Instead of granting the power to Congress, permission was given to the States to impose duties, with consent of that body, to encourage their own manufactures; and thus in the true spirit of justice, imposing the burden on those, who were to be benefited. But giving to precedents, whatever weight may be claimed, the committee feel confident, that in this case there are none in point, previous to the adoption of the present Tariff system. Every instance which has been cited, may fairly be referred to the legitimate power of Congress to impose duties on imports for revenue. It is a necessary incident of such duties to act as an encouragement to manufactures, whenever imposed on articles, which may be manufactured in our own country. In this incidental manner Congress has the power of encouraging manufactures; and the committee readily concede, that in the passage of an impost bill, that body may, in modifying the details, so arrange the provisions of the bill, as far as it may be done consistently with its proper object, as to aid manufactures. To this extent Congress may constitutionally go, and has gone from the commencement of the government, which will fully explain the precedents cited from the early stages of its operation. Beyond this, *they* never advanced until the commencement of the present system, the inequality and oppression of which, your committee will next proceed to consider.

The committee feel, on entering upon this branch of the subject, the painful character of the duty they must perform. They would desire never to speak of our country, as far as the action of the General Government is concerned, but as one great whole, having a common interest, which all its parts ought zealously to promote. Previously to the adoption of the Tariff system, such was the unanimous feeling of this State; but in speaking of its operation it will be impossible to avoid the discussion of sectional interest, and the use of sectional language. On its au-

thors however, and not on us, who are compelled to adopt this course in self-defence by the injustice and oppression of their measures—be the censure. So partial are the effects of the system, that its burdens are exclusively on one side and its benefits on the other. It imposes on the agricultural interest of the South, including the South West, and that portion of our commerce and navigation engaged in foreign trade, the burden, not only of sustaining the system itself, but that also of sustaining government. In stating the case thus strongly, it is not the intention of the committee to exaggerate. If exaggeration were not unworthy of the gravity of the subject, the reality is such as to render it unnecessary.

That the manufacturing States, even in their own opinions bear no share of the burden of the Tariff in reality—we may infer with the greatest certainty from their own conduct. The fact, that they incessantly demand an increase of duties, and consider every addition as a blessing, and a failure to obtain one, a curse, is the strongest confession, that whatever burden it imposes, in reality falls, not on them, but on others. Men ask not for burdens, but for benefits. The tax paid by the duty on imports by which, with the exception of the receipts from the sale of public lands, the government is wholly supported, and which, in its gross amount, is annually equal to about $23,000,000, is then in truth no tax on them. Whatever portion of it they advance, as consumers of the articles, on which it is imposed, returns to them from the labour of others, with usurious interest, through an artfully contrived system. That such are the facts, the committee will proceed to demonstrate, by other arguments, than the confession of the party of its acts, conclusive as that ought to be considered.

If the duty were imposed upon exports, instead of imports, no one would doubt its partial operation. It would clearly fall on those engaged in rearing products for foreign markets, and as Rice, Tobacco and Cotton, constitute the great mass of our exports, such a duty would, of necessity, mainly fall on the Southern States, where they are exclusively cultivated; and to prove that the burthen of the Tariff also falls on them almost exclusively, it is only necessary to shew, that, as far as their interest is concerned, there is little or no difference between an export and an import duty. We export to import. The object is, an exchange of the fruits of our labour, for those of other countries. We have, from soil and climate, a facility in rearing certain great agricultural staples, while other and older countries, with a dense population, and capital greatly accumulated, have equal facility in manufacturing various articles suited to our use; and thus a foundation is laid for an exchange of the products of labour, mutually advantageous. A duty, whether it be laid on imports or exports, must fall upon this exchange, and on which ever laid in our country, must in reality be paid by the American producer of the articles exchanged. Such must be the operation of all taxes on sales and exchanges. The owner in reality pays it, whether laid on the vendor or purchaser. It matters not in the sale of a tract of land, or any other article, if a tax be imposed on the sale, whether it be paid by him who sells or him who buys, the amount must, in must cases, be deducted from the price. Nor can it

alter, in this particular, the operation of such a tax, if imposed on the exchanges of communities instead of individuals. Such exchanges are but the aggregate of sales of the individuals of the respective countries, and must, if taxed, be governed by the same rules. Nor is it material whether the exchange be barter or sale, direct of circuitous; in every case it must fall on the producer. To the growers of Rice, Cotton and Tobacco, it is the same whether the government takes one-third of the Salt, Sugar, Iron, Coffee, Cloth, and other articles they may need in exchange, for the liberty of bringing them home; in both cases he gets a third less than he ought, a third of his labour is taken, yet the one is an import and the other an export duty. It is true, that a tax on imports, by raising the price of the articles imported, may, in time, produce the supply at home, and thus give a new direction to the exchanges of a country, but it is also true, that a tax on the exports, by diminishing at home the price of the raw material, may have the same effect, and with no greater burden to the grower. Whether the situation of the South will be materially benefitted [sic] by this new direction to its exchanges, will be considered hereafter; but whatever portion of our foreign exchanges may in fact remain in any stage of this process of changing her market, must be governed by the rule laid down. Whatever duty may be imposed to bring it about, must fall on the foreign trade which remains, and be paid by the South almost exclusively; as much so as an equal amount of duty on their exports.

Let us now trace the operation of the system in some of its prominent details, in order to understand with greater precision, the extent of the burden it imposes on us, and the benefits which it confers, at our expense, on the manufacturing States.

The committee is the discussion of this point will not aim at minute accuracy. They have neither the means nor the time requisite for that purpose, nor do they deem it necessary, if they had, to estimate the fractions of gain or loss on either side, in transactions of such great magnitude. The exports of domestic produce in round numbers, may be estimated at averaging $53,000,000, annually, of which, the States growing Cotton, Rice and Tobacco, produce about $35,000,000. The average value of the exports of Cotton, Tobacco and Rice, for the last four years, exceed[s] $35,500,000, to which if we add Flour, Lumber, Corn, and various other articles, exported from the same States, but which cannot be distinguished on the Custom House books from exports of the same description from the other States, the amount must be equal to that stated. Taking it at that sum, the exports of the Southern or staple States, and of the other States, will then stand as $37,000,000 to $16,000,000, considerably exceeding the proportion of two to one, while their population, estimated in federal numbers, is the reverse, the former sending to the House of Representatives 76 members, and the latter 137. It follows that one-third of the Union exports near two two-thirds of the domestic products. Such then is the amount of labour which our country annually exchanges with the rest of the world, and such our proportion. The government is supported almost entirely by a tax on this exchange, in the shape of an import duty, the gross amount of which is annually about $23,000,000 as has been already stated. Previous to the passing of the act of the last session, this tax averaged about 37½ per cent. on the value of the imports. What addition that has made, it is difficult with the present data to establish with precision; but it is certainly short of the truth to state it to be an average increase of 7½ percent. Thus making the present duty to average at least 45 per cent. which on $37,000,000 the amount of our share of the exports will give the sum of [$]16,650,000 as our share of the general contributions to the Treasury.

Let us take another and perhaps more simple and striking view of this important point. Exports and imports must be equal in a series of years. This is a principle universally conceded. Let it then be supposed for the purpose of illustration, that the United States were organized, into two separate and distinct Custom House establishments; one for the staple States, and the other for the rest of the Union; and that all commercial intercourse between the two sections were taxed, in the same manner and to the same extent with that now imposed on the commerce with the rest of the world. The foreign commerce under the circumstances supposed, would be carried on from each section, direct with the rest of the world; and the imports of the Southern Custom House establishment, on the principle, that imports and exports must be equal, would amount annually to $37,000,000, which at 45 per cent. the average amount of the impost duty would give an annual revenue of $16,650,000, without increasing the burden on the people of these State one cent. This would be the amount of revenue on the exchange of that portion of their products, which go abroad; but if we take into the estimate the duty which would accrue on the exchange of the products with the manufacturing States, which now in reality is paid by the southern States in the shape of increased prices, as a bounty to the manufactories, but which on the supposition would be paid, as a part of their revenue at the Custom House, many millions more would have been added.

But it is contended that the consumers really pay the impost, and, as the manufacturing States consume a full share, in proportion to their population, of the articles imported, they must also contribute their full share to the Treasury of the Union. The committee will not deny that the consumers pay the duties, and will take it for granted that the consumption of imported articles is in proportion to population. The manufacturing States however, indemnify themselves, and more than indemnify themselves for the increased price, they pay on the articles they consume, as has already been proved, by their confession, in a form which cannot deceive, by their own acts. Nor is it difficult to trace the operation by which it is effected. The very acts of Congress imposing burdens on them, as consumers, give them the means, through the monopoly, which affords the manufacturers in the home market, not only of indemnifying themselves for the increased price on the imported articles, which they consume, but in a great measure of commanding the industry of the rest of the Union. The argument urged by them for the adoption of the system, and with much success is, that the price of property

and products in the manufacturing States must be thereby increased, which clearly proves the beneficial operation on the system on them. It is by this very increase of price, which must be paid by their fellow citizens of the South, that the indemnity to the manufacturers, is effected; and by means of this the fruits of our toil and labour, which on every principle of justice, ought to belong to ourselves, are transferred from us to them. The maxim that the consumers pay, strictly applies to us. We are mere consumers, and destitute of all means of transferring the burden from ourselves to others. We may be assured, that the large amount paid into the Treasury, under the duties on imports, is really derived from the labor of some portion of our citizens. The government has no mines. Some one must bear the burden of its support. This unequal lot is ours. We are the serffs [sic] of the system, out of whose labor is raised, not only the money that is paid into the Treasury, but the funds out of which are drawn the rich reward of the manufacturer and his associates in interest. Their encouragement is our discouragement. The duty on imports which is mainly paid out of our labour gives them the means of selling to us at a higher price, while we cannot, to compensate the loss, dispose of our products at the least advance. It is then not a subject of wonder, when properly understood, that one section of country though blessed by a kind Providence with a genial sun and prolific soil, from which spring the richest products, should languish in poverty and sink into decay; while the rest of the Union though less fortunate in natural advantages is flourishing in prosperity beyond example.

The assertion, that the encouragement of the industry of the manufacturing States, is in fact discouragement to ours, was not made without due deliberation. It is susceptible of the clearest proof.

We cultivate certain great staples for the supply of the general market of the world; and they manufacture almost exclusively for the home market. Their object in the Tariff is to keep down foreign competition, in order to obtain a monopoly of the domestic market. The effect on us is to compel us to purchase at a higher price, both what we purchase from them and from others, without receiving a corresponding increase of price for what we sell. The price, at which we can afford to cultivate, must depend on the price at which we receive our supplies. The lower the latter, the lower we may dispose of our products with profit; and in the same degree our capacity of meeting competition is increased; on the contrary, the higher the price of our supplies, the less the profit at the same price, and the less consequently the capacity for meeting competition. If, for instance, Cotton can be cultivated at ten cents a pound, under an increase of 45 per cent. for what is purchased in return, it is clear, we could cultivate it as profitably at 5½ cents, if the 45 per cent. were not added, and our capacity of meeting the competition of foreigners in the general market of the world would be increased in the same proportion. If we can now, with the increased prices under the Tariff, retain our commerce, we would be able with a reduction of 45 per cent. in the prices of our supplies, to drive out all competition, and thus add annually to the consumption of our cotton at least 300,000 bales, with a corresponding increase of our annual revenue. The case then, fairly stated between us and the manufacturing States, is, that the Tariff gives them a prohibition against foreign competition in our own market, in the sale of their goods, and deprives us of the benefit of a competition of purchasers for our raw material. They who say, that they cannot compete with foreigners at their own doors without an advantage of nearly fifty per cent, expect us to meet them abroad, under a disadvantage equal to their encouragement. But the oppression, great as it is to us, will not stop at this point. The trade between us and Europe, has heretofore been a mutual exchange of products. Under the existing duties, the consumption of European fabrics must in a great measure cease in our country, and the trade must become, on their part a cash transaction. But he must be ignorant of the principles of commerce, and the policy of Europe, particularly England, who does not see, that it is impossible to carry on a trade of such vast extent on any other basis but that of mutual exchange of products; and if it were not impossible, such a trade would not long be tolerated. We already see indications of the commencement of a commercial warfare, the termination of which cannot be conjectured, though our fate may easily be. The last remains of our great and once flourishing agriculture must be annihilated in the conflict. In the first instance we will be thrown on the home market, which cannot consume a fourth of our products; and instead of supplying the world, as we should with a free trade, we shall be compelled to abandon the cultivation of three-fourths of what we now raise, and receive for the residue, whatever the manufacturers, (who will then have their policy consummated, by the entire possession of their market, both exports and imports,) may choose to give. Forced with an immense sacrifice of capital to abandon our ancient and favorite pursuit, to which our soil, climate, habits and peculiar labor are adapted, we should be compelled without experience or skill, and with a population untried in such pursuits, to attempt to become the rivals instead of the customers of the manufacturing States. The result is not doubtful. If they, by superior capital and skill, should keep down successful competition on our part, we should be doomed to toil at our unprofitable agriculture, selling at the prices, which a single and limited market might give. But on the other hand, if our necessity should triumph over their capital and skill, if, instead of raw cotton, we should ship to the manufacturing States, cotton yarn, and cotton goods, the thoughtful must see, that it would immediately bring about a state of things, which could not long continue. Those who now make war on our gains would then make it on our labour. They would not tolerate, that those, who now cultivate our plantations and furnish them with the material and the market for the products of their arts, should, by becoming their rivals, take bread out of the mouths of their wives and children. The committee will not pursue this painful subject, but as they clearly see, that the system if not arrested, must bring the country to this hazardous extremity, neither prudence nor patriotism would permit them to pass it by, without giving warning of an event so full of danger.

It has been admitted in the argument that the consumption of the manufacturing States, in proportion to population, was as great as ours. How they with their limited means of payment, if estimated by the exports of their own products, could consume as much as we, with our ample exports, has been partially explained, but it demands a fuller consideration: Their population in round numbers may be estimated at 8,000,000 and ours at 4,000,000, while the value of their products exported compared to ours is as sixteen to thirty-seven millions of dollars. If to the aggregate of these sums, be added the profits of our foreign trade and navigation, it will give the amount of the fund out of which is annually paid the price of foreign articles consumed in this country. This profit, at least so far as it constitutes a portion of the fund out of which the price of foreign articles is paid, is represented by the difference between the value of the exports and imports, both estimated at our own ports, and, taking the average of the last five years, amount[s] to about $4,000,000. The foreign trade of the country being principally in the hands of the manufacturing States, we will add this sum to their means of consumption, which will raise theirs to $20,000,000, and will place the relative means of consumption of the two sections, as twenty, to 37,000,000 of dollars; while on the supposition of equal consumption would amount to thirty-eight and ours to nineteen millions of dollars. Their consumption would thus exceed their capacity to consume, if judged by the value of their exports, and the profits of their foreign commerce, by eighteen millions; while ours judged the same way would fall short by the same sum. The inquiry which naturally presents itself on this statement is, how is this great change in the relative condition of the parties, to our disadvantage, effected. The committee will proceed to explain this. It obviously grows out of their connection with us. If they were entirely separate, without political or commercial connection, it is manifest, that the consumption of the manufacturing States of foreign articles could not exceed twenty millions, the sum at which the value of their exports, of domestic products, and the profits of their foreign trade is estimated. It would in fact be much less as the profits of foreign navigation and commerce which have been added to their means, depend almost exclusively on the great staples of the south, and would be deducted from their means if no connection existed. On the contrary it is equally manifest, that the means of the south to consume the products of other countries, would not be materially affected, in the state supposed. Let us then inquire, what are the causes growing out of this connexion, by which so great a change is made. They may be comprehended under three, the custom house, the appropriations, and the monopoly of the manufacturers, under the Tariff system, all which are so intimately blended, as to constitute one system, which its advocates, by a perversion of all that is associated with the name, call the American System. The Tariff is the soul of the system. It has already been proved that our contribution through the Custom House to the Treasury of the Union, amounts annually to $16,650,000 which leads to the inquiry,

what becomes of the amount of the products of our labour, placed, by the operation of the system at the disposal of Congress. One point is certain, a very small share returns to us, out of whose labor it is extracted. It would require much investigation to state with precision, the proportion of the public revenue disbursed annually in the southern and other States respectively; but the committee feel a thorough conviction on an examination of the annual appropriation acts, that a sum much less than two millions of dollars falls to our share of the disbursements, and that it would be a moderate estimate to place our contribution, above what we receive back, through all the appropriations at fifteen millions; constituting to that great amount an annual, continued and uncompensated draft on the industry of the southern States, through the Custom House alone. This sum deducted from the $37,000,000, the amount of our products annually exported and added to the [$]20,000,000, the amount of the exports of the other States, with the profit of foreign trade and navigation, would reduce our means of consumption to $22,000,000 and raise theirs to $35,000,000, still leaving $3,000,000 to be accounted for; this may be readily explained, by the operation of the remaining branch of the system, the monopoly, afforded to the manufacturers in our own market, *which* empowers them to force their goods on us at a price equal to the foreign article of the same description, with the addition of the duty, thus receiving in exchange, our products to be shipped on their account, and thereby increasing their means of diminishing ours in the same proportion. But this constitutes but a small part of our loss under this branch. In addition to the $37,000,000 of our products, which are shipped to foreign markets, a very large amount is annually sent to the other States for their own use and consumption. The article of cotton alone is estimated at 150,000 bales, which valued at $30 per bale, would amount to $4,500,000 and constitutes a part of this forced exchange.

Such is the process with the amount in part of the transfer of our property annually to other sections of the country, estimated on the supposition, that each section consumes of imported articles an amount in proportion to its population; but the committee are aware that they have rated our share of the consumption far higher, than the advocates of the system have placed it. Some of them rate it as low as $5,000,000 annually, not perceiving by thus reducing ours and adding to that of the manufacturing States, in the same proportion, they demonstrably prove how oppressive the system is to us and gainful to them, instead of showing, as they suppose, how little we are affected by its operation. Our very complaint is, that we are not permitted to consume the fruits of our labour; but that through an artful and complex system, in violation of every principle of justice they are transferred from us to others. It is indeed wonderful, that those who profit by our loss, (blinded as they are by self-interest,) never thought to enquire, when reducing our consumption as low as they have, what became of the immense amount of the product of our industry, which was annually sent out in exchange with the rest of the world; and if *we* did not consume its proceeds,

who did, and by what means. If, in the ardent pursuit of gain, such a thought had occurred it would seem impossible, that all the sophistry of self-interest, delusive as it is, could disguise from their view our deep oppression, under the operation of the system. Your committee do not intend to represent, that the commercial connexion between us and the manufacturing States is wholly sustained by the Tariff system. A great, natural, and profitable commercial communication would exist between us without the aid of monopoly on their part, which with mutual advantage, would transfer a large amount of their products to us, and an equal amount of ours to them, as the means of carrying on their commercial operations with other countries. But even this legitimate commerce, is made unequal and burthen some by the Tariff system, which by raising the price of capital and labour in the manufacturing States, raises in a corresponding degree the price of all articles in the same quarter, as well those protected as those not protected. That such would be the effect, we know has been much urged, in argument to reconcile all classes in those States to the system, and with such success, as to leave us no room to doubt its correctness; and yet, such is [sic] the strange contradictions in which the advocates of an unjust cause must ever involve themselves, when they attempt to sustain it by reason, that, the very persons who urge the adoption of the system in one quarter by holding out the temptation of high prices for *all* they make, turn round and gravely inform us that its tendency is to depress and not to advance prices. The capitalist, the farmer, the wool grower, the mechanic and labourer in the manufacturing States are all to receive higher rates, while we who consume, are to pay less for the products of their labour and capital. The obvious absurdity of these arguments leaves no room to doubt that those who advance them, are conscious that the proof of the partial and oppressive operation of the system, is unanswerable, if it be conceded that we pay inconsequence of it higher prices for what we consume. If it were possible to meet that conclusion on other grounds, it could not be, that men of sense would venture to encounter such palpable contradictions; for so long as the wages of labour and the rate of interest, constitute the principal elements of price as they ever must, the one or the other argument, that addressed to us or that to the manufacturing States must be false. But in order to have a clear conception of this important point, the committee propose to consider more fully the assertion, that it is the tendency of high duties, by affording protection to reduce instead of increasing prices; and if they are not greatly mistaken, it will prove, on examination, to be utterly erroneous. Before entering into the discussion, and in order to avoid misapprehension, the committee will admit that it is perhaps for a country to find itself in such a situation in regard to its manufacturing capacities, that the interposition of the Legislature, by encouraging their development, may effect a permanent reduction of prices—but a comparison of the elements which constitute price here and, in England, will demonstrate, that such a result cannot take place in this country.

In the United States, the wages of labor are one hundred and fifty per cent higher than in England. The profits of capital are one hundred per cent. higher—while the price of the raw material is higher in England only by the cost of the freight, which is certainly not above twenty-five per cent. Combining these elements in their due proportion, and making every plausible allowance in favor of our own manufacturers, and the result will be, that the manufactured article here must cost more than eighty per cent. higher than the same article in England. The circumstances of the country, therefore, are not such as to permit us to calculate on a reduction of prices, as the result of the protecting system—but an enhancement of them by the erection of an artificial monopoly. It is therefore clearly our interest that such a monopoly should not be created, and that our market should afford a free and open competition to all the world. The effect would be a reduction of price on all we consume.

Having answered the argument in the abstract, the committee will not swell their report by considering the various instances which have been quoted to shew that prices have not advanced since the commencement of the system. We know that they would instantly fall nearly fifty per cent. if the duties were removed, and that is sufficient for us to know. Many and conclusive reasons might be urged to show why prices have declined, since the period referred to; the fall of the price of raw materials; the increase of capital and competition; the effects of the return of peace; the immense reduction in the circulating medium by subtracting from circulation a vast amount of paper, both in this country and in Europe; the improvements in the mechanical arts; and the great improvements in the use of steam, and in the art of spinning and weaving.

We are told by those who pretend to understand our interest better than we do ourselves, that excess of production, and not the tariff, is the evil that afflicts us; and that our true remedy is a reduction of the quantity of cotton, rice, and tobacco which we raise, and not a repeal of the tariff. They assert that low prices are necessary consequences of excess of supply, and that the only proper correction is in diminishing the quantity. We should feel more disposed to respect the spirit in which the advice is offered, if those from whom it comes, accompanied it with the weight of their example. They also complained much of low prices, but instead of diminishing the supply as a remedy, they demanded an enlargement of their market by the exclusion of all competition in the home market. *Our market is the world*; and as we cannot imitate their example by enlarging it for our products to the exclusion of others, we must decline to follow their advice; which in truth instead of alleviating would greatly increase our embarrassment. We have no monopoly in the supply of our products. Three-fourths of the globe may produce them. Should we reduce our production to raise prices, others stand ready by increasing theirs, to take our place; instead of raising prices, we should only diminish our share of the supply. We are thus compelled to produce, be the price what it may, under the penalty of losing our market. Once lost, it may be lost forever. And lose it we must, if we continue to be compelled as we now are, on the one hand by the general competition of the world to sell low, and on the other, by the tariff to buy high. We cannot withstand this double action. Our ruin must follow. In fact our only permanent and safe remedy is, not the rise in the price of what we sell, from which we can receive no aid from our government; but is a reduction in the price of what we buy; which is prevented by the interference of the government. Give us a free and open competition in the general markets of the world. If, under all our discouragements, by the acts of our own government, we are still able to contend with these against the world, can it be doubted if the impediment were removed we should force out all of our fellow citizens of the other States, but by our industry, enterprise and natural advantages.

But while the system prevents this great enlargement of our foreign market, and endangers what we have left, its advocates attempt to console us by the growth of the home market for our products, which, according to this calculation, is to compensate us amply for all our losses; though in the leading article of our products, cotton, the home market consumes but a sixth, and with an absolute prohibition would not consume more than a fifth. In the other articles, rice and tobacco, it is even much less.

But brilliant prospects are held out of a great export trade in cotton goods, which we are told is to demand an immense amount of the raw material. To what countries are the goods to be shipped? Not to Europe, for there we will meet prohibition for prohibition; not to the southern portion of this continent, for already they have been taught to imitate our prohibitory policy. The most sanguine will not expect extensive or profitable markets in the other portions of the globe. But admitting that no other impediment existed, our system itself is an effectual barrier against extensive exports of our manufactured articles. The very means which secures the domestic market, must lose the foreign. High prices are an effectual stimulus, when enforced by a monopoly, as in our own market, but they are fatal to competition in the open and free market of the world. Besides, when manufactured articles are exported, they must follow the same law, to which the products of the soil are subject, when they are also exported. They will be sent out in order to be exchanged with the products of other countries; if these products be taxed on the introduction, as a back return, it has been demonstrated that like all other taxes on exchange, it must be paid by the producer. The nature of the operation will be seen, if it be supposed, in their exchange with us, instead of receiving our products free of duty, the manufacturer[s] had to pay forty-five per cent. on the back return of the cotton and other products, which they receive from us in exchange. If to these insuperable impediments to a large export trade, be added, that our country rears the products of almost every soil and climate, and that scarcely an article [*sic*] that can be imported, but what may come in competition with some of the products of our arts or our soil, and consequently ought to be excluded on the principles of the system, it must be apparent that the system itself, when perfected, will essentially exclude all exports, unless we should charitably export for the supply of the wants of others, without

expectation of a return. The loss of the exports, and with it the imports also, must in truth be the end of the system. If we export, we must import, and the most simple and efficient system to secure the home market, would in fact be to prohibit exports, and as *duties are not prohibition*, we may yet witness this modification of the American system.

The committee deemed it more satisfactory to explain the operation of the system on the southern States generally, than its peculiar operation on this. In fact they had not the data, had they the inclination, to separate the oppression under which this State labors, from that of the other staple States. The fate of one must be that of all.

The committee have considered the question in its relative effects on the staple and manufacturing States, comprehending under the latter all the States who advocate the Tariff system. It is not for them to determine whether all those States have equal interest in its continuance. It is manifest that their situation is very different. While in some the manufacturing interest wholly prevails, others are divided between that and the commercial and navigating interest, and in a third, the agricultural interest greatly predominates; as is the case with all the western States. It is difficult to conceive what real interest the last can have in the system. They manufacture but little and must consequently draw their supplies principally from aboard or from the manufacturing States, and, in either case, must pay the increased price in consequence of the duties, while at the same time the tariff must necessarily diminish, if not destroy, their trade with us. From the nature of our commercial connexion with them our loss must precede theirs, but theirs will with certainty follow, unless compensation for the loss of our trade can be found somewhere in the system. Its authors have informed us that it consists of two parts, of which *prohibition* is the essence of one, and *appropriation* of the other. In both capacities, it impoverishes us, and in both, enriches the manufacturing States. The agricultural States of the west are differently affected. As a protective system, they lose in common with us; and it will remain for them to determine, whether an adequate compensation can be found in *appropriation*, for the steady and rich return which a free exchange of the produce of their fertile soil with the staple States must give, provided the latter be left in full possession of their natural advantages.

It remains to be considered, in tracing the effects of the system, whether the gains of one section of the country will be equal to the loss of the other. If such were the fact—if all we lose be gained by the citizens of the other section, we would at least have the satisfaction of thinking, that however unjust and oppressive, it was but a transfer of property, without diminishing the wealth of the community. Such, however, is not the fact, and to its other mischievous consequences, we must add, that it destroys much more than it transfers. Industry cannot be forced out of its natural channel, without loss. The exact amount of loss, from such intermeddling, may be difficult to ascertain, but it is not therefore the less certain. The committee will not undertake to estimate the millions which are annually lost to our country under the existing system; but some idea may be formed of its magnitude, by stating that it is at least equal to the difference between the profits of our manufactures and the duty imposed for their protection, when it is not prohibitory. The lower the profit [and] the higher the duty, if [it is] not prohibitory, the greater the loss. If, with these certain data, the evidence reported by the Committee on Manufactures at the last session of Congress, be examined, a correct opinion may be formed of the extent of the loss of the country, provided the manufacturers have fairly stated the case. With a duty of almost fifty per cent. on the leading articles of consumption (if we are to credit the testimony reported,) the manufacturers did not receive generally a profit equal to the legal rate of interest, which would give a loss of about forty per cent. on their products. It is different with the foreign articles of the same description. On such, at least, the country loses nothing. There the duty passes into the treasury, lost indeed to the Southern planters, out of whose labor directly or indirectly it must for the most part be paid; but transferred through appropriations; and well may its advocates affirm, that they constitute an essential feature of the American system. Let this conduit, through which it is so profusely supplied be intercepted, and we feel confident, that scarcely a State, except those really manufacturing, would tolerate its burden. A total prohibition of importation by destroying the revenue and thereby the means of making appropriations, would in a short period destroy it. But the excess of its loss over its gains, leads to the consolatory reflection, that's its abolition would relieve us much more than it would embarrass the manufacturing States. We have suffered too much to desire to see others afflicted, even for our relief, when it can possibly be avoided. We should rejoice to see our manufactures flourish on any constitutional principle consistent with justice and the public liberty. It is not against them, but the means by which they have been forced to our ruin, that we object. As far as a moderate system, the national revenue would be based on our labours, and be paid by our industry. With such constitutional and moderate protection the manufacturer ought to be satisfied. His loss would not be so great as might be supposed. If low duties would be followed by low prices, they would also diminish the cost of manufacturing, and thus the reduction on the prices of the article. Be that, however, as it may, the General Government cannot proceed beyond this point of protection, consistently with its powers, and with justice to the whole. If the manufacturing States deem farther protection necessary, it is in their power to afford it to their citizens within their own limits, against foreign competition to any extent, that they may judge expedient. The Constitution authorizes them to lay an impost duty, with the consent of Congress, which doubtless would be given; and if this be not sufficient, they have the additional power of giving a direct bounty for their encouragement, which the ablest writers on the subject concede to be the least burdensome and most efficient mode, if indeed encouragement be in any case expedient. Thus those who are to be benefited will bear the burden as they ought; and those who believe that it is wise and just to protect manufactures by legislation, may have the satisfaction of doing it at their own expense, and not at

the expense of the citizens of other States, who entertain precisely the opposite opinion.

The committee having presented its views on the partial and oppressive operation of the system, will now proceed to discuss the next position which they proposed. That its tendency is to corrupt the government and destroy the liberties of the country.

If there be a political proposition universally true, one which springs from the nature of man, and is independent of circumstances, it is, that irresponsible power is inconsistent with liberty and must corrupt those who exercise it. On this great principle our political system rests. We consider all powers as delegated from the people and to be controlled by those who are interested in their just and proper exercise; and our governments, both State and General, are but a system of judicious contrivances to bring this fundamental principle into fair practical operation. Among the most permanent of these is the responsibility of representatives to their constituents, through frequent periodical elections. Without such a check in their powers, however clearly they may be defined and distinctly prescribed, our liberty would be but a mockery. The government, instead of being devoted to the general good, would speedily become but the instrument to aggrandize those who might be entrusted with its administration. On the other hand, if laws were uniform in their operation; if that which imposed a burden on one, imposed it alike on all; or that which acted beneficially for one, should act so for all, the responsibility of representatives to their constituents, would alone be sufficient to guard against abuse and tyranny, provided the people be sufficiently intelligent to understand their interests, and the motives and conduct of their public agents. But if it be supposed that from diversity of interest in the several classes of the people and sections of the country, laws acted differently, so that the same law, though couched in general terms and apparently fair, shall in reality transfer the power and prosperity of one class or section to another in such case responsibility to constituents, which is but the means of enforcing the fidelity of representatives to them, must prove wholly insufficient to preserve the purity of public agents, or the liberty of the country. It would in fact be inapplicable to the evil. The disease would be in the community itself; in the constituents, not in the representatives. The opposing interest of the community would engender necessarily opposing hostile parties, organized in this very diversity of interest; the stronger of which, if the government provided no efficient check, would exercise unlimited and unrestrained power over the weaker. The relations of equality between them would thus be destroyed, and in its place there would be substituted the relation of sovereign and subject, between the stronger and the weaker interest, in its most odious and oppressive form. That this is a possible state of society even when the representative system prevails, we have high authority. Mr. Hamilton, in the 51st No. of the Federalist, says, "It is of the greatest importance in a republic not only to guard society against the oppression of its rulers, but to guard one part of the society against the injustice of the other part. Different interests necessarily ex-

ist indifferent classes of citizens. If a majority be united by a common interest, the rights of the minority will be insecure." Again, "in a society under the forms of which, the stronger faction can readily unite and oppress the weaker, anarchy may be said as truly to reign as in a state of nature, where the weaker individual is not secured against the violence of the stronger." We have still higher authority, the unhappy existing examples, of which we are the victims. The committee have labored to little purpose if they have not demonstrated, that the very case which Mr. Hamilton so forcibly describes, does now exist in our country, under the name of the "American System"; which if not speedily arrested must be followed by all the consequences that never fail to spring from the exercise of irresponsible power. On the great and vital point, the industry of the country, which comprehends nearly all the other interests, two great sections of the Union are opposed. We want free trade, they, restrictions. We want moderate taxes, frugality in the government, economy, accountability, and a rigid application of the public money, to the payment of the public debt and the objects authorized by the Constitution; in all these particulars, if we may judge by experience, their views of their interest are the opposite. They act and feel on all questions connected with the American System, as sovereigns; as those always do who impose burdens on others for their own benefit; and we, on the contrary, like those on whom such burdens are imposed. In a word, to the extent stated, the country is divided and organized into two great opposing parties, one sovereign and the other subject; marked by all the characteristics which must accompany that relation, under whatever form it may exist. That our industry is controlled by the many, instead of one, by a majority in Congress elected by a majority in the community having an opposing interest, instead of hereditary rulers, forms not the slightest mitigation of the evil. In fact, instead of mitigating, it aggravates. In our case one opposing branch of industry cannot prevail without associating others, and thus instead of a single act of oppression we must bear many. The history of the woolens' bill will illustrate the truth of this position. The woolen manufacturers found they were too feeble to enforce their exactions alone, and of necessity resorted to the expedient, (which will ever be adopted in such cases,) of associating their interests till a majority was formed; the result of which was in this case, that instead of increased duties on woolens alone, which would have been the case if that interest alone governed us, we have to bear increased duties on more than a dozen of the leading articles of consumption. It would be weakness to attempt to disguise the fact, on a full knowledge of which, and of the danger which it threatens, the hope of deriving some means of security depends; that different and opposing interest do, and must ever exist in this county, against the danger of which representation affords not the slightest protection. Laws so far from being uniform in their operation, are scarcely ever so. It requires the greatest wisdom and moderation to form over any country, a system of equal laws; and it is this very opposition of interest, which in all associations of men for common purposes, be they public or private, constitutes the

main difficulty in forming and administering free and just governments. Liberty comprehends the idea of responsible power, that those who make and execute the laws should be controlled by those on whom they operate; that the governed should govern. Thus to prevent rulers from abusing their trust, constituents must controul [*sic*] them through elections; and so to prevent the major from oppressing the minor interests of society, the constitution must provide (as the committee hope to prove it does,) a check founded on the same principle, and equally efficacious. In fact the abuse of delegated power, and the tyranny of the greater over the less interests of society, are the two great dangers, and the only two, to be guarded against; if they be effectually guarded liberty must be eternal. Of the two, the latter is the greater danger, and most difficult to check. It is less perceptible. Every circumstance of life teaches us the liability of delegated power to abuse. We cannot appoint an agent without being admonished of the fact; and therefore it has become well understood, and is sufficiently guarded against in our political institutions. Not so with the other and greater danger. Though it exists in all associations, the law, the courts, and the government itself, are checks to its extreme abuse in most cases of price and subordinate companies, which prevents them from displaying their real tendency. But let it be supposed that there was no paramount authority, no court, no government to control, what sober individual, who intended to act honestly, would place his property in joint stock with any number of individuals however respectable, to be disposed of by the unchecked will of the majority, whether acting in a body as stockholders, or through representation by a direction? Who does not see, that sooner or later, a major and a minor interest would spring up, and that the former would in a short time monopolize all the advantages of the concern. And what is government itself but a joint stock company which comprehends every interest, and which as there can be no higher power to restrain its natural operation, if not checked by its peculiar organization, must follow the same law? The actual condition of man in every country at this and all preceding periods, attests the truth of the remark. No government based on the naked principle, that the majority ought to govern, however true the maxim in its proper sense and under proper restrictions, ever preserved its liberty, even for a single generation. The history of all has been the same, injustice, violence and anarchy, succeeded by the government of one, or a few, under which the people seek refuge, from the more oppressive despotism of the majority. Those governments only, which provide checks, which limit and restrain within proper bounds the power of the majority, have had a prolonged existence, and been distinguished for virtue, power and happiness. Constitutional government, and the government of the majority, are utterly incompatible, it being the sole purpose of a constitution to impose limitations and checks upon the majority. An unchecked majority is a despotism—and government is free, and will be permanent in proportion to the number, complexity and efficiency of the checks, by which it powers are controlled.

The committee entertain no doubt, that the present disordered state of our political system, originated in the diversity of the interests of the several sections of the country. This very diversity the Constitution itself recognizes; and to it owes one of its most distinguished and peculiar features, the division of the sovereign power between the State and General Government. Our short experience before the formation of the present government had conclusively shewn, that while there were powers which were in their nature local and peculiar, and which could not be exercised at all, without oppression to some of the parts; so also there were those which in their operation necessarily affected the whole and could not therefore be exercised by any one of the parts, without affecting injuriously the others. To a certain extent we have a community of interest which can only be justly and fairly supervised by concentrating the will and authority of the whole in one General Government; while at the same time the States have distinct and separate interests. Which can not be consolidated in the general power, without injustice and oppression. Thence the division of the sovereign power; and it is upon this distribution of power, that the whole system of our government rests. In drawing the line between the General and State Governments, the great difficulty consisted in determining correctly to which the various political powers belonged. This difficult duty was however performed with so much success, that to this day there is an almost uniform acquiescence in the correctness with which it was executed. It would be extraordinary if a system thus based, with profound wisdom, on the diversity of geographical interest, should make no provision against the danger of their conflict. The framers of our constitutions [*sic*] have not exposed themselves to the imputations of such weakness. When their work is fairly examined it will be found, that they have provided, with admirable skill, the most effective remedy, and that if it has not prevented the approach of the dangers, the fault is not theirs, but ours, in neglecting to make the proper application of it. The powers of the General Government are particularly enumerated, and specifically delegated; all others are expressly reserved to the States and the people. Those of the General Government are intended to act uniformly on all the parts, the residue are left to the States, by whom alone from the nature of these powers, they can be justly and fairly exercised.

Our system, then consists of two distinct and independent sovereignties. The general powers conferred on the General Government, are subject to its sole and separate control, and the States cannot, without violating the Constitution, interpose their authority to check, or in any manner counteract its movements, so long, as they are confined to its proper sphere; so also the peculiar and local powers, reserved to the States, are subject to their exclusive control, nor can the General Government interfere with them, without on its part, also violating the Constitution. In order to have a full and clear conception of our institutions, it will be proper to remark, that there is in our system a striking distinction between the government and the sovereign power. Whatever may be the true doctrine in regard to the sovereignty of the States individually, it is unquestionably clear that while the government of the union is vested in its legislative, executive, and political departments, the actual sovereign power, resides in the several States, who created it, in their separate and distinct political character. But by an express provision of the Constitution it may be amended or changed, by three-fourths of the States; and each State by assenting to the Constitution with this provision, has surrendered its original rights as a sovereign, which made its individual consent necessary to any change in the political condition, and has placed this important power in the hands of three-fourths of the States; in which the sovereignty of the union under the Constitution does now actually reside. Not the least portion of this high sovereign authority, resides in Congress or any of the departments of the General Government. They are but the creatures of the Constitution, appointed, but to execute its provisions, and therefore, any attempt in all or any of the departments to exercise any power definitely, which in its consequences may alter the nature of the instrument or change the condition of the parties to it, would be an act of the highest political usurpation. It is thus that our political system, recognizing the opposition of geographical interests in the community, has provided the most efficient check against its dangers. Looking to facts and not mere hypothesis, the Constitution has made us a community only to the extent of our common interest, leaving the States distinct and independent, as to their peculiar interests, and has drawn the line of separation with consummate skill. The great question however is, what means are provided by our system for the purpose of enforcing this fundamental provision: If we look to the practical operation of the system, we will find, on the side of the States, not a solitary constitutional means resorted to, in order to protect their reserved rights, against the encroachment of the General Government, while the latter has from the beginning, adopted the most efficient, to prevent that of the States on their authority. The 25th section of the Judiciary Act, passed in 1789, provides an appeal from the States [sic] Courts to the Supreme Court of the United States, in all cases in the decision of which the construction of the Constitution, the laws of Congress, or treaties of the United States may be involved; this giving to that high tribunal the right of final interpretation, and the power in reality of nullifying the Acts of the State Legislatures, whenever in their opinion they may conflict with the power delegated to the General Government. A more ample and complete protection against the encroachments of the States by their Legislatures cannot be imagined; and for this purpose, this high power may be considered indispensable and constitutional; but by a strange misconception of the nature of our system, in fact, of the nature of government, it has been regarded, not only as affording protection to the General Government against the States, but also to the States against the General Government; and as the only means provided by the Constitution of restraining the State and General Government within their respective spheres; and consequently of deciding on the extent of the powers of each, even where a State in its highest sovereign capacity, is at issue with the General Government on the question, whether a particular power be delegated, or not. Such a construction of the powers of the Federal Court, which would raise one of the departments of the General Government, above the sovereign parties, who created the Constitution, would enable it in practice to alter at pleasure the relative powers of the States and General Government. The most erroneous and dangerous doctrine, in regard to the powers of the Federal Court, has been ably refuted by Mr. Madison in his report to the Virginia Legislature, in 1800, that the committee avail themselves at once of his argument and authority. Speaking of the rights of the State to interpret the Constitution for itself in the last resort he says: "that it has been objected that the judicial authority is to be regards, as the sole expositor of the Constitution; on this objection it might be observed—1st. That there may be instances of usurped powers," (the case of the Tariff is a striking illustration of its truth,) "Which the forms of the Constitution could never draw within the control of the judicial department: secondly, that if the decision of the judiciary, be raised above the authority of the sovereign parties to the Constitution, the decisions of the other departments, not carried by the forms of the Constitution before the judiciary, must be equally authoritative and final with the decision of that department. But the proper answer to the objection is, that the resolution of the General Assembly, related to those, great and extraordinary cases, in which all the forms of the Constitution may prove ineffectual against infractions, dangerous to the essential rights of the parties to it. The resolution supposes, that dangerous powers not delegated, may not only be usurped and executed by the other departments, but that the judicial department also may exercise, or sanction dangerous powers beyond the grant of the Constitution, to judge, whether the compact has been dangerously violated, must extend to violations by one delegated authority as well as by another—by the judiciary as well by the Executive, or the Legislature.

"However true therefore it may be, that the judicial is, in all questions submitted to it, by the forms of the Constitution to decide in the last resort, this resort must necessarily be deemed the last in relation to the authorities of the other departments of the government, not in relation to the rights of the parties to the constitutional compact, from which the judicial as well as the other departments hold their delegated trusts. On any other hypothesis, the delegation of judicial power would annul the authority delegating it; and the concurrence of this department with the others in usurped powers, might subvert for ever and beyond the possible reach of any rightful remedy, the very Constitution, which all were constituted to preserve."

Although this constitutional mode of restraining the encroachments of the General Government, was thus early and clearly pointed out by Mr. Madison, an effort has been made to substitute for it what has been called a rigid rule of construction, which would inhibit the exercise of all powers not plainly delegated, or that were not obviously necessary and proper as means, to their execution. A government like ours of divided powers, must necessarily give great importance to a proper system of construction, but it is perfectly clear that no system of the kind, however, perfect, can prescribe bounds to the encroachment of power. They constitute in fact, but an appeal by the minority to the justice of the majority, and if such appeals were sufficient to restrain the avarice, and ambition of those, who are invested with power, then would a system of technical construction be sufficient. But on such a supposition, reason and justice might alone be relied on, without the aid of any constitutional or artificial restraint whatever. Universal experience, in all ages and countries however, teaches that power can only be met with power, and not by reason and justice, and that all restrictions on authority, unsustained by an equal antagonist power, must forever prove wholly insufficient in practice. Such also has been the decisive proof of our own short experience. From the beginning, a great and powerful minority gave every force, of which it was susceptible, to construction, as a means of restraining a majority of Congress to the exercise of its proper powers; and though that original minority, through the force of circumstances, has had the advantage of becoming a majority; and to possess, in consequence, the administration of the General Government, during the greater portion of its existence, yet we this day witness, under these most favourable circumstances, an extension of the powers of the General Government in spite of mere construction, to a point so extreme as to leave few powers to the State worth possessing. In fact, that very power of construction, on which reliance is placed, to preserve the rights of the States, has been wielded, as it ever will and must be if not checked, to destroy those rights. If the minority has a right to select its rule of construction, a majority will exercise the same, but with this striking difference, that the power of the former will be a mere nullity, against that of the latter. But that protection which the minor interest ever fails to find, in any technical system of construction, where alone in practice it has heretofore been sought, it may find in the reserved rights of the States themselves, if they be properly called into action; and there only will it ever be found of sufficient efficacy. The constitutional power to protect their rights as members of the confederacy, results necessarily, by the most simple and demonstrable arguments, from the very nature of the relation subsisting between the States and General Government. If it be conceded, as it must by every one who is the least conversant with our institutions, that the sovereign power is divided between the States and General Government, and that the former holds its reserved rights, in the same high sovereign capacity, which the latter does its delegated rights; it will be impossible to deny to the States the right of deciding on the infraction of their rights, and the proper remedy to be applied for the correction. The right of judging, in such cases, is an essential attribute of sovereignty of which the States cannot be divested, without losing their sovereignty itself; and being reduced to a subordinate corporate condition. In fact, to divide power, and to give to one of the parties the exclusive right of judging of the portion allotted to each,

is in reality not to divide at all; and to reserve such exclusive right to the General Government, (it matters not by what department it be exercised,) is in fact to constitute it one great consolidated government, with unlimited powers, and to reduce the States to mere corporations. It is impossible to understand the force of terms, and to deny these conclusions. The opposite opinion can be embraced only on hasty and imperfect views of the relation existing between the States and the General Government. But the existence of the right of judging of their powers, clearly established from the sovereignty of the States, as clearly implies a veto, or controul on the action of the General Government on contested points of authority; and this very controul is the remedy, which the Constitution has provided to prevent the encroachment of the General Government on the reserved right of the States; and by the exercise of which, the distribution of power between the General and State Governments, may be preserved forever inviolate, as is established by the Constitution; and thus afford effectual protection to the great minor interest of the community, against the oppression of the majority.

Nor does this important conclusion stand on the deduction of reason alone, it is sustained by the highest contemporary authority. Mr. Hamilton in the number of the Federalist, already cited, remarks, "that in a single republic all the powers surrendered by the people are submitted to the administration of a single government; and usurpations are guarded against by a division of the government into districts [*sic*; distinct] and separate departments. In the compound republic of America, the power surrendered by the people, is first divided between two distinct governments; and then the portion allotted to each, sub-divided among districts [*sic*; distinct] and separate departments. Hence a double security arises to the rights of the people. The different governments will controul each other; at the same time that each will be controlled by itself."

He thus clearly affirms the control of the States over the General Government, which he traces to the division of the sovereign power under our political system, and by comparing this control to the veto, which the several departments in most of our constitutions respectively exercised over the acts of each other, clearly indicates it as his opinion, that the control between the States and General Government is of the same character. Mr. Madison is still more explicit. In his report already alluded to, he says: "The resolution having taken this view of the federal compact, proceeds to infer, 'that in case of a deliberate, palpable, and dangerous exercise of other powers, not granted by the said compact, the States, who are parties thereto, have the right, and are in duty bound, to interpose for arresting the progress of the evil, and for maintaining within their respective limits, the authorities, rights, and liberties appertaining to them." It appears to your committee to be a plain principle, founded in common sense, illustrated by common practice, and essential to the nature of compacts, that where resort can be had to no tribunal superior to the authorities of the parties, the parties themselves must be the rightful judges in the last resort, whether the bargain made has been pursued or violated. The Constitution

of the United States, was formed by the sanction of the States, given by each in its sovereign capacity. It adds to the stability and dignity, as well as to the authority of the Constitution, that it rests on this legitimate and solid foundation. The States then being parties to the constitutional company, and in the sovereign capacity, it follows of necessity, that there can be no tribunal above their authority to decide in the last resort, whether the compact made by them be violated, and consequently that as the parties to it, they must themselves decide in the last resort, such questions as may be of sufficient magnitude to regain [*sic*; require] their interposition." To these the no less explicit opinion of Mr. Jefferson may be added, who in the Kentucky resolutions on the same subject, states that, "the government created by this compact was not made the exclusive, or final judge of the extent of the power delegated to itself, since that would have made its discretion and not the Constitution the measure of its powers; but that as in all other cases of compact among parties, having no common judge, each party has one [*sic*] equal right to judge for itself, as well of infractions as of the mode and measure of redress."

Time and experience confirmed his opinion on this all important point. This illustrious citizen, nearly a quarter of a century afterwards, in the year 1821, expressed himself in this emphatic manner. "It is a fatal heresy," he says, "to suppose that either our state governments are superior to the federal, or the federal to the state; neither is authorized, literally, to decide what belongs to itself, or its co-partner in government"; "in differences of opinion between their different sets of public servants, the appeal is to neither, but to their employers, peaceably assembled by their representatives in Convention." If to these authorities, which so explicitly affirm the right of the States in their sovereign capacity, to decide both on the infraction of their rights, and the remedy, there be added the solemn decisions of the Legislatures of two leading States, Virginia and Kentucky, and the implied sanction of a majority of the States in the important political revolution, which shortly followed, and brought Mr. Jefferson into power on this very ground, it will be scarcely possible to add to the weight of authority, by which this fundamental principle in our system is sustained.

The committee having thus established the constitutional right of the States to interpose in order to protect their powers, it cannot be necessary to bestow, much time, in order to meet possible objections; particularly as they must be raised, not against the soundness of the argument by which the position is sustained, which they deem unanswerable, but against apprehended consequences; which, even if true, would not be so much an objection to the conclusion of the committee, as to the Constitution itself, but which they are persuaded, will be found, on investigation, destitute of solidarity. Under these impressions the committee proposed to discuss the objections with all possible brevity.

It is objected in the first place, that the rights of the State, to interpose, rests [sic] on mere inference without any express provision in the Constitution, and that it is not to be supposed if the Constitution contemplated the exercise of a power of such high importance, that it would have been left to interference alone. In answer, the committee would ask those, who raise the objection, if the power of the Supreme Court to declare a law unconstitutional, is not among the very highest and most important, that can be exercised by any department of the government, and where they can find any express provision to justify its exercise? Like the power in question, it also rests on mere inference, but an inference so clear, that no express provision could render it more certain. The simple facts, that the Judges must decide according to Law, and that the Constitution is paramount to the Law, imposes a necessity on the Court to declare the latter void, whenever it comes into conflict with the former; so from the fact, that the sovereign power is divided, and that the States hold their portion in the same sovereign capacity with the General Government, by like necessity, then is [deduced?] the right of judging of the infraction of their sovereignty, as well as of the remedy. The deduction in the one case is not clearer than the other; but if we refer to the nature of our Constitution, the right of the State stands on stronger grounds than that of the court.

In the distribution of powers between the General and State Governments, the Constitution professes to enumerate those assigned to the former, in whatever department they may be vested; while the powers of the latter are reserved in general terms, without an attempt at enumeration. It therefore raises a presumption against the powers of the court to declare a law unconstitutional, that the power is not enumerated among those belonging to the judiciary. While the omission to enumerate amongst the powers of the States, that [power] to interfere and protect their rights, being strictly in accord with the principles on which the framers formed the Constitution, raises not the slightest presumption against its existence.

It is next objected to the power that it places the minority over the majority, in opposition to the whole theory of government, and that its consequences must be feebleness, anarchy, and finally disunion.

It is impossible to impose any limitation on sovereign power; without encountering from its supporters this very objection; and we accordingly find that the history of every country which has attempted to establish free institutions, proves, that on this point the opposing parties, the advocates of power and of freedom have ever separated. It constitutes the essence of the controversy between the Patricians and Plebans of the Roman republic; of the Tories and Whigs in England; of the Ultras and Liberals in France; and finally of the Federalists and Republicans in our own country, as illustrated by Mr. Madison's Report; and if it were proposed to give to Russia or Austria a representation of the people, it would form the point of controversy, between the imperial and popular parties. It is in fact not at all surprising, that to a people unacquainted with the nature of liberty, and inexperienced in its blessing, all limitation on the supreme power should appear incompatible with its nature, and as tending to feebleness and anarchy.

Nature has not permitted us to doubt the necessity of supreme power in every community. All see and feel it, and are instinctively impelled to its support; but it requires some effort of reason to perceive, that if not controlled, such power must necessarily lead to abuse; and still higher efforts to understand that it may be checked without destroying its supremacy. With us however who know from our own experience and that of other free nations, the truth of both these positions; and also that power can be rendered useful and secure by being properly checked, it is indeed strange that any intelligent citizen should consider limitation in sovereignty, as incompatiable with its nature; or should fear danger from any check properly lodged, which may be necessary to secure any distinct and important interest. That there are such interests represented by the States, and that on principle the State alone can protect them has been proved; and it only remains in order to meet the objection to prove, that for this purpose the States may be safely entrusted with the power. If the committee do not greatly mistake, it never has in any country, or under any institutions, been lodged, where it was less liable to abuse. The great number by whom it must be exercised, a majority of the people of one of the States, the solemnity of the mode, the delay, the deliberation, are all calculated to allay excitement, to impress on the people of the State, a deep and solemn tone, highly favorable to calm investigation. Under such circumstances, it would be impossible for a party to preserve a majority in the State, unless the violation of its rights be "palpable, deliberate, and dangerous." The attitude in which the State would be placed, in relation to a majority of the States; the force of public opinion which would be brought to bear on her, the deep reverence for the General Government, the strong influence of the General Government, the strong influence of that portion of her citizens, who aspire to office or distinction in the Union, and above all the local parties which must ever exist in the States, and which [sic] in this case must ever throw the powerful influence of the minority in the State, on the side of the General Government; and would stand ready to take advantage of an error in the side of the majority. So powerful are these causes, that nothing but the truth and a deep sense of oppression on the part of the people of the State, will ever authorize the exercise of the power; and, if it should be attempted under other circumstances, those in power would be speedily replaced by others, who would make a merit of closing the controversy, by yielding the point in dispute. But in order to understand more fully, what its operation would be, we must take into the estimate, the effect which a recognition of the power, would have on the administration both of the General and State Governments. On the former, it would necessarily produce, in the exercise of doubtful power, the most marked moderation. On the latter a feeling of conscious security would effectually prevent jealousy, animosity and hatred, and thus give scope to the natural attachment to our institutions. But withhold this protective power from the State, and the reverse of all these happy consequences must follow, which however the committee will not undertake to describe, as the living example of discord, hatred, and jealousy, threatening anarchy and dissolution, must impress on every beholder a more vivid picture, than what they could possibly draw. The continuance of this unhappy state must end in the loss of all affection, leaving the government to be sustained by force instead of patriotism. In act to him who will daily reflect, it must be apparent, that where there are important, separate interests to preserve, there is no alternative but a veto or military force. If these deductions be correct as cannot be doubted, then under that state of moderation and security, followed by mutual kindness which must accompany the acknowledgment of the right, the necessity of exercising a veto would rarely exist; and the possibility of abuse on the part of the State, would almost be wholly removed. Its acknowledged existence would thus supercede [sic] its exercise. But suppose in this the committee to be mistaken, still there exists a sufficient remedy for the disease. As high as is the power of the States in their individual sovereign capacity, it is not the highest power to our system. There is a still higher power, placed above all by the express consent of all, the creating and preserving power, deposited in the hands of three-fourths of the United States, which under the character of the amending power, can modify the whole system at pleasure, and to the final decision of which, it would be political heresy to object. Give then the veto to the States and admit its liability to abuse by them; and what is the effect, but to create the presumption against the constitutionality of the disputed powers exercised by the General Government, which if the presumption be well founded must compel them to abandon it, but if not, the General Government may remove it by invoking this high power to decide the question in the form of an amendment to the Constitution. If the decision be favourable to the General Government, a disputed constructive power, will be converted into a certain and express grant. On the other hand, if it be adverse, the refusing to grant will be tantamount to inhibiting its exercise; and thus in either case the controversy will be peaceably determined. Such is the sum of its effects. And ought not a sovereign State in protecting the minor and local interests of the country, to have a power to compel a decision? Without it, can the system itself exist? Let us examine the case. To compel the State to appeal against the acts of the General Government, by proposing an amendment to the Constitution, would be perfectly idle. The very complaint is that a majority of the States, through the General Government by force of construction urge powers not delegated, and by their exercise, increase their wealth and power at the expense of a minority. How absurd then to compel one of the injured States, to attempt a remedy by proposing an amendment to be ratified by three-fourths of the States, when there is by supposition a majority opposed to it. Nor would it be less absurd to expect the General Government to propose an amendment, in order to settle the point disputed, unless compelled to that course by the State. On their part there can be no inducement. They have a more summary mode of assuming the power by construction. The consequence is clear. Neither would appeal to the amending power; the one because it would be useless; and the other because it could effect its object without it. Under the operation of this supreme controlling power to whose interposition no one can object, all controversy between the States and General Government would be thus adjusted; and the Constitution would gradually acquire by its constant interposition in important cases, all the perfection of which the work of men is susceptible. It is this that the creative will become the preserving power; and we may rest assured, that it is no less true in politics, than in divinity that the power which creates can alone preserve, and that preservation is perpetual creation. Such will be the operation of the veto of the State.

If indeed it had the effect of placing the State over the General Government the objection would be fatal. For it the majority cannot be trusted with the supreme power, neither can the minority; and to transfer if from the former to the latter, would be but the repetition of the old error of taking shelter under a monarchy or aristocracy, against the more oppressive tyranny of a majority in an ill constructed republic. But is not the consequence of proper checks to change places between the majority and the minority. It leaves the power controlled still supreme as is exemplified in our political institutions, by the operation of acknowledged checks. The powers of the judiciary to declare an act of Congress, or of a State legislature unconstitutional, is a powerful, and for its appropriate purpose an efficient one; but who acquainted with the nature of our government, ever supposed it really vested (when confined to its proper object,) a Supreme power in the Court over Congress or the State Legislatures? Such could be neither the intention nor its proper effect. The check was given to the Judiciary to protect the supremacy of the Constitution over the acts of the Legislation, and not to set up a supreme power in the Courts. The Constitution has provided another check, which will still further illustrate the nature of its operation. Among the various interests which exist under our complex system, that of large and small States are among the most prominent and among the most carefully guarded in the organization of our government. To settle the relative weight of the States in the system; and to secure to each the means of maintaining this proper political consequence in its operation, were amongst the most difficult duties in framing the Constitution. No one subject occupied greater space in the proceedings of the Convention. In its final adjustment, the large States had assigned to them a preponderating influence in the House of Representatives, but to compensate which, and to secure their political rights against their preponderance, the small States had an equality assigned them in the Senate, while in the constitution of the Executive branch, the two were blended. To secure the consequence allotted to each, as well as to insure due deliberation in legislation, a veto is allowed to each in the passage of bills; but it would be absurd to suppose, that this veto placed either above the other; or was incompatible with the portion of the sovereign power allotted to the House, the Senate or the President.

It is thus that our system has provided appropriate checks, with a veto to ensure the supremacy of the Constitution over the laws; and to preserve the due importance of the States, considered in reference to large and small, without creating discord or weakening

the beneficient energy of the government, and so in the division of sovereign authority between the General and State Governments, and in granting an efficient power to the latter, to protect by a veto the minor against the major interests of the community, the framers of the Constitution acted in strict conformity with the principle which invariably prevails, throughout the whole system whenever separate interests exist. They were in truth no ordinary men. They were wise and practical men, enlightened by history and their own enlarged experience, acquired in conducting our country through a most important revolution; and understood profoundly the nature of man and of government. They saw and felt that there existed in our nature the necessity of a government, which to effect the object of the government must have adequate powers. They saw the selfish predominate over the social feelings, and that without a government with such powers, universal conflict and anarchy must prevail among the component parts of society; but they also clearly saw, that our nature remaining unchanged by change of condition, that unchecked power from this very predominance of the selfish over the social feeling, which rendered government necessary, would of necessity lead to corruption and oppression on the past of those invested with its exercise. Thus the necessity of government and of checks originate in the same great principle of our nature, through which the very selfishness, which would impel those who have power, to desire more than their own, will also, with great energy impel those, on whom power may operate to demand their own; and in [sic] the balance of these opposing tendencies from different conditions, but originating in the same principle of action, the one impelling to excess, the other restraining within the bounds of moderation and justice, liberty and happiness must forever depend. This great principle guided the framers of the Constitution in constructing our political system. This is not an opposing interest, throughout the whole that is not counterpoised. Have the rulers a separate interest from the people? To check its abuse, the relation of representative and constituent is created between them, through periodical elections, by which the fidelity of rulers to their trusts is secured. Have the States as members of the Union, distinct political interests in reference to their magnitude? Their relative weight is carefully settled, and each class has its appropriate means with a veto to protect its political consequence. May there be a conflict between the Constitution and the laws, whereby the rights of citizens may be affected? To preserve the ascendancy of the Constitution, a power is vested in the Supreme Court to declare the law unconstitutional in such cases. Is there in a geographical point of view separate interests? To meet this a peculiar organization is provided in the division of the sovereign power between the State and General Governments? Is there danger growing out of this division, that the State[s] may encroach on the general powers through the acts of their legislatures? To the Supreme Court is also assigned adequate power to check such encroachment. May the General Government on the other hand encroach on the rights reserved to the States? To the States in their sovereign

capacity is reserved the power to arrest such encroachment. And finally may this power be abused by the States in interfering improperly with the powers delegated to the General Government? There remains still higher power created supreme over all, invested with the ultimate power over all interest, to enlarge, to modify or rescind at pleasure, whose interposition the majority may invoke; and to oppose whose decision would be rebellion. On this the whole system rests.

That there exists a case which would justify the interposition of this State, and thereby compel the General Government to abandon an unconstitutional power, or to make an appeal to the amending power to confer it by express grant, the committee does not in the least doubt; and they are equally clear in the existence of a necessity to justify its exercise, if the General Government should continue to persist in its improper assumption of powers, belonging to the State; which brings them to the last point which they propose to consider. When would it be proper to exercise this high power? If they were to judge only by the magnitude of the interest and urgency of the case, they would without hesitation recommend the exercise of this power without delay. But they deeply feel the obligation of respect for the other members of the confederacy, and of great moderation and forbearance in the exercise, even of the most unquestionable right, between parties who stand connected by the closest and most sacred political union. With these sentiments, they deem it advisable after presenting the views of the Legislature in this solemn manner, to allow time for further consideration and reflection, in the hope that a returning sense of justice on the part of the majority, when they have come to reflect on the wrongs, which this and other staple States have suffered, and are suffering, may repeal the obnoxious and unconstitutional acts, and thereby prevent the necessity of interposing the sovereign power of this State.

The Committee is further induced at this time to recommend this course, under the hope, that the great political revolution which will displace from power on the 4th of March next, those who acquired authority by setting the will of the people at defiance; and which will bring in an eminent citizen, [Andrew Jackson,] distinguished for his services to his country and his justice and patriotism, may be followed up under his influence with a complete restoration of the pure principles of our government.

But in thus recommending delay, the committee wish it to be distinctly understood, that neither doubts of the power of the State, nor apprehension of consequences, constitute the smallest part of their motives. They would be unworthy of the name of Freemen, of Americans, of Carolinians, if danger, however great, could cause them to shrink from the maintainance [sic] of their constitutional rights; but they deem it preposterous to anticipate danger, under a system of laws, where a sovereign party to the compact, which formed the government, exercises a power, which after the fullest investigation of the Constitution itself, and which is essential to the preservation of her sovereignty.

The committee deem it not only the right of the State, but the duty of her representatives under the solemn sanction of an oath, to interpose if no other remedy be applied. They interpret the oath of the Constitution, not simply to impose an obligation to abstain from violation, but if possible to prevent it in others. In their opinion, he is as guilty of violating that sacred instrument, who permits an infraction, when in his power to prevent it, as he who is actually guilty of the infraction. The one may be bolder and the other more timid, but the sense of duty must be equally weak on both.

With these views the committee are solemnly of impression if the system be persevered in, after due forbearance on the part of the State, that it will be her sacred duty to interpose her veto; a duty to herself, to the Union, to present, and to future generations, and to the cause of liberty over the world, to arrest the progress of a power, which, if not arrested, must in its consequences, corrupt the public morals, and destroy the liberty of the country.

To avert these calamities, to restore the Constitution to its original purity, and to allay the differences which have been unhappily produced between various States, and between the States and General Government, we solemnly appeal to the justice and good feeling of those States heretofore opposed to us; and earnestly invoke the council and co-operation of those States, similarly situated with our own. Not doubting their good will and support; and sustained by a deep sense of the righteousness of its cause—the committee trusts that under Divine Providence the exertions of the State will be crowned with success.

See also: **Vol. I**: American System; Calhoun, John Caldwell; Clay, Henry; Clay's Compromise; Force Act; Jackson, Andrew; Nullification; South Carolina *Exposition* and *Protest*; Tariff of 1816; Tariff of 1824; Tariff of 1828 (Tariff of Abominations); Tariff of 1832; Tariff of 1833 (Compromise Tariff). **Vol. III**: Tariff of 1824; Tariff of 1828 (Tariff of Abominations); Tariff of 1832; Tariff of 1833 (Compromise Tariff).

South Carolina *Protest*

After the Special Committee of the House of Representatives on the Tariff reported the Exposition *to the general assembly, South Carolina's state legislators declared their position on the constitutionality of the Tariff of 1828. The legislature drafted a formal complaint on December 19, 1828, and the state's two senators then submitted the South Carolina* Protest *to the U.S. Senate. Congress failed to act on the document and tensions continued to escalate until 1832, when the passage of another tariff bill, having failed to adequately address the issue by lowering duty rates, forced South Carolina to employ a different tactic.*

The Senate and House of Representatives of South Carolina, now met, and sitting in General Assembly, through the Hon. William Smith and the Hon. Robert Y. Hayne, their representatives in the Senate of the United States, do, in the name and on behalf of the good people of the said commonwealth, solemnly protest against the system of protecting duties, lately adopted by the federal government, for the following reasons:

1. Because the good people of this commonwealth believe that the powers of Congress were delegated to it in trust for the accomplishment of certain specified objects which limit and control them, and that every exercise of them for any other purposes, is a violation of the Constitution as unwarrantable as the undisguised assumption of substantive, independent powers not granted or expressly withheld.

2. Because the power to lay duties on imports is, and in its very nature can be, only a means of effecting objects specified by the Constitution; since no free government, and least of all a government of enumerated powers, can of right impose any tax, any more than a penalty, which is not at once justified

by public necessity, and dearly within the scope and purview of the social compact; and since the right of confining appropriations of the public money to such legitimate and constitutional objects is as essential to the liberties of the people as their unquestionable privilege to be taxed only by their own consent.

3. Because they believe that the tariff law passed by Congress at its last session, and all other acts of which the principal Object is the protection of manufactures, or any other branch of domestic industry, if they be considered as the exercise of a power in Congress to tax the people at its own good will and pleasure, and to apply the money raised to objects not specified in the Constitution, is a violation of these fundamental principles, a breach of a well-defined trust; and a perversion of the high powers vested in the federal government for federal purposes only.

4. Because such acts, considered in the light of a regulation of commerce, are equally liable to objection; since, although the power to regulate commerce may, like other powers, be exercised so as to protect domestic manufactures, yet it is clearly distinguishable from a power to do so, both in the nature of the thing and in the common acceptation of the terms; and because the confounding of them would lead to the most extravagant results, since the encouragement of domestic industry implies an absolute control over all the interests, resources, and pursuits of a people, and is inconsistent with the idea of any other than simple, consolidated government

5. Because, from the contemporaneous exposition of the Constitution in the numbers of the Federalist, (which is cited only because the Supreme Court has recognized its authority,) it is clear that the power to regulate commerce was considered by the Convention as only incidentally connected with the encouragement of agriculture and manufactures; and because the power of laying imposts and duties on imports was not understood to justify, in any case, a prohibition of foreign commodities; except as a means of extending commerce, by coercing foreign nations to a fair reciprocity in their intercourse with us, or for some other bona fide commercial purpose.

6. Because, whilst the power to protect manufactures is nowhere expressly granted to Congress, nor can be considered as necessary and proper to carry into effect any specified power, it seems to be expressly reserved to the states, by the 10th section of the 1st article of the Constitution.

7. Because, even admitting Congress to have a constitutional right to protect manufactures by the imposition of duties, or by regulations, of commerce, designed principally for that purpose, yet a tariff of which the operation is grossly unequal and oppressive, is such an abuse of power as is incompatible with the principles of a free government and the great ends of civil society, justice, and equality of rights and protection.

8. Finally, because South Carolina, from her climate, situation, and peculiar institutions, is, and must ever continue to be, wholly dependent upon agriculture and commerce, not only for her prosperity, but for her very existence as a state; because the valuable products of her soil—the blessings by which Divine Providence seems to have designed to compensate for the

great disadvantages under which she suffers in other respects—are among the very few that can be cultivated with any profit by slave labor; and if, by the loss of her foreign commerce, these products Should be confined to an inadequate market, the fate of this fertile state would be poverty and utter desolation; her citizens, in despair, would emigrate to more fortunate regions, and the whole frame and constitution of her civil polity be impaired and deranged, if not dissolved entirely.

Deeply impressed with these considerations, the representatives of the good people of this Commonwealth, anxiously desiring to live in peace with their fellow-citizens, and to do all that in them lies to preserve and perpetuate the union of the states, and liberties of which it is the surest pledge, but feeling it to be their bounden duty to ex-

pose and resist all encroachments upon the true spirit of the Constitution, lest an apparent acquiescence in the system of protecting duties should be drawn into precedent—do, in the name of the commonwealth of South Carolina, claim to enter upon the Journal of the Senate their protest against it as unconstitutional, oppressive, and unjust.

See also: **Vol. I**: American System; Calhoun, John Caldwell; Clay, Henry; Clay's Compromise; Force Act; Jackson, Andrew; Nullification; South Carolina *Exposition* and *Protest*; Tariff of 1816; Tariff of 1824; Tariff of 1828 (Tariff of Abominations); Tariff of 1832; Tariff of 1833 (Compromise Tariff). **Vol. III**: Tariff of 1824; Tariff of 1828 (Tariff of Abominations); Tariff of 1832; Tariff of 1833 (Compromise Tariff).

South Carolina Ordinance of Nullification

South Carolina adopted a more militant stance after the passage of the Tariff of 1832 because Congress had failed to address the state's formal protest and devise a new tax schedule equitable to all regions of the country. On November 24, 1832, a convention held at Columbia, South Carolina, approved the following Ordinance of Nullification, which invalidated federal law and forbade the collection of duties in the state.

An ordinance to nullify certain acts of the Congress of the United States, purporting to be laws laying duties and imposts on the importation of foreign commodities.

Whereas the Congress of the United States by various acts, purporting to be acts laying duties and imposts on foreign imports, but in reality intended for the protection of domestic manufactures and the giving of bounties to classes and individuals engaged in particular employments, at the expense and to the injury and oppression of other classes and individuals, and by wholly exempting from taxation certain foreign commodities, such as are not produced or manufactured in the United States, to afford a pretext for imposing higher and excessive duties on articles similar to those intended to be protected, bath exceeded its just powers under the constitution, which confers on it no authority to afford such protection, and bath violated the true meaning and intent of the constitution, which provides for equality in imposing the burdens of taxation upon the several States and portions of the confederacy: And whereas the said Congress, exceeding its just power to impose taxes and collect revenue for the purpose of effecting and accomplishing the specific objects and purposes which the constitution of the United States authorizes it to effect and accomplish, both raised and collected unnecessary revenue for objects unauthorized by the constitution.

We, therefore, the people of the State of South Carolina, in convention assembled, do declare and ordain and it is hereby declared and ordained, that the several acts and parts of acts of the Congress of the United States, purporting to be laws for the imposing of duties and imposts on the importation of foreign commodities, and now having actual operation and effect within the United States, and, more especially, an act entitled "An act in alteration of the several acts imposing duties on imports," approved on the nineteenth day of May, one thousand eight hundred and twenty-eight and also an act entitled "An act to alter and amend the several acts imposing duties on imports," approved on the fourteenth day of July, one thousand eight hundred and thirty-two, are unauthorized by the constitution of the United States, and violate the true meaning and intent thereof and are null, void, and no law, nor binding upon this State, its officers or citizens; and all promises, contracts, and obligations, made or entered into, or to be made or entered into, with purpose to secure the duties imposed by said acts, and all judicial proceedings which shall be hereafter had in affirmance thereof, are and shall be held utterly null and void.

And it is further ordained, that it shall not be lawful for any of the constituted authorities, whether of this State or of the United States, to enforce the payment of duties imposed by the said acts within the limits of this State; but it shall be the duty of the legislature to adopt such measures and pass such acts as may be necessary to give full effect to this ordinance, and to prevent the enforcement and arrest the operation of the said acts and parts of acts of the Congress of the United States within the limits of this State, from and after the first day of February next, and the duties of all other constituted authorities, and of all persons residing or being within the limits of this State, and they are hereby required and enjoined to obey and give effect to this ordinance, and such acts and measures of the legislature as may be passed or adopted in obedience thereto.

And it is further ordained, that in no case of law or equity, decided in the courts of this State, wherein shall be drawn in question the authority of this ordinance, or the validity of such act or acts of the legislature as may be passed for the purpose of giving effect thereto, or the validity of the aforesaid acts of Congress, imposing duties, shall any appeal be taken or allowed to the Supreme Court of the United States, nor shall any copy of the record be permitted or allowed for that purpose; and if any such appeal shall be attempted to be taken, the courts of this State shall proceed to execute and enforce their judgments according to the laws and usages of the State, without reference to such attempted appeal, and the person or persons attempting to take such appeal may be dealt with as for a contempt of the court.

And it is further ordained, that all persons now holding any office of honor, profit, or trust, civil or military, under this State (members of the legislature excepted), shall, within such time, and in such manner as the legislature shall prescribe, take an oath well and truly to obey, execute, and enforce this ordinance, and such act or acts of the legislature as may be passed in pursuance thereof, according to the true intent and meaning of the same, and on the neglect or omission of any such person or persons so to do, his or their office or offices shall be forthwith vacated, and shall be filled up as if such person or persons were dead or had resigned; and no person hereafter elected to any office of honor, profit, or trust, civil or military (members of the legislature excepted), shall, until the legislature shall otherwise provide and direct, enter on the execution of his office, or be he any respect competent to discharge the duties thereof until he shall, in like manner, have taken a similar oath; and no juror shall be impaneled in any of the courts of this State, in any cause in which shall be in question this ordinance, or any act of the legislature passed in pursuance thereof, unless he shall first, in addition to the usual oath, have taken an oath that he will well and truly obey, execute, and enforce this ordinance, and such act or acts of the legislature as may be passed to carry the same into operation and effect, according to the true intent and meaning thereof.

And we, the people of South Carolina, to the end that it may be fully understood by the government of the United States, and the people of the co-States, that we are determined to maintain this our ordinance and declaration, at every hazard, do further declare that we will not submit to the application of force on the part of the federal government, to reduce this State to obedience, but that we will consider the passage, by Congress, of any act authorizing the employment of a military or naval force against the State of South Carolina, her constitutional authorities or citizens; or any act abolishing or closing the ports of this State, or any of them, or otherwise obstructing the free ingress and egress of vessels to and from the said ports, or any other act on the part of the federal government, to coerce the State, shut up her ports, destroy or harass her commerce or to enforce the acts hereby declared to be null and void, otherwise than through the civil tribunals of the country, as inconsistent with the longer continuance of South Carolina in the Union; and that the people of this State will henceforth hold themselves absolved from all further obligation to maintain or preserve their political connection with the people of the other States; and will forthwith proceed to organize a separate government, and do all other acts and things which sovereign and independent States may of right do.

Done in convention at Columbia, the twenty-fourth day of November, in the year of our Lord one thousand eight hundred and thirty-two, and in the fifty-seventh year of the Declaration of the Independence of the United States of America.

See also: **Vol. I**: American System; Calhoun, John Caldwell; Clay, Henry; Clay's Compromise; Force Act; Jackson, Andrew; Nullification; South Carolina *Exposition* and *Protest*; Tariff of 1816; Tariff of 1824; Tariff of 1828 (Tariff of Abominations); Tariff of 1832; Tariff of 1833 (Compromise Tariff). **Vol. III**: Tariff of 1824; Tariff of 1828 (Tariff of Abominations); Tariff of 1832; Tariff of 1833 (Compromise Tariff).

Proclamation to the People of South Carolina

President Andrew Jackson issued the following proclamation to the people of South Carolina after their legislature passed the Ordinance of Nullification in November 1832. Jackson outlined the actions taken at the convention held in Columbia and argued that despite differences over the tariff, the most pressing issue remained the preservation of the Union. He appealed to the citizens of the state to resist this violation of the Constitution before the situation worsened.

Whereas, a convention assembled in the state of South Carolina have passed an ordinance by which they declare "that the several acts and parts of acts of the Congress of the United States purporting to be laws for the imposing of duties and imposts on the importation of foreign commodities and now having actual operation and effect within the United States, and more especially" two acts for the same purposes passed on the 29th of May, 1829, and on the 14th of July, 1832, are unauthorized by the Constitution of the United States, and violate the true meaning and intent thereof, and are null and void and no law, nor binding on the citizens of that state or its officers; and by the said ordinance it is further declared to be unlawful for any of the constituted authorities of the state or of the United States to enforce the payment of the duties imposed by the said acts within the same state, and that it is the duty of the legislature to pass such laws as may be necessary to give full effect to the said ordinance; and

Whereas, by the said ordinance it is further ordained that in no case of law or equity decided in the courts of said state wherein shall be drawn in question the validity of the said ordinance, or of the acts of the legislature that may be passed to give it effect, or of the said laws of the United States, no appeal shall be allowed to the Supreme Court of the United States, nor shall any copy of the record be permitted or allowed for that purpose, and that any person attempting to take such appeal shall be punished as for contempt of court; and, finally, the said ordinance declares that the people of South Carolina will maintain the said ordinance at every hazard, and that they will consider the passage of any act by Congress abolishing or closing the ports of the said state or otherwise obstructing the free ingress or egress of vessels to and from the said ports, or any other act of the federal government to coerce the state, shut up her ports, destroy or harass her commerce, or to enforce the said acts, otherwise than through the civil tribunals of the country, as inconsistent with the longer continuance of South Carolina in the Union, and that the people of the said state will thenceforth hold themselves absolved from all further obligation to maintain or preserve their political connection with the people of the other states, and will forthwith proceed to organize a separate government and do all other acts and things which sovereign and independent states may of right do; and

Whereas, the said ordinance prescribes to the people of South Carolina a course of conduct in direct violation of their duty as citizens of the United States, contrary to the laws of their country, subversive of its Constitution, and having for its object the destruction of the Union . . . to preserve this bond of our political existence from destruction, to maintain inviolate this state of national honor and prosperity, and to justify the confidence my fellow citizens have reposed in me, I, Andrew Jackson, President of the United States,

have thought proper to issue this my proclamation, stating my views of the Constitution and laws applicable to the measures adopted by the convention of South Carolina and to the reasons they have put forth to sustain them, declaring the course which duty will require me to pursue, and appealing to the understanding and patriotism of the people, warn them of the consequences that must inevitably result from an observance of the dictates of the convention.

Strict duty would require of me nothing more than the exercise of those powers with which I am now or may hereafter be invested for preserving the peace of the Union and for the execution of the laws; but the imposing aspect which opposition has assumed in this case, by clothing itself with state authority and the deep interest which the people of the United States must all feel in preventing a resort to stronger measures while there is a hope that anything will be yielded to reasoning and remonstrance, perhaps demand, and will certainly justify, a full exposition to South Carolina and the nation of the views I entertain of this important question, as well as a distinct enunciation of the course which my sense of duty will require me to pursue.

The ordinance is founded, not on the indefeasible right of resisting acts which are plainly unconstitutional and too oppressive to be endured but on the strange position that any one state may not only declare an act of Congress void but prohibit its execution; that they may do this consistently with the Constitution; that the true construction of that instrument permits a state to retain its place in the Union and yet be bound by no other of its laws than those it may choose to consider as constitutional. It is true, they add, that to justify this abrogation of a law it must be palpably contrary to the Constitution; but it is evident that to give the right of resisting laws of that description, coupled with the uncontrolled right to decide what laws deserve that character, is to give the power of resisting all laws; for as by the theory there is no appeal, the reasons alleged by the state, good or bad, must prevail. If it should be said that public opinion is a sufficient check against the abuse of this power, it may be asked why it is not deemed a sufficient guard against the passage of an unconstitutional act by Congress?

There is, however, a restraint in this last case which makes the assumed power of a state more indefensible, and which does not exist in the other. There are two appeals from an unconstitutional act passed by Congress—one to the judiciary, the other to the people and the states. There is no appeal from the state decision in theory, and the practical illustration shows that the courts are closed against an application to review it, both judges and jurors being sworn to decide in its favor. But reasoning on this subject is superfluous when our social compact, in express terms, declares that the laws of the United States, its Constitution, and treaties made under it are the supreme law of the land, and, for greater caution, adds "that the judges in every state shall be bound thereby, anything in the constitution or laws of any state to the contrary notwithstanding." And it may be asserted without fear of refutation that no federative government could exist without a similar provision.

Look for a moment to the consequence. If South Carolina considers the revenue laws unconstitutional and has a right to prevent their execution in the port of Charleston, there would be a clear constitutional objection to their collection in every other port; and no revenue could be collected anywhere, for all imposts must be equal. It is no answer to repeat that an unconstitutional law is no law so long as the question of its legality is to be decided by the state itself, for every law operating injuriously upon any local interest will be perhaps thought, and certainly represented, as unconstitutional, and, as has been shown, there is no appeal.

If this doctrine had been established at an earlier day, the Union would have been dissolved in its infancy. The excise law in Pennsylvania, the embargo and nonintercourse law in the Eastern states, the carriage tax in Virginia were all deemed unconstitutional, and were more unequal in their operation than any of the laws now complained of; but, fortunately, none of those states discovered that they had the right now claimed by South Carolina. The war into which we were forced to support the dignity of the nation and the rights of our citizens might have ended in defeat and disgrace, instead of victory and honor, if the states who supposed it a ruinous and unconstitutional measure had thought they possessed the right of nullifying the act by which it was declared and denying supplies for its prosecution. Hardly and unequally as those measures bore upon several members of the Union, to the legislatures of none did this efficient and peaceable remedy, as it is called, suggest itself. The discovery of this important feature in our Constitution was reserved to the present day. To the statesmen of South Carolina belongs the invention, and upon the citizens of that state will unfortunately fall the evils of reducing it to practice.

If the doctrine of a state veto upon the laws of the Union carries with it internal evidence of its impracticable absurdity, our constitutional history will also afford abundant proof that it would have been repudiated with indignation had it been proposed to form a feature in our government. . . .

Under the Confederation, then, no state could legally annul a decision of the Congress or refuse to submit to its execution; but no provision was made to enforce these decisions. Congress made requisitions, but they were not complied with. The government could not operate on individuals. They had no judiciary, no means of collecting revenue.

But the defects of the Confederation need not be detailed. Under its operation we could scarcely be called a nation. We had neither prosperity at home nor consideration abroad. This state of things could not be endured, and our present happy Constitution was formed but formed in vain if this fatal doctrine prevails. It was formed for important objects that are announced in the Preamble, made in the name and by the authority of the people of the United States, whose delegates framed and whose conventions approved it. The most important among these objects—that which is placed first in rank, on which all the others rest—is "to form a more perfect union."

Now, is it possible that even if there were no express provision giving supremacy to the Constitution and laws of the United States over those of the states, can it be conceived that an instrument made for the purpose of "forming a more perfect union" than that of the Confederation could be so constructed by the assembled wisdom of our country as to substitute for that Confederation a form of government dependent for its existence on the local interest, the party spirit of a state or of a prevailing faction in a state? Even man of plain, unsophisticated understanding who hears the question will give such an answer as will preserve the Union. . . .

I consider, then, the power to annul a law of the United States, assumed by one state, incompatible with the existence of the Union, contradicted expressly by the letter of the Constitution, unauthorized by its spirit, inconsistent with every principle on which it was founded, and destructive of the great object for which it was formed.

After this general view of the leading principle, we must examine the particular application of it which is made in the ordinance.

The Preamble rests its justification on these grounds: It assumes as a fact that the obnoxious laws, although they purport to be laws for raising revenue, were in reality intended for the protection of manufactures, which purpose it asserts to be unconstitutional; that the operation of these laws is unequal; that the amount raised by them is greater than is required by the wants of the government; and, finally, that the proceeds are to be applied to objects unauthorized by the Constitution. These are the only causes alleged to justify an open opposition to the laws of the country and a threat of seceding from the Union if any attempt should be made to enforce them. The first virtually acknowledges that the law in question was passed under a power expressly given by the Constitution to lay and collect imposts; but its constitutionality is drawn in question from the *motives* of those who passed it. However apparent this purpose may be in the present case, nothing can be more dangerous than to admit the position that an unconstitutional purpose entertained by the members who assent to a law enacted under a constitutional power shall make that law void.

For how is that purpose to be ascertained? Who is to make the scrutiny? How often may bad purposes be falsely imputed, in how many cases are they concealed by false professions, in how many is no declaration of motive made? Admit this doctrine and you give to the states an uncontrolled right to decide; and every law may be annulled under this pretext. If, therefore, the absurd and dangerous doctrine should be admitted that a state may annul an unconstitutional law, or one that it deems such, it will not apply to the present case.

The next objection is that the laws in question operate unequally. This objection may be made with truth to every law that has been or can be passed. The wisdom of man never yet contrived a system of taxation that would operate with perfect equality. If the unequal operation of a law makes it unconstitutional, and if all laws of that description may be abrogated by any state for that cause, then indeed is the federal Constitution unworthy of the slightest effort for its presentation.

We have hitherto relied on it as the perpetual bond of our Union; we have received it as the work of the assembled wisdom of the nation; we have trusted to it as to the sheet anchor of our safety in the stormy times of conflict with a foreign or domestic foe; we have looked to it with sacred awe as the palladium of our liberties; and with all the solemnities of religion have pledged to each other our lives and fortunes here and our hopes of happiness hereafter in its defense and support. Were we mistaken, my countrymen, in attaching this importance to the Constitution of our country? . . .

Our Constitution does not contain the absurdity of giving power to make laws and another to resist them. The sages whose memory will always be reverenced have given us a practical and, as they hoped, a permanent constitutional compact. The father of his country did not affix his revered name to so palpable an absurdity. Nor did the states, when they severally ratified it, do so under the impression that a veto on the laws of the United States was reserved to them or that they could exercise it by implication. Search the debates in all their conventions, examine the speeches of the most zealous opposers of federal authority, look at the amendments that were proposed; they are, all silent-not a syllable uttered, not a vote given, not a motion made to correct the explicit supremacy given to the laws of the Union over those of the states, or to show that implication, as is now contended, could defeat it.

No; we have not erred. The Constitution is still the object of our reverence, the bond of our Union, our defense in danger, the source of our prosperity in peace. It shall descend, as we have received it, uncorrupted by sophistical construction, to our posterity; and the sacrifices of local interests, of state prejudices, of personal animosities that were made to bring it into existence will again be patriotically offered for its support.

The two remaining objections made by the ordinance to these laws are that the sums intended to be raised by them are greater than are required, and that the proceeds will be unconstitutionally employed. . . .

The ordinance, with the same knowledge of the future that characterizes a former objection, tells you that the proceeds of the tax will be unconstitutionally applied. If this could be ascertained with certainty, the objection would with more propriety be reserved for the law so applying the proceeds, but surely cannot be urged against the laws levying the duty.

These are the allegations contained in the ordinance. Examine them seriously, my fellow citizens; judge for yourselves. I appeal to you to determine whether they are so clear, so convincing, as to leave no doubt of their correctness; and even if you should come to this conclusion, how far they justify the reckless, destructive course which you am directed to pursue. Review these objections and the conclusions drawn from them once more. What are they? Every law, then, for raising revenue, according to the South Carolina ordinance, may be rightfully annulled unless it be so framed as no law ever will or can be framed. Congress have a right to pass laws for raising revenue and each state has a right to oppose their execution—two rights directly opposed to each other; and yet is this absurdity supposed to be con-

tained in an instrument drawn for the express purpose of avoiding collisions between the states and the general government by an assembly of the most enlightened statesmen and purest patriots ever embodied for a similar purpose.

In vain have these sages declared that Congress shall have power to lay and collect taxes, duties, imposts, and excises; in vain have they provided that they shall have power to pass laws which shall be necessary and proper to carry those powers into execution, that those laws and that Constitution shall be the "supreme law of the land, and that the judges in every state shall be bound thereby, anything in the constitution or laws of any state to the contrary notwithstanding"; in vain have the people of the several states solemnly sanctioned these provisions, made them their paramount law, and individually sworn to support them whenever they were called on to execute any office. Vain provisions! Ineffectual restrictions! Vile profanation of oaths! Miserable mockery of legislation!—if a bare majority of the voters in any one state may, on a real or supposed knowledge of the intent with which a law has been passed, declare themselves free from its operation; say, here it gives too little; there, too much, and operates unequally; here it suffers articles to be free that ought to be taxed; there it taxes those that ought to be free; in this case the proceeds are intended to be applied to purposes which we do not approve; in that, the amount raised is more than is wanted.

Congress, it is true, are invested by the Constitution with the right of deciding these questions according to their sound discretion. Congress is composed of the representatives of all the states and of all the people of all the states. But we, part of the people of one state, to whom the Constitution has given no power on the subject, from whom it has expressly taken it away; *we*, who have solemnly agreed that this Constitution shall be our law; *we*, most of whom have sworn to support it—*we* now abrogate this law and swear, and force others to swear, that it shall not be obeyed; and we do this not because Congress have no right to pass such laws—this we do not allege—but because they have passed them with improper views. They are unconstitutional from the motives of those who passed them, which we can never with certainty know; from their unequal operation, although it is impossible, from the nature of things, that they should be equal; and from the disposition which we presume may be made of their proceeds, although that disposition has not been declared. This is the plain meaning of the ordinance in relation to laws which it abrogates for alleged unconstitutionality.

But it does not stop there. It repeals in express terms an important part of the Constitution itself and of laws passed to give it effect which have never been alleged to be unconstitutional. The Constitution declares that the judicial powers of the United States extend to cases arising under the laws of the United States, and that such laws, the Constitution, and treaties shall be paramount to the state constitutions and laws. The judiciary act prescribes the mode by which the case may be brought before a court of the United States by appeal when a state tribunal shall decide against this provision of the Constitution. The ordinance declares there shall be no appeal-makes the state law paramount to the Constitution and laws of the United States, forces judges and jurors to swear that they will disregard their provisions, and even makes it penal in a suitor to attempt relief by appeal. It further declares that it shall not be lawful for the authorities of the United States or of that state to enforce the payment of duties imposed by the revenue laws within its limits.

Here is a law of the United States, not even pretended to be unconstitutional, repealed by the authority of a small majority of the voters of a single state. Here is a provision of the Constitution which is solemnly abrogated by the same authority.

On such expositions and reasonings the ordinance grounds not only an assertion of the right to annul the laws of which it complains but to enforce it by a threat of seceding from the Union if any attempt is made to execute them.

This right to secede is deduced from the nature of the Constitution, which, they say, is a compact between sovereign states who have preserved their whole sovereignty and therefore are subject to no superior; that because they made the compact they can break it when in their opinion it has been departed from by the other states. Fallacious as this course of reasoning is, it enlists state pride and finds advocates in the honest prejudices of those who have not studied the nature of our government sufficiently to see the radical error on which it rests. . . .

The Constitution of the United States, then, forms a *government*, not a league; and whether it be formed by compact between the states or in any other manner, its character is the same.

It is a government in which all the people are represented, which operates directly on the people individually, not upon the states; they retained all the power they did not grant. But each state, having expressly parted with so many powers as to constitute, jointly with the other states, a single nation, cannot, from that period, possess any right to secede, because such secession does not break a league but destroys the unity of a nation; and any injury to that unity is not only a breach which would result from the contravention of a compact but it is an offense against the whole Union.

To say that any state may at pleasure secede from the Union is to say that the United States are not a nation, because it would be a solecism to contend that any part of a nation might dissolve its connection with the other parts, to their injury or ruin, without committing any offense. Secession, like any other revolutionary act, may be morally justified by the extremity of oppression; but to call it a constitutional right is confounding the meaning of terms, and can only be done through gross error or to deceive those who are willing to assert a right, but would pause before they made a revolution or incur the penalties consequent on a failure.

Because the Union was formed by a compact, it is said the parties to that compact may, when they feel themselves aggrieved, depart from it; but it is precisely because it is a compact that they cannot. A compact is an agreement or binding obligation. It may by its terms have a sanction or penalty for its breach, or it may not. If it contains no sanction, it may be broken with no other consequence than moral guilt; if it have a sanction, then the breach incurs the designated or implied penalty. A league between independent nations generally has no sanction other than a moral one; or if it should contain a penalty, as there is no common superior it cannot be enforced. A government, on the contrary, always has a sanction, express or implied; and in our case it is both necessarily implied and expressly given. An attempt by force of arms to destroy a government is an offense, by whatever means the constitutional compact may have been formed; and such government has the right by the law of self-defense to pass acts for punishing the offender, unless that right is modified, restrained, or resumed by the constitutional act. In our system, although it is modified in the case of treason, yet authority is expressly given to pass all laws necessary to carry its powers into effect, and under this grant provision has been made for punishing acts which obstruct the due administration of the laws.

It would seem superfluous to add anything to show the nature of that Union which connects us, but as erroneous opinions on this subject are the foundation of doctrines the most destructive to our peace, I must give some further development to my views on this subject. No one, fellow citizens, has a higher reverence for the reserved rights of the states than the magistrate who now addresses you. No one would make greater personal sacrifices or official exertions to defend them from violation; but equal care must be taken to prevent, on their part, an improper interference with or resumption of the rights they have vested in the nation. The line has not been so distinctly drawn as to avoid doubts in some cases of the exercise of power.

Men of the best intentions and soundest views may differ in their construction of some parts of the Constitution; but there are others on which dispassionate reflection can leave no doubt.

Of this nature appears to be the assumed right of secession. It rests, as we have seen, on the alleged undivided sovereignty of the states and on their having formed in this sovereign capacity a compact which is called the Constitution, from which, because they made it, they have the right to secede. Both of these positions are erroneous, and some of the arguments to prove them so have been anticipated.

The states severally have not retained their entire sovereignty. It has been shown that in becoming parts of a nation, not members of a league, they surrendered many of their essential parts of sovereignty. The right to make treaties, declare war, levy taxes, exercise exclusive judicial and legislative powers were all of them functions of sovereign power. The states, then, for all these important purposes, were no longer sovereign. The allegiance of their citizens was transferred, in the first instance, to the government of the United States; they became American citizens and owed obedience to the Constitution of the United States and to laws made in conformity with the powers it vested in Congress. . . .

This, then, is the position in which we stand. A small majority of the citizens of one state in the Union have elected delegates to a state convention; that convention has ordained that all the revenue laws of the United States must be repealed, or that they are no longer a member of the Union. The governor of that state has recommended to the legislature the raising of an army to carry the secession into effect, and that he may be empowered to give clearances to vessels in the name of the state. No act of violent opposition to the laws has yet been committed, but such a state of things is hourly apprehended. And it is the intent of this instrument to proclaim, not only that the duty imposed on me by the Constitution "to take care that the laws be faithfully executed" shall be performed to the extent of the powers already vested in me by law, or of such others as the wisdom of Congress shall devise and intrust to me for that purpose, but to warn the citizens of South Carolina who have been deluded into an opposition to the laws of the danger they will incur by obedience to the illegal and disorganizing ordinance of the convention; to exhort those who have refused to support it to persevere in their determination to uphold the Constitution and laws of their country; and to point out to all the perilous situation into which the good people of that state have been led, and that the course they am urged to pursue is one of ruin and disgrace to the very state whose rights they affect to support. . . .

Disunion by armed force is *treason*. Are you really ready to incur its guilt? If you are, on the heads of the instigators of the act be the dreadful consequences; on their heads be the dishonor, but on yours may fall the punishment. On your unhappy state will inevitably fall all the evils of the conflict you force upon the government of your country. It cannot accede to the mad project of disunion, of which you would be the first victims. Its first magistrate cannot, if he would, avoid the performance of his duty. . . .

Fellow citizens of the United States,

the threat of unhallowed disunion, the names of those once respected by whom it is uttered, the array of military force to support it, denote the approach of a crisis in our affairs on which the continuance of our unexampled prosperity, our political existence, and perhaps that of all free governments may depend. The conjuncture demanded a free, a full and explicit enunciation, not only of my intentions, but of my principles of action; and as the claim was asserted of a right by a state to annul the laws of the Union, and even to secede from it at pleasure, a frank exposition of my opinions in relation to the origin and form of our government and the construction I give to the instrument by which it was created seemed to be proper.

Having the fullest confidence in the justness of the legal and constitutional opinion of my duties which has been expressed, I rely with equal confidence on your undivided support in my determination to execute the laws, to preserve the Union by all constitutional means, to arrest, if possible, by moderate and firm measures the necessity of a recourse to force; and if it be the will of Heaven that the recurrence of its primeval curse on man for the shedding of a brother's blood should fall upon our land, that it be not called down by any offensive act on the part of the United States.

Fellow citizens, the momentous case is before you. On your undivided support of your government depends the decision of the great question it involves—whether your sacred Union will be preserved and the blessing it secures to us as one people shall be perpetuated.

See also: **Vol. I**: American System, Calhoun, John Caldwell; Clay, Henry; Clay's Compromise; Force Act; Jackson, Andrew; Nullification; South Carolina *Exposition* and *Protest*; Tariff of 1816; Tariff of 1824; Tariff of 1828 (Tariff of Abominations); Tariff of 1832; Tariff of 1833 (Compromise Tariff). **Vol. III**: Tariff of 1824; Tariff of 1828 (Tariff of Abominations); Tariff of 1832; Tariff of 1833 (Compromise Tariff).

Andrew Jackson's Message to Congress on the Nullification Crisis

After issuing the Proclamation to the People of South Carolina, President Andrew Jackson waited for a response from the state. In January 1833, he received further reports indicating that the legislature had not only nullified the Tariff of 1828 and the Tariff of 1832 but that they had also rescinded all tariff laws including those passed for revenue only. The state, in effect, refused to pay for any portion of the federal burden and reasserted its sovereignty. Jackson notified Congress that the Ordinance of Nullification, scheduled to take effect on February 1, allowed little time for a political resolution. Recognizing the limitations of the executive branch, he indicated that Congress must handle the situation. After Congress received this message, Henry Clay proposed the Compromise Tariff of 1833, an act that Jackson signed into law on March 2, 1833. South Carolina suspended the February 1 deadline while Congress worked on reducing the tariff to an acceptable rate.

The following written message was received from the President of the United States, by Mr. Donelson, his Secretary:

Gentlemen of the Senate and House of Representatives of the United States:

In my annual message, at the commencement of your present session, I adverted to the opposition to the revenue laws in a particular quarter of the United States, which threatened not merely to thwart their execution, but to endanger the integrity of the Union.

And, although I then expressed my reliance that it might be overcome by the prudence of the officers of the United States and the patriotism of the people, I stated that, should the emergency arise rendering the execution of the existing laws impracticable from any cause whatever, prompt notice should be given to Congress, with the suggestion of such views and measures as might be necessary to meet it.

Events which have occurred in the

quarter then alluded to, or which have come to my knowledge subsequently, present this emergency.

Since the date of my last message, I have had officially transmitted to me by the Governor of South Carolina, which I now communicate to Congress, a copy of the ordinance passed by the Convention which assembled at Columbia, in the State of South Carolina, in November last, declaring certain acts of Congress therein mentioned, within the limits of that State to be absolutely null and void, and making it the duty of the Legislature to pass such laws as would be necessary to carry the same into effect from and after the first February next.

The consequences to which this extraordinary defiance of the just authority of the Government might too surely lead, were clearly foreseen, and it was impossible for me to hesitate as to my own duty in such an emergency.

The ordinance has been passed, however, without any certain knowledge of the recommendation which, from a view of the interests of the nation at large, the Executive had determined to submit to Congress; and a hope was indulged that, by frankly explaining his sentiments, and the nature of those duties which the crisis would devolve upon him, the authorities of South Carolina might be induced to retrace their steps. In this hope, I determined to issue my proclamation of the 10th of December last, a copy of which I now lay before Congress.

I regret to inform you that these reasonable expectations have not been realized, and that the several acts of the Legislature of South Carolina, which I now lay before you, and which have, all and each of them, finally passed, af-

ter a knowledge of the desire of the administration to modify laws complained of, are too well calculated, both in their positive enactments and in the spirit of opposition which they obviously encourage, wholly to obstruct the collection of the revenue within the limits of that State.

Up to this period, neither the recommendation of the Executive in regard to our financial policy and impost system, nor the disposition manifested by Congress promptly to act upon this subject, nor the unequivocal expression of the public will in all parts of the Union, appears to have produced any relaxation in the measures of opposition adopted by the State of South Carolina; nor is there any reason to hope that the ordinance and laws will be abandoned.

I have no knowledge that an attempt has been made, or that it is in contemplation, to re-assemble either the Convention or the Legislature; and it will be perceived that the interval before the first of February is too short to admit of the preliminary steps necessary for that purpose. It appears, moreover, that the State authorities are actively organizing their military resources, and providing the means, and giving the most solemn assurances of protection and support to all who shall enlist in opposition to the revenue laws.

A recent proclamation of the present Governor of South Carolina has openly defied the authority of the Executive of the Union, and general orders from the head quarters of the State announced his determination to accept the services of volunteers, and his belief, should their country need their services, they will be found at the post of honor and duty, ready to lay down their lives in her defence. Under these orders, the forces referred to are directed to "hold themselves in readiness to take the field at a moment's warning;" and in the city of Charleston, within a collection district and a port of entry, a rendezvous has been opened for the purpose of enlisting men for the magazine and municipal guard. Thus South Carolina presents herself in the attitude of hostile preparation, and ready even for military violence, if need be, to enforce her laws for preventing the collection of the duties within her limits.

Proceedings thus announced and matured must be distinguished from menaces of unlawful resistance by irregular bodies of people, who, acting under temporary delusion, may be restrained by reflection, and the influence of public opinion, from the commission of actual outrage. In the present instance, aggression may be regarded as committed when it is officially authorized, and the means of enforcing it fully provided.

Under these circumstances, there can be no doubt that it is the determination of the authorities of South Carolina fully to carry into effect their ordinance and laws after the first of February. It therefore becomes my duty to bring the subject to the serious consideration of Congress, in order that such measures as they, in their wisdom, may deem fit, shall be seasonably provided; and that it may be thereby understood that, while the Government is disposed to remove all just cause of complaint, as far as may be practicable consistently with a proper regard to the interests of the community at large, it is, nevertheless, determined that the supremacy of the laws shall be maintained.

In making this communication, it appears to me to be proper not only that I should lay before you the acts and proceedings of South Carolina, but that I should also fully acquaint you with those steps which I have already caused to be taken for the due collection of the revenue, and with my views of the subject generally, that the suggestions which the Constitution required me to make, in regard to your future legislation, may be better understood.

This subject having early attracted the anxious attention of the Executive, as soon as it was probable that the authorities of South Carolina seriously mediated resistance to the faithful execution of the revenue laws, it was deemed advisable that the Secretary of the Treasury should, particularly, instruct the officers of the United States in that part of the Union as to the nature of the duties prescribed by the existing laws.

Instructions were accordingly issued on the 6th of November to the collectors in that State, pointing out their respective duties, and enjoining upon each a firm and vigilant, but discreet, performance of them in the emergency then apprehended.

I herewith transmit copies of these instructions, and of the letter addressed to the district attorney requesting his co-operation. These instructions were dictated in the hope that, as the opposition to the laws by the anomalous proceeding of nullification, was represented to be of a pacific nature, to be pursued, substantially, according to the forms of the Constitution, and without resorting, in any event, to force or violence, the measures of its advocates would be taken in conformity with that profession; and, on such supposition, the means afforded by the existing laws would have been adequate to meet any emergency likely to arise.

It was, however, not possible altogether to suppress apprehension of the excesses to which the excitement prevailing in that quarter might lead: but it certainly was not foreseen that the meditated obstruction to the laws would so soon openly assume its present character.

Subsequently to the date of these instructions, however, the ordinance of the Convention was passed, which, if complied with by the people of the State, must effectually render inoperative the present revenue laws within her limits.

That ordinance declares and ordains, "that the several acts, and parts of acts, of the Congress of the United States, purporting to be laws for the imposing of duties and imposts on the importation of foreign commodities, and now having operation and effect within the United States; and, more especially, "An act in alteration of the several acts imposing duties on imports," approved on the 19th of May, 1828; and also an act entitled "An act to alter and amend the several acts imposing duties on imports," approved on the 14th July, 1832, are unauthorized by the Constitution of the United States, and violate the true intent and meaning thereof, and are null and void, and no law, nor binding upon the State of South Carolina, its officers, and citizens; and all promises, contracts, and obligations made or entered into, or to be made or entered into, and all judicial proceeding which shall be hereafter had in affirmance thereof, are

and shall be held utterly null and void."

It also ordains "that it shall not be lawful for any of the constituted authorities of the State of South Carolina or of the United States, to enforce the payment of duties imposed by the said acts within the limits of the State, but that it shall be the duty of the Legislature as may be passed for the purpose of giving effect hereto, or the validity of the aforesaid acts of Congress imposing duties, shall any appeal be taken or allowed to the Supreme Court of the United States, nor shall any copy of the record be permitted or allowed for that purpose; and the person or persons attempting to take such appeal may be dealt with as for a contempt of court."

It likewise ordains, "that all persons holding any office of honor, profit, or trust, civil or military, under the State, shall, within such time, and in such manner as the Legislature shall prescribe, take an oath well and truly to obey, execute, and enforce this ordinance, and such act or acts of the Legislature as may be passed in pursuance thereof, according to the true intent and meaning of the same; and on the neglect or omission of any such person or persons so to do, his or their office or offices shall be forthwith vacated, and shall be filled up as if such person or persons were dead, or had resigned; and no person hereafter elected to any office of honor, profit, or trust, civil or military, shall until the Legislature shall otherwise provide and direct, enter on the execution of his office, or be, in any respect, competent to discharge the duties thereof, until he shall, in like manner, have taken a similar oath; and no juror in which shall be in question this ordinance, or any act of the Legislature passed in pursuance thereof, unless he shall first, in addition to the usual oath, have taken an oath that he will well and truly obey, execute, and enforce, this ordinance, and such act or acts of the Legislature as may be passed to carry the same into operation and effect, according to the true intent and meaning thereof."

The ordinance concludes: "And we, the people of South Carolina, to the end that it may be fully understood by the Government of the United States, and the people of the co-States, that we are determined to maintain this ordinance and declaration at every hazard, do further declare that we will not submit to the application of force on the part of the Federal Government to reduce this State to obedience; but that we will consider the passage, by Congress, of any act authorizing the employment of a military or naval force against the State of South Carolina, her constituted authorities, or citizens; or any act abolishing or closing the ports of this State, or any of them, or otherwise obstructing the free ingress and egress of vessels to and from the said ports; or any other act on the part of the Federal Government to coerce the State, shut up her ports, destroy or harass her commerce, or to enforce the acts hereby declared to be null and void, otherwise than through the civil tribunals of the country, as inconsistent with the longer continuance of South Carolina in the Union; and that the people of this State will thenceforth hold themselves absolved from all further obligation to maintain or preserve their political connexion with the people of the other States, and will forthwith proceed to organize a separate

government, and to do all other sets and things which sovereign and independent States may of right do."

This solemn denunciation of the laws and authority of the United States has been followed up by a series of acts, on the part of the authorities of that State, which manifest a determination to render inevitable a resort to those measures of self-defence which the paramount duty of the Federal Government requires; but, upon the adoption of which, that State will proceed to execute the purpose it has avowed in this ordinance, or withdrawing from the Union.

On the 27th of November, the Legislature assembled at Columbia; and, on their meeting, the Governor laid before them the ordinance of the Convention. In his message on that occasion, he acquaints them that "this ordinance has thus become a part of the fundamental law of South Carolina;" that "the die has been at least cast, and South Carolina has at length appealed to her ultimate sovereignty as a member of this confederacy, and has planted herself on her reserved rights. The rightful exercise of this power is not a question which we shall any longer argue. It is sufficient that she has willed it, and that the act is done; nor is its strict compatibility with our constitutional obligation to all laws passed by the General Government, within the authorized grants of power, to be drawn in question, when this interposition is exerted in a case in which the compact has been palpably, deliberately, and dangerously violated. That it brings up a conjuncture of deep and momentous interest, is neither to be concealed nor denied. This crisis presents a class of duties which is referable to yourselves. You have been commanded by the people, in their sovereignty, to take care that, within the limits of their State, their will shall be obeyed. "The measure of legislation," he says, "which you have to employ at this crisis, is the precise amount of such enactments as may be necessary to render it utterly impossible to collect, within our limits, the duties imposed by the protective tariffs thus nullified." He proceeds:

"That you should arm every citizen with a civil process by which he may claim, if he pleases, a restitution of his goods, seized under the existing imposts, on his giving security to abide the issue of a suit at law, and, at the same time, define what shall constitute treason against the State, and, by a bill of pains and penalties, compel obedience, and punish disobedience to your own laws, are points too obvious to require any discussion. In one word, you must survey the whole ground. You must look to and provide for all possible contingencies. In your own limits, your own courts of judicature must not only be supreme, but you must look to the ultimate issue of any conflict of jurisdiction and power between them and the courts of the United States.

The Governor also asks for power to grant clearances, in violation of the laws of the Union; and, to prepare for the alternative which must happen unless the United States shall passively surrender their authority, and the Executive, disregarding his oath, refrain from executing the laws of the Union, he recommends a thorough revision of the militia system, and that the Governor "be authorized to accept, for the defence of Charleston and its dependencies, the services of two thousand volunteers, either by companies or files;" and that they be formed into a legionary brigade, consisting of infantry, riflemen, cavalry, field and heavy artillery; and that they be "armed and equipped, from the public arsenals, completely for the field; and that appropriations be made for supplying all deficiencies in our munitions of war." In addition to those volunteer drafts, he recommends that the Governor be authorized "to accept the services of ten thousand volunteers from the other divisions of the State, to be organized and arranged in regiments and brigades; the officers to be selected by the commander-in chief; and that this whole force be called the *State Guard*."

A request has been regularly made of the Secretary of State of South Carolina for authentic copies of the acts which have been passed for the purpose of enforcing the ordinance: but, up to the date of the latest advices, that request had not been complied with; and, on the present occasion, therefore, reference can only be made to those acts as published in the newspapers of the State.

The acts to which it is deemed proper to invite the particular attention of the Congress, are,

1st. "An act to carry into effect, in part, an ordinance to nullify certain acts of the Congress of the United States, purporting to be laws laying duties on the importation of foreign commodities," passed in Convention of this State, at Columbia, on the 24th November, 1822.

This act provides, that any goods seized or detained, under pretence of securing the duties, or for the non-payment of duties, or under any process, order, or decree, or other pretext, contrary to the intent and meaning of the ordinance, may be recovered by the owner or consignee by "an act of replevin." That, in case of refusing to deliver them, or removing them so that the replevin cannot be executed, the sheriff may seize the personal estate of the offender to double the amount of the goods: and, if any attempt shall be made to retake or seize them, it is the duty of the sheriff to recapture them. And that any person who shall disobey the process, or remove the goods, or any one who shall attempt to retake or seize the goods under pretence of securing the duties, or for non-payment of duties, shall be fined and imprisoned, besides being liable for any other offences involved in the act.

It also provides that any person arrested or imprisoned on any judgment or decree obtained in any Federal Court for duties, shall be entitled to the benefit secured by the habeas corpus act of the State in cases of unlawful arrest, and may maintain an action for damages; and that, if any estate shall be sold under such judgment or decrees, the sale shall be held illegal. It also provides, that any jailor who receives a person committed on any process or other judicial proceedings to enforce the payment of duties, and any one who hires his house as a jail to receive such persons, shall be fined and imprisoned. And, finally, it provides that persons paying duties may recover them back with interest.

The next is called "An act to provide for the security and protection of the people of the State of South Carolina."

This act provides, that, if the Government of the United States, or any officer thereof, shall, by the employment of naval or military force, attempt to coerce the State of South Carolina into submission to the acts of Congress declared by the ordinance null and void, or to resist the enforcement of the ordinance, or of the laws passed in pursuance thereof, or in case of any armed or forcible resistance thereto, the Governor is authorized to resist the same, and to order into service the whole, or so much of the military force of the State as he may deem necessary; and that in case of any overt act of coercion, or intention to commit the same, manifested by an unusual assemblage of naval or military forces in or near the State, or the occurrence of any circumstances indicating that armed force is about to be employed against the State or in resistance to its laws, the Governor is authorized to accept the services of such volunteers, and call into service such portions of the militia, as may be required to meet the emergency.

The act also provides for accepting the service of the volunteers, and organizing the militia, embracing all free white males between the ages of sixteen and sixty, and for the purchase of arms, ordinance, and ammunition. It also declares that the power conferred on the Governor shall be applicable to all cases of insurrection or invasion, or imminent danger thereof, and to cases where the laws of the State shall be opposed, and the execution thereof forcibly resisted, by too powerful to be suppressed by the power vested in the sheriffs and other civil officers; and declares it to be the duty of the Governor, in every such case, to call forth such proportions of militia and volunteers as may be necessary promptly to suppress such combinations, and cause the laws of the State to be executed.

No. 9, is "An act concerning the oath

required by the ordinance passed in Convention at Columbia, on the 24th of November, 1832." This act prescribes the form of the oath, which is, to obey and execute the ordinance and all acts passed by the Legislature in pursuance thereof; and directs the time and manner of taking it by the officers of the State, civil, judiciary, and military.

It is believed that other sets have been passed, embracing provisions for enforcing the ordinance, but I have not yet been able to procure them.

I transmit however, a copy of Governor Hamilton's message to the Legislature of South Carolina, of Governor Hayne's inaugural address to the same body, as also of his proclamation, and a general order of the Governor and commander-in-chief, dated the 20th of December, giving public notice that the services of volunteers will be accepted under the act already referred to.

If these measures cannot be defeated and overcome by the power conferred by the Constitution and the Federal Government, the Constitution must be considered as incompetent to its own defence, the supremacy of the laws is at an end, and the rights and liberties of the citizens can no longer receive protection from the Government of the Union. They not only abrogate the acts of Congress, commonly called the tariff acts of 1828 and 1832, but they prostrate and sweep away, at once, and without exception, every act, and every part of every act, imposing any amount whatever of duty on any foreign merchandise; and virtually, every existing act which has ever been passed authorizing the collection of the revenue, including the act of 1816, and, also, the collection law of 1799, the constitutionality of which has never been ques-

tioned. It is not only those duties which are charged to have been imposed for the protection of manufactures that are thereby repealed, but all others, though laid for the purpose of revenue merely, and upon articles in no degree suspected of being objects of protection. The whole revenue system of the United States in South Carolina is obstructed and overthrown; and the Government is absolutely prohibited from collecting any part of the public revenue within the limits of that State. Henceforth, not only the citizens of South Carolina and of the United States, but the subjects of foreign states, may import any description or quantity of merchandise into the ports of South Carolina, without the payment of any duty whatsoever. That the State is thus relieved from the payment of any part of the public burthens, and duties and imports are not only rendered not uniform throughout the United States, but a direct and ruinous preference is given to the ports of that State over those of all the other States of the Union, is manifest violation of the positive provisions of the Constitution.

In point of duration, also, those aggressions upon the authority of Congress, which, by the ordinance, are made part of the fundamental law of South Carolina, are absolute, indefinite, and without limitation. They neither prescribes the period when they shall cease, not indicate any conditions upon which those who have thus undertaken to arrest the operation of the laws are to retrace their steps, and rescind their measures. They offer to the United States no alternative but unconditional submission. If the scope of the ordinance is to be received as the scale of concession, their demands can be satisfied only by a repeal of the whole system of revenue laws, and by abstaining from the collection of any duties and imports whatsoever.

It is true, that in the address to the people of the United States by the Convention of South Carolina, after announcing "the fixed and final determination of the State in relation to the protecting system," they say "that it remains for us to submit a plan of taxation, in which we would be willing to acquiesce, in a liberal spirit of concession, provided we are met in due time, and in a becoming spirit, by the States interested in manufactures." In the opinion of the Convention, an equitable plan would be, that "the whole list of protected articles should be imported free of all duty, and that the revenue derived from import duties shall be raised exclusively from the unprotected articles, or that whenever a duty is imposed upon protected articles imported, an excise duty of the same rate shall be imposed upon all similar articles manufactured in the United States." The address proceeds to state, however, that "they are willing to make a large offering to preserve the Union, and with a distinct declaration that it is a concession on our part, we will consent that the same rate of duty may be imposed upon the protected articles that shall be imposed upon the unprotected, provided that no more revenue raised than is necessary to meet the demands of the Government for constitutional purposes, and provided also that a duty substantially uniform be imposed upon all foreign imports."

It is also true, that, in his message to the Legislature, when urging the ne-

cessity of providing "means of securing their safety by ample resources for repelling force by force," the Governor of South Carolina observes, that he "cannot but think that, on a calm and dispassionate review by Congress, and the functionaries of the General Government, of the true merits of this controversy the arbitration, by a call of a Convention of all the States, which we sincerely and anxiously seek and desire, will be accorded to us."

From the diversity of terms indicated in these two important documents, taken in connexion with the progress of recent events in that quarter, there is too much reason to apprehend, without in any manner doubting the intentions of those public functionaries, that neither the terms proposed in the address of the Convention, not those alluded to in the message of the Governor would appease the excitement which has led to the present excesses. It is obvious, however, that, should the latter be insisted on, they present an alternative which the General Government, of itself, can by no possibility grant, since, by an express provision of the Constitution, Congress can call a convention for the purpose of proposing amendments only "on the application of the Legislatures of two-thirds of the States." And it is not perceived that the terms presented in the address are more practicable than those referred to in the message.

It will not escape attention that the conditions on which it is said, in the address of the Convention, they "would be willing to acquiesce," form on part of the ordinance. While this ordinance bears all the solemnity of a fundamental law, is to be authoritative upon all within the limits of South Carolina, and is absolute and unconditional in its terms, the address conveys only the sentiments of the Convention in no binding or practical form; one is the act of the State, the other only the expression of the opinions of the members of the Convention. To limit the effect of that solemn act by any terms or conditions whatever, they should have been embodied in it, and made of import no less authoritative than the act itself. By the positive enactments of the ordinance, the execution of the laws of the Union is absolutely prohibited; and the address offers no other prospect of their being again restored, even in the modified form proposed than what depends upon the improbable contingency, that, amid changing events and increasing excitement, the sentiments of the present members of the Convention, and of their successors, will remain the same.

It is to be regretted, however, that these conditions, even if they had been offered in the same binding form, are so undefined, depend upon so many contingencies, and are so directly opposed to the known opinions and interests of the great body of the American people, as to be almost hopeless of attainment. The majority of the States, and of the people, will certainly not consent that the protecting duties shall be wholly abrogated, never to be re-enacted at any future time, or in any possible contingency. As little practicable is it to provide that "the same rate of duty shall be imposed upon the protected articles that shall be imposed upon the unprotected;" which, moreover, would be severely oppressive to the poor, and, in time of war, would add greatly to its rigors. And though there can be no objection to the prin-

ciple, properly understood, that no more revenue shall be raised than is necessary for the constitutional purposes of the Government; which principle has been already recommended by the Executive as the true basis of taxation; yet it is very certain that South Carolina alone cannot be permitted to decide what these constitutional purposes are.

The period which constitutes the due time in which the terms proposed in the address are to be accepted, would seem to present scarcely less difficulty than the terms themselves. Though the revenue laws are already declared to be void in South Carolina, as well as the bonds taken under them, and the judicial proceedings for carrying them into effect, yet, as the full action and operation of the ordinance are to be suspended until the first of February, the interval may be assumed as the time within which it is expected that the most complicated portion of the national legislation, a system of long standing, and affecting great interest in the community, is to be rescinded and abolished. If this be required, it is clear that a compliance is impossible.

In the uncertainty, then, that exists as to the duration of the ordinance, and of the enactments for enforcing it, it becomes imperiously the duty of the Executive of the United States, acting with a proper regard to all the great interests committed to his care, to treat those acts as absolute and unlimited. They are so, as far as his agency is concerned. He cannot either embrace or lead to the performance of the conditions. He has already discharged the only part in his power, by the recommendation in his annual message. The rest is with Congress and the people;

and until they have acted, his duty will require him to look to the existing state of things, and act under them according to his high obligations.

By these various proceedings, therefore, the State of South Carolina has forced the General Government, unavoidably, to decide the new and dangerous alternative of permitting a State to obstruct the execution of the laws within its limits, or seeing it attempt to execute a threat of withdrawing from the Union. That portion of the people at present exercising the authority of the State, solemnly assert their right to do either, and as solemnly announce their determination to do one or the other.

In my opinion, both purposes are to be regarded as revolutionary in their character and tendency, and subversive of the supremacy of the laws and of the integrity of the Union. The result of each is the same; since a State in which, by an usurpation of power, the constitutional authority of the Federal Government is openly defied and set aside, wants only the form to be independent of the Union.

The right of the people of a single State to absolve themselves at will, and without the consent of the other States, from their most solemn obligations, and hazard the liberties and happiness of the millions composing this Union, cannot be acknowledged. Such authority is believed to be utterly repugnant both to the principles upon which the General Government is constituted, and to the objects which it is expressly formed to attain.

Against all acts which may be alleged to transcend the constitutional power of the Government, or which may be inconvenient or oppressive in their operation, the Constitution itself has prescribed the modes of redress. It is the acknowledged attribute of free institutions that, under them, the empire of reason and law is substituted for the power of the sword. To no other source can appeals for supposed wrongs be made, consistently with the obligations of South Carolina; to no other can such appeals be made with safety at any time; and to their decisions, when constitutionality pronounced, it becomes the duty, no less of the public authorities than of the people, in every case to yield to a patriotic submission.

That a State, or any other great portion of the people, suffering under long and intolerable oppression, and having tried all constitutional remedies, without the hope of redress, may have a natural right, when their happiness can be no otherwise secured, and when they can do so without greater injury to others, to absolve themselves from their obligations to the Government, and appeal to the last resort, needs not, on the present occasion, be denied.

The existence of this right, however, must depend upon the causes which may justify its exercise. It is the *ultima ratio*, which presupposes that the proper appeals to all other means of redress have been made in good faith, and which can never be rightfully resorted to unless it be unavoidable. It is not the right of the State, but of the individual, and of all the individuals of the State. It is the right of mankind generally to secure, by all the means in their power, the blessings of liberty and happiness; but when, for these purposes, any body of men have voluntarily associated themselves under a particular form of government, no portion of them can dissolve the association without acknowledging the relative right in the remainder to decide whether that dissolution can be permitted consistently with the general happiness. In this view, it is a right dependent upon the power to enforce it. Such a right, though it may be admitted to pre-exist, and cannot be wholly surrendered, is necessarily subjected to limitations in all free governments, and in compacts of all kinds, freely and voluntarily entered into, and in which the interest and welfare of the individual become identified with those of the community to create a scared obligation; and in compacts of civil government, involving the liberties and happiness of millions of mankind, the obligation cannot be less.

Without adverting to the particular theories to which the federal compact has given rise, both as to its formation and the parties to it, and without inquiring whether it be merely federal, or social, or national, it is sufficient that it must be admitted to be a company, and to possess the obligations incident to a compact; to be "a compact by which power is created on the one hand, and obedience exacted on the other; a compact freely, voluntarily, and solemnly, entered into by the several States, and the people thereof, respectively; a compact by which the Federal Government is bound to the several States, and to every citizen of the United States." To this compact, in whatever mode it may have been done, the people of South Carolina have freely and voluntarily given their assent; and to the whole and every part of it, they are, upon every principle of good faith, inviolably bound. Under this obligation they are bound, and

should be required, to contribute their portion of the public expense, and to submit to all the laws made by the common consent, in pursuance of the Constitution, for the common defence and general welfare, until they can be changed in the mode which the compact has provided for the attainment of those great ends of the Government and of the Union. Nothing less than causes which would justify revolutionary remedy, can absolve the people from this obligation; and for nothing less can the Government permit it to be done without violating its own obligations, by which, under the compact, it is bound to the other States, and to every citizen of the United States.

These deductions plainly flow from the nature of the federal company, which is one of the limitations, not only upon the powers originally possessed by the parties thereto, but also upon those conferred on the Government, and every department thereof. It will be freely conceded that, by the principles of our system, all power is vested in the people; but to be exercised in the mode, and subject to the checks, which the people themselves have prescribed. These checks are, undoubtedly, only different modifications of the same great popular principle which lies at the foundation of the whole, but are not, on that account, to be less regarded or less obligatory.

Upon the power of Congress, the veto of the Executive, and the authority of the judiciary, which is to extend to all cases in law and equity arising under the Constitution and laws of the United States made in pursuance thereof, are the obvious checks; and the sound action of public opinion, with the ultimate power of amendment, are the salutary and only limitation upon the powers of the whole.

However it may be alleged that a violation of the compact, by the measures of the Government, can affect the obligations of the parties, it cannot even be pretended that such violation can be predicted of those measures until all the constitutional remedies shall have been fully tried. If the Federal Government exercise powers not warranted by the Constitution, and immediately affecting individuals, it will scarcely be denied that the proper remedy is a recourse to the judiciary. Such, undoubtedly, is the remedy for those who deem the acts of Congress laying duties and imports and providing for their collection, to be unconstitutional. The whole operation of such laws is upon the individuals importing the merchandise. A State is absolutely prohibited from laying imports or duties on imports or exports, without the consent of Congress, and cannot become a party, under these laws, without importing in her own name, or wrongfully interposing her authority against them. By thus interposing, however, she cannot rightfully obstruct the operation of the laws upon individuals. For their disobedience to, or violation of, the laws, the ordinary remedies through the judicial tribunal would remain. And in a case where an individual should be prosecuted for any offence against the laws, he could not set up, in justification of his act, a law of the State, which, being unconstitutional, would therefore be regarded as null and void. The law of a State cannot authorize the commission of a crime against the United States, or any other act which, according to the supreme law of the Union, would be oth-

erwise unlawful. And it is equally clear, that, if there be any case in which a State, as such, is affected by the law beyond the scope of judicial power, the remedy consists in appeals to the people, either to effect a change in the representation, or to procure relief by an amendment of the Constitution. But the measure of the Government are to be recognized as valid, and, consequently, supreme, until these remedies shall have been effectually tried; and any attempt to subvert those measures, or to render the laws subordinate to State authority, and, afterwards, to resort to constitutional redress, is worse than evasive. It would not be a proper resistance to "a government of unlimited powers," as has been sometimes pretended, but unlawful opposition to the very limitations on which the harmonious action of the Government, and all its parts, absolutely depends. South Carolina has appealed to none of these remedies, but, in effect, has defied them all. While threatening to separate from the Union if any attempt be made to enforce the revenue laws otherwise then through the civil tribunals of the country, she has not only not appealed in her own name to those tribunals which the Constitution has provided for all cases in law or equity arising under the Constitution and laws of the United States, but has endeavored to frustrate their proper action on her citizens, by drawing the cognizance of cases under the revenue laws to her own tribunals, especially prepared and fitted for the purpose of enforcing the acts passed by the State to obstruct these laws, and both the judges and jurors of which will be bound, by the imports of oaths previously taken, to treat the Constitution and laws of the United States in this respect as a nullity. Nor has the State made the proper appeal to public opinion, and to the remedy of amendment. For, without waiting to learn whether the other States will consent to a Convention, or, if they do, will construe or amend the Constitution to suit her views, she has, of her own authority, altered the import of that Instrument, and given immediate effect to the change. In fine, she has set her own cause, and has passed at once all intermediate steps to measures of avowed resistance, which, unless they be submitted to, can be enforced only by the sword.

In deciding upon the course which a high sense of duty to all the people of the United States imposes upon the authorities of the Union in this emergency, it cannot be overlooked that there is no sufficient cause for the acts of South Carolina, or for her thus placing in jeopardy the happiness of so many millions of people. Misrule and oppression, to warrant the disruption of the free institutions of the Union of these States, should be great and lasting, defying all other remedy. For causes of minor character, the Government could not submit to such a catastrophe, without a violation of its most sacred obligations to the other States of the Union, who have submitted their destiny to its hands.

There is, in the present instance, no such cause, either in degree of misrule or oppression complained of, or in the hopelessness of redress by constitutional means. The long sanction they have received from the proper authorities and from the people, not less than the unexampled growth and increasing prosperity of so many millions of free-men, attest that no such oppression as would justify or even palliate such a resort, can be justly imputed with to the present policy or past measures of the Federal Government. The same made of collecting duties, and for the same general objects, which began with the foundation of the Government, and which has conducted the country through its subsequent steps to its present evitable condition of happiness and renown, has not been changed. Taxation and representation, the greatest principle of the American revolution, have continually gone hand in hand: and at all times, and in every instance, no tax of any kind has been imposed without their participation; and, in some instance, which have been complained of, no revenue has been raised beyond the necessary wants of the country, and the authorized expenditures of the Government. And as soon as the burthen of the public debt is removed, those charged with the administration have promptly recommended a corresponding reduction of revenue.

That this system, thus pursued, has resulted in no such oppression upon South Carolina, needs no further proof than the solemn and official declaration of the late chief magistrate of that State in his address to the Legislature. In that he says, that "the occurrences of the past year, in connexion with our domestic concerns, are to be reviewed with a sentiment of fervent gratitude of the Great Disposer of human events; that tributes of grateful acknowledgment are due for the various and multiplied blessings he has been pleased to bestow on our people; that abundant harvests in every quarter of the State have crowned the exertions of agricultural labor; that health, almost beyond former precedent, has blessed our homes; and that there is not less reason for thankfulness in surveying our social condition." It would, indeed, be difficult to imagine oppression there, as for abundant harvests, and varied and multiplied blessings with which a kind Providence had favored them.

Independently of these considerations, it will not escape observation, that South Carolina still claims to be a component part of the Union, to participate in the national councils, and to share in the public benefits, without contributing to the public burdens—thus asserting the dangerous anomaly of continuing in an association without acknowledging any other obligation to its laws than what depends upon her own will.

In this posture of affairs, the duty of the Government seems to be plain. It inculcates a recognition of that State as a member of the Union, and subject to its authority; a vindication of the just power of the Constitution; the preservation of the integrity of the Union; and the execution of the laws by all constitutional means.

The Constitution, which his oath of office obliges him to support, declares that the Executive *"shall take care that the laws be faithfully executed;"* and, in providing that he shall, from time to time, give to Congress information of the state of the Union, and recommend to their consideration such measures as he shall judge necessary and expedient, imposed the additional obligation of recommending to Congress such more efficient provision for executing the laws, as may, from time to time, be found expedient.

The same instrument confers on Congress the power not merely to lay and collect taxes, duties, imposts, and excises, to pay the debts and provide for the common defence and general welfare; but "to make all laws which shall be necessary and proper for carrying into effect the foregoing powers, and all other powers vested by the Constitution in the Government of the United States, or in any department or officer thereof;" and, also, to provide for calling forth the militia for executing the laws of the Union. In all cases similar to the present, the duties of the Government become the measure of its powers; and whenever it fails to exercise a power necessary and proper to the discharge of the duty prescribed by the Constitution, it violates the public trusts not less than it would in transcending its proper limits. To refrain, therefore, from the high and solemn duties thus enjoined, however painful the performance may be, and thereby tacitly permit the rightful authority of the Government to be condemned, and its laws obstructed by a single State, would neither comport with its own safety, nor the rights of the great body of the American people.

It being thus shown to be the duty of the Executive to execute the laws by all constitutional means, it remains to consider the extent of those already at his disposal, and what it may be proper further to provide.

In the instructions of the Secretary of the Treasury to the collectors in South Carolina, the provisions and regulations made by the act of 1799, and also the fines, penalties, and forfeitures, for their enforcement, are particularly detailed and explained. It may be well apprehended, however, that these provisions may prove inadequate to meet such an open, powerful, organized opposition, as is to be commenced after the first of February next.

Subsequently to the date of these instructions, and to the passage of the ordinance, information has been received, from sources entitled to be relied on, that, owing to the popular excitement in the State, and the effect of the ordinance declaring the execution of the revenue laws unlawful, a sufficient number of persons, in whom confidence might be placed, could not be induced to accept the office of inspector, to oppose, with any probability of success, the force which will, no doubt, be used when an attempt is made to remove vessels and their cargoes from the custody of the officers of the customs; and, indeed, that it would be impracticable for the collector, with the aid of any number of inspectors whom he may be authorized to employ, to preserve the custody against such an attempt.

The removal of the custom-house from Charleston to Castle Pinckney was deemed a measure of necessary precaution; and, though the authority to give that direction is not questioned, it is nevertheless apparent that a similar precaution cannot be observed in regard to the ports of Georgetown and Beaufort, each of which, under the present laws, remains a port of entry, and exposed to the obstructions meditated in that quarter.

In considering the best means of avoiding or of preventing the apprehended obstruction to the collection of the revenue, and the consequences which may ensure, it would appear to be proper and necessary to enable the officers of the customs to preserve the custody of vessels and their cargoes, which, by the existing laws, they are required to take, until the duties to which they are liable shall be paid or secured. The mode by which it is contemplated to deprive them of that custody, is the process of replevin, and that of *capias in withernam,* in the nature of a distress from the State tribunals organized by the ordinance.

Against the proceeding in the nature of a distress, it is not perceived that the collector can interpose any resistance whatever; and against the process of replevin authorized by the law of the State, he, having no common law power, can only oppose such inspectors as he is by statute authorized, and may find it practicable to employ; and these, from the information already adverted to, are shown to be wholly inadequate.

The respect which that process deserves, must therefore be considered.

If the authorities of South Carolina has not obstructed the legitimate action of the courts of the United States, or if they had permitted the State tribunals to administer the law according to their oath under their Constitution and the regulations of the laws of the Union, the General Government might have been content to look to them for maintaining the custody, and to encounter the other inconveniences arising out of the recent proceedings. Even in that case, however, the process of replevin from the courts of the States would be irregular and unauthorized. It has been decided by the Supreme Court of the United States that the courts of the United States have exclusive jurisdiction of all seizures made on land or water for a breach of the laws of the United States, and any intervention of a State authority, which, by taking the thing seized out of the hands of the United States' officer, might obstruct the exercise of this jurisdiction, is unlawful; that, in such case, the court of the United States having cognizance of the seizure, may enforce a re-delivery of the thing by attachment or other summary process; that the question under such a seizure, whether a forfeiture has been actually incurred, belongs exclusively to the courts of the United States, and it depends on the final decree, whether the seizure is to be deemed rightful or tortuous; and that not until the seizure be finally judged wrongful and without probable cause by the courts of the United States, can the party proceed at common law for damages in the State courts.

But, by making it "unlawful for any of the constituted authorities, whether of the United States or of the State, to enforce the laws for the payment of duties, and declaring that all judicial proceedings which shall be hereafter had in affirmance of the contracts made with purpose to secure the duties imposed by the said acts, are, and shall be held utterly null and void," she has, in effect, abrogated the judicial tribunals within her limits in this respect; has virtually denied the United States access to the courts established by their own laws; and declared it unlawful for the judges to discharge those duties which they are sworn to perform. In lieu of these, she has substituted those State tribunals already adverted to, the judges whereof are not merely forbidden to allow an appeal or permit a copy of their record, but are previously sworn to disregard the laws of the Union, and enforce those only of South Carolina; and, thus deprived of the

function essential to the judicial character, or inquiring into the validity of the law and the right of the matter, become merely ministerial instruments in aid of the concerted obstruction of the laws of the Union.

Neither the process nor the authority of these tribunals, thus constituted, can be respected, consistently with the supremacy of the laws or the rights and security of the citizen. If they be submitted to, the protection due from the Government to its officers and citizens is withheld, and there is, at once, an end, not only to the laws, but to the Union itself.

Against such a force as the sheriff may, and which, by the replevin law of South Carolina, it is his duty to exercise, it cannot be expected that a collector can retain his custody with the aid of the inspectors. In such case, it is true, it would be competent to institute suits in the United States' courts against those engaged in the unlawful proceeding; or the property might be seized for a violation of the revenue laws, and, being libeled in the proper courts, an order might be made for its re-delivery, which would be committed to the marshal for execution. But, in that case, the 4th section of the act, in broad and unqualified terms, makes it the duty of the sheriff "to prevent such recapture or seizure, or to re-deliver the goods, as the case may be," "even under any process, order, or decrees, or other pretext, contrary to the true intent and meaning of the ordinance aforesaid." It is thus the duty of the sheriff to oppose the process of the courts of the United States, and, for that purpose, if need be, to employ the whole power of the county. And the act expressly reserves to him all power, which, independently of its provisions, he could have used. In this reservation, it obviously contemplates a resort to other means than those particularly mentioned.

It is not to be disguised that the power which it is thus enjoined upon the sheriff to employ, is nothing less than the *posse comitatis*, in all the rigor of the ancient common law. This power, though it may be used against unlawful resistance to judicial process, is, in its character, forcible, and analogous to that conferred upon the marshals by the act of 1795. It is, in fact, the embodying of the whole mass of the population, under the command of a single individual, to accomplish, by their forcible aid, what could not be effected peaceably and by the ordinary means. It may properly be said to be a relict of those ages in which the laws could be defended rather by physical than moral force, and, in its origin, was conferred upon the sheriffs of England to enable them to defend their county against any of the king's enemies when they came into the land, as well as for the purpose of executing process. In early, and less civilized, times it was intended to include "the aid and attendance of all knights and others who were bound to have harness." It includes the right of going with arms and military equipment, and embraces larger classes and greater masses of population than can be compelled by the laws of most of the States to perform militia duty. If the principles of the common law are recognized in South Carolina, (and from this act it would seem they are,) the power of summoning the *posse comitatis* will compel, under the penalty of fine and imprisonment, every man over the age of fifteen, and able to travel, to turn out, at the call of the sheriff, and with such weapons as may be necessary; and it may justify beating, and even killing, such as may resist. The use of the *posse comitatis* is, therefore, a direct application of force, and cannot be otherwise regarded than as the employment of the whole militia force of the county, and in an equally efficient form, under a different name. No proceeding which resorts to this power, to the extent contemplated by the act, can be properly denominated peaceable.

The act of South Carolina, however, does not rely altogether upon this forcible remedy. For even attempting to resist of destroy—though by the aid only of the ordinary officers of the customs—the process of replevin, the collector and all concerned are subjected to a further proceeding in the nature of a distress of their personal effects; and are, moreover, made guilty of a misdemeanor, and liable to be punished by a fine or not less than one thousand, not more than five thousand dollars, and to imprisonment not exceeding two years, and not less than six months; and for even attempting to execute the order of the court for retaking property, the marshal, and all assisting, would be guilty of a misdemeanor, and liable to a fine or not less than three thousand dollars, not more than ten thousand, and to imprisonment not exceeding two years, nor less than one, and, in case of goods should be retaken under such process, it is made the absolute duty of the sheriff to retake them.

It is not to be supposed that, in the face of these penalties, aided by the powerful force of the county, which would doubtless be brought to sustain the State officers, either that the collector would retain the custody in the first instance, or that the marshal could summon sufficient aid to retake the property pursuant to the order or other process of the court.

It is, moreover, obvious that in this conflict between the powers of the officers of the United States and of the State, (unless the latter be passively submitted to,) the destruction to which the property of the officers of the customs would be exposed, the commission of actual violence, and the loss of lives, would be scarcely avoidable.

Under these circumstances, and the provisions of the acts of South Carolina, the execution of the laws is rendered impracticable even through the ordinary judicial tribunals of the United States. There would certainly be fewer difficulties, and less opportunity of actual collision between the officers of the United States and of the State, and the collection of the revenue would be more effectually secured—if indeed it can be done in any other way—by placing the custom-house beyond the immediate power of the county.

For this purpose, it might be proper to provide that whenever, by any unlawful combination or obstruction in any State, or in any port, it should become impracticable faithfully to collect the duties the President of the United States should be authorized to alter and abolish such of the districts and ports of entry as should be necessary, and to establish the custom-house at some secure place within some port or harbor of such State; and, in such cases, it should be the duty of the collector to reside at such place, and to detain all vessels and cargoes until the duties imposed by law should be properly secured or paid in case, deducting interest; that, in such cases, it should be unlawful to take the vessel and cargo from the custody of the proper officer of the customs, unless by process from the ordinary judicial tribunals of the United States; and that, in case of an attempt otherwise to take the property by a force too great to be overcome by the officers by the employment of the land and naval forces and militia, under provisions similar to those authorized by the 11th section of the act of the 9th of January, 1809.

This provision, however, would not shield the officers and citizens of the United States, acting under the laws, from suits and prosecutions, in the tribunals of the States which might thereafter be brought against them; nor would it protect their property from the proceeding by distress; and it may well be apprehended that it would be insufficient to insure a proper respect to the process of the constitutional tribunals in prosecutions for offences against the United States, and to protect the authorities of the United States, whether judicial or ministerial, in the performance of their duties. It would, moreover, be inadequate to extend the protection due from the Government to that portion of the people of South Carolina, against outrage and oppression of any kind, who may manifest their attachment, and yield obedience to the laws of the Union.

It may therefore be desirable to revive, with some modifications better adapted to the occasion, the 6th section of the act of the 3d March, 1815, which expired on the 4th March, 1817, by the limitation of that of 27th April, 1816, and to provide that, in any case where suit shall be brought against any individual in the courts of the States, for any act done under the laws of the United States, he should be authorized to remove the said cause, by petition, into the circuit court of the United States, without any copy of the record, and that the court should proceed to hear and determine the same as if it had been originally instituted therein. And that in all cases of injuries to the persons or property of individuals for disobedience to the ordinance and laws of South Carolina, in pursuance thereof, redress may be sought in the courts of the United States. It may be expedient, also, by modifying the resolution of the 3d March, 1791, to authorize the marshals to make the necessary provision for the safe keeping of prisoners committed under the authority of the United States.

Provisions less than these, consisting, as they do, for the most part, rather of a revival of the policy of former acts called for by the existing emergency, than of the introduction of any unusual or rigorous enactments, would not cause the laws of the Union to be properly respected or enforced. It is believed these would prove inadequate, unless the military forces of the State of South Carolina, authorized by the late act of the Legislature, should be actually embodied and called out in aid of their proceedings, and of the provisions of the ordinance generally. Even in that case, however, it is believed that no more will be necessary than a few modifications of its terms, to adapt the act of 1795 to the present emergency, as, by that act, the provisions of the law of 1792, were accommodated to the crisis then existing; and by conferring authority upon the President to give it operation during the session of Congress, and without the ceremony of a proclamation, whenever it shall be officially made known to him by the authority of any State, or by the courts of the United States, that, within the limits of such State, the laws of the United States will be openly opposed, and their execution obstructed by the actual employment of military force, or by any unlawful means whatsoever, too great to be otherwise overcome.

In closing this communication, I should do injustice to my own feelings not to express my confident reliance upon the disposition of each department of the Government to perform its duty, and to co-operate in all measures necessary in the present emergency.

The crisis undoubtedly invokes the fidelity of the patriot and the sagacity of the statesman, not more in removing such portion of the public burden as may be necessary, than in preserving the good order of society, and in the maintenance of well regulated liberty.

While a forbearing spirit may, and I trust will, be exercised towards the errors of our brethren in a particular quarter, duty to the rest of the Union demands that open and organized resistance to the laws should not be executed with impunity.

The rich inheritance bequeathed by our fathers has devolved upon us the sacred obligation of preserving it by the same virtues which conducted them through the eventful scenes of the revolution, and ultimately crowned their struggle with the noblest model of civil institutions. They bequeathed to us a Government of laws, and a federal Union founded upon the great principle of popular representation. After a successful experiment of forty-four years, at a moment when the Government and the Union are the objects of the hopes of the friends of civil liberty throughout the world, and in the midst of public and individual prosperity unexampled in history, we are called to decide whether these laws possess any force, and that Union the means of self-preservation. The decision of this question by an enlightened and patriotic people cannot be doubtful. For myself, fellow citizens, devoutly relying upon that kind Providence which has hitherto watched over our destines, and actuated by a profound reverence for those institutions I have so much cause to love, and for the American people, whose partiality honored me with their highest trust, I have determined to spare no effort to discharge the duty which, in this conjuncture, is devolved upon me. That a similar spirit will actuate the Representatives of the American people is not to be questioned; and I fervently pray that the Great Ruler of nations may so guide your deliberations, and our joint measures, as that they may prove salutary examples, not only to the present, but to future times; and solemnly proclaim that the Constitution and the laws are supreme, and the *Union indissoluble.*

Andrew Jackson
Washington, January 16, 1833.

See also: **Vol. I**: American System; Calhoun, John Caldwell; Clay, Henry; Clay's Compromise; Force Act; Jackson, Andrew; Nullification; South Carolina *Exposition* and *Protest*; Tariff of 1816; Tariff of 1824; Tariff of 1828 (Tariff of Abominations); Tariff of 1832; Tariff of 1833 (Compromise Tariff). **Vol. III**: Tariff of 1824; Tariff of 1828 (Tariff of Abominations); Tariff of 1832; Tariff of 1833 (Compromise Tariff).

Force Act

The passage of the Compromise Tariff of 1833 coincided with the passage of the Force Act. This measure authorized the president to use military force, if necessary, to ensure the collection of the tariff duties in the port of Charleston and throughout the state of South Carolina. Jackson signed both acts into law at the same time. South Carolina responded by rescinding the Ordinance of Nullification, but then nullified the Force Act purely on principle.

An Act further to provide for the collection of duties on imports.

Be it enacted by the Senate and House of Representatives of the United States of America, in Congress assembled, That whenever, by reason of unlawful obstructions, combinations, or assemblages of persons, it shall become impracticable, in the judgment of the President, to execute the revenue laws, and collect the duties on imports in the ordinary way, in any collection district, it shall and may be lawful for the President to direct that the custom-house for such district be established and kept in any secure place within some port or harbour of such district, either upon land or on board any vessel; and, in that case, it shall be the duty of the collector to reside at such place, and there to detain all vessels and cargoes arriving within the said district until the duties imposed on said cargoes, by law, be paid in cash, deducting interest according to existing laws; and in such cases it shall be unlawful to take the vessel or cargo from the custody of the proper officer of the customs, unless by process from some court of the United States; and in case of any attempt otherwise to take such vessel or cargo by any force, or combination, or assemblage of persons too great to be overcome by the officers of the customs, it shall and may be lawful for the President of the United States, or such person or persons as he shall have empowered for that purpose, to employ such part of the land or naval forces, or militia of the United States, as may be deemed necessary for the purpose of preventing the removal of such vessel or cargo, and protecting the officers of the customs in retaining the custody thereof.

SEC. 2. And be it further enacted, That the jurisdiction of the circuit courts of the United States shall extend to all cases, in law or equity, arising under the revenue laws of the United States, for which other provisions are not already made by law; and if any person shall receive any injury to his person or property for or on account of any act by him done, under any law of the United States, for the protection of the revenue or the collection of duties on imports, he shall be entitled to maintain suit for damage therefor in the circuit court of the United States in the district wherein the party doing the injury may reside, or shall be found. And all property taken or detained by any officer or other person under authority of any revenue law of the United States, shall be irrepleviable, and shall be deemed to be in the custody of the law, and subject only to the orders and decrees of the courts of the United States having jurisdiction thereof. And if any person shall dispossess or rescue, or attempt to dispossess or rescue, any property so taken or detained as aforesaid, or shall aid or assist therein, such person shall be deemed guilty of a misdemeanour, and shall be liable to such punishment of certain crimes against the United States, approved the thirtieth day of April, Anno Domini one thousand seven hundred and ninety; for the willful obstruction or resistance of officers in the service of process.

SEC. 3. And be it further enacted, That in any case where suit or prosecution shall be commenced in a court of any state, against any officer of the United States, or other person, for or on account of any act done under the revenue laws of the United States, or under colour thereof, or for or on account of any right, authority, or title, set up or claimed by such officer, or other person under any such law of the United States, it shall be lawful for the defendant in such suit or prosecution, at any time before trial, upon a petition to the circuit court of the United States, in and for the district in which the defendant shall have been served with process, setting forth the nature of said suit or prosecution, and verifying the said petition by affidavit, together with a certificate signed by an attorney or counsellor at law of some court of record of the state in which such suit shall have been commenced, or of the United States, setting forth that, as counsel for the petitioner, he has examined the proceedings against him, and has carefully inquired into all the matters set forth in the petition, and that he believes the same to be true; which petition, affidavit, and certificate, shall be presented to the said circuit court, if in session, and if not, to the clerk thereof, at his office, and shall be filed in said office, if the suit were commenced in the court below by summons, to issue a writ of certiorari to the state court, requiring said court to send to the said circuit court the record and proceedings in such cause; or if it were commenced by capias, he shall issue a writ of habeas corpus cum cause, a duplicate of which said writ shall be delivered to the clerk of the state court, or left at his office by the marshal of the district, or his deputy, or some person duly authorized thereto; and, thereto, and, thereupon it shall be the duty of the said state court to stay all further proceedings in such cause, and the said suit or prosecution, upon delivery of such process, or leaving the same as aforesaid, shall be deemed and taken to be moved to the said circuit court, and any further proceedings, trial or judgment therein in the state court shall be wholly null and void. And if the defendant in any such suit be in actual custody on mesne process therein, it shall be the duty of the marshal, by virtue of the writ of habeas corpus cum cause, to take the body of the defendant into his custody, to be dealt with in the said cause according to the rules of law and the order of the circuit court, or of any judge thereof, in vacation. And all attachments made and all bail and other security given upon such suit, or prosecution, shall be and continue in like force and effect, as if the same suit or prosecution had proceeded to final judgment and execution in the state court. And if, upon the removal of any such suit, or prosecution, it shall be made to appear to the said circuit court that no copy of the record and proceedings therein, in the state court, can be obtained, it shall be lawful for said circuit court to allow and require the plaintiff to proceed *de novo*, and to file declaration of his cause of action, and the parties may thereupon proceed as in actions originally brought in said circuit court; and on failure of so proceeding, judgment of *non pros.* may be rendered against the plaintiff with costs for the defendant.

SEC. 4. And be it further enacted, That in any case in which any party is, or may be by law, entitled to copies of the record and proceedings in any suit or prosecution in any state court, to be used in any court of the United States, if the clerk of said state court shall, upon demand, and the payment or tender of the legal fees, refuse or neglect to deliver to such party certified copies of such record and proceedings, the court of the United States in which such record and proceedings may be needed, on proof, by affidavit, that the clerk of such state court has refused or neglected to deliver copies thereof, on demand as aforesaid, may direct and allow such record to be supplied by affidavit, or otherwise, as the circumstances of the case may require and allow; and, thereupon, such proceeding, trial, and judgment, may be had in the said court of the United States, and all such processes awarded, as if certified copies of such records and proceedings had been regularly before the said court.

SEC. 5. And be it further enacted, That whenever the President of the United States shall be officially informed, by the authorities of any state, or by a judge of any circuit or district court of the United States, in the state, that, within the limits of such state, any law or laws of the United States, or the execution thereof, or of any process from the courts of the United States, is obstructed by the employment of military force, or by any other unlawful means, too great to be overcome by the ordinary course of judicial proceeding, or by the powers vested in the marshal by existing laws, it shall be lawful for him, the President of the United States, forthwith to issue his proclamation, declaring such fact or information, and requiring all such military and other force forthwith to disperse; and if at any time after issuing such proclamation, any such opposition or obstruction shall be made, in the manner or by the means aforesaid, the President shall be, and hereby is, authorized, promptly to employ such means to suppress the same, and to cause the said laws or process to be duly executed, as are authorized and provided in the cases therein mentioned by the act of the twenty-eighth of February, one thousand seven hundred and ninety-five, entitled "An act to provide for calling forth the militia to execute the laws of the Union, suppress insurrections, repel invasions, and to repeal the act now in force for that purpose;" and also, by the act of the third of March, one thousand eight hundred and seven, entitled "An act authorizing the employment of the land and naval forces of the United States in cases of insurrection."

SEC. 6. And be it further enacted, That in any state where the jails are not allowed to be used for the imprisonment of persons arrested or committed under the laws of the United States, or where houses are not allowed to be so used, it shall and may be lawful for any marshal, under the direction of the judge of the United States for the proper district, to use other convenient places, within the limits of said state, and to make such other provision as he may deem expedient and necessary for that purpose.

SEC. 7. And be it further enacted, That either of the justices of the Supreme Court, or a judge of any district of the United States, in addition to the authority already conferred by law, shall have power to grant writs of habeas corpus in all cases of a prisoner or prisoners, in jail or confinement, where he or they shall be committed or confined on, or by any authority or law, for any act done, or omitted to be done, in pursuance of a law of the United States, or any order, process, or decree, of any judge or court thereof, any thing in any act of Congress to the contrary notwithstanding. And if any person or persons to whom such writ of habeas corpus may be directed, shall refuse to obey the same, or shall neglect or refuse to make return, or shall made a false return thereto, in addition to the remedies already given by law, he or they shall be deemed and taken to be guilty of a misdemeanor, and shall, on the conviction before any court of competent jurisdiction, be punished by fine, not exceeding one thousand dollars, and by imprisonment, not exceeding six months, or by either, according to the nature and aggravation of the case.

SEC. 8. And be it further enacted, That the several provisions contained in the first and fifth sections of this act, shall be in force until the end of the next session of Congress, and no longer.

APPROVED, March 2, 1833.

See also: **Vol. I**: American System; Calhoun, John Caldwell; Clay, Henry; Clay's Compromise; Force Act; Jackson, Andrew; Nullification; South Carolina *Exposition* and *Protest*; Tariff of 1816; Tariff of 1824; Tariff of 1828 (Tariff of Abominations); Tariff of 1832; Tariff of 1833 (Compromise Tariff). **Vol. III**: Tariff of 1824; Tariff of 1828 (Tariff of Abominations); Tariff of 1832; Tariff of 1833 (Compromise Tariff).

Walker's Report

On December 3, 1845, Secretary of the Treasury Robert J. Walker submitted his report on the state of the finances to the Twenty-ninth Congress. Walker noted that the revenue from tariff duties had decreased during the past year and he attributed the change to the high rates passed under the Tariff of 1842. He recommended that Congress reduce the tax on non-luxury items to the lowest point that yielded the highest revenue. He also argued for a revenue-only tariff instead of continuing the protectionist policy of the last three decades. Walker's controversial report helped Democrats pass the Tariff of 1846, also known as Walker's Tariff, which reduced the average rate from 33 to 25 percent while taxing luxury items at rates of up to 100 percent. The report revived the debate over free trade in the United States.

The receipts of the first quarter of this year are less by $2,011,885.90 than the receipts of the same quarter last year. Among the causes of decrease is the progressive diminution of the importation of many highly protected articles and the substitution of rival domestic products. For the nine months ending June 30, 1843, since the present tariff, the average of duties upon dutiable imports was equal to 37.84 1-10 per cent; for the year ending June 30, 1844, 33.85 9-10 per cent; and for the year ending June 30, 1845, 29.90 per cent, showing a great diminution in the average percentage, owing in part to increased importation of some articles bearing the lighter duties and decreased importation of others bearing the higher duty.

The revenue from *ad valorem* duties last year exceeded that realized from specific duties, although the average of the *ad valorem* duties was only 23.57 per cent, and the average of the specific duties 41.30, presenting another strong proof that lower duties increase the revenue. Among the causes tending to augment the revenue are increased emigration and the annexation of Texas. The estimates for the expenditures of 1846 are based chiefly upon appropriations made by Congress. The estimated expenditures of 1847 are founded upon data furnished by the several departments and are less by $4,108,238.65 than those of the preceding year.

These estimates are submitted in the full conviction that whenever Congress, guided by an enlightened economy, can diminish the expenditures without injury to the public interest, such retrenchment will be made, so as to lighten the burden of taxation and hasten the extinguishment of the public debt, reduced on the 1st of October last to $17,075,445.52.

In suggesting improvements in the revenue laws the following principles have been adopted:

First. That no more money should be collected than is necessary for the wants of the Government, economically administered.

Second. That no duty be imposed on any article above the lowest rate which will yield the largest amount of revenue.

Third. That below such rate discrimination may be made, descending in the scale of duties, or, for imperative reasons, the article may be placed in the list of those free from all duty.

Fourth. That the maximum revenue duty should be imposed on luxuries.

Fifth. That all minimums and all specific duties should be abolished and *ad valorem* duties substituted in their place, care being taken to guard against fraudulent invoices and undervaluation, and to assess the duty upon the actual market value.

Sixth. That the duty should be so imposed as to operate as equally as possible throughout the Union, discriminating neither for nor against any class or section.

No horizontal scale of duties is recommended, because such a scale would be a refusal to discriminate for revenue and might sink that revenue below the wants of the Government. Some articles will yield the largest revenue at duties that would be wholly or partially prohibitory in other cases. Luxuries, as a general rule, will bear the highest revenue duties; but even some very costly luxuries, easily smuggled, will bear but a light duty for revenue, whilst other articles, of great bulk and weight, will bear a higher duty for revenue. There is no instance within the knowledge of this department of any horizontal tariff ever having been enacted by any one of the nations of the world. There must be discrimination for revenue or the burden of taxation must be augmented in order to bring the same amount of money into the treasury. It is difficult, also, to adopt any arbitrary maximum to which an inflexible adherence must be demanded in all cases. Thus, upon brandy and spirits, a specific duty, varying as an equivalent *ad valorem* from 180 to 261 per cent, yields a large revenue; yet no one would propose either of these rates as a maximum. These duties are too high for revenue, from the encouragement they present for smuggling these baneful luxuries; yet a duty of 20 per cent upon brandy and spirits would be far below the revenue standard, would greatly diminish the income on these imports, require increased burdens upon the necessaries of life, and would revolt the moral sense of the whole community. There are many other luxuries which will bear a much higher duty for revenue than 20 per cent, and the only true maximum is that which experience demonstrates will bring in each case the largest revenue at the lowest rate of duty. Nor should maximum revenue duties be imposed upon all articles, for this would yield too large an income and would prevent all discrimination within the revenue standard and require necessaries to be taxed as high as luxuries. But, whilst it is impossible to adopt any horizontal scale of duties, or even any arbitrary maximum, experience proves that, as a general rule, a duty of 20 per cent *ad valorem* will yield the largest revenue. There are, however, a few exceptions above as well as many below this standard. Thus, whilst the lowest revenue duty on most luxuries exceeds 20 per cent, there are many costly articles of small bulk, easily smuggled, which would bring, perhaps, no revenue at a duty as high as 20 per cent; and even at the present rate of 7½ per cent they yield, in most cases, a small revenue; whilst coal, iron, sugar, and molasses—articles of great bulk and weight—yielded last year six millions of revenue, at an average rate of duty exceeding 60 per cent *ad valorem*. These duties are far too high for revenue upon all these articles and ought to be reduced to the revenue standard; but if Congress desire to obtain the largest revenue from duties on these articles, those duties at the lowest rate for revenue, would exceed 20 per cent *ad valorem*.

There are appended to this report tables, prepared with great care and labor, showing the rates of duty each year on each of these four articles and the equivalent *ad valorem* from the organization of the Government down to the present period, with the revenue collected every year upon each, from which tables Congress will be enabled to judge how far the present rates exceed the lowest revenue duties, and how much they must be reduced so as to yield a revenue equal to that now obtained from these articles.

It is believed that sufficient means can be obtained at the lowest revenue duties on the articles now subjected to duty; but if Congress desire a larger revenue, it should be procured by taxing the free articles rather than transcend, in any case, the lowest revenue duties. It is thought, however, that, without exceeding the limit in any case, an adequate revenue will still be produced and permit the addition to the free list of salt and guano. In one of his annual messages Mr. Jefferson recommended to Congress "the suppression of the duties on salt." A large portion of this duty is exhausted in heavy expenses of measuring salt and in large sums paid for fishing bounties and allowances in lieu of the drawback of the duty, both which expenditures would fall with a repeal of the duty; which repeal, therefore, can cause no considerable reduction of the revenue. Salt is a necessary of life and should be as free from tax as air or water. It is used in large quantities by the farmer and planter, and to the poor this tax operates most oppressively, not only in the use of the article itself, but as combined with salted provisions. The salt made abroad by solar evaporation is almost pure and wholesome and as conservative of health should be exempt from taxation.

The duty on cotton bagging is equivalent to 55.20 per cent *ad valorem* on the Scotch bagging and to 123.11 per cent on the gunny bag, and yet the whole revenue from these duties has fallen to $66,064.50. Nearly the entire amount, therefore, of this enormous tax makes no addition to the revenue, but inures to the benefit of about 30 manufacturers. As five-sixths of the cotton crop is exported abroad, the same proportion of the bagging around the bale is exported and sold abroad at a heavy loss, growing out of a deduction for tare. Now, as duties are designed to operate only on the domestic consumption there ought to be a drawback of the whole duty on cotton bagging reexported around the bale, on the same principles on which drawbacks are allowed in other cases. The cotton planting is the great exporting interest and suffers from the tariff in the double capacity of consumer and exporter. Cotton is the great basis of our foreign exchange, furnishing most of the means to purchase imports and supply the revenue. It is thus the source of two-thirds of the revenue and of our foreign freight and commerce, upholding our commercial marine and maritime power. It is also a bond of peace with foreign nations, constituting a stronger preventive of war than armies or navies, forts or armaments. At present prices our cotton crop will yield an annual product of $72,000,000 and the manufactured fabric $504,000,000, furnishing profits abroad to thousands of capitalists and wages to hundreds of thousands of the working classes, all

of whom would be deeply injured by any disturbance, growing out of a state of war, to the direct and adequate supply of the raw material. If our manufacturers consume 400,000 bales it would cost them $12,000,000 whilst selling the manufactured fabric for $84,000,000, and they should be the last to unite in imposing heavy taxes upon that great interest which supplies them with the raw material out of which they realize such large profits. Accompanying the drawback of the duty on cotton bagging should be the repeal of the duty on foreign cotton, which is inoperative and delusive and not desired by the domestic producer.

The condition of our foreign relations, it is said, should suspend the production of the tariff. No American patriot can desire to arrest our onward career in peace and prosperity; but if, unhappily, such should be the result, it would create an increased necessity for reducing our present high duties in order to obtain sufficient revenue to meet increased expenditures. The duties for the quarter ending the 30th of September, 1844, yielded $2,011,885.90 more of revenue than the quarter ending 30th September, 1845, showing a very considerable decline of the revenue, growing out of a diminished importation of the highly protected articles and the progressive substitution of the domestic rivals. Indeed, many of the duties are becoming dead letters, except for the purpose of prohibition, and, if not reduced, will ultimately compel their advocates to resort to direct taxation to support the Government. In the event of war nearly all the high duties would become prohibitory, from the increased risk and cost of importations; and if there be, indeed, in the opinion of any, a serious danger of such an occurrence, it appeals most strongly to their patriotism to impose the lowest revenue duties on all articles as the only means of securing at such a period any considerable income from the tariff.

The whole power to collect taxes, whether direct or indirect, is conferred by the same clause of the Constitution. The words are, "The Congress shall have power to lay and collect taxes, duties, imposts, and excises." A direct tax or excise, not for revenue but for protection, clearly would not be within the legitimate object of taxation, and yet it would be as much so as a duty imposed for a similar purpose. The power is "to lay and *collect* taxes, duties, imposts, and excises." A duty must be laid only that it may be *collected*, and if it is so imposed that it can not be collected, in whole or in part, it violates the declared object of the granted power. To lay all duties so high that none of them could be collected would be a prohibitory tariff. To lay a duty on any one article so high that it could not be collected would be a prohibitory tariff upon that article. If a duty of 100 per cent were imposed upon all or upon a number of articles, so as to diminish the revenue upon all or any of them, it would operate as a partial prohibition. A partial and a total prohibition are alike in violation of the true object of the taxing power. They only differ in degree and not in principle. If the revenue limit may be exceeded 1 per cent, it may be exceeded 100. If it may be exceeded upon any one article, it may be exceeded on all; and there is no escape from this conclusion, but in contending that Congress may lay duties on all articles

so high as to collect no revenue and operate as a total prohibition.

The Constitution declares that "all bills for raising revenue shall originate in the House of Representatives." A tariff bill, it is conceded, can only originate in the House, because it is a bill for *raising revenue*. That is the only proper object of such a bill. A tariff is a bill to "lay and collect taxes." It is a bill for "raising revenue," and whenever it departs from that object, in whole or in part, either by total or partial prohibition, it violates the purpose of the granted power.

In arranging the details of the tariff, it is believed that the maximum revenue duties should be imposed upon luxuries. It is deemed just that taxation, whether direct or indirect, should be as nearly as practicable in proportion to property. If the whole revenue were raised by a tax upon property, the poor, and especially those who live by the wages of labor, would pay but a very small portion of such tax; whereas by the tariff, the poor, by the consumption of various imports or domestic articles enhanced in price by the duties, pay a much larger share of the taxes than if they were collected by an assessment in proportion to property. To counteract as far as possible this effect of the tariff—to equalize its operation and make it approximate as nearly as may be to a system of taxes in proportion to property—the duties upon luxuries, used almost exclusively by the rich, should be fixed at the highest revenue standard. This would not be discriminating in favor of the poor, however just that might be within the revenue limit; but it would mitigate, as far as practicable, that discrimination against the poor which results from every tariff by compelling them to pay a larger amount of taxes than if assessed and collected on all property in proportion to its value. In accordance with these principles, it is believed that the largest practicable portion of the aggregate revenue should be raised by maximum revenue duties upon luxuries, whether grown, produced, or manufactured at home or abroad.

An appeal has been made to the poor by the friends of protection on the ground that it augments the wages of labor. In reply it is contended that the wages of labor have not augmented since the tariff of 1842, and that in some cases they have diminished.

When the number of manufactories is not great, the power of the system to regulate the wages of labor is inconsiderable; but as the profit of capital invested in manufactures is augmented by the protective tariff there is a corresponding increase of power until the control of such capital over the wages of labor becomes irresistible. As this power is exercised from time to time, we find it resisted by combinations among the working classes, by turning out for higher wages or for shorter time, by trades unions, and in some countries, unfortunately, by violence and bloodshed. But the Government, by protective duties, arrays itself on the side of the manufacturing system, and by thus augmenting its wealth and power soon terminates in its favor the struggle between man and money—between capital and labor. When the tariff of 1842 was enacted the maximum duty was 20 per cent. By that act the average of duties on the protected articles was more than double. But the wages of labor did not increase in a corresponding ratio or in any ratio

whatever. On the contrary, whilst wages in some cases have diminished, the prices of many articles used by the working classes have greatly appreciated.

A protective tariff is a question regarding the enhancement of the profits of capital. That is its object and not to augment the wages of labor, which would reduce those profits. It is a question of percentage and is to decide whether money vested in our manufactures shall, by special legislation, yield a profit of 10, 20, or 30 per cent, or whether it shall remain satisfied with a dividend equal to that accruing from the same capital invested in agriculture, commerce, or navigation.

The present tariff is unjust and unequal, as well in its details as in the principles upon which it is founded. On some articles the duties are entirely prohibitory and on others there is a partial prohibition. It discriminates in favor of manufactures and against agriculture by imposing many higher duties upon the manufactured fabric than upon the agricultural product out of which it is made. It discriminates in favor of the manufacturer and against the mechanic by many higher duties upon the manufacture than upon the article made out of it by the mechanic. It discriminates in favor of the manufacturer and against the merchant by injurious restrictions upon trade and commerce, and against the shipbuilding and navigating interest by heavy duties on almost every article used in building or navigating vessels. It discriminates in favor of manufactures and against exports, which are as truly the product of American industry as manufactures. It discriminates in favor of the rich and against the poor by high duties upon nearly all the necessaries of life and by minimums and specific duties, rendering the tax upon the real value much higher on the cheaper than upon the finer article.

Minimums are a fictitious value assumed by law instead of the real value, and the operation of all minimums may be illustrated by a single example. Thus, by the tariff of 1842, a duty of 30 per cent *ad valorem* is levied on all manufactures of cotton, but the law further provides that cotton goods "not dyed, colored, printed, or stained, not exceeding in value 20 cents per square yard, shall be valued at 20 cents per square yard." If, then, the real value of the cheapest cotton goods is but 4 cents a square yard, it is placed by law at the false value of 20 cents per square yard, and the duty levied on the fictitious value—raising it five times higher on the cheap article consumed by the poor, than upon the fine article purchased by the more wealthy. Indeed, by House Document No. 306, of the first session of the Twenty-eighth Congress, this difference, by actual importation, was 65 per cent between the cheaper and the finer article of the 20 per cent minimum, 131 per cent on the 30 per cent minimum, 48½ per cent on the 35 per cent minimum, 84 per cent on the 60 per cent minimum, and 84 per cent on the 75 per cent minimum. This difference is founded on actual importation and shows an average discrimination against the poor on cotton imports of 82 per cent beyond what the tax would be if assessed upon the actual value. The operation of the specific duty presents a similar discrimination against the poor and in favor of the rich. Thus, upon salt: The duty is not upon the value, but it is 8 cents a bushel, whether the article be coarse or fine—showing, by the same document, from actual importation, a discrimination of 64 per cent against the cheap and in favor of the finer article; and this, to a greater or less extent, is the effect of all specific duties. When we consider that $2,892,621.74 of the revenue last year was collected by minimum duties and $13,311,085.46 by specific duties, the discrimination against the cheaper article must amount, by estimates founded on the same document, to a tax of $5,108,422 exacted by minimums and specific duties annually from the poorer classes, by raising thus the duties on the cheaper articles above what they would be if the duty were assessed upon the actual value. If direct taxes were made specific, they would be intolerable. Thus, if an annual tax of $30 was assessed on all houses, without respect to their actual value, making the owner of the humble tenement or cabin pay a tax of $30 and the owner of the costly mansion a tax of but $30 on their respective houses, it would differ only in degree but not in principle from the same unvarying specific duty on cheap as on fine articles. If any discrimination should be made, it should be the reverse of the specific duty and of the minimum principle, by establishing a maximum standard, above which value the duties on the finer article should be higher and below which they should be lower on the cheaper article. The tax upon the actual value is the most equal and can only be accomplished by *ad valorem* duties. As to fraudulent invoices and undervaluations, these dangers are believed to be arrested effectually by the stringent provisions and severe penalty of the seventeenth section of the tariff of 1842, and now one-half the revenue is collected from *ad valorem* duties.

At least two-thirds of the taxes imposed by the present tariff are paid, not into the treasury, but to the protected classes. The revenue from imports last year exceeded $27,000,000. This, in itself, is a heavy tax; but the whole tax imposed upon the people by the present tariff is not less than $81,000,000—of which $27,000,000 are paid to the Government upon the imports and $54,000,000 to the protected classes in enhanced prices of similar domestic articles.

This estimate is based upon the position that the duty is added to the price of the import and also of its domestic rival. If the import is enhanced in price by the duty, so must be the domestic rival; for, being like articles, their price must be the same in the same market. The merchant advances in cash the duty on the import and adds the duty, with a profit upon it and other charges, to the price—which must therefore be enhanced to that extent unless the foreign producer had first deducted the duty from the price. But this is impossible, for such now is and long has been the superabundance of capital and active competition in Europe that a profit of 6 per cent in any business is sufficient to produce large investments of money in that business; and if, by our tariff, a duty of 40 per cent be exacted on the products of such business, and the foreign producer deducts that duty from his previous price, he must sustain a heavy loss. This loss would also soon extend beyond the sales for our consumption to sales to our merchants of articles to be re-exported by them from our ports with a drawback of the duty, which would bring down their price throughout the markets of the world. But this the foreign producer could not afford. The duty therefore must be added to the price and paid by the consumer—the duty constituting as much a part of the price as the cost of production.

If it be true that when a duty of 40 per cent is imposed by our tariff, the foreign producer first deducts the duty from the previous price on the sale to our merchant, it must be equally true with a duty of 100 per cent, which is exactly equal to the previous price, and, when deducted, would reduce the price to nothing.

The occasional fall in price of some articles after a tariff is no proof that this was the effect of the tariff, because, from improved machinery, diminished prices of the raw material, or other causes, prices may fall even after a tariff, but they would in such cases have fallen much more but for the tariff. The truest comparison is between the present price of the same article at home and abroad, and to the extent that the price is lower in the foreign market than in our own, the duty, if equal to that difference, must to that extent enhance the price and in the same ratio with the lower duty. The difference in price at home or abroad is generally about equal to the difference in the cost of production, and presents, in a series of years, the surest measure of the effect of the duty—the enhancement in price being equal to that difference if the duty be higher than that difference or equal to it; or if the duty be lower, then the enhancement is equal to the duty; and if the article is produced, like cotton, more cheaply here than abroad, the duty is inoperative. The great argument for the tariff is that foreign labor being cheaper than our own, the cost of foreign productions, it is said, is lessened to that extent, and that we must make up this difference by an equivalent duty and a corresponding enhancement of price in our own market both of the foreign article and of its rival domestic product, thus rendering the duty a tax on all consumers for the benefit of the protected classes. If the marshal were sent by the Federal Government to collect a direct tax from the whole people, to be paid over to manufacturing capitalists to enable them to sustain their business or realize a profit, it would be the same in effect as the protective duty, which, when analyzed in its simplest elements and reduced to actual results, is a mere subtraction of so much money from the people to increase the resources of the protected classes. Legislation for classes is against the doctrine of equal rights, repugnant to the spirit of our free institutions, and, it is apprehended by many, may become but another form for privileged orders, under the name of protection, instead of privilege—indicated here not by rank or title, but by profits and dividends extracted from the many, by taxes upon them, for the benefit of the few.

No prejudice is felt by the Secretary of the Treasury against manufacturers. His opposition is to the protective system and not to classes or individuals. He doubts not that the manufacturers are sincerely persuaded that the system which is a source of so much profit to them is beneficial also to the country. He entertains a contrary opinion and claims for the opponents of the system a settled conviction of its injurious effects. Whilst a due regard to the just and equal rights of all classes forbids a discrimination in favor of the manufacturers by duties above the lowest revenue limit, no disposition is felt to discriminate against them by reducing such duties as operate in their favor below that standard. Under revenue duties it is believed they would still receive a reasonable profit—equal to that realized by those engaged in other pursuits—and it is thought they should desire no more, at least through the agency of governmental power. Equal rights and profits, so far as laws are made, best conform to the principles upon which the Constitution was founded, and with an undeviating regard to which all its functions should be exercised—looking to the whole country and not to classes or sections.

Soil, climate, and other causes vary very much in different countries, the pursuits which are most profitable in each; and the prosperity of all of them will be best promoted by leaving them unrestricted by legislation, to exchange with each other those fabrics and products which they severally raise most cheaply. This is clearly illustrated by the perfect free trade which exists among all the states of the Union and by the acknowledged fact that any one of these states would be injured by imposing duties upon the products of the others. It is generally conceded that reciprocal free trade among nations would best advance the interests of all. But it is contended that we must meet the tariffs of other nations by countervailing restrictions. That duties upon our exports by foreign nations are prejudicial to us is conceded, but whilst this injury is slightly felt by the manufacturer, its weight falls almost exclusively upon agriculture, commerce, and navigation. If those interests which sustain the loss do not ask countervailing restrictions, it should not be demanded by the manufacturers, who do not feel the injury, and whose fabrics, in fact, are not excluded by the foreign legislation of which they complain. That agriculture, commerce, and navigation are injured by foreign restrictions constitutes no reason why they should be subject to still severer treatment, by additional restrictions and countervailing tariffs enacted at home. Commerce, agriculture, and navigation, harassed as they may be by foreign restrictions, diminishing the amount of exchangeable products which they could otherwise purchase abroad, are burdened with heavier impositions at home. Nor will augmented duties here lead to a reduction of foreign tariffs; but the reverse, by furnishing the protected classes there with the identical argument used by the protected classes here against reduction. By countervailing restrictions we injure our own fellow-citizens much more than the foreign nations at whom we propose to aim their force, and in the conflict of opposing tariffs we sacrifice our own commerce, agriculture, and navigation. As well might we impose monarchical or aristocratic restrictions on our own Government or people because that is the course of foreign legislation. Let our commerce be as free as our political institutions. Let us, with revenue duties only, open our ports to all the world, and nation after nation will soon follow our example. If we reduce our tariff, the party opposed to the corn laws of England would soon prevail and admit all our agricultural products at all times freely into her ports in exchange for her exports. And

if England would now repeal her duties upon our wheat, flour, Indian corn, and other agricultural products, our own restrictive system would certainly be doomed to overthrow. If the question is asked, Who shall begin this work of reciprocal reduction? it is unanswered by the fact that England has already abated her duties upon most of our exports. She has repealed the duty upon cotton and greatly reduced the tariff upon our breadstuffs, provisions, and other articles, and her present bad harvest, if accompanied by a reduction of our tariff, would lead to the repeal of her corn laws and the unrestricted admission at all times of our agricultural products. The manufacturing interest opposed reciprocal free trade with foreign nations. It opposes the Zoll-Verein treaty, and it is feared that no other treaty producing a reciprocal reduction of our own and foreign tariffs will receive its support. If that interest preferred a reciprocal exchange of our own for foreign fabrics at revenue duties, it would not have desired a tariff operating, without exception, against all nations that adopted low as well as high tariffs; nor would it have opposed every amendment proposing, when the tariff of 1842 was under consideration, a reduction of our duties upon the exports of such nations as would receive, free of duty, our flour and other agricultural products. If that interest desired reciprocal free trade with other nations, it would have desired a very different tariff from that of 1842. It would have sought to confine the high duties to those cases where the foreign importer would sell his imports for cash only, and admitted a drawback of one-half of the duty where American exports would be taken abroad in exchange—not an actual barter of foreign imports for an equal amount in value of our products, but without any barter, where a sum equal to the value of their exports was used in purchasing here an equal amount in value of any of our products; and the shipment made abroad of these products upon the same principle under which a drawback of duties is now allowed on the re-exportation of foreign imports. This would be less simple and is not recommended in lieu of that absolute reduction of the duties which will accomplish the same object of unrestricted exchange. But such a provision would be a self-executing reciprocity law and should be desired by those believing in countervailing tariffs against foreign nations, but in reciprocal free trade with all—thus enabling our farmers and planters to sell their products for cheaper foreign manufactures, getting more for what they sell and paying less for what they purchase in exchange. It seems strange that while the profit of agriculture varies from 1 to 8 per cent, that of manufactures is more than double. The reason is that whilst the high duties secure nearly a monopoly of the home market to the manufacturer, the farmer and planter are deprived to a great extent of the foreign market by this duties. The farmer and planter are to a great extent forbidden to buy in the foreign market and confined to the domestic articles enhanced in price by the duties. The tariff is thus a double benefit to the manufacturer and a double loss to the farmer and planter—a benefit to the former in nearly a monopoly of the home market and in enhanced prices of their fabrics, and a loss to the latter in the payment of those high prices and a total or partial exclusion from the foreign market. The true question is whether the farmer and planter shall to a great extent supply our people with cheap manufactures, purchased abroad with their agricultural products, or whether this exchange shall be forbidden by high duties on such manufactures and their supply thrown, as a monopoly, at large prices by high tariffs into the hands of our own manufacturers. The number of manufacturing capitalists who derive the benefit from the heavy taxes extracted by the tariff from 20,000,000 of people does not exceed 10,000. The whole number (including the working classes engaged in our manufactures) deriving any benefit from the tariff does not exceed 400,000, of whom not more than 40,000 have been brought into this pursuit by the last tariff. But this small number of 40,000 would still have been in the country, consuming our agricultural products, and in the attempt to secure them as purchasers, so small in number and not consuming one-half the supply of many counties, the farmer and planter are asked to sacrifice the markets of the world, containing a population of 800,000,000, disabled from purchasing our products by our high duties on all they would sell in exchange. The farmer and planter have the home market without a tariff, and they would have the foreign market also to a much greater extent but for the total or partial prohibition of the last tariff.

We have more fertile lands than any other nation, can raise a greater variety of products, and, it may be said, could feed and clothe the people of nearly all the world. The home market of itself is wholly inadequate for such products.

They must have the foreign market, or a large surplus, accompanied by great depression in price, must be the result. The States of Ohio, Indiana, and Illinois, if cultivated to their fullest extent, could of themselves raise more than sufficient food to supply the entire home market. Missouri or Kentucky could more than supply it with hemp; already the State of Mississippi raises more cotton than is sufficient for all the home market; Louisiana is rapidly approaching the same point as to sugar; and there are lands enough adapted to that product in Louisiana, Texas and Florida to supply with sugar and molasses nearly all the markets of the world. If cotton is depressed in price by the tariff, the consequence must be a comparative diminution of the product and the raising in its place to a great extent hemp, wheat, corn, stock, and provisions, which otherwise would be supplied by the teeming products of the West. The growing West in a series of years must be the greatest suffers by the tariff, in depriving them of the foreign market and that of the cotton-growing states. We demand, in fact, for our agricultural products specie from nearly all the world, by heavy taxes upon all their manufactures; and their purchases from us must therefore be limited, as well as their sales to us enhanced in price. Such a demand for specie, which we know in advance cannot be complied with, is nearly equivalent to a decree excluding most of our agricultural products from foreign markets. Such is the rigor of our restrictions that nothing short of a famine opens freely the ports of Europe for our breadstuffs. Agriculture is our chief employment; it is best adapted to our situation; and, if not depressed by the tariff, would be the most profitable. We can raise a larger surplus of agricultural products and a greater variety than almost any other nation and at cheaper rates. Remove, then, from agricultural all our restrictions, and by its own unfettered power it will break down all foreign restrictions, and, ours being removed, would feed the hungry and clothe the poor of our fellow-men throughout all the densely peopled nations of the world. But now we will take nothing in exchange for these products but specie, except at very high duties, and nothing but a famine breaks down all foreign restrictions and opens for a time the ports of Europe to our breadstuffs. If, on a reduction of our duties, England repeals her corn laws, nearly all Europe must follow her example or give to her manufacturers advantages which cannot be successfully encountered in most of the markets of the world. The tariff did not raise the price of our breadstuffs, but a bad harvest in England does—giving up for the time that foreign market which we would soon have at all times by that repeal of the corn laws which must follow the reduction of our duties. But whilst breadstuffs rise with a bad harvest in England, cotton almost invariably falls; because the increased sum which, in that event, England must pay for our breadstuffs we will take, not in manufactures, but only in specie; and not having it to spare, she brings down, even to a greater extent, the price of our cotton. Hence the result that a bad harvest in England reduces the aggregate price of our exports, often turns the exchanges against us, carrying our specie abroad, and inflicting a serious blow on our prosperity. Foreign nations cannot for a series of years import more than they export; and if we close our markets against their imports by high duties, they must buy less of our exports or give a lower price, or both.

Prior to the 30th of June, 1842, a credit was given for the payment of duties, since which date they have been collected in cash. Before the cash duties and the tariff of 1842 our trade in foreign imports re-exported abroad afforded large and profitable employment to our merchants and freight to our commercial marine, both for the inward and outward voyage; but since the last tariff this trade is being lost to the country, as is proved by the tables hereto annexed. The total amount of foreign imports re-exported during the three years since the last tariff, both of free and dutiable goods, is $33,384,394—being far less than in any three years (except during the war) since 1793, and less than was re-exported in any one of eight several years. The highest aggregate of any three years was $173,108,813 and the lowest aggregate $41,315,705—being in the years 1794, 1795, and 1796. Before 1820 the free goods are not distinguished in this particular from the dutiable goods, but since that date the returns show the following result: During the three years since the tariff of 1842 the value of dutiable imports re-exported was $12,590,811—being less than in any one of seven years preceding since 1820—the lowest aggregate of any three years since that date being $14,918,444 and the highest $57,727,293. Even before the cash duties, for five years preceding the high tariff of 1828, the value of dutiable goods re-exported was $94,796,241, and for the five years

succeeding that tariff, $66,784,192—showing a loss of $28,012,049 of our trade in foreign exports after the tariff of 1828. The diminution of this most valuable branch of commerce has been the combined result of cash duties and of the high tariff of 1842. If the cash duties are retained, as it is believed they should be, the only sure method of restoring this trade is the adoption of the warehousing system, by which the foreign imports may be kept in store by the Government until they are required for re-exportation abroad or consumption at home—in which latter contingency, and at the time when, for that purpose, they are taken out of these stores for consumption, the duties are paid, and, if re-exported, they pay no duty, but only the expense of storage. Under the present system the merchant introduces foreign imports of the value of $100,000. He must now, besides the advance for the goods, make a further advance in cash, in many cases, of $50,000 for the duties. Under such a system but a small amount of goods will be imported for drawbacks, and the higher the duty the larger must be the advance and the smaller the imports for re-exportation.

The imports, before payment of duties under the same regulations now applied to our imports in transit to Canada, may be taken from warehouse to warehouse—from the East to the Lakes, and to Pittsburg[h], Cincinnati, and Louisville—from New Orleans to Natchez, Vicksburg, Memphis, and St. Louis—and warehoused in these and other interior ports, the duties remaining unpaid until the goods are taken out of the warehouse and out of the original package at such ports for consumption; thus carrying our foreign commerce into the interior, with all the advantage of augmented business and cheaper supplies throughout the country. It will introduce into our large ports on or near the seaboard assorted cargoes of goods, to be re-exported with our own, to supply the markets of the world. It will cheapen prices to the consumer by deducting the interest and profit that are now charged upon the advance of duty—building up the marts of our own commerce and giving profitable employment to our own commercial marine. It will greatly increase our revenue by augmenting our imports, together with our exports, and is respectfully recommended to Congress as an important part of the whole system now proposed for their consideration.

The act of the 3d of March last allowing a drawback on foreign imports exported from certain of our ports to Canada and also to Santa Fe and Chihuahua, in Mexico, has gone to some extent into effect under regulations prescribed by this department and is beginning to produce the most happy results, especially in an augmented trade in the supply of foreign exports to Canada from our own ports. Indeed, this law must soon give to us the whole of this valuable trade during the long period when the St. Lawrence is closed by ice, and a large proportion of it at all seasons. The result would be still more beneficial if Canada were allowed to carry all her exports to foreign nations *in transitu* through our own railroads, rivers, and canals, to be shipped from our own ports. Such a system, whilst it would secure to us this valuable trade, would greatly enlarge the business on our rivers, lakes, railroads, and canals, as well as aug-

ment our commerce; and would soon lead to the purchase by Canada not only of our foreign exports, but also, in many cases, of our domestic products and fabrics to complete an assortment. In this manner our commercial relations with Canada would become more intimate, and more and more of her trade every year would be secured to our people.

Connected with this department and the finances is the question of the sales of the public lands. The proceeds of these sales, it is believed, should continue to constitute a portion of the revenue, diminishing to that extent the amount required to be raised by the tariff. The net proceeds of these sales paid into the Treasury during the last fiscal year was $2,077,022.30, and from the first sales in 1787 up to the 30th of September last was $118,607,335.91. The average annual sales have been much less than 2,000,000 of acres, yet the aggregate net proceeds of the sales in 1834, 1835, 1836 and 1837 was $51,268,617.82. Those large sales were almost exclusively for speculation, and this can only be obviated at all times by confining the sales to settlers and cultivators in limited quantities, sufficient for farms or plantations. The price at which the public lands should be sold is an important question to the country, but especially to the people of the new states, living mostly remote from the seaboard, and who have scarcely felt the presence of the Government in local expenditures, but chiefly in the exhaustion of their means for purchases of public lands and for customs. The public lands are not of the same value, yet they are all fixed at one varying price, which is far above the value of a large portion of these lands. The quantity now subject to entry at the minimum price of $1.25 per acre is 133,307,457 acres and 109,035,345 in addition, to which the Indian title has been extinguished—being an aggregate of 242,342,802 acres, and requiring a century and a quarter to complete the sales at the rate they have progressed heretofore, without including any of the unsold lands of Texas or Oregon or the vast region besides to which the Indian title is not yet extinguished. It is clear, then, that there is a vast and annually increasing surplus of public lands, very little of which will be sold within any reasonable period at the present price, and in regard to which the public interest would be promoted and the revenue augmented by reducing the price. The reduction of the price of the public lands in favor of settlers and cultivators would enhance the wages of labor. It is an argument urged in favor of the tariff that we ought to protect our labor against when is called the "pauper labor" of Europe. But whilst the tariff does not enhance the wages of labor, the sales of the public lands at low prices and in limited quantities to settlers and cultivators would accomplish this object. If those who live by the wages of labor could purchase 320 acres of land for $80, 160 acres for $40, or 80 acres for $20, or 40-acre lot for $10, the power of the manufacturing capitalist in reducing the wages of labor would be greatly diminished; because when these lands were thus reduced in price those who live by the wages of labor could purchase farms at these low rates and cultivate the soil for themselves and families instead of working for others twelve hours a day in manufactories. Reduce the price

which the laborer must pay for the public domain; bring thus the means of purchase within his power; prevent all speculation and monopoly in the public lands; confine the sales to settlers and cultivators in limited quantities; preserve these hundreds of millions of acres for ages to come as homes for the poor and oppressed; reduce the taxes by reducing the tariff and bringing down the prices which the poor are thus compelled to pay for all the necessaries and comforts of life, and more will be done for the benefit of American labor than if millions were added to the profits of manufacturing capital by the enactment of a protective tariff.

The Secretary of the Treasury, on coming into office, found the revenues deposited with banks. The law establishing the Independent Treasury was repealed, and the Secretary had no power to re-establish that system. Congress had not only repeals that law, but, as a substitute, had adopted the present system of deposit banks and prohibited changing any one of those for another bank except for specified reasons. No alternative was left but to continue the existing system until Congress should think proper to change it. That change, it is hoped, will now be made by a return to the Treasury of the Constitution. One of the great evils of banks is the constant expansion and contraction of the currency, and this evil is augmented by the deposits of the revenue with banks, whether state or national. The only proper course for the Government is to keep its own money separate from all banks and bankers, in its own treasury—whether in the mint, branch mints, or other government agencies—and to use only gold and silver coin in all receipts and disbursements. The business of the country will be more safe when an adequate supply of specie is kept within our limits and its circulation encouraged by all the means within the power of the Government. If this Government and the states and the people unite in suppressing the use of specie, an adequate supply, for want of a demand, cannot be kept within our limits and the condition of the business and currency of the country will be perilous and uncertain. It will be completely within the power of the banks, whose paper will constitute the exclusive circulation of the whole community. Nor will it be useful to establish a constitutional treasury if it is to receive or disburse the paper of banks. Separation from banks in that case would only be nominal and no addition would be made to the circulation of gold and silver.

Various forms of paper credit have been suggested as connected with the operations of the constitutional treasury, but they are all considered as impairing one of the great objects of such a treasury—namely, an augmented circulation of specie. If paper, in whatever form or from whatever source it may issue, should be introduced as a circulation by the constitutional treasury, it would, precisely to that extent, diminish its use as a means of circulating gold and silver.

The constitutional treasury could be rendered a most powerful auxiliary of the mint in augmenting the specie circulation. The amount of public money which can be placed in the mint is now limited by law to $1,000,000, and to that extent it is now used as a depository and as a means of increasing our coinage. It is suggested that this limi-

tation may be so modified as to permit the use of our mint and branch mints for a much larger sum, in connection with the constitutional treasury. The amount of public money received at New York greatly exceeds that collected at all other points and would of itself seem to call for a place of public deposit there; in view of which, the location of a branch of the mint of the United States at that city would be most convenient and useful. The argument used against a constitutional treasury, of the alleged insecurity of the public funds in the hands of individuals, and especially the vast amount collected at New York, will be entirely obviated by such an establishment. The mint of the United States has now been in existence fifty-two years. It has had the custody of upward of $114,000,000, and during this long period of time there never has been a loss of any of its specie in the mint by the Government. The mint at Philadelphia is now conducted with great efficiency by the able and faithful officer at the head of that establishment, whose general supervisory authority, without leaving the parent mint, might still be wisely extended to the branch at New York. Besides the utility of such a branch as a place for keeping safely and disbursing the public money, it is believed that the coinage might be greatly augmented by the existence of a branch of the mint at that great city. It is there that two-thirds of the revenue is annually collected—the whole of which, under the operation of the constitutional treasury, would be received in specie. Of that amount a very large sum would be received in coin of other countries, and especially in foreign gold coins—all which could be speedily converted, upon the spot, into our own coins of gold and silver. The amount, also, of such foreign coin brought by emigrants to the city of New York is very considerable, a large portion of which would find its way to the branch of the mint for recoinage. The foreign gold coins do not, and it is feared will not, circulate generally as a currency, notwithstanding they are made a tender by law. The rate at which these coins are fixed by law is not familiar to the people; the denomination of such coin is inconvenient; the parts into which it is divided are not decimal; the rates at which it is taken vary in different parts of the Union. It is inconvenient in the way of ready transfer in counting; it is more difficult, in common use, to distinguish the genuine from the counterfeit foreign coin; and the stamp upon it is not familiar to the people—from all which causes a foreign coin does not and will not circulate generally as a currency among the people. In many of the banks nearly the whole of their specie is kept in every variety of foreign gold coin, and when it is tendered by them in payment of their notes, the great body of the people, not being familiar with these coins, do not receive them; and thus the circulation of a gold currency is, to a great extent, defeated. If these coins were converted at our mint or branch mints into the eagle, the half-eagle, and quarter-eagle, we should speedily have a large supply of American gold coin, and it would very soon be brought into common use as a currency, and this give to it greater stability and greater security to all of the business of the country. A considerable amount of foreign gold coin has, during the present year, under the di-

rections of this department, been converted into American gold coin; but the process would be much more rapid if aided by the organization of the constitutional treasury and the establishment of a branch of the mint at the great commercial emporium of the Union. With the mint and branch mints as depositories, the sums remaining in the hands of other receivers of public money, whether of lands or customs, would be inconsiderable, and the Government could be readily protected from all losses of such sums by adequate bonds and the power by law to convict and punish as criminals all who embezzle the public moneys.

It is believed, under such a system, that no defaults would take place, and that the public moneys would be safely kept and disbursed in gold and silver. This Government is made, by the Constitution, the guardian of a specie currency. That currency can only be coined and its value regulated by this Government. It is one of its first duties to supply such a currency by an efficient mint and by general regulations of the coinage; but in vain will it attempt to perform that duty, if, when coin is made or regulated in value, this Government dispenses with its use and expels it from circulation, or drives it out of the country by substituting the paper of banks in all the transactions of the Government.

There is nothing which will advance so surely the prosperity of the country as an adequate supply of specie, diffused throughout every portion of the Union and constituting to a great extent the ordinary circulation everywhere among the people. It is a currency that will never break nor fall; it will neither expand not contract beyond the legitimate business of the country; it will lead to no extravagant speculations at one time, to be followed by certain depression at another; nor will labor ever be robbed of its reward by the depreciation of such currency. There is no danger that we shall have too much gold and silver in actual circulation, or too small an amount of bank paper, or that any injury ever will be inflicted upon the business of the country by a diminution of the circulation of the paper of banks and the substitution in its place to that extent of gold and silver. Even their most ardent advocates must admit that banks are subject to periodical expansions and contractions, and that this evil would be increased by giving them the funds of the Government to loan and by receiving and disbursing nothing but their paper.

It is believed that the permanent interest of every class of the people will be advanced by the establishment of the constitutional treasury, and that the manufacturers especially will derive great benefit from its adoption. It will give stability to all their operations and insure them to a great extent against those fluctuations, expansions, and contractions of the currency so prejudicial to their interests. By guarding against inflations of the currency it will have a tendency to check periodical excesses of foreign importations purchased in fact upon credit; while loans from banks, or dangerous enlargements of their business, and excessive issues of their paper will be greatly diminished. Whilst a sound and stable currency guards the manufacturer against excessive importations from abroad, it protects him from disasters at home and from those ruinous revul-

sions in which so many thousands are reduced to bankruptcy. The tariff, if followed, as in the absence of adequate checks it certainly soon will be, by an inflated currency, whilst it thus enhances the expenses of manufacturing at home, will speedily and certainly raise prices up to the whole amount of the duty, so as to repeal the operation of that duty in favor of the manufacturer, and enable the foreign importer again to flood the market at the enhanced prices arising from an inflated currency. But soon the revulsion comes, and all are overwhelmed in a common ruin. The currency is reduced below the wants of the country by a sudden and ruinous contraction; and the labor and industry of years are required to repair the mischief. Stability, both in the tariff and the currency, is what the manufacturer should most desire. Let the tariff be permanently adjusted by a return to reasonable and moderate revenue duties which, even when imposed truly and in good faith for that purpose, will yield sufficient advantage to afford reasonable profits; and let this permanent system (and none other can be permanent) be established and accompanied by a stable currency, and the manufacturer, in a series of years, will derive the greatest benefits from the system. The present system cannot be permanent. It is too unequal and unjust, too exorbitant and oppressive, and too clearly in conflict with the fundamental principles of the Constitution. If the manufacturer thinks that this system can be permanent, let him look to the constant changes which have attended all attempts to establish and continue a protective tariff. The first tariff was based in part upon the principle of very moderate protection to domestic manufactures, and the result has been, as appears by the table hereto annexed, that the tariff has been changed and modified thirty times since that period, being more than once, on an average, for every Congress since the Government was founded; and one of these tariffs was in itself a system of successive biennial changes, operating through a period of ten years. Of these changes, fourteen have been general and sixteen special. From 1816 onward these changes have been most frequent, and it is vain to expect permanency from anything but a revenue tariff. Stability is what the manufacturer should desire, and especially that the question should be taken out of the arena of politics by a just and permanent settlement. A great number of tables, illustrative of the effects of the tariff, compiled from official documents, accompany this report. Some of these tables exhibit the operation of each of our tariffs from the organization of the Government to the present period. In order to enable the Secretary to comply with the direction of the acts of Congress, requiring him in his annual report to suggest "plans for improving or increasing the revenues" and to give "information to Congress in adopting modes of raising" the revenue, two circulars were issued, published, and generally distributed propounding various questions connected with this subject, and requesting replies. Some answers have been received from friends as well as opponents of the tariff, but the Secretary regrets that the manufacturers, with very few exceptions, have declines answering these questions or communicating any information as regards their profits

and surplus or in relation to the wages of labor. An abstract of all that is deemed useful in these replies, together with a copy of both the circulars, is appended to this report.

The coast survey is rapidly progressing, having been extended eastward to the eastern coast of Massachusetts, and southward nearly to the dividing line of Maryland and Virginia on the Chesapeake. Two new centers of operation have been opened, under the sanction of this department, in North Carolina and on the Gulf of Mexico, from which the work may be spread until the parts unite. Important positions for forts, navy yards, harbors, and lighthouses present themselves along this interesting portion of the coast of Louisiana, Mississippi, and Alabama, and the islands guarding the interior channel between Mobile and New Orleans. Great economy exists in the administration of the fund appropriated for the coast survey, and every effort is made by the superintendent to press the work onward to a completion; and his report in detail will be hereafter submitted to Congress. Three charts, resulting from the survey, have been published within the past year, and five more are nearly ready for publication. This great work is most honorable to the science of our country, most useful to our navy and commercial marine, and, in connection with our lighthouses, must decrease the cost of freight and insurance as well as the risk of life and property. Great attention has been given by this department to the very important subject of our lighthouse system. The various improvements suggested by experience at home or abroad, the relative advantages of gas or oil, of reflectors, lenticular and revolving lights, the location and construction of the buildings as well as the mode of keeping the lights, are all being fully and carefully investigated, and a report, it is believed, will be ready during the present session of Congress. From the Chesapeake to the capes of Florida, and thence westward, our coast is badly lighted, as well as the Great Lakes of the Northwest; and numerous wrecks, often accompanied with loss of life and property, seem to require the interposition of Congress.

Such portions of the charts of the exploring expedition as were placed under the charge of this department were distributed for the benefit of our whale ships. These valuable charts embrace the survey of many hitherto almost unexplored regions and islands of the Pacific as well as a part of the coast of Oregon, and must be eminently useful for many purposes, but especially to our seaman and merchants engaged in the whale fishery. In pursuance of a resolution of Congress a report is in progress of preparation as regards the banks and currency, and also in relation to statistics; and these, with all other reports required from this department, will be presented at the earliest practicable period of the present session.

In presenting his annual report, in obedience to the law, the Secretary of the Treasury submits his views with undissembled diffidence, consoled by the reflection that all his errors of judgment will be corrected by the superior wisdom of the two Houses of Congress, guided and directed by that overruling Providence which has blessed the unexampled progress of this great and happy Union.

R.J. Walker
Secretary of the Treasury

Hon. John W. Davis,
Speaker of the House of Representatives

See also: **Vol. I**: Free trade; Walker, Robert John; Walker's Report. **Vol. III**: Tariff of 1846 (Walker's Tariff).

John Sherman's 1865 Speech in Favor of Increased Tariffs

Senator John Sherman of Ohio delivered the following speech in the U.S. Senate on February 27, 1865, in support of the Tariff of 1865, which the Republican Congress passed during the last weeks of the Civil War. Sherman argued for a high protective tariff that would safeguard both cotton farmers and manufacturers. He excluded certain raw materials and foodstuffs. The act passed Congress despite efforts by the railroads to lower the cost of imported iron needed for the construction of rail lines.

The first object of legislation in regard to customs duties should be, not to tax articles which do not come within the class of raw materials or food, but, on the contrary, to tax those articles alone which can be taxed without injuriously affecting our trade with other countries, and to tax such articles only to such an extent as will not injuriously affect their consumption by our own people.

Upon this principle, and another equally simple, not to impose duties on the raw materials of industry and the first articles of food, was based the policy of Sir Robert Peel, which reduced the number of articles charged with duties from one thousand one hundred and sixty-three in 1841 to forty-four in 1862; and, sir, if we were at peace, with our currency restored to its normal condition, I should be very willing to discriminate in favor of our own commerce and manufactures. Although representing an interior state chiefly engaged in agriculture, yet I have always felt that the prosperity of one industry and section finally inured to the benefit of the whole nation and of every part. I therefore have supported the present tariff law, framed with a distinct view to discriminate in favor of our home industry, and I would not only so far modify the present as to increase the revenue. If by lowering the duty we can increase the revenue, it should be done. If by increasing the duties on any article we can increase the revenue without diminishing in a greater degree the consumption of that article, it ought to be done. During war, when our industry is fully employed in repairing the waste of war, increased importation may become a vast injury by exhausting us of gold and food, which must then be sent to pay for luxuries. Then we send abroad that which we most need, and receive that which we can do without. The true principle for a nation in our condition, struggling for its existence, is so to frame its tariff laws as to produce the greatest revenue from the least importation. When the war ceases, our armies will be disbanded and our soldiers will return to their ordinary pursuits of industry; then the English rule should be applied of levying the requisite duties on the fewest articles, and with a view to increase our commerce and protect our industry.

With the general statement, I approach the consideration of the bill. I am not entirely satisfied with it, but I am sure it will improve the present law and add some new sources of revenue. When the machinery of collecting is perfected, which can only be done by experience, the whole of these taxes will be revised. They will be arranged into classes and schedules, and simplified. Its success will depend mainly upon the Commissioner of Internal Revenue. If he will perform his duty, and require his subordinates to do theirs, we shall realize during this calendar year $3,000,000 of internal revenue, which will be an ample basis of public credit, and will go far to reduce the public debt. If military and naval forces complete their great duty within

this year, our present system of national finance will, I confidently trust, very soon enable us to commence the permanent reduction of our national debt, and resume specie payments within a period equal to that required in Great Britain after her wars with Napoleon. We have resources in this country, when united and at peace, far greater than those of any nation of modern times. Our accumulated wealth is not to be compared with that of Great Britain and France, but a bountiful Providence has given us sources of wealth far greater than either of these powerful nations ever had. The cotton now coming through our lines already affects the price of exchange. Petroleum is already exported to the amount of thirty-one million gallons a year. Our mineral resources are scarcely touched. Our young sister Nevada is exciting our fancy with mountains of gold and silver; and dry statistics inform us of a product there of gold and silver equal to the product of the world fifty years ago. The South is to be opened to the new industry, and millions of laborers from Europe and Asia are meeting on our favored shores to help develop our resources. We have taken our place among the great nations; but as we have attained our military position only after hard, exacting toil of military discipline, and after defects and discouragements, we can maintain our financial position only by the hard processes of taxes and economy. I wish to see the evil predictions of our enemies, at home and abroad, all belied. They prophesied disunion. They prophesied bankruptcy; we will see them begging for our bonds, our cotton, petroleum, and gold. Then we can provide for our public debt. Then we can restore our commerce on the high seas, now driven by British pirates to take refuge under foreign flags. Then we may revive old doctrines about the American continent being no longer the home of European kings. Now our duty is dry, hard, exacting; but it will be the more cheering when in the future our self-sacrificing patriotism in this great crisis shall have enabled our country to enter upon its new career without a stain upon its financial honor.

See also: **Vol. I**: Civil War (American); Lincoln, Abraham; Morrill, Justin S.; Protectionism; Reconstruction; Tariff of 1864; Tariff of 1866. **Vol. III**: Tariff of 1865.

Grover Cleveland's 1887 State of the Union Address

In 1887 the federal treasury had a surplus of $94 million, prompting President Grover Cleveland to push for a tariff reduction. The tariff became a major campaign issue in the upcoming election, especially after December 6, 1887, when Cleveland deviated from established precedent by devoting his entire State of the Union address to the subject. His Republican opponent, Benjamin Harrison, argued that such a reduction would lead to higher taxes and unemployment. Cleveland lost the 1888 election to Harrison, in large part because of the tariff issue.

To the Congress of the United States:

You are confronted at the threshold of your legislative duties with a condition of the national finances which imperatively demands immediate and careful consideration.

The amount of money annually extracted, through the operation of present laws, from the industries and necessities of the people largely exceeds the sum necessary to meet the expenses of the Government.

When we consider that the theory of our institutions guarantees to every citizen the full enjoyment of all the fruits of his industry and enterprise, with only such deduction as may be his share toward the careful and economical maintenance of the Government which protects him, it is plain that the exaction of more than this is indefensible extortion and a culpable betrayal of American fairness and justice. This wrong inflicted upon those who bear the burden of national taxation, like other wrongs, multiples a brood of evil consequences. The public Treasury, which should only exist as a conduit conveying the people's tribute to its legitimate objects of expenditure, becomes a hoarding place for money needlessly withdrawn from trade and the people's use, thus crippling our national energies, suspending our country's development, preventing investment in productive enterprise, threatening financial disturbance, and inviting schemes of public plunder.

This condition of our Treasury is not altogether new, and it has more than once of late been submitted to the people's representatives in the Congress, who alone can apply a remedy. And yet the situation still continues, with aggravated incidents, more than ever presaging financial convulsion and widespread disaster.

It will not do to neglect this situation because its dangers are not now palpably imminent and apparent. They exist none the less certainly, and await the unforeseen and unexpected occasion when suddenly they will be precipitated upon us.

On the 30th day of June, 1885, the excess of revenues over public expenditures, after complying with the annual retirement of the sinking-fund act, was $17,859,735.84; during the year ended June 30, 1886, such excess amounted to $49,405,545.20, and during the year ended June 30, 1887, it reached the sum of $55,567,849.54.

The annual contributions to the sinking fund during the three years above specified, amounting in the aggregate to $138,058,320.94, and deducted from the surplus as stated, were made by calling in for that purpose outstanding 3 per cent bonds of the Government. During the six months prior to June 30, 1887, the surplus revenue had grown so large by repeated accumulations, and it was feared the withdrawal of this great sum of money needed by the people would so affect the business of the country, that the sum of $79,864,100 of such surplus was applied to the payment of the principal

and interest of the 3 per cent bonds still outstanding, and which were then payable at the option of the Government. The precarious condition of financial affairs among the people still needing relief, immediately after the 30th day of June, 1887, the remainder of the 3 per cent bonds then outstanding, amounting with principal and interest to the sum of $18,877,500, were called in and applied to the sinking-fund contribution for the current fiscal year. Notwithstanding these operations of the Treasury Department, representations of distress in business circles not only continued, but increased, and absolute peril seemed at hand. In these circumstances the contribution to the sinking fund for the current fiscal year was at once completed by the expenditure of $27,684,283.55 in the purchase of Government bonds not yet due bearing 4 and 4½ per cent interest, the premium paid thereon averaging about 24 per cent for the former and 8 per cent for the latter. In addition to this, the interest accruing during the current year upon the outstanding bonded indebtedness of the Government was to some extent anticipated, and banks selected as depositories of public money were permitted to somewhat increase their deposits.

While the expedients thus employed to release to the people the money lying idle in the Treasury served to avert immediate danger, our surplus revenues have continued to accumulate, the excess for the present year amounting on the 1st day of December to $55,238,701.19, and estimated to reach the sum of $113,000,000 on the 30th of June next, at which date it is expected that this sum added to the prior accumulations, will swell the surplus in the Treasury to $140,000,000.

There seems to be no assurance that, with such a withdrawal from use of the people's circulating medium, our business community may not in the near future be subjected to the same distress which was quite lately produced from the same cause. And while the functions of our National Treasury should be few and simple, and while its best condition would be reached, I believe, by its entire disconnection with private business interests, yet when, by a perversion of its purposes, it idly holds money uselessly subtracted from the channels of trade, there seems to be reason for the claim that some legitimate means should be devised by the Government to restore in an emergency, without waste or extravagance, such money to its place among the people.

If such an emergency arises, there now exists no clear and undoubted executive power of relief. Heretofore the redemption of 3 per cent bonds, which were payable at the option of the Government, has afforded a means for the disbursement of the excess of our revenues; but these bonds have all been retired, and there are no bonds outstanding the payment of which we have a right to insist upon. The contribution to the sinking fund which furnishes the occasion for expenditure in the purchase of bonds has already been made for the current year, so that there is no outlet in that direction.

In the present state of legislation the only pretense of any existing executive power to restore at this time any part of our surplus revenues to the people by its expenditure consists in the supposition that the Secretary of the Treasury may enter the market and purchase the bonds of the Government not yet due, at a rate of premium to be agreed upon. The only provision of law from which such a power could be derived is found in an appropriation bill passed a number of years ago, and it is subject to the suspicion that it was intended as temporary and limited in its application, instead of conferring a continuing discretion and authority. No condition ought to exist which would justify the grant of power to a single official, upon his judgment of its necessity, to withhold from or release to the business of the people, in an unusual manner, money held in the Treasury, and thus affect at his will the financial situation of the country; and if it is deemed wise to lodge in the Secretary of the Treasury the authority in the present juncture to purchase bonds, it should be plainly vested, and provided, as far as possible, with such checks and limitations as will define this official's right and discretion and at the same time relieve him from undue responsibility.

In considering the question of purchasing bonds as a means of restoring to circulation the surplus money accumulating in the Treasury, it should be borne in mind that premiums must of course be paid upon such purchase, that they may be a large part of these bonds held as investments which can not be purchased at any price, and that combinations among holders who are willing to sell may unreasonably enhance the cost of such bonds to the Government.

It has been suggested that the present bonded debt might be refunded at a less rate of interest and the difference between the old and new security paid in cash, thus finding use for the surplus in the Treasury. The success of this plan, it is apparent, must depend upon the volition of the holders of the present bonds; and it is not entirely certain that the inducement which must be offered them would result in more financial benefit to the Government than the purchase of bonds, while the latter proposition would reduce the principal of the debt by actual payment instead of extending it.

The proposition to deposit the money held by the Government in banks throughout the country for use by the people is, it seems to me, exceedingly objectionable in principle, as establishing too close a relationship between the operations of the Government Treasury and the business of the country and too extensive a commingling of their money, thus fostering an unnatural reliance in private business upon public funds. If this scheme should be adopted, it should only be done as a temporary expedient to meet an urgent necessity. Legislative and executive effort should generally be in the opposite direction, and should have a tendency to divorce, as much and as fast as can be safely done, the Treasury Department from private enterprise.

Of course it is not expected that unnecessary and extravagant appropriations will be made for the purpose of avoiding the accumulation of an excess of revenue. Such expenditure, besides the demoralization of all just conceptions of public duty which it entails, stimulates a habit of reckless improvidence not in the least consistent with the mission of our people or the high and beneficent purposes of our Government.

I have deemed it my duty to thus bring to the knowledge of my countrymen, as well as to the attention of their representatives charged with the responsibility of legislative relief, the gravity of our financial situation. The failure of the Congress heretofore to provide against the dangers which it was quite evident the very nature of the difficulty must necessarily produce caused a condition of financial distress and apprehension since your last adjournment which taxes to the utmost all the authority and expedients within executive control; and these appear now to be exhausted. If disaster results from the continued inaction of Congress, the responsibility must rest where it belongs.

Though the situation thus far considered is fraught with danger which should be fully realized, and though it presents features of wrong to the people as well as peril to the country, it is but a result growing out of a perfectly palpable and apparent cause, constantly reproducing the same alarming circumstances—a congested National Treasury and a depleted monetary condition in the business of the country. It need hardly be stated that while the present situation demands a remedy, we can only be saved from a like predicament in the future by the removal of its cause.

Our scheme of taxation, by means of which this needless surplus is taken from the people and put into the public Treasury, consists of a tariff or duty levied upon importations from abroad and internal-revenue taxes levied upon the consumption of tobacco and spirituous and malt liquors. It must be conceded that none of the things subjected to internal-revenue taxation are, strictly speaking, necessaries. There appears to be no just complaint of this taxation by the consumers of these articles and there seems to be nothing so well able to bear the burden without hardship to any portion of the people.

But our present tariff laws, the vicious, inequitable, and illogical source of unnecessary taxation, ought to be at once revised and amended. These laws, as their primary and plain effect, raise the price to consumers of all articles imported and subject to duty by precisely the sum paid for such duties. Thus the amount of the duty measures the tax paid by those who purchase for use these imported articles. Many of these things, however, are raised or manufactured in our own country, and the duties now levied upon foreign goods and products are called protection to these home manufactures, because they render it possible for those of our people who are manufacturers to make these taxed articles and sell them for a price equal to that demanded for the imported foods that have paid customs duty. So it happens that while a comparatively few use the imported articles, millions of our people, who never used and never saw any of the foreign products, purchase and use things of the same kind made in this country, and pay therefore nearly or quite the same enhanced price which the duty adds to the imported articles. Those who buy imports pay the duty charged thereon into the public Treasury, but the great majority of our citizens, who buy domestic articles of the same class, pay a sum at least approximately equal to this duty to the home manufacturer. This reference to the operation of our tariff laws is not made by way of instruction, but in order that we may be constantly reminded of the manner in which they impose a burden upon those who consume domestic products as well as those who consume imported articles, and thus create a tax upon all our people.

It is not proposed to entirely relieve the country of this taxation. It must be extensively continued as the source of the Government's income; and in a readjustment of our tariff the interests of American labor engaged in manufacture should be carefully considered, as well as the preservation of our manufacturers. It may be called protection or by any other name, but relief from the hardships and dangers of our present tariff laws should be devised with especial precaution against imperiling the existence of our manufacturing interests. But this existence should not mean a condition which, without regard to the public welfare or a national exigency, must always insure the realization of immense profits instead of moderately profitable returns. As the volume and diversity of our national activities increase, new recruits are added to those who desire a continuation of the advantages which they conceive the present system of tariff taxation directly affords them. So stubbornly have all efforts to reform the present condition been resisted by those of our fellow-citizens thus engaged that they can hardly complain of the suspicion, entertained to a certain extent, that there exists an organized combination all along the line to maintain their advantage.

We are in the midst of centennial celebrations, and with becoming pride we rejoice in American skill and ingenuity, in American energy and enterprise, and in the wonderful natural advantages and resources developed by a century's national growth. Yet when an attempt is made to justify a scheme which permits a tax to be laid upon every consumer in the land for the benefit of our manufacturers, quite beyond a reasonable demand for governmental regard, it suits the purposes of advocacy to call our manufactures infant industries still needing the highest and greatest degree of favor and fostering care that can be wrung from Federal legislation.

It is also said that the increase in the price of domestic manufactures resulting from the present tariff is necessary in order that higher wages may be paid to our workingmen employed in manufactories than are paid for what is called the pauper labor of Europe. All will acknowledge the force of an argument, which involves the welfare, and liberal compensation of our laboring people. Our labor is honorable in the eyes of every American citizen; and as it lies at the foundation of our development and progress, it is entitled, without affection or hypocrisy, to the utmost regard. The standard of our laborers' life should not be measured by that of any other country less favored, and they are entitled to their full share of all our advantages.

By the last census it is made to appear that of the 17,392,099 of our population engaged in all kinds of industries 7,670,493 are employed in agriculture, 4,074,238 in professional and personal service (2,934,876 of whom are domestic servants and laborers), while 1,810,256 are employed in trade and transportation and 3,837,112 are classed as employed in manufacturing and mining.

For present purposes, however, the last number given should be considerably reduced. Without attempting to enumerate all, it will be conceded that there should be deducted from those which it includes 375,143 carpenters and joiners, 285,401 milliners, dressmakers, and seamstresses, 172,726 blacksmiths, 133,756 tailors and tailoresses, 102,473 masons, 76,241 butchers, 41,309 bakers, 22,083 plasterers, and 4,891 engaged in manufacturing agricultural implements, amounting in the aggregate to 1,214,023, leaving 2,623,089 persons employed in such manufacturing industries as are claimed to be benefited by a high tariff.

To these the appeal is made to save their employment and maintain their wages by resisting a change. There should be no disposition to answer such suggestions by the allegation that they are in a minority among those who labor, and therefore should forego an advantage in the interest of low prices for the majority. Their compensation, it may be affected by the operation of tariff laws, should at all times be scrupulously kept in view; and yet with slight reflection they will not overlook the fact that they are consumers with the rest; that they too have their own wants and those of their families to supply from their earnings, and that the price of the necessaries of life, as well as the amount of their wages, will regulate the measure of their welfare and comfort.

But the reduction of taxation demanded should be so measured as not to necessitate or justify either the loss of employment by the workingman or the lessening of his wages; and the profits still remaining to the manufacturer after a necessary readjustment should furnish no excuse for the sacrifice of the interests of his employees, either in their opportunity to work or in the diminution of their compensation. Nor can the worker in manufactures fail to understand that while a high tariff is claimed to be necessary to allow the payment of remunerative wages, it certainly results in a very large increase in the price of nearly all sorts of manufactures, which, in almost countless forms, he needs for the use of himself and his family. He receives at the desk of his employer his wages, and perhaps before he reaches his home is obliged, in a purchase for family use of an article which embraces his own labor, to return in the payment of the increase in price which the tariff permits the hard-earned compensation of many days of toil.

The farmer and the agriculturist who manufacture nothing, but who pay the increased price which the tariff imposes, upon every agricultural implement, upon all he wears and upon all he uses and owns, except the increase of his flocks and herds and such things as his husbandry produces from the soil, is invited to aid in maintaining the present situation; and he is told that a high duty on imported wool is necessary for the benefit of those who have sheep to shear, in order that the price of their wool may be increased. They, of course, are not reminded that the farmer who has no sheep is by this scheme obliged, in his purchase of clothing and woolen goods, to pay a tribute to his fellow farmer as well as to the manufacturer and the merchant; not is any mention made of the fact that the sheep owners themselves and their household must wear clothing and use other articles manufactured from the wool they sell at tariff prices,

and thus as consumers must return their shape of this increased price to the tradesman.

I think it may be fairly assumed that a large proportion of the sheep owned by the farmers throughout the country are found in small flocks numbering from twenty-five to fifty. The duty on the grade of imported wool which these sheep yield is 10 cents each pound if of the value of 30 cents or less, and 12 cents if of the value of more than 30 cents. If the liberal estimate of six pounds be allowed for each fleece the duty thereon would be 60 or 72 cents, and this may be taken as the utmost enhancement of its price to the farmer by reason of this duty. Eighteen dollars would thus represent the increased price of the wool from twenty-five sheep and $36 that from the wool of fifty sheep; and at present values this addition would amount to about one-third of its price. If upon its sale the farmer receives this or a less tariff profit, the wool leaves his hands charged with precisely that sum, which in all its changes will adhere to it until it reaches the consumer. When manufactured into cloth and other goods and materials for use its cost is not only increased to the extent of the farmer's tariff profit, but a further sum has been added for the benefits of the manufacturer under the operation of other tariff laws. In the meantime the day arrives when the farmer finds it necessary to purchase woolen goods and material to clothe himself and family for the winter. When he faces a tradesman for that purpose he discovers that he is obliged not only to return in the way of increased prices, his tariff profit on the wool he sold, and which then perhaps lies before him in manufactured form, but that he must add a considerable sum thereto to meet a further increase in cost caused by a tariff duty on the manufacturer. Thus in the end he is aroused to the fact that he has paid upon a moderate purchase, as the result of the tariff scheme, which, when he sold his wool seemed so profitable, an increase in price more than sufficient to sweep away all the tariff profit he received upon the wool he produced and sold.

When the number of farmers engaged in wool raising is compared with all the farmers in the country, and the small proportion they bear to our population is considered; when it is made apparent that, in the case of a large part of those who own sheep, the benefit of the present tariff on wool is illusory, and, above all, when it must be conceded that the increase of the cost of living caused by such a tariff becomes a burden upon those with moderate means and the poor, the employed and the unemployed, the sick and well, and the young and old, and that it constitutes a tax which, with a relentless grasp, is fastened upon the clothing of every man, woman and child in the land, reasons are suggested why the removal or the reduction of this duty should be included in a revision of our tariff laws.

In speaking of the increase cost of the consumer of our home manufactures resulting from a duty laid upon imported articles of the same description, the fact is not overlooked that competition among our domestic producers sometimes has the effect of keeping the price of their products below the highest limit allowed by such duties. But it is notorious that this competition is too often strangled by combinations quite prevalent at this time, and frequently called trusts, which have for their object the regulation of the supply and price of commodities made and sold by members of the combination. The people can hardly hope for any consideration in the operation of these selfish schemes.

If, however, in the absence of such combination, a healthy and free competition reduces the price of any particular dutiable article of home production below the limit which it might otherwise reach under our tariff laws, and if, with such reduced price, its manufacture continued to thrive, it is entirely evident that one thing had been discovered which should be carefully scrutinized in an effort to reduce taxation.

The necessity of combination to maintain the price of any commodity to the tariff point furnishes proof that someone is willing to accept lower prices for such commodities, and that such prices are remunerative; and lower prices produced by competition prove the same thing. Thus where either of these conditions exist a case would seem to be presented for an easy reduction of taxation. The considerations which have been presented touching our tariff laws are intended only to enforce an earnest recommendation that the surplus revenues of the government be prevented by the reduction of our customs duties, and at the same time to emphasize a suggestion that in accomplishing this purpose we may discharge double duty to our people by granting to them a measure of relief from tariff taxation in quarters where it is most needed and from sources where it can be most fairly and justly accorded.

Nor can the presentation made of such considerations be, with any degree of fairness, regarded as evidence of unfriendliness toward our manufacturing interests, or any lack of appreciation of their value and importance. These interests constitute a leading and most substantial element of our national greatness and furnish the proud proof of our country's progress. But if in the emergency that presses upon us our manufacturers are asked to surrender something for the public good and to avert disaster, their patriotism, as well as a grateful recognition of advantages already afforded, should lead them to willing co-operation. No demand is made that they should forego all the benefits of governmental regard, but they cannot fail to be admonished of their duty as well as their enlightened self-interest and safety, when they are reminded of the fact that financial panic and collapse, to which the present conditions tends, afford no greater shelter or protection to our manufactures than to our other important enterprises. Opportunity for safe, careful and deliberate reform is now afforded; and none of us should be unmindful of a time when an abused and irritated people, heedless of those who have resisted timely and reasonable relief, may insist upon a radical and sweeping rectification of their wrongs. The difficulty attending a wise and fair revision of our tariff laws is not underestimated. It will require on the part of the Congress great labor and care, and especially a broad and national contemplation of the subject, and a patriotic disregard of such local and selfish claims as are unreasonable and reckless of the welfare of the entire country.

Under our present laws more than four thousand articles are subject to duty. Many of these do not in any way compete with our own manufactures, and many are hardly worth attention as subjects of revenue. A considerable reduction can be made in the aggregate by adding them to the free list. The taxation of luxuries presents no features of hardship; but the necessaries of life used and consumed by all the people, the duty upon which adds to the cost of living in every home, should be greatly cheapened.

The radical reduction of the duties imposed upon raw material used in manufactures or its free importation is of course an important factor in any effort to reduce the price of these necessaries; it would not only relieve them from the increased cost caused by the tariff on such material, but the manufactured product being thus cheapened, that part of the tariff now laid on such products, as a compensation to our manufactures for the present price of raw material, could be accordingly modified. Such reduction or free importation would serve beside to largely reduce the revenue. It is not apparent how such a change can have any injurious effect upon our manufactures. On the contrary, it would appear to give them a better chance in foreign markets with the manufacturers of other countries, who cheapen their wares by free material. Thus our people might have the opportunity of extending their sales beyond the limits of home consumption—saving them from the depression, interruption in business and loss caused by a glutted domestic market, and affording their employees more certain and steady labor, with its resulting quiet and contentment.

The question thus imperatively

presented for solution should be approached in a spirit higher than partisanship and considered in the light of that regard for patriotic duty which should characterize the action of those intrusted with the weal of a confiding people. But the obligation to the declared party policy and principle is not wanting to urge prompt and effective action. Both of the great political parties now represented in the Government have, by repeated and authoritative declarations, condemned the condition of our laws which permits the collection from the people of unnecessary revenue, and have, in the most solemn manner, promised its correction; and neither as citizens or partisans are our countrymen in a mood to condone the deliberate violation of these pledges.

Our progress toward a wise conclusion will not be improved by dwelling upon the theories of protection and free trade. This savors too much of bandying epithets. It is a condition which confronts us—not a theory. Relief from this condition may involve a slight reduction of the advantages which we award our home productions, but the entire withdrawal of such advantages should not be contemplated. The question of free trade is absolutely irrelevant; and the persistent claim made in certain quarters, that all efforts to relieve the people from unjust and unnecessary taxation are schemes of so-called free-traders, is mischievous and far removed from any consideration for the public good.

The simple and plain duty which we owe the people is to reduce taxation to the necessary expenses of an economical operation of the Government, and to restore to the business of the country the money which we hold in the treasury through the perversion of governmental powers. These things can and should be done with safety to all our industries, without danger to the opportunity for remunerative labor which our working men need, and with benefit to them and all our people, by cheapening the means of their subsistence and increasing the measure of their comforts.

The Constitution provides that the President "shall from time to time give to Congress information of the state of the Union." It has been the custom of the Executive, in compliance with this provision, to annually exhibit to the Congress, at the opening if its session, the general condition of the country, and to detail with some particularity the operations of the different Executive Departments. It would be especially agreeable to follow this course at the present time and to call attention to the valuable accomplishments of these Departments during the last fiscal year; but I am so much impressed with the paramount importance of the subject to which this communication has thus far been devoted that I shall forego the addition of any other topic, and only urge upon your immediate consideration the "state of the Union" as shown in the present condition of our Treasury and our general fiscal situation, upon which every element of our safety and prosperity depends.

The reports of the heads of Departments, which will be submitted, contain full and explicit information touching the transaction of the business intrusted to them and such recommendations relating to legislation in the public interest as they deem advisable. I ask for these reports and recommendations the deliberate examination and action of the legislative branch of the Government.

There are other subjects not embraced in the departmental reports demanding legislative consideration, and which I should be glad to submit. Some of them, however, have been earnestly presented in previous messages, and as to them I beg leave to repeat prior recommendations.

As the law makes no provision for any report from the Department of State, a brief history of the transactions of that important Department, together with other matters which it may hereafter be deemed essential to commend to the attention of the Congress, may furnish the occasion for a future communication.

See also: **Vol. I**: American Free Trade League (AFTL); American Protective Tariff League (APTL); American Reciprocal Tariff League (ARTL); Boston Home Market Club; Carnegie, Andrew; Democratic Party; Industrial Revolution; Labor; Merchants Association of New York (MANY); Mills, Roger Q.; Mills Bill; National Association of Manufacturers (NAM); Reagan, John Henninger; Robber barons; Tariff of 1883 (Mongrel Tariff); Trusts. **Vol. III**: Tariff of 1890 (McKinley Tariff).

Benjamin Harrison's 1889 State of the Union Address

On December 3, 1889, Benjamin Harrison presented his First Annual Message to Congress. In the address, Harrison devoted only two paragraphs to the tariff issue, whereas his predecessor, Grover Cleveland, had devoted his entire speech to the topic of reducing tariff rates. Harrison's inattention to the tariff led to worsening economic conditions. When Harrison and Cleveland ran against each other again in 1892, Cleveland regained the White House. Included below is the portion of Harrison's 1889 address that discusses the tariff.

I recommend a revision of our tariff law, both in its administrative features and in the schedules. The need of the former is generally conceded, and an agreement upon the evils and inconveniences to be remedied and the best methods for their correction will probably not be difficult. Uniformity of valuation at all our ports is essential, and effective measures should be taken to secure it. It is equally desirable that questions affecting rates and classifications should be promptly decided.

The preparation of a new schedule of customs duties is a matter of great delicacy because of its direct effect upon the business of the country, and of great difficulty by reason of wide divergence of opinion as to the objects that may be promoted by such legislation. Some disturbances of business may perhaps result from the consideration of this subject by Congress, but this temporary ill effect will be reduced to the minimum by prompt action and by the assurance which the country already enjoys that any necessary changes will be so made as not to impair the just and reasonable protection of our home industries. The inequalities of the law should be adjusted, but the protective principle should be maintained and fairly applied to the products of our farms as well as our shops. These duties necessarily have relation to other things besides the revenues. We cannot limit their effects by fixing our eyes on the public treasury alone. They have a direct relation to home production, to work, to wages, and to the commercial independence of our country, and the wise and patriotic legislator should enlarge the field of his vision to include all of these. The necessary reduction in our public revenues, I am sure, can be made without making the smaller burden more onerous than the larger by reason of the disabilities and limitations which the process of reduction puts upon both capital and labor. The free list can very safely be extended by placing thereon articles that do not offer injurious competition to such domestic products as our home labor can supply. The removal of the internal tax upon tobacco would relieve an important agricultural product from a burden which was imposed only because our revenue from customs duties was insufficient for the public needs. If safe provision against fraud can be devised, the removal of tax upon spirits used in arts and in manufactures would also offer an unobjectionable method of reducing the surplus.

See also: **Vol. I**: American Free Trade League (AFTL); American Protective Tariff League (APTL); American Reciprocal Tariff League (ARTL); Boston Home Market Club; Carnegie, Andrew; Democratic Party; Industrial Revolution; Labor; McKinley, William; Merchants Association of New York (MANY); Mills, Roger Q.; Mills Bill; National Association of Manufacturers (NAM); Reagan, John Henninger; Republican Party; Robber barons; Trusts. **Vol. III**: Tariff of 1890 (McKinley Tariff).

Samuel J. Randall's 1888 Speech on Tariff Benefits for the Wealthy

Congressman Samuel J. Randall of Pennsylvania delivered the following tariff speech in the House of Representatives on May 18, 1888, during the great tariff debate. Randall argued that the high protectionist tariff benefited the wealthy while penalizing the common people. He pointed out that foreign luxuries purchased by the rich, such as statuary and fine paintings, remained on the free list. He also illustrated how the rich could purchase finished products from abroad cheaply because the tariff rate on these items remained much lower than the rates on raw materials imported to manufacture the same items in the United States. Randall called for a tariff revision that would adjust the rates accordingly.

The declared purpose of this bill is to secure "free raw materials to stimulate manufactories."

In execution of this idea, the bill places on the free list a large number of articles which are really manufactured articles, such as salt, sawed and dressed lumber, glue, various oils and chemicals, china, clay, etc. These constitute the products of large and useful industries throughout the United States in which millions of capital are invested, and employing many thousands of working people. At the same time the bill leaves or puts upon the dutiable list, lead, iron, zinc and nickel ores, and coal which might be called raw material. Further than this the bill not only makes so-called "raw materials" free, but places on the free list the manufactured products of these materials. The manufacture of such articles is made impossible in this country, except by reducing American labor to a worse condition than that of labor in Europe. It goes even further, and placed or leaves dutiable certain so-called raw materials, such as iron ore, lead, coal, paper, paints, etc., while placing on the free list articles made from these materials, such as hoop iron and cotton ties, tin plates, machinery, books and pamphlets, etc.

In other words, the bill leaves or makes dutiable the raw material and puts on the free list the articles manufactured from it; thus not only placing an insurmountable barrier in the way of making such articles here, but actually protecting the foreign manufacturer and laborer against our own, and imposing for their benefit a burden upon the consumer in this country. Again, the bill places lower rates on some manufactured articles than on the raw materials used in making them. For instance, type metal, 15 per cent; pig lead, 45 per cent; carpet, 30 per cent; yarns used in their manufacture, 40 per cent. It leaves an internal revenue tax of more than 100 per cent on alcohol used in the arts, amounting to as much as the entire amount of duty collected on raw wool. This article enters as a material in a vast number of important and needful articles which the committee have even made free or have so reduced the rates thereon that the duty will be less than the tax on alcohol consumed in their manufacture.

In some cases the difference between the duty imposed by the bill on the so-called raw material and the articles made from them is so small as to destroy these industries, except upon the condition of leveling the wages of home labor to that of Europe. This was so in the case of pig lead and red lead, which is made from it, and of pig iron and steel blooms and steel rails.

Such legislation would leave the ore in the mines, or the pig lead in the smelting works, or the pig iron to rust at the furnaces, while foreigners would supply our market with these manufactured products. In a large number of articles throughout the schedule the reductions proposed by the bill are so large that the effect might be to destroy or restrict home production and increase enormously foreign importation, thus increasing customs revenue instead of reducing it, as claimed by the advocates of the bill. Particular mention in this connection is made of earthen and chine ware, glass, leaf tobacco, manufactures of cotton, flax, hemp and jute, carpets, brushes, leather, gloves, manufactures of India rubber and pipes.

Mr. Randall asserted that instead of the bill reducing customs revenues $64,000,000, as was claimed, it would be fair to estimate that its effect would be to largely increase the revenue instead of reducing it, while the amount of material wealth it would destroy in incalculable.

Those supporting the bill, he said, hold themselves out as the champions of the farmer, while they take from him the protection duties on his wool, hemp, flax, meats, vegetables, etc. And what do they give him in return? They profess to give the manufacturer better rates than he now has. If this be so, how is the farmer to be benefited, or where does he get compensation for the loss of his protective duties?

Much has been said about removing taxes on necessaries and imposing them upon luxuries. What does this bill propose? It gives olive oil to the epicure and taxes castor oil 5 per cent. It gives free tin plates to the Standard Oil Company and to the great meat canning monopolies, and imposes a duty of 100 per cent on rice; it gives the sugar trust free bone black and proposes prohibitory duties on grocery grades of sugar; it imposes a duty of 40 per cent on the "poor man's blanket" and only 30 per cent on the Axminster carpet of the rich. It admits free of duty the fine animals imported by the gentlemen of the turf; makes free the paintings and the statuary of the railway millionaire and the coal baron.

Mr. Randall said he yielded to no man on his side of the House in his desire for continued Democratic control in the administration of the Federal Government. He did not believe the adoption of the committee's bill would make such results certain, and added:

"I cannot be coerced into any particular action upon economic questions by the direction of a party caucus. The period of the political caucus has departed, never to return, and yet we should confer and have unity, if it is possible.

"In these matters I speak only for myself. My convictions on the tariff are strong and founded, as I think, upon principle, and upon information and intelligent comprehension of the subject. When any one here enters upon the task of involving caucus power or other modes of coercion I can only say to him, if he acts with good purpose, that it will prove a fruitless undertaking; or if with ill motive, then I consign to him all the natural contempt which such self-constituted superciliousness deserves."

In conclusion, Mr. Randall quoted from the earliest statesmen in support of his views upon the tariff, and said: "If Jackson could say he was confirmed in his opinions by the opinions of Jefferson, Madison and Monroe, how much more am I confirmed in my opinions by his great authority added to that of the founders and builders of the Democratic party? I warn the party

that it is not safe to abandon the principles so fundamental to our institutions and so necessary to maintenance of our industrial system; principles which attest the wisdom of those who established them by the fruits they have borne, the full fruition of which, however, can only be realized in the extension of diversified industries to all parts of the country, not in the North and East alone, but in the West and South as well. A new era of industrial enterprise has already dawned upon the South; no section of the country possesses greater natural advantages that the South, with her genial climate, her limitless raw materials, her mines of coal and iron, with abundant labor ready to develop them. Considering what has been there achieved in a single decade, what may not a century bring forth from her under a system calculated to favor the highest industrial development? When I read the history of my country and consider the past and present, and reflect on what is before us, I cannot believe that the idea that went down in the convulsions of 1861 will ever again dominate the destinies of the Republic."

See also: **Vol. I**: American Free Trade League (AFTL); American Protective Tariff League (APTL); American Reciprocal Tariff League (ARTL); Boston Home Market Club; Carnegie, Andrew; Cleveland, Stephen Grover; Democratic Party; Industrial Revolution; Labor; McKinley, William; Merchants Association of New York (MANY); Mills, Roger Q.; Mills Bill; National Association of Manufacturers (NAM); Reagan, John Henninger; Republican Party; Robber barons; Tariff of 1883 (Mongrel Tariff); Trusts. **Vol. III**: Tariff of 1890 (McKinley Tariff).

William McKinley's 1888 Speech on Tariff Benefits for Labor

During the great tariff debate of 1888, politicians on both sides of the issue presented their arguments to people throughout the United States. William McKinley, U.S. Representative from Ohio, delivered the following speech before the Chautauqua Society of Georgia. McKinley argued that a revenue tariff would lead to lower wages for American workers and would not result in the United States being able to increase its share in foreign markets, as promised by his opponents. Efforts by men like McKinley ensured the continuation of the policy of protection throughout the remainder of the nineteenth century.

One of the striking differences between a revenue tariff and a protective tariff is that the former sends the money of its people abroad for foreign supplies and seeks out the foreign market. The latter keeps the money at home among our own people, circulating through the arteries of trade and creates a market at home, which is always the best, because the most reliable.

Surely a new era of industrial development has come to the South. Nothing should be permitted to check or retard it. To her, Nature has been most prodigal with her gifts. Her hills and valleys have been made the store houses of richest treasure. Coal and iron mines wait impatiently the touch of labor and capital, and tempt both with a promise of lavish profit.

Raw materials are found at every turn to invite the skilled artisan to transform them into the finest products for the highest uses of man. She possesses the fibres in richest abundance; her skilled labor should weave the fabric.

It is said that there is nothing grown in any of the states, except Florida, that Georgia cannot profitably produce. She has coal, iron deposits, marble and building stone, cotton and the cereals. Nothing but her own folly, nothing but blindness to her highest and best interests can keep her from the front rank of the industrial states of the Union. Whether we discuss this question from principle, from statistics, or experience, we must reach the same conclusion; all lead to the same conviction.

One of the chief complaints against the protective system is its alleged hindrance to foreign trade and the foreign market for our own products. It is argued that if we could import raw material from other countries free, and manufacture such raw material into products for use, we could export them at great profit, and thus secure a standing in the markets of the world. This theory, is wholly, as I believe, illusory. It is without substance. We have an example of free raw material in a certain line of manufactures—that of leather for boots, shoes, etc. In 1872 hides and skins were made free, so that our manufacturers could import them without custom house burdens. They have had "free trade" in their raw material now for sixteen years. This industry has been an exceptionally successful one, and yet you cannot avoid being surprised when I say to you that in these sixteen years we have been able to export but 2 per cent of the leather production of this country.

But if free raw material be necessary to secure an export trade and the foreign markets, then I answer that our manufacturers today have substantial free trade in foreign raw materials which they make into finished products in the United States, provided they export it. Sections 3019, 3020, 3021 and 3022 of the United States Statutes provide for the remission of duties on all foreign materials used in manufacturing for the export trade. The law is positive that all articles manufactured for export from imported material upon which duties have been paid shall, when exported, be entitled to a drawback of 90 per cent of the duties paid on such raw materials. Some use has been made of these laws. The remission of duties in 1884 paid upon imported material manufactured for foreign markets amounted to $2,356,638. On some articles the drawback is equal to the duty paid, but in no instance, where articles are imported to be manufactured here and sent abroad, is the duty to exceed 10 per cent.

And yet we are gravely told by the tariff reformer that we cannot reach foreign markets on account of the high tariff on the raw materials, when, in fact, for foreign trade foreign raw materials are practically free. This principle was recognized as early as the administration of George Washington, and has been enlarged and made applicable to all imported materials, the drawbacks varying from 60 to 100 per cent. What becomes, then, of the cry for free raw materials in the presence of this fact? The truth is: we are not so much concerned about foreign markets as we are about the home market. The latter is the best, and we have not yet been able to control it, and, until we do, that should be our chief concern. But if any of our people are sighing for a foreign market, and value it more highly than our own, they can import foreign raw material practically free of duty, and, after advancing it into higher forms of manufacture, can go out and possess the world's markets. Taxes on raw materials do not stand in their way, and it is hypocrisy to claim otherwise. "The markets of the world," in our present condition, are a snare and a delusion. We will reach them whenever we can undersell competing nations, and not sooner. Tariffs do not keep us out, and free trade will not make it easier to enter them.

Upon what terms can we adopt a revenue tariff system in this country? In one way only, by accepting European conditions and submitting to all of the discomforts and disadvantages of our commercial rivals. The chief obstruction in the way of a revenue tariff are the wages paid American working men, and any return to that policy involves a reduction of the cost of labor. We cannot afford to have cheap labor in the United States. Cheap labor means cheap men and dear money. I would rather elevate and improve the condition of my fellow citizen than increase the value of money and the power of "money bags." This is a republic of free and equal citizenship. The Government is in the hands of the masses, and not of the few. This is our boast, and it is a proud one. The condition of the masses, their well-being, their intelligence, their preparation for the civil duties which rest upon them depend largely upon the scale of industrial wages. It is essential, therefore, that the best possible wages attainable shall be secured and maintained. This is vital and fundamental. We cannot, without grave danger and serious disturbance—we ought not under any circumstances—adopt a policy which would scale down the wages and diminish the comforts of the American working men. Their welfare and independence, their progress and elevation are closely related to the welfare and independence and progress of the Republic. We have got no pampered class

in this country, and we want none. We want the field kept open. No narrowing of the avenues, no lowering of our standard. We want no barriers raised against a higher and better civilization. The gateway of opportunity must be open to all, to the end that they may be first who deserve to be first, whether born in poverty or reared in luxury. We do not want the masses excluded from competing for the first rank among their countrymen and for the Nation's greatest honors, and we do not mean they shall be.

Free trade, or a revenue tariff, will, of necessity, shut them out. It has no respect for labor. It holds it as the mere machinery of capital. It would have cheap men that it might have cheap merchandise. With all its boast of love for the struggling millions, it is infinitely more interested in cutting down the wages of labor than in saving 25 cents on a blanket; more intent in reducing the purchasing power of a man's labor than the cost of his coat. Things are not always dearest when their price is nominally the highest. The price is not the only measure, but the wherewith to buy it is an essential factor. Few men before me but have found in the course of their lives more than once that that which was cheapest, when measured by mere price, was the dearest when they were without money and employment, or when their products could find no market, and, finding it, commanded no price at all commensurate with the labor which is interested most in this question of protection. The man with money can seek other avenues of profit and investment, or can wait for his dividends, but the laborer cannot wait for his dinner, and the United States do not want citizens who make Presidents and Senates and the House of Representatives to be in a condition of dependence and destitution. That is not the sort of citizenship we want. We are different from any other nation, and it is that difference which makes us the best. Our political system rests upon a principle different from that of any other. If we had wanted it otherwise we would not have left home, but would have remained the obedient child of an impervious parent. We would not have turned away from the mother country. We would have remained one of her dependencies. We would not have fought our way through blood and sacrifice to independence. We separated to set up for ourselves a free and independent political society, and that policy is the best for us which best subserves the purposes of our organization, our citizenship and civilization. It is ours to work out our own destiny, and, in doing so, furnish an example of a free and progressive people, whose industrial policy has made it possible to satisfy the best and the highest aspirations of men, and which closes no field to human endeavor. We would wish for all mankind the beneficence of our system and the opportunities which it presents. I bid them level their condition up to ours; we will not level ours down to theirs. We will remove all restrictions from international trade, as we have removed all restrictions from interstate trade, whenever they will raise their labor and their conditions to our standard.

Men of Georgia, upon this great industrial question there should be no North, nor South. To us of every section have been intrusted the interests of our country—our whole country. To others have been confided the care of other nations and other people. We will not interfere with them; we bid them not interfere with us. My fellow citizens, in this conflict, influenced by patriotism, national interest and national pride, let us be Americans.

See also: **Vol. I**: American Free Trade League (AFTL); American Protective Tariff League (APTL); American Reciprocal Tariff League (ARTL); Boston Home Market Club; Carnegie, Andrew; Cleveland, Stephen Grover; Democratic Party; Industrial Revolution; Labor; McKinley, William; Merchants Association of New York (MANY); Mills, Roger Q.; Mills Bill; National Association of Manufacturers (NAM); Reagan, John Henninger; Republican Party; Robber barons; Tariff of 1883 (Mongrel Tariff); Trusts. **Vol. III**: Tariff of 1890 (McKinley Tariff).

Inaugural Address of William Howard Taft

After being sworn in as the twenty-seventh president of the United States on March 4, 1909, William Howard Taft outlined the policies of the new administration in his inaugural speech. Against the advice of his predecessor, Theodore Roosevelt, Taft called Congress into special session to address the tariff issue. He encouraged Congress to reduce the rates on most items and grant the executive branch authority to increase the maximum rates on imports from foreign countries that discriminated against American products. He also noted that the recent Panic of 1907 had resulted in the collection of less revenue than expenditures, and asked Congress to keep that in mind when adjusting the tariff rates. When Congress finally passed the Payne-Aldrich Tariff they raised rates on 220 items, reduced them on 654 items, and left 1,150 items unchanged.

My Fellow-Citizens:

Anyone who has taken the oath I have just taken must feel a heavy weight of responsibility. If not, he has no conception of the powers and duties of the office upon which he is about to enter, or he is lacking in a proper sense of the obligation which the oath imposes.

The office of an inaugural address is to give a summary outline of the main policies of the new administration, so far as they can be anticipated. I have had the honor to be one of the advisers of my distinguished predecessor, and, as such, to hold up his hands in the reforms he has initiated. I should be untrue to myself, to my promises, and to the declarations of the party platform upon which I was elected to office, if I did not make the maintenance and enforcement of those reforms a most important feature of my administration. They were directed to the suppression of the lawlessness and abuses of power of the great combinations of capital invested in railroads and in industrial enterprises carrying on interstate commerce. The steps which my predecessor took and the legislation passed on his recommendation have accomplished much, have caused a general halt in the vicious policies which created popular alarm, and have brought about in the business affected a much higher regard for existing law.

To render the reforms lasting, however, and to secure at the same time freedom from alarm on the part of those pursuing proper and progressive business methods, further legislative and executive action are needed. Relief of the railroads from certain restrictions of the antitrust law have been urged by my predecessor and will be urged by me. On the other hand, the administration is pledged to legislation looking to a proper federal supervision and restriction to prevent excessive issues of bonds and stock by companies owning and operating interstate commerce railroads.

Then, too, a reorganization of the Department of Justice, of the Bureau of Corporations in the Department of Commerce and Labor, and of the Interstate Commerce Commission, looking to effective cooperation of these agencies, is needed to secure a more rapid and certain enforcement of the laws affecting interstate railroads and industrial combinations.

I hope to be able to submit at the first regular session of the incoming Congress, in December next, definite suggestions in respect to the needed amendments to the antitrust and the interstate commerce law and the changes required in the executive departments concerned in their enforcement.

It is believed that with the changes to be recommended American business can be assured of that measure of stability and certainty in respect to those things that may be done and those that are prohibited which is essential to the life and growth of all business. Such a plan must include the right of the people to avail themselves of those methods of combining capital and effort deemed necessary to reach the highest degree of economic efficiency, at the same time differentiating between combinations based upon legitimate economic reasons and those formed with the intent of creating monopolies and artificially controlling prices.

The work of formulating into practical shape such changes is creative work of the highest order, and requires all the deliberation possible in the interval. I believe that the amendments to be proposed are just as necessary in the protection of legitimate business as in the clinching of the reforms which properly bear the name of my predecessor.

A matter of most pressing importance is the revision of the tariff. In accordance with the promises of the platform upon which I was elected, I shall call Congress into extra session to meet on the 15th day of March, in order that consideration may be at once given to a bill revising the Dingley Act. This should secure an adequate revenue and adjust the duties in such a manner as to afford to labor and to all industries in this country, whether of the farm, mine or factory, protection by tariff equal to the difference between the cost of production abroad and the cost of production here, and have a provision which shall put into force, upon executive determination of certain facts, a higher or maximum tariff against those countries whose trade policy toward us equitably requires such discrimination. It is thought that there has been such a change in conditions since the enactment of the Dingley Act, drafted on a similarly protective principle, that the measure of the tariff above stated will permit the reduction of rates in certain schedules and will require the advancement of few, if any.

The proposal to revise the tariff made in such an authoritative way as to lead the business community to count upon it necessarily halts all those branches of business directly affected; and as these are most important, it disturbs the whole business of the country. It is imperatively necessary, therefore, that a tariff bill be drawn in good faith in accordance with promises made before the election by the party in power, and as promptly passed as due consideration will permit. It is not that the tariff is more important in the long run than the perfecting of the reforms in respect to antitrust legislation and interstate commerce regulation, but the need for action when the revision of the tariff has been determined upon is more immediate to avoid embarrassment of business. To secure the needed speed in the passage of the tariff bill, it would seem wise to attempt no other legislation at the extra session. I venture this as a suggestion only, for the course to be taken by Congress, upon the call of the Executive, is wholly within its discretion.

In the mailing of a tariff bill the prime motive is taxation and the securing thereby of a revenue. Due largely to the business depression which followed the financial panic of 1907, the revenue from customs and other sources has decreased to such an extent that the expenditures for the current fiscal year will exceed the receipts by $100,000,000. It is imperative that such a deficit shall not continue, and the framers of the tariff bill must, of course, have in mind the total revenues likely to be produced by it and so arrange the duties as to secure an adequate income. Should it be impossible to do so by import duties, new kinds of taxation must be adopted, and among these I recommend a graduated inheritance tax as correct in principle and as certain and easy of collection.

The obligation on the part of those responsible for the expenditures made to carry on the Government, to be as economical as possible, and to make the burden of taxation as light as possible, is plain, and should be affirmed in every declaration of government policy. This is especially true when we are face to face with a heavy deficit. But when the desire to win the popular approval leads to the cutting off of expenditures really needed to make the Government effective and to enable it to accomplish its proper objects, the result is as much to be condemned as the waste of government funds in unnecessary expenditure. The scope of a modern government in what it can and ought to accomplish for its people has been widened far beyond the principles laid down by the old "laissez faire" school of political writers, and this widening has met popular approval.

In the Department of Agriculture the use of scientific experiments on a large scale and the spread of information derived from them for the improvement of general agriculture must go on.

The importance of supervising business of great railways and industrial combinations and the necessary investigation and prosecution of unlawful business methods are another necessary tax upon Government which did not exist half a century ago.

The putting into force of laws which shall secure the conservation of our resources, so far as they may be within the jurisdiction of the Federal Government, including the most important work of saving and restoring our forests and the great improvement of waterways, are all proper government functions which must involve large expenditure if properly performed. While some of them, like the reclamation of lands, are made to pay for themselves, others are of such an indirect benefit that this cannot be expected of them. A permanent improvement, like the Panama Canal, should be treated as a distinct enterprise, and should be paid for by the proceeds of bonds, the issue of which will distribute its cost between the present and future generations in accordance with the benefits derived. It may well be submitted to the serious consideration of Congress whether the deepening and control of the channel of a great river system, like that of the Ohio or of the Mississippi, when definite and practical plans for the enterprise have been approved and determined upon, should not be provided for in the same way.

Then, too, there are expenditures of Government absolutely necessary if our country is to maintain its proper place among the nations of the world, and is to exercise its proper influence in defense of its own trade interests in the maintenance of traditional American policy against the colonization of European monarchies in this hemisphere, and in the promotion of peace and international morality. I refer to the cost of maintaining a proper army, a proper navy, and suitable fortifications upon the mainland of the United States and in its dependencies.

We should have an army so organized and so officered as to be capable in time of emergency, in cooperation with the national militia and under the provisions of a proper national volunteer law, rapidly to expand into a force sufficient to resist all probable invasion from abroad and to furnish a respectable expeditionary force if necessary in the maintenance of our traditional American policy which bears the name of President Monroe.

Our fortifications are yet in a state of only partial completeness, and the number of men to man them is insufficient. In a few years however, the usual annual appropriations for our coast defenses, both on the mainland and in the dependencies, will make them sufficient to resist all direct attack, and by that time we may hope that the men to man them will be provided as a necessary adjunct. The distance of our shores from Europe and Asia of course reduces the necessity for maintaining under arms a great army, but it does not take away the requirement of mere prudence—that we should have an army sufficiently large and so constituted as to form a nucleus out of which a suitable force can quickly grow.

What has been said of the army may be affirmed in even a more emphatic way of the navy. A modern navy can not be improvised. It must be built and in existence when the emergency arises which calls for its use and operation. My distinguished predecessor has in many speeches and messages set out with great force and striking language the necessity for maintaining a strong navy commensurate with the coast line, the governmental resources, and the foreign trade of our Nation; and I wish to reiterate all the reasons which he has presented in favor of the policy of maintaining a strong navy as the best conservator of our peace with other nations, and the best means of securing respect for the assertion of our rights, the defense of our interests, and the exercise of our influence in international matters.

Our international policy is always to promote peace. We shall enter into any war with a full consciousness of the awful consequences that it always entails, whether successful or not, and we, of course, shall make every effort consistent with national honor and the highest national interest to avoid a resort to arms. We favor every instrumentality, like that of the Hague Tribunal and arbitration treaties made with a view to its use in all international controversies, in order to maintain peace and to avoid war. But we should be blind to existing conditions and should allow ourselves to become foolish idealists if we did not realize that, with all the nations of the world armed and prepared for war, we must be ourselves in a similar condition, in order to prevent other nations from taking advantage of us and of our inability to defend our interests and assert our rights with a strong hand.

In the international controversies that are likely to arise in the Orient growing out of the question of the open door and other issues the United States can maintain her interests intact and can secure respect for her just demands. She will not be able to do so, however, if it is understood that she never intends to back up her assertion of right and her defense of her interest by anything but mere verbal protest and diplomatic note. For these reasons the expenses of the army and navy and of coast defenses should always be considered as something which the Government must pay for, and they should not be cut off through mere consideration of economy. Our Government is able to afford a suitable army and a suitable navy. It may maintain them without the slightest danger to the Republic or the cause of free institutions, and fear of additional taxation ought not to change a proper policy in this regard.

The policy of the United States in the Spanish war and since has given it a position of influence among the nations that it never had before, and should be constantly exerted to securing to its bona fide citizens, whether native or naturalized, respect for them as such in foreign countries. We should make every effort to prevent humiliating and degrading prohibition against any of our citizens wishing temporarily to sojourn in foreign countries because of race or religion.

The admission of Asiatic immigrants who cannot be amalgamated with our population has been made the subject either of prohibitory clauses in our treaties and statutes or of strict administrative regulation secured by diplomatic negotiation. I sincerely hope that we may continue to minimize the evils likely to arise from such immigration without unnecessary friction and

265

by mutual concessions between self-respecting governments. Meantime we must take every precaution to prevent, or failing that, to punish outbursts of race feeling among our people against foreigners of whatever nationality who have by our grant a treaty right to pursue lawful business here and to be protected against lawless assault or injury.

This leads me to point out a serious defect in the present federal jurisdiction, which ought to be remedied at once. Having assured to other countries by treaty the protection of our laws for such of their subjects or citizens as we permit to come within our jurisdiction, we now leave to a state or a city, not under the control of the Federal Government, the duty of performing our international obligations in this respect. By proper legislation we may, and ought to, place in the hands of the Federal Executive the means of enforcing the treaty rights of such aliens in the courts of the Federal Government. It puts our Government in a pusillanimous position to make definite engagements to protect aliens and then to excuse the failure to perform those engagements by an explanation that the duty to keep them is in States or cities, not within our control. If we would promise we must put ourselves in a position to perform our promise. We cannot permit the possible failure of justice, due to local prejudice in any State or municipal government, to expose us to the risk of a war which might be avoided if federal jurisdiction was asserted by suitable legislation by Congress and carried out by proper proceedings instituted by the Executive in the courts of the National Government.

One of the reforms to be carried out during the incoming administration is a change of our monetary and banking laws, so as to secure greater elasticity in the forms of currency available for trade and to prevent the limitations of law from operating to increase the embarrassment of a financial panic. The monetary commission, lately appointed, is giving full consideration to existing conditions and to all proposed remedies, and will doubtless suggest one that will meet the requirements of business and of public interest.

We may hope that the report will embody neither the narrow dew of those who believe that the sole purpose of the new system should be to secure a large return on banking capital or of those who would have greater expansion of currency with little regard to provisions for its immediate redemption or ultimate security. There is no subject of economic discussion so intricate and so likely to evoke differing views and dogmatic statements as this one. The commission, in studying the general influence of currency on business and of business on currency, have wisely extended their investigations in European banking and monetary methods. The information that they have derived from such experts as they have found abroad will undoubtedly be found helpful in the solution of the difficult problem they have in hand.

The incoming Congress should promptly fulfill the promise of the Republican platform and pass a proper postal savings bank bill. It will not be unwise or excessive paternalism. The promise to repay by the Government will furnish an inducement to savings deposits which private enterprise can not supply and at such a low rate of interest as not to withdraw custom from existing banks. It will substantially increase the funds available for investment as capital in useful enterprises. It will furnish absolute security which makes the proposed scheme of government guaranty of deposits so alluring, without its pernicious results.

I sincerely hope that the incoming Congress will be alive, as it should be, to the importance of our foreign trade and of encouraging it in every way feasible. The possibility of increasing this trade in the Orient, in the Philippines, and in South America are known to everyone who has given the matter attention. The direct effect of free trade between this country and the Philippines will be marked upon our sales of cottons, agricultural machinery, and other manufactures. The necessity of the establishment of direct lines of steamers between North and South America has been brought to the attention of Congress by my predecessor and by Mr. Root before and after his noteworthy visit to that continent, and I sincerely hope that Congress may be induced to see the wisdom of a tentative effort to establish such lines by the use of mail subsidies.

The importance of the part which the Departments of Agriculture and of Commerce and Labor may play in ridding the markets of Europe of prohibitions and discriminations against the importation of our products is fully understood, and it is hoped that the use of the maximum and minimum feature of our tariff law to be soon passed will be effective to remove many of those restrictions.

The Panama Canal will have a most important bearing upon the trade between the eastern and far western sections of our country, and will greatly increase the facilities for transportation between the eastern and the western seaboard, and may possibly revolutionize the transcontinental rates with respect to bulky merchandise. It will also have a most beneficial effect to increase the trade between the eastern seaboard of the United States and the western coast of South America, and, indeed, with some of the important ports on the east coast of South America reached by rail from the west coast.

The work on the canal is making most satisfactory progress. The type of the canal as a lock canal was fixed by Congress after a full consideration of the conflicting reports of the majority and minority of the consulting board, and after the recommendation of the War Department and the Executive upon those reports. Recent suggestion that something had occurred on the Isthmus to make the lock type of the canal less feasible than it was supposed to be when the reports were made and the policy determined on led to a visit to the Isthmus of a board of competent engineers to examine the Gatun dam and locks, which are the key of the lock type. The report of that board shows nothing has occurred in the nature of newly revealed evidence which should change the views once formed in the original discussion. The construction will go on under a most effective organization controlled by Colonel Goethals and his fellow army engineers associated with him, and will certainly be completed early in the next administration, if not before.

Some type of canal must be constructed. The lock type has been selected. We are all in favor of having it built as promptly as possible. We must not now, therefore, keep up a fire in the rear of the agents whom we have authorized to do our work on the Isthmus. We must hold up their hands, and speaking for the incoming administration I wish to say that I propose to devote all the energy possible and under my control to pushing of this work on the plans which have been adopted, and to stand behind the men who are doing faithful, hard work to bring about the early completion of this, the greatest constructive enterprise of modern times.

The governments of our dependencies in Porto Rico and the Philippines are progressing as favorably as could be desired. The prosperity of Porto Rico continues unabated. The business conditions in the Philippines are not all that we could wish them to be, but with the passage of the new tariff bill permitting free trade between the United States and the archipelago, with such limitations on sugar and tobacco as shall prevent injury to domestic interests in those products, we can count on an improvement in business conditions in the Philippines and the development of a mutually profitable trade between this country and the islands. Meantime our Government in each dependency is upholding the traditions of civil liberty and increasing popular control which might be expected under American auspices. The work which we are doing there redounds to our credit as a nation.

I look forward with hope to increasing the already good feeling between the South and the other sections of the country. My chief purpose is not to effect a change in the electoral vote of the Southern States. That is a secondary consideration. What I look forward to is an increase in the tolerance of polit-ical views of all kinds and their advocacy throughout the South, and the existence of a respectable political opposition in every State; even more than this, to an increased feeling on the part of all the people in the South that this Government is their Government, and that its officers in their states are their officers.

The consideration of this question can not, however, be complete and full without reference to the negro race, its progress and its present condition. The thirteenth amendment secured them freedom; the fourteenth amendment due process of law, protection of property, and the pursuit of happiness; and the fifteenth amendment attempted to secure the negro against any deprivation of the privilege to vote because he was a negro. The thirteenth and fourteenth amendments have been generally enforced and have secured the objects for which they are intended. While the fifteenth amendment has not been generally observed in the past, it ought to be observed, and the tendency of Southern legislation today is toward the enactment of electoral qualifications which shall square with that amendment. Of course, the mere adoption of a constitutional law is only one step in the right direction. It must be fairly and justly enforced as well. In time both will come. Hence it is clear to all that the domination of an ignorant, irresponsible element can be prevented by constitutional laws which shall exclude from voting both negroes and whites not having education or other qualifications thought to be necessary for a proper electorate. The danger of the control of an ignorant electorate has therefore passed. With this change, the interest which many of the Southern white citizens take in the welfare of the negroes has increased. The colored men must base their hope on the results of their own industry, self-restraint, thrift, and business success, as well as upon the aid and comfort and sympathy which they may receive from their white neighbors of the South.

There was a time when Northerners who sympathized with the negro in his necessary struggle for better conditions sought to give him the suffrage as a protection to enforce its exercise against the prevailing sentiment of the South. The movement proved to be a failure. What remains is the fifteenth amendment to the Constitution and the right to have statutes of States specifying qualifications for electors subjected to the test of compliance with that amendment. This is a great protection to the negro. It never will be repealed, and it never ought to be repealed. If it had not passed, it might be difficult now to adopt it; but with it in our fundamental law, the policy of Southern legislation must and will tend to obey it, and so long as the statutes of the States meet the test of this amendment and are not otherwise in conflict with the Constitution and laws of the United States, it is not the disposition or within the province of the Federal Government to interfere with the regulation by Southern States of their domestic affairs. There is in the South a stronger feeling than ever among the intelligent well-to-do, and influential element in favor of the industrial education of the negro and the encouragement of the race to make themselves useful members of the community. The progress which the negro has made in the last fifty years, from slavery, when its statistics are reviewed, is marvelous, and it furnishes every reason to hope that in the next twenty-five years a still greater improvement in his condition as a productive member of society, on the farm, and in the shop, and in other occupations may come.

The negroes are now Americans. Their ancestors came here years ago against their will, and this is their only country and their only flag. They have shown themselves anxious to live for it and to die for it. Encountering the race feeling against them, subjected at times to cruel injustice growing out of it, they may well have our profound sympathy and aid in the struggle they are making. We are charged with the sacred duty of making their path as smooth and easy as we can. Any recognition of their distinguished men, any appointment to office from among their number, is properly taken as an encouragement and an appreciation of their progress, and this just policy should be pursued when suitable occasion offers.

But it may well admit of doubt whether, in the case of any race, an appointment of one of their number to a local office in a community in which the race feeling is so widespread and acute as to interfere with the ease and facility with which the local government business can be done by the appointee is of sufficient benefit by way of encouragement to the race to outweigh the recurrence and increase of race feeling which such an appointment is likely to engender. Therefore the Executive, in recognizing the negro race by appointments, must exercise a careful discretion not thereby to do it more harm than good. On the other hand, we must be careful not to encourage the mere pretense of race feeling manufactured in the interest of individual political ambition.

Personally, I have not the slightest race prejudice or feeling, and recognition of its existence only awakens in my heart a deeper sympathy for those who have to bear it or suffer from it, and I question the wisdom of a policy which is likely to increase it. Meantime, if nothing is done to prevent it, a better feeling between the negroes and the whites in the South will continue to grow, and more and more of the white people will come to realize that the future of the South is to be much benefited by the industrial and intellectual progress of the negro. The exercise of political franchises by those of this race who are intelligent and well to do will be acquiesced in, and the right to vote will be withheld only from the ignorant and irresponsible of both races.

There is one other matter to which I shall refer. It was made the subject of great controversy during the election and calls for at least a passing reference now. My distinguished predecessor has given much attention to the cause of labor, with whose struggle for better things he has shown the sincerest sympathy. At his instance Congress has passed the bill fixing the liability of interstate carriers to their employees for injury sustained in the course of employment, abolishing the rule of fellow-servant and the common-law rule as to contributory negligence, and substituting therefor the so-called rule of "comparative negligence." It has also passed a law fixing the compensation of government employees for injuries sustained in the employ of the Government through the negligence of the superior. It has also passed a model child-labor law for the District of Columbia. In previous administrations an arbitration law for interstate commerce railroads and their employees, and laws for the application of safety devices to save the lives and limbs of employees of interstate railroads had been passed. Additional legislation of this kind was passed by the outgoing Congress.

I wish to say that insofar as I can I hope to promote the enactment of further legislation of this character. I am strongly convinced that the Government should make itself as responsible to employees injured in its employ as an interstate-railway corporation is made responsible by federal law to its employees; and I shall be glad, whenever any additional reasonable safety device can be invented to reduce the loss of life and limb among railway employees, to urge Congress to require its adoption by interstate railways.

Another labor question has arisen which has awakened the most excited discussion. That is in respect to the power of the federal courts to issue injunctions in industrial disputes. As to that, my convictions are fixed. Take away from the courts, if it could be taken away, the power to issue injunctions in labor disputes, and it would create a privileged class among the laborers and save the lawless among their number from a most needful remedy available to all men for the protection of their business against lawless invasion. The proposition that business is not a property or pecuniary right which can be protected by equitable injunction is utterly without foundation in precedent or reason. The proposition is usually linked with one to make the secondary boycott lawful. Such a proposition is at variance with the American instinct, and will find no support, in my judgment, when submitted to the American people. The secondary boycott is an instrument of tyranny, and ought not to be made legitimate.

The issue of a temporary restraining order without notice has in several instances been abused by its inconsiderate exercise, and to remedy this the platform upon which I was elected recommends the formulation in a statute of the conditions under which such a temporary restraining order ought to issue. A statute can and ought to be framed to embody the best modern practice, and can bring the subject so closely to the attention of the court as to make abuses of the process unlikely in the future. The American people, if I understand them, insist that the authority of the courts shall be sustained, and are opposed to any change in the procedure by which the powers of a court may be weakened and the fearless and effective administration of justice be interfered with.

Having thus reviewed the questions likely to recur during my administration, and having expressed in a summary way the position which I expect to take in recommendations to Congress and in my conduct as an Executive, I invoke the considerate sympathy and support of my fellow-citizens and the aid of the Almighty God in the discharge of my responsible duties.

William Howard Taft's Winona Speech

During the presidential election campaign of 1908, William Howard Taft promised to lower tariff rates if elected. Once elected, he called Congress into a special session to consider the issue. The House of Representatives produced a bill that lowered most rates, but the Senate added over 800 amendments, forcing committee members from both chambers to work out a compromise bill—the Payne-Aldrich Tariff of 1909. Republicans opposed the measure as having fallen short of their intended goals but President Taft signed the bill into law anyway. In a speech at Winona, Minnesota, on September 17, 1909, Taft defended Payne-Aldrich as "the best tariff bill" ever passed. The following is an excerpt of the speech.

As long ago as August 1906, in the congressional campaign in Maine, I ventured to announce that I was a tariff revisionist and thought that the time had come for a readjustment of the schedules. I pointed out that it had been ten years prior to that time that the Dingley Bill had been passed; that great changes had taken place in the conditions surrounding the productions of the farm, the factory, and the mine, and that under the theory of protection in that time the rates imposed in the Dingley Bill in many instances might have become excessive; that is,

might have been greater than the difference between the cost of production abroad and the cost of production at home, with a sufficient allowance for a reasonable rate of profit to the American producer. I said that the party was divided on the issue, but that in my judgment the opinion of the party was crystallizing and would probably result in the near future in an effort to make such revision. I pointed out the difficulty that there always was in a revision of the tariff, due to the threatened disturbance of industries to be affected and the suspension of business, in a way which made it unwise to have too many revisions.

In the summer of 1907 my position on the tariff was challenged, and I then entered into a somewhat fuller discussion of the matter. It was contended by the so-called standpatters that rates beyond the necessary measure of protection were not objectionable because behind the tariff wall competition always reduced the prices and thus saved the consumer. But I pointed out in that speech what seems to me as true today as it then was, that the danger of excessive rates was in the temptation they created to form monopolies in the protected articles, and thus to take advantage of the excessive rates by increasing the prices, and therefore, and in order to avoid such a danger, it was wise at regular intervals to examine the question of what the effect of the rates had been upon the industries in this country, and whether the conditions with respect to the cost of production here had so changed as to warrant a reduction in the tariff, and to make a lower rate truly protective of the industry.

It will be observed that the object of the revision under such a statement was not to destroy protected industries in this country but it was to continue to protect them where lower rates offered a sufficient protection to prevent injury by foreign competition. That was the object of the revision as advocated by me, and it was certainly the object of the revision as promised in the Republican platform.

I want to make as clear as I can this proposition, because, in order to determine whether a bill is a compliance with the terms of that platform, it must be understood what the platform

means. A free trader is opposed to any protective rate because he thinks that our manufacturers, our farmers, and our miners ought to withstand the competition of foreign manufacturers and miners and farmers, or else go out of business and find something else more profitable to do. Now, certainly the promises of the platform did not contemplate the downward revision of the tariff rates to such a point that any industry theretofore protected should be injured. Hence, those who contend that the promise of the platform was to reduce prices by letting in foreign competition are contending for a free trade and not for anything that they had the right to infer from the Republican platform.

The Ways and Means Committee of the House, with Mr. Payne at its head, spent a full year in an investigation, assembling evidence in reference to the rates under the tariff, and devoted an immense amount of work in the study of the question where the tariff rates could be reduced and where they ought to be raised with a view to maintaining a reasonably protective rate, under the principles of the platform, for every industry that deserved protection. They found that the determination of the question, what was the actual cost of production and whether an industry in this country could live under a certain rate and withstand threatened competition from abroad, was most difficult. The manufacturers were prone to exaggerate the injury which a reduction in the duty would give and to magnify the amount of duty that was needed; while the importers, on the other hand, who were interested in developing the importation from foreign shores, were quite likely to be equally biased on the other side.

Mr. Payne reported a bill—the Payne Tariff Bill—which went to the Senate and was amended in the Senate by increasing the duty on some things and decreasing it on others. The difference between the House bill and the Senate bill was very much less than the newspapers represented. It turns out upon examination that the reductions in the Senate were about equal to those in the House, though they differed in character.

Now, there is nothing quite so difficult as the discussion of a tariff bill, for the reason that it covers so many different items, and the meaning of the terms and the percentages are very hard to understand. The passage of a new bill, especially where a change in the method of assessing the duties has been followed, presents an opportunity for various modes and calculations of the percentages of increases and decreases that are most misleading and really throw no light at all upon the changes made.

One way of stating what was done is to say what the facts show—that under the Dingley law there were 2,024 items. This included dutiable items only. The Payne law leaves 1,150 of these items unchanged. There are decreases in 654 of the items and increases in 220 of the items. Now, of course, that does not give a full picture, but it does show the proportion of decreases to have been three times those of the increases. . . .

Now, the promise of the Republican platform was not to revise everything downward, and in the speeches which have been taken as interpreting that platform which I made in the campaign, I did not promise that everything should go downward. What I promised was that there should be many decreases, and that in some few things increases would be found to be necessary; but that on the whole I conceived that the change of conditions would make the revision necessarily downward—and that, I contend, under the showing which I have made, has been the result of the Payne Bill. I did not agree, nor did the Republican Party agree, that we would reduce rates to such a point as to reduce prices by the introduction of foreign competition. That is what the free traders desire. That is what the revenue tariff reformers desire; but that is not what the Republican platform promised, and it is not what the Republican Party wished to bring about.

To repeat the statement with which I opened this speech, the proposition of the Republican Party was to reduce rates so as to maintain a difference between the cost of production abroad and the cost of production here, insuring a reasonable profit to the manufacturer on all articles produced in this country; and the proposition to reduce rates and prevent their being excessive was to avoid the opportunity for monopoly and the suppression of competition, so that the excessive rates could be taken advantage of to force prices up.

Now, it is said that there was not a reduction in a number of the schedules where there should have been. It is said that there was no reduction in the cotton schedule. There was not. The House and the Senate took evidence and found from cotton manufacturers and from other sources that the rates upon the lower class of cottons were such as to enable them to make a decent profit—but only a decent profit—and they were contented with it; but that the rates on the higher grades of cotton cloth, by reason of court decisions, had been reduced so that they were considerably below those of the cheaper grades of cotton cloth, and that by undervaluations and otherwise the whole cotton schedule had been made unjust and the various items were disproportionate in respect to the varying cloths.

Hence, in the Senate, a new system was introduced attempting to make the duties more specific rather than ad valorem in order to prevent by judicial decision or otherwise a disproportionate and unequal operation of the schedule. Under this schedule it was contended that there had been a general rise of all the duties on cotton. This was vigorously denied by the experts of the Treasury Department. At last, the Senate, in conference, consented to a reduction amounting to about 10 percent on all the lower grades of cotton, and this reduced the lower grades of cotton substantially to the same rates as before and increased the higher grades to what they ought to be under the Dingley law and what they were intended to be.

Now, I am not going into the question of evidence as to whether the cotton duties were too high and whether the difference between the cost of production abroad and at home, allowing for a reasonable profit to the manufacturer here, is less than the duties which are imposed under the Payne Bill. It was a question of evidence which Congress passed upon, after they heard the statements of cotton manufacturers and such other evidence as they could

avail themselves of. I agree that the method of taking evidence and the determination was made in a general way and that there ought to be other methods of obtaining evidence and reaching a conclusion more satisfactory. . . .

On the whole, however, I am bound to say that I think the Payne Tariff Bill is the best tariff bill that the Republican Party ever passed; that in it the party has conceded the necessity for following the changed conditions and reducing tariff rates accordingly. This is a substantial achievement in the direction of lower tariffs and downward revision, and it ought to be accepted as such. Critics of the bill utterly ignore the very tremendous cuts that have been made in the iron schedule which heretofore has been subject to criticism in all tariff bills. . . .

The high cost of living, of which 50 percent is consumed in food, 25 percent in clothing, and 25 percent in rent and fuel, has not been produced by the tariff, because the tariff has remained the same while the increases have gone on. It is due to the change of conditions the world over. Living has increased everywhere in cost—in countries where there is free trade and in countries where there is protection—and that increase has been chiefly seen in the cost of food products. In other words, we have had to pay more for the products of the farmer—for meat, for grain, for everything that enters into food. Now, certainly no one will contend that protection has increased the cost of food in this country, when the fact is that we have been the greatest exporters of food products in the world. It is only that the demand has increased beyond the supply, that farmlands have not been opened as rapidly as the population, and the demand has increased.

I am not saying that the tariff does not increase prices in clothing and in building and in other items that enter into the necessities of life, but what I wish to emphasize is that the recent increases in the cost of living in this country have not been due to the tariff. We have a much higher standard of living in this country than they have abroad, and this has been made possible by higher income for the workingman, the farmer, and all classes. Higher wages have been made possible by the encouragement of diversified industries, built up and fostered by the tariff.

Now, the revision downward of the tariff that I have favored will not, I hope, destroy the industries of the country. Certainly it is not intended to. All that it is intended to do, and that is what I wish to repeat, is to put the tariff where it will protect industries here from foreign competition but will not enable those who will wish to monopolize to raise prices by taking advantage of excessive rates beyond the normal difference in the cost of production.

If the country desires free trade, and the country desires a revenue tariff and wishes the manufacturers all over the country to go out of business, and to have cheaper prices at the expense of the sacrifice of many of our manufacturing interests, then it ought to say so and ought to put the Democratic Party in power if it thinks that party can be trusted to carry out any affirmative policy in favor of a revenue tariff. Certainly in the discussions in the Senate there was no great manifestation on the part of our Democratic friends in favor of reducing rates on necessities. They voted to maintain the tariff rates on everything that came from their particular sections. If we are to have free trade, certainly it cannot be had through the maintenance of Republican majorities in the Senate and House and a Republican administration.

See also: **Vol. I**: Aldrich, Nelson W.; Atkinson, Edward; Payne, Sereno E.; Payne-Aldrich Tariff (Tariff of 1909); Personal income tax (Sixteenth Constitutional Amendment); Taft, William Howard; Trade associations; U.S. Chamber of Commerce. **Vol. III**: Tariff of 1909 (Payne-Aldrich Tariff).

William Howard Taft's 1912 Acceptance Speech

In the presidential campaign of 1912, Republicans renominated William How-ard Taft as their candidate despite opposition from the supporters of Theodore Roosevelt, who formed the "Bull Moose" Party after losing the nomination. In his acceptance speech, delivered on August 1, 1912, Taft defended his sign-ing of the Payne-Aldrich Tariff and blamed the recent economic troubles on an increase in the gold supply and urbanization. Portions of this speech are included below.

The statement has been widely cir-culated and has received considerable support from political opponents that the tariff act of 1909 is a chief factor in creating the high cost of living. This is not true. A careful investigation will show that the phenomenon of in-creased prices and cost of living is worldwide in it extent and quite as much in evidence in other countries of advanced civilization and progressive tendencies as in our own. Bitter com-plaints of the burden of increased prices and cost of living have been made not only in this country, but even in countries of Asia and Africa. Disor-der and even riots have occurred in several European cities because of the unprecedented cost of food products. In our own country, changes have been manifested without regard to lower or higher duties in the tariff act of 1909. Indeed, the most notable increase in prices has been in the case of products where no duties are imposed, and in some instances in which they were di-minished or removed by the recent tar-iff act.

It is difficult to understand how any legislation or promise in a political platform can remedy this universal condition. I have recommended the creation of a commission to study this subject and to report upon all possible methods for alleviating the hardship of which people complain, but great economic tendencies, notable among which are the practically universal movement from the country to the city and the increased supply of gold have been the most potent factors in causing high prices. These facts every careful student of the situation must admit.

See also: **Vol. I**: Aldrich, Nelson W.; Atkinson, Edward; Payne, Sereno E.; Payne-Aldrich Tariff (Tariff of 1909); Personal income tax (Sixteenth Constitutional Amendment); Roosevelt, Theodore; Taft, William Howard; Trade associations; U.S. Chamber of Commerce; Wilson, Thomas Woodrow. **Vol. III**: Tariff of 1909 (Payne-Aldrich Tariff).

Theodore Roosevelt's Bull Moose Acceptance Speech

After failing to secure the nomination of the Republican Party in 1912, former president Theodore Roosevelt helped form the National Progressive, or "Bull-Moose," Party. Roosevelt had decided to run for the presidency again mainly because of his disagreement with Taft over the tariff issue. In his acceptance speech he advocated the formation of a Tariff Commission that would determine rates on a scientific basis. The following is an excerpt of Roosevelt's acceptance speech before the National Progressive Convention on August 6, 1912.

I believe in a protective tariff, but I believe in it as a principle, approached from the standpoint of the interests of the whole people, and not as a bundle of preferences to be given to favored individuals. In my opinion, the American people favor the principle of a protective tariff, but they desire such a tariff to be established primarily in the interests of the wage-worker and the consumer. The chief opposition to our tariff at the present moment comes from the general conviction that certain interests have been improperly favored by over-protection. I agree with this view. The commercial and industrial experience of this country has demonstrated the wisdom of the protective policy, but it has also demonstrated that in the application of that policy certain clearly recognized abuses have developed. It is not merely the tariff that should be revised, but the method of tariff-making and of tariff administration. Wherever nowadays an industry is to be protected it should be on the theory that such protection will serve to keep up the wages and the standard of living of the wage-worker in that industry will full regard for the interest of the consumer. To accomplish this the tariff to be levied should as nearly as is scientifically possible approximate the differential between the cost of production at home and abroad. This difference is chiefly, if not wholly, in labor cost. No duty should be permitted to stand as regards any industry unless the workers receive their full share of the benefits of that day.

In other words, there is no warrant for protection unless a legitimate share of the benefits gets into the pay envelope of the wage-worker.

The practice of undertaking a general revision of all the schedules at one time and of securing information as to conditions in the different industries and as to rates of duty desired chiefly from those engaged in the industries, who themselves benefit directly from the rates they propose, has been demonstrated to be not only iniquitous but futile. It has afforded opportunity for practically all of the abuses which have crept into our tariff-making and our tariff administration. The day of the log-rolling tariff must end. The progressive thought of the country has recognized this fact for several years, and the time has come when all genuine Progressives should insist upon a thorough and radical change in the method of tariff-making.

The first step should be the creation of a permanent commission of non-partisan experts whose business shall be to study scientifically all phases of tariff-making and of tariff effects. This commission should be large enough to cover all the different and widely varying branches of American industry. It should have ample powers to enable it to secure exact and reliable information. It should have authority to examine closely all correlated subjects, such as the effect of any given duty o the consumers of the article on which the duty is levied; that is, it should directly consider the question as to what any duty costs the people in the price

of living. It should examine into the wages and conditions of labor and life of the workmen in any industry, so as to insure out refusing protection to any industry unless the showing as regards the share labor receives therefore in satisfactory. This commission would be wholly different from the present unsatisfactory Tariff Board, which was created under a provision of law which failed to give it the powers indispensable if it was to do the work it should do.

It will be well for us to study the experience of Germany in considering this question. The German Tariff Commission has proved conclusively the efficiency and wisdom of this method of handling tariff questions. The reports of a permanent expert and non-partisan tariff commission would at once strike a most powerful blow against the chief iniquity of the old log-rolling method of tariff-making. One of the principal difficulties with the old method has been that it was impossible for the public generally, and especially for those members of Congress not directly connected with the committees handling a tariff bill, to secure anything like adequate and impartial information on the particular subjects under consideration. The reports of such a tariff commission would at once correct this evil and furnish to the general public full, complete and disinterested information on every subject treated in a tariff bill. With such reports it would no longer be possible to construct a tariff bill in secret or to jam it through either House of Congress without the fullest and most illuminating discussion. The path of the tariff "joker" would be rendered infinitely difficult.

As a further means of disrupting the old crooked log-rolling method of tariff-making, all future revisions of the tariff should be made schedule by schedule as changing conditions may require. This as a great obstacle will be thrown in the way of the trading of votes which has marked so scandalously the enactment of every tariff bill of recent years. The tariff commission should render reports at the call of Congress or of either branch of Congress and to the President. Under the Constitution, Congress is the tariff-making power. It should not be the purpose in creating a tariff commission to take anything way from this power of Congress, but rather to afford a wise means of giving to Congress the widest and most scientific assistance possible, and of furnishing it and the public with the fullest disinterested information. Only by this means can the tariff be taken out of politics. The creation of such a permanent tariff commission, and the adoption of the policy of schedule by schedule revision, will do more to accomplish this highly desired object than any other means yet devised.

The Democratic platform declares for a tariff for revenue only, asserting that a protective tariff is unconstitutional. To say that a protective tariff is unconstitutional, as the Democratic platform insists, is only excusable on a theory of the Constitution which would make it unconstitutional to legislate in any shape or way for the betterment of social and industrial conditions. The abolition of the protective tariff or the substitution for it of a tariff for revenue only, as proposed by the Democratic platform, would plunge this country into the most widespread industrial depression we have yet seen, and this depression would continue for an indefinite period. There is no hope from the standpoint of our people from action such as the Democrats propose. The one and only chance to secure stable and favorable business conditions in this country, while at the same time guaranteeing fair play to farmer, consumer, business man and wage-worker, lies in the creation of such a commission as I herein advocate. Only by such a commission and only by such activities of the commission will it be possible for us to get a reasonably quick revision of the tariff schedule by schedule—a revision which shall be downwards and not upwards, and at the same time secure a square deal not merely to the manufacturer, but to the wage-worker and to the general consumer.

See also: **Vol. I**: Aldrich, Nelson W.; Atkinson, Edward; Payne, Sereno E.; Payne-Aldrich Tariff (Tariff of 1909); Personal income tax (Sixteenth Constitutional Amendment); Taft, William Howard; Trade associations; U.S. Chamber of Commerce; Wilson, Thomas Woodrow. **Vol. III**: Tariff of 1909 (Payne-Aldrich Tariff).

Woodrow Wilson's Democratic Nomination Acceptance Speech

During the 1912 presidential election, all three candidates addressed the issue of the tariff in their acceptance speeches. Woodrow Wilson addressed the Democratic Convention on August 7, 1912, after receiving the party's nomination. He called for a revenue-only tariff that would foster competition among manufacturers.

The tariff question, as dealt with in our time at any rate, has not been business. It has been politics. Tariff schedules have been made up for the purpose of keeping as large a number as possible of the rich influential manufacturers of the country in a good humor with the Republican party, which desired their constant financial support. The tariff has become a system of favors, which the phraseology of the schedule was often deliberately contrived to conceal. It becomes a matter of business, of legitimate business, only when the partnership and understanding it represents is between the leaders of Congress and the whole people of the United States, instead of between the leaders of Congress and small groups of manufacturers demanding special recognition and consideration. That is why the general idea of representative government becomes a necessary part of the tariff question. Who, when you come down to the hard facts of the matter, have been represented in recent years when our tariff schedules were being discussed and determined, not on the floor of Congress, for that is not where they have been determined—in the committee rooms and conferences? That is the heart of the whole affair. Will you, can you bring the whole people into the partnership or not? No one is discontented with representative government; it falls under only when it ceases to be representative. It is at bottom a question of good faith and morals.

How does the present tariff look in

the light of it? I say nothing for the moment about the policy of protection, conceived and carried out as a disinterested statesman might conceive it. Our own clear conviction, as Democrats, is, that in the last analysis the only safe and legitimate object of tariff duties, as of every other kind, is to raise revenue for the support of the Government; but that is not my present point. We denounce the Payne-Aldrich tariff act as the most conspicuous example ever afforded the country of the special favors and monopolistic advantages which the leaders of the Republic party have so often shown themselves willing to extend to those to whom they looked for campaign contributions. Tariff duties, as they have employed them, have not been a means of setting up an equitable system of protection. They have been, on the contrary, a method of fostering special privilege. They have made it easy to establish monopoly in our domestic markets. Trusts have owned their origin and secure power to them. The economic freedom of our people, our untrammeled energy in manufacture, depend upon their reconsideration from top to bottom in an entirely different spirit.

We do not ignore the fact that the business of a country like ours is exceedingly sensitive to changes in legislation of this kind. It has been built up, however ill-advisedly, upon the tariff schedules written in the way I have indicated, and its foundations must not be too radically or too suddenly disturbed. When we act we should act with caution and prudence, like men who know what they are about, and not like those in love with a theory. It is obvious that the changes

we make should be made only at such a rate and in such a way as will least interfere with the normal and healthful course of commerce and manufacture. But we shall not on that account act with timidity, as if we did not know our minds, for we are certain of our ground and of our object. There should be an immediate revision and it should be downward, unhesitatingly and steadily downward.

It should begin with the schedules which have been most obviously used to kill competition and to raise prices in the United States, arbitrarily and without regard to the prices pertaining elsewhere in the markets of the world; and it should, before it is finished or intermitted, be extended to every item in every schedule which affords any opportunity for monopoly, for special privilege to limited groups of beneficiaries or for subsidized control of any kind in the markets or the enterprise of the country, until special favors of every sort shall have been absolutely without, and every part of our laws of taxation shall have been transformed from a system of governmental patronage into a system of just and reasonable charges which shall fall where they will create the least burden. When we shall have done that, we can fix questions of revenue and business adjustment in a new spirit and with clear minds. We shall then be partners with all the business men of the country, and a day of freer, more stable prosperity shall have dawned. There has been no more demoralizing in our politics in our time than the influence of tariff legislation, the influence of the idea that Government was the grand dispenser of favors, the make and unmake of fortunes and of opportunities such as certain men have sought in order to control the movement of trade and industry throughout the continent. It has made the Government a prize to be captured and parties the means of affecting the capture. It has made the business men of one of the most virile and enterprising nations in the world timid, fretful, full of alarms; has robbed them of self-confidence and manly force, until they have cried out that they could do nothing without the assistance of the Government at Washington. It has made them feel that their lives depended upon the Ways and Means Committee of the House and the Finance Committee of the Senate (in these later years particularly the Finance Committee of the Senate). They have insisted very anxiously that these committees should be made up only of their "friends," until the country in its turn grew suspicious and wondered how those committees were being guided and controlled—by what influences and plans of personal advantage.

Government cannot be wholesomely conducted in such an atmosphere. Its very honesty is in jeopardy. Favors are never conceived in the general interest; they are always for the benefit of the few, and the few who seek and obtain them have only themselves to blame if presently they seem to be distrusted.

See also: **Vol. I**: Aldrich, Nelson W.; Atkinson, Edward; Payne, Sereno E.; Payne-Aldrich Tariff (Tariff of 1909); Personal income tax (Sixteenth Constitutional Amendment); Roosevelt, Theodore; Taft, William Howard; Trade associations; U.S. Chamber of Commerce; Wilson, Thomas Woodrow. **Vol. III**: Tariff of 1909 (Payne-Aldrich Tariff).

Joseph Ridgway Grundy's Speech in Favor of the Hawley-Smoot Tariff

During the congressional debates over the controversial Hawley-Smoot Tariff bill, Senator Joseph Ridgway Grundy gave the following speech to the Manufacturers' Club of Philadelphia on January 25, 1930. Advocating passage of the bill, Grundy argued that manufacturing interests would greatly benefit from the measure. He served as the president of and lobbyist for the Pennsylvania Manufacturer's Association from 1909 to 1930. Grundy became a junior senator on December 11, 1929, after being appointed to fill a vacancy, and remained at that post until December 1, 1930, during which time Congress passed the Hawley-Smoot Tariff. His efforts to secure the passage of that bill led many, including New York Governor Franklin D. Roosevelt, to refer to the bill as the Grundy-Smoot-Hawley Tariff Act during the 1932 presidential campaign.

To me it seems most fitting that my first public appearance since my appointment as a United States Senator should be within the Manufacturers' Club. I have always been interested in all of those things for which the club stands, and over a long period of years I frequently have had the privilege of participating in the activities as an individual. In addition to that, because of the part my father had in the affairs of the club's earlier years, it always will hold a place of deep sentimental attachment to my heart.

The outstanding policy for which the club has stood, in which we have had a common interest, is the protective-tariff principle, and we have been in entire agreement that upon that policy of government the whole industrial structure of this county has been reared. It was that principle, and the issues revolving around it, that brought this club into existence; and for nearly half a century it has defended, espoused, and advanced the protective doctrine with increasing prestige and a constantly widening sphere of influence.

It was that interest in a protective tariff, with all that it means to labor and industry alike, and hence to all business and trade, especially in such a predominately industrial State as Pennsylvania—together with certain moral obligations to my fellow citizens of Pennsylvania which I felt I had assumed in the national campaign of 1928—that took me to Washington just about a year ago.

Recounts Experiences at National Capital

Washington is the great theatre of national events—sometimes tragic, often humorous, but invariably interesting and always instructive, if one goes upon that principle that in every situation, and from all people, there is something valuable that may be learned. As you may have heard, my own experiences there were somewhat varied and sometimes hectic. Certainly their outcome could not have been predicted and was beyond the realm of remote thought at the time I went to Washington, in January, 1929. But in many respects they afforded opportunity for learning, and it is concerning some of my observations, and the conclusions drawn from them, that I want to speak to-night.

The first thought that I would like to present to you has to do with the distinct and divergent functions of the respective divisions of government under our system; in which we have the municipal, county, and State units

upon the one hand and the Federal Government upon the other.

These constitute the two grand divisions of government under our Constitution. In a political, governmental, and economic sense this is the arrangement of authority and obligation under which we carry out the difficult and intricate job of doing our national housekeeping. And in seeking to set forth what I conceive to be the complementary but definitely separated general functions of these two grand divisions of government, I do not think I could illustrate with a more homely simile than by likening the situation to the broad arrangement of responsibilities which prevails in the average American home.

There the duties of the wife and the mother, while of the most important character, largely are localized to the home and have to do with all the cares under which the various phases of the family life are carried on. She has the care of the children and, in a major sense, the supervision of their education and upbringing. Upon the wife and mother fall the thousand and one things of an administrative character which go to make up the daily routine of maintaining and managing the average home.

It seems to me that in a general way this is analogous to and illustrative of the broad field of public authority and responsibility encompassed by that division of government which is organized and expressed in the local forms which range from the smallest political units to that of the State. As with the cares and duties of the wife and mother in the home, these smaller subdivisions of government relate to the personal side of our existence and pertain to the safeguarding of health, life, and property and to the maintenance of community life and society as organized.

American Opportunity Envy of Whole World

To continue the illustration further, however, it is the part of the husband and father in the family to go out into the world, to form the necessary contacts in whatever the field selected, and then to carry on those activities which deal with the material things of life, so as not only to provide income for the current expenses of existence but also to add to the capital account as a competence for future years. This, I feel, is that part of the maintenance of family life which is analogous to the Federal Government's position in our constitutional scheme of things.

For with its authority to make treaties with foreign governments, its right to regulate navigation and commerce with the rest of the world, its power to lay taxes upon imports, great prerogatives of far-reaching effect exist. And it has been the wise and intelligent use of these powers, in the development of our natural resources, in encouraging industry, and in retaining within this country the business and money needed in supplying our people with the requirements of daily consumption, that there has been built up here a Nation whose opportunities and prosperity in the past 70 years have been the wonder and envy of the world.

It is of the husbandly part of the picture—or the Federal Government's place in the national scheme of things—that I want to speak to-night.

I have said that when these hus-

bandly powers of the Government are intelligently used, results of great benefit have accrued to our people. From that standpoint, surveying the situation as it has developed since the formation of our Government, I should say that in a broad economic sense, in the last 150 years, we have passed through two distinct periods and are now in a third.

It will be remembered that with the adoption of the Constitution and the enactment of the legislation which quickly followed it the young Nation was off to a flying start. During the ensuing 25 years or so the Federal Government was relieved of any great exertion in what I have described as the husbandly role, due to the fact that the Napoleonic Wars which convulsed Europe, coupled with our own War of 1812, created a period of feverish prosperity and development here that was not unlike the experiences which our country passed through during the recent World War.

Country Failed to Hold Early Gains

It was not ordained, however, that the first flush of our national existence and development—that earliest era of the encouragement of individual energy and initiative, and the establishment, protection, and expansion of our newly created industries and productive activities—was to last. For, from 1815 practically continuously to the outbreak of the Civil War, he whom we might designate as the "man of the American home"—the National Government—not only failed to consolidate and retain what had been gained in the first 25 years of our national existence, but permitted such retrogression that by 1860 our national income was woefully insufficient to our current requirements, our credit was at lowest ebb, and financial and industrial disaster prevailed or impended on every side.

The outbreak of the Civil War brought about a return, upon a larger and more energetic scale, of that general progress and development which had marked our earliest years as a Nation. Large sums of money were required to prosecute the conflict for the preservation of the Union, and as one of the means thereto higher and higher taxes were laid upon imports, thus out of the necessities of war applying the Hamiltonian theory and stimulating domestic manufacture.

During most of the 70 years that have intervened the wise application of those governmental principles to the development of our natural resources, to the production in this country of the commodities necessary to meet our daily requirements, this keeping the money of that commerce within the United States, resulted not only in the employment of all our people, but attracted millions of workers to our shores. The consequences were that communities were built up, utilities developed, and transportation systems established as they exist nowhere else in the world; and while from the beginning of Colonial times to 1860 our population reached only 30,000,000, the pending census is expected to show a population of 115,000,000.

In constantly increasing measure we have had a greater and more diffused enjoyment of material prosperity than has existed in any other country in the world. All of this, however, has not been brought about without marked changes in our economic conditions and relationships, which is the especial subject of my thought to-night.

Industry Based on Protective Principle

With the development and expansion which came with the Civil War our industrial structure continued to be in the form of individual units, with the more or less close relationships between employer and employees; and this condition continued throughout the succeeding 40 years. This period embraced the Civil War tariffs and those which immediately followed: the unfortunate and backward revision of 1883 (the consequences of which brought the Manufacturers' Club into existence); the well-balanced and protective McKinley tariff of 1890; and the widely disastrous Democratic revision known as the Wilson bill in 1894. Productive enterprises existed in the form of small units, and in large measure the employers themselves came from the ranks of the employed, as a consequence of energy, application, and the saving of surplus earnings.

In all the aspects of its progress and development, therefore, I would characterize the era, particularly from 1860 to the removal of the Wilson bill from the statute books in 1897, as the first period of new economic life, and during that period the enactment of all our constructive tariff legislation was with the aim of creating new and more diversified enterprises, and of protecting those already in existence.

It was approximately with the enactment of the Dingley Tariff of 1897 that we came into what I would describe as the second period of internal economic life—the period of the passing of many of the small and individual industrial units, with the intimate contacts between the owner and his employees; the period of larger enterprises in corporate form, and consolidations of many enterprises in like character into single big business.

This continued not only throughout the years of the Payne-Aldrich Tariff, which supplanted the Dingley law in 1909, but also throughout the life of the Underwood-Simmons Act; for, during a major part of the period that this Democratic tariff was in existence, 1913–1922, the World War gave us an artificial protection, and, at the same time, a war-time prosperity under which some of our industrial development was pushed to a productive capacity considerably in excess of domestic peace-time demands.

Industry Expands Under Protection

I think it may be said with a fair degree of accuracy that, throughout both the first and the second periods of our economic history, our constructive and protective legislation was the consequence of the educational work carried on, and the strenuous efforts put forth, by domestic industry, plus an enlightened and forward-looking statesmanship in both branches of Congress, without much direct help from labor.

I do not make that statement in any spirit of the slightest derogation of labor, for it is self-evident that the party of protection could not have been so frequently successful in the elections without the votes of our working people. And particularly the employees of our industrial plants, our mines, our transportation systems, etc. As a matter of fact, if for no other reason than that of intelligent self-interest, the workers of the United States, as a body, always have been for tariff protection of their wage scales, and only upon rare occasions have they permitted other issues to obscure or minimize that which is the most important of all to them. But what I do mean to say is that it had been largely left to industry to appear before the tariff committees of Congress with the evidence and arguments in support of the retention or enactment of protective legislation.

Thus we have come to the close of the second period in this economic history and the opening of the third. And it is to be noted that up to the point to which this brings us we always have had a situation in which our industries and their labor, being concentrated within the United States—and our financial institutions—practically were united in their support of the protective principle under which our great industrial structure has been erected and by which it and our wage scale and our standard of living are sustained.

I would not attempt to fix the exact time when the transition from the second to the third of these economic periods really took on a substantial momentum; but if I were called upon to define in general terms the difference between the change from the first to the second period, I should say that the first change was evolutionary in character, in that it was a logical and natural development in the course of our national economic progress and expansion; while the more recent change is revolutionary in its nature, because it brings wholly new considerations into our national economy and involved a large-scale abandonment of the historical principle most vital to the preservation and expansion of our internal development and to the labor employed therein.

The third and present era in our economic history might be described as the period of migration of American capital (and in some instances the complete removal of domestic industrial plants) to foreign countries.

For, as a consequence of the stimulus given our industries by the World War, the continued trend toward consolidations and mergers, and certainly to some extent because there is available in foreign countries ample supplies of cheap labor, a progressively large number of our big corporations are going abroad with their surplus capital and either erecting factories or purchasing existing plants. From there they not only are supplying such foreign trade as they previously may have built up from their American mills, but also are seeking to sell here, in competition with American industry and domestic labor, the products manufactured with their cheaper labor abroad.

The results are at least threefold. In the first place, many of these corporations which previously were most active supporters of the protective-tariff principle, no longer have that interest. Upon the contrary, in many instances, because they are bidders for the American market from abroad they actually are in the same position as the exporting foreign manufacturer, and, like the latter, now are opposed to a tariff which would adequately protect American industry and labor. Secondly, to the extent that they employ abroad have diminished the amount of employment that otherwise would have been available to American labor. And thirdly, to the extent that they can land competitive products here which have been made by foreign labor, and at a price advantage over similar domestic products, they diminish the demand for American labor by American mills and factories.

Capital is liquid and is bound to flow into channels of largest profits consistent with security. Labor, upon the other hand, is more or less fixed and permanent. Where it settles it usually stays unless the means of existence are withdrawn. Furthermore, even if American labor were inclined to be migratory, it is evident that it could not profit itself by following American capital into the low-wage countries of Europe and elsewhere. By reason of the very economic facts which govern the situation, therefore, the battle ground of domestic labor is right here in the highest wage country in the world; and the protective tariff is labor's fight in a way that it never has been before.

Labor Fully Alive to Foreign Menace

In making that statement I do not mean that tariff protection is labor's fight alone. But I do mean that in this third period of our economic history labor has more at stake and a greater concern in protection than ever before. That labor itself recognizes this fact was amply demonstrated in the tariff hearings of the pending revision. No more intelligent or comprehensive presentations were made than those offered by the representative of labor. And in contending aggressively against the existing foreign-value basis of our tariff and for a domestic base of valuation for the ad valorem rates; likewise for the exclusion of products enjoying the protection of American patents or trade-marks and manufactured abroad; and for other recommendations looking to more effective protection and a stricter administration of our tariffs, labor has shown not only a keen realization of its dependence upon the tariff but also has demonstrated a most thorough understanding of the entire subject.

It has been with intelligent understanding, therefore, that labor has analyzed the working of the protective system during the past 70 years. It has seen that the development of industry has brought two consequences; increased domestic competition in the production of commodities has resulted in cheapening them to the consumer, while the growth and expansion of industry has increased the demand for labor to such an extent that the scale of wages in this country is from two and a half to ten times the wages prevailing in competitive foreign countries.

Labor also keenly realized that since the World War much industry which is designed to supply United States markets, and operating under the most modern American manufacturing methods, has been established in countries where the lowest production costs prevail because they have the lowest wage scales. It should understand, also, that vastly greater inroads would have been made in the American market were foreign goods better known and trade routes to domestic distributors better developed.

Apparently labor realizes that many of our existing tariff duties are not suf-

ficient to equalize foreign and domestic production costs, and it recognizes, too, that legislation enacted at the instance of labor to restrict immigration is not in itself proving effective in preserving the United States industrial field if capital is to go abroad ad employ this excluded labor at wages far below those prevailing here and then send the products of that labor into this country under tariff duties that are too low to afford protection.

Foreign-Value Rate A Mere Gesture

I think labor very clearly sees also that in so far as protection is attempted in the form of ad valorem rates, the presumed protection is nothing more than a gesture, so long as we apply those rates to a foreign value and thus leave it to the foreigner virtually to determine the amount of duty he will pay upon landing his products in this market.

The issue, however, is industry's fight also, for in this tariff question the interests of industry and of labor are so absolutely interwoven that what advantages one benefits the other, and what hurts either injures both.

In such a situation the need for a continuation and expansion of the splendid work carried on by the Manufacturers' Club for nearly half a century is more urgent than ever before. Great as its achievements have been in the past, and as widely as its good influences have been extended, its future still is before it and its largest works remain yet to be done.

It is the husbandly side of our constitutional system—the Federal Government—that must, in addition to a hoped-for protective tariff, provide a curb upon those phases of our third economic era which threaten grave injury to our industries and labor alike. So long as I shall continue to be in the Senate, therefore, I assure you that I shall assiduously seek such remedies. And in that, as in all similar work, I certainly shall hope for the aid and co-operation of such groups as this, as well as those representative of every other phase of our political, economic, and social life.

I thank you.

See also: **Vol. I**: American farmers; Hoover, Herbert; Hull, Cordell; Great Depression; Hawley, Willis C.; Hawley-Smoot Tariff (Tariff of 1930); Reciprocal Trade Agreements Act (RTAA); Roosevelt, Franklin D.; Smoot, Reed. **Vol. III**: Tariff of 1930 (Hawley-Smoot Tariff).

Protest of American Economists over the Hawley-Smoot Tariff

The proposed Hawley-Smoot Tariff Act of 1930 received criticism from various aspects of the political and economic community. Mississippi Senator Byron Patton (Pat) Harrison presented one such protest into the official record of Congress on Monday, May 5, 1930. The originators of the protest included Paul H. Douglass of the University of Chicago, Irving Fisher of Yale University, and Frank W. Taussig of Swarthmore College, along with 1,025 other signers representing the economic community of the United States. The petition argued that higher protective duties in a time of economic crisis would ultimately hurt all segments of American society, not only through higher consumer costs but also in the trade barriers they would produce between the United States and other nations. Such barriers would impede the marketing of agricultural surpluses and basic goods manufactured in the United States, causing further unemployment and hindering the open trade that would foster world peace.

The undersigned American economists and teachers of economics strongly urge that any measure which provides for a general upward revision of tariff rates be denied passage by Congress, or if passed, be vetoed by the President.

We are convinced that increased protective duties would be a mistake. They would operate, in general, to increase the prices which domestic consumers would have to pay. By raising prices they would encourage concerns with higher costs to undertake production, thus compelling the consumer to subsidize waste and inefficiency in industry. At the same time they would force him to pay higher rates of profit to established firms which enjoyed lower production costs. A higher level of protection, such as is contemplated by both the House and Senate bills, would therefore raise the cost of living and injure the great majority of our citizens.

Few people could hope to gain from such a change. Miners, construction, transportation and public utility workers, professional people and those employed in banks, hotels, newspaper offices, in the wholesale and retail trades, and scores of other occupations would clearly lose, since they produce no products which could be protected by tariff barriers.

The vast majority of farmers, also, would lose. Their cotton, corn, lard, and wheat are export crops and are sold in the world market. They have no important competition in the home market. They can not benefit, therefore, from any tariff which is imposed upon the basic commodities which they produce. They would lose through the increased duties on manufactured goods, however, and in a double fashion. First, as consumers they would have to pay still higher prices for the products, made of textiles, chemicals, iron, and steel, which they buy. Second, as producers, their ability to sell their products would be further restricted by the barriers placed in the way of foreigners who wished to sell manufactured goods to us.

Our export trade, in general, would suffer. Countries can not permanently buy from us unless they are permitted to sell to us, and the more we restrict the importation of goods from them by means of ever higher tariffs the more we reduce the possibility of our exporting to them. This applies to such exporting industries as copper, automobiles, agricultural machinery, typewriters, and the like fully as much as it does to farming. The difficulties of these industries are likely to be increased still further if we pass a higher tariff. There are already many evidences that such action would inevitably provoke other countries to pay us back in kind by levying retaliatory duties against our goods. There are few more ironical spectacles than that of the American Government as it seeks, on the one hand, to promote exports thorough the activity of the Bureau of Foreign and Domestic Commerce, while, on the other hand, by increasing tariffs it makes exportation ever more difficult. President Hoover has well said, in his message to Congress on April 16, 1929, "It is obviously unwise protection which sacrifices a greater amount of employment in exports to gain a less amount of employment from imports."

We do not believe that American manufacturers, in general, need higher tariffs. The report of the President's committee on recent economic changes has shown that industrial efficiency has increased, that costs have fallen, that profits have grown with amazing rapidity since the end of the war. Already our factories supply our people with over 96 percent of the manufactured goods which they consume, and our producers look to foreign markets to absorb the increasing output of their machines. Further barriers to trade will serve them not well, but ill.

Many of our citizens have invested their money in foreign enterprises. The Department of Commerce has estimated that such investments, entirely aside from the war debts, amounted to between $12,555,000,000 and $14,555,000,000 on January 1, 1929. These investors, too, would suffer if protective duties were to be increased, since such action would make it still more difficult for their foreign creditors to pay them the interest due them.

America is now facing the problem of unemployment. Her labor can find work only if her factories can sell their products. Higher tariffs would not promote such sales. We can not increase employment by restricting trade. American industry, in the present crisis, might well be spared the burden of adjusting itself to new schedules of protective duties.

Finally, we would urge our Government to consider the bitterness which a policy of higher tariffs would inevitably inject into our international relations. The United States was ably represented at the World Economic Conference which was held under the auspices of the League of Nations in 1927. This conference adopted a resolution announcing that "the time has come to put an end to the increase in tariffs and to move in the opposite direction." The higher duties proposed in our pending legislation violate the spirit of this agreement and plainly invite other nations to compete with us in raising further barriers to trade. A tariff war does not furnish good soil for the growth of world peace.

See also: **Vol. I**: American farmers; Hoover, Herbert; Hull, Cordell; Great Depression; Hawley, Willis C.; Hawley-Smoot Tariff (Tariff of 1930); Reciprocal Trade Agreements Act (RTAA); Roosevelt, Franklin D.; Smoot, Reed. **Vol. III**: Tariff of 1930 (Hawley-Smoot Tariff).

Daniel Frederic Steck's Iowa Speech against the Hawley-Smoot Tariff

Just prior to President Herbert Hoover's signing into law the Hawley-Smoot Tariff of 1930, both Democrats and Republicans engaged in heated and passionate debates over the merits of the proposed legislation. Iowa Senator Daniel Frederic Steck delivered the following speech before a group of farmers in his home state on June 12, 1930. He argued that the Hawley-Smoot Tariff, if passed, would benefit manufacturers, not the farmers who Hoover had originally targeted for assistance. He informed the audience that he opposed the legislation for that reason. Steck ran for reelection in November 1930 but failed to regain the seat he had held since 1926.

The past four years have been of extreme importance to Iowa and to all the great agricultural States. For many years the rights and needs of agriculture have been discussed in party platforms and by the party candidates for political offices, but only during the past four years has there been any real attempt to translate promises into legislation. During these years we have had three fights for the McNary-Haugen bills—the export debenture, the Federal Farm Board, and the revision of the tariff.

Entering the Senate in April, 1926, it has been my privilege to take a part in all these fights. Shortly after I entered the Senate the McNary-Haugen bill, containing the equalization-fee plan, came up for the first time. I supported it and during the debate spoke in favor of its passage. (This bill was defeated.)

At that time (June 8, 1926), commenting on the causes of the depression of agriculture, I said: "In my opinion, the present agriculture problem is based upon two conditions, both economically unsound. First, the farmer sells in competition with the world and buys in a protected market. In other words, the tariff does not add to his income and does contribute materially to his expenditure. Second, the farmer has no orderly method of marketing, and so is unable to get a stable price for his products." That was my judgment then and is my judgment now. In the fight for the McNary-Haugen bills we were trying to provide the farmer with a plan of orderly marketing, and I am still convinced that that plan was the most sound and workable plan which has received the consideration of Congress. Twice the Congress passed these bills and twice they were vetoed by President Coolidge. Then came the general election and the nomination of Mr. Hoover at Kansas City. Many good Republicans claim that the farmers were ignored and their interests betrayed at his convention. Whether this be true is a question for Republicans to decide. It was their convention and theirs is the responsibility. However that may be, the fact is that the McNary-Haugen plan was thrown overboard and in its stead we were promised a Federal Farm Board with broad powers and practically unlimited funds. Also we were promised a revision of the tariff in the interests of agriculture, a revision which was to mitigate the forces working to the detriment of agriculture and place agriculture on a parity with other industry.

Mr. Hoover became President Hoover and within a few weeks after this inauguration he called Congress into special session to accomplish these two things—farm relief and limited changes in the tariff.

The Congress speedily passed the act creating the Federal Farm Board and it has been in operation for about a year. I was impatient to get some plan which promised relief to our farmers and

voted for its passage. I sincerely hope it will prove a real help. I believe the board is making a good-faith effort to accomplished the purpose of the act and want it to be given a fair opportunity to prove itself before it is condemned. It was regrettable that the United States Chamber of Commerce recently passed a resolution condemning the Farm Board, and I have been happy to see the chambers of commerce of so many of our Iowa cities repudiating this hasty and ill-advised action of the national chamber.

After passing the bill creating the Farm Board the Congress took up the tariff. Tariff bills and all revenue measures must originate in the House of Representatives. The House Committee on Ways and Means held hearings for six months and reported a bill which the House passed practically unchanged and within a few days. Everyone remembers the storm of protest that went up when the terms of the bill became known to the country. Instead of a limited revision as promised and reccommended by the President, the House bill was a general revision of the present law. And instead of being a revision in favor of agriculture, it placed agriculture in a worse position than it had been under the act of 1922. The protests against the House bill were from nearly every group and from every section of the country. Republican newspapers vied with Democratic newspapers in condemning it. It had no defenders except certain great industrial leaders in whose behalf and at whose behest it was written. Not even the Republican Congressmen by whose votes it was passed defended it.

Everyone looked to the Senate to rewrite the bill to comply with the President's promises and wishes. The Senate Finance Committee after long hearings reported a bill which was better than the House bill, but which in comparison with the existing law was outrageous and undefendable. In fact no Senator has had the courage to defend it on the floor of the Senate from the day it was reported to the day of its passage.

The Senate started to work on it. There were over 20,000 items in the bill. To have carefully considered each item would have taken two years or more. For a time it looked as if most of the glaring abuses would be eliminated. The Democrats, together with the Republican Senators from agriculture States, were successful in reducing many industrial rates and raising many on agricultural products. We were also successful in adding the debenture plan to the bill. Then Mr. Grundy was appointed to the Senate from Pennsylvania. He had been maintaining an extensive lobby in Washington for months. He moved his lobby into the Senate Office Building and went to work. To Grundy and to Senators Smoot, Watson, and others to a lesser degree can be given the credit for the bill which finally passed the Senate. I voted against it. The bill then went to conference, where we lost most of the remaining victories won in behalf of agriculture and the consumer.

Months ago I stated that I would vote against the bill unless it was fairer to agriculture and to the consumer than the present law. I can not believe that any fair-minded person with a knowledge of the provisions of the bill will claim that it is as fair to those groups of our people as is the present law, or that it carried out the promises

and wishes of the President. The President may sign it. I hope not. If he does, it will be because it is the work of a Republican Congress and not because the bill meets with his personal approval.

It is impractical to mention all the increases in industrial rates which will increase the costs of living, but some of the outstanding ones are: Lumber, cement, brick, sugar, shoes and leather goods, cotton goods and clothing, woolen goods and clothing, aluminum cooking utensils, etc., farm tools, crockery and chinaware, window glass, pig iron, metal household and kitchen utensils, women's and men's felt and straw hats, linen table cloths and handkerchiefs, and wool blankets and carpets.

It is true that the rates on many agriculture products were raised, but it is also true that most of these rates can not be made effective. If we had been able to retain the debenture clause in the bill most of these rates could have been made effective, but that was stricken out by Republican votes in both the House and the Senate. Without the debenture, and producing a surplus as we do of most farm products, these rates are not effective and can not be made effective.

On many farm products where the tariff would be effective we were defeated in our fight to get fair and necessary rates. A fair rate on dairy products was refused.

The farmer's request that he be given the case in market was refused.

The farmer's request that he be given the vegetable oils was refused.

His request that he be given the starch market was denied.

His request that he be given the frozen and dried egg market was refused.

His request for a proper protection on flaxseed was refused as was his request for a real protective duty on linseed.

There are some of the reasons I voted against the tariff bill. I worked and voted to keep down industrial rates and to secure fair rates on agriculture products. I led the fight in the Senate for an 8-cent duty on blackstrap molasses. I was one of the leaders in the fight against a duty on shoes and leather goods, and took an active part in many other contests.

The present method of making a tariff bill is essentially selfish and sectional and I fought for the interest of my State, particularly the consumers and our greatest industry, agriculture. I believe nearly everyone who has watched this tariff bill in the making is convinced that never again should there be a general revision by Congress. The tariff should be taken out of politics and the power to fix rates lodged in a nonpartisan tariff commission. I introduced an amendment to bring this about, but it failed of passage. I am certain however that some such plan as I suggested will be adopted in the near future.

I believe in a protective tariff. Our country is definitely and I believe everlastingly committed to this economic policy; but I am opposed to a prohibitive tariff and believing as I do that most of the new rates in the present bill are prohibitive rather than protective I could not give my consent to its becoming a law.

Among other important matters before the Congress during the past four years of particular interest to Iowa have been:

The fights of limit immigration.

The bill providing for the construction of Boulder Dam.

The improvement of our two border rivers—the upper Mississippi and the upper Missouri.

Labor legislation.

Legislation for veterans of all wars.

I took a leading part in the two principal immigration controversies. I favored a drastic limitation in the number of immigrants but opposed the national origins quota plan because it reduced the percentage of immigrants coming from northern and western Europe, especially Germany and the Scandinavian countries, and increased the percentage of those coming from southern and eastern Europe and Asia, especially Italy. The basic racial stock of our people comes from northern and western Europe and while I firmly believe that the future of our country will be best served by limiting future immigration almost entirely to the peoples of Norway, Sweden, Denmark, Holland, Germany, England, Ireland, and other Nordic peoples whence has come the bulk of those who have built and maintained our country and its institutions, and whose people more nearly and most easily fit into our manner of living and our form of government. Also, I voted and fought for an amendment to our immigration laws which would drastically limit immigration from Mexico because the class of people we get from that country can not be merged with our people and because all immigrants aggravate our already serious unemployment situation.

I was one of two mid-western Senators who opposed the construction of Boulder Dam by the Federal Government. In the first place, I am fundamentally opposed to Government construction, ownership, and operation of our public utilities. Also I am opposed to taxing our people for projects which create millions of acres of agricultural lands to be operated in competition with our Iowa farms, when the country's available farm acreage is already producing a great surplus of agricultural products.

Ever since coming to the Senate I have fought for the construction of a 9-foot channel on the upper Mississippi River and the improvement of the upper Missouri from Kansas City to Sioux City. In the session of Congress commencing December, 1929, Senator Stewart and I took the lead in the fight to improve the upper Missouri. We put it over at that session, and the project is now underway.

The fight for a 9-foot channel on the upper Mississippi has gone on for years. In 1928 we passed legislation ordering a survey, and at this session of the Congress we have secured an amendment to the rivers and harbors bill which adopts the 9-foot channel as a Federal project and authorizes an appropriation of seven and one-half millions of dollars to initiate the work. I took an active part in this fight, and feel that we have won a distinct victory for Iowa and other middle western States.

Much important legislation has been before Congress during my term of service. The Labor Board for the settlement of controversies between employer and employee was created. We passed the unemployment bills, the Couzens resolution holding up railroad consolidation, the convict labor bill, and the bill to regulate motor-bus lines. All these bills and others in which labor was interested received my active support.

Many bills have been passed during my four years in the Senate in the interests of our veterans. All have had my support. We have passed many special bills granting pensions to our veterans of the Civil War and the widows of Civil War veterans and have increased their regular pensions. As a member of the Senate Pensions Committee I have helped in drawing and passing all those bills. Also we have liberalized the Spanish war pension legislation and have passed several bills for the hospitalization and compensation of our World War veterans. We have increased the number of hospitals and the number of beds in existing hospitals. We passed the emergency officers' retirement bill and the Reed-Snell resolution looking toward the enactment of a universal draft act. All these and many other similar bills had my active support in the committee and on the Senate floor.

In conclusion, let me say that while I am a Democrat, and, I believe, a good one, yet I have sincerely tried to represent Iowa without regard to partisanship. I have voted in what I believe to be the best interest of all of the people of Iowa and the Nation. In following this course I have at times voted contrary to the majority of my party as represented in the Senate. Also, I have refused to blindly follow any group or organization and on a few occasions have voted contrary to the desires of some of the farm organizations, of organized labor, of the American League, of the commercial and industrial organizations, and others, although I have been glad to agree with such groups and organizations whenever in my judgment their wishes were consistent with my general policy of trying to honestly and impartially represent the best interest of our people as a whole.

I have no apology for any vote I have cast. Each vote was cast after a careful consideration of the question involved and represented my best judgment. I know I have not pleased every individual with all my votes. Indeed, I have not tried to do so. But I hope that my efforts on the whole merit and have the approval of the great majority of the people I have had the honor to represent.

See also: **Vol. I**: American farmers; Hoover, Herbert; Hull, Cordell; Great Depression; Hawley, Willis C.; Hawley-Smoot Tariff (Tariff of 1930); Reciprocal Trade Agreements Act (RTAA); Roosevelt, Franklin D.; Smoot, Reed. **Vol. III**: Tariff of 1930 (Hawley-Smoot Tariff).

Herbert Hoover's Statement of Intention to Approve the Hawley-Smoot Tariff Act

On the morning of June 16, 1930, Herbert Hoover indicated his intention to sign the Hawley-Smoot Tariff into law, which he did the following day at 12:59 P.M. In the following address he explains why this tariff benefits the economy and the country. He first defends the tariff as a promise made by the Republican Party at its convention in 1928. He also compares this tariff to those of the recent past, claiming that it merely continues a tradition already established by previous legislation and actually lowers the rates on more items than did the 1922 Fordney-McCumber Tariff. Hoover supported the innovative flexible provision in the bill that allowed the Tariff Commission to consider dutiable items on an individual basis. Finally, he asserts that the country needs a strong tariff to ensure economic recovery and to regain its strength in the world market.

I shall approve the tariff bill. This legislation has now been under almost continuous consideration by Congress for nearly 15 months. It was undertaken as the result of pledges given by the Republican Party at Kansas City. Its declarations embraced these obligations:

"The Republican Party believes that the home market built up under protective policy belongs to the American farmer, and it pledges its support of legislation which will give this market to him to the full extent of his ability to supply it. * * *

"There are certain industries which can not now successfully compete with foreign producers because of lower foreign wages and a lower cost of living abroad, and we pledge the next Republican Congress to an examination and where necessary a revision of these schedules to the end that the American labor in these industries may again command the home market, may maintain its standard of living, and may count upon steady employment in its accustomed field."

Platform promises must not be empty gestures. In my message of April 16, 1929, to the special session of the Congress I accordingly recommended an increase in agricultural protection, a limited revision of other schedules to take care of the economic changes necessitating increases or decreases since the enactment of the 1922 law, and I further recommended a reorganization both of the Tariff Commission and of the method of executing the flexible provisions.

A statistical estimate of the bill by the Tariff Commission shows that the average duties collected under the 1922 law were about 13.8 per cent of the value of all imports, both free and dutiable, while if the new law had been applied it would have increased this percentage to about 16 per cent.

This compares with the average level of the tariff under the McKinley law of 23 per cent: the Wilson law of 20.9 per cent; the Dingley law of 25.8 per cent; the Payne-Aldrich law of 19.3 per cent; and the Fordney-McCumber law of 13.83 per cent.

Under the Underwood law of 1913 the amounts were disturbed by war conditions, varying 6 per cent to 14.8 per cent.

The proportion of imports which will be free of duty under the new law is estimated at from 61 to 63 per cent. This compares with averages under the McKinley law of 52.4 per cent; the Wilson law of 49.4 per cent; the Dingley law of 45.2 per cent; the Payne-Aldrich law of 53.5 per cent; and the Fordney-McCumber law of 63.8 per cent.

Under the Underwood law of 1913 disturbed conditions varied the free list

from 60 to 73 per cent, averaging 66.3 per cent.

The increases in tariff are largely directed to the interest of the farmer. Of the increases, it is stated by the Tariff Commission that 93.73 per cent are upon products of agricultural origin measured in value, as distinguished from 6.25 per cent upon commodities of strictly nonagricultural origin. The average rate upon agricultural raw materials shows an increase from 38.10 per cent to 48.92 per cent in contrast to dutiable articles of strictly other than agricultural origin which show an average increase of from 31.02 per cent to 34.31 per cent. Compensatory duties have necessarily been given on products manufactured from agricultural raw materials and protective rates added to these in some instances.

The extent of rate revision as indicated by the Tariff Commission is that in value of the total imports the duties upon approximately 22.5 per cent have been increased, and 77.5 per cent were untouched or decreased. By number of the dutiable items mentioned in the bill, out of the total of about 3,300 there were about 890 increased, 235 decreased, and 2,170 untouched. The number of items increased was, therefore 27 per cent of all dutiable items, and compares with 83 per cent of the number of items which were increased in the 1922 revision.

This tariff law is like all other tariff legislation, whether framed primarily upon a protective or a revenue basis. It contains many compromises between sectional interests and between different industries. No tariff bill has ever been enacted or ever will be enacted under the present system that will be perfect. A large portion of the items are always adjusted with good judgment, but it is bound to contain some inequalities and inequitable compromises. There are items upon which duties will prove too high and others upon which duties will prove to be too low.

Certainly no President, with his other duties, can pretend to make that exhaustive determination of the complex facts which surround each of those 3,300 items, and which has required the attention of hundreds of men in Congress for nearly a year and a third. That responsibility must rest upon the Congress in a legislative-rate revision.

On the administrative side I have insisted, however, that there should be created a new basis for the flexible tariff, and it has been incorporated in this law. Thereby the means are established for objective and judicial review of these rates upon principles laid down by the Congress, free from pressures inherent in legislative action. Thus, the outstanding step of this tariff legislation has been the reorganization of the largely inoperative flexible provision of 1922 into a form which should render it possible to secure prompt and scientific adjustment of serious inequities and inequalities which may prove to have been incorporated in the bill.

This new provision has even a larger importance. If a perfect tariff bill were enacted to-day, the increased rapidity of economic change and the constant shifting of our relations to industries abroad, will create a continuous stream of items which would work hardship upon some segment of the American people except for the provision of this relief. Without a workable flexible provision we would require even more frequent congressional tariff revision

than during the past. With it the country should be freed from further general revision for many years to come. Congressional revisions are not only disturbing to business but with all their necessary collateral surroundings in lobbies, logrolling, and the activities of group interests, are disturbing to public confidence.

Under the old flexible provisions the task of adjustment was imposed directly upon the President, and the limitations in the law which circumscribed it were such that action was long delayed and it was largely inoperative, although important benefits were brought to the dairying, flax, glass, and other industries through it.

The new flexible provision established the responsibility for revisions upon a reorganized Tariff Commission, composed of members equally of both parties as a definite rate-making body acting through semijudicial methods of open hearings and investigation by which items can be taken up one by one upon direction or upon application of aggrieved parties. Recommendations are to be made to the President, he being given authority to promulgate or veto the conclusions of the commission. Such revision can be accomplished without disturbance to business, as they concern but one item at a time, and the principles laid down assure a protective basis.

The principle of a protective tariff for the benefit of labor, industry, and the farmer is established in the bill by the requirement that the commission shall adjust the rates so as to cover the differences in cost of production at home and abroad—and it authorized to increase or decrease the duties by 50 per cent to effect this end. The means and methods of ascertaining such differences by the commission are provided in such fashion as should expedite prompt and effective action if grievances develop.

When the flexible principle was first written into law in 1922, by tradition and force of habit the old conception of legislative revision was so firmly fixed that the innovation was bound to be used with caution and in a restricted field, even had it not been largely inoperative for other reasons. Now, however, and particularly after the record of the last 15 months, there is a growing and widespread realization that in this highly complicated and intricately organized and rapidly shifting modern economic world, the time has come when a more scientific and business-like method of tariff revision must be devised. Toward this the new flexible provision takes a long step.

These provisions meet the repeated demands of statesmen and industrial and agricultural leaders over the past 25 years. It complies in full degree with the proposals made 20 years ago by President Roosevelt. It now covers proposals which I urged in 1922.

If, however, by any chance the flexible provisions now made should prove insufficient for effective action, I shall ask for further authority for the commission, for I believe that public opinion will give whole-hearted support to the carrying out of such a protective system free from the vices which have characterized every tariff revision in the past.

The complaints from some foreign countries that these duties have been placed unduly high can be remedied, if justified, by proper application to the Tariff Commission.

It is urgent that the uncertainties in the business world which have been added to by the long-extended debate of the measure should be ended. They can be ended only by completion of this bill. Meritorious demands for further protection to agriculture and labor which have developed since the tariff of 1922 would not end if this bill fails of enactment. Agitation for legislative tariff revision would necessarily continue before the country. Nothing would contribute to retard business recovery more than this continued agitation.

As I have said, I do not assume the rate structure in this or any other tariff bill is perfect, but I am convinced that the disposal of the whole question is urgent. I believe that the flexible provisions can within reasonable time remedy inequalities; that this provision is a progressive advance and gives great hope of taking the tariff away from politics, lobbying, and logrolling; that the bill gives protection to agriculture for the market of its products and to several industries in need of such protection for the wage of their labor; that with returning normal conditions our foreign trade will continue to expand.

See also: **Vol. I**: American farmers; Hoover, Herbert; Hull, Cordell; Great Depression; Hawley, Willis C.; Hawley-Smoot Tariff (Tariff of 1930); Reciprocal Trade Agreements Act (RTAA); Roosevelt, Franklin D.; Smoot, Reed. **Vol. III**: Tariff of 1930 (Hawley-Smoot Tariff).

Andrew W. Mellon's Defense of the Hawley-Smoot Tariff for Economic Recovery

After the passage of the Hawley-Smoot Tariff, members of President Hoover's cabinet addressed various concerns. When asked if the new tariff bill would adversely affect American business, or perhaps impede economic recovery in that sector, Treasury Secretary Andrew W. Mellon replied with the following statement.

I do not believe that it will. It seems to me that fears and criticisms have been greatly exaggerated. Whenever a new protective tariff law has been enacted gloomy prophecies have been made. They have failed to materialize as far back as I can remember, and my memory goes back many years. The rates in the bill as it passed the House a year ago were higher than in the bill recently signed by the President. Yet business at that time did not take alarm. There seems to be no reason why it should now. I know of no industry that is seriously hurt, while those industries which needed additional protection and received it are benefited.

I have canvassed the situation with the Secretary of Commerce, and the no-tion that this law is going to destroy our foreign trade expressed in some quarters is certainly without foundation. The United States will continue to buy a vast quantity of foreign products and to sell the products of its farms, mines, and factories all over the world. In so far as imports are concerned, foreign nations that do business with us would do well to remember that the all-important factor is the maintenance of the high purchasing power and standard of living of the American people.

The enactment of this measure brings to an end 15 months of uncertainty. American industries know now where they stand and will, I am confident, adjust themselves without difficulty to new conditions. There seems to be an impression that the new bill makes a sweeping revision upward of existing rates. While it is true that there is a sharp increase in rates applicable to the agricultural schedule, generally speaking, other rates can not be said to have been advanced sufficiently to alter substantially our existing economic position. In fact, only a comparatively few of the major items have been changed. I do not mean to imply that the bill is free from defects. No tariff bill is. But this measure at least by its own terms provides the means whereby inequalities and errors may be adjusted. I look upon the flexible provisions as highly important. I believe that they offer the opportunity not only to correct errors and to adjust rates to meet new and changing conditions, but that they lay a foundation for a businesslike method of tariff revision, free from the pull of sectional and political interests that seem to make a scientific and well-balanced revision by the legislative body almost impossible. If these provisions are intelligently and courageously applied, they should go a long way toward making another legislative revision of the tariff unnecessary for many years to come. This of itself is of inestimable benefit to business, for there is nothing more unfavorable to prosperity than uncertainty and frequent necessity to adjust economic conditions to legislative enactments. In short, it seems to me that the final enactment of the tariff law, far from placing a new obstacle in the way of business recovery, removes one by eliminating the uncertainty of the last 15 months, and by its promise of more businesslike revision in the future makes a definite contribution to business stability.

See also: **Vol. I**: American farmers; Hoover, Herbert; Hull, Cordell; Great Depression; Hawley, Willis C.; Hawley-Smoot Tariff (Tariff of 1930); Reciprocal Trade Agreements Act (RTAA); Roosevelt, Franklin D.; Smoot, Reed. **Vol. III**: Tariff of 1930 (Hawley-Smoot Tariff).

James Watson's Radio Address in Support of the Hawley-Smoot Tariff

As soon as President Hoover signed the Hawley-Smoot Tariff of 1930 into law, Democrats vehemently attacked the bill. In response to the opposition, Senator James Watson of Indiana spoke on the subject of the tariff during a radio address delivered on June 20. The following is his speech in support of the measure.

The principal arguments of Democratic orators in both House and Senate during the consideration of the Smoot-Hawley tariff law so recently enacted consisted altogether of denunciation. For over a hundred years that has been the line of attack pursued by opponents of the protective system. Every bill proposed has been "the most infamous," "the most outrageous," and "the most un-American" law ever enacted on the subject. A Niagara flood of such denunciation marked the passage of the Dingley law, and the Payne-Aldrich law, and the Fordney-McCumber law, and precisely the same sort of fusillade was indulged in to a limitless extent during the passage of the law just enacted.

The condition in the country now is quite similar to that which existed after the passage of the Fordney-McCumber law. Then there were 4,000,000 men out of employment, the factories were closed and operatives idle and capital in hiding. Then, as now, there was uncertainty throughout the country and people were filled with fear because of it.

I want now to take up the Democratic Campaign textbook of 1922, the one they used throughout the political contest that year, the one that all speakers took for their information and inspiration throughout that campaign, and to read from page 22 of that book to show you the conditions that obtained then obtain now and that the Democrats were saying precisely the things then about the law that they are saying now about this law. The Fordney-McCumber Act had just been passed when these things were written, precisely as the present law has just been enacted and is receiving the same character of attack as the one that followed the passage of that law—regular machine-gun attack of denunciation.

I read: "The Fordney-McCumber profiteers' tariff bill is the worst tariff bill ever passed by an American Congress." This is exactly what they have said about every other protective tariff bill ever passed in this country. "This is the opinion not only of Democrats but of the leading Republican newspapers, the commercial and trade papers, the most prominent Republican businessmen, and even of some Republican Senators and Representatives." And that was true then and the same is true now. Those who denounced it then either did not understand it or were filled with fear regarding it, just as those who are opposing it now are in the state of mind concerning it which is the result of a lack of understanding of its fundamental principles. It is true that many leading Republican business men have been opposing this tariff, just as they have opposed many tariff acts in the past, but always their predictions have been swallowed up by the prosperity produced by the passage of these acts just as will occur in this instance.

SOME OBJECTIONS

Some of the main objections urged against the Fordney-McCumber tariff bill are:

"It puts an additional tax upon the people of the United States of $3,000,000,000 to $4,000,000,000, according to how the special privilege class in whose interest it was passed takes advantage of its provisions." Although challenged time and again to say why they had arrived at $3,000,000,000 to $4,000,000,000 nobody ever answered. They had just as well said $10,000,000,000 to $15,000,000,000 because there was not the slightest foundation for the assertion. In fact, instead of levying tribute on the people to the extent of billions, it reduced the cost of living, it opened all the factories, it set all the idle men to work, it brought all the hidden capital into the open, and it resulted in a degree of prosperity never enjoyed by this or any other land until the crash in the stock market last October.

And again: "It will not yield the Government itself more than $250,000,000 in revenue under the most favorable circumstances." The answer to which is that last year it provided $604,000,000 of revenue. Nothing more need to be said on that item. And every other prophecy carried in that book about that law was just as rational as this one."

And again I read:

"It gives to special privilege and profiteering classes an amount of protection estimated as high as $6,000,000,000."

Our friends have grown modest in the last eight years. Then, they proclaimed with unusual vehemence that we had fleeced the American people of $6,000,000,000 by the passage of that law. The highest that any one of them put the fleecing at this year was at $1,000,000,000 by the passage of this law. That assertion was utterly baseless before and is utterly baseless now. It was a wild, unsupported blast based on no fact and utterly without a scintilla of truth on which to found it. Exactly the reverse was true because all of the people, without regard to rank, or class, or section, or occupation, were greatly benefited by that act during its entire life.

And again: "It will greatly increase the cost of living." During the entire consideration of that law the cry was daily raised that we bear now, namely, that an increased tariff would result in increased prices to the consumer. It will be recalled that then, as is being done right now, tables were put out showing how many billions of dollars in increased cost of living would be loaded on the backs of the consuming public by the tariff of 1922.

Capper's Weekly recently published some Government figures which show the relationship between such claims and the facts. During the period 1918–1930 food, clothing, fuel, light, and house furnishings were at their high point for the period in 1920, miscellaneous items entering into the cost of living in 1921, and rent only, upon which there is no tariff, in 1924. Basing the index number of 1913 at 100, clothing sank in wholesale price from 287.5 in 1920 two years after the close of the World War to 160.5 in 1929. House furnishings sank from 292.7 in 1920 to 197.7 in 1929.

Facts like these of course, will have no effect on the fervent imagination of the foes of the protective policy. No, as they did either years ago, they are putting out mathematical tables trying to prove that increases in the tariff law result in heavy increases in the cost of living, despite the fact that over and over again it has been demonstrated that increased competitive activity

within the United States under tariff encouragement, always has decreased and not increased the cost of living. Moreover, our tariff history has demonstrated beyond all peradventure that a protective tariff provides, rather than destroys, the means of earning that living.

And again, the Democratic textbook of 1922, in summarizing all of the dire effects that were sure to follow the passage of the Fordney-McCumber bill, recited the following additional cause of woe to the American people:

"It will prevent the collection of $11,000,000,000 foreign indebtedness." It really is a source of mirth to contemplate a proposition of that kind. The truth is that settlements have been made with all of our foreign creditors except Russia, and the fact that we set up a tariff against imports into this country from those countries had not a thing in the world to do with the collection of these debts. This shows how far afield the opponents of the tariff always have gone in making wild assertions about the results of a tariff law.

MORE MISTAKES

And the next is a favorite charge of the opponents of the protective tariff system, repeated so many times during the last discussion in Congress that it became almost a daily matter during the entire time: "It is practically an embargo upon foreign products, and will destroy what is left of our foreign trade, already reduced one-half under this administration." Such was the Democratic assertion. What were the uncontrovertible facts? We increased our imports under the Fordney-McCumber law, right in the teeth of these dismal assertions, from $3,112,000,000 in 1922, to $4,400,000,000 in 1929, or $1,287,000,000 of an increase in what we bought from other people, while our exports during the same period rose from $3,831,777,000 in 1922, to $5,241,262,000 in 1929, or an increase of $1,409,485,000 in what we sold to other people. In other words, despite all these doleful prophecies of woe, our total foreign commerce rose $6,944,524,000 in 1922, to $9,641,389,000 in 1929, or a total increase of $2,696,865,000 in what we brought from and sold to the other people of the world.

And yet this remarkable Campaign Textbook of 1922, so replete with unfulfilled prophecies, solemnly recited on page 25 that: "In surrendering the American people to the selfishness and greed of some 4,000 representatives of privilege and monopoly, the bill automatically closes foreign markets not only as a source of supply for American consumers but as a selling price for our surplus products, agricultural and manufactured." How could such fantastical propositions ever originate in the brains of men as able as our fellow Senators and as wise as our colleagues who have daily repeated such assertions for the last six months? Those prophecies were utterly groundless before and they are utterly groundless now. Not one of them was fulfilled by succeeding events and not one of them will be now. And yet these same Senators for months have stood upon the same floor to utter these same wild predictions as to the results of the Smoot-Hawley law. And this same Democratic Textbook solemnly asserted that the Fordney law was "practically an embargo upon foreign products" and that it "will destroy what is left of our foreign trade."

Is it not possible for them to learn anything from experience or to glean either knowledge or wisdom from demonstrated facts?

And again, we were told in that Democratic bible of 1922, from which every text for campaign sermons that year, that "this tariff law will work irreparable injury to labor by reducing production and creating a surplus of labor with consequent wage reduction." And yet the simple truth is that exactly the reverse occurred in every phase of this prediction.

Labor instead of being injured was greatly benefited, evidenced by the fact that deposits in savings banks during the operation of that law increased from $10,000,000,000 to $16,000,000,000 in the United States, and the representatives of labor swarmed the corridors of the Capitol from the beginning to the end of the consideration of the present tariff law demanding that it be enacted in the interest of protection to the laboring classes of the country. There was no surplus of labor until the crash in the stock market, nor have there been wage reductions for, notwithstanding the present unfortunate situation in the country, President Hoover secured promises from the heads of the great labor organizations that they would not strike during the continuance of the present depressed condition of the country and also pledges from the employers of labor that they would not reduce wages even under extreme conditions.

And again this marvelous collection of prophecies recites: "It contains an unconstitutional clause delegating the legislative powers of Congress to the President," and yet the very clause was held constitutional by the Supreme Court of the United States and was reenacted in the present law giving to the President additional power.

And another dire prediction contained in that Campaign Textbook was to the effect that "This presidential clause will create endless corruption in determining fluctuating valuations." Never was a more groundless assertion made in the history of any tariff legislation. Exactly the reverse has occurred in every instance and nowhere at any time have any charges of this kind been made by anybody since the passage of that law.

And the last prophecy to which I desire to call attention sums up all the sad conditions and sorrowful situations that will fall upon the American people because of the passage of that law.

"It will prevent any natural or normal revival of industry of business," it says, "and bring about intolerable conditions of living for the American people." That statement is so fantastical as to be grotesque, and one wonders how citizens of the United States at all familiar with the history of the tariff laws of the Nation and their results could possibly have been brought to write such a sentence, or make such a prediction, even under the stress of political battle. Not one single thing thus set forth happened in this country, or to our people, as a result of the passage of that act, and every single prophecy therein made turned out to be utterly false, refuted by indisputable facts and by the experience of every American citizen.

And yet precisely the same predictions are now being made with reference to the passage of this law and its results that were then made with reference to the passage of that law and its results. None of them proved true then, and none of them will prove true now. Two and two always makes four, like causes always produce like results under like circumstances, and no tariff law ever enacted in American history produced any of the results set forth by these calamity howlers and these purveyors of woe.

And yet it is passing strange that after all of this terrible arraignment of the act of 1922 by the entire Democratic Party, by every Democratic stumper and orator throughout the country, by the Democratic press and Democratic literature of every kind and character, the rates imposed by that act became the standard by which these same Democrats measured tariff revision throughout the whole period of Congress was discussing the Smoot-Hawley tariff law. Practically the sole question that guided them throughout was: "Is the proposed rate higher than the one carried in the past law?"— meaning the Fordney-McCumber law.

If it was higher they voted against it, if it was lower they were willing to raise it to that level. In but very few instances did they ask to change a single one of the rates carried in the Fordney-McCumber law, but struck at every proposal to increase these rates. Verily the stone rejected by the builders became the head of the corner, and the "infamous" Fordney-McCumber tariff law of 1922 that they deluged with their epithets and submerged beneath their curses became the standard by which they were willing to measure all rates in 1930. No more glaring inconsistency has ever been brought to light in the entire tariff-making history of the United States.

FOREIGN PROTESTS

Our Democratic friends have rolled under their tongues as sweet morsels for months the protests uttered by representatives of foreign nations against the passage of the law just enacted. This is an old practice by those nations. When the Dingley law was under consideration 31 nations protests vigorously and said that it would destroy our trade with them. When the Payne-Aldrich tariff bill was under consideration 40 nations voiced their protest.

During the months that the Fordney-McCumber bill was up for action, 37 nations vehemently expressed their resentment through their representatives. Consuls from those nations held a meeting in New York to protest against the passage of the act. They did not want to meet on American soil and be subject to that criticism, and so they hired a boat and went out beyond the harbor limits, where they held a banquet and spoke with the utmost freedom about what was going to happen under the proposed tariff law. Two foreign ambassadors made open speeches in this country, one protesting that our commerce with his country would practically cease, and the other uttering dire threats to the effect that his country would no longer buy from this country if we passed the law. And for months newspapers and magazines teemed with articles written by writers from foreign countries inveighing in caustic terms against the protective tariff system in general and against the passage of the then pending law in particular. It is the same old story.

But let it be remembered that 68 per cent of all the imports coming into this country under the Fordney-McCumber law came in free of duty, and that practically the same per cent will come in free of any tariff exaction under the existing law. All this talk about isolation, therefore, becomes idle if not farcical in the light of that fact.

And furthermore, let it be remembered that every nation protesting against the passage of this act has raised its own tariff rates within the last 12 years and in multiplied thousands of instances higher than the rates carried in our own law. And thus, while they protest vehemently against our people protecting themselves by a law of this character, they openly and boldly pass more drastic ones themselves. And yet these are the same people that have filled our papers with these threats of reprisals.

My fellow citizens, it is an old story, but let us remember that this law was enacted for the benefit of our people, our own farmers and not for the benefit of the citizens of any other country on earth. It is the American policy for which we stand and which has brought our country to its present high position among the nations of the world.

SOME PAST HISTORY

The Democrats filibustered the McKinley bill of 1890 until three weeks before the election and then permitted it to be passed. This enabled them to go out on the stump and make every conceivable kind of charge that could be made because of the shortness of the time in which to make them. The great flood of denunciation that was poured out upon the American people had its effect because the only possible way in which to demonstrate the falsity of charges of this kind is by the actual operations of the law itself, and three weeks was not sufficient for that demonstration to be made.

The Democrats filibustered the tariff bill of 1922, having it in the Senate five straight months, and until six weeks before the election that year. They then filled the newspapers with their clamors about the effects of the passage of that act. All their campaign speakers terrorized audiences by telling them of the horrible things that were about to break before them because of the passage of that tariff act. They cast a gloom over the whole American people by their recital of the doleful conditions that were about to come upon our citizens because of the enactment of that "most infamous" of all tariff laws.

Six weeks is not a sufficient time for a tariff law to vindicate itself or to justify the wisdom of its sponsors, and so the Republican Party suffered at the polls because the people believed many of these dire prophecies and those vehement assertions.

The law just passed was held in the Senate almost nine months, and it is now but four months and a half until the election occurs this fall. During this time all the Democratic newspapers will be filled with those same dismal forebodings and these same gloomy prophecies and we shall have dinned into our ears over and over again from every stump in the country and from every Democratic orator throughout the land the sad prediction of the blighting and withering results of this "infamous" tariff law we have just fastened upon the helpless people of our country.

Whether or not four months will afford time and opportunity for this tariff law to vindicate the wisdom of its provisions and the soundness of its rates can not now be foretold, but that vindication is just as sure to come later on as day is to follow night. It always has been so in the past and it always will be so in the future while protective tariffs continue to be essential to protect American labor and American capital from Niagara floods of importations from abroad.

SALIENT FACTS

The rates in this bill are no higher than they were in any other tariff bill passed in 40 years and are lower than those imposed by the McKinley law, and no higher than those provided by the Wilson law.

The simple truth is that the total increase in duties under the pending bill amounts to but $6,736,551 for the different items designated as the nonagricultural group while all the other increases are those imposed upon agricultural products. That is, putting it differently, but 6.25 per cent of the total increase is upon nonagricultural products while 93.75 per cent represent increases in duties based upon agricultural raw materials.

This Congress literally has executed the wish of the President in calling the special session of Congress last year, namely, to aid agriculture as far as possible by the imposition of additional tariff duties on agricultural products, and at the same time to help those industries that were being injured by large imports of competitive products from abroad. These two objects have been accomplished and the immediate future will show conclusively the wisdom of this action.

This bill is a wholesome piece of legislation for three reasons particularly, first, it disposed of the whole matter after 18 months of consideration and thus gives business a clear view of where it stands and dispels the clouds of uncertainty that during all this time have hovered over the industries of the country. Secondly, it provides higher rates for the protection of agriculture and thus will give a third of the people of the country added prosperity and increased purchasing power. Third, it gives added authority to the President through the flexible provisions it provides to deal with the inequities and inequalities which inhere in every tariff bill because of the very character of the legislation, and which will enable him to meet changed conditions and shifting costs of conversion as they occur from time to time throughout the world. The country has operated under the protective tariff throughout 125 of the 150 years of its existence. Our business is adjusted to it and the policy must be continued if we are to hold our place among the nations of the world. A large number of the Democrats recognize this, witnessed by the fact that five of them voted for this bill directly and all of them voted to protect the particular products of their own State thus showing that they favor it for local reasons if not as a national policy. We doubtless shall travel a bumpy road for a few weeks, just as we always have after the enactment of any tariff measure but soon we shall be in the open with a clear way before us and normal prosperity will be resumed in the country largely because of the passage of the Smoot-Hawley tariff law.

See also: **Vol. I**: American farmers; Hoover, Herbert; Hull, Cordell; Great Depression; Hawley, Willis C.; Hawley-Smoot Tariff (Tariff of 1930); Reciprocal Trade Agreements Act (RTAA); Roosevelt, Franklin D.; Smoot, Reed. **Vol. III**: Tariff of 1930 (Hawley-Smoot Tariff).

Franklin D. Roosevelt's 1932 Campaign Radio Speech

During the presidential campaign of 1932, Democratic nominee Franklin D. Roosevelt repeatedly argued that the passage of the Hawley-Smoot Tariff, signed into law by President Hoover two years earlier, had exacerbated the Great Depression. He addressed the issue in numerous campaign speeches, including one given in Sioux City, Iowa, on September 29, 1932. His remarks, broadcast throughout the nation on radio, forced Hoover to defend his policy during the remaining weeks of the campaign. Many Americans accepted Roosevelt's argument and voted Hoover out of office in November 1932.

Mr. Chairman, my friends in Sioux City, my friends in this great State, and, indeed, all of you through the country who are listening on the radio tonight, let me tell you first of all that I appreciate this remarkable welcome that you have given me, and I appreciate, too, the performance put on by the mounted patrol of my fellow Shriners.

Two weeks ago, when I was heading toward the Coast, I presented before an audience in the City of Topeka, what I conceived to be the problem of agriculture in these United States, with particular reference to the Middle West and West, and what the Government of the Nation can do to meet that problem of ours.

I have been highly gratified to receive from all parts of the country and particularly from farm leaders themselves, assurances of their hearty support and promises of cooperation, in the efforts that I proposed to improve the deplorable condition into which agriculture has fallen. The meeting of this farm problem of ours is going to be successful only if two factors are present.

The first is a sympathetic Administration in Washington, and the second is the hearty support and patient co-operation of agriculture itself and its leaders.

I cannot avoid a word concerning this plight of agriculture—what it means to all. It means that the product of your labor brings just half of what it brought before the war. It means that no matter how hard you work and how long and how carefully you save, and how much efficiency you apply to your business, you face a steadily diminishing return. As a farm leader said to me, you have been caught like a man in a deep pit, helpless in the grip of forces that are beyond your control. Still, my friends, it has meant that in spite of the maxims that we have learned when we were in school, that we ought to work and save, to be prudent and be temperate, in spite of all of the rest of the homely virtues, the return on these virtues has belied the hopes and the promises on which you and I were raised.

That is one of the tragic consequences of this depression. The things that we were taught have not come true. We were taught to work and we have been denied the opportunity to work. We were taught to increase the products of our labor and we have found that while the products increase the return has decreased. We were taught to bring forth the fruits of the earth, and we have found that the fruits of the earth have found no market.

The results of our labor, my friends, have been lost in the smash of an economic system that was unable to fulfill its purposes.

It is a moral as well as an economic question that we face—moral because we want to reestablish the standards that in times past were our goal. We want the opportunity to live in comfort, reasonable comfort, out of which we may build our spiritual values. The consequences of poverty bring a loss of spiritual and moral values. And even more important is the loss of the opportunity that we hope to give to the younger generation. We want our children to have a chance for an education, for the sound development of American standards to be applied in their daily lives at play and work. Those opportunities can come only if the condition of agriculture is made more prosperous.

Now, the farmer—and when I speak of the farmer I mean not only you who live in the corn belt, but also those in the East and the Northwest who are in the dairy business, those in the South who are raising cotton, and those on the plains who are raising cattle and sheep, and those in the many sections of the country who are raising cattle, all kinds of things, small fruits and big fruits—in other words, the farmer in the broad sense, has been attacked during this past decade simultaneously from two sides. On the one side the farmer's expenses, chiefly in the form of increased taxes, have been going up rather steadily during the past generation, and on the other side, he has been attacked by a constantly depreciating farm dollar during the past twelve years, and it seems to be nothing less than old-fashioned horse sense to seek means to circumvent both of these attacks at the same time. That means, first, for us to seek relief for him from the burden of his expense account and, second, to try to restore the purchasing power of his dollar by getting for him higher prices for the products of the soil.

Now, those two great purposes are, quite frankly, the basis of my farm policy, and I have definitely connected both of them with the broadest aspects of a new national economy, something that I like to label in simpler words, "A New Deal," covering every part of the Nation, and covering industry and business as well as farming, because I recognize, first of all, that from the soil itself springs our ability to restore our trade with the other Nations of the world.

First of all, I want to discuss with you one of the angles of the mounting expenses of agriculture in practically every community and in every State—the problem of taxes which we have to pay.

Let us examine the proportion of our expenditures that goes to the various divisions of Government. Half of what you and I pay for the support of the Government—in other words, on the average in this country fifty cents out of every dollar—goes to local government, that is, cities, townships, counties and lots of other small units; and the other half, the other fifty cents, goes to the State and Nation.

This fifty cents that goes to local government, therefore, points to the necessity for attention to local government. As a broad proposition you and I know we are not using our present agencies of local government with real economy and efficiency. That means we must require our public servants to give a fuller measure of service for what they are paid. It means we must eliminate useless office holders. It means every public official, every employee of local government must determine that he

owes it to the country to cooperate in the great purpose of saving the taxpayers' money.

But it means more than that, my friends. I am going to speak very frankly to you. There are offices in most States that are provided for in the Constitution and laws of some of the States, offices that have an honorable history but are no longer necessary for the conduct of Government. We have too many tax layers, and it seems to me relief can come only through resolute, courageous cutting.

Some of you will ask why I, a candidate for the office of president of the United States, am talking to you about changes in local government. Now, it is perfectly clear that the president has no legal or constitutional control over the local government under which you people live. The President has, nevertheless, my friends, the right and even the duty of taking a moral leadership in this national task because it is a national problem, because in its scope it covers every State, and any problem that is national in this broader sense creates a national moral responsibility in the President of the United States himself.

And I propose to use this position of high responsibility to discuss up and down the country, in all seasons and at all times, the duty of reducing taxes, or increasing the efficiency of Government, of cutting out the underbrush around out governmental structure, of getting the most public service for every dollar paid in taxation. That I pledge you, and nothing I have said in the campaign transcends in importance this covenant with the taxpayers of the United States.

Now, of the other half dollar of your

taxes, it is true that part goes to the support of State Governments. I am not going to discuss that end. In this field also I believe that substantial reductions can be made. While the President rightly has no authority over State budgets, he has the same moral responsibility of national leadership for generally lowered expenses, and therefore for generally lowered taxes.

It is in the field of the Federal Government that the office of President can, of course, make itself most directly and definitely felt. Over 30 percent of your tax dollar goes to Washington, and in their field also, items such as the interest can be accomplished. There are, of course, items such as the interest on the public debt which must be paid each year, and which can be reduced only through a reduction of the debt itself, by the creation of a surplus in the place of the present deficit in the national treasury, and it is perhaps worth while that I should tell you that I spent nearly eight years in Washington during the Administration of Woodrow Wilson, and that during those eight years I had a fair understanding of the problem of the national expenses, and that I knew first hand many of the details of actual administration of the different departments. Later in this campaign, I proposed to analyze the enormous increase in the growth of what you and I call bureaucracy. We are not getting an adequate return for the money we are spending in Washington, or to put it another way, we are spending altogether too much money for Government services that are neither practical nor necessary. And then, in addition to that, we are attempting too many functions. We need to sim-

plify what the Federal Government is giving to the people.

I accuse the present Administration of being the greatest spending Administration in peace times in all our history. It is an Administration that has piled bureau on bureau, commission on commission, and has failed to anticipate the dire needs and the reduced earning power of the people. Bureaus and bureaucrats, commissions and commissioners have been retained at the expense of the taxpayer.

Now, I read in the past few days in the newspapers that the President is at work on a plan to consolidate and simplify the Federal bureaucracy. My friends, four long years ago, in the campaign of 1928, he, as a candidate, proposed to do this same thing. And today, once more a candidate, he is still proposing, and I leave you to draw your own inferences.

And on my part I ask you very simply to assign to me the task of reducing the annual operating expenses of your national Government.

Now I come to the other half of the farmer's problem, the increase of the purchasing power of the farm dollar. I have already gone at length into the emergency proposals relating to our major crops, and now I want to discuss in more detail a very importance factor, a thing known as the tariff, and our economic relationship to the rest of this big round world.

From the beginning of our Government, one of the most difficult questions in our economic life has been the tariff. But it is a fact that it is now so interwoven with our whole economic structure, and that structure is such an intricate and delicate pattern of causes and effects, that tariff revision must be undertaken, with scrupulous care and only on the basis of established facts.

I have to go back in history a little way. In the course of his 1928 campaign, the present Republican candidate for President with great boldness laid down the propositions that high tariffs interfere only slightly, if at all, with our export or our import trade, that they are necessary to the success of agriculture and afford essential farm relief; that they do not interfere with the payments of debts by other Nations to us, and that they are absolutely necessary to the economic formula which he proposed at that time as the road to the abolition of poverty. And I must pause here for a moment to observe that the experience of the past four years has unhappily demonstrated the error, the gross, fundamental, basic error of every single one of those propositions—but four years ago!—that every one of them has been one of the effective causes of the present depression; and finally that no substantial progress toward recovery from this depression, either here or abroad, can be had without a forthright recognition of those errors.

And so I am asking effective action to reverse the disastrous policies which were based on them. As I have elsewhere remarked, the 1928 Republican leadership prosperity promise was based on the assertion that although our agriculture was producing a surplus far in excess of our power to consume, and that, due to the mass and automatic machine production of today, our industrial production had also passed far beyond the point of domestic consumption, nevertheless, we should press forward to increase industrial production as the only means

of maintaining prosperity and employment. And the candidate of that year insisted that, although we could nor consume all those things at home, there was some kind of unlimited market for our rapidly increasing surplus in export trade, and he boldly asserted that on this theory we were on the verge of the greatest commercial expansion in history. I do not have to tell you the later history of that.

And then, in the spring of 1929, ostensibly for the purpose of enacting legislation for the relief of agriculture, a special session of Congress was called, and the disastrous fruit of that session was the notorious and indefensible Grundy-Smoot-Hawley tariff.

As to the much-heralded purpose of that special session for the relief of agriculture, the result, my friends, was a ghastly jest. The principal cash crops of our farms are produced much in excess of our domestic requirements. And we know that no tariff on a surplus crop, no matter how height the wall—1,000 percent, if you like—has the slightest effect on raising the domestic price of that crop. Why, the producers of all those crops are so effectively thrust outside the protection of our tariff walls as if there were no tariff at all. But we still know that the tariff does protect the price of industrial products and raises them above world prices, as the farmer with increasing bitterness has come to realize. He sells on a free trade basis; he buys in a protected market. The higher industrial tariffs go, my friends, the greater is the burden of the farmer.

Now, the first effect of the Grundy tariff was to increase or sustain the cost of all that agriculture buys, but the harm to our whole farm production did not stop there.

The destructive effect of the Grundy tariff on export markets has not been confined to agriculture. It has ruined our export trade in industrial products as well. Industry, with its foreign trade cut off, naturally began to look to the home market—a market supplied for the greater part by the purchasing power of farm families—but for reasons that you and I know, it found that the Grundy tariff had reduced the buying power of the farmer.

So what happened? Deprived of any American market, the other industrial Nations in order to support their own industries, and take care of their own employment problem, had to find new outlets. In that quest they took to trade agreements with other countries than ourselves and also to the preservation of their own domestic markets against importations by trade restrictions of all kinds. An almost frantic movement toward self-contained nationalism began among other Nations of the world, and of course the direct result was a series of retaliatory and defensive measures on their part, in the shape of tariffs and embargoes and import quotas and international arrangements. Almost immediately international commerce began to languish. The export markets for our industrial and agricultural surplus began to disappear altogether.

In the year 1929, a year before the enactment of the Grundy tariff, we exported 54.8 percent of all the cotton produced in the United States—more than one-half. That means, Mr. Cotton Grower, that in 1929 every other row of your cotton was sold abroad. And you, the growers of wheat, exported 17 percent of your wheat, but your great foreign market had been largely sacrificed; and so, with the grower of rye, who was able to disposed of 20 percent of his crop to foreign markets. The grower of leaf-tobacco had a stake of 41 percent of his income overseas, and one-third of the lard production, 33 percent, was exported in the year 1929. Where does that come in? Well, it concerns the corn grower because some of us, even from the East, know that corn is exported in the shape of lard.

How were your interests taken care of? Oh, they gave you a tariff on corn—chicken feed—literally and figuratively, but those figures show how vitally you are interested in the preservation, perhaps I had better say the return, of our export trade.

Now, the ink on the Hawley-Smoot-Grundy tariff bill was hardly dry before foreign Nations commenced their program of retaliation. Brick for brick they built their walls against us. They learned the lesson from us. The villainy we taught them they practiced on us.

And the Administration in Washington had reason to know that would happen. It was warned. While the bill was before Congress, our State Department received 160 protests from 33 other nations, many of whom after the passage of the bill erected their own tariff walls to the detriment or destruction of much of our export trade.

Well, what is the result? In two years, from 1930 to May, 1932, to escape the penalty on the introduction of American-made goods, American manufacturers have established in foreign countries 258 separate factories; 48 of them in Europe; 12 in Latin American; 28 in the Far East, and 71 across the border in Canada. The Prime Minister of Canada said in a recent speech that a factory is moving every day of the year from the United States into Canada, and he assured those at the recent conferences at Ottawa that the arrangements made there with Great Britain and other colonies would take $250,000,000 of Canadian trade that would otherwise go to the United States. So you see, my friends, what that tariff bill did there was to put more men on the street here, and to put more people to work outside our borders.

Now, there was a secondary and perhaps even more disastrous effect of Grundyism. Billions of dollars of debts are due to this country from abroad. If the debtor Nations cannot export goods, they must try to pay in gold. But we started such a drain on the gold reserves of the other Nations as to force practically all of them off the gold standard. What happened? The value of the money of each of these countries relative to the value of our dollar declined alarmingly and steadily. It took more Argentine pesos to buy an American plow. It took more English shillings to buy an American bushel of wheat, or an American bale of cotton.

Why, they just could not buy goods with their money. These goods then were thrown back upon our markets and prices fell still more.

And so, summing up, this Grundy tariff has largely extinguished the export markets for our industrial and our farm surplus; it has prevented the payment of public and private debts to us and the interest thereon, increasing taxation to meet the expense of our Government, and finally it has driven our factories abroad.

The process still goes on, my friends. Indeed, it may be only in its beginning.

The Grundy tariff still retains its grip on the throat of international commerce.

There is no relief in sight, and certainly there can be no relief if the men in Washington responsible for this disaster continue in power. And I say to you, in all earnestness and sincerity, that unless and until this process is reversed throughout the world, there is no hope for full economic recovery, or for true prosperity in this beloved country of ours.

The essential trouble is that the Republican leaders thought they had a good patent on the doctrine of unscaleable tariff walls and that no other Nation could use the same idea. Well, either that patent has expired or else never was any good anyway; or else, one other alternative, all the other Nations have infringed on our patent and there is no court to which we can take our case. It was a stupid, blundering idea, and we know it today and we know it has brought disaster.

Do not expect our adroit Republican friends to admit this. They do not. On the contrary, they have adopted the boldest alibi in the history of politics. Having brought this trouble on the world, they now seek to avoid all responsibility by blaming the foreign victims for their own economic blundering. They say that all of our troubles come from abroad and that the Administration is not in the least to be held to answer. This excuse is a classic of impertinence. If ever a condition was more clearly traceable to two specific American-made causes, it is the depression of this country and the world. Those two causes are interrelated. The second one, in point of time, is the Grundy tariff. The first one is the fact that by improvident loans to "backward and crippled countries," the policy of which was specifically recommended by the President, we financed practically our entire export trade and the payment of interest and principal to us by our debtors, and even in part, the payment of German reparations.

When we began to diminish that financing in 1929 the economic structure of the world began to totter.

If it be fair to ask, What does the Democratic Party propose to do in the premises?

The platform declares in favor of a competitive tariff which means one which will put the American producers on a market equality with their foreign competitors, one that equalizes the difference in the cost of production, not a prohibitory tariff back of which domestic producers may combine to practice extortion of the American public.

I appreciate that the doctrine thus announced is not widely different from that preached by Republican statesmen and politicians, but I do know this, that the theory professed by them is that the tariff should equalize the difference in the cost of production as between this country and competitive countries, and I know that in practice that theory is utterly disregarded. The rates that are imposed are far in excess of any such difference, looking to total exclusion of imports—in other words, prohibitory rates.

Of course the outrageously excessive rates in that bill as it became law, must come down. But we should not lower them beyond a reasonable point, a point indicated by common sense and facts. Such revision of the tariff will injure no legitimate interest. Labor need

have no apprehensions concerning such a course, for labor knows by long and bitter experience that the highly protected industries pay not one penny higher wages than the non-protected industries, such as the automobile industry, for example.

But, my friends, how is reduction to be accomplished? In view of present world conditions, international negotiation is the first, the most practical, the most common-sense, and the most desirable method. We must consent to the reduction to some extent of some of our duties in order to secure a lowering of foreign tariff walls over which a larger measure of our surplus may be sent.

I have not the fear that possesses some timorous minds that we should get the worst of it in such reciprocal arrangements. I ask if you have no faith in our Yankee tradition of good old-fashioned trading? Do you believe that our early instincts for successful barter have degenerated or atrophied? I do not think so. I have confidence that the spirit of the stalwart traders still permeates our people, that the red blood of the men who sailed our Yankee clipper ships around the Horn and Cape of Good Hope in the China trade still courses in our veins. I cannot picture Uncle Sam as a supine, white-livered, flabby-muscled old man, cooling his heels in the shade of our tariff walls. We may not have the astuteness in some forms of international diplomacy that our more experienced European friends have, but when it comes to good old-fashioned barter and trade—whether it be goods or tariff—my money is on the American. My friends, there cannot and shall not be any foreign dictation of our tariff policies, but I am willing and ready to sit down around the table with them.

And next, my friends, the Democrats propose to accomplish the necessary reduction through the agency of the Tariff Commission.

I need not say to you that one of the most deplorable features of tariff legislation is the log-rolling process by which it has been effected in Republican and Democratic Congresses. Indefensible rates are introduced through an understanding, usually implied rather than expressed among members, each of whom is interested in one or more individual items. Yet, it is a case of you scratch my back and I will scratch yours. Now, to avoid that as well as other evils in tariff making, a Democratic Congress in 1916 passed, and a Democratic President approved, a bill creating a bipartisan Tariff Commission, charged with the duty of supplying the Congress with accurate and full information upon which to base tariff rates. That Commission functioned as a scientific body until 1922, when by the incorporation of the so-called flexible provisions of the Act it was transformed into a political body. Under those flexible provisions—reenacted in the Grundy tariff of 1930—the Commission reports not to a Congress but to the President, who is then empowered on its recommendation to raise or lower the tariff rates by as much as 50 percent. At the last session of Congress—this brings us down to date—by the practically unanimous action of the Democrats of both houses, aided by liberal-minded Republicans led by Senator Norris, of Nebraska, a bill was passed by the Congress, but vetoed by the President, which, for the purpose of preventing log-rolling pro-

vided that if a report were made by the Tariff Commission on a particular item, with a recommendation as to the rates of duty, a bill to make effective that rate would not be subject to amendment in the Congress so as to include any other items not directly affected by the change proposed in the bill. And in that way each particular tariff rate proposed would be judged on its merits alone. If that bill had been signed by the President of the United States, log-rolling would have come to an end.

I am confident in the belief that under such a system rates adopted would generally be so reasonable that there would be very little opportunity for criticism or even caviling as to them. I am sure that it is not that any duties are imposed that complaint is made, for despite the effort, repeated in every campaign, to stigmatize the Democratic Party as a free trade party, there never has been a tariff act passed since the Government came into existence, in which the duties were not levied with a view to giving the American producer an advantage over his foreign competitor. I think you will agree with me that the difference in our day between the two major parties in respect to their leadership on the subject of the tariff is that the Republican leaders, whatever may be their profession, would put the duties so high as to make them practically prohibitive—and on the other hand that the Democratic leaders would put them as low as the preservation of the prosperity of American industry and American agriculture will permit.

Another feature of the bill to which reference has been made, a feature designed to obviate tariff log-rolling, contemplated the appointment of a public counsel who should be heard on all applications for changes in rates whether for increases sought by producers, sometimes greedy producers, or for decreases asked by importers, equally often actuated by purely selfish motives. And I hope some such change may speedily be enacted. It will have my cordial approval because, my friends, it means that the average citizen would have some representation.

Now, just a few words in closing. I want to speak to you of one other factor which enters into the dangerous emergency in which you farmers find yourselves at this moment. For more than a year I have spoken in my State and in other States of the actual calamity that impends on account of farm mortgages. Ever since my nomination on the first day of July, I have advocated immediate attention and immediate action looking to the preservation of the American home to the American farmer. But I recognize that I am not at the head of the National Administration nor shall I be until the March 4th next. Today I read in the papers that for the first time, so far as I know, the Administration of President Hoover has discovered the fact that there is such a thing as a farm mortgage or a home mortgage.

I do not have to tell you that, with the knowledge of conditions in my State which ranks fifth or sixth among the agricultural States of the Union and with the knowledge I have gleaned on this trip from coast to coast, I realize to the full the seriousness of the farm mortgage situation. And at least we can take a crumb of hope from his proposal for just another conference, a conference of some kind at least to discuss the situation. Seriously, my friends, all that I can tell you is that with you I deplore, I regret the inexcusable, the reprehensible delay of Washington, not for months alone, but for years. I have already been specific on this subject, upon mortgages, in my Topeka speech. All that I can promise you between now and the fourth of March is that I will continue to preach the plight of the farmer who is losing his home. All I can do is to promise you that when the authority of administration and recommendation to Congress is placed in my hands I will do everything in my power to bring the relief that is so long overdue. I shall not wait until the end of a campaign, I shall not wait until I have spent four years in the White House.

See also: **Vol. I**: American farmers; Hoover, Herbert; Hull, Cordell; Great Depression; Hawley, Willis C.; Hawley-Smoot Tariff (Tariff of 1930); Reciprocal Trade Agreements Act (RTAA); Roosevelt, Franklin D.; Smoot, Reed. **Vol. III**: Tariff of 1930 (Hawley-Smoot Tariff).

Herbert Hoover's Response to Franklin D. Roosevelt

In the presidential election campaign of 1932, Democratic nominee Franklin D. Roosevelt, during a speech in Sioux City, Iowa, blamed President Herbert Hoover for the Great Depression. Roosevelt argued that the passage of the Hawley-Smoot Tariff had hurt international trade and deepened economic difficulties. Hoover responded to the charges in a campaign speech in Cleveland, Ohio, on October 15, 1932, which is excerpted below.

I spoke at Des Moines about agriculture. My remarks this evening will be largely directed to employment and to the wage and salary earners. I propose to review what the Administration has done and the measures and policies it has in action together with the relation of these policies to those of our opponents. As President of the United States, I have the duty to speak to workers, but I also have a certain personal right to speak.

When I talk to you tonight about labor I speak not out of academic imaginings but from sharp personal experience. I have looked at these human problems, not only from the fireside of one who has returned from a day's work with his own hands but I know the problem that haunts the employer through the night, desperate to find the money with which to meet the week's pay roll. In public service during years I have had to look at these problems from the point of view of the national welfare as a whole.

The people of a free nation have a right to ask their government, "Why has our employment been interrupted? What measures have been taken in our protection? What has been done to remove the obstacles from the return of our work to us?" They not only have a right to ask these questions but to have an answer. I am here tonight to give that answer.

During the past three years our economic system has received the most terrific shock and dislocation which, had not strong action been taken by your government, would have imperiled the Republic and the whole hope of recovery. It has affected business, industry, employment, and agriculture alike. It is appropriate to report that while many of our measures are directed to the protection and assistance of particular groups, yet all are in the same boat and all must come to shore together. And how are they to get to shore? By listening to those who manifestly display a lack of knowledge of the character of the storm and of the primary problems of navigation? By boring holes in the bottom of the boat? By throwing overboard the measures designed to meet the storm and which are proving their effectiveness?

Our opponents have been going up and down the land repeating the statement that the sole or major origins of this disruption of this world-wide hurricane came from the United States through the wild floatation of securities and the stock market speculation in New York three years ago, together with the passage of the Smoot-Hawley tariff bill, which took place 9 months after the storm broke.

I proposed to discuss this assertion.

First. Because it can be proved absolutely untrue.

Second. Because the United States did not bring this calamity upon the world. The United States is not the oppressor of the world.

Third. Because it can be demonstrated to be founded upon a complete misunderstanding of what has happened in the world.

Fourth. Because any party which exhibits such a lack of economic understanding upon which to base national politics should not be trusted with the fate of 25,000,000 American families. They should not be trusted to command the battle against the most gigantic economic emergency with which our people have ever been confronted, and to bring that battle to victorious issue in the reestablishment of the functioning of our economic machine.

This thesis of the opposition as to the origin of our troubles is a wonderful explanation for political purposes. I would be glad, indeed, if all the enormous problems in the world could be simplified in such a fashion. If that were all that has been the matter with us, we could have recovered from this depression two years ago instead of fighting ever since that time against the most destructive force which we have ever met in the whole history of the United States—and I am glad to say fighting victoriously.

Nowhere do I find the slightest reference in all the statements of the opposition party to the part played by the greatest war in history, the inheritances from it, the fears and panics and dreadful economic catastrophes which have developed from these causes in foreign countries, or the idea that they may have had the remotest thing to do with the calamity against which this administration is fighting day and night.

The leaders of the Democratic Party appear to be entirely in ignorance of the effect of the killing or incapacitating of 40,000,000 of the best youth of the earth, or of the stupendous cost of war—a sum of $300,000,000,000, or a sum nearly equal to the value of all the property in the United States, or the stupendous inheritance of debt, with its subsequent burden of taxes on scores of nations, with their stifling effect upon recuperation of industry and commerce or paralyzing effect upon world commerce by the continued instability of currencies and budgets.

Democratic leaders have apparently not yet learned of the political instability that arose all over Europe from the harsh treaties which ended the war from time to time paralyzed confidence. They have apparently never heard of the continuing economic dislocation from the transfer on every frontier of great masses of people from their former economic setting.

They apparently have not heard of the continuing dislocation of the stream of economic life which has been caused by the carving of 12 new nations from 3 old empires. These nations have a rightful aspiration to build their own separate economic systems; they naturally have surrounded themselves with tariffs and other national protections and have thereby diverted the long-established currents of trade. I presume, however, that if our Democrat leaders should hear of these nine new tariff walls introduced into the world some 14 years ago they would lay them at the door of the Smoot-Hawley bill passed 12 years later.

They apparently have not heard of the increase of standing armies of the world from two to five million men, with consequent burdens upon the taxpayer and the constant threat to the peace of the world.

Democratic leaders apparently ignore the effect upon us of the revolution among 300,000,000 people in China or the agitations amongst 160,000,000 people in Russia. They have ignored the effect of Russia's dumping into the world the commodities taken from its necessitous people in a desperate effort to secure money with which to carry on—shall I call it—a new deal.

The Democratic leaders apparently have never heard that there has been gigantic over-production of rubber in the Indies, of sugar in Cuba, of coffee in Brazil, of cocoa in Ecuador, of copper in the Congo, of lead in Burma, overproduction of zinc in Australia, overproduction of oil from new discoveries in the United States, Russia, Sumatra, and Venezuela; and likewise the effect of the introduction into the world of gigantic areas of new wheatlands in the Argentine and in Canada; new cotton lands in Egypt. In each and every case these enormous overproductions, far beyond consumption even in boom times, have crashed into the immutable law of supply and demand and brought collapse in prices and with it a train of bankruptcies and destruction of buying power for American goods.

They appear not to recognize that these forces finally generated economic strangulations, fears, and panic, the streams of which precipitated another long series of world-wide disasters.

The Democratic leaders apparently never hear that there followed revolutions in Spain and Portugal, Brazil, the Argentine, Chile, Peru, Ecuador, Siam, with attempts at revolution in a dozen other countries, resulting in their partial or practical repudiation of debt and the constant decrease in buying power for our goods.

They seem not to know that the further accumulation of all these causes and dislocations finally placed a strain upon the weakened economic systems of Europe until one by one they collapsed in failure of their gold standards and the partial or total repudiation of debts. They would hold the American people ignorant that every one of these nations in their financial crises imposed direct or indirect restrictions on the import of goods in order to reduce expenditures of their people. They call these "reprisals" against the Smoot-Hawley tariff bill.

They apparently have never heard of the succeeding jeopardy in which our Nation was put through these destructions of world commerce, or the persistent dumping of securities into the American market from these panic-stricken countries; the gigantic drains upon our gold and exchange; or the consequent fear that swept over our people, causing them to draw from our bank resources $1,500,000,000, all of which contracted credit, resulted in demand for payment of debts right and left, and thwarted our every effort for industrial recovery.

Yet in the face of all these tremendous facts, our Democratic friends leave the impression with the American people that the prime cause of this disaster was the boom in flotations and stock prices and a small increase in American tariffs.

Such an impression is unquestionably sought by the Democratic candidate when he says:

"That bubble burst first in the land of its origin—the United States. The major collapse abroad followed. It was not simultaneous with ours."

I do not underrate the distressing losses to millions of our people or the weakening of our strength from the mania of speculation and flotation of securities, but I may incidentally remark that the state governments have the primary responsibility to protect their citizens in these matters and that the vast majority of such transactions originated or took place in the State of New York.

But as to the accuracy of the statement I have quoted I may call your attention to a recent bulletin of the highly respected National Bureau of Economic Research, in which it is shown that this depression in the world began in 11 countries, having a population of 600,000,000 people, before it even appeared in our country, instead of the bubble having "first burst in the United States." Their report shows that the depression in eight other countries, with a population of another 600,000,000 people, started at the same time with ours. In fact, the shocks from the continued economic earthquakes in these other countries carried our prices far below the values they would otherwise have sunk to, with all its train of greatly increased losses, perils, and unemployment.

Our opponents demand to know why the governmental leaders of business men over the world did not foresee the approach of these disintegrating forces. That answer is simple. The whole world was striving to overcome them, but finally they accumulated until certain countries could no longer stand the strain, and their people, suddenly overtaken by fear and panic, through hoarding and exporting their capital for safety, brought down their own houses and these disasters spread like a prairie fire through the world. No man can foresee the coming fear or panic, or the extent of this effect. I did not notice any Democratic Jeremiahs.

So much for the beginnings and forces moving in this calamity.

I now come to the amazing statements that the tariff bill of 1930 has borne a major influence in this debacle.

I quote from the Democratic candidate:

"The Hawley-Smoot tariff is one of the most important factors in the present world-wide depressions."

"The tariff has done so much to destroy foreign trade as to make foreign trade virtually impossible."

I shall analyze the accuracy of these statements not only because I should like to get before my countrymen a picture of the lack of understanding which the Democratic Party has of world trade, but also for the further reasons that it is of vital importance to labor that, as our opponents have this obsession, it means that if they are intrusted with control of our government they intend to break down the protective tariff which is the very first line of defense of the American standard of living against these new forces.

It requires a collection of dull facts to demonstrate the errors in these bald assertions by Democratic leaders.

At the beginning I may repeat that this tariff bill was not passed until nine months after the economic depression began in the United States and also not until 20 other countries had already gone into the depression.

The Democratic Party seldom mentions that 66 per cent of our imports are free of duty, but that is the fact. From half to two-thirds of the trade of the world is in nondutiable goods—that is, mostly raw materials; another part is in luxuries, upon which all nations collect tariffs for revenue; another part, and probably less than one-third of the whole, is in competitive goods so far as the importing nation is concerned and therefore subject to protective tariffs.

The trade of the world has distressingly diminished under the impact of these successive dislocations abroad. But the decrease is almost exactly the same in the free goods everywhere as in the dutiable goods. That is the case in the United States.

If the Smoot-Hawley tariff reduced our imports of dutiable goods, what was it that reduced the two-thirds of non-dutiable goods?

If we explore a little further, we would find from the Tariff Commission that the total duties collected in a comparable year represent 16 per cent of the total imports, this being an increase from 13.8 per cent of the previous tariffs. In other words, the effect of the new tariff shows an increase of 2.2 per cent. This is the margin with which they say we have pulled down foreign governments, created tyrannies, financial shocks, and revolutions.

I may mention that upon the same basis the McKinley duties were 23 per cent; the Dingley duties were 25.8 per cent; the Payne-Aldrich duties were 19.3 per cent of the whole of our imports—all compared with the 16 per cent of the present tariff—and yet they produced in foreign countries no revolutions, no financial crises, and did not destroy the whole world, nor destroy American foreign trade.

And I may explore the facts further. The 5-year average of the import trade of the United States before the depression was about 12 per cent of the whole world import trade. This they would say that 2.2 per cent increased applied to one-eighth of the world's imports has produced this catastrophe.

I can explore this in still another direction. I remind you that we levy tariffs upon only one-third of our imports. I also remind you that the actual increases made in the Smoot-Hawley Act covered one-quarter of the dutiable imports. I may also remind you that our import trade is only one-eighth of the import trade of the world. So they would have us believe this world catastrophe and this destruction of foreign trade happened because the United States increased tariffs on one-fourth of one-third of one-eighth of the world's imports. Thus we pulled down the world, so they tell us, by increased on less than 1 per cent of the goods being imported by the world.

And I may explore the responsibility of the tariffs still further. My opponent has said that it—

"Started such a drain on the gold reserves of the principal countries as to force practically all of them off the gold standard."

At Des Moines I defended the American people from this guilt. I pointed out that it happens there had been no drain of gold from Europe, which is the center of this disturbance, but on the contrary, that Europe's gold holdings have increased every year since the Smoot-Hawley tariff was passed.

My fellow citizens, I could continue for hours in an analysis of mistaken statements and misinformation from the opposition. But I assure you that this country is not to blame for the catastrophes that have come on the world. The American people did not originate the age-old controversies of Europe. We did not inaugurate the Great War or the panics in Europe.

No, my friends, the increase of duties collected by the United States by 2.2 per cent calculated on all the goods we import did not bring about the debacle in the world. If every country in the world were to increase the duty upon their imports by 2.2 per cent tomorrow, but if at the same time they would also adopt domestic policies which would bring about release of the energies and progress of their people— if they would support confidence in the world, then the world's, as well as our own, international commerce would thrive and boom beyond any dimensions that we ever dreamed of.

I dwell on this point, not only because I believe it is important to correct current misstatements of our opponents but because the policies of our opponents are founded upon misconceptions of the utmost gravity for the future of the United States. If it were not a matter of such utter gravity for the future of the United States, I should treat them not in a sense of seriousness but in a sense of humor. There is a vital determination before the American people as to whether there shall be placed in power over the destinies of 120,000,000 of people a party which so lacks a penetration into the forces active in the world and the dangers and responsibilities that arise from them. . . .

I wish for a moment to return to the tariff. There is no measure in the whole economic gamut more vital to the American workingman and the farmer today than the maintenance of the protective tariff. I stand on that principle of protection. Our opponents are opposed to that principle. They propose "a competitive tariff for revenue." They propose to do this in the face of the fact that in the last year currencies of competing nations have depreciated by going off the gold standard and consequently wages have been lowered in 30 competing countries. This is a flat issue which every farmer and workman in the United States should consider from the point of view of his home and his living.

That it is the intention of the Democratic candidate to reduce the tariffs—on all commodities—must be clear from these typical expressions in respect to the present tariff used in this campaign—"Wicked and exorbitant tariff," "its outrageous rates," "almost prohibitive tariffs," "the notorious and indefensible Smoot-Hawley tariff," "the excessive rates of that bill must come down," "until the tariff is lowered," "our policy calls for lower tariffs."

Do you want to compete with laborers whose wages in his own money are only sufficient to buy from one-eighth to one-third of the amount of bread and butter which you can buy at the present rate of wages? That is the plain question. It does not require a great deal of ingenious argument to support its correct answer. It is true we have the most gigantic market in the world today, surrounded by nations clamoring to get in. But it has been my belief—and it is still my belief—that we should protect this market for our own labor; not surrender it to the labor of foreign countries as the Democratic party proposes to do.

See also: **Vol. I**: American farmers; Hoover, Herbert; Hull, Cordell; Great Depression; Hawley, Willis C.; Hawley-Smoot Tariff (Tariff of 1930); Reciprocal Trade Agreements Act (RTAA); Roosevelt, Franklin D.; Smoot, Reed. **Vol. III**: Tariff 1930 (Hawley-Smoot Tariff).

The General Agreement on Tariffs and Trade, 1947, As Amended through 1966

In the post–World War II period, the industrialized nations of the world, led by the United States, moved toward free trade as a means of securing world peace. The signatories of the General Agreement on Tariffs and Trade (GATT) sought to reduce tariff barriers. Between 1947 and 1967 members participated in five rounds of negotiations and decreased rates by 73 percent. Since 1967, members have engaged in two additional rounds in which the range of topics has expanded to include such issues as the environment. The more structured World Trade Organization, formed in 1995, formally replaced the voluntary association of GATT.

TABLE OF CONTENTS

BODY OF DOCUMENT

THE GENERAL AGREEMENT ON TARIFFS AND TRADE

PREAMBLE

The Governments of the COMMONWEALTH OF AUSTRALIA, the KINGDOM OF BELGIUM, the UNITED STATES of BRAZIL, BURMA, CANADA, CEYLON, the REPUBLIC OF CHILE, the REPUBLIC of CHINA, the REPUBLIC OF CUBA, the CZECHOSLOVAK REPUBLIC, the FRENCH REPUBLIC, INDIA, LEBANON, the GRAND-DUCHY OF LUXEMBURG, the KINGDOM OF THE NETHERLANDS, NEW ZEALAND, the KINGDOM OF NORWAY, PAKISTAN,

SOUTHERN RHODESIA, SYRIA, the UNION OF SOUTH AFRICA, the UNITED KINGDOM of GREAT BRITAIN AND NORTHERN IRELAND, and the UNITED STATES of AMERICA:

Recognizing that their relations in the field of trade and economic endeavour should be conducted with a view to raising standards of living, ensuring full employment and a large and steadily growing volume of real income and effective demand, developing the full use of the resources of the world and expanding the production and exchange of goods, Being desirous of contributing to these objectives by entering into reciprocal and mutually advantageous arrangements directed to the substantial reduction of tariffs and other barriers to trade and to the elimination of discriminatory treatment in international commerce,

Have through their Representatives agreed as follows:

PART I

Article I
General Most-Favoured-Nation Treatment

1. With respect to customs duties and charges of any kind imposed on or in connection with importation or exportation or imposed on the international transfer of payments for imports or exports, and with respect to the method of levying such duties and charges, and with respect to all rules and formalities in connection with importation and exportation, and with respect to all matters referred to in paragraphs 2 and 4 of Article III, any advantage, favour, privilege or immunity granted by any contracting party to any product originating in or destined for any other country shall be accorded immediately and unconditionally to the like product originating in or destined for the territories of all other contracting parties.

2. The provisions of paragraph 1 of this Article shall not require the elimination of any preferences in respect of import duties or charges which do not exceed the levels provided for in paragraph 4 of this Article and which fall within the following descriptions:
   a. Preferences in force exclusively between two or more of the territories listed in Annex A, subject to the conditions set forth therein;
   b. Preferences in force exclusively between two or more territories which on July 1, 1939, were connected by common sovereignty or relations of protection or suzerainty and which are listed in Annexes B, C and D, subject to the conditions set forth therein;
   c. Preferences in force exclusively between the United States of America and the Republic of Cuba;
   d. Preferences in force exclusively between neighbouring countries listed in Annexes E and F.

3. The provisions of paragraph 1 shall not apply to preferences between the countries formerly a part of the Ottoman Empire and detached from it on July 24, 1923, provided such preferences are approved under paragraph 5 of Article XXV, which

shall be applied in this respect in the light of paragraph 1 of Article XXIX.

4. The margin of preference on any product in respect of which a preference is permitted under paragraph 2 of this Article but is not specifically set forth as a maximum margin of preference in the appropriate Schedule annexed to this Agreement shall not exceed:

   a. in respect of duties or charges on any product described in such Schedule, the difference between the most-favoured-nation and preferential rates provided for therein; if no preferential rate is provided for, the preferential rate shall for the purposes of this paragraph be taken to be that in force on April 10, 1947, and, if no most-favoured-nation rate is provided for, the margin shall not exceed the difference between the most-favoured-nation and preferential rates existing on April 10, 1947;

   b. in respect of duties or charges on any product not described in the appropriate Schedule, the difference between the most-favoured nation and preferential rates existing on April 10, 1947.

   In the case of the contracting parties named in Annex G, the date of April 10, 1947, referred to in subparagraphs (a) and (b) of this paragraph shall be replaced by the respective dates set forth in that Annex.

Article II
Schedules of Concessions

1.

   a. Each contracting party shall accord to the commerce of the other contracting parties treatment no less favourable than that provided for in the appropriate Part of the appropriate Schedule annexed to this Agreement.

   b. The products described in Part I of the Schedule relating to any contracting party, which are the products of territories of other contracting parties, shall, on their importation into the territory to which the Schedule relates, and subject to the terms, conditions or qualifications set forth in that Schedule, be exempt from ordinary customs duties in excess of those set forth and provided for therein. Such products shall also be exempt from all other duties or charges of any kind imposed on or in connection with importation in excess of those imposed on the date of this Agreement or those directly and mandatorily required to be imposed thereafter by legislation in force in the importing territory on that date.

   c. The products described in Part II of the Schedule relating to any contracting party which are the products of territories entitled under Article I to receive preferential treatment upon importation into the territory to which the Schedule relates shall, on their importation into such territory, and subject to the terms, conditions or qualifications set forth in that Schedule, be exempt from ordinary customs duties in excess of those set forth and provided for in Part II of that Schedule. Such products shall also be exempt from all other duties or charges of any kind imposed on or in connection with importation in excess of those imposed on the date of this Agreement or those directly and mandatorily required to be imposed thereafter by legislation in force in the importing territory on that date. Nothing in this Article shall prevent any contracting party from maintaining its requirements existing on the date of this Agreement as to the eligibility of goods for entry at preferential rates of duty.

2. Nothing in this Article shall prevent any contracting party from imposing at any time on the importation of any product:

   a. a charge equivalent to an internal tax imposed consistently with the provisions of paragraph 2 of Article III in respect of the like domestic product or in respect of an article from which the imported product has been manufactured or produced in whole or in part;

   b. any anti-dumping or countervailing duty applied consistently with the provisions of Article VI;

   c. fees or other charges commensurate with the cost of services rendered.

3. No contracting party shall alter its method of determining dutiable value or of converting currencies so as to impair the value of any of the concessions provided for in the appropriate Schedule annexed to this Agreement.

4. If any contracting party establishes, maintains or authorizes, formally or in effect, a monopoly of the importation of any product described in the appropriate Schedule annexed to this Agreement, such monopoly shall not, except as provided for in that Schedule or as otherwise agreed between the parties which initially negotiated the concession, operate so as to afford protection on the average in excess of the amount of protection provided for in that Schedule. The provisions of this paragraph shall not limit the use by contracting parties of any form of assistance to domestic producers permitted by other provisions of this Agreement.

5. If any contracting party considers that a product is not receiving from another contracting party the treatment which the first contracting party believes to have been contemplated by a concession provided for in the appropriate Schedule annexed to this Agreement, it shall bring the matter directly to the attention of the other contracting party. If the latter agrees that the treatment contemplated was that claimed by the first contracting party, but declares that such treatment cannot be accorded because a court or other proper authority has ruled to the effect that the product involved cannot be classified under the tariff laws of such contracting party so as to permit the treatment contemplated in this Agreement, the two contracting parties, together with any other contracting parties substantially interested, shall enter promptly into further negotiations with a view to a compensatory adjustment of the matter.

6.

   a. The specific duties and charges included in the Schedules relating to contracting parties members of the International Monetary Fund, and margins of preference in specific duties and charges maintained by such contracting parties, are expressed in the appropriate currency at the par value accepted or provisionally recognized by the Fund at the date of this Agreement. Accordingly, in case this par value is reduced consistently with the Articles of Agreement of the International Monetary Fund by more than twenty per centum, such specific duties and charges and margins of preference may be adjusted to take account of such reduction; Provided that the CONTRACTING PARTIES (i.e., the contracting parties acting jointly as provided for in Article XXV) concur that such adjustments will not impair the value of the concessions provided for in the appropriate Schedule or elsewhere in this Agreement, due account being taken of all factors which may influence the need for, or urgency of, such adjustments.

b. Similar provisions shall apply to any contracting party not a member of the Fund, as from the date on which such contracting party becomes a member of the Fund or enters into a special exchange agreement in pursuance of Article XV.

7. The Schedules annexed to this Agreement are hereby made an integral part of Part I of this Agreement.

PART II

Article III
National Treatment on Internal Taxation and Regulation

1. The contracting parties recognize that internal taxes and other internal charges, and laws, regulations and requirements affecting the internal sale, offering for sale, purchase, transportation, distribution or use of products, and internal quantitative regulations requiring the mixture, processing or use of products in specified amounts or proportions, should not be applied to imported or domestic products so as to afford protection to domestic production.

2. The products of the territory of any contracting party imported into the territory of any other contracting party shall not be subject, directly or indirectly, to internal taxes or other internal charges of any kind in excess of those applied, directly or indirectly, to like domestic products. Moreover, no contracting party shall otherwise apply internal taxes or other internal charges to imported or domestic products in a manner contrary to the principles set forth in paragraph 1.

3. With respect to any existing internal tax which is inconsistent with the provisions of paragraph 2, but which is specifically authorized under a trade agreement, in force on April 10, 1947, in which the import duty on the taxed product is bound against increase, the contracting party imposing the tax shall be free to postpone the application of the provisions of paragraph 2 to such tax until such time as it can obtain

release from the obligations of such trade agreement in order to permit the increase of such duty to the extent necessary to compensate for the elimination of the protective element of the tax.

4. The products of the territory of any contracting party imported into the territory of any other contracting party shall be accorded treatment no less favourable than that accorded to like products of national origin in respect of all laws, regulations and requirements affecting their internal sale, offering for sale, purchase, transportation, distribution or use. The provisions of this paragraph shall not prevent the application of differential internal transportation charges which are based exclusively on the economic operation of the means of transport and not on the nationality of the product.

5. No contracting party shall establish or maintain any internal quantitative regulation relating to the mixture, processing or use of products in specified amounts or proportions which requires, directly or indirectly, that any specified amount or proportion of any product which is the subject of the regulation must be supplied from domestic sources. Moreover, no contracting party shall otherwise apply internal quantitative regulations in a manner contrary to the principles set forth in paragraph 1.

6. The provisions of paragraph 5 shall not apply to any internal quantitative regulation in force in the territory of any contracting party on July 1, 1939, April 10, 1947, or March 24, 1948, at the option of that contracting party; Provided that any such regulation which is contrary to the provisions of paragraph 5 shall not be modified to the detriment of imports and shall be treated as a customs duty for the purpose of negotiation.

7. No internal quantitative regulation relating to the mixture, processing or use of products in specified amounts or proportions shall be applied in such a manner as to allocate any such amount or proportion among external sources of supply.

8.

   a. The provisions of this Article shall not apply to laws, regulations or requirements governing the procurement by governmental agencies of products purchased for governmental purposes and not with a view to commercial resale or with a view to use in the production of goods for commercial sale.

   b. The provisions of this Article shall not prevent the payment of subsidies exclusively to domestic producers, including payments to domestic producers derived from the proceeds of internal taxes or charges applied consistently with the provisions of this Article and subsidies effected through governmental purchases of domestic products.

9. The contracting parties recognize that internal maximum price control measures, even though conforming to the other provisions of this Article, can have effects prejudicial to the interests of contracting parties supplying imported products. Accordingly, contracting parties applying such measures shall take account of the interests of exporting

345

contracting parties with a view to avoiding to the fullest practicable extent such prejudicial effects.

10. The provisions of this Article shall not prevent any contracting party from establishing or maintaining internal quantitative regulations relating to exposed cinematograph films and meeting the requirements of Article IV.

Article IV
Special Provisions relating to Cinematograph Films

If any contracting party establishes or maintains internal quantitative regulations relating to exposed cinematograph films, such regulations shall take the form of screen quotas which shall conform to the following requirements:

a. Screen quotas may require the exhibition of cinematograph films of national origin during a specified minimum proportion of the total screen time actually utilized, over a specified period of not less than one year, in the commercial exhibition of all films of whatever origin, and shall be computed on the basis of screen time per theatre per year or the equivalent thereof;

b. With the exception of screen time reserved for films of national origin under a screen quota, screen time including that released by administrative action from screen time reserved for films of national origin, shall not be allocated formally or in effect among sources of supply;

c. Notwithstanding the provisions of sub-paragraph (b) of this Article,

any contracting party may maintain screen quotas conforming to the requirements of sub-paragraph (a) of this Article which reserve a minimum proportion of screen time for films of a specified origin other than that of the contracting party imposing such screen quotas; Provided that no such minimum proportion of screen time shall be increased above the level in effect on April 10, 1947;

d. Screen quotas shall be subject to negotiation for their limitation, liberalization or elimination.

Article V
Freedom of Transit

1. Goods (including baggage), and also vessels and other means of transport, shall be deemed to be in transit across the territory of a contracting party when the passage across such territory, with or without transshipment, warehousing, breaking bulk, or change in the mode of transport, is only a portion of a complete journey beginning and terminating beyond the frontier of the contracting party across whose territory the traffic passes. Traffic of this nature is termed in this Article "traffic in transit".

2. There shall be freedom of transit through the territory of each contracting party, via the routes most convenient for international transit, for traffic in transit to or from the territory of other contracting parties. No distinction shall be made which is based on the flag of vessels, the place of origin, departure, entry, exit or destination, or on any circumstances relating to the ownership of

goods, of vessels or of other means of transport.

3. Any contracting party may require that traffic in transit through its territory be entered at the proper custom house, but, except in cases of failure to comply with applicable customs laws and regulations, such traffic coming from or going to the territory of other contracting parties shall not be subject to any unnecessary delays or restrictions and shall be exempt from customs duties and from all transit duties or other charges imposed in respect of transit, except charges for transportation or those commensurate with administrative expenses entailed by transit or with the cost of services rendered.

4. All charges and regulations imposed by contracting parties on traffic in transit to or from the territories of other contracting parties shall be reasonable, having regard to the conditions of the traffic.

5. With respect to all charges, regulations and formalities in connection with transit, each contracting party shall accord to traffic in transit to or from the territory of any other contracting party treatment no less favourable than the treatment accorded to traffic in transit to or from any third country.

6. Each contracting party shall accord to products which have been in transit through the territory of any other contracting party treatment no less favourable than that which would have been accorded to such products had they been transported from their place of origin to their destination without going through the territory of such other contracting party. Any contracting party shall, however, be free to maintain its requirements of direct consignment existing on the date of this Agreement, in respect of any goods in regard to which such direct consignment is a requisite condition of eligibility for entry of the goods at preferential rates of duty or has relation to the contracting party's prescribed method of valuation for duty purposes.

7. The provisions of this Article shall not apply to the operation of aircraft in transit, but shall apply to air transit of goods (including baggage).

Article VI
Anti-dumping and Countervailing Duties

1. The contracting parties recognize that dumping, by which products of one country are introduced into the commerce of another country at less than the normal value of the products, is to be condemned if it causes or threatens material injury to an established industry in the territory of a contracting party or materially retards the establishment of a domestic industry. For the purposes of this Article, a product is to be considered as being introduced into the commerce of an importing country at less than its normal value, if the price of the product exported from one country to another

a. is less than the comparable price, in the ordinary course of trade, for the like product when destined for consumption in the exporting country, or,

b. in the absence of such domestic price, is less than either

i. the highest comparable price

for the like product for export to any third country in the ordinary course of trade, or

ii. the cost of production of the product in the country of origin plus a reasonable addition for selling cost and profit.

Due allowance shall be made in each case for differences in conditions and terms of sale, for differences in taxation, and for other differences affecting price comparability.

2. In order to offset or prevent dumping, a contracting party may levy on any dumped product an anti-dumping duty not greater in amount than the margin of dumping in respect of such product. For the purposes of this Article, the margin of dumping is the price difference determined in accordance with the provisions of paragraph 1.

3. No countervailing duty shall be levied on any product of the territory of any contracting party imported into the territory of another contracting party in excess of an amount equal to the estimated bounty or subsidy determined to have been granted, directly or indirectly, on the manufacture, production or export of such product in the country of origin or exportation, including any special subsidy to the transportation of a particular product. The term "countervailing duty" shall be understood to mean a special duty levied for the purpose of offsetting any bounty or subsidy bestowed, directly or indirectly, upon the manufacture, production or export of any merchandise.

4. No product of the territory of any contracting party imported into the territory of any other contracting party shall be subject to anti-dumping or countervailing duty by reason of the exemption of such product from duties or taxes borne by the like product when destined for consumption in the country of origin or exportation, or by reason of the refund of such duties or taxes.

5. No product of the territory of any contracting party imported into the territory of any other contracting party shall be subject to both anti-dumping and countervailing duties to compensate for the same situation of dumping or export subsidization.

6.

a. No contracting party shall levy any anti-dumping or countervailing duty on the importation of any product of the territory of another contracting party unless it determines that the effect of the dumping or subsidization, as the case may be, is such as to cause or threaten material injury to an established domestic industry, or is such as to retard materially the establishment of a domestic industry.

b. The CONTRACTING PARTIES may waive the requirement of subparagraph (a) of this paragraph so as to permit a contracting party to levy an anti-dumping or countervailing duty on the importation of any product for the purpose of offsetting dumping or subsidization which causes or threatens material injury to an industry in the territory of another contracting party exporting the product concerned to the territory of the importing contracting party. The CON-

TRACTING PARTIES shall waive the requirements of sub-paragraph (a) of this paragraph, so as to permit the levying of a countervailing duty, in cases in which they find that a subsidy is causing or threatening material injury to an industry in the territory of another contracting party exporting the product concerned to the territory of the importing contracting party.

c. In exceptional circumstances, however, where delay might cause damage which would be difficult to repair, a contracting party may levy a countervailing duty for the purpose referred to in sub-paragraph (b) of this paragraph without the prior approval of the CONTRACTING PARTIES; Provided that such action shall be reported immediately to the CONTRACTING PARTIES and that the countervailing duty shall be withdrawn promptly if the CONTRACTING PARTIES disapprove.

7. A system for the stabilization of the domestic price or of the return to domestic producers of a primary commodity, independently of the movements of export prices, which results at times in the sale of the commodity for export at a price lower than the comparable price charged for the like commodity to buyers in the domestic market, shall be presumed not to result in material injury within the meaning of paragraph 6 if it is determined by consultation among the contracting parties substantially interested in the commodity concerned that:

a. the system has also resulted in the sale of the commodity for export at a price higher than the comparable price charged for the like commodity to buyers in the domestic market, and

b. the system is so operated, either because of the effective regulation of production, or otherwise, as not to stimulate exports unduly or otherwise seriously prejudice the interests of other contracting parties.

Article VII
Valuation for Customs Purposes

1. The contracting parties recognize the validity of the general principles of valuation set forth in the following paragraphs of this Article, and they undertake to give effect to such principles, in respect of all products subject to duties or other charges or restrictions on importation and exportation based upon or regulated in any manner by value. Moreover, they shall, upon a request by another contracting party review the operation of any of their laws or regulations relating to value for customs purposes in the light of these principles. The CONTRACTING PARTIES may request from contracting parties reports on steps taken by them in pursuance of the provisions of this Article.

2.

a. The value for customs purposes of imported merchandise should be based on the actual value of the imported merchandise on which duty is assessed, or of like merchandise, and should not be based on the value of merchan-

349

dise of national origin or on arbitrary or fictitious values.

b. "Actual value" should be the price at which, at a time and place determined by the legislation of the country of importation, such or like merchandise is sold or offered for sale in the ordinary course of trade under fully competitive conditions. To the extent to which the price of such or like merchandise is governed by the quantity in a particular transaction, the price to be considered should uniformly be related to either (i) comparable quantities, or (ii) quantities not less favourable to importers than those in which the greater volume of the merchandise is sold in the trade between the countries of exportation and importation.

c. When the actual value is not ascertainable in accordance with sub-paragraph (b) of this paragraph, the value for customs purposes should be based on the nearest ascertainable equivalent of such value.

3. The value for customs purposes of any imported product should not include the amount of any internal tax, applicable within the country of origin or export, from which the imported product has been exempted or has been or will be relieved by means of refund.

4.

a. Except as otherwise provided for in this paragraph, where it is necessary for the purposes of paragraph 2 of this Article for a contracting party to convert into its own currency a price expressed in the currency of another country, the conversion rate of exchange to be used shall be based, for each currency involved, on the par value as established pursuant to the Articles of Agreement of the International Monetary Fund or on the rate of exchange recognized by the Fund, or on the par value established in accordance with a special exchange agreement entered into pursuant to Article XV of this Agreement.

b. Where no such established par value and no such recognized rate of exchange exist, the conversion rate shall reflect effectively the current value of such currency in commercial transactions.

c. The CONTRACTING PARTIES, in agreement with the International Monetary Fund, shall formulate rules governing the conversion by contracting parties of any foreign currency in respect of which multiple rates of exchange are maintained consistently with the Articles of Agreement of the International Monetary Fund. Any contracting party may apply such rules in respect of such foreign currencies for the purposes of paragraph 2 of this Article as an alternative to the use of par values. Until such rules are adopted by the CONTRACTING PARTIES, any contracting party may employ, in respect of any such foreign currency, rules of conversion for the purposes of paragraph 2 of this Article which are designed to reflect effectively the value of such foreign currency in commercial transactions.

d. Nothing in this paragraph shall be construed to require any contracting party to alter the method of converting currencies for customs purposes which is applicable in its territory on the date of this Agreement, if such alteration would have the effect of increasing generally the amounts of duty payable.

5. The bases and methods for determining the value of products subject to duties or other charges or restrictions based upon or regulated in any manner by value should be stable and should be given sufficient publicity to enable traders to estimate, with a reasonable degree of certainty, the value for customs purposes.

Article VIII
Fees and Formalities
connected with Importation
and Exportation

1.

a. All fees and charges of whatever character (other than import and export duties and other than taxes within the purview of Article III) imposed by contracting parties on or in connexion with importation or exportation shall be limited in amount to the approximate cost of services rendered and shall not represent an indirect protection to domestic products or a taxation of imports or exports for fiscal purposes.

b. The contracting parties recognize the need for reducing the number and diversity of fees and charges referred to in sub-paragraph (a).

c. The contracting parties also recognize the need for minimizing the incidence and complexity of import and export formalities and for decreasing and simplifying import and export documentation requirements.

2. A contracting party shall, upon request by another contracting party or by the CONTRACTING PARTIES, review the operation of its laws and regulations in the light of the provisions of this Article.

3. No contracting party shall impose substantial penalties for minor breaches of customs regulations or procedural requirements. In particular, no penalty in respect of any omission or mistake in customs documentation which is easily rectifiable and obviously made without fraudulent intent or gross negligence shall be greater than necessary to serve merely as a warning.

4. The provisions of this Article shall extend to fees, charges, formalities and requirements imposed by governmental authorities in connexion with importation and exportation, including those relating to:

a. consular transactions, such as consular invoices and certificates;
b. quantitative restrictions;
c. licensing;
d. exchange control;
e. statistical services;
f. documents, documentation and certification;
g. analysis and inspection; and
h. quarantine, sanitation and fumigation.

Article IX
Marks of Origin

1. Each contracting party shall accord to the products of the territories of other contracting parties treatment with regard to marking requirements no less favourable than the treatment accorded to like products of any third country.
2. The contracting parties recognize that, in adopting and enforcing laws and regulations relating to marks of origin, the difficulties and inconveniences which such measures may cause to the commerce and industry of exporting countries should be reduced to a minimum, due regard being had to the necessity of protecting consumers against fraudulent or misleading indications.
3. Whenever it is administratively practicable to do so, contracting parties should permit required marks of origin to be affixed at the time of importation.
4. The laws and regulations of contracting parties relating to the marking of imported products shall be such as to permit compliance without seriously damaging the products, or materially reducing their value, or unreasonably increasing their cost.
5. As a general rule, no special duty or penalty should be imposed by any contracting party for failure to comply with marking requirements prior to importation unless corrective marking is unreasonably delayed or deceptive marks have been affixed or the required marking has been intentionally omitted.
6. The contracting parties shall cooperate with each other with a view

to preventing the use of trade names in such manner as to misrepresent the true origin of a product, to the detriment of such distinctive regional or geographical names of products of the territory of a contracting party as are protected by its legislation. Each contracting party shall accord full and sympathetic consideration to such requests or representations as may be made by any other contracting party regarding the application of the undertaking set forth in the preceding sentence to names of products which have been communicated to it by the other contracting party.

Article X
Publication and Administration of Trade Regulations

1. Laws, regulations, judicial decisions and administrative rulings of general application, made effective by any contracting party, pertaining to the classification or the valuation of products for customs purposes, or to rates of duty, taxes or other charges, or to requirements, restrictions or prohibitions on imports or exports or on the transfer of payments therefor, or affecting their sale, distribution, transportation, insurance, warehousing, inspection, exhibition, processing, mixing or other use, shall be published promptly in such a manner as to enable governments and traders to become acquainted with them. Agreements affecting international trade policy which are in force between the government or a governmental agency of any contracting party and the government

or governmental agency of any other contracting party shall also be published. The provisions of this paragraph shall not require any contracting party to disclose confidential information which would impede law enforcement or otherwise be contrary to the public interest or would prejudice the legitimate commercial interests of particular enterprises, public or private.

2. No measure of general application taken by any contracting party effecting an advance in a rate of duty or other charge on imports under an established and uniform practice, or imposing a new or more burdensome requirement, restriction or prohibition on imports, or on the transfer of payments therefor, shall be enforced before such measure has been officially published.

3.

   a. Each contracting party shall administer in a uniform, impartial and reasonable manner all its laws, regulations, decisions and rulings of the kind described in paragraph 1 of this Article.

   b. Each contracting party shall maintain, or institute as soon as practicable, judicial, arbitral or administrative tribunals or procedures for the purpose, inter alia, of the prompt review and correction of administrative action relating to customs matters. Such tribunals or procedures shall be independent of the agencies entrusted with administrative enforcement and their decisions shall be implemented by, and shall govern the practice of, such agencies unless an appeal is lodged with a court or tribunal of superior jurisdiction within the time prescribed for appeals to be lodged by importers; Provided that the central administration of such agency may take steps to obtain a review of the matter in another proceeding if there is good cause to believe that the decision is inconsistent with established principles of law or the actual facts.

   c. The provisions of sub-paragraph (b) of this paragraph shall not require the elimination or substitution of procedures in force in the territory of a contracting party on the date of this Agreement which in fact provide for an objective and impartial review of administrative action even though such procedures are not fully or formally independent of the agencies entrusted with administrative enforcement. Any contracting party employing such procedures shall, upon request, furnish the CONTRACTING PARTIES with full information thereon in order that they may determine whether such procedures conform to the requirements of this sub-paragraph.

Article XI
General Elimination of Quantitative Restrictions

1. No prohibitions or restrictions other than duties, taxes or other charges, whether made effective through quotas, import or export licences or other measures, shall be instituted or maintained by any contracting party on the importation of any product of the territory of any other

contracting party or on the exportation or sale for export of any product destined for the territory of any other contracting party.

2. The provisions of paragraph I of this Article shall not extend to the following:

a. Export prohibitions or restrictions temporarily applied to prevent or relieve critical shortages of foodstuffs or other products essential to the exporting contracting party;

b. Import and export prohibitions or restrictions necessary to the application of standards or regulations for the classification, grading or marketing of commodities in international trade;

c. Import restrictions on any agricultural or fisheries product, imported in any form, necessary to the enforcement of governmental measures which operate:

i. to restrict the quantities of the like domestic product permitted to be marketed or produced, or, if there is no substantial domestic production of the like product, of a domestic product for which the imported product can be directly substituted; or

ii. to remove a temporary surplus of the like domestic product, or, if there is no substantial domestic production of the like product, of a domestic product for which the imported product can be directly substituted, by making the surplus available to certain groups of domestic consumers free of charge or at prices below the current market level; or

iii. to restrict the quantities permitted to be produced of any animal product the production of which is directly dependent, wholly or mainly, on the imported commodity, if the domestic production of that commodity is relatively negligible.

Any contracting party applying restrictions on the importation of any product pursuant to sub-paragraph (c) of this paragraph shall give public notice of the total quantity or value of the product permitted to be imported during a specified future period and of any change in such quantity or value. Moreover, any restrictions applied under (i) above shall not be such as will reduce the total of imports relative to the total of domestic production, as compared with the proportion which might reasonably be expected to rule between the two in the absence of restrictions. In determining this proportion, the contracting party shall pay due regard to the proportion prevailing during a previous representative period and to any special factors which may have affected or may be affecting the trade in the product concerned.

Article XII
Restrictions to Safeguard the Balance of Payments

1. Notwithstanding the provisions of paragraph 1 of Article XI, any contracting party, in order to safeguard its external financial position and its balance of payments, may restrict

the quantity or value of merchandise permitted to be imported, subject to the provisions of the following paragraphs of this Article.

2.

a. Import restrictions instituted, maintained or intensified by a contracting party under this Article shall not exceed those necessary:

i. to forestall the imminent threat of, or to stop, a serious decline in its monetary reserves, or

ii. in the case of a contracting party with very low monetary reserves, to achieve a reasonable rate of increase in its reserves.

Due regard shall be paid in either case to any special factors which may be affecting the reserves of such contracting party or its need for reserves, including, where special external credits or other resources are available to it, the need to provide for the appropriate use of such credits or resources.

b. Contracting parties applying restrictions under sub-paragraph (a) of this paragraph shall progressively relax them as such conditions improve, maintaining them only to the extent that the conditions specified in that sub-paragraph still justify their application. They shall eliminate the restrictions when conditions would no longer justify their institution or maintenance under that sub-paragraph.

3.

a. Contracting parties undertake, in carrying out their domestic policies, to pay due regard to the need for maintaining or restoring equilibrium in their balance of payments on a sound and lasting basis and to the desirability of avoiding an uneconomic employment of productive resources. They recognize that, in order to achieve these ends, it is desirable so far as possible to adopt measures which expand rather than contract international trade.

b. Contracting parties applying restrictions under this Article may determine the incidence of the restrictions on imports of different products or classes of products in such a way as to give priority to the importation of those products which are more essential.

c. Contracting parties applying restrictions under this Article undertake:

i. to avoid unnecessary damage to the commercial or economic interests of any other contracting party;

ii. not to apply restrictions so as to prevent unreasonably the importation of any description of goods in minimum commercial quantities the exclusion of which would impair regular channels of trade; and

iii. not to apply restrictions which would prevent the importation of commercial samples or prevent compliance with patent, trade mark, copyright, or similar procedures.

d. The contracting parties recognize that, as a result of domestic policies directed towards the achievement and maintenance of full and productive employment or towards the development of economic resources, a contracting party may experience a high level of demand for imports involving a threat to its monetary reserves of the sort referred to in paragraph 2(a) of this Article. Accordingly, a contracting party otherwise complying with the provisions of this Article shall not be required to withdraw or modify restrictions on the ground that a change in those policies would render unnecessary restrictions which it is applying under this Article.

4.

a. Any contracting party applying new restrictions or raising the general level of its existing restrictions by a substantial intensification of the measures applied under this Article shall immediately after instituting or intensifying such restrictions (or, in circumstances in which prior consultation is practicable, before doing so) consult with the CONTRACTING PARTIES as to the nature of its balance of payments difficulties, alternative corrective measures which may be available, and the possible effect of the restrictions on the economies of other contracting parties.

b. On a date to be determined by them, the CONTRACTING PARTIES shall review all restrictions still applied under this Article on that date. Beginning one year after that date, contracting parties applying import restrictions under this Article shall enter into consultations of the type provided for in sub-paragraph (a) of

this paragraph with the CONTRACTING PARTIES annually.

c.

i. If, in the course of consultations with a contracting party under sub-paragraph (a) or (b) above, the CONTRACTING PARTIES find that the restrictions are not consistent with the provisions of this Article or with those of Article XIII (subject to the provisions of Article XIV), they shall indicate the nature of the inconsistency and may advise that the restrictions be suitably modified.

ii. If, however, as a result of the consultations, the CONTRACTING PARTIES determine that the restrictions are being applied in a manner involving an inconsistency of a serious nature with the provisions of this Article or with those of Article XIII (subject to the provisions of Article XIV) and that damage to the trade of any contracting party is caused or threatened thereby, they shall so inform the contracting party applying the restrictions and shall make appropriate recommendations for securing conformity with such provisions within a specified period of time. If such contracting party does not comply with these recommendations within the specified period, the CONTRACTING PARTIES may release any contracting party the trade of which is adversely affected by the restrictions from such obligations under this Agreement towards the contracting party applying the restrictions as they determine to be appropriate in the circumstances.

d. The CONTRACTING PARTIES shall invite any contracting party which is applying restrictions under this Article to enter into consultations with them at the request of any contracting party which can establish a prima facie case that the restrictions are inconsistent with the provisions of this Article or with those of Article XIII (subject to the provisions of Article XIV) and that its trade is adversely affected thereby. However, no such invitation shall be issued unless the CONTRACTING PARTIES have ascertained that direct discussions between the contracting parties concerned have not been successful. If, as a result of the consultations with the CONTRACTING PARTIES, no agreement is reached and they determine that the restrictions are being applied inconsistently with such provisions, and that damage to the trade of the contracting party initiating the procedure is caused or threatened thereby, they shall recommend the withdrawal or modification of the restrictions. If the restrictions are not withdrawn or modified within such time as the CONTRACTING PARTIES may prescribe, they may release the contracting party initiating the procedure from such obligations under this Agreement towards the contracting party applying the restrictions as they determine to be appropriate in the circumstances.

e. In proceeding under this paragraph, the CONTRACTING PARTIES shall have due regard to any special external factors adversely affecting the export trade of the contracting party applying restrictions.

f. Determinations under this paragraph shall be rendered expeditiously and, if possible, within sixty days of the initiation of the consultations.

5. If there is a persistent and widespread application of import restrictions under this Article, indicating the existence of a general disequilibrium which is restricting international trade, the CONTRACTING PARTIES shall initiate discussions to consider whether other measures might be taken, either by those contracting parties the balances of payments of which are under pressure or by those the balances of payments of which are tending to be exceptionally favourable, or by any appropriate intergovernmental organization, to remove the underlying causes of the disequilibrium. On the invitation of the CONTRACTING PARTIES, contracting parties shall participate in such discussions.

Article XIII
Non-discriminatory
Administration of
Quantitative Restrictions

1. No prohibition or restriction shall be applied by any contracting party on the importation of any product of

the territory of any other contracting party or on the exportation of any product destined for the territory of any other contracting party, unless the importation of the like product of all third countries or the exportation of the like product to all third countries is similarly prohibited or restricted.

2. In applying import restrictions to any product, contracting parties shall aim at a distribution of trade in such product approaching as closely as possible the shares which the various contracting parties might be expected to obtain in the absence of such restrictions, and to this end shall observe the following provisions:

   a. Wherever practicable, quotas representing the total amount of permitted imports (whether allocated among supplying countries or not) shall be fixed, and notice given of their amount in accordance with paragraph 3 (b) of this Article;

   b. In cases in which quotas are not practicable, the restrictions may be applied by means of import licences or permits without a quota;

   c. Contracting parties shall not, except for purposes of operating quotas allocated in accordance with sub-paragraph (d) of this paragraph, require that import licences or permits be utilized for the importation of the product concerned from a particular country or source;

   d. In cases in which a quota is allocated among supplying countries, the contracting party applying the restrictions may

seek agreement with respect to the allocation of shares in the quota with all other contracting parties having a substantial interest in supplying the product concerned. In cases in which this method is not reasonably practicable, the contracting party concerned shall allot to contracting parties having a substantial interest in supplying the product shares based upon the proportions, supplied by such contracting parties during a previous representative period, of the total quantity or value of imports of the product, due account being taken of any special factors which may have affected or may be affecting the trade in the product. No conditions or formalities shall be imposed which would prevent any contracting party from utilizing fully the share of any such total quantity or value which has been allotted to it, subject to importation being made within any prescribed period to which the quota may relate.

3.

   a. In cases in which import licences are issued in connection with import restrictions, the contracting party applying the restrictions shall provide, upon the request of any contracting party having an interest in the trade in the product concerned, all relevant information concerning the administration of the restrictions, the import licences granted over a recent period and the distribution of such licences among supplying countries; Provided that there shall be no obligation to supply information as to the names of importing or supplying enterprises.

b. In the case of import restrictions involving the fixing of quotas, the contracting party applying the restrictions shall give public notice of the total quantity or value of the product or products which will be permitted to be imported during a specified future period and of any change in such quantity or value. Any supplies of the product in question which were en route at the time at which public notice was given shall not be excluded from entry; Provided that they may be counted so far as practicable, against the quantity permitted to be imported in the period in question, and also, where necessary, against the quantities permitted to be imported in the next following period or periods; and Provided further that if any contracting party customarily exempts from such restrictions products entered for consumption or withdrawn from warehouse for consumption during a period of thirty days after the day of such public notice, such practice shall be considered full compliance with this sub-paragraph.

c. In the case of quotas allocated among supplying countries, the contracting party applying the restrictions shall promptly inform all other contracting parties having an interest in supplying the product concerned of the shares in the quota currently allocated, by quantity or value, to the various supplying countries and shall give public notice thereof.

4. With regard to restrictions applied in accordance with paragraph 2 (d) of this Article or under paragraph 2 (c) of Article XI, the selection of a representative period for any product and the appraisal of any special factors affecting the trade in the product shall be made initially by the contracting party applying the restriction; Provided that such contracting party shall, upon the request of any other contracting party having a substantial interest in supplying that product or upon the request of the CONTRACTING PARTIES, consult promptly with the other contracting party or the CONTRACTING PARTIES regarding the need for an adjustment of the proportion determined or of the base period selected, or for the reappraisal of the special factors involved, or for the elimination of conditions, formalities or any other provisions established unilaterally relating to the allocation of an adequate quota or its unrestricted utilization.

5. The provisions of this Article shall apply to any tariff quota instituted or maintained by any contracting party, and, in so far as applicable, the principles of this Article shall also extend to export restrictions.

Article XIV
Exceptions to the Rule of Non-discrimination

1. A contracting party which applies restrictions under Article XII or under Section B of Article XVIII may, in the application of such restric-

tions, deviate from the provisions of Article XIII in a manner having equivalent effect to restrictions on payments and transfers for current international transactions which that contracting party may at that time apply under Article VIII or XIV of the Articles of Agreement of the International Monetary Fund, or under analogous provisions of a special exchange agreement entered into pursuant to paragraph 6 of Article XV.

2. A contracting party which is applying import restrictions under Article XII or under Section B of Article XVIII may, with the consent of the CONTRACTING PARTIES, temporarily deviate from the provisions of Article XIII in respect of a small part of its external trade where the benefits to the contracting party or contracting parties concerned substantially outweigh any injury which may result to the trade of other contracting parties.

3. The provisions of Article XIII shall not preclude a group of territories having a common quota in the International Monetary Fund from applying against imports from other countries, but not among themselves, restrictions in accordance with the provisions of Article XII or of Section B of Article XVIII on condition that such restrictions are in all other respects consistent with the provisions of Article XIII.

4. A contracting party applying import restrictions under Article XII or under Section B of Article XVIII shall not be precluded by Articles XI to XV or Section B of Article XVIII of this Agreement from applying measures to direct its exports in such a manner as to increase its earnings of currencies which it can use without deviation from the provisions of Article XIII.

5. A contracting party shall not be precluded by Articles XI to XV, inclusive, or by Section B of Article XVIII, of this Agreement from applying quantitative restrictions:

a. having equivalent effect to exchange restrictions authorized under Section 3 (b) of Article VII of the Articles of Agreement of the International Monetary Fund, or

b. under the preferential arrangements provided for in Annex A of this Agreement, pending the outcome of the negotiations referred to therein.

Article XV
Exchange Arrangements

1. The CONTRACTING PARTIES shall seek co-operation with the International Monetary Fund to the end that the CONTRACTING PARTIES and the Fund may pursue a co-ordinated policy with regard to exchange questions within the jurisdiction of the Fund and questions of quantitative restrictions and other trade measures within the jurisdiction of the CONTRACTING PARTIES.

2. In all cases in which the CONTRACTING PARTIES are called upon to consider or deal with problems concerning monetary reserves, balances of payments or foreign exchange arrangements, they shall consult fully with the International Monetary Fund. In such consultations, the CONTRACTING PAR-

TIES shall accept all findings of statistical and other facts presented by the Fund relating to foreign exchange, monetary reserves and balances of payments, and shall accept the determination of the Fund as to whether action by a contracting party in exchange matters is in accordance with the Articles of Agreement of the International Monetary Fund, or with the terms of a special exchange agreement between that contracting party and the CONTRACTING PARTIES. The CONTRACTING PARTIES, in reaching their final decision in cases involving the criteria set forth in paragraph 2 (a) of Article XII or in paragraph 9 of Article XVIII, shall accept the determination of the Fund as to what constitutes a serious decline in the contracting party's monetary reserves, a very low level of its monetary reserves or a reasonable rate of increase in its monetary reserves, and as to the financial aspects of other matters covered in consultation in such cases.

3. The CONTRACTING PARTIES shall seek agreement with the Fund regarding procedures for consultation under paragraph 2 of this Article.

4. Contracting parties shall not, by exchange action, frustrate the intent of the provisions of this Agreement, nor, by trade action, the intent of the provisions of the Articles of Agreement of the International Monetary Fund.

5. If the CONTRACTING PARTIES consider, at any time, that exchange restrictions on payments and transfers in connexion with imports are being applied by a contracting party in a manner inconsistent with the exceptions provided for in this Agreement for quantitative restrictions, they shall report thereon to the Fund.

6. Any contracting party which is not a member of the Fund shall, within a time to be determined by the CONTRACTING PARTIES after consultation with the Fund, become a member of the Fund, or, failing that, enter into a special exchange agreement with the CONTRACTING PARTIES. A contracting party which ceases to be a member of the Fund shall forthwith enter into a special exchange agreement with the CONTRACTING PARTIES. Any special exchange agreement entered into by a contracting party under this paragraph shall thereupon become part of its obligations under this Agreement.

7.

a. A special exchange agreement between a contracting party and the CONTRACTING PARTIES under paragraph 6 of this Article shall provide to the satisfaction of the CONTRACTING PARTIES that the objectives of this Agreement will not be frustrated as a result of action in exchange matters by the contracting party in question.

b. The terms of any such agreement shall not impose obligations on the contracting party in exchange matters generally more restrictive than those imposed by the Articles of Agreement of the International Monetary Fund on members of the Fund.

8. A contracting party which is not a member of the Fund shall furnish

such information within the general scope of section 5 of Article VIII of the Articles of Agreement of the International Monetary Fund as the CONTRACTING PARTIES may require in order to carry out their functions under this Agreement.

9. Nothing in this Agreement shall preclude:

   a. the use by a contracting party of exchange controls or exchange restrictions in accordance with the Articles of Agreement of the International Monetary Fund or with that contracting party's special exchange agreement with the CONTRACTING PARTIES, or

   b. the use by a contracting party of restrictions or controls on imports or exports, the sole effect of which, additional to the effects permitted under Articles XI, XII, XIII and XIV, is to make effective such exchange controls or exchange restrictions.

Article XVI
Subsidies

Section A—Subsidies in General

1. If any contracting party grants or maintains any subsidy, including any form of income or price support, which operates directly or indirectly to increase exports of any product from, or to reduce imports of any product into, its territory, it shall notify the CONTRACTING PARTIES in writing of the extent and nature of the subsidization, of the estimated effect of the subsidization on the quantity of the affected product or products imported into or exported from its territory and of the circumstances making the subsidization necessary. In any case in which it is determined that serious prejudice to the interests of any other contracting party is caused or threatened by any such subsidization, the contracting party granting the subsidy shall, upon request, discuss with the other contracting party or parties concerned, or with the CONTRACTING PARTIES, the possibility of limiting the subsidization.

Section B—Additional Provisions on Export Subsidies

2. The contracting parties recognize that the granting by a contracting party of a subsidy on the export of any product may have harmful effects for other contracting parties, both importing and exporting, may cause undue disturbance to their normal commercial interests, and may hinder the achievement of the objectives of this Agreement.

3. Accordingly, contracting parties should seek to avoid the use of subsidies on the export of primary products. If, however, a contracting party grants directly or indirectly any form of subsidy which operates to increase the export of any primary product from its territory, such subsidy shall not be applied in a manner which results in that contracting party having more than an equitable share of world export trade in that product, account being taken of the shares of the contracting parties in such trade in the product during a previous representative period, and any special factors

which may have affected or may be affecting such trade in the product.

4. Further, as from 1 January 1958 or the earliest practicable date thereafter, contracting parties shall cease to grant either directly or indirectly any form of subsidy on the export of any product other than a primary product which subsidy results in the sale of such product for export at a price lower than the comparable price charged for the like product to buyers in the domestic market. Until 31 December 1957 no contracting party shall extend the scope of any such subsidization beyond that existing on 1 January 1955 by the introduction of new, or the extension of existing, subsidies.

5. The CONTRACTING PARTIES shall review the operation of the provisions of this Article from time to time with a view to examining its effectiveness, in the light of actual experience, in promoting the objectives of this Agreement and avoiding subsidization seriously prejudicial to the trade or interests of contracting parties.

Article XVII
State Trading Enterprises

1.
   a. Each contracting party undertakes that if it establishes or maintains a State enterprise, wherever located, or grants to any enterprise, formally or in effect, exclusive or special privileges, such enterprise shall, in its purchases or sales involving either imports or exports, act in a manner consistent with the general principles of non-discriminatory treatment prescribed in this Agreement for governmental measures affecting imports or exports by private traders.

   b. The provisions of sub-paragraph (a) of this paragraph shall be understood to require that such enterprises shall, having due regard to the other provisions of this Agreement, make any such purchases or sales solely in accordance with commercial considerations, including price, quality, availability, marketability, transportation and other conditions of purchase or sale, and shall afford the enterprises of the other contracting parties adequate opportunity, in accordance with customary business practice, to compete for participation in such purchases or sales.

   c. No contracting party shall prevent any enterprise (whether or not an enterprise described in sub-paragraph (a) of this paragraph) under its jurisdiction from acting in accordance with the principles of subparagraphs (a) and (b) of this paragraph.

2. The provisions of paragraph 1 of this Article shall not apply to imports of products for immediate or ultimate consumption in governmental use and not otherwise for resale or use in the production of goods for sale. With respect to such imports, each contracting party shall accord to the trade of the other contracting parties fair and equitable treatment.

3. The contracting parties recognize that enterprises of the kind described in paragraph 1 (a) of this Ar-

ticle might be operated so as to create serious obstacles to trade; thus negotiations on a reciprocal and mutually advantageous basis designed to limit or reduce such obstacles are of importance to the expansion of international trade.

4.

a. Contracting parties shall notify the CONTRACTING PARTIES of the products which arc imported into or exported from their territories by enterprises of the kind described in paragraph 1 (a) of this Article.

b. A contracting party establishing, maintaining or authorizing an import monopoly of a product, which is not the subject of a concession under Article II, shall, on the request of another contracting party having a substantial trade in the product concerned, inform the CONTRACTING PARTIES of the import mark-up on the product during a recent representative period, or, when it is not possible to do so, of the price charged on the resale of the product.

c. The CONTRACTING PARTIES may, at the request of a contracting party which has reason to believe that its interests under this Agreement are being adversely affected by the operations of an enterprise of the kind described in paragraph 1 (a), request the contracting party establishing, maintaining or authorizing such enterprise to supply information about its operations related to the carrying out of the provisions of this Agreement.

d. The provisions of this paragraph shall not require any contracting party to disclose confidential information which would impede law enforcement or otherwise be contrary to the public interest or would prejudice the legitimate commercial interests of particular enterprises.

Article XVIII
Governmental Assistance to Economic Development

1. The contracting parties recognize that the attainment of the objectives of this Agreement will be facilitated by the progressive development of their economies, particularly of those contracting parties the economies of which can only support low standards of living and are in the early stages of development.

2. The contracting parties recognize further that it may be necessary for those contracting parties, in order to implement programmes and policies of economic development designed to raise the general standard of living of their people, to take protective or other measures affecting imports, and that such measures are justified in so far as they facilitate the attainment of the objectives of this Agreement. They agree, therefore, that those contracting parties should enjoy additional facilities to enable them (a) to maintain sufficient flexibility in their tariff structure to be able to grant the tariff protection required for the establishment of a particular industry and (b) to apply quantitative restrictions for balance of payments purposes in a manner which takes full account of the con-

tinued high level of demand for imports likely to be generated by their programmes of economic development.

3. The contracting parties recognize finally that, with those additional facilities which are provided for in Sections A and B of this Article, the provisions of this Agreement would normally be sufficient to enable contracting parties to meet the requirements of their economic development. They agree, however, that there may be circumstances where no measure consistent with those provisions is practicable to permit a contracting party in the process of economic development to grant the governmental assistance required to promote the establishment of particular industries with a view to raising the general standard of living of its people. Special procedures are laid down in Sections C and D of this Article to deal with those cases.

4.

   a. Consequently, a contracting party the economy of which can only support low standards of living and is in the early stages of development shall be free to deviate temporarily from the provisions of the other Articles of this Agreement, as provided in Sections A, B and C of this Article.

   b. A contracting party the economy of which is in the process of development, but which does not come within the scope of sub-paragraph (a) above, may submit applications to the CONTRACTING PARTIES under Section D of this Article.

5. The contracting parties recognize that the export earnings of contracting parties, the economies of which are of the type described in paragraph 4 (a) and (b) above and which depend on exports of a small number of primary commodities, may be seriously reduced by a decline in the sale of such commodities. Accordingly, when the exports of primary commodities by such a contracting party are seriously affected by measures taken by another contracting party, it may have resort to the consultation provisions of Article XXII of this Agreement.

6. The CONTRACTING PARTIES shall review annually all measures applied pursuant to the provisions of Sections C and D of this Article.

Section A

7.

   a. If a contracting party coming within the scope of paragraph 4 (a) of this Article considers it desirable, in order to promote the establishment of a particular industry with a view to raising the general standard of living of its people, to modify or withdraw a concession included in the appropriate Schedule annexed to this Agreement, it shall notify the CONTRACTING PARTIES to this effect and enter into negotiations with any contracting party with which such concession was initially negotiated, and with any other contracting party determined by the CONTRACTING PARTIES to have a substantial interest therein. If agreement is reached between such contracting parties concerned, they shall be free to modify or withdraw concessions under the appropriate Schedules to this Agreement in order to give effect to such agreement, including any compensatory adjustments involved.

b. If agreement is not reached within sixty days after the notification provided for in subparagraph (a) above, the contracting party which proposes to modify or withdraw the concession may refer the matter to the CONTRACTING PARTIES, which shall promptly examine it. If they find that the contracting party which proposes to modify or withdraw the concession has made every effort to reach an agreement and that the compensatory adjustment offered by it is adequate, that contracting party shall be free to modify or withdraw the concession if, at the same time, it gives effect to the compensatory adjustment. If the CONTRACTING PARTIES do not find that the compensation offered by a contracting party proposing to modify or withdraw the concession is adequate, but find that it has made every reasonable effort to offer adequate compensation, that contracting party shall be free to proceed with such modification or withdrawal. If such action is taken, any other contracting party referred to in sub-paragraph (a) above shall be free to modify or withdraw substantially equiva-

lent concessions initially negotiated with the contracting party which has taken the action.

Section B

8. The contracting parties recognize that contracting parties coming within the scope of paragraph 4 (a) of this Article tend, when they are in rapid process of development, to experience balance of payments difficulties arising mainly from efforts to expand their internal markets as well as from the instability in their terms of trade.

9. In order to safeguard its external financial position and to ensure a level of reserves adequate for the implementation of its programme of economic development, a contracting party coming within the scope of paragraph 4 (a) of this Article may, subject to the provisions of paragraphs 10 to 12, control the general level of its imports by restricting the quantity or value of merchandise permitted to be imported; Provided that the import restrictions instituted, maintained or intensified shall not exceed those necessary:

a. to forestall the threat of, or to stop, a serious decline in its monetary reserves, or

b. in the case of a contracting party with inadequate monetary reserves, to achieve a reasonable rate of increase in its reserves. Due regard shall be paid in either case to any special factors which may be affecting the reserves of the contracting party or its need for reserves, including, where special external credits or other resources are available to it, the need to provide for the appropriate use of such credits or resources.

10. In applying these restrictions, the contracting party may determine their incidence on imports of different products or classes of products in such a way as to give priority to the importation of those products which are more essential in the light of its policy of economic development; Provided that the restrictions are so applied as to avoid unnecessary damage to the commercial or economic interests of any other contracting party and not to prevent unreasonably the importation of any description of goods in minimum commercial quantities the exclusion of which would impair regular channels of trade; and Provided further that the restrictions are not so applied as to prevent the importation of commercial samples or to prevent compliance with patent, trade mark, copyright or similar procedures.

11. In carrying out its domestic policies, the contracting party concerned shall pay due regard to the need for restoring equilibrium in its balance of payments on a sound and lasting basis and to the desirability of assuring an economic employment of productive resources. It shall progressively relax any restrictions applied under this Section as conditions improve, maintaining them only to the extent necessary under the terms of paragraph 9 of this Article and shall eliminate them when conditions no longer justify such maintenance;

Provided that no contracting party shall be required to withdraw or modify restrictions on the ground that a change in its development policy would render unnecessary the restrictions which it is applying under this Section.

12.

a. Any contracting party applying new restrictions or raising the general level of its existing restrictions by a substantial intensification of the measures applied under this Section, shall immediately after instituting or intensifying such restrictions (or, in circumstances in which prior consultation is practicable, before doing so) consult with the CONTRACTING PARTIES as to the nature of its balance of payments difficulties, alternative corrective measures which may be available, and the possible effect of the restrictions on the economies of other contracting parties.

b. On a date to be determined by them, the CONTRACTING PARTIES shall review all restrictions still applied under this Section on that date. Beginning two years after that date, contracting parties applying restrictions under this Section shall enter into consultations of the type provided for in subparagraph (a) above with the CONTRACTING PARTIES at intervals of approximately, but not less than, two years according to a programme to be drawn up each year by the CONTRACTING PARTIES; Provided that no consultation under this sub-paragraph shall take place within two years after the conclusion of a consultation of a general nature under any other provision of this paragraph.

c.

i. If, in the course of consultations with a contracting party under sub-paragraph (a) or (b) of this paragraph, the CONTRACTING PARTIES find that the restrictions are not consistent with the provisions of this Section or with those of Article XIII (subject to the provisions of Article XIV), they shall indicate the nature of the inconsistency and may advise that the restrictions be suitably modified.

ii. If, however, as a result of the consultations, the CONTRACTING PARTIES determine that the restrictions are being applied in a manner involving an inconsistency of a serious nature with the provisions of this Section or with those of Article XIII (subject to the provisions of Article XIV) and that damage to the trade of any contracting party is caused or threatened thereby, they shall so inform the contracting party applying the restrictions and shall make appropriate recommendations for securing conformity with such provisions within a specified period. If such contracting party does not comply with these recommendations within the specified period, the CONTRACTING PARTIES may release any contracting party the trade of which is adversely affected by the restrictions from such obligations under this Agreement towards the contracting party applying the restrictions as they determine to be appropriate in the circumstances.

d. The CONTRACTING PARTIES shall invite any contracting party which is applying restrictions under this Section to enter into consultations with them at the request of any contracting party which can establish a prima facie case that the restrictions are inconsistent with the provisions of this Section or with those of Article XIII (subject to the provisions of Article XIV) and that its trade is adversely affected thereby. However, no such invitation shall be issued unless the CONTRACTING PARTIES have ascertained that direct discussions between the contracting parties concerned have not been successful. If, as a result of the consultations with the CONTRACTING PARTIES no agreement is reached and they determine that the restrictions are being applied inconsistently with such provisions, and that damage to the trade of the contracting party initiating the procedure is caused or threatened thereby, they shall recommend the withdrawal or modification of the restrictions. If the restrictions are not withdrawn or modified within such time as the CONTRACTING PARTIES may prescribe, they may release the contracting party initiating the procedure from such obligations under this Agreement towards the contracting party applying the restrictions as they determine to be appropriate in the circumstances.

e. If a contracting party against which action has been taken in accordance with the last sentence of sub-paragraph (c) (ii) or (d) of this paragraph, finds that the release of obligations authorized by the CONTRACTING PARTIES adversely affects the operation of its programme and policy of economic development, it shall be free, not later than sixty days after such action is taken, to give written notice to the Executive Secretary 1 to the CONTRACTING PARTIES of its intention to withdraw from this Agreement and such withdrawal shall take effect on the sixtieth day following the day on which the notice is received by him.

f. In proceeding under this paragraph, the CONTRACTING PARTIES shall have due regard to the factors referred to in paragraph 2 of this Article. Determinations under this paragraph shall be rendered expeditiously and, if possible, within sixty days of the initiation of the consultations.

Section C

13. If a contracting party coming within the scope of paragraph 4 (a) of this Article finds that governmental assistance is required to promote the establishment of a particular industry with a view to raising the general standard of living of its people, but that no measure consistent with the other provisions of this Agreement is practicable to achieve that objective, it may have recourse to the provisions and procedures set out in this Section.

14. The contracting party concerned shall notify the CONTRACTING PARTIES of the special difficulties which it meets in the achievement of the objective outlined in paragraph 13 of this Article and shall indicate the specific measure affecting imports which it proposes to introduce in order to remedy these difficulties. It shall not introduce that measure before the expiration of the time-limit laid down in paragraph 15 or 17, as the case may be, or if the measure affects imports of a product which is the subject of a concession included in the appropriate Schedule annexed to this Agreement, unless it has secured the concurrence of the CONTRACTING PARTIES in accordance with the provisions of paragraph 18; Provided that, if the industry receiving assistance has already started production, the contracting party may, after informing the CONTRACTING PARTIES, take such measures as may be necessary to prevent, during

that period, imports of the product or products concerned from increasing substantially above a normal level.

15. If, within thirty days of the notification of the measure, the CONTRACTING PARTIES do not request the contracting party concerned to consult with them, that contracting party shall be free to deviate from the relevant provisions of the other Articles of this Agreement to the extent necessary to apply the proposed measure.

16. If it is requested by the CONTRACTING PARTIES to do so, the contracting party concerned shall consult with them as to the purpose of the proposed measure, as to alternative measures which may be available under this Agreement, and as to the possible effect of the measure proposed on the commercial and economic interests of other contracting parties. If, as a result of such consultation, the CONTRACTING PARTIES agree that there is no measure consistent with the other provisions of this Agreement which is practicable in order to achieve the objective outlined in paragraph 13 of this Article, and concur in the proposed measure, the contracting party concerned shall be released from its obligations under the relevant provisions of the other Articles of this Agreement to the extent necessary to apply that measure.

17. If, within ninety days after the date of the notification of the proposed measure under paragraph 14 of this Article, the CONTRACTING PARTIES have not concurred in such measure, the contracting party concerned may introduce the measure proposed after informing the CONTRACTING PARTIES.

18. If the proposed measure affects a product which is the subject of a concession included in the appropriate Schedule annexed to this Agreement, the contracting party concerned shall enter into consultations with any other contracting party with which the concession was initially negotiated, and with any other contracting party determined by the CONTRACTING PARTIES to have a substantial interest therein. The CONTRACTING PARTIES shall concur in the measure if they agree that there is no measure consistent with the other provisions of this Agreement which is practicable in order to achieve the objective set forth in paragraph 13 of this Article, and if they are satisfied:

a. that agreement has been reached with such other contracting parties as a result of the consultations referred to above, or

b. if no such agreement has been reached within sixty days after the notification provided for in paragraph 14 has been received by the CONTRACTING PARTIES, that the contracting party having recourse to this Section has made all reasonable efforts to reach an agreement and that the interests of other contracting parties are adequately safeguarded. The contracting party having recourse to this Section shall thereupon be released from its obligations under the relevant provisions of the other

Articles of this Agreement to the extent necessary to permit it to apply the measure.

19. If a proposed measure of the type described in paragraph 13 of this Article concerns an industry the establishment of which has in the initial period been facilitated by incidental protection afforded by restrictions imposed by the contracting party concerned for balance of payments purposes under the relevant provisions of this Agreement, that contracting party may resort to the provisions and procedures of this Section; Provided that it shall not apply the proposed measure without the concurrence of the CONTRACTING PARTIES.

20. Nothing in the preceding paragraphs of this Section shall authorize any deviation from the provisions of Articles I, II and XIII of this Agreement. The provisos to paragraph 10 of this Article shall also be applicable to any restriction under this Section.

21. At any time while a measure is being applied under paragraph 17 of this Article any contracting party substantially affected by it may suspend the application to the trade of the contracting party having recourse to this Section of such substantially equivalent concessions or other obligations under this Agreement the suspension of which the CONTRACTING PARTIES do not disapprove; Provided that sixty days' notice of such suspension is given to the CONTRACTING PARTIES not later than six months after the measure has been introduced or changed substantially to the detriment of the contracting party affected. Any such contracting party shall afford adequate opportunity for consultation in accordance with the provisions of Article XXII of this Agreement.

Section D

22. A contracting party coming within the scope of sub-paragraph 4 (b) of this Article desiring, in the interest of the development of its economy, to introduce a measure of the type described in paragraph 13 of this Article in respect of the establishment of a particular industry may apply to the CONTRACTING PARTIES for approval of such measure. The CONTRACTING PARTIES shall promptly consult with such contracting party and shall, in making their decision, be guided by the considerations set out in paragraph 16. If the CONTRACTING PARTIES concur in the proposed measure the contracting party concerned shall be released from its obligations under the relevant provisions of the other Articles of this Agreement to the extent necessary to permit it to apply the measure. If the proposed measure affects a product which is the subject of a concession included in the appropriate Schedule annexed to this Agreement, the provisions of paragraph 18 shall apply.

23. Any measure applied under this Section shall comply with the provisions of paragraph 20 of this Article.

Article XIX
Emergency Action on Imports
of Particular Products

1.

a. If, as a result of unforeseen developments and of the effect of the obligations incurred by a contracting party under this Agreement, including tariff concessions, any product is being imported into the territory of that contracting party in such increased quantities and under such conditions as to cause or threaten serious injury to domestic producers in that territory of like or directly competitive products, the contracting party shall be free, in respect of such product, and to the extent and for such time as may be necessary to prevent or remedy such injury, to suspend the obligation in whole or in part or to withdraw or modify the concession.

b. If any product, which is the subject of a concession with respect to a preference, is being imported into the territory of a contracting party in the circumstances set forth in sub-paragraph (a) of this paragraph, so as to cause or threaten serious injury to domestic producers of like or directly competitive products in the territory of a contracting party which receives or received such preference, the importing contracting party shall be free, if that other contracting party so requests, to suspend the relevant obligation in whole or in part or to withdraw or modify the concession in respect of the product,

to the extent and for such time as may be necessary to prevent or remedy such injury.

2. Before any contracting party shall take action pursuant to the provisions of paragraph 1 of this Article, it shall give notice in writing to the CONTRACTING PARTIES as far in advance as may be practicable and shall afford the CONTRACTING PARTIES and those contracting parties having a substantial interest as exporters of the product concerned an opportunity to consult with it in respect of the proposed action. When such notice is given in relation to a concession with respect to a preference, the notice shall name the contracting party which has requested the action. In critical circumstances, where delay would cause damage which it would be difficult to repair, action under paragraph 1 of this Article may be taken provisionally without prior consultation, on the condition that consultation shall be effected immediately after taking such action.

3.

a. If agreement among the interested contracting parties with respect to the action is not reached, the contracting party which proposes to take or continue the action shall, nevertheless, be free to do so, and if such action is taken or continued, the affected contracting parties shall then be free, not later than ninety days after such action is taken, to suspend, upon the expiration of thirty days from the day on which written notice of such suspension is received by the CONTRACTING PARTIES, the application to the trade of the contracting party taking such action, or, in the case envisaged in paragraph 1 (b) of this Article, to the trade of the contracting party requesting such action, of such substantially equivalent concessions or other obligations under this Agreement the suspension of which the CONTRACTING PARTIES do not disapprove.

b. Notwithstanding the provisions of sub-paragraph (a) of this paragraph, where action is taken under paragraph 2 of this Article without prior consultation and causes or threatens serious injury in the territory of a contracting party to the domestic producers of products affected by the action, that contracting party shall, where delay would cause damage difficult to repair, be free to suspend, upon the taking of the action and throughout the period of consultation, such concessions or other obligations as may be necessary to prevent or remedy the injury.

Article XX
General Exceptions

Subject to the requirement that such measures are not applied in a manner which would constitute a means of arbitrary or unjustifiable discrimination between countries where the same conditions prevail, or a disguised restriction on international trade, nothing in this Agreement shall be construed to prevent the adoption or enforcement by any contracting party of measures:

a. necessary to protect public morals;
b. necessary to protect human, animal or plant life or health;
c. relating to the importation or exportation of gold or silver;
d. necessary to secure compliance with laws or regulations which are not inconsistent with the provisions of this Agreement, including those relating to customs enforcement, the enforcement of monopolies operated under paragraph 4 of Article II and Article XVII, the protection of patents, trade marks and copyrights, and the prevention of deceptive practices;
e. relating to the products of prison labour;
f. imposed for the protection of national treasures of artistic, historic or archaeological value;
g. relating to the conservation of exhaustible natural resources if such measures are made effective in conjunction with restrictions on domestic production or consumption;
h. undertaken in pursuance of obligations under any intergovernmental commodity agreement which conforms to criteria submitted to the CONTRACTING PARTIES and not disapproved by them or which is itself so submitted and not so disapproved;
i. involving restrictions on exports of domestic materials necessary to ensure essential quantities of such materials to a domestic processing industry during periods when the domestic price of such materials is held below the world price as part of a governmental stabilization plan; Provided that such restrictions shall not operate to increase the exports of or the protection afforded to

such domestic industry, and shall not depart from the provisions of this Agreement relating to non-discrimination;

j. essential to the acquisition or distribution of products in general or local short supply; Provided that any such measures shall be consistent with the principle that all contracting parties are entitled to an equitable share of the international supply of such products, and that any such measures, which are inconsistent with the other provisions of this Agreement shall be discontinued as soon as the conditions giving rise to them have ceased to exist. The CONTRACTING PARTIES shall review the need for this subparagraph not later than 30 June 1960.

Article XXI
Security Exceptions

Nothing in this Agreement shall be construed

a. to require any contracting party to furnish any information the disclosure of which it considers contrary to its essential security interests; or
b. to prevent any contracting party from taking any action which it considers necessary for the protection of its essential security interests
  i. relating to fissionable materials or the materials from which they are derived;
  ii. relating to the traffic in arms, ammunition and implements of war and to such traffic in other goods and materials as is carried on directly or indirectly for the pur-

pose of supplying a military establishment;
  iii. taken in time of war or other emergency in international relations; or
c. to prevent any contracting party from taking any action in pursuance of its obligations under the United Nations Charter for the maintenance of international peace and security.

Article XXII
Consultation

1. Each contracting party shall accord sympathetic consideration to, and shall afford adequate opportunity for consultation regarding, such representations as may be made by another contracting party with respect to any matter affecting the operation of this Agreement.
2. The CONTRACTING PARTIES may, at the request of a contracting party, consult with any contracting party or parties in respect of any matter for which it has not been possible to find a satisfactory solution through consultation under paragraph 1.

Article XXIII
Nullification or Impairment

1. If any contracting party should consider that any benefit accruing to it directly or indirectly under this Agreement is being nullified or impaired or that the attainment of any objective of the Agreement is being impeded as the result of
  a. the failure of another contracting party to carry out its obligations under this Agreement, or
  b. the application by another con-

tracting party of any measure, whether or not it conflicts with the provisions of this Agreement, or

c. the existence of any other situation, the contracting party may, with a view to the satisfactory adjustment of the matter, make written representations or proposals to the other contracting party or parties which it considers to be concerned. Any contracting party thus approached shall give sympathetic consideration to the representations or proposals made to it.

2. If no satisfactory adjustment is effected between the contracting parties concerned within a reasonable time, or if the difficulty is of the type described in paragraph 1(c) of this Article, the matter may be referred to the CONTRACTING PARTIES. The CONTRACTING PARTIES shall promptly investigate any matter so referred to them and shalt make appropriate recommendations to the contracting parties which they consider to be concerned, or give a ruling on the matter, as appropriate. The CONTRACTING PARTIES may consult with contracting parties, with the Economic and Social Council of the United Nations and with any appropriate inter-governmental organization in cases where they consider such consultation necessary. If the CONTRACTING PARTIES consider that the circumstances are serious enough to justify such action, they may authorize a contracting party or parties to suspend the application to any other contracting party or parties of such concessions or other obligations under

this Agreement as they determine to be appropriate in the circumstances. If the application to any contracting party of any concession or other obligation is in fact suspended, that contracting party shall then be free, not later than sixty days after such action is taken, to give written notice to the Executive Secretary to the CONTRACTING PARTIES of its intention to withdraw from this Agreement and such withdrawal shall take effect upon the sixtieth day following the day on which such notice is received by him.

PART III

Article XXIV
Territorial Application—
Frontier Traffic—Customs
Unions and Free-trade Areas

1. The provisions of this Agreement shalt apply to the metropolitan customs territories of the contracting parties and to any other customs territories in respect of which this Agreement has been accepted under Article XXVI or is being applied under Article XXXIII or pursuant to the Protocol of Provisional Application. Each such customs territory shall, exclusively for the purposes of the territorial application of this Agreement, be treated as though it were a contracting party; Provided that the provisions of this paragraph shall not be construed to create any rights or obligations as between two or more customs territories in respect of which this Agreement has been accepted under Article XXVI or is being applied under Article XXXIII or

pursuant to the Protocol of Provisional Application by a single contracting party.

2. For the purposes of this Agreement a customs territory shall be understood to mean any territory with respect to which separate tariffs or other regulations of commerce are maintained for a substantial part of the trade of such territory with other territories.

3. The provisions of this Agreement shalt not be construed to prevent:

   a. Advantages accorded by any contracting party to adjacent countries in order to facilitate frontier traffic;

   b. Advantages accorded to the trade with the Free Territory of Trieste by countries contiguous to that territory, provided that such advantages are not in conflict with the Treaties of Peace arising out of the Second World War.

4. The contracting parties recognize the desirability of increasing freedom of trade by the development, through voluntary agreements, of closer integration between the economies of the countries parties to such agreements. They also recognize that the purpose of a customs union or of a free-trade area should be to facilitate trade between the constituent territories and not to raise barriers to the trade of other contracting parties with such territories.

5. Accordingly, the provisions of this Agreement shall not prevent, as between the territories of contracting parties, the formation of a customs union or of a free-trade area or the adoption of an interim agreement necessary for the formation of a customs union or of a free-trade area; Provided that:

   a. with respect to a customs union, or an interim agreement leading to the formation of a customs union, the duties and other regulations of commerce imposed at the institution of any such union or interim agreement in respect of trade with contracting parties not parties to such union or agreement shall not on the whole be higher or more restrictive than the general incidence of the duties and regulations of commerce applicable in the constituent territories prior to the formation of such union or the adoption of such interim agreement, as the case may be;

   b. with respect to a free-trade area, or an interim agreement leading to the formation of a free-trade area, the duties and other regulations of commerce maintained in each of the constituent territories and applicable at the formation of such free-trade area or the adoption of such interim agreement to the trade of contracting parties not included in such area or not parties to such agreement shall not be higher or more restrictive than the corresponding duties and other regulations of commerce existing in the same constituent territories prior to the formation of the free-trade area, or interim agreement, as the case may be; and

   c. any interim agreement referred to in sub-paragraphs (a) and (b) shall include a plan and schedule for the formation of such a customs union or of such a free-trade area within a reasonable length of time.

6. If, in fulfilling the requirements of sub-paragraph 5 (a), a contracting party proposes to increase any rate of duty inconsistently with the provisions of Article II, the procedure set forth in Article XXVIII shall apply. In providing for compensatory adjustment, due account shall be taken of the compensation already afforded by the reductions brought about in the corresponding duty of the other constituents of the union.

7.
   a. Any contracting party deciding to enter into a customs union or free-trade area, or an interim agreement leading to the formation of such a union or area, shall promptly notify the CONTRACTING PARTIES and shall make available to them such information regarding the proposed union or area as will enable them to make such reports and recommendations to contracting parties as they may deem appropriate.

   b. If, after having studied the plan and schedule included in an interim agreement referred to in paragraph 5 in consultation with the parties to that agreement and taking due account of the information made available in accordance with the provisions of sub-paragraph (a), the CONTRACTING PARTIES find that such agreement is not likely to result in the formation of a customs union or of a free-trade area within the period contemplated by the parties to the agreement or that such period is not a reasonable one, the CONTRACTING PARTIES shall make recommendations to the parties to the agreement. The parties shall not maintain or put into force, as the case may be, such agreement if they are not prepared to modify it in accordance with these recommendations.

   c. Any substantial change in the plan or schedule referred to in paragraph 5 (c) shall be communicated to the CONTRACTING PARTIES, which may request the contracting parties concerned to consult with them if the change seems likely to jeopardize or delay unduly the formation of the customs union or of the free-trade area.

8. For the purposes of this Agreement:
   a. A customs union shall be understood to mean the substitution of a single customs territory for two or more customs territories, so that
      i. duties and other restrictive regulations of commerce (except, where necessary, those permitted under Articles XI, XII, XIII, XIV, XV and XX) are eliminated with respect to substantially all the trade between the constituent territories of the union or at least with respect to substantially all the trade in products originating in such territories, and,
      ii. subject to the provisions of paragraph 9, substantially the same duties and other

regulations of commerce are applied by each of the members of the union to the trade of territories not included in the union;

b. A free-trade area shall be understood to mean a group of two or more customs territories in which the duties and other restrictive regulations of commerce (except, where necessary, those permitted under Articles XI, XII, XIII, XIV, XV and XX) are eliminated on substantially all the trade between the constituent territories in products originating in such territories.

9. The preferences referred to in paragraph 2 of Article I shall not be affected by the formation of a customs union or of a free-trade area but may be eliminated or adjusted by means of negotiations with contracting parties affected. This procedure of negotiations with affected contracting parties shall, in particular, apply to the elimination of preferences required to conform with the provisions of paragraph 8 (a) (i) and paragraph 8 (b).

10. The CONTRACTING PARTIES may by a two-thirds majority approve proposals which do not fully comply with the requirements of paragraphs 5 to 9 inclusive, provided that such proposals lead to the formation of a customs union or a free-trade area in the sense of this Article.

11. Taking into account the exceptional circumstances arising out of the establishment of India and Pakistan as independent States and recognizing the fact that they have long constituted an economic unit, the contracting parties agree that the provisions of this Agreement shall not prevent the two countries from entering into special arrangements with respect to the trade between them, pending the establishment of their mutual trade relations on a definitive basis.

12. Each contracting party shall take such reasonable measures as may be available to it to ensure observance of the provisions of this Agreement by the regional and local governments and authorities within its territory.

Article XXV
Joint Action by the Contracting Parties

1. Representatives of the contracting parties shall meet from time to time for the purpose of giving effect to those provisions of this Agreement which involve joint action and, generally, with a view to facilitating the operation and furthering the objectives of this Agreement. Wherever reference is made in this Agreement to the contracting parties acting jointly they are designated as the CONTRACTING PARTIES.

2. The Secretary-General of the United Nations is requested to convene the first meeting of the CONTRACTING PARTIES, which shall take place not later than March 1, 1948.

3. Each contracting party shall be entitled to have one vote at all meetings of the CONTRACTING PARTIES.

4. Except as otherwise provided for in this Agreement, decisions of the CONTRACTING PARTIES shall be taken by a majority of the votes cast.

5. In exceptional circumstances not elsewhere provided for in this Agreement, the CONTRACTING PARTIES may waive an obligation imposed upon a contracting party by this Agreement; Provided that any such decision shall be approved by a two-thirds majority of the votes cast and that such majority shall comprise more than half of the contracting parties. The CONTRACTING PARTIES may also by such a vote

   i. define certain categories of exceptional circumstances to which other voting requirements shall apply for the waiver of obligations, and

   ii. prescribe such criteria as may be necessary for the application of this paragraph.

Article XXVI
Acceptance, Entry into Force and Registration

1. The date of this Agreement shall be 30 October 1947.
2. This Agreement shall be open for acceptance by any contracting party which, on 1 March 1955, was a contracting party or was negotiating with a view to accession to this Agreement.
3. This Agreement, done in a single English original and in a single French original, both texts authentic, shall be deposited with the Secretary-General of the United Nations, who shall furnish certified copies thereof to all interested governments.
4. Each government accepting this Agreement shall deposit an instrument of acceptance with the Execu-

tive Secretary to the CONTRACTING PARTIES, who will inform all interested governments of the date of deposit of each instrument of acceptance and of the day on which this Agreement enters into force under paragraph 6 of this Article.

5.

   a. Each government accepting this Agreement does so in respect of its metropolitan territory and of the other territories for which it has international responsibility, except such separate customs territories as it shall notify to the Executive Secretary to the CONTRACTING PARTIES at the time of its own acceptance.

   b. Any government, which has so notified the Executive Secretary under the exceptions in subparagraph (a) of this paragraph, may at any time give notice to the Executive Secretary that its acceptance shall be effective in respect of any separate customs territory or territories so excepted and such notice shall take effect on the thirtieth day following the day on which it is received by the Executive Secretary.

   c. If any of the customs territories, in respect of which a contracting party has accepted this Agreement, possesses or acquires full autonomy in the conduct of its external commercial relations and of the other matters provided for in this Agreement, such territory shall, upon sponsorship through a declaration by the responsible contracting party establishing the above-mentioned fact, be deemed to be a contracting party.

6. This Agreement shall enter into force, as among the governments which have accepted it, on the thirtieth day following the day on which instruments of acceptance have been deposited with the Executive Secretary to the CONTRACTING PARTIES on behalf of governments named in Annex H, the territories of which account for 85 per centum of the total external trade of the territories of such governments, computed in accordance with the applicable column of percentages set forth therein. The instrument of acceptance of each other government shall take effect on the thirtieth day following the day on which such instrument has been deposited.

7. The United Nations is authorized to effect registration of this Agreement as soon as it enters into force.

Article XXVII
Withholding or Withdrawal of Concessions

Any contracting party shall at any time be free to withhold or to withdraw in whole or in part any concession, provided for in the appropriate Schedule annexed to this Agreement, in respect of which such contracting party determines that it was initially negotiated with a government which has not become, or has ceased to be, a contracting party. A contracting party taking such action shall notify the CONTRACTING PARTIES and, upon request, consult with contracting parties which have a substantial interest in the product concerned.

Article XXVIII
Modification of Schedules

1. On the first day of each three-year period, the first period beginning on 1 January 1958 (or on the first day of any other period that may be specified by the CONTRACTING PARTIES by two-thirds of the votes cast) a contracting party (hereafter in this Article referred to as the "applicant contracting party") may, by negotiation and agreement with any contracting party with which such concession was initially negotiated and with any other contracting party determined by the CONTRACTING PARTIES to have a principal supplying interest (which two preceding categories of contracting parties, together with the applicant contracting party, are in this Article hereinafter referred to as the "contracting parties primarily concerned"), and subject to consultation with any other contracting party determined by the CONTRACTING PARTIES to have a substantial interest in such concession, modify or withdraw a concession included in the appropriate Schedule annexed to this Agreement.

2. In such negotiations and agreement, which may include provision for compensatory adjustment with respect to other products, the contracting parties concerned shall endeavour to maintain a general level of reciprocal and mutually advantageous concessions not less favourable to trade than that provided for in this Agreement prior to such negotiations.

3.

   a. If agreement between the contracting parties primarily concerned cannot be reached before 1 January 1958 or before the expiration of a period envisaged in paragraph 1 of this Article, the contracting party which proposes to modify or withdraw the concession shall, nevertheless, be free to do so and if such action is taken any contracting party with which such concession was initially negotiated, any contracting party determined under paragraph 1 to have a principal supplying interest and any contracting party determined under paragraph 1 to have a substantial interest shall then be free not later than six months after such action is taken, to withdraw, upon the expiration of thirty days from the day on which written notice of such withdrawal is received by the CONTRACTING PARTIES, substantially equivalent concessions initially negotiated with the applicant contracting party.

b. If agreement between the contracting parties primarily concerned is reached but any other contracting party determined under paragraph 1 of this Article to have a substantial interest is not satisfied, such other contracting party shall be free, not later than six months after action under such agreement is taken, to withdraw, upon the expiration of thirty days from the day on which written notice of such withdrawal is received by the CONTRACTING PARTIES, substantially equivalent concessions initially negotiated with the applicant contracting party.

4. The CONTRACTING PARTIES may, at any time, in special circumstances, authorize a contracting party to enter into negotiations for modification or withdrawal of a concession included in the appropriate Schedule annexed to this Agreement subject to the following procedures and conditions:

a. Such negotiations and any related consultations shall be conducted in accordance with the provisions of paragraphs 1 and 2 of this Article.

b. If agreement between the contracting parties primarily concerned is reached in the negotiations, the provisions of paragraph 3 (b) of this Article shall apply.

c. If agreement between the contracting parties primarily concerned is not reached within a period of sixty days after negotiations have been authorized, or within such longer period as the CONTRACTING PARTIES may have prescribed, the applicant contracting party may refer the matter to the CONTRACTING PARTIES.

d. Upon such reference, the CONTRACTING PARTIES shall promptly examine the matter and submit their views to the contracting partiesprimarily concerned with the aim of achieving a settlement. If a settlement is reached, the provisions of paragraph 3 (b) shall apply as if agreement between the contracting parties primarily concerned had been reached. If no settlement is reached between the contracting parties primarily concerned, the applicant contracting party shall be free to modify or withdraw the concession, unless the CONTRACTING PARTIES determine that the applicant contracting party has unreasonably failed to offer adequate compensation. If such action is taken, any contracting party with which the concession was initially negotiated, any contracting party determined under paragraph 4 (a) to have a principal supplying interest and any contracting party determined under paragraph 4 (a) to have a substantial interest, shall be free, not later than six months after such action is taken, to modify or withdraw, upon the expiration of thirty days from the day on which written notice of such withdrawal is received by the CONTRACTING PARTIES, substantially equivalent concessions initially negotiated with the applicant contracting party.

5. Before 1 January 1958 and before the end of any period envisaged in paragraph 1 a contracting party may elect by notifying the CONTRACTING PARTIES to reserve the right, for the duration of the next period, to modify the appropriate Schedule in accordance with the procedures of paragraphs 1 to 3. If a contracting party so elects, other contracting parties shall have the right, during the same period, to modify or withdraw, in accordance with the same procedures, concessions initially negotiated with that contracting party.

Article XXVIII-bis
Tariff Negotiations

1. The contracting parties recognize that customs duties often constitute serious obstacles to trade; thus negotiations on a reciprocal and mutually advantageous basis, directed to the substantial reduction of the general level of tariffs and other charges on imports and exports and in particular to the reduction of such high tariffs as discourage the importation even of minimum quantities, and conducted with due regard to the objectives of this Agreement and the varying needs of individual contracting parties, are of great importance to the expansion of international trade. The CONTRACTING PARTES may therefore sponsor such negotiations from time to time.

2.

   a. Negotiations under this Article may be carried out on a selective product-by-product basis or by the application of such multilateral procedures as may be accepted by the contracting parties concerned. Such negotiations may be directed towards the reduction of duties, the binding of duties at then existing levels or undertakings that individual duties or the average duties on specified categories of products shall not exceed specified levels. The binding against increase of low duties or of duty-free treatment shall, in principle, be recognized as a concession equivalent in value to the reduction of high duties.

   b. The contracting parties recognize

that in general the success of multilateral negotiations would depend on the participation of all contracting parties which conduct a substantial proportion of their external trade with one another.

3. Negotiations shall be conducted on a basis which affords adequate opportunity to take into account:

a. the needs of individual contracting parties and individual industries;

b. the needs of less-developed countries for a more flexible use of tariff protection to assist their economic development and the special needs of these countries to maintain tariffs for revenue purposes; and

c. all other relevant circumstances, including the fiscal, developmental, strategic and other needs of the contracting parties concerned.

Article XXIX
The Relation of this Agreement to the Havana Charter

1. The contracting parties undertake to observe to the fullest extent of their executive authority the general principles of Chapters I to VI inclusive and of Chapter IX of the Havana Charter pending their acceptance of it in accordance with their constitutional procedures.

2. Part II of this Agreement shall be suspended on the day on which the Havana Charter enters into force.

3. If by September 30, 1949, the Havana Charter has not entered into force, the contracting parties shall meet before December 31, 1949, to agree whether this Agreement shall be amended, supplemented or maintained.

4. If at any time the Havana Charter should cease to be in force, the CONTRACTING PARTIES shall meet as soon as practicable thereafter to agree whether this Agreement shall be supplemented, amended or maintained. Pending such agreement, Part II of this Agreement shall again enter into force; Provided that the provisions of Part II other than Article XXIII shall be replaced, mutatis mutandis, in the form in which they then appeared in the Havana Charter; and Provided further that no contracting party shall be bound by any provisions which did not bind it at the time when the Havana Charter ceased to be in force.

5. If any contracting party has not accepted the Havana Charter by the date upon which it enters into force, the CONTRACTING PARTIES shall confer to agree whether, and if so in what way, this Agreement in so far as it affects relations between such contracting party and other contracting parties, shall be supplemented or amended. Pending such agreement the provisions of Part II of this Agreement shall, notwithstanding the provisions of paragraph 2 of this Article, continue to apply as between such contracting party and other contracting parties.

6. Contracting parties which are Members of the International Trade Organization shall not invoke the provisions of this Agreement so as to prevent the operation of any provision of the Havana Charter. The

application of the principle under-lying this paragraph to any contract-ing party which is not a Member of the International Trade Organiza-tion shall be the subject of an agree-ment pursuant to paragraph 5 of this Article.

Article XXX
Amendments

1. Except where provision for modifi-cation is made elsewhere in this Agreement, amendments to the pro-visions of Part I of this Agreement or to the provisions of Article XXIX or of this Article shall become ef-fective upon acceptance by all the contracting parties, and other amendments to this Agreement shall become effective, in respect of those contracting parties which ac-cept them, upon acceptance by two-thirds of the contracting parties and thereafter for each other contracting party upon acceptance by it.
2. Any contracting party accepting an amendment to this Agreement shall deposit an instrument of acceptance with the Secretary-General of the United Nations within such period as the CONTRACTING PARTIES may specify. The CONTRACTING PARTIES may decide that any amendment made effective under this Article is of such a nature that any contracting party which has not accepted it within a period specified by the CONTRACTING PARTIES shall be free to with-draw from this Agreement, or to re-main a contracting party with the consent of the CONTRACTING PARTIES.

Article XXXI
Withdrawal

Without prejudice to the provisions of paragraph 12 of Article XVIII, of Arti-cle XXIII or of paragraph 2 of Article XXX, any contracting party may with-draw from this Agreement, or may separately withdraw on behalf of any of the separate customs territories for which it has international responsibil-ity and which at the time possesses full autonomy in the conduct of its external commercial relations and of the other matters provided for in this Agreement. The withdrawal shall take effect upon the expiration of six months from the day on which written notice of with-drawal is received by the Secretary-General of the United Nations.

Article XXXII
Contracting Parties

1. The contracting parties to this Agreement shall be understood to mean those governments which are applying the provisions of this Agreement under Articles XXVI or XXXIII or pursuant to the Protocol of Provisional Application.
2. At any time after the entry into force of this Agreement pursuant to par-agraph 6 of Article XXVI, those con-tracting parties which have accepted this Agreement pursuant to para-graph 4 of Article XXVI may decide that any contracting party which has not so accepted it shall cease to be a contracting party.

Article XXXIII
Accession

A government not party to this Agree-ment, or a government acting on behalf of a separate customs territory possessing full autonomy in the conduct of its external commercial relations and of the other matters provided for in this Agreement, may accede to this Agreement, on its own behalf or on behalf of that territory, on terms to be agreed between such government and the CONTRACTING PARTIES. Decisions of the CONTRACTING PARTIES under this paragraph shall be taken by a two-thirds majority.

Article XXXIV
Annexes

The annexes to this Agreement are hereby made an integral part of this Agreement.

Article XXXV
Non-application of the Agreement between particular Contracting Parties

1. This Agreement, or alternatively Article II of this Agreement, shall not apply as between any contracting party and any other contracting party if:
   a. the two contracting parties have not entered into tariff negotiations with each other, and
   b. either of the contracting parties, at the time either becomes a contracting party, does not consent to such application.
2. The CONTRACTING PARTIES may review the operation of this Article in particular cases at the request of any contracting party and make appropriate recommendations.

PART IV
TRADE AND DEVELOPMENT

Article XXXVI
Principles and Objectives

1. The contracting parties,
   a. recalling that the basic objectives of this Agreement include the raising of standards of living and the progressive development of the economies of all contracting parties, and considering that the attainment of these objectives is particularly urgent for less-developed contracting parties;
   b. considering that export earnings of the less-developed contracting parties can play a vital part in their economic development and that the extent of this contribution depends on the prices paid by the less-developed contracting parties for essential imports, the volume of their exports, and the prices received for these exports;
   c. noting, that there is a wide gap between standards of living in less-developed countries and in other countries;
   d. recognizing that individual and joint action is essential to further the development of the economies of less-developed contracting parties and to bring about a rapid advance in the standards of living in these countries;
   e. recognizing that international trade as a means of achieving economic and social advancement should be governed by such rules and procedures—and measures in conformity with such rules and procedures—as are consistent with the objectives set forth in this Article;

f. noting that the CONTRACTING PARTIES may enable less-developed contracting parties to use special measures to promote their trade and development; agree as follows.

2. There is need for a rapid and sustained expansion of the export earnings of the less-developed contracting parties.

3. There is need for positive efforts designed to ensure that less-developed contracting parties secure a share in the growth in international trade commensurate with the needs of their economic development.

4. Given the continued dependence of many less-developed contracting parties on the exportation of a limited range of primary products, there is need to provide in the largest possible measure more favourable and acceptable conditions of access to world markets for these products, and wherever appropriate to devise measures designed to stabilize and improve conditions of world markets in these products, including in particular measures designed to attain stable, equitable and remunerative prices, thus permitting an expansion of world trade and demand and a dynamic and steady growth of the real export earnings of these countries so as to provide them with expanding resources for their economic development.

5. The rapid expansion of the economies of the less-developed contracting parties will be facilitated by a diversification of the structure of their economies and the avoidance of an excessive dependence on the export of primary products. There is, therefore, need for increased access in the largest possible measure to markets under favourable conditions for processed and manufactured products currently or potentially of particular export interest to less-developed contracting parties.

6. Because of the chronic deficiency in the export proceeds and other foreign exchange earnings of less-developed contracting parties, there are important inter-relationships between trade and financial assistance to development. There is, therefore, need for close and continuing collaboration between the CONTRACTING PARTIES and the international lending agencies so that they can contribute most effectively to alleviating the burdens these less-developed contracting parties assume in the interest of their economic development.

7. There is need for appropriate collaboration between the CONTRACTING PARTIES, other intergovernmental bodies and the organs and agencies of the United Nations system, whose activities relate to the trade and economic development of less-developed countries.

8. The developed contracting parties do not expect reciprocity for commitments made by them in trade negotiations to reduce or remove tariffs and other barriers to the trade of less-developed contracting parties.

9. The adoption of measures to give effect to these principles and objectives shall be a matter of conscious and purposeful effort on the part of the contracting parties both individually and jointly.

Article XXXVII
Commitments

1. The developed contracting parties shall to the fullest extent possible—that is, except when compelling reasons, which may include legal reasons, make it impossible—give effect to the following provisions:

   a. accord high priority to the reduction and elimination of barriers to products currently or potentially of particular export interest to less-developed contracting parties, including customs duties and other restrictions which differentiate unreasonably between such products in their primary and in their processed forms;

   b. refrain from introducing, or increasing the incidence of, customs duties or non-tariff import barriers on products currently or potentially of particular export interest to less-developed contracting parties; and

   c.
      i. refrain from imposing new fiscal measures, and
      ii. in any adjustments of fiscal policy accord high priority to the reduction and elimination of fiscal measures, which would hamper, or which hamper, significantly the growth of consumption of primary products, in raw or processed form, wholly or mainly produced in the territories of less-developed contracting parties, and which are applied specifically to those products.

2.
   a. Whenever it is considered that effect is not being given to any of the provisions of sub-paragraph (a), (b) or (c) of paragraph 1, the matter shall be reported to the CONTRACTING PARTIES either by the contracting party not so giving effect to the relevant provisions or by any other interested contracting party.

   b.
      i. The CONTRACTING PARTIES shall, if requested so to do by any interested contracting party, and without prejudice to any bilateral consultations that may be undertaken, consult with the contracting party concerned and all interested contracting parties with respect to the matter with a view to reaching solutions satisfactory to all contracting parties concerned in order to further the objectives set forth in Article XXXVI. In the course of these consultations, the reasons given in cases where effect was not being given to the provisions of sub-paragraph (a), (b) or (c) of paragraph 1 shall be examined.

      ii. As the implementation of the provisions of sub-paragraph (a), (b) or (c) of paragraph 1 by individual contracting parties may in some cases be more readily achieved where action is taken jointly with other developed contracting parties, such consultation might, where appropriate, be directed towards this end.

      iii. The consultations by the CONTRACTING PARTIES might also, in appropriate cases, be directed towards agreement on joint action designed to further the objectives of this Agreement as envisaged in paragraph 1 of Article XXV.

3. The developed contracting parties shall:

   a. make every effort, in cases where a government directly or indirectly determines the resale price of products wholly or mainly produced in the territories of less-developed contracting parties, to maintain trade margins at equitable levels;

   b. give active consideration to the adoption of other measures designed to provide greater scope for the development of imports from less-developed contracting parties and collaborate in appropriate international action to this end;

   c. have special regard to the trade interests of less-developed contracting parties when considering the application of other measures permitted under this Agreement to meet particular problems and explore all possibilities of constructive remedies before applying such measures where they would affect essential interests of those contracting parties.

4. Less-developed contracting parties agree to take appropriate action in implementation of the provisions of Part IV for the benefit of the trade of other less-developed contracting parties, in so far as such action is consistent with their individual present and future development, financial and trade needs taking into account past trade developments as well as the trade interests of less-

developed contracting parties as a whole.

5. In the implementation of the commitments set forth in paragraphs 1 to 4 each contracting party shall afford to any other interested contracting party or contracting parties full and prompt opportunity for consultations under the normal procedures of this Agreement with respect to any matter or difficulty which may arise.

Article XXXVIII
Joint Action

1. The contracting parties shall collaborate jointly, within the framework of this Agreement and elsewhere, as appropriate, to further the objectives set forth in Article XXXVI.

2. In particular, the CONTRACTING PARTIES shall:

   a. where appropriate, take action, including action through international arrangements, to provide improved and acceptable conditions of access to world markets for primary products of particular interest to less-developed contracting parties and to devise measures designed to stabilize and improve conditions of world markets in these products including measures designed to attain stable, equitable and remunerative prices for exports of such products;

   b. seek appropriate collaboration in matters of trade and development policy with the United Nations and its organs and agencies, including any institutions that may be created on the basis of recommendations by the

United Nations Conference on Trade and Development;

c. collaborate in analysing the development plans and policies of individual less-developed contracting parties and in examining trade and aid relationships with a view to devising concrete measures to promote the development of export potential and to facilitate access to export markets for the products of the industries thus developed and, in this connexion, seek appropriate collaboration with governments and international organizations, and in particular with organizations having competence in relation to financial assistance for economic development, in systematic studies of trade and aid relationships in individual less-developed contracting parties aimed at obtaining a clear analysis of export potential, market prospects and any further action that may be required;

d. keep under continuous review the development of world trade with special reference to the rate of growth of the trade of less-developed contracting parties and make such recommendations to contracting parties as may, in the circumstances, be deemed appropriate;

e. collaborate in seeking feasible methods to expand trade for the purpose of economic development, through international harmonization and adjustment of national policies and regulations, through technical and commercial standards affecting production, transportation and

marketing, and through export promotion by the establishment of facilities for the increased flow of trade information and the development of market research; and

f. establish such institutional arrangements as may be necessary to further the objectives set forth in Article XXXVI and to give effect to the provisions of this Part.

ANNEXES

Annex A
List of Territories Referred to in Paragraph 2 (a) of Article I

United Kingdom of Great Britain and Northern Ireland

Dependent territories of the United Kingdom of Great Britain and Northern Ireland

Canada

Commonwealth of Australia

Dependent territories of the Commonwealth of Australia

New Zealand

Dependent territories of New Zealand

Union of South Africa including South West Africa

Ireland

India (as on April 10, 1947)

Newfoundland

Southern Rhodesia

Burma

Ceylon

Certain of the territories listed above have two or more preferential rates in force for certain products. Any such territory may, by agreement with the other contracting parties which are principal suppliers of such products at the most-favoured-nation rate, substitute for such preferential rates a single preferential rate which shall not on the whole be less favourable to suppliers at the most-favoured-nation rate than the preferences in force prior to such substitution.

The imposition of an equivalent margin of tariff preference to replace a margin of preference in an internal tax existing on April 10, 1947 exclusively between two or more of the territories listed in this Annex or to replace the preferential quantitative arrangements described in the following paragraph, shall not be deemed to constitute an increase in a margin of tariff preference.

The preferential arrangements referred to in paragraph 5 (b) of Article XIV are those existing in the United Kingdom on April 10, 1947, under contractual agreements with the Governments of Canada, Australia and New Zealand, in respect of chilled and frozen beef and veal, frozen mutton and lamb, chilled and frozen pork, and bacon. It is the intention, without prejudice to any action taken under sub-paragraph (h) of Article XX, that these arrangements shall be eliminated or replaced by tariff preferences, and that negotiations to this end shall take place as soon as practicable among the countries substantially concerned or involved.

The film hire tax in force in New Zealand on April 10, 1947, shall, for the purposes of this Agreement, be treated as a customs duty under Article I. The renters' film quota in force in New Zealand on April 10, 1947, shall, for the purposes of this Agreement, be treated as a screen quota under Article IV.

The Dominions of India and Pakistan have not been mentioned separately in the above list since they had not come into existence as such on the base date of April 10, 1947.

Annex B
List of the French Union
Referred to in Paragraph 2 (b)
of Article I

France

French Equatorial Africa (Treaty Basin of the Congo and other territories)

French West Africa

Cameroons under French Trusteeship

French Somali Coast and Dependencies

French Establishments in Oceania

French Establishments in the Condominium of the New Hebrides

Indo-China

Madagascar and Dependencies

Morocco (French zone)

New Caledonia and Dependencies

Saint-Pierre and Miquelon

Togo under French Trusteeship

Tunisia

Annex C
List of Territories Referred to
in Paragraph 2 (b) of Article I
as respects the Customs
Union of Belgium,
Luxembourg and The
Netherlands

The Economic Union of Belgium and Luxemburg

Belgian Congo
Ruanda Urundi
Netherlands
New Guinea
Surinam
Netherlands Antilles
Republic of Indonesia

For imports into the territories constituting the Customs Union only.

Annex D
List of Territories Referred to in Paragraph 2 (b) of Article I as respects the United States of America

United States of America (customs territory)

Dependent territories of the United States of America

Republic of the Philippines

The imposition of an equivalent margin of tariff preference to replace a margin of preference in an internal tax existing on April 10, 1947, exclusively between two or more of the territories listed in this Annex shall not be deemed to constitute an increase in a margin of tariff preference.

Annex E
List of Territories Covered by Preferential Arrangements Between Chile and Neighbouring Countries Referred to in Paragraph 2 (d) of Article I

Preferences in force exclusively between Chile on the one hand, and

1. Argentina
2. Bolivia
3. Peru

on the other hand.

Annex F
List of Territories Covered by Preferrential Arrangements Between Lebanon and Syria and Neighbouring Countries Referred to in Paragraph 2 (d) of Article I

Preferences in force exclusively between the Lebano-Syrian Customs Union, on the one hand, and

1. Palestine
2. Transjordan

on the other hand.

Annex G
Dates Establishing Maximum Margins of Preference Referred to in Paragraph 4 of Article I

Australia	October 15, 1946
Canada	July 1, 1939
France	January 1, 1939
Lebano-Syrian Customs Union	November 30, 1938
Union of South Africa	July 1, 1938
Southern Rhodesia	May 1, 1941

Annex H
Percentage Shares of Total External Trade To Be Used for The Purpose of Making The Determination Referred to in Article XXVI (based on the average of 1949–1953)

If, prior to the accession of the Government of Japan to the General Agreement, the present Agreement has been accepted by contracting parties the external trade of which under column I accounts for the percentage of such trade specified in paragraph 6 of Article XXVI, column I shall be applicable for the purposes of that paragraph. If the present Agreement has not been so accepted prior to the accession of the Government of Japan, column II shall be applicable for the purposes of that paragraph.

	Column I (Contracting parties on 1 March 1955)	Column II (Contracting parties on 1 March 1955 and Japan)
Australia	3.1	3.0
Austria	0.9	0.8
Belgium-Luxemburg	4.3	4.2
Brazil	2.5	2.4
Burma	0.3	0.3
Canada	6.7	6.5
Ceylon	0.5	0.5
Chile	0.6	0.6
Cuba	1.1	1.1
Czechoslovakia	1.4	1.4
Denmark	1.4	1.4
Dominican Republic	0.1	0.1
Finland	1.0	1.0
France	8.7	8.5
Germany, Federal Republic	5.3	5.2
Greece	0.4	0.4
Haiti	0.1	0.1
India	2.4	2.4
Indonesia	1.3	1.3
Italy	2.9	2.8
Netherlands, Kingdom of the	4.7	4.6
New Zealand	1.0	1.0
Nicaragua	0.1	0.1
Norway	1.1	1.1
Pakistan	0.9	0.8
Peru	0.4	0.4
Rhodesia and Nyasaland	0.6	0.6
Sweden	2.5	2.4
Turkey	0.6	0.6
Union of South Africa	1.8	1.8
United Kingdom	20.3	19.8
United States of America	20.6	20.1
Uruguay	0.4	0.4
Japan	—	2.3
	100.0	100.0

Note: These percentages have been computed taking into account the trade of all territories in respect of which the General Agreement on Tariffs and Trade is applied.

Annex I
Notes and Supplementary Provisions

Ad Article I

Paragraph 1

The obligations incorporated in paragraph 1 of Article I by reference to paragraphs 2 and 4 of Article in and those incorporated in paragraph 2 (b) of Article II by reference to Article VI shall be considered as falling within Part II for the purposes of the Protocol of Provisional Application.

The cross-references, in the paragraph immediately above and in paragraph 1 of Article I, to paragraphs 2 and 4 of Article III shall only apply after Article III has been modified by the entry into force of the amendment provided for in the Protocol Modifying Part II and Article XXVI of the General Agreement on Tariffs and Trade, dated September 14, 1948.

Paragraph 4

The term "margin of preference" means the absolute difference between the most-favoured-nation rate of duty and the preferential rate of duty for the like product, and not the proportionate relation between those rates. As examples:

1. If the most-favoured-nation rate were 36 per cent ad valorem and the preferential rate were 24 per cent ad valorem, the margin of preference would be 12 per cent ad valorem, and not one-third of the most-favoured-nation rate;
2. If the most-favoured-nation rate were 36 per cent ad valorem and the preferential rate were expressed as two-thirds of the most-favoured-nation rate, the margin of preference would be 12 per cent ad valorem;
3. If the most-favoured-nation rate were 2 francs per kilogramme and the preferential rate were 1.50 francs per kilogramme, the margin of preference would be 0.50 franc per kilogramme.

The following kinds of customs action, taken in accordance with established uniform procedures, would not be contrary to a general binding of margins of preference:

i. The re-application to an imported product of a tariff classification or rate of duty, properly applicable to such product, in cases in which the application of such classification or rate to such product was temporarily suspended or inoperative on April 10, 1947; and
ii. The classification of a particular product under a tariff item other than that under which importations of that product were classified on April 10, 1947, in cases in which the tariff law clearly contemplates that such product may be classified under more than one tariff item.

Ad Article II

Paragraph 2 (a)

The cross-reference, in paragraph 2 (a) of Article II, to paragraph 2 of Article III shall only apply after Article III has been modified by the entry into force of the amendment provided for in the Protocol Modifying Part II and Article XXVI of the General Agreement on

Tariffs and Trade, dated September 14, 1948.

Paragraph 2 (b)

See the note relating to paragraph 1 of Article I.

Paragraph 4

Except where otherwise specifically agreed between the contracting parties which initially negotiated the concession, the provisions of this paragraph will be applied in the light of the provisions of Article 31 of the Havana Charter.

Ad Article III

Any internal tax or other internal charge, or any law, regulation or requirement of the kind referred to in paragraph 1 which applies to an imported product and to the like domestic product and is collected or enforced in the case of the imported product at the time or point of importation, is nevertheless to be regarded as an internal tax or other internal charge, or a law, regulation or requirement of the kind referred to in paragraph 1, and is accordingly subject to the provisions of Article III.

Paragraph 1

The application of paragraph 1 to internal taxes imposed by local governments and authorities within the territory of a contracting party is subject to the provisions of the final paragraph of Article XXIV. The term "reasonable measures" in the last-mentioned paragraph would not require, for example, the repeal of existing national legislation authorizing local governments to impose internal taxes which, although technically inconsistent with the letter of Article III, are not in fact inconsistent with its spirit, if such repeal would result in a serious financial hardship for the local governments or authorities concerned. With regard to taxation by local governments or authorities which is inconsistent with both the letter and spirit of Article III, the term "reasonable measures" would permit a contracting party to eliminate the inconsistent taxation gradually over a transition period, if abrupt action would create serious administrative and financial difficulties.

Paragraph 2

A tax conforming to the requirements of the first sentence of paragraph 2 would be considered to be inconsistent with the provisions of the second sentence only in cases where competition was involved between, on the one hand, the taxed product and, on the other hand, a directly competitive or substitutable product which was not similarly taxed.

Paragraph 5

Regulations consistent with the provisions of the first sentence of paragraph 5 shall not be considered to be contrary to the provisions of the second sentence in any case in which all of the products subject to the regulations are produced domestically in substantial quantities. A regulation cannot be justified as being consistent with the provisions of the second sentence on the ground that the proportion or amount allocated to each of the products which are the subject of the regulation constitutes an equitable relationship between imported and domestic products.

Ad Article V

Paragraph 5

With regard to transportation charges, the principle laid down in paragraph 5 refers to like products being transported on the same route under like conditions.

Ad Article VI

Paragraph 1

1. Hidden dumping by associated houses (that is, the sale by an importer at a price below that corresponding to the price invoiced by an exporter with whom the importer is associated, and also below the price in the exporting country) constitutes a form of price dumping with respect to which the margin of dumping may be calculated on the basis of the price at which the goods are resold by the importer.
2. It is recognized that, in the case of imports from a country which has a complete or substantially complete monopoly of its trade and where all domestic prices are fixed by the State, special difficulties may exist in determining price comparability for the purposes of paragraph 1, and in such cases importing contracting parties may find it necessary to take into account the possibility that a strict comparison with domestic

prices in such a country may not always be appropriate.

Paragraphs 2 and 3

1. As in many other cases in customs administration, a contracting party may require reasonable security (bond or cash deposit) for the payment of anti-dumping or countervailing duty pending final determination of the facts in any case of suspected dumping or subsidization.
2. Multiple currency practices can in certain circumstances constitute a subsidy to exports which may be met by countervailing duties under paragraph 3 or can constitute a form of dumping by means of a partial depreciation of a country's currency which may be met by action under paragraph 2. By "multiple currency practices" is meant practices by governments or sanctioned by governments.

Paragraph 6 (b)

Waivers under the provisions of this sub-paragraph shall be granted only on application by the contracting party proposing to levy an anti-dumping or countervailing duty, as the case may be.

Ad Article VII

Paragraph 1

The expression "or other charges" is not to be regarded as including internal taxes or equivalent charges imposed on or in connexion with imported products.

Paragraph 2

1. It would be in conformity with Article VII to presume that "actual value" may be represented by the invoice price, plus any non-included charges for legitimate costs which are proper elements of "actual value" and plus any abnormal discount or other reduction from the ordinary competitive price.
2. It would be in conformity with Article VII, paragraph 2 (b), for a contracting party to construe the phrase "in the ordinary course of trade . . . under fully competitive conditions", as excluding any transaction wherein the buyer and seller are not independent of each other and price is not the sole consideration.
3. The standard of "fully competitive conditions" permits a contracting party to exclude from consideration prices involving special discounts limited to exclusive agents.
4. The wording of sub-paragraphs (a) and (b) permits a contracting party to determine the value for customs purposes uniformly either (1) on the basis of a particular exporter's prices of the imported merchandise, or (2) on the basis of the general price level of like merchandise.

Ad Article VIII

1. While Article VIII does not cover the use of multiple rates of exchange as such, paragraphs 1 and 4 condemn the use of exchange taxes or fees as a device for implementing multiple currency practices; if, however, a contracting party is using multiple currency exchange fees for balance of payments reasons with the approval of the International Monetary Fund, the provisions of paragraph 9 (a) of Article XV fully safeguard its position.
2. It would be consistent with paragraph 1 if, on the importation of products from the territory of a contracting party into the territory of another contracting party, the production of certificates of origin should only be required to the extent that is strictly indispensable.

Ad Articles XI, XII, XIII, XIV and XVIII

Throughout Articles XI, XII, XIII, XIV and XVIII, the terms "import restrictions" or "export restrictions" include restrictions made effective through state-trading operations.

Ad Article XI

Paragraph 2 (c)

The term "in any form" in this paragraph covers the same products when in an early stage of processing and still perishable, which compete directly with the fresh product and if freely imported would tend to make the restriction on the fresh product ineffective.

Paragraph 2, last sub-paragraph

The term "special factors" includes changes in relative productive efficiency as between domestic and foreign producers, or as between different foreign producers but not changes artificially brought about by means not permitted under the Agreement.

Ad Article XII

The CONTRACTING PARTIES shall make provision for the utmost secrecy in the conduct of any consultation under the provisions of this Article.

Paragraph 3 (c) (i)

Contracting parties applying restrictions shall endeavour to avoid causing serious prejudice to exports of a commodity on which the economy of a contracting party is largely dependent.

Paragraph 4 (b)

It is agreed that the date shall be within ninety days after the entry into force of the amendments of this Article effected by the Protocol Amending the Preamble and Parts II and III of this Agreement. However, should the CONTRACTING PARTIES find that conditions were not suitable for the application of the provisions of this sub-paragraph at the time envisaged, they may determine a later date; Provided that such date is not more than thirty days after such time as the obligations of Article VIII, Sections 2, 3 and 4, of the Articles of Agreement of the International Monetary Fund become applicable to contracting parties, members of the Fund, the combined foreign trade of which constitutes at least fifty per centum of the aggregate foreign trade of all contracting parties.

Paragraph 4 (e)

It is agreed that paragraph 4 (e) does not add any new criteria for the imposition or maintenance of quantitative restrictions for balance of payments reasons. It is solely intended to ensure that all external factors such as changes in the terms of trade, quantitative restrictions, excessive tariffs and subsidies, which may be contributing to the balance of payments difficulties of the contracting party applying restrictions, will be fully taken into account.

Ad Article XIII

Paragraph 2 (d)

No mention was made of "commercial considerations" as a rule for the allocation of quotas because it was considered that its application by governmental authorities might not always be practicable. Moreover, in cases where it is practicable, a contracting party could apply these considerations in the process of seeking agreement, consistently with the general rule laid down in the opening sentence of paragraph 2.

Paragraph 4

See note relating to "special factors" in connexion with the last sub-paragraph of paragraph 2 of Article XI.

Ad Article XIV

Paragraph 1

The provisions of this paragraph shall not be so construed as to preclude full consideration by the CONTRACTING PARTIES, in the consultations provided for in paragraph 4 of Article XII and in paragraph 12 of Article XVIII, of the nature, effects and reasons for discrimination in the field of import restrictions.

Paragraph 2

One of the situations contemplated in paragraph 2 is that of a contracting party holding balances acquired as a result of current transactions which it finds itself unable to use without a measure of discrimination.

Ad Article XV

Paragraph 4

The word "frustrate" is intended to indicate, for example, that infringements of the letter of any Article of this Agreement by exchange action shall not be regarded as a violation of that Article if, in practice, there is no appreciable departure from the intent of the Article. Thus, a contracting party which, as part of its exchange control operated in accordance with the Articles of Agreement of the International Monetary Fund, requires payment to be received for its exports in its own currency or in the currency of one or more members of the International Monetary Fund will not thereby be deemed to contravene Article XI or Article XIII. Another example would be that of a contracting party which specifies on an import licence the country from which the goods may be imported, for the purpose not of introducing any additional element of discrimination in its import licensing system but of enforcing permissible exchange controls.

Ad Article XVI

The exemption of an exported product from duties or taxes borne by the like product when destined for domestic consumption, or the remission of such duties or taxes in amounts not in excess of those which have accrued, shall not be deemed to be a subsidy.

Section B

1. Nothing in Section B shall preclude the use by a contracting party of multiple rates of exchange in accordance with the Articles of Agreement of the International Monetary Fund.
2. For the purposes of Section B, a "primary product" is understood to be any product of farm, forest or fishery, or any mineral, in its natural form or which has undergone such processing as is customarily required to prepare it for marketing in substantial volume in international trade.

Paragraph 3

1. The fact that a contracting party has not exported the product in question during the previous representative period would not in itself preclude that contracting party from establishing its right to obtain a share of the trade in the product concerned.
2. A system for the stabilization of the domestic price or of the return to domestic producers of a primary product independently of the movements of export prices, which results at times in the sale of the product for export at a price lower than the comparable price charged for the like product to buyers in the domestic market, shall be considered not to involve a subsidy on exports within the meaning of paragraph 3 if the CONTRACTING PARTIES determine that:
   a. the system has also resulted, or is so designed as to result, in the sale of the product for export at a price higher than the compara-

ble price charged for the like product to buyers in the domestic market; and

b. the system is so operated, or is designed so to operate, either because of the effective regulation of production or otherwise, as not to stimulate exports unduly or otherwise seriously to prejudice the interests of other contracting parties. Notwithstanding such determination by the CONTRACTING PARTIES, operations under such a system shall be subject to the provisions of paragraph 3 where they are wholly or partly financed out of government funds in addition to the funds collected from producers in respect of the product concerned.

Paragraph 4

The intention of paragraph 4 is that the contracting parties should seek before the end of 1957 to reach agreement to abolish all remaining subsidies as from 1 January 1958; or, failing this, to reach agreement to extend the application of the standstill until the earliest date thereafter by which they can expect to reach such agreement.

Ad Article XVII

Paragraph 1

The operations of Marketing Boards, which are established by contracting parties and are engaged in purchasing or selling, are subject to the provisions of sub-paragraphs (a) and (b).

The activities of Marketing Boards which are established by contracting parties and which do not purchase or sell but lay down regulations covering private trade are governed by the relevant Articles of this Agreement.

The charging by a state enterprise of different prices for its sales of a product in different markets is not precluded by the provisions of this Article, provided that such different prices are charged for commercial reasons, to meet conditions of supply and demand in export markets.

Paragraph 1 (a)

Governmental measures imposed to ensure standards of quality and efficiency in the operation of external trade, or privileges granted for the exploitation of national natural resources but which do not empower the government to exercise control over the trading activities of the enterprise in question, do not constitute "exclusive or special privileges".

Paragraph 1 (b)

A country receiving a "tied loan" is free to take this loan into account as a "commercial consideration" when purchasing requirements abroad.

Paragraph 2

The term "goods" is limited to products as understood in commercial practice, and is not intended to include the purchase or sale of services.

Paragraph 3

Negotiations which contracting parties agree to conduct under this paragraph may be directed towards the reduction of duties and other charges on imports and exports or towards the conclusion of any other mutually satisfactory arrangement consistent with the provisions of this Agreement. (See paragraph 4 of Article II and the note to that paragraph.)

Paragraph 4 (b)

The term "import mark-up" in this paragraph shall represent the margin by which the price charged by the import monopoly for the imported product (exclusive of internal taxes within the purview of Article III, transportation, distribution, and other expenses incident to the purchase, sale or further processing, and a reasonable margin of profit) exceeds the landed cost.

Ad Article XVIII

The CONTRACTING PARTIES and the contracting parties concerned shall preserve the utmost secrecy in respect of matters arising under this Article.

Paragraphs 1 and 4

1. When they consider whether the economy of a contracting party "can only support low standards of living", the CONTRACTING PARTIES shall take into consideration the normal position of that economy and shall not base their determination on exceptional circumstances such as those which may result from the temporary existence of exceptionally favourable conditions for the staple export product or products of such contracting party.
2. The phrase "in the early stages of development" is not meant to apply

only to contracting parties which have just started their economic development, but also to contracting parties the economies of which are undergoing a process of industrialization to correct an excessive dependence on primary production.

Paragraphs 2, 3, 7, 13 and 22

The reference to the establishment of particular industries shall apply not only to the establishment of a new industry, but also to the establishment of a new branch of production in an existing industry and to the substantial transformation of an existing industry, and to the substantial expansion of an existing industry supplying a relatively small proportion of the domestic demand. It shall also cover the reconstruction of an industry destroyed or substantially damaged as a result of hostilities or natural disasters.

Paragraph 7 (b)

A modification or withdrawal, pursuant to paragraph 7 (b), by a contracting party, other than the applicant contracting party, referred to in paragraph 7 (a), shall be made within six months of the day on which the action is taken by the applicant contracting party, and shall become effective on the thirtieth day following the day on which such modification or withdrawal has been notified to the CONTRACTING PARTIES.

Paragraph 11

The second sentence in paragraph 11 shall not be interpreted to mean that a contracting party is required to relax or remove restrictions if such relaxation or removal would thereupon produce conditions justifying the intensification or institution, respectively, of restrictions under paragraph 9 of Article XVIII.

Paragraph 12 (b)

The date referred to in paragraph 12 (b) shall be the date determined by the CONTRACTING PARTIES in accordance with the provisions of paragraph 4 (b) of Article XII of this Agreement.

Paragraphs 13 and 14

It is recognized that, before deciding on the introduction of a measure and notifying the CONTRACTING PARTIES in accordance with paragraph 14, a contracting party may need a reasonable period of time to assess the competitive position of the industry concerned.

Paragraphs 15 and 16

It is understood that the CONTRACTING PARTIES shall invite a contracting party proposing to apply a measure under Section C to consult with them pursuant to paragraph 16 if they are requested to do so by a contracting party the trade of which would be appreciably affected by the measure in question.

Paragraphs 16, 18, 19 and 22

1. It is understood that the CONTRACTING PARTIES may concur in a proposed measure subject to specific conditions or limitations. If the measure as applied does not conform to the terms of the concurrence it will to that extent be deemed a measure in which the CONTRACTING PARTIES have not concurred. In cases in which the CONTRACTING PARTIES have concurred in a measure for a specified period, the contracting party concerned, if it finds that the maintenance of the measure for a further period of time is required to achieve the objective for which the measure was originally taken, may apply to the CONTRACTING PARTIES for an extension of that period in accordance with the provisions and procedures of Section C or D, as the case may be.

2. It is expected that the CONTRACTING PARTIES will, as a rule, refrain from concurring in a measure which is likely to cause serious prejudice to exports of a commodity on which the economy of a contracting party is largely dependent.

Paragraphs 18 and 22

The phrase "that the interests of other contracting parties are adequately safeguarded" is meant to provide latitude sufficient to permit consideration in each case of the most appropriate method of safeguarding those interests. The appropriate method may, for instance, take the form of an additional concession to be applied by the contracting party having recourse to Section C or D during such time as the deviation from the other Articles of the Agreement would remain in force or of the temporary suspension by any other contracting party referred to in paragraph 18 of a concession substantially equivalent to the impairment due to the introduction of the measure in question. Such contracting party would have the right to safeguard its interests through such a temporary suspension of a concession; Provided that this right will not be exercised when, in the case of a measure imposed by a contracting party coming within the scope of paragraph 4 (a), the CONTRACTING PARTIES have determined that the extent of the compensatory concession proposed was adequate.

Paragraph 19

The provisions of paragraph 19 are intended to cover the cases where an industry has been in existence beyond the "reasonable period of time" referred to in the note to paragraphs 13 and 14, and should not be so construed as to deprive a contracting party coming within the scope of paragraph 4(a) of Article XVIII, of its right to resort to the other provisions of Section C, including paragraph 17, with regard to a newly established industry even though it has benefited from incidental protection afforded by balance of payments import restrictions.

Paragraph 21

Any measure taken pursuant to the provisions of paragraph 21 shall be withdrawn forthwith if the action taken in accordance with paragraph 17 is withdrawn or if the CONTRACTING PARTIES concur in the measure proposed after the expiration of the ninety-day time limit specified in paragraph 17.

Ad Article XX

Sub-paragraph (h)

The exception provided for in this sub-paragraph extends to any commodity agreement which conforms to the principles approved by the Economic and Social Council in its resolution 30 (IV) of 28 March 1947.

Ad Article XXIV

Paragraph 9

It is understood that the provisions of Article I would require that, when a product which has been imported into the territory of a member of a customs union or free-trade area at a preferential rate of duty is re-exported to the territory of another member of such union or area, the latter member should collect a duty equal to the difference between the duty already paid and any higher duty that would be payable if the product were being imported directly into its territory.

Paragraph 11

Measures adopted by India and Pakistan in order to carry out definitive trade arrangements between them, once they have been agreed upon, might depart from particular provisions of this Agreement, but these measures would in general be consistent with the objectives of the Agreement.

Ad Article XXVIII

The CONTRACTING PARTIES and each contracting party concerned should arrange to conduct the negotiations and consultations with the greatest possible secrecy in order to avoid premature disclosure of details of prospective tariff changes. The CONTRACTING PARTIES shall be informed immediately of all changes in national tariffs resulting from recourse to this Article.

Paragraph 1

1. If the CONTRACTING PARTIES specify a period other than a three-year period, a contracting party may act pursuant to paragraph 1 or paragraph 3 of Article XXVIII on the first day following the expiration of such other period and, unless the CONTRACTING PARTIES have again specified another period, subsequent periods will be three-year periods following the expiration of such specified period.

2. The provision that on 1 January 1958, and on other days determined pursuant to paragraph 1, a contracting party "may . . . modify or withdraw a concession" means that on such day, and on the first day after the end of each period, the legal obligation of such contracting party under Article II is altered; it does not mean that the changes in its customs tariff should necessarily be made effective on that day. If a tariff change resulting from negotiations undertaken pursuant to this Article is delayed, the entry into force of any compensatory concessions may be similarly delayed.

3. Not earlier than six months, nor later than three months, prior to 1 January 1958, or to the termination date of any subsequent period, a contracting party wishing to modify or withdraw any concession embodied in the appropriate Schedule, should notify the CONTRACTING PARTIES to this effect. The CONTRACTING PARTIES shall then determine the contracting party or contracting parties with which the negotiations or consultationsreferred to in paragraph 1 shall take place. Any contracting party so determined shall participate in such negotiations or consultations with the applicant contracting party with the aim of reaching agreement before the end of the period. Any extension of the assured life of the Schedules shall relate to the Schedules as modified after such negotiations, in accordance with paragraphs 1, 2 and 3 of Article XXVIII. If the CONTRACTING PARTIES are arranging for multilateral tariff negotiations to take place within the period of six months before 1 January 1958, or before any other day determined pursuant to paragraph 1, they shall include in the arrangements for such negotiations suitable procedures for carrying out the negotiations referred to in this paragraph.

4. The object of providing for the participation in the negotiations of any contracting party with a principal supplying interest, in addition to any contracting party with which the concession was initially negotiated, is to ensure that a contracting party with a larger share in the trade affected by the concession than a contracting party with which the concession was initially negotiated

shall have an effective opportunity to protect the contractual right which it enjoys under this Agreement. On the other hand, it is not intended that the scope of the negotiations should be such as to make negotiations and agreement under Article XXVIII unduly difficult nor to create complications in the application of this Article in the future to concessions which result from negotiations thereunder. Accordingly, the CONTRACTING PARTIES should only determine that a contracting party has a principal supplying interest if that contracting party has had, over a reasonable period of time prior to the negotiations, a larger share in the market of the applicant contracting party than a contracting party with which the concession was initially negotiated or would, in the judgment of the CONTRACTING PARTIES, have had such a share in the absence of discriminatory quantitative restrictions maintained by the applicant contracting party. It would therefore not be appropriate for the CONTRACTING PARTIES to determine that more than one contracting party, or in those exceptional cases where there is near equality more than two contracting parties, had a principal supplying interest.

5. Notwithstanding the definition of a principal supplying interest in note 4 to paragraph 1, the CONTRACTING PARTIES may exceptionally determine that a Contracting party has a principal supplying interest if the concession in question affects trade which constitutes a major part of the total exports of such contracting party.

6. It is not intended that provision for participation in the negotiations of any contracting party with a principal supplying interest, and for consultation with any contracting party having a substantial interest in the concession which the applicant contracting party is seeking to modify or withdraw, should have the effect that it should have to pay compensation or suffer retaliation greater than the withdrawal or modification sought, judged in the light of the conditions of trade at the time of the proposed withdrawal or modification, making allowance for any discriminatory quantitative restrictions maintained by the applicant contracting party.

7. The expression "substantial interest" is not capable of a precise definition and accordingly may present difficulties for the CONTRACTING PARTIES. It is, however, intended to be construed to cover only those contracting parties which have, or in the absence of discriminatory quantitative restrictions affecting their exports could reasonably be expected to have, a significant share in the market of the contracting party seeking to modify or withdraw the concession.

Paragraph 4

1. Any request for authorization to enter into negotiations shall be accompanied by all relevant statistical and other data. A decision on such request shall be made within thirty days of its submission.

2. It is recognized that to permit certain contracting parties, depending in large measure on a relatively

small number of primary commodities and relying on the tariff as an important aid for furthering diversification of their economies or as an important source of revenue, normally to negotiate for the modification or withdrawal of concessions only under paragraph 1 of Article XXVIII, might cause them at such a time to make modifications or withdrawals which in the long run would prove unnecessary. To avoid such a situation the CONTRACTING PARTIES shall authorize any such contracting party, under paragraph 4, to enter into negotiations unless they consider this would result in, or contribute substantially towards, such an increase in tariff levels as to threaten the stability of the Schedules to this Agreement or lead to undue disturbance of international trade.

3. It is expected that negotiations authorized under paragraph 4 for modification or withdrawal of a single item, or a very small group of items, could normally be brought to a conclusion in sixty days. It is recognized, however, that such a period will be inadequate for cases involving negotiations for the modification or withdrawal of a larger number of items and in such cases, therefore, it would be appropriate for the CONTRACTING PARTIES to prescribe a longer period.

4. The determination referred to in paragraph 4 (d) shall be made by the CONTRACTING PARTIES within thirty days of the submission of the matter to them unless the applicant contracting party agrees to a longer period.

5. In determining under paragraph 4

(d) whether an applicant contracting party has unreasonably failed to offer adequate compensation, it is understood that the CONTRACTING PARTIES will take due account of the special position of a contracting party which has bound a high proportion of its tariffs at very low rates of duty and to this extent has less scope than other contracting parties to make compensatory adjustment.

Ad Article XXVIII bis

Paragraph 3

It is understood that the reference to fiscal needs would include the revenus aspect of duties and particularly duties imposed primarily for revenue purpose, or duties imposed on products which can be substituted for products subject to revenue duties to prevent the avoidance of such duties.

Ad Article XXIX

Paragraph 1

Chapters VII and VIII of the Havana Charter have been excluded from paragraph 1 because they generally deal with the organization, functions and procedures of the International Trade Organization.

Ad Part IV

The words "developed contracting parties" and the words "less-developed contracting parties" as used in Part IV are to be understood to refer to developed and less-developed countries which are parties to the General Agreement on Tariffs and Trade.

Ad Article XXXVI

Paragraph 1

This Article is based upon the objectives set forth in Article I as it will be amended by Section A of paragraph 1 of the Protocol Amending Part I and Articles XXIX and XXX when that Protocol enters into force.

Paragraph 4

The term "primary products" includes agricultural products, vide paragraph 2 of the note ad Article XVI, Section B.

Paragraph 5

A diversification programme would generally include the intensification of activities for the processing of primary products and the development of manufacturing industries, taking into account the situation of the particular contracting party and the world outlook for production and consumption of different commodities.

Paragraph 8

It is understood that the phrase "do not expect reciprocity" means, in accordance with the objectives set forth in this Article, that the less-developed contracting parties should not be expected, in the course of trade negotiations, to make contributions which are inconsistent with their individual development, financial and trade needs, taking into consideration past trade developments.

This paragraph would apply in the event of action under Section A of Article XVIII, Article XXVIII, Article XXVIII bis (Article XXIX after the amendment set forth in Section A of paragraph 1 of the Protocol Amending Part I and Articles XXIX and XXX shall have become effective), Article XXXIII, or any other procedure under this Agreement.

Ad Article XXXVII

Paragraph 1 (a)

This paragraph would apply in the event of negotiations for reduction or elimination of tariffs or other restrictive regulations of commerce under Articles XXVIII, XXVIII bis (XXIX after the amendment set forth in Section A of paragraph 1 of the Protocol Amending Part I and Articles XXIX and XXX shall have become effective), and Article XXXIII, as well as in connexion with other action to effect such reduction or elimination which contracting parties may be able to undertake.

Paragraph 3 (b)

The other measures referred to in this paragraph might include steps to promote domestic structural changes, to encourage the consumption of particular products, or to introduce measures of trade promotion.

PROTOCOL OF PROVISIONAL APPLICATION OF THE GENERAL AGREEMENT ON TARIFFS AND TRADE

1. The Governments of the COMMONWEALTH OF AUSTRALIA, the KINGDOM OF BELGIUM (in respect of its metropolitan territory), CANADA, the FRENCH REPUBLIC (in respect of its metropolitan terri-

tory), the GRAND-DUCHY OF LUXEMBURG, the KINGDOM OF THE NETHERLANDS (in respect of its metropolitan territory), the UNITED KINGDOM OF GREAT BRITAIN AND NORTHERN IRELAND (in respect of its metropolitan territory), and the UNITED STATES OF AMERICA, undertake, provided that this Protocol shall have been signed on behalf of all the foregoing Governments not later than 15 November 1947, to apply provisionally on and after 1 January 1948:

a. Parts I and III of the General Agreement on Tariffs and Trade, and

b. Part II of that Agreement to the fullest extent not inconsistent with existing legislation.

2. The foregoing Governments shall make effective such provisional application of the General Agreement, in respect of any of their territories other than their metropolitan territories, on or after 1 January 1948, upon the expiration of thirty days from the day on which notice of such application is received by the Secretary-General of the United Nations.

3. Any other government signatory to this Protocol shall make effective such provisional application of the General Agreement, on or after 1 January 1948, upon the expiration of thirty days from the day of signature of this Protocol on behalf of such Government.

4. This Protocol shall remain open for signature at the Headquarters of the United Nations (a) until 15 November 1947, on behalf of any government named in paragraph 1 of this Protocol which has not signed it on this day, and (b) until 30 June 1948, on behalf of any other Government signatory to the Final Act adopted at the conclusion of the Second Session of the Preparatory Committee of the United Nations Conference on Trade and Employment which has not signed it on this day.

5. Any government applying this Protocol shall be free to withdraw such application, and such withdrawal shall take effect upon the expiration of sixty days from the day on which written notice of such withdrawal is received by the Secretary-General of the United Nations.

6. The original of this Protocol shall be deposited with the Secretary-General of the United Nations, who will furnish certified copies thereof to all interested Governments.

IN WITNESS WHEREOF the respective Representatives, after having communicated their full powers, found to be in good and due form, have signed the Protocol.

DONE at Geneva, in a single copy, in the English and French languages, both texts authentic, this thirtieth day of October one thousand nine hundred and forty-seven.

See also: **Vol. I**: Bretton Woods Conference; Cold War; Dollar Gap; Eisenhower, Dwight D. (Ike); Escape clause; European Community (EC); Free trade; Great Depression; Hull, Cordell; International Monetary Fund (IMF); Kennedy Round; Reciprocal Trade Agreements Act (RTAA); Roosevelt, Franklin D.; Tokyo Round; Truman, Harry S; Uruguay Round; World War I; World War II.

Alliance for Progress

On March 13, 1961, President John F. Kennedy addressed members of Congress and the diplomatic corps of the Latin American republics at a White House reception held in the East Room. Kennedy advocated the development of stronger economic ties with Latin America as a means of shoring up fledgling democratic regimes throughout the region. Although the Alliance for Progress failed to achieve all of its goals, it did improve relations between the United States and its southern neighbors, at least temporarily.

It is a great pleasure for Mrs. Kennedy and for me, for the Vice President and Mrs. Johnson, and for the Members of Congress, to welcome the Ambassadorial Corps of our Hemisphere, our long time friends, to the White House today. One hundred and thirty-nine years ago this week the United States, stirred by the heroic struggle of its fellow Americans, urged the independence and recognition of the new Latin American Republics. It was then, at the dawn of freedom throughout this hemisphere, that Bolivar spoke of his desire to see the Americas fashioned into the greatest region in the world, "greatest," he said, "not so much by virtue of her area and her wealth, as by her freedom and her glory."

Never in the long history of our hemisphere has this dream been nearer to fulfillment, and never has it been in greater danger.

The genius of our scientists has given us the tools to bring abundance to our land, strength to our industry, and knowledge to our people. For the first time we have the capacity to strike off the remaining bonds of poverty and ignorance—to free our people for the spiritual and intellectual fulfillment which has always been the goal of our civilization.

Yet at this very moment of maximum opportunity, we confront the same forces which have imperiled America throughout its history—the alien forces which once again seek to impose the despotisms of the Old World on the people of the New.

I have asked you to come here today so that I might discuss these challenges and these dangers.

We meet together as firm and ancient friends, united by history and experience and by our determination to advance the values of American civilization. For this New World of ours is not a mere accident of geography. Our continents are bound together by a common history, the endless exploration of new frontiers. Our nations are the product of a common struggle, the revolt from colonial rule. And our people share a common heritage, the quest for the dignity and the freedom of man.

The revolutions which gave us birth ignited, in the words of Thomas Paine, "a spark never to be extinguished." And across vast, turbulent continents these American ideals still stir man's struggle for national independence and individual freedom. But as we welcome the spread of the American revolution to other lands, we must also remember that our own struggle—the revolution which began in Philadelphia in 1776, and in Caracas in 1811— is not yet finished. Our hemisphere's mission is not yet completed. For our unfulfilled task is to demonstrate to the entire world that man's unsatisfied aspiration for economic progress and social justice can best be achieved by free men working within a framework of democratic institutions. If we can do this in our own hemisphere, and for our own people, we may yet realize the prophecy of the great Mexican patriot,

Benito Juarez, that "democracy is the destiny of future humanity."

As a citizen of the United States let me be the first to admit that we North Americans have not always grasped the significance of this common mission, just as it is also true that many in your own countries have not fully understood the urgency of the need to lift people from poverty and ignorance and despair. But we must turn from these mistakes—from the failures and the misunderstandings of the past to a future full of peril, but bright with hope.

Throughout Latin America, a continent rich in resources and in the spiritual and cultural achievements of its people, millions of men and women suffer the daily degradations of poverty and hunger. They lack decent shelter or protection from disease. Their children are deprived of the education or the jobs which are the gateway to a better life. And each day the problems grow more urgent. Population growth is outpacing economic growth—low living standards are further endangered and discontent—the discontent of a people who know that abundance and the tools of progress are at last within their reach—that discontent is growing. In the words of Jose Figueres, "once dormant peoples are struggling upward toward the sun, toward a better life."

If we are to meet a problem so staggering in its dimensions, our approach must itself be equally bold—an approach consistent with the majestic concept of Operation Pan America. Therefore I have called on all people of the hemisphere to join in a new Alliance for Progress—*Alianza para Progreso*—a vast cooperative effort, unparalleled in magnitude and nobility of purpose, to satisfy the basic needs of the American people for homes, work and land, health and schools—*techo, trabajo y tierra, salud y escuela*.

First, I propose that the American Republics begin on a vast new Ten Year Plan for the Americas, a plan to transform the 1960's into a historic decade of democratic progress.

These 10 years will be the years of maximum progress-maximum effort, the years when the greatest obstacles must be overcome, the years when the need for assistance will be the greatest.

And if we are successful, if our effort is bold enough and determined enough, then the close of this decade will mark the beginning of a new era in the American experience. The living standards of every American family will be on the rise, basic education will be available to all, hunger will be a forgotten experience, the need for massive outside help will have passed, most nations will have entered a period of self-sustaining growth, and though there will be still much to do, every American Republic will be the master of its own revolution and its own hope and progress.

Let me stress that only the most determined efforts of the American nations themselves can bring success to this effort. They, and they alone, can mobilize their resources, enlist the energies of their people, and modify their social patterns so that all, and not just a privileged few, share in the fruits of growth. If this effort is made, then outside assistance will give vital impetus to progress; without it, no amount of help will advance the welfare of the people.

Thus if the countries of Latin America are ready to do their part, and I am sure they are, then I believe the United States, for its part, should help provide resources of a scope and magnitude sufficient to make this bold development plan a success—just as we helped to provide, against equal odds nearly, the resources adequate to help rebuild the economies of Western Europe. For only an effort of towering dimensions can ensure fulfillment of our plan for a decade of progress.

Secondly, I will shortly request a ministerial meeting of the Inter-American Economic and Social Council, a meeting at which we can begin the massive planning effort which will be at the heart of the Alliance for Progress.

For if our Alliance is to succeed, each Latin nation must formulate long-range plans for its own development, plans which establish targets and priorities, ensure monetary stability, establish the machinery for vital social change, stimulate private activity and initiative, and provide for a maximum national effort. These plans will be the foundation of our development effort, and the basis for the allocation of outside resources.

A greatly strengthened IA-ECOSOC, working with the Economic Commission for Latin America and the Inter-American Development Bank, can assemble the leading economists and experts of the hemisphere to help each country develop its own development plan—and provide a continuing review of economic progress in this hemisphere.

Third, I have this evening signed a request to the Congress for $500 million as a first step in fulfilling the Act of Bogotá. This is the first large-scale Inter-American effort, instituted by my predecessor President Eisenhower, to attack the social barriers which block economic progress. The money will be used to combat illiteracy, improve the productivity and use of their land, wipe out disease, attack archaic tax and land tenure structures, provide educational opportunities, and offer a broad range of projects designed to make the benefits of increasing abundance available to all. We will begin to commit these funds as soon as they are appropriated.

Fourth, we must support all economic integration which is a genuine step toward larger markets and greater competitive opportunity. The fragmentation of Latin American economies is a serious barrier to industrial growth. Projects such as the Central American common market and free trade areas in South America can help to remove these obstacles.

Fifth, the United States is ready to cooperate in serious, case-by-case examinations of commodity market problems. Frequent violent change in commodity prices seriously injure the economies of many Latin American countries, draining their resources and stultifying their growth. Together we must find practical methods of bringing an end to this pattern.

Sixth, we will immediately step up our Food for Peace emergency program, help establish food reserves in areas of recurrent drought, help provide school lunches for children, and offer feed grains for use in rural development. For hungry men and women cannot wait for economic discussions or diplomatic meetings—their need is urgent—and their hunger rests heavily on the conscience of their fellow men.

Seventh, all the people of the hemi-sphere must be allowed to share in the expanding wonders of science—wonders which have captured man's imagination, challenged the powers of his mind, and given him the tools for rapid progress. I invite Latin American scientists to work with us in new projects in fields such as medicine and agriculture, physics and astronomy, and desalinization, to help plan for regional research laboratories in these and other fields, and to strengthen cooperation between American universities and laboratories.

We also intend to expand our science teacher training programs to include Latin American instructors, to assist in establishing such programs in other American countries, and translate and make available revolutionary new teaching materials in physics, chemistry, biology, and mathematics, so that the young of all nations may contribute their skills to the advance of science.

Eighth, we must rapidly expand the training of those needed to man the economies of rapidly developing countries. This means expanded technical training programs, for which the Peace Corps, for example, will be available when needed. It also means assistance to Latin American universities, graduate schools, and research institutes.

We welcome proposals in Central America for intimate cooperation in higher education—cooperation which can achieve a regional effort or increased effectiveness and excellence. We are ready to help fill the gap in trained manpower, realizing that our ultimate goal must be a basic education for all who wish to learn.

Ninth, we reaffirm our pledge to come to the defense of any American nation whose independence is endangered. As its confidence in the collective security system of the OAS spreads, it will be possible to devote to constructive use a major share of those resources now spent on the instruments of war. Even now, as the government of Chile has said, the time has come to take the first steps toward sensible limitations of arms. And the new generation of military leaders has shown an increasing awareness that armies cannot only defend their countries—they can, as we have learned through our own Corps of Engineers, they can help to build them.

Tenth, we invite our friends in Latin America to contribute to the enrichment of life and culture in the United States. We need teachers of your literature and history and tradition, opportunities for our young people to study in your universities, access to your music, your art, and the thought of your great philosophers. For we know we have much to learn.

In this way you can help bring a fuller spiritual and intellectual life to the people of the United States—and contribute to understanding and mutual respect among the nations of the hemisphere.

With steps such as these, we propose to complete the revolution of the Americas, to build a hemisphere where all men can hope for a suitable standard of living, and all can live out their lives in dignity and in freedom.

To achieve this goal political freedom must accompany material progress. Our Alliance for Progress is an alliance of free governments, and it must work to eliminate tyranny from a hemisphere in which it has no rightful place. Therefore let us express our spe-cial friendship to the people of Cuba and the Dominican Republic—and the hope they will soon rejoin, the society of free men, uniting with us in common effort.

This political freedom must be accompanied by social change. For unless necessary social reforms, including land and tax reform, are freely made—unless we broaden the opportunity for all of our people—unless the great mass of Americans share in increasing prosperity—then our alliance, our revolution, our dream, and our freedom will fail. But we call for social change by free men change in the spirit of Washington and Jefferson, of Bolivar and San Martin and Martin—not change which seeks to impose on men tyrannies which we cast out a century and a half ago. Our motto is what it has always been—progress yes, tyranny no—*progreso sí, tiranía no!*

But our greatest challenge comes from within—the task of creating an American civilization where spiritual and cultural values are strengthened by an ever-broadening base of material advance—where, within the rich diversity of its own traditions, each nation is free to follow its own path towards progress.

The completion of our task will, of course, require the efforts of all governments of our hemisphere. But the efforts of governments alone will never be enough. In the end, the people must choose and the people must help themselves.

And so I say to the men and women of the Americas—to the *campesino* in the fields, to the *obrero* in the cities, to the *estudiante* in the schools—prepare your mind and heart for the task ahead—call forth your strength and let each devote his energies to the betterment of all, so that your children and our children in this hemisphere can find an ever richer and a freer life.

Let us once again transform the American continent into a vast crucible of revolutionary ideas and efforts—a tribute to the power of the creative energies of free men and women—an example to all the world that liberty and progress walk hand in hand. Let us once again awaken our American revolution until it guides the struggle of people everywhere—not with an imperialism of force or fear—but the rule of courage and freedom and hope for the future of man.

See also: **Vol. I**: Kennedy, John F.; Latin America.

The Enterprise for the Americas Initiative

Hoping to establish stronger ties with Latin America that would offset the economic development of the European Community, President George Herbert Walker Bush proposed the Enterprise for the Americas Initiative in the East Room of the White House on June 27, 1990. The initiative ultimately led to the signing of the North American Free Trade Agreement (NAFTA) between the United States, Canada, and Mexico in 1992.

Thank you all very much for coming to the White House, and it is my pleasure to welcome so many distinguished guests with such strong interests in the vital Latin American and Caribbean region. Let me recognize the many members of the diplomatic corps that are here and extend to you a warm welcome—from Latin America, particularly, and the Caribbean, Europe, Japan. Members of our Cabinet—Nick Brady and Secretary Baker, Carla Hills, Secretary Mosbacher—delighted you're here. Chairman of the Council of Economic Advisers, Mike Boskin, is here. Bill Webster, welcome. And of course, we're delighted to see Alan Greenspan, Chairman of the Federal Reserve Board, here and then an old friend,

Barber Conable, of the World Bank, and Richard Erb, from the IMF. And Ricky Iglesias, an old friend of the Bushes, and we welcome him, of the IDB, and so many leading lights in the business and financial communities. To all of you, then, a welcome.

In the past 12 months, every one of us, from the man in the White House to the man on the street, has been fascinated by the tremendous changes, the positive changes, taking place around the world. Freedom has made great gains not just in Eastern Europe but right here in the Americas; and we've seen a resurgence of democratic rule, a rising tide of democracy, never before witnessed in the history of this beloved hemisphere. And with one exception, Cuba, the transition to democracy is moving towards completion, and we can all sense the excitement that the day is not far off when Cuba joins the ranks of world democracies and makes the Americas fully free.

With one exception, that's the case. But the political transformation sweeping the rest of Latin America and the Caribbean has its parallel in the economic sphere. Throughout the region, nations are turning away from the statist economic policies that stifle growth and are now looking to the power of the free market to help this hemisphere realize its untapped potential for progress. A new leadership has emerged, backed by the strength of the people's mandate, leadership that understands that the future of Latin America lies with free government and free markets. In the words of Colombia's courageous leader, Virgilio Barco—President Barco: "The long-running match between Karl Marx and Adam Smith is finally coming to an end" with the "recognition that open economies with access to markets can lead to social progress."

For the United States, these are welcome developments, developments that we're eager to support. But we recognize that each nation in the region must make its own choices. There is no blueprint, no one-size-fits-all approach, to reform. The primary responsibility for achieving economic growth lies with each individual country. Our challenge in this country is to respond in ways that support the positive changes now taking place in the hemisphere. We must forge a genuine partnership for free-market reform.

Back in February, I met in Cartagena [Colombia] with heads of the three An-

dean nations, and I came away from that meeting convinced that the U.S. must review its approach not only to that region but to Latin America and the Caribbean as a whole. And I asked Treasury Secretary Brady to lead a review of U.S. economic policy towards this vital region, to make a fresh assessment, if you will, of the problems and opportunities we'll encounter in the decade ahead. And that review is now complete, and the results are in, and the need for new economic initiatives is clear and compelling.

All signs point to the fact that we must shift the focus of our economic interaction towards a new economic partnership because prosperity in our hemisphere depends on trade, not aid. And I've asked you here today to share with you some of the ideas, some of the ways we can build a broad-based partnership for the nineties—to announce the new Enterprise for the Americas Initiative that creates incentives to reinforce Latin America's growing recognition that free-market reform is the key to sustained growth and political stability.

The three pillars of our new initiative are trade, investment, and debt. To expand trade, I propose that we begin the process of creating a hemispherewide free trade zone; to increase investment, that we adopt measures to create a new flow of capital into the region; and to further ease the burden of debt, a new approach to debt in the region with important benefits for our environment.

Let's begin with trade. In the 1980's, trade within our hemisphere trailed the overall pace of growth in world trade. One principal reason for that: over-restrictive trade barriers that wall off the economies of our region from each other and from the United States at great cost to us all. These barriers are the legacy of the misguided notion that a nation's economy needs protection in order to thrive. The great economic lesson of this century is that protectionism still stifles progress and free markets breed prosperity. To this end, we've formulated a three-point trade plan to encourage the emerging trend toward free-market reform that are now gathering forces in the Americas.

First, as we enter the final months of the current Uruguay round of the world trade talks, I pledge close cooperation with the nations of this hemisphere. The successful completion of the Uruguay round remains the most effective way of promoting long-term trade growth in Latin America and the increased integration of Latin nations into the overall global trading system. Our aim in the Uruguay round is free and fair trade, and through these talks we are seeking to strengthen existing trade rules and to expand them to areas that do not now have agreed rules of fair play. And to show our commitment to our neighbors in Latin America and the Caribbean, we will seek deeper tariff reductions in this round on products of special interest to them.

Second, we must build on the trend we see toward free markets and make our ultimate aim a free trade system that links all of the Americas: North, Central, and South. And we look forward to the day when not only are the Americas the first fully free, democratic hemisphere but when all are equal partners in a free trade zone stretching from the port of Anchorage to the Tierra del Fuego.

I'm announcing today that the U.S. stands ready to enter into free trade agreements with other markets in Latin America and the Caribbean, particularly with groups of countries that have associated for purposes of trade liberalization. And the first step in this process is the now-announced free trade agreement with Mexico. We must all recognize that we won't bring down barriers to free trade overnight; changes so far-reaching may take years of preparation and tough negotiations. But the payoff in terms of prosperity is worth every effort, and now is the time to make a comprehensive free trade zone for the Americas our long-term goal.

And third, I understand that some countries aren't yet ready to take that dramatic step to a full free trade agreement. And that's why we're prepared to negotiate with any interested nation in the region bilateral framework agreements to open markets and develop closer trade ties. Such agreements already exist with Mexico and Bolivia. Framework agreements will enable us to move forward on a step-by-step basis to eliminate counterproductive barriers to trade and towards our ultimate goal of free trade. And that's a prescription for greater growth and a higher standard of living in Latin America and, right here at home, new markets for American products and more jobs for American workers.

Promoting free trade is just one of three key elements in our new Enterprise for the Americas Initiative. And our second pillar is increased investment.

The competition for capital today is fierce, and the key to increased investment is to be competitive, to turn around the conditions that have discouraged both foreign and domestic

417

investment—reduce the regulatory burden, clear away the thicket of bureaucratic barriers that choke off Latin America's aspiring entrepreneurs.

In one large Latin city, for instance, it takes almost 300 days to cut through the red tape to open a small garment shop. In another country, the average overseas caller has to make five phone calls to get through, and the wait for a new telephone line can be as long as 5 years. And that's got to change.

Investment reform is essential to make it easier to start new business ventures and make it possible for international investors to participate and profit in Latin American markets. In order to create incentives for investment reform, the United States is prepared to take the following steps:

First, the United States will work with the Inter-American Development Bank to create a new lending program for nations that take significant steps to remove impediments to international investment. The World Bank could also contribute to this effort.

And second, we propose the creation of a new investment fund for the Americas. This fund, administered by the IDB, could provide up to $300 million a year in grants in response to market-oriented investment reforms in progress in privatization. The U.S. intends to contribute $100 million to the fund, and we will seek matching contributions from Europe and Japan.

But in order to create an attractive climate for new investment, we must build on our successful efforts to ease the debt burden. That's the third pillar of this new Enterprise for the Americas Initiative.

Many nations have already undertaken painful economic reforms for the sake of future growth, but the investment climate remains clouded, weighted down by the heavy debt burden. Under the Brady plan, we are making significant progress. The agreements reached with Mexico and Costa Rica and Venezuela are already having a positive impact on investment in those countries. Mexico, to take just one example, has already seen a reversal of the destructive capital flight that drained so many Latin American nations of precious investment resources. That's critical. If we restore confidence, capital will follow.

As one means of expanding our debt strategy, we propose that the IDB add its efforts and resources to those of the International Monetary Fund and the World Bank to support commercial bank debt reduction in Latin America and the Caribbean, and as in the case of World Bank and IMF, IDB funds should be directly linked to economic reform.

While the Brady plan has helped nations reduce commercial bank debt, for nations with high levels of official debt—debt owed to governments rather than private financial institutions—the burden remains heavy. And today, across Latin America, official debt owed to the U.S. Government amounts to nearly $12 billion, with $7 billion of that amount in concessional loans. And in many cases, the heaviest official debt burdens fall on some of the region's smallest nations, countries like Honduras and El Salvador and Jamaica.

That's a problem we must address today. As the key component in addressing the region's debt problem, I am proposing a major new initiative to reduce Latin America and the Caribbean's official debt to the United States for countries that adopt strong economic and investment reform programs with the support of international institutions.

Our debt reduction program will deal separately with concessional and commercial types of loans. On the concessional debt, loans made from AID or Food for Peace accounts, we will propose substantial debt reductions for the most heavily burdened countries. And we will also sell a portion of outstanding commercial loans to facilitate these debt-for-equity and debt-for-nature swaps in countries that have set up such programs. These actions will be taken on a case-by-case basis.

One measure of prosperity and the most important long-term investment any nation can make is environmental well-being. As part of our Enterprise for the Americas Initiative, we will take action to strengthen environmental policies in this hemisphere. Debt-for-nature swaps are one example, patterned after the innovative agreements reached by some Latin American nations and their commercial creditors. We will also call for the creation of environmental trusts, where interest payments owed on restructured U.S. debt will be paid in local currency and set aside to fund environmental projects in the debtor countries.

These innovative agreements offer a powerful new tool for preserving the natural wonders of this hemisphere that we share. From the vistas of the unspoiled Arctic to the beauties of the barrier reef off Belize to the rich rain forests of the Amazon, we must protect this living legacy that we hold in trust. For an increasing number of our neigh-

bors, the need for free-market reform is clear. These nations need economic breathing room to enact bold reforms, and this official debt initiative is one answer, a way out from under the crushing burden of debt that slows the process of reform.

I know there is some concern that the revolutionary changes we've witnessed this past year in Eastern Europe will shift our attention away from Latin America; but I want to assure all of you here today, as I've assured many democratic leaders in Central and South America and the Caribbean and Mexico, the United States will not lose sight of the tremendous challenges and opportunities right here in our own hemisphere. And indeed, as we talk with the leaders of the G-24 about the emerging democracies in Europe— I've been talking to them also about their supporting democracy and economic freedom in Central America. Our aim is a closer partnership between the Americas and our friends in Europe and in Asia.

Two years from now, our hemisphere will celebrate the 500th anniversary of an epic event: Columbus' discovery of America, our New World. And we trace our origins, our shared history, to the time of Columbus' voyage and the courageous quest for the advancement of man. Today the bonds of our common heritage are strengthened by the love of freedom and a common commitment to democracy. Our challenge, the challenge in this new era of the Americas, is to secure this shared dream and all its fruits for all the people of the Americas—North, Central, and South.

The comprehensive plan that I've just outlined is proof positive the

United States is serious about forging a new partnership with our Latin American and Caribbean neighbors. We're ready to play a constructive role at this critical time to make ours the first fully free hemisphere in all of history. Thank you all for coming, and God bless the peoples of the Americas. Thank you very, very much, indeed.

See also: **Vol. I**: Bush, George Herbert Walker; Free Trade Area of the Americas (FTAA); Kennedy, John F.; Latin America; North American Free Trade Agreement (NAFTA).

Presidential Debate over the North American Free Trade Agreement

During the presidential debates of 1992, the issue of NAFTA figured into the different positions of the presidential nominees. During one of the debates between Republican nominee (and incumbent president) George Bush, Democratic nominee William Jefferson Clinton, and Independent candidate H. Ross Perot, all three men discussed the proposed signing of NAFTA. The following is an excerpt from the debate held in East Lansing, Michigan on October 19, 1992.

JIM LEHRER. Good evening. Welcome to this third and final debate among the three major candidates for President of the United States: Governor Bill Clinton, the Democratic nominee; President George Bush, the Republican nominee; and independent candidate Ross Perot.

I am Jim Lehrer, of "The Mac-Neil/Lehrer NewsHour" on PBS. I will be the moderator for this debate, which is being sponsored by the Commission on Presidential Debates. It will be 90 minutes long. It is happening before an audience on the campus of Michigan State University in East Lansing.

The format was conceived by and agreed to by representatives of the Bush and Clinton campaigns. And it is somewhat different than those used in the earlier debates. I will ask questions for the first half under rules that permit follow-ups. A panel of three other journalists will ask questions in the second half under rules that do not. As always, each candidate will have 2 minutes, up to 2 minutes, to make a closing statement. The order of those as well as that for the formal questioning were all determined by a drawing.

Gentlemen, again, welcome. And again, good evening. . . .

NAFTA

Mr. LEHRER. Mr. Perot, based on your experience at General Motors, where do you come down on this? This has been thrown about, back and forth during this campaign from the very beginning about jobs and CAFE standards.

Mr. PEROT. Well, everybody's nibbling around the edges. Let's go to the center of the bull's eye to the core problem. Believe me, everybody on the factory floor all over this country knows it. You implement that NAFTA, the Mexican trade agreement, where they pay people $1 an hour, have no health care, no retirement, no pollution controls, et cetera, et cetera, et cetera, and you're going to hear a giant sucking sound of jobs being pulled out of this country right at a time when we need the tax base to pay the debt and pay down the interest on the debt and get our house back in order. We have got to proceed very carefully on that.

See, there's a lot I don't understand. I do understand business. I do understand creating jobs. I do understand how to make things work. And I've got a long history of doing that. Now, if you want to go to the core problem that faces everybody in manufacturing in this country, it's that agreement that's about to be put into practice.

But here, very simply, everybody says it will create jobs. Yes, it will create bubble jobs. Now, watch this. Listen very carefully to this: One-time surge while we build factories and ship machine tools and equipment down there. Then year after year for decades they will have jobs. And I finally thought I didn't understand it. I called all the experts, and they said, "Oh, it will be disruptive for 12 to 15 years." We haven't got 12 days, folks. We cannot lose those jobs. They were saying Mexican jobs will eventually come to $7.50 an hour and ours will eventually go down to $7.50 an hour. It makes you feel real good to hear that, right?

Let's think it through, here. Let's be careful. I'm for free trade philosophically, but I have studied these trade agreements until the world has gone flat, and we don't have good trade agreements across the world. I hope we'll have a chance to get into that tonight, because I can get right to the center of the bull's eye and tell you why we're losing whole industries in this country. Excuse me.

Mr. LEHRER. Just for the record, though, Mr. Perot, I take it then for your answer you do not have a position on whether or not enforcing the CAFE standards will cost jobs in the auto industry.

Mr. PEROT. Oh, no. It will cost jobs. But that's not—let me say this: I'd rather, if you gave me two bad choices—

Mr. LEHRER. Okay.

Mr. PEROT. I'd rather have some jobs left here than just see everything head south, see?

Mr. LEHRER. So that means no—[laughter]—in other words, you

agree with President Bush, is that right?

Mr. PEROT. No, I'm saying our principal need now is to stabilize the tax base, which is the job base, and create a growing, dynamic base. Now, please, folks, if you don't hear anything else I say, remember millions of people at work are our tax base. One quick point: If you confiscate the Forbes 400 wealth, take it all, you cannot balance the budget this year. Kind of gets your head straight about where the taxes year-in and year-out have got to come from. Millions and millions of people at work.

Mr. LEHRER. I wanted—yes, sir.

President BUSH. Well, I'm caught in the middle of NAFTA. Ross says, with great conviction, he opposes the North American free trade agreement. I am for the North American free trade agreement. My problem with Governor Clinton, once again, is that one time he's going to make up his mind, he will see some merit in it. But then he sees a lot of things wrong with it. And then the other day, he says he's for it; however, then we've got to pass other legislation. When you're President of the United States, you cannot have this pattern of saying, "Well, I'm for it, but I'm on the other side of it." And it's true on this, and it's true on CAFE.

Look, if Ross were right and we get a free trade agreement with Mexico, why wouldn't they have gone down there now? You have a differential in wages right now.

I just have an honest philosophical difference. I think free trade is going to expand our job opportunity. I think it is exports that have saved us when we're in a global slowdown, a connected, global slowdown, a recession in some countries. It's free trade, fair trade that needs to be our hallmark, and we need more free trade agreements, not fewer.

Mr. LEHRER. Governor, a quick answer on trade, and I want to go on to something else.

Governor CLINTON. I'd like to respond to that. You know, Mr. Bush was very grateful when I was among the Democrats who said he ought to have the authority to negotiate an agreement with Mexico. Neither I nor anybody else, as far as I know, agreed to give him our proxy to say that whatever he did was fine for the workers of this country and for the interests of this country.

I am the one who is in the middle on this. Mr. Perot says it's a bad deal. Mr. Bush says it's a hunky-dory deal. I say, on balance, it does more good than harm if we could get some protection for the environment so that the Mexicans have to follow their own environmental standards, their own labor law standards, and if we have a genuine commitment to reeducate and retrain the American workers who lose their jobs and reinvest in this economy.

I have a realistic approach to trade. I want more trade. I know there are some good things in that agreement, but it can sure be made better.

Let me just point out, just today in the *Los Angeles Times*, Clyde Prestowitz, who was one of President Reagan's leading trade advisers, and a lifelong conservative Republican, endorsed my candidacy because he knows that I'll have a free and fair trade policy, a hard-headed realistic policy, and not get caught up in rubber-stamping everything the Bush administration did. If I wanted to do that, why would I run for President, Jim? Anybody else can run the middle class down and run the economy in a ditch. I want to change it.

President BUSH. I think he made my case. On the one hand, it's a good deal, but on the other hand, I'd make it better. You can't do that as President. You can't do it on the war, where he says, "Well, I was with the minority, but I guess I would have voted with the majority."

This is my point tonight: We're talking about 2 weeks from now you've got to decide who is going to be President. And there is this pattern that has plagued him in the primaries and now about trying to have it both ways on all these issues. You can't do that. If you make a mistake, say you made a mistake and go on about your business, trying to serve the American people. Right now we heard it. Ross is against it. I am for it. He says, "On the one hand, I'm for it, and on the other hand, I may be against it."

Mr. LEHRER. Governor—

Governor CLINTON. That's what's wrong with Mr. Bush. His whole deal is, you've got to be for it or against it, and you can't make it better. I believe we can be better. I think the American people are sick and tired of either-or solutions, people being pushed in the corner, polarized to extremes. I think they want somebody with common sense, who can do what's best for the American people. I'd be happy to discuss these other issues, but I can't believe he is accusing me of getting on both sides.

He said trickle-down economics was voodoo economics. Now, he's its biggest practitioner. Let me just say—

President BUSH. I've always said trickle-down Government is bad.

Governor CLINTON. I could run this string out a long time, but remember this, Jim: Those 209 Americans last Thursday night in Richmond told us they wanted us to stop talking about each other and start talking about Americans and their problems and their promises. I think we ought to get back to that. I'll be glad to answer any question you have, but this election ought to be about the American people.

Mr. LEHRER. Mr. Perot?

Mr. PEROT. Is there an equal time rule here tonight?

President BUSH. Yes.

Mr. PEROT. Or do you just keep lunging in at will? I thought we were going to have equal time, but maybe I just have to interrupt the other two. Is that the way it works this—

Mr. LEHRER. No. Mr. Perot, you're doing fine. Go ahead. Whatever you want to say, say it.

FOREIGN LOBBYISTS

Mr. PEROT. Now that we've talked all around the problem about free trade, let's go again to the center of the bull's eye.

Mr. LEHRER. Wait a minute. I was going to ask—I thought you wanted to respond to what we were talking about.

Mr. PEROT. I do. I do. I just want to make—these foreign lobbyists, this whole thing. Our country has sold out to foreign lobbyists. We don't have free trade. Both parties have foreign lobbyists on leave in key roles in their campaigns. If there's anything more unwise than that, I don't know what it is. Every debate, I bring this up, and nobody ever addresses it.

I would like for them to look you in the eye and tell you why they have people representing foreign countries working on their campaigns. And you know, you've seen the list; I've seen the list. We won't go into the names. But no wonder they—if I had those people around me all day every day telling me it was fair and free, I might believe it. But if I look at the facts as a businessman, it's so tilted. The first thing you ought to do is just say, "Guys, if you like these deals so well, we'll give you the deal you gave us." Now, Japanese couldn't un-load the cars in this country if they had the same restrictions we had, and on and on and on and on and on.

I suggest to you that the core problem—one country spent $400 million lobbying in 1988—our country. And it goes on and on. And you look at a Who's Who in these campaigns around the two candidates. They're foreign lobbyists taking leaves. What do you think they're going to do when the campaign's over? Go back to work at 30,000 bucks a month representing some other country. I don't believe that's in the American people's interest.

I don't have a one of them, and I haven't taken a penny of foreign money, and I never will.

Mr. LEHRER. Mr. President, how do you respond to that? Mr. Perot has made that charge several times, the fact that you have people working in your campaign who are paid foreign lobbyists.

President BUSH. Most people that are lobbying are lobbying the Congress. I don't think there's anything wrong with an honest person who happens to represent an interest of another country for making his case. That's the American way. What you're assuming is that that makes the recipient of the lobbying corrupt or the lobbyists themselves corrupt. I don't agree with that.

But if I found somebody that had a conflict of interest that would try to illegally do something as a foreign registered lobby, the laws cover this. I don't know why—I've never understood quite why Mr. Perot was so upset about it, because one of the guys he used to have working for him, I believe, had foreign accounts. Could be wrong, but I think so.

Mr. PEROT. Soon as I found it out, he went out the door, too.

President BUSH. Well, I think you've got to look at the integrity and the honor of the people that are being lobbied and those that are lobbyists. The laws protect the American taxpayer in this regard. If the laws are violated so much—but to suggest if somebody represents a foreign country on anything, that makes him corrupt or against the taxpayer, I don't agree with it.

Mr. PEROT. One quick relevant specific. We're getting ready to dismantle the airlines industry in our country, and none of you know it. I doubt, in all candor, if the President knows it. But this deal that we're doing with BAC and USAir and KLM and Northwest—now, guess who is on the President's campaign big time? A guy from Northwest. This deal is terribly destructive to the U.S. airline industry. One of the largest industries in the world is the travel and tourist business. We won't be making airplanes in this country 10 years from now if we let deals like this go through.

If the press has any interest tonight, I'll detail it to you. I won't take 10 minutes tonight; all these things take a few minutes. But that's happening as we sit here today. We hammerlock the American companies, American Airlines, Delta, the last few great we have, because we're trying to do this deal with these two European companies. Never forget, they've got Airbus over there, and it's a government-owned, privately owned consortium across Europe. They're dying to get the commercial airline business. Japan is trying to get the commercial airline business. I don't think there are any villains inside Government on this issue, but there sure are a lot of people who don't understand business. And maybe you need somebody up there who understands when you're getting your pocket picked.

Mr. LEHRER. Governor, I'm sorry, but that concludes my time with—

Governor CLINTON. Boy, I had a great response to that.

Mr. LEHRER. All right. Go ahead, quickly. Just very briefly.

Governor CLINTON. I think Ross is right and that we do need some more restrictions on lobbyists. We ought to make them disclose the people they've given money to when they're testifying before congressional committees. We ought to close the lawyers' loophole; they ought to have to disclose when they're really lobbying. We ought to have a much longer period of time, about 5 years, between the time when people can leave executive branch offices and then go out and start lobbying for foreign interest. I agree with that.

We've wrecked the airline industry already because there's all these leveraged buyouts and all these terrible things that have happened to the airline industry. We're going to have a hard time rebuilding it. But the real thing we've got to have is a competitive economic strategy. Look what's happening to McDonnell Douglas. Even Boeing is losing market share because we let the Europeans spend 25 to 40 billion dollars on Airbus without an appropriate competitive response.

What I want America to do is to trade more, but to compete and win by investing in competitive ways. And we're in real trouble on that.

Mr. LEHRER. I'm going to be in real trouble if I don't bring out—it's about time—

President BUSH. I promise it's less than 10 seconds.

Mr. LEHRER. Okay.

President BUSH. I heard Governor Clinton congratulate us on one thing. First time he said something pleasant about this administration. Productivity in this country is up. It is way up. Productivity is up, and that's a good thing. There are many other good ones, but I was glad he acknowledged that.

Mr. PEROT. I've volunteered—now, look, I'm just kind of a, you know, cur dog here. I was put on the ballot by the people, not special interest, so I have to stand up for myself. Now, Jim, let me net it out. On the second debate, I offered, since both sides want the enterprise zones but can't get together, I said I'll take a few days off and go to Washington and hold hands with you, and we'll get it done. I'll take a few days off, hold hands with you, and get this airline thing straightened out, because that's important to this country.

That's kind of pathetic I have to do it, and nobody's called me yet to come up, I might mention— [laughter]—but if they do, if they do, it's easy to fix. If you all want the enterprise zones, why don't we pass the dang thing and do it? Right? . . .

See also: **Vol. 1**: Bush, George Herbert Walter; Clinton, William Jefferson (Bill); Fast-track legislation; Free Trade Area of the Americas (FTAA); Gore, Albert Arnold Jr.; Kennedy, John F.; Latin America; North American Free Trade Agreement (NAFTA); Perot, Henry Ross; Salinas de Gortari, Carlos.

Gore-Perot Debate over the Ratification of the North American Free Trade Agreement

After winning the election of 1992, Democratic President William Jefferson Clinton decided to support the ratification of NAFTA. Independent Party candidate H. Ross Perot continued to argue that the agreement would result in the loss of American jobs and capital as industries moved outside of the United States in an effort to lower costs and increase profits. Vice President Albert Gore confronted Perot in a debate broadcast on Larry King Live *on November 9, 1993. Gore argued that high protective tariffs tended to destroy trade and that the elimination of tariff barriers would encourage American-owned companies to return to the United States. Eight days after the debate Congress ratified NAFTA and the northern portion of the Western Hemisphere became a free-trade zone.*

LARRY KING LIVE ANNOUNCER: Welcome to a special edition of Larry King Live. The North American Free Trade Agreement. A deal to knock down trade barriers between Mexico, Canada, and the United States. Good or bad for Americans? Tonight, Vice President Al Gore meets Ross Perot, as Larry King and CNN present The NAFTA Debate. Now, from Washington, Larry King.

LARRY KING, Host: Good evening. We need to tell you off the top about some ground rules that have been agreed to by the vice president, Mr. Perot, and CNN. We have no studio audience here. Neither the vice president nor Mr. Perot have any staffers in the studio, nor may they talk with any assistants during the telecast. No representatives of either side are in the control room while we are on the air. Our guests may use notes, visual aids if they wish. We have no debate clock. This is no formal statement-and-rebuttal format. There's no time limit on questions or answers. The program will go 90 minutes.

To be fair about deciding who got to sit where, we tossed a coin earlier today.

The vice president won and chose the inside seat. Viewer calls will be screened and chosen by the producer of this program, who will make every effort to assure balance. The call-in number in the United States is (202) 408-1666. Overseas, (202) 408-4821. We'll give you those numbers again later. We'll start with the vice president. We're going to wing back and forth, and then include your phone calls.

When President Bush signed this in San Antonio, he was on our show, and then a few nights later I was with you and then-president-then-governor, now President-Elect, Clinton, asked about this, NAFTA, and the president said, to the best of my memory, "Well, I'm basically for it. I want to see the side agreements and I want to hear what the unions object to, and then I'll come back and sort of let you know." But it was not a definitive yes. What changed?

Vice President AL GORE: Well, we negotiated two side agreements that protect labor and protect the environment. And, not until the two side agreements were completed did we agree to support NAFTA. Now, this is a good deal for our country, Larry, and let me explain why.

KING: But, you were hedging earlier?

Vice Pres. GORE: Well, we said from the very beginning that we wanted to improve the basic arrangement, which we did with the side agreements. And the reason why this is so important can be illustrated by the story of a good friend of mine that I grew up with, named Gordon Thompson, who lives in Elmwood, Tennessee, with his wife Sue and his son Randy. He makes tires for a living. He's a member of the United Rubber Workers, and he's for this because he's taken the time to look at how it affects his job and his family. We make the tires in the world, but we have a hard time selling them in Mexico because they have a 20 percent tax, collected at the border, on all of the tires that we try to sell.

Now, when they make tires and sell them into the United States, the tax at the border is zero. So it's a one-way street. NAFTA changes that. It makes it even-Steven.

KING: So he'll make more tires.

Vice Pres. GORE: Well, his job will be more secure, they'll make more tires, they'll be able to sell more tires. His son will have a better chance of going into that line of work, if that's what he should decide he wants to do, and, remember this—I mean, people think, "Well, they don't buy tires." Mexico bought 750,000 new cars last year. The Big Three sold them only 1,000, because they have the same barriers against our cars. Those barriers will be eliminated

430

by NAFTA. We'll sell 60,000, not 1,000, in the first year after NAFTA. Every one of those cars has four new tires and one spare. We'll create more jobs with NAFTA.

KING: Weren't you a free trader always, Ross?

ROSS PEROT: I am a free trader now.

KING: Do you favor some sort of NAFTA?

Mr. PEROT: Absolutely.

KING: Then what's your rub?

Mr. PEROT: The problem is this is not good for the people of either country.

KING: Either country?

Mr. PEROT: You have my—yes. I think the important thing for everybody watching this show tonight is to remember, this is not an athletic contest. This is not a question of who wins, whether I win or the vice president wins. This is a question of do the people of the United States and the people of Mexico win? Now, that's the important issue, and I'm sure we're in agreement on that. My concern is very simple. I look at many years experience in maquiladora programs, and—

KING: These are the—

Mr. PEROT:—here is what I see. This—we have a lot of experience in Mexico. I've been accused of looking in the rear-view mirror. That's right. I'm looking back at reality, and here is what I see after many years. Mexican workers' life, standard of living and pay, has gone

down, not up. After many years of having U.S. companies in Mexico, this is the way Mexican workers live all around big new U.S. plants. Now, just think if you owned a big U.S. company and you went down to see your new plant, and you found slums all around it, your first reaction would be, "Why did you build a plant in the middle of slums?" And your plant manager would say, "Oh, there were no slums here when we built the plant." And you say, "Well, why are they here now?" They said, "This is where the workers work."

KING: Your agreement would have been a different NAFTA, right?

Vice Pres. GORE: And I would suggest—

Mr. PEROT: This would be a NAFTA that gives the people—now, what are the rules here? Do I answer his questions or yours?

KING: Well, mine, or both. This is freewheeling now.

Mr. PEROT: OK, but, the point being, this is—there it is. Here it is on a more personal basis. Livestock in this country, and animals, have a better life than good, decent, hardworking Mexicans working for major U.S. companies. And here's one just to look at.

KING: Now, all this—

Mr. PEROT: Now, here's a good, decent man working his heart out, making his cardboard shack. And the cardboard came from boxes that were used to ship the goods down there.

Vice Pres. GORE: Can I say something about this picture?

Mr. PEROT: This—I didn't interrupt you.

KING: OK, now, guys.

Mr. PEROT: Now, maybe it just—

KING: Is this—now, your concept would have been what, Ross? If this was a bad deal, what would you—

Mr. PEROT: All I'm saying is if after 10 active years—this has been in effect since the '60s, but let's say 10 active years, you would think the standard of living of the Mexican worker would begin to come up. Instead, it continues to go down, by design. Thirty-six families own over half the country—

KING: So, you're—

Mr. PEROT: Eighty-five million people work for them in poverty, U.S. companies, because it is so difficult to do business in this country, can't wait to get out of this country and go somewhere else, and, if possible, get labor that costs one-seventh of what it costs the United States.

Vice Pres. GORE: How would you change it? How would you change it?

Mr. PEROT: Very simply. I would go back and study—first, we look at this. It doesn't work.

Vice Pres. GORE: Well, what specific changes would you make in it?

Mr. PEROT: I can't—unless you let me finish, I can't answer your question. Now, you asked me and I'm trying to tell you.

Vice Pres. GORE: Right. Well, you brought your charts tonight, so I want to know what specific changes you would like to make in the treaty.

KING: That's a fair question. If you're against it—let him respond, OK?

Mr. PEROT: How can I answer if you keep interrupting me?

KING: All right.

Vice Pres. GORE: Go ahead. Go ahead.

Mr. PEROT: OK. Now, first, study the things that work. The European Community has had a similar experience. They got to Spain, Portugal, countries like that, where the wages were different, people didn't have rights, so on and so forth, and they made them come up the economic scale. In 1904, Theodore Roosevelt wrote a beautiful simple statement. And, basically, he said something very similar to what Congressman Gephardt recently said. He said, "Under no circumstances can we lower the standard of living of the working American." Therefore, any trade agreement we enter into must require a social tariff, I would say, that makes it an even playing field, then gives Mexico an incentive to raise the standard of living with those people, which it does not have now.

Vice Pres. GORE: OK, can I respond now?

Mr. PEROT: They have lowered the standard of living for those people.

KING: OK.

Vice Pres. GORE: OK. Now, so, your basic response is you would change it by raising tariffs—

Mr. PEROT: Now, I just started, but you interrupted.

Vice Pres. GORE:—on Mexico—

Mr. PEROT: That's the first thing I would do.

KING: Well, let's do it one by one.

Vice Pres. GORE: All right.

Mr. PEROT: It's the first thing I would do.

Vice Pres. GORE: OK, now, I've heard Mr. Perot say in the past, as the carpenter says, "Measure twice and cut once." We've measured twice on this. We have had a test of our theory, and we've had a test of this theory. Over the last five years, Mexico's tariffs have begun to come down because they've made a unilateral decision to bring them down some, and, as a result, there has been a surge of exports from the United States into Mexico, creating an additional 400,000 jobs, and we can create hundreds of thousands more if we continue this trend. We know this works. If it doesn't work, you know, we give six months' notice and we're out of it. But, we've also had a test of his theory.

KING: When?

Vice Pres. GORE: In 1930, when the proposal by Mr. Smoot and Mr. Hawley was to raise tariffs across the board to protect our workers. And, I brought some pictures too. You brought some pictures?

KING: [crosstalk]—of protectionist?

Vice Pres. GORE: This is a picture of Mr. Smoot and Mr. Hawley. They look like pretty good fellas. They sounded reasonable at the time. A lot of people believed them. The Congress passed the Smoot-Hawley Protection Bill. He wants to raise tariffs on Mexico. They raised tariffs, and it was one of the principal causes—many economists say the principal cause—of the Great Depression in this country and around the world. Now, I framed this so you can put it on your wall if you want to.

Mr. PEROT: Thank you. Thank you. Thank you.

KING: Would raising tariffs produce another—

Mr. PEROT: You're talking two totally different unrelated situations. Now, you do need to measure twice and cut once, but then, if you have a program that is failing, you should not institutionalize it. See, the Mexican program has failed. It's failed the people of Mexico; it's failed the people of the United States. These numbers they give of exports from the United States are not realistic numbers. For example, they count in the government figures automobile parts going into Mexico to be put into cars made by U.S. car companies in Mexico and shipped back to the United States to be sold as if Mexican consumers bought those parts. But it didn't happen.

Then, if you take a—let's just say you have a piece of glass crystal, that you spend $100 making it in this country. You're going to send it to Mexico to have $10 of additional work done to it. They count it as a $100 export, and then they count it as a hundred—you come into Mexico from the U.S., then they count it as $110 import back in the United States. Now, then, when you look at how they count, the real export figures to Mexican consumers are tiny. The used factory equipment coming from U.S. factories going into Mexico, new factories going to Mexico—

KING: Are not bought?

Mr. PEROT: No. No, no. It's a—Zenith moves equipment from the U.S. into Mexico. That's used equipment. Then we count that as if Mexican consumers bought it. Nobody bought anything. Old equipment just came to Mexico.

Vice Pres. GORE: Let me respond to that if I can because, unfortunately, there's a grain of truth to that, but it's so tiny that it's—I mean, it's not a half-truth, it doesn't quite rise to that level. There are a few things in that category, but the vast majority, 80 to 90 percent, are exports that stay in Mexico and are bought there. Here's what's happened to our trade surplus, and these figures are net figures. It takes into account everything that he's talking about in that small category. In 1987, before Mexico started lowering its taxes at the border, its tariffs, we had a $5.7 billion trade deficit with Mexico. After five years, the goods we make and sell into Mexico, the volume has been growing twice as fast as the goods they make and sell in the United States. So, last year we had a $5.4 billion trade surplus. Now, if that trend continued for another two years, and NAFTA will, by removing those barriers, greatly accelerate it, we will have a larger trade surplus with Mexico than with any country in the entire world.

KING: Why are trade unions so opposed to it then?

Vice Pres. GORE: Well, some of them—

KING: I mean, it's your friend who makes the tire, and he's a union member, he's going to benefit from this. Why are the unions aligned with Ross Perot? Why do we have this alignment of Ross Perot, unions, Jesse Jackson, Pat Buchanan, and Ralph Nader?

Vice Pres. GORE: Because some of them make the same mistake that, with all due respect, Mr. Perot makes. They confuse the bad trade deals in the past with this one, which is the first time we've been able to get one that's even-Steven with zero on zero taxes on both sides. You know, I told you about my friend Gordon Thompson. The international president of his union opposes NAFTA. Gordon Thompson has taken the time to look at the facts, and he supports NAFTA. Let me tell you who else has taken the time. Every living former president of the United States, in both parties. The two-termers and the one-termers. Every former secretary of state, every former secretary of defense, secretary of treasury. Every living Nobel Prize winner in economics, conservatives, liberals, every one in between. They'd never agreed on anything—

KING: Well, that fact—

Vice Pres. GORE: Wait, let me just finish this one point. And distinguished Americans from Colin Powell to Tip O'Neil to Rush Limbaugh, Ross Perot, Jr., the head of his business, Mort Meyerson, Orville Swindle, the head of United We Stand, the last time, and Ross Perot, Sr., supported it until he started running for president and attempting to bring out the politics of fear.

KING: Ross?

Mr. PEROT: Will I be able to speak—

KING: You sure may.

Mr. PEROT:—for a second or two? From time to time?

KING: You may, you—you're on.

Mr. PEROT: Because there's a lot of inaccuracies here. Let's go to the Big Picture and skip the personal stuff. People who don't make anything can't buy anything. Let's start with that. We are 85 percent of the market. Canada is 11 percent of the buying power.

KING: Of the total of the three markets.

Mr. PEROT: And Mexico is only 4 percent. People who don't make anything cannot buy anything. Never forget that. Now, then, let's look at these exports. See, here's Mexico, 4 percent; Canada, 11 percent; the United States, 85 percent. We're the biggest buyer of goods and services in the world. Please

remember that tonight, that's one of our aces. Now, then, here's the real export story. You get down here, these are the phony exports down here. Here are the real exports here, about $7.7 billion. You take this thing into pieces. You take this big number here and take it right down to here, and that's what you're really talking about. And, just remember this. If you want to trade, you trade with people who make money. You don't trade with people who oppress their workers and they don't have any money.

Now, it's true—let's—Now, a good deal will sell itself, folks, just plain talk. Four former presidents came out for it and couldn't sell it. All the secretaries of state came out for it and couldn't sell it. We had satellite going across 200 auditoriums across the country. That didn't sell it. Got Lee Iacocca for it. That didn't sell it. Thirty million dollars coming out of Mexico, and that is rotten and that is wrong, and that didn't sell it. Thirty, thirty-five million dollars coming out of corporate America to try to get out of this country, go south of the border and hire that cheap labor, and that didn't sell it.

KING: Let me know when you—

Mr. PEROT: This dog just didn't hunt. Now, today they don't have the votes in the House of Representatives. We're in the third quarter. They can get them because they're buying them big-time with your tax money. We're working the halls night and day to make sure it doesn't happen. You can play a key role in it. But, sure, they all tried to sell it to you, and the fact that they couldn't demonstrates that this deal is not good for our country.

KING: All right, let me get a break and then—but, it doesn't impress you that every former president supports this?

Mr. PEROT: It impresses me that they couldn't do it.

Vice. Pres. GORE:—But it's not over with, yet.

LARRY KING, Anchor:—[unintelligible] that they support it?

Mr. PEROT: That they showed—those are the guys that cut the worst trade deal in history. He's already talked about it.

Vice. Pres. GORE: It's not—it's not over.

Mr. PEROT:—Wait just a minute, now! They did the Japanese deals, they did the Chinese deals—

KING:—We'll have the vice—

Mr. PEROT:—that cost you two million jobs.

Vice. Pres. GORE:—Do you think they fooled Colin Powell? Do you think they fooled Colin Powell?

Mr. PEROT: He's a great soldier, doesn't know anything about business.

KING: We'll have the vice president respond—

Vice. Pres. GORE:—Do you think they fooled Lee Iacocca?

Mr. PEROT: They must have.

KING:—with Vice President Gore and Ross Perot after this.

[commercial break]

LARRY KING, Host: We're back on "Larry King Live." We'll be going to your phone calls in about 15 minutes. And we're going to cover as much of this as possible. We're going to be getting to jobs and other aspects of it. But I want the vice president to respond to Mr. Perot, who's made some charges here that this is being bought.

Vice. Pres. GORE: Well, all of the—there's been more money spent against the NAFTA than for it, for sure. You can just look at the commercials. Every dollar that has been spent lobbying for it has been publicly disclosed. That is not true of the other side, and I would like to suggest to Mr. Perot—

KING:—You say they're hiding the—

Vice. Pres. GORE: Well, I think it would be a good idea, seriously, if you would publicly disclose the finances of your organization lobbying against it. They have not released the money spent, the contributors, where it's coming from, how much of it is Mr. Perot's, where the rest of it is coming from. But there was another statement I wanted to respond to also. And that is that Mexico doesn't buy a lot of products, that they're too poor to buy a lot of products. There's a big misunderstanding in the minds of some people about that. They are buying a lot of products. In fact, they're our second largest customer for manufacturing goods. They will be one of the largest customers overall if the trends continue. They already are. Seventy percent of everything that they buy from a foreign country comes from the United States because we're so close to them and because they prefer our products.

KING: And this treaty would increase jobs here?—

Vice. Pres. GORE:—Oh, no question about it—

KING:—Because there was an announcement today that it would be minimal either way.

Vice. Pres. GORE: There have been 23 studies of the impact of NAFTA on jobs in the United States. Twenty-two of them have shown that it will cause an increase in jobs in the United States. The one that didn't showed that there would be a decline in illegal immigration, and they counted all of the illegal immigrants as holding jobs. And when they were taken out of the picture, they said that was a decline. Everybody else says it increases jobs in the United States.

KING: On those points, Ross—

Mr. PEROT: OK. Government studies are kind of like weather forecasters before balloons, even, and certainly before radar.

KING: You don't trust them.

Mr. PEROT: Let me give you three. Let me give you three. Now we're back down to common sense. Number one—you remember in the tax and budget summit when they said, "Watch my lips, no new taxes"? Then they gave you a big tax increase and they told you if you would pay it they would balance the budget, pay off the debt, and we'd live happily ever after. See? Now then, the new president had to raise taxes again because that one didn't work. And you picked up the difference.

Now, let's go to Medicare. When Medicare was first conceived in 1965—

Vice. Pres. GORE:—Are we talking about NAFTA, or—

Mr. PEROT: I'm talking about government forecasts.

Vice. Pres. GORE: Well, can we talk about NAFTA?

Mr. PEROT: Excuse me, Larry, I don't interrupt. May I finish?

KING: No, but he brought up a specific point—

Mr. PEROT:—Could I finish?

KING: Yeah, but of course.

Mr. PEROT: I'm saying all government forecasts—how come the facts are—

Vice. Pres. GORE:—Well, I don't want to sit here and listen to you just take shots at President Clinton on other subjects.

Mr. PEROT: Well, excuse me, I haven't taken a shot at it. He wasn't here in 1965. I'm saying—

Vice. Pres. GORE: Well, no, but you talked about—

Mr. PEROT: No, the, the—

Vice. Pres. GORE:—We tried to reverse trickle-down economics, and we're proud that we did.

Mr. PEROT: The, the tax and budget summit occurred before he became president.

Vice. Pres. GORE: Yeah, you went on

from that, though. Why don't we talk about NAFTA?

Mr. PEROT: Excuse me. All I said was he had to raise taxes again. That's hardly a cheap shot.

Vice. Pres. GORE: Well, on the wealthy, on the wealthy.

Mr. PEROT: Oh, my goodness!

KING: Back to the point.

Mr. PEROT: That's the campaign promise.

KING: Let's try to stay on point. He says—

Mr. PEROT: I agree, I agree—

KING: He says—are you spending more money than the other side?

Mr. PEROT: Larry, I would really like to finish. I don't interrupt him, and if I could finish—

KING: OK.

Mr. PEROT: Let me give these two examples. We've talked about the inability to forecast the debt—right?—and the fact that we have to keep paying more taxes. Then when Medicare came along in 1965, they said it would cost us $9 billion in 1990. It cost us $109 billion. Then, when Medicaid came along, they said it would cost $1 billion in 1990. It cost $76 billion in 1990.

KING: Meaning that you don't trust any government forecast?

Mr. PEROT: I'm saying they basically come out with phony numbers. He's talking about exports—

KING:—You're saying—

Vice. Pres. GORE:—Can I respond?

KING: Hold it. You're saying the forecasts on NAFTA are phony?

Mr. PEROT: Yes. Then let's take the next one. We say that we're spending more money against NAFTA than they're spending for it? That is not even close to truth. It is a matter of record how much record how much Mexico has spent. It is a matter of record how much USA/NAFTA has spent. You take—

Vice. Pres. GORE:—Why isn't it a matter of record—

Mr. PEROT:—I, I—

Vice. Pres. GORE:—how much you all spent. Can that be a matter of public record? Can you release those numbers?

Mr. PEROT: I really would appreciate being able to speak.

KING: All right, go ahead, it was a question he raised before—

Mr. PEROT:—I really would—

Vice. Pres. GORE: It's a fair question, isn't it?

Mr. PEROT: Excuse me—

Vice. Pres. GORE: I raised it earlier.

Mr. PEROT: It was my understanding tonight we'd have a format where you would ask the questions.

KING: OK.

Mr. PEROT: I would be able—I am not able to finish.

KING: But if he makes a statement—I'm just trying to balance so that he answers yours—

Mr. PEROT: Well, excuse me, I would like—I would like to finish a sentence, just once before the program's over.

Now, we are not able to buy time. If you are anti-NAFTA, you cannot buy time on the networks. We have had to go buy local station time. We cannot buy network time because the networks won't sell it. That's the covers on how much you're spending. We didn't run 10-page supplements in the *New York Times*, et cetera, et cetera.

Vice. Pres. GORE: OK, now, I'd like to respond to that, OK?

KING: Let him finish, he's got one more thing.

Vice. Pres. GORE: All right, go ahead. I do want to respond.

KING: For the benefit of both of you, our time is equal, you both have spoken equally tonight in time. We're keeping time in the control room so that we're fair.

Mr. PEROT: All right. And on the manufacturing goods, second largest manufacturing goods—second largest manufacturing goods, they send all this phony turn-around stuff and count it as though we sold it to Mexican citizens.

Now, people who don't make any money can't buy anything. When you look at the Mexican worker, and you go to the *Miami Herald*, and you look at the man who works for Zenith in Mexico, and you compare him to his counterpart who works for Zenith in the United States, this poor man makes $8.50 a day. You know what his dream is? To someday have an outhouse. You know what his big dream is? To some day have running water. You know why these people are desperate for running water. Because

Mexico ignores their pollution and environmental laws—

KING:—But this all is without NAFTA.

Vice. Pres. GORE: Yeah, that's all happening now.

Mr. PEROT:—Excuse me, excuse me, but this is the prelude to NAFTA. They have strong environmental laws that they don't enforce—now, just one second—

Vice. Pres. GORE:—Let me respond to that—

KING:—Let him respond to that, and then we'll have—

Vice. Pres. GORE:—OK. First of all, you will notice, and the audience will notice, that he does not want to publicly release how much money he's spending, how much money he's received from other sources to campaign against NAFTA. I would like to see those public releases that other side has made.

Now, let me come to the point—he talked about accuracy of forecasts and numbers. I watched on this program, right here at this desk, when the war against Iraq was about to take place, and you told Larry King, "This is a terrible mistake because it will lead to the death of 40,000 American troops."

You said you had talked to the person who had "ordered the caskets." You were wrong about that. You said on "Larry King" just before the election that after Election Day, there would be 100 banks that would fail, costing the taxpayers $100 billion. You were wrong about that. Now, the politics of negativism and fear only go so far.

KING:—All right—

Vice. Pres. GORE:—You started out as—

KING:—take a break, and I'll have Ross respond. We'll come back on "Larry King Live"—

Mr. PEROT:—That has nothing to do with—but we'll have to fool with it, and I'll be happy to.

KING: OK, we'll come right back on "Larry King Live." We've got a lot to go, your calls, too. Don't go away.

[*commercial break*]

KING: [in progress]—President finish his statement and Mr. Perot respond, and then we'll get to some specifics and your phone calls.

Vice Pres. GORE: Well, you're getting to the key issue there because Bill Clinton and I were elected to do something about what's happening to working men and women to this country.

KING: Correct.

Vice Pres. GORE: They've been losing their jobs. There has been unfair competition from foreign countries that don't let our products in even though we buy their products. This will help to stop that. Some people want to stay with the status quo, just keep things the way they are. We want to open up these barriers. And let me give you a specific example. Valmont Electric Company in Danville, Illinois, less than a year ago was

trying to sell products into Mexico. They've got a 13 percent tax at the border. We have zero tax coming the other way. They closed down in Danville, 400 jobs lost. They opened up in Mexico with 100 jobs down there, and now they ship their products duty free back into the United States through the Alliance Airport, which is the free trade zone that Mr. Perot's company has set up for—it's kind of a private free trade zone outside of Dallas—

KING: You're saying Mr. Perot—

Vice Pres. GORE: And they take Valmont Electric's products and distribute them through the United States duty free. Now, if we passed NAFTA, that 13 percent tax that they have at their border would be gone, and companies like Valmont could stay here in the United States, sell their products in Mexico, and not have to go down there to get over the barrier.

KING: Are you saying that Mr. Perot is personally benefiting by attacking NAFTA?

Vice Pres. GORE: I think he has set it up so that he will benefit financially either way. But if NAFTA passes—I mean, if NAFTA is defeated, this family business that has a free trade zone outside of Dallas will continue to distribute products coming from Mexico into the rest of the United States. What is the deal with Alliance?

Mr. PEROT: I think what the—I'll explain it, but we see here tonight is why our country is four trillion dollars in debt, going a billion dollars in debt every working day. Nobody ever focuses on the real problems. Now, I'm going to try to say this as simply as I can. Alliance Airport is in Fort Worth, Texas, not in Mexico. Alliance Airport is owned by the city of Fort Worth, not my son.

Do you shake head on that?

Vice Pres. GORE: No, the—

Mr. PEROT: Alliance Airport, check the FAA, is owned by the city of Fort Worth.

Vice Pres. GORE: You don't have ownership of Alliance Carter [—] an Incorporated.

Mr. PEROT: The airport. Now, I'm going to—please.

KING: Let him finish.

Mr. PEROT: Let's have an unnatural event and try not to interrupt me. Now, my son owns land adjoining the airport. Now, the purpose of that land is to build factories and warehouses to be—so that industrial goods can be moved by rail and by air. Just—now, watch my lips. The jobs will be created in Texas. Texas is in the United States. The workers will be United States citizens. They will be paid U.S. wages. It is a job creator in the United States of America. And all of this other silly putty throw up—for example, the free trade zone concept goes back to the 1930s. It is nothing new about the free trade zone concept. You have to apply to the U.S. government to get it, and if it didn't make sense I guess they wouldn't have given

it to him. But it is not aimed at doing business with Mexico.

Vice Pres. GORE: You're not involved in it?

Mr. PEROT: Mexico will be a tiny little pipe of this whole operation. Okay, if—I am putting my country's interest far ahead of my business interest.

KING: You would do better with NAFTA?

Mr. PEROT: I would—no. When I'm in a room with corporate America, the first thing they say is, "Perot, why don't you keep your mouth shut. You could with your resources make more money than anybody else." Here is the NAFTA game.

Buy U.S. manufacturing companies cheap right after NAFTA passes that are labor intensive that make good products that have marginal profits, close the factories in the U.S., move the factories to Mexico, take advantage of the cheap labor, run your profits through the roof, sell the company stock at a profit, go get another one.

Vice Pres. GORE: That's what they do now. That's what they're doing right now.

KING: Are they doing that now?

Vice Pres. GORE: And they're using Alliance Carter Incorporated in part to do it.

Mr. PEROT: Oh, come on, come on. You're talking about something like a trickle of water coming over Niagara Falls as opposed to the gusher. You know it.

Vice Pres. GORE: Now, you say it's your son's business but isn't—

Mr. PEROT: Now, do you guys never do anything but propaganda?

Vice Pres. GORE: Isn't your business also—

Mr. PEROT: Would you even know the truth if you saw it?

Vice Pres. GORE: Oh, yes—

Mr. PEROT: I don't believe you would. We've been up here too long.

Vice Pres. GORE: Let me ask you a question.

Mr. PEROT: Please let me finish. This is not "Crossfire," is it, Larry?

KING: No.

Mr. PEROT: May I finish?

Vice Pres. GORE: And then I'd like to ask a question.

Mr. PEROT: All right, I have tried to explain with countless interruptions that this creates jobs in the United States. I am extremely proud of what my son is doing. I want to answer the question that he jumped in to ask. I own a minority interest in the airport. This—everything I'm doing makes it next to impossible for my family to ever do anything south of the border, and I could care less, okay?

KING: You do no business in Mexico or going to?

Mr. PEROT: I have no—look, I will put my country's interest in front of making money.

Vice Pres. GORE: Let me know when I can respond.

Mr. PEROT: And I don't ever want to make money at the expense of other people. Now, I got interrupted a minute ago when you shifted it back—

KING: One other thing could finish with.

Vice Pres. GORE: No, I'd like to respond on this.

KING: The financing of the anti-NAFTA campaign, it had not been answered and he asked it.

Mr. PEROT: Okay, fine, I'll answer it. See, again, he throws up propaganda. He throws up gorilla dust that makes no sense.

KING: What is it then?

Mr. PEROT: May I finish?

KING: Yeah.

Mr. PEROT: Okay. Most of the television time I bought during the campaign. That is a matter of public record. I have had two television shows since the campaign in the spring. They cost about $400,000 a piece. Those were network shows. Then we just did a NAFTA show, but we have to buy the time locally. I don't have the figures yet on what that cost me or I'd be glad to tell you.

KING: You're spending—

Mr. PEROT: I had to buy—no, I buy the television time because I don't want to take the members money for that. They understand that, they approve of that.

Vice Pres. GORE: Can I—it's not all his money, and we don't know because they do not—

Mr. PEROT: No, but television time—I just told you.

Vice Pres. GORE: Well, but—see, they do not release the records, but I accept your response because you have said that now—

Mr. PEROT: If it makes you feel better to see the checks and the bills from the network—

Vice Pres. GORE: It's okay for you interrupt but not me?

KING: Okay, all right—

Vice Pres. GORE: Now, hold on. You just said that you would—

KING: Let's go back to jobs.

Vice Pres. GORE: You just said that you would release the records, and I appreciate that. Now, this—

Mr. PEROT: It has nothing to do with what's going to happen to our country.

Vice Pres. GORE: Well, we need to know who's trying to influence it.

Mr. PEROT: I am paying for it, it's that simple.

KING: We got the answer.

Vice Pres. GORE: Now, on this—this Alliance business is connected to the jobs issue.

KING: Why is it important?

Vice Pres. GORE: Well, because right now we've got these barriers that we cannot surmount to sell into Mexico. We have been trying for years to get an even relationship so that their tariffs, their barriers, their taxes at the border will be eliminated. A lot of companies now have an incentive to leave the United States and locate down there. We heard about auto parts. Right now there is 13 percent tax at the border collected by Mexico on U.S. auto parts.

KING: All right, all right—

Vice Pres. GORE: Wait a minute, let me finish. This is important, Larry. And there is less than one half of one percent tariff the other way. That big growing market down there, in a few years they're going to buying a million cars a year. In order to sell into that market, these companies now have an incentive to pull up stakes and move down there. This business, which is not just his son's business, and there's nothing dishonorable about it at all. But here is the brochure for it, and here is the prospectus. And here are the two principles—what look like the principle investors there, Mr. Perot and the American eagle. And in the prospectus it says— okay, see it there. And in the prospectus it says that this is an ideal national distribution center for products coming out of Mexico. Plus, they have—he has lobbied the taxpayers to spend more than 200 million dollars in taxpayer funds in this project—

Mr. PEROT: Who is he?

Vice Pres. GORE: That takes you and your business.

Mr. PEROT: No, I'm not lobbying anybody.

Vice Pres. GORE: There's nothing illegal about it.

Mr. PEROT: I haven't done it. I don't— I haven't lobbied anybody.

Vice Pres. GORE: You've never hired a lobbyist?

Mr. PEROT: I—in my life? You mean on the airport?

Vice Pres. GORE: Both.

KING: No, on the airport.

Vice Pres. GORE: On the airport.

Mr. PEROT: I don't hire lobbyists. This is my son's project. I went to the air show and haven't been out there—oh, probably been 18 months since I've been out there.

KING: What's the relevance?

Vice Pres. GORE: Well, the relevance is that if the free trade—if NAFTA is defeated then—

KING: What?

Vice Pres. GORE: Then this free trade zone that he has is still in business. If it's good enough for him, why isn't it good enough for the rest of the country?

KING: Do you say he's doing this for personal profit?

Vice Pres. GORE: I said before that I think he is in a position to benefit either way. And he was in favor of NAFTA, again, made speeches in favor of it, wrote in favor of it in your book before you started running for president. You started getting a response from people—

KING: Let's ask this then, what turned you against it if you were in favor of it?

Mr. PEROT: Well, conceptually I am for free trade. I am, if we ever get back to the subject, for a good agreement with Mexico. I am deeply concerned about the 85 million people who live in poverty and don't have any rights. I am deeply concerned about workers who when they go on strike U.S. companies call in goons, bring in the state police, shoot several workers, kill one, injure dozens, put the workers back to work and cut wages 45 percent. Those are things that are wrong. We can do this right. I am not in favor of a one political party country. The PRI runs the country. President Salinas will pick his successor. President Salinas went to the 36 families who own over 54 percent of the gross domestic product and asked them for 25 million dollars a piece. Fortunately for their families one of them leaked it to the New York Times and they didn't have to pay. That's Mexico. He will pick his successor not the Mexican people. Read the state department's annual report on human rights; a journalist being killed, people in the opposing political parties being put in prison and killed and tortured. This is not a free society, and yet for some reason the same people who are willing to put our troops at risk around the world to make sure people are protected, once we get to Mexico, ignore all of that.

KING: Are you not anyone that supports a fascist kind of state?

Mr. PEROT: I'm saying this is not—I'm concerned any agreement we do should give the Mexican people a decent life and over a period of time should give them some purchasing power. If I'm going to do business with somebody—let's just say the U.S. is going to do business with another country, let's do business with a country whose people can buy things. Let's go—

KING: You don't think President Salinas is a progressive.

Mr. PEROT: President Salinas is almost out of office. I'm worried to death about who follows him.

Vice Pres. GORE: Can I respond on that?

Mr. PEROT: When you treat people the way they treat people, it's a matter of time until they lose power. And they've had it for a lot of years, and they keep it by force. But whether it's labor and management or countries and people, you oppress people long enough and you got to change, and that will happen.

Vice Pres. GORE: Let me respond to this because some of what he is saying here is true. Mexico is not yet a full democracy. They do not yet have full protection for human rights. They do not yet have the kind of living standard and labor standards and environmental protection standards that we would like them to see, but they've been making tremendous progress. And the progress has been associated with this new relationship to the United States. The decisions in Mexico will ultimately be made by the people in Mexico. The question is whether or not we will have the ability to influence what they and their government decide. The best way to eliminate our influence down there is to defeat NAFTA. The best way to preserve it is to enter into this bargain, continue the lowering of the barriers. We've got a commitment that they're going to raise their minimum wage with productivity. We've got an agreement for the first time in history to use trade sanctions to compel the enforcement of their environmental standards. As they begin to develop and locate better jobs farther south, we cut down on illegal immigration. Now, one of the reasons why all of the living former presidents and the other folks that I mentioned are supporting this is because this is the kind of choice that comes along only once every 40 or 50 years. This is a major choice for our country of historic proportions. Sometimes we do something right; the creation of NATO, the Louisiana Purchase, Thomas Jefferson did the right thing there, the purchase of Alaska. These were all extremely controversial choices, but they made a difference for our country. This is such a choice—if we make—if we should happen to give into the politics of fear and make the wrong choice, the consequences would be catastrophic. If we make the right choice, we have a chance to encourage Mexico to continue on the path they have been traveling.

KING: Ross is not saying he wants the status quo. He wants a different treaty, am I correct?

Vice Pres. GORE: He wants to raise tariffs on Mexico.

Mr. PEROT: Just a second. Let's look at reality—

KING:—And then we'll take our first call. Go ahead.

Mr. PEROT: Let's look at reality instead of theory. There's a major U.S. chemical plant in Mexico that digs holes in the ground, dumps the chemical waste in those holes, bulldozes over those holes, and contaminates the water supply for the people in that area. A disproportionate number of the babies born in the shantytown around that plant are born without a brain. Now, I don't care if you're poor or rich. If your baby is born without a brain because a U.S. company is willing to take advantage of workers to that extent, that's wrong. Now, if there's any question about it, the xylene, the chemical xylene, in the water content in a ditch coming out of that plant is 53,000 times the amount permitted in the United States. This outfit, big Democratic group—backing the Democratic Party—here's the videotape that shows them digging the holes, putting the chemicals in the ground. It shows one child whose foot is horribly burned from chemicals, and it shows the classic worker abuse—

Vice Pres. GORE:—Can I respond? Can I respond?

Mr. PEROT: I pass it on to Vice President Gore—

Vice. Pres. GORE:—Yeah, thank you—

Mr. PEROT: Because I know he cares, and I'm not—I'm not trying to play doctor with you.

Vice Pres. GORE: I agree with you on this, I agree with you on this.

Mr. PEROT: I know you care deeply about these things.

Vice Pres. GORE: Yeah, can I answer?

Mr. PEROT: I know you're a good man, but the laws are on the books, they're not enforced.

Vice Pres. GORE: Yeah—

KING: NAFTA would what? Change them? Not change them?

Mr. PEROT: Well, they have this little side agreement, but the facts are Mexico is so sensitive about its sovereignty they're not about to let us go down there and get into the middle of their—the Rio Grande River, all right folks, the Rio Grande River is the most polluted river in the Western Hemisphere—

Vice Pres. GORE:—Wait a minute. Can I respond to this first?

KING: Yeah, let him respond—

Mr. PEROT: The Tijuana River is the most—they've had to close it—

KING: But all of this is without NAFTA, right?

Vice Pres. GORE: Yeah, and let me respond to this, if I could, would you—

Mr. PEROT:—Larry, Larry, this is after years of U.S. companies going to Mexico, living free—

KING:—But they could do that without NAFTA.

Mr. PEROT: But we can stop that without NAFTA and we can stop that with a good NAFTA.

Vice Pres. GORE: How do you stop that without NAFTA?

Mr. PEROT: Just make—just cut that out. Pass a few simple laws on this, make it very, very clear.

Vice Pres. GORE: Pass a few simple laws on Mexico?

Mr. PEROT: No.

Vice Pres. GORE: How do you stop it without NAFTA?

Mr. PEROT: Give me your whole mind.

Vice Pres. GORE: Yeah, I'm listening. I haven't heard the answer, but go ahead.

Mr. PEROT: That's because you haven't quit talking.

Vice Pres. GORE: Well, I'm listening. How do you stop it without NAFTA?

Mr. PEROT: OK, are you going to listen? Work on it. Now, very simple—just tell every company south of the border if they operate that way they cannot ship their goods into the U.S. at any price period, and they will become choir boys overnight. See, Mexico is a country that can't buy anything. Japan, everybody else in the world is going to flood into Mexico if NAFTA is passed so that they can get cheap labor—

KING: OK, I gotta get a break in and—

Vice Pres. GORE:—When we come back I want to respond to this.

KING: The vice president will respond and then we'll go to your phone calls on "Larry King Live." We'll be right back.

[commercial break]

Vice. Pres. GORE: [off-mike] Are you going to give me a chance to respond to this?

KING: OK—[on-mike] OK, if we keep responding and responding, we're never going to get some calls, but I'll have the vice president respond on the Stefan Chemical, and then quickly to calls. Quick.

Vice Pres. GORE: Oh, thank you. Well, if we defeat NAFTA, we'll lose all leverage over the enforcement of Mexico's environmental laws.

KING: Ross says we just pass a law to—

Vice Pres. GORE: That wouldn't affect Mexican companies or the investments from other countries. But the problem has been not so much their laws, but the enforcement of their laws. We can probably agree on that. This side agreement that we negotiated gives us the ability to use trade sanctions to compel the enforcement of their environmental laws.

KING: Let me get some calls in—

Vice Pres. GORE:—A major step forward—

KING:—and by the way, I must tell our audience that we're keeping kind of score, so we're fair. We always try to be fair, and each party has had equal time right to this minute in talking. We go to Washington, D.C., as we begin phone calls. Hello?

WASHINGTON, D.C., CALLER: Hello. My question is for Mr. Perot.

KING: Yes.

WASHINGTON, D.C., CALLER: How can the United States expect to compete on a long-term basis in an increasingly interdependent economic world, while Europe and the Pac Rim nations unite through their own respective trade alignments?

Mr. PEROT: Very simple—we've got the most productive workforce in the world.

We're the biggest buyer of goods and services in the world.

We're the market everybody wants to sell to. Our problem is we do the world's dumbest trade agreements. You go back to the agreements we've done all over the world, you'd be amazed that adults did them. We're about to do another one, but the American people have stopped it and it's dead in the House of Representatives. It's time we draw a line in the sand, and we've done it.

Now, here's the key—you want to buy and sell with people who have money. You want to trade with partners who have money, but then if you make a one-sided deal with Japan, they get all the benefits, we get all the problems. Then, you come to Mexico. It's an emerging nation. You want to help it. You put in this tariff that as they raise the standard of living of their people, the tariff goes away. If anybody wants to do things like destroy people's life by dumping chemicals and all that and polluting the Rio Grande River and destroying the Tijuana River and the beaches in San Diego—and the life in San Diego pretty soon—you just say you can't ship your good to the U.S.

KING:—Ross, his question was—

Mr. PEROT:—You can help Mexico and do it—

KING:—Ross—

Mr. PEROT:—No—You can't compete—go put your primary effort with people who have money to spend. Then, because we want to help emerging nations, help nations like Mexico. But you're primary effort has to be—and be-

lieve me, you say, does everybody want to do business with us? More than anything else in the world, because we buy a lot.

KING: Please try to limit answers, so we can get our calls in.

Vice. Pres. GORE: I'd like to respond to that quickly. Could I?

KING: Yeah.

Vice. Pres. GORE: Let me give you a quick example. Mattel just announced that if NAFTA is passed, it will move a plastics factory from Asia to Mexico. Instead of getting the plastic from China, it will get the plastic from the United States. With NAFTA, we will enlarge what is already the largest consumer market in the world with the addition of a country that buys 70 percent of all of its foreign products from the United States of America. It will position us to compete effectively with the rest of the world. That's why a lot of these other countries are a little nervous about it.

One of the trade officials in Japan described this as 'sneaky protectionism' and raised a lot of questions about it. It will benefit us in our trading relationship with Asia and Europe, and we're right now in the middle of the negotiations with the GATT—that's the larger world trade agreement. If we pass NAFTA, we will be able to use the leverage to drop the barriers against our products in other countries.

KING: Fairview Heights, Ill., hello?

ILLINOIS CALLER: Hello, Larry. Vice President Gore, I understand the United States will spend $7 billion to clean up the pollution left by multi-national companies in Mexico, much of it polluting our rivers. I would like to know why we're going to spend that money, and couldn't be better spent here at home?

Vice. Pres. GORE: Well, Mexico will join in, so will the Inter-American Bank, and so will the polluters who have caused the problem. And we should clean up that pollution that Mr. Perot was talking about so eloquently earlier whether we have NAFTA or not. With NAFTA, we will have the cooperation of Mexico and other countries in this hemisphere in doing that.

KING: Aren't you—

Mr. PEROT:—May I cut in briefly?

KING: Yeah, sorry.

Mr. PEROT: It will cost us several billion dollars in tariff losses. It will cost us at least $15 billion and probably more to build infrastructure. And we will have a $20–40 billion bill on pollution alone. Now, guess who's going to pay that? All you hard-working taxpayers that still have jobs, go look in the mirror and ask yourselves why the government's policies have caused four out of five of you to have to lower your standard of living. Ask yourselves why your government sent two million jobs to Asia alone, manufacturing jobs, in the 1980s. [To Vice Pres. Gore] Now, you agree with that number?

Vice. Pres. GORE: All of that happened before NAFTA—

Mr. PEROT:—You agree with two million, or not?

Vice. Pres. GORE:—and before we took office.

Mr. PEROT:—That's not the point. Is it a good number?

Vice. Pres. GORE: Oh, we've lost a lot of jobs to lousy trade deals in the past because they weren't fair, they weren't fair.

Mr. PEROT: Well, we agree that we've made—

Vice. Pres. GORE:—Let me finish, now—

Mr. PEROT:—Excuse me, excuse me.

Vice. Pres. GORE: Thank you very much. I'll let you finish. I like that line.

I appreciate that. The fact is that we have the opportunity with NAFTA to stop this kind of stuff. All of the problems that Mr. Perot talks about will be made worse if NAFTA is defeated. We have an opportunity to make all of them better if we pass NAFTA.

Listen, Larry—the whole world is poised, waiting for America's response to Mexico's decision to say "yes." We have knocked on their door for 20 years trying to get them to stop being protectionist—

KING:—Are you saying this embarrasses us if we—

Vice Pres. GORE:—Well, of course it does, but it's far more important than just embarrassment. It diminishes our ability, it would diminish our ability to open other markets overseas. The GATT round would probably not be completed if NAFTA were defeated.

KING: All right, I've got an exact break here. We'll come right back, half hour to go. We'll take your phone calls. Don't go away.

[commercial break]

LARRY KING, Anchor: We're back with the NAFTA debate on Larry King Live and back to your phone calls for Vice President Al Gore and Ross Perot. Nanamo, British Columbia. Hello.

CALLER: Hi. It's Nanimo. I'd like to know what Mr. Perot and Mr. Gore have both learned from the previous free trade agreement between Canada and the U.S.

KING: Both learned? Ross?

[Mr.] PEROT: Well, just by watchin' it. First thing, thousands of people joined United We Stand America out of Canada. I couldn't figure out why so I checked—they were mad at NAFTA. Then I watched the election—the Conservative Party had 155 seats and the prime minister. There's a message here for both political parties in the United States. After the dust cleared, they had two seats in parliament, no prime minister. The reason—

KING: NAFTA?

Mr. PEROT: Reason—NAFTA. Why? Huge numbers of manufacturing jobs left Canada, came into the United States because of a 15 percent wage differential. We pay our workers less than Canada. Now, when you've got a seven-to-one wage differential between the United States and Mexico,

you will hear the giant sucking sound—

Vice Pres. GORE: Now, wait—

Mr. PEROT:—there's a political lesson, there's a business lesson—

KING:—a quick—I'm going to ask you to limit the answers so we can move on.

Vice Pres. GORE: But this is an important question and it's important to realize that only one of the parties in that election campaigned against the basic NAFTA treaty—that was the socialists. They lost seats. They only got nine seats out of 258 and now the person who won has been talking with the—President Clinton. This has been a good deal for both Canada and the United States. Both have gained jobs; both have gained trade flows; both have become more competitive in the world marketplace as a result.

Mr. PEROT: And there is a tooth fairy and there is an Easter Bunny.

KING: Bethesda, Maryland. Hello.

CALLER: Good evening, Larry. I'd like to ask the vice president specifically to answer, in terms of a time limit, how long—how many years? Five, eight, 10 years will it be before we see these new jobs in America that are supposed to be out there?

KING: Job swing, how long?

Vice Pres. GORE: Well, we're already seeing a great many new jobs. We have seen 400,000 new jobs just in the last five years because of Mexico's unilateral decision to lower the barriers to U.S. products. We'll see 200,000 jobs, it is estimated, over the next several years—

KING: But there'll be a dip first, right?

Vice Pres. GORE:—in the wake of NAFTA. No, no, no. We think—absolutely not.

KING: Unions are wrong?

Vice Pres. GORE: Oh yes, I think they're wrong.

KING: The trade unions are wrong about fearing a dip?

Vice Pres. GORE: Absolutely. Now, there is always, in our economy, a churning of the economy—

KING: Five hundred thousand jobs—

Vice Pres. GORE:—with or without NAFTA, that is the case, but the net change is positive with NAFTA. Now, there are all kinds of estimates—virtually all of them show job gains, as I've said before. Some of them show very large job gains, but the importance of NAFTA goes beyond that because again, it gives us the ability to open up markets in the rest of the world because other countries—let me give you a specific example to illustrate this. Computers in the United States will—

KING: A business he knows—

Vice Pres. GORE:—we sell into Mexico—they have a 20 percent tariff on our computers. After NAFTA, they will have a zero percent tariff on our computers, but the 20 percent will still apply to Asia and to Europe, so with the transportation advantage and a 20 percent price advantage, who are they going to buy their computers from? They're going to buy lots of them from us.

Now, that gives us an advantage and when you sell more products, you make more products. When you make more products, you hire more people.

Mr. PEROT: Quickly. If you believe that, I've got a lot of stuff in the attic I can sell you. Second, if this is all true, why is corporate America downsizing? If this is all true, why do we have the largest number of college graduates this year unable to find jobs since at any time in the '40s? If this is all true, why is that everywhere I go in a hotel, I've got a college graduate comin' up to the room, bringin' food, carrying bags, so on and so forth, waiting till they get their job? If this is all true, why isn't our economy booming? You see, it just doesn't fit, folks. Just go—

Vice Pres. GORE:—I'd like to answer—

KING: OK.

Mr. PEROT:—look at reality.

Vice Pres. GORE: I'd like to answer the question if I could.

KING: OK.

Mr. PEROT: We—

Vice Pres. GORE:—no, because, see while we have a $5.6 billion trade surplus with Mexico, we have a $49 billion deficit with Japan, a $19 billion deficit with China, a $9 billion deficit with Taiwan—those are trade problems. Mexico is a trade opportunity. If we use the opportunity to pry open the markets in the rest of the world, we'll change this. All of the problems that he talks about? That's what we want to change. We don't accept the status quo. We want to fight for working men and women and NAFTA is part of it.

KING: Zaghreb, Croatia, hello.

CALLER: Good evening. My question is this. Mr. Perot, since you obviously have many, many criticisms about the NAFTA agreement, can you give us specific answers as to an alternative to it? If you don't like it, tell us what, really, we should be doing?

KING: Can you over-view a treaty you would sign?

Mr. PEROT: Yes, I will do it again. First, we've got to have a clear understanding with Mexico that we can only do business with a country that gives its people a decent standard of living and respects human rights. Because we are all humans—every human life is precious.

KING:—and that would be the first part of it?

Mr. PEROT:—every human life is precious. If you don't treat your workers fairly and if you don't treat your people fairly, history teaches us that that produces stress that will take maybe a century to cure. It's in Mexico's interest to do that. Then, their workers will come up the economic scale; we'll put in a social tariff that drops as they bring their workers' pay and benefits up. If we pass NAFTA and we pass health care and your competitor goes to Mexico, you will either have to go to Mexico or go out of business. I can give you a whole list of things like that.

KING: You would have a tariff that swings?

Mr. PEROT: The way we're set now. No, it's a social tariff—as they bring their people up, we drop the tariff. When it's head-to-head competition and their people have equal pay and benefits as ours—

KING: What's wrong with that?

Mr. PEROT:—there is no tariff and we've brains and wits and off we go. That's good for Mexico and it protects our people.

KING: Why is that bad?

Vice Pres. GORE: Well, it—it kind of goes back to the Smoot-Hawley idea—

Mr. PEROT:—oh, come on—

Vice Pres. GORE:—seriously, for this reason—for this reason. The idea that we can isolate ourselves from the rest of the world and only do business with "perfect" countries that do everything the way we want them to do is pretty unrealistic. His proposal, as I understand it, is to raise tariffs and call it a social tariff and use that to keep products out from any country that doesn't meet our standards in all things.

Mr. PEROT:—I said Mexico—

Vice Pres. GORE:—now, let me finish, please. Now, you take—

Mr. PEROT:—tiny little market—

Vice Pres. GORE:—that kind of approach to Mexico and you defeat NAFTA, you've lost the partnership we've been building with Mexico for a generation and more. But beyond that, here's the central point. We have to realize that we, unilaterally, cannot change the entire world. We can't force every country in the world that we want to trade with to meet our standards in everything that we would like to see them meet.

Now, the fundamental—the guts of this whole thing is the reason why some people listen to what he's saying is that they think if a country has wages lower than we have, then it's fundamentally unfair to trade with them even when it's totally even in all other respects. If that were the case— if low wages were the determinant of where you locate businesses, then Haiti would be an economic powerhouse; Bangladesh would be a powerhouse. We have problems—trade problems— with countries that have wages higher than we have, like Germany and they have fewer barriers than we do and higher wages because, Larry, the secret is productivity—our working men and women are the most productive of any nation on the face of the Earth. You give us the opportunity to sell our products unimpeded, without these trade barriers and—that we've been having to deal with, into these other countries—we'll knock the socks off the worker of any other country in this world.

KING: Why doesn't that make sense to you?

Mr. PEROT: Well, it wouldn't make sense to most people over six years old.

KING: Why?

Mr. PEROT: If I have to explain it to the audience, they'd probably—I don't think I will. Bangladesh and Haiti? They all got that. Well, I won't waste your time on that one. You understand that that—

Vice Pres. GORE: No, but they have the lowest wages.

Mr. PEROT: That's not the point. Everybody out there understands why Bangladesh and Haiti are not like Mexico, so I won't waste my time. Secondly—

Vice Pres. GORE:—but tell me, I mean, humor me if you would and—

Mr. PEROT:—no, I won't. I don't think I can. Now, next thing. It's pretty simple stuff. We've been out-traded by everybody. All we've got to do is explain very nicely to Mexico that they out-traded us on this deal. We've got to make a fair deal with them. They'll huff and puff for a few days. They'll be back. We'll make a good deal. For a very simple reason. They need us. We don't need them. Now then, we go to Japan—send a horse trader over to Japan.

Send somebody that knows how to negotiate and just explain to them that they was the most one-sided trade deals in the world. We've got to reopen 'em; we've got to make 'em fair and they'd say "What do you mean?" I say "We'll just take the same deal we gave you." They would look at you like "Good gracious sakes alive! You mean, you want the same deal we've had for years?" That's fair. Then you start to negotiate and say, well, a fall-back position—"We'll just take the deals that ya'll made with Europe because they're a whole lot better than the ones you made with the U.S." You know what the problem is folks? It's foreign lobbyists—are wreckin' this whole thing. Right here, *Time* magazine just says it all—it says "In spite of Clinton's protests, the influence-peddling machine in Washington is back in high gear." The headline, Time magazine—"A Lobbyist's Paradise."

Vice Pres. GORE: I'd like to respond to that.

KING: OK.

Mr. PEROT: We are being sold out by foreign lobbyists. We've got 33 of them working on this in the biggest lobbying effort in the history of our country to ram NAFTA down your throat.

KING: All right, let him respond.

Vice Pres. GORE: I'd like to respond.

Mr. PEROT: The good news is it ain't working.

KING: OK, Ross.

Mr. PEROT: I'll turn it over to the others.

Vice Pres. GORE: OK, thank you.

KING: And we've got another call.

Vice Pres. GORE: One of President Clinton's first acts in office was to put limits on the lobbyists and new ethics laws, and we're working for lobby law reform right now. But, you know, we had a little conversation about this earlier, but every dollar that's been spent for NAFTA has been publicly disclosed. We don't know yet—

KING: He says—

Vice Pres. GORE: Tomorrow—perhaps tomorrow we'll see, but the reason

why, and I say this respectfully, because I served in the Congress and I don't know of any single individual who lobbied the Congress more than you did, or people in your behalf did, to get tax breaks for your companies. And it's legal.

Mr. PEROT: You're lying. You're lying now.

Vice Pres. GORE: You didn't lobby the Ways and Means Committee for tax breaks for yourself and your companies?

Mr. PEROT: What do you have in mind? What are you talking about?

Vice Pres. GORE: Well, it's been written about extensively and again, there's nothing illegal about it.

Mr. PEROT: Well that's not the point. I mean, what are you talking about?

Vice Pres. GORE: Lobbying the Congress. You know a lot about it.

Mr. PEROT: I mean, spell it out, spell it out.

Vice Pres. GORE: You didn't lobby the Ways and Means Committee. You didn't have people lobbying the Ways and Means Committee for tax breaks?

Mr. PEROT: What are you talking about?

Vice Pres. GORE: In the 1970's.

Mr. PEROT: Well, keep going.

Vice Pres. GORE: Well, did you or did you not? I mean, it's not—

Mr. PEROT: Well, you're so general I can't pin it down. I mean, 1970—

[*crosstalk*]

Vice Pres. GORE: I'm not charging anything illegal. It's this blunderbust attack on all lobbyists.

[*crosstalk*]

Mr. PEROT: Wait just a minute. Wait just a minute. Let's talk about the lobbying reforms—that's the biggest sham in history. All you had to do was take a pledge. The pledge is like a pledge to quit drinking. We don't have lobbying reform under Clinton. We will get it, but we don't have it yet. And this stuff they've come up with is nothing, and if you look at who's running all these economic negotiations, it's a who's who of former foreign lobbyists now in the Clinton administration.

KING: McLean, Virginia, hello.

CALLER: Sir, this is for Mr. Perot.

KING: Yeah, go ahead.

CALLER: Sir, over the past five years, and I think you probably know this, the U.S. has nearly tripled its electronics exports to Mexico, worth about $6 billion. Now that's produced a lot of high-tech, good paying jobs in America. Now if Congress does the right thing and passes NAFTA and removes the tariffs on these products, how can you believe that this wouldn't increase our exports, create more jobs, create more exports for America?

Mr. PEROT: Well I think you're seeing, counted in that figure, every piece of electronics that goes to Mexico, does a turn-around in an assembly plant, and comes back to the United States. I am certain you're seeing all the radios that go down and get put in cars that come back to United States. If we strip it down to the real electric products that the Mexican people buy that stay in Mexico, it would be a fraction of that sum.

Vice Pres. GORE: Did you see the Wal-Mart that opened in Mexico City on the news?

KING: Largest one in the—

Vice Pres. GORE: Largest one in the world, if I understand it. They have 72 cash registers ringing constantly with people in that—in Mexico taking American products out of that store. We have this image of them being so poor that they can't possibly buy any electronic equipment or anything else that we make. They are poorer than we are. But you know what? They spend more per person on American products than any other country except. [crosstalk] Let me finish, let me finish, because this is very important. Japan, if you take everything that Japan buys, only 2 percent of it comes from the United States. If you take everything that Mexico buys, it's 800 percent larger, and if you take what they buy from foreign countries, 70 percent of everything they buy from other countries come from us. They prefer American products. If we lower those trade barriers and get rid of them altogether, we will have an export surge into Mexico and we'll have a partnership with Mexico that will help us remove the trade barriers in the rest of the world.

KING: Fairfax, Virginia, hello. I should bring it down. Fairfax, Virginia, with Vice President Al Gore and Ross Perot, hello.

CALLER: Companies can come into Mexico by, you know, thousands and set up manufacturing of products using the cheap Mexican labor, and I think that that is the biggest threat to the loss of U.S. jobs. Is this correct?

Vice Pres. GORE: No, it's not correct, because American workers are more than five times more productive than their counterparts in Mexico because they have better tools, they have better training, they have a better infrastructure.

There are lots and lots of companies that moved down to Mexico and decided that they would rather move back to the United States. I've got a whole long list of them. General Motors is one of them that moved down while Mr. Perot was on the board. He may have voted against that, but they have—I don't know, but they now moved, started moving jobs back from Mexico, back to the United States. Let me give you another example. Norm Cohen in Charlotte, North Carolina, is in the textile business. 15 years ago, he tried to sell his products in Mexico—he had the price, he had the quality, he couldn't sell. Why not? He went in and investigated. His Mexican counterparts got a little mail-out from the Mexican government every month with a listing of all the foreign companies, including American companies that wanted to sell in competition into Mexico.

They were given an opportunity to put an "X" beside the name of any company they didn't want to compete with. He got some investors and opened up a company in Mexico. Now NAFTA not only eliminates the taxes at the border, it eliminates practices like that "x marks the spot," and if NAFTA passes, Norm Cohen has plans right now to shut that factory in Mexico down and move 150 jobs back to Charlotte, North Carolina.

KING: Want to respond?

Mr. PEROT: If I have to.

KING: Don't have to.

Mr. PEROT: First off, the whole textile thing is a joke. Talk to anybody in the textile business and they will tell you if their competitors go to Mexico, they will have to go to Mexico. They will also tell that the Mexicans have spent a fortune building textile plants and are building them now in Cuba, where labor is next to nothing. Next, the GM bringing back jobs into this country is a sham used in the union negotiation. Next, the Mexican—the U.S. worker is five times more productive than the Mexican worker—big joke of the century. The Mexican worker is a good worker, he is an industrious worker. He quickly gets up to 70 percent as productive, and after three to five years, is 90 percent as productive, and only makes 1/7 as much. You cannot compete with that in the good ol' USA, particularly with our benefits, retirement, and so on and so forth. It's just that simple. It's a tilted deck.

KING: Mexico City, hello.

Vice Pres. GORE: It's not just that simple.

CALLER: Hi. The subject has come up about the possibility of Japanese taking over if NAFTA doesn't go through. I'm American; I've been living in Mexico City for many years. There are thousands of Japanese here. They are waiting. They are lurking. What are you people doing? Why [call cuts off]

Vice Pres. GORE: Let me answer that.

KING: What's the finish of it, ma'am? All right, I didn't hear the end of it.

Vice Pres. GORE: Yeah, she said what are you doing, why don't you wake up.

Mr. PEROT: Does he get to answer first every time?

KING: I think the question was for him.

Vice Pres. GORE: You go ahead and answer.

Mr. PEROT: No, you go ahead.

Vice Pres. GORE: I'd like to answer it, but you go first.

Mr. PEROT: Let him go ahead, he can have it. I know—as long as I get a brief follow up.

KING: Well, I think the question was for you.

Mr. PEROT: It will only take a minute to kill this snake, go ahead.

KING: Go ahead, kill it.

Vice Pres. GORE: You're talking about the question, not me, right?

Mr. PEROT: No, the question. Absolutely. Excuse me.

KING: Go ahead, it's for you.

Mr. PEROT: It's just this basic. There's a constant in the Clinton administration. Any time they get cornered, they go into what I call "the sky is falling routine"—the presidency is at stake, the Japanese are coming.

KING: No, the question was—she says there are Japanese—

Mr. PEROT:—next thing we'll have is "The British are coming." You know, the ghosts are coming. Look, the Japanese cannot just wander into Mexico, do anything they want to do, dump across our border unless we're stupid enough to let them. Now, if our foreign lobbyists stay wired in the way they are now, we'll probably say "Ooh, this is wonderful." I can tell you about Japanese deals that have been cut through our foreign lobbyists. I can tell you a deal that's buried in this agreement that gives a $17 million benefit to Honda—it's buried. I can show it to you in print. It's there big time. I can show you a deal—

KING: Benefits a single company?

Mr. PEROT:—you bet. I can show you a deal on Tennessee whiskey that'll make you just wonder what the heck is going on. The sky is not falling, the Japanese are our friends—

Vice Pres. GORE: Well, let me respond—

Mr. PEROT:—they're not a threat.

KING: OK. All right.

Vice Pres. GORE: Let me respond. Both automobile manufacturers, including Honda in Marysville, Ohio, Nissan in Tennessee, Saturn in Tennessee, all of the companies in Detroit—they benefit because that Mexican tariff is brought down to zero. Every other American from Tennessee—whiskey benefits—every American business potentially benefits if they want to sell in Mexico—

Mr. PEROT: And they—

Vice Pres. GORE: Hold on, hold on, because I want to respond to her question. This is extremely important. President Salinas has a trade mission to Japan the month after the vote on NAFTA. If we don't take this deal, you can bet that Japan will try to take this deal. They'll be in there in a New York minute. Europe will try to get this deal. They are concerned about us taking this deal.

　　Listen, we—Larry, we ought to thank our lucky stars that the Mexican people have had the vision and courage to strike out on the American path toward the ideas of Thomas Jefferson, toward democracy, toward free markets, and now they just want to know "Can we take 'yes' for an answer?"

KING: In the interest of time, Ross, is there—are there things about this treaty you like?

Mr. PEROT: Oh, sure, but here's the Honda deal—

KING:—are there any—is there anything about it—

Mr. PEROT: Here it is, folks, as they say—it's in the book. There's the Honda deal. Here is the Tennessee whiskey deal.

KING: Al, is there anything about the deal you don't like?

Mr. PEROT:—now, stay with me one second. Here is the deal on Tennessee whiskey. Only in the state of Tennessee, authorized to produce only in the state of Tennessee—

Vice Pres. GORE: No—

Mr. PEROT:—this is foreign lobbying big-time. This is what's wrong with our country. This is what you and I will clear up through government reform.

KING: That's protection of a brand name. I mean, that's protection of a brand name. One of the things about this treaty is it protects intellectual property.

Mr. PEROT: Why just that brand name?

Vice Pres. GORE: Well, it's not just that brand name. If you'll look at the line above it, it says "Bourbon Whiskey." That doesn't have—that's not a brand name.

Mr. PEROT: Stay with me. Tennessee whiskey—

Vice Pres. GORE:—and Tennessee whiskey—

Mr. PEROT:—authorized to produce only in the state of Tennessee—

Vice Pres. GORE: No, but that refers to the other one. It recognizes—it deals with all bourbon—

KING: Bourbon is only from Kentucky, right?

Mr. PEROT:—caught in the middle of the act, folks. No place to run, no place to hide.

KING: I think Bourbon is only—

Vice Pres. GORE: It's two different brand names.

KING: Is there anything about—

Vice Pres. GORE: Excuse me. Just so you're clear about that. Those are brand names and one of the things we've been trying to get in our trade dealings with other countries is protection for what's called intellectual property. And it's a good thing, too, because Mexicans now prefer U.S. brand name products. That's why they're going in and out of that Wal-Mart so fast.

KING: All right, there's a six-month out if it's turned down, right?

Vice Pres. GORE: Yeah, that—

KING:—let me, let me—

Vice Pres. GORE:—now, let's talk about that for a minute. If we don't—if I'm wrong and he's right, then you give six months notice and you're out of it.

KING: Ross, what's wrong with that?

Mr. PEROT: Now, here's the way we get out of it. If the House of Representatives lets this go through, the whole House of Representatives is running in 1994 and a third of the Senate, we've got a little song we sing.

"We'll remember in November" when we step into that little booth. If we have to, we the peo-

ple, the owners of this country, we'll clean this mess up in Washington in '94.

KING: Are you saying you will—

Mr. PEROT:—and. And. We'll make sure that we put the six-month tail on this thing in 1995 and if you think these guys will, you believe in the tooth fairy.

Vice Pres. GORE:—well—

KING: Ross, are you saying that you're going to work against congressmen who vote for it?

Mr. PEROT: I'm not—our people are really angry about this. Working people all across the United States are extremely angry. There is no way to stop 'em. They are not going to tolerate having their jobs continued to be shipped all over the world—

Vice Pres. GORE: I'd like to say something about that.

Mr. PEROT:—we've got to have a climate in this country where we can create jobs in the good old U.S.A.

KING: OK—[blocked]

[crosstalk]

Mr. PEROT:—that is one thing that the president and vice president should do for us and they're not.

Vice Pres. GORE: Excuse me. I'd like to say something about that. Because that's a direct political threat against anybody who votes for this. This is a choice between the politics of fear and the politics of hope. It's a choice between the past and the future. It's a choice between pessimism and optimism. It's a choice between the status quo—leave things as they are—enact new tariffs on Mexico and I don't know who else, or move forward into the future with confidence. We're not scared. We're not a nation of quitters. We're not a nation that is afraid to compete in the world marketplace and when we face a choice as important as this one, it is extremely important that we make the right decision. This is a fork in the road. The whole world is watching.

KING: What's going to happen in eight days?

Mr. PEROT: I love the way these guys turn around on a dime. They've been out making speeches that everybody ought to get a depression check every time they get their eyes checked or their glasses checked and the president's made a stream of speeches telling us how insecure we are. Now, suddenly, they figure out that we are a strong, proud people and—

Vice Pres. GORE: We are—

Mr. PEROT:—and we are not going to let this trade agreement go through and create further damage to this great country. We—let me make sure I say this before we go off the air tonight. I'll give you one reason that will just stick— why we can't continue to do these agreements.

KING: Thirty seconds for each.

Mr. PEROT: If we keep shifting our manufacturing jobs across the border and around the world and de-industrializing our country, we will not be able to defend this great country and that is a risk we will never take.

Vice Pres. GORE: He started off as head of United We Stand. I'm afraid he's going to end up as head of Divided We Fall. Everything that he is worried about will get worse if NAFTA is defeated. We want jobs for America's working men and women. We want to get rid of the barriers that have prevented us from selling what we make in other countries. This is an historic opportunity to do that.

KING: Thank you both for this historic evening. The vote in Congress is eight days away. You'll be hearing lots more about it. Thanks to Ross Perot and Vice President Al Gore. For everyone here at "Larry King Live" and for the superb staff that put this all together, the best in the business. Thanks for joining us and good night.

See also: **Vol. I**: Bush, George Herbert Walker; Clinton, William Jefferson (Bill); Fast-track legislation; Free Trade Area of the Americas (FTAA); Gore, Albert Arnold Jr.; Kennedy, John F.; Latin America; North American Free Trade Agreement (NAFTA); Perot, Henry Ross; Salinas de Gortari, Carlos.